MASS MEDIA AND SOCIETY

EDITED BY **Alan Wells** NEWCOMB COLLEGE, TULANE UNIVERSITY

 National Press Books Palo Alto, California

To Lois, Erica, and Danette

CONTENTS

PREFACE

In the seventies the mass media are more pervasive than ever before, both in the rich countries
of the world and in the poor. The transistor radio
is common deep in Africa, Asia, and Latin America,
and it accompanies our own "tuned in" youth
wherever they go. Communications satellites circle
the globe, and more spectacular technologies are
probably just around the corner. The Age of
Aquarius is a media age.

The last few years have seen a growth of interest
in how the media work, how they affect our daily
lives, and how the public might ensure the fulfillment of the media's staggering potential. In the
United States, critics on both the "left" and the
"right" have expressed alarm over the growing
political impact of television and the press, the
management of news, and the effects of the media
on our quality of life. Perhaps as never before,
mass communication is a public issue, an issue that
demands the fullest understanding of the mass
media industries and their effect on our society. In
selecting material for *Mass Media and Society* I have
kept this need for critical understanding in mind.

This volume is designed to serve as a basic text
for general liberal arts courses in mass communications offered by general social science, sociology,
political science, journalism, and communications
departments in two- and four-year colleges. The
emphasis has therefore been on selecting factual or
controversial essays rather than complicated technical articles whenever possible. Only a minimum
number of overtly scholarly articles and material
published more than five years ago is included. The
remaining selections are primarily recent articles
from magazines written for the layman. For the
communications specialist the book may offer a
convenient source of nontechnical work by media
practitioners and also suggest an approach to the
study of mass media that takes into account
the organizational structure of the media industry.
Communications "insiders," creative artists, and
public service-oriented media personnel of the
future should find in this book much to trouble
them but also much to inspire them.

I would like to acknowledge the encouragement
and guidance of my colleague Thomas Ktsanes in
the crucial formative stage of this volume and the
efforts of my students who helped gauge the value
of this and much discarded material. William Rivers
provided encouragement and valuable criticism.
Finally, I have to thank the authors and publishers
who permitted their work to be re-printed here,
Maryknoll Communications, which allowed me to
use portions of my book, *The Global Metropolis*, in
my introductions, and National Press Books for
judging the volume worthwhile. Of course, the final
selection of material and its setting in this book are
my own responsibility.

MASS MEDIA AND SOCIETY

Introduction

Introduction

Today's mass media—radio, television, and the press—comprise part of modern man's environment. This communications web, which has been aptly called the "noosphere," serves as a background for many of our activities. Like the rest of our environment it is often taken for granted or, alternatively, blamed for all of our ills. This volume attempts to avoid these extremes by taking the media seriously without assuming that everything can be explained by their affects. This does not mean that we want to remain impartial, if impartiality means accepting the mass media as a socially innocuous phenomena. Far from it. I view the operation of the media, especially in the United States, as far from satisfactory, and my selections reflect this. However, I wish to remain critical while avoiding blanket condemnations. Objective criticism requires both the imagination of perceptive journalism and the more disciplined eye of the social scientist.

I agree with Nicholas Johnson, perhaps the most dynamic commissioner to serve on the Federal Communications Commission, that "the wave of renewed interest in the impact of ownership"—and I would add the critical study of mass communication in general—is a healthy sign in our society. He adds:

> All will gain from intelligent inquiry by Congress, the Executive, the regulatory commissions—and especially the academic community, the American People generally, and the media themselves. For, as the Supreme Court has noted, nothing is more important in a free society than "the widest possible dissemination of information from diverse and antagonistic sources." And if we are unwilling to discuss *this* issue fully today, we may find ourselves discussing none that matter very much tomorrow."[1]

I agree. This collection is designed to provide the groundwork for this vitally important public evaluation of mass media at a time that the media themselves have been made, at least temporarily, a major political issue.

Modern mass media are a very contemporary phenomena and are changing rapidly. Today's youth are fully attuned to television, while their parents grew up with radio, and their grandparents may still marvel at the novelty of the broadcast voice. In much of the world, however, this media revolution is taking place in a single generation, and the entire globe may be on the threshold of new media breakthroughs in the age of satellites and advanced electronics. For this reason the study of the media and their impact on society must be constantly updated.

The American public today probably spends more time occupied with the mass media than with any other single activity, including gainful employment, which itself often is accompanied by the sounds of radio. Even college students when they accurately log their media exposure average around six hours of media contact per day, which is more than most spend in the classroom. We know from

[1]Nicholas Johnson, "The Media Barons and the Public Interest," *The Atlantic Monthly*, June, 1968, p. 51.

social psychology that experiences shape character, and that the media must therefore be an integral component in the development of the self. Thus if we are to understand society and the people that comprise it we must grasp the part played by the media.

The book begins with an examination of the media industries in the United States and treats them as complex organizations having their own inner dynamics and interests. It is shown that newspapers, radio, and television, despite their claims that freedom of thought and the public use of the airwaves prevail, are organized and consequently operated as private corporate businesses within the context of the U.S. economy as a whole. The media corporations are interlocked with each other and other corporations. They are seldom autonomous and competing voices; nor is their prime concern the "public interest."

The next two sections deal with the government agencies that regulate the media and the advertising business which supports them. Together these help comprise the dominant commercial media system as it operates in the U.S. today. Regulation, although seen as a major threat by newspapers and broadcasters, has not been particularly harsh, nor has it greatly changed the basic mode of media operation. Because other sources of finance have not been firmly established, the mass media have had to rely almost entirely on advertising revenue. This means that those who desire to promote cultural and educational programming must inevitably compromise their goals, for the prime task of the media is to sell goods to the public. If they fail in this, they cannot survive.

The selections in Part IV outline the basic social psychology of mass communications and their impact on audiences. This includes an outline of the basic communication process, detailed analysis of the flow of information from gatherer to audience, and the impact of media messages on the receiver's opinions and behavior. Part V also deals with the impact of communications but at the mass rather than individual level. The first section considers the ability of the media to shape the overall life styles and consumer preferences of the public. This is followed by the media's propaganda potential, that is, their ability to fashion ideology and shape behavior. Finally, a section is devoted to an examination of the far reaching revolutionary potential of the mass media as proposed by communication's leading guru, H. Marshall McLuhan.

Selections in the final section, Part VI, deal with two public issues in which the media are implicated. The first group of articles is concerned with the media's part in fostering a climate in which crime and violence appear to flourish. Would a different way of using our communication system help produce a more tranquil and just society? The final set of articles are addressed to questions about the changing political impact of the media: If politics becomes just another part of show business, how will our society be affected? The section concludes with an examination of the national debate stimulated by Vice President Spiro Agnew's attacks on partisan reporting and editorializing—two perennial political issues—which he levelled against his media critics.

No single collection of readings, of course, could do justice to the task of examining fully the relation between the mass media and society. The subject is too vast and complex. In the introductions I have included some material not included in the articles. The introductions and the references in the essays should provide leads for continued study and a deeper understanding of the media. The selections, written by outstandingly perceptive and creative men and women, should make readers sensitive to the media which engulf us all. It is hoped that they will become and remain a conscious public, for nothing less will make the press, radio, and television serve the public interest.

THE STRUCTURE OF
MEDIA INDUSTRIES

Part I

INTRODUCTION

A. The Press

The modern newspaper was the first medium of communication with a genuinely mass character.[1] Although some societies have used writing for more than 2000 years, the development of printing had to await the complex technological development of the printing press and the production of uniform paper. Four hundred years more elapsed before social conditions were ready for the daily newspaper. During the American Revolution there was no mass press, only irregular pamphlets for the elites. It was not until the 1830's that the population concentration in cities and the spread of mass literacy provided a market for a mass press.

Once the imaginative newspaper pioneers discovered that with the aid of advertising revenues they could produce a cheap product like the penny press, they found a ready market in the large metropolitan centers. Like the later electronic media, the founders of the press initially enjoyed bonanza conditions while their audience rapidly grew. Their progress was greatly aided by improved city transportation and the development of the telegraph. The latter permitted rapid news-gathering, and collective services utilizing the wire were organized as early as 1848.

By the 1880's the period of easy entry for the would-be newspaper tycoon was over, and the industry entered into a period of intense competition. This period witnessed the spread of "Yellow Journalism," the unprincipled use of sensationalism and gimmickry, as major chains, including Pulitzer and Hearst, battled for supremacy and the small papers for survival. Socially and politically influential reformers responded with threats to regulate the news industry. These warnings were heeded, and the papers adopted a series of self-imposed reforms and set up standards for journalism.

Newspaper circulation out-paced population growth as mass transport improved, literacy became more widespread, and the nation became more urban. But in terms of the number of papers sold per household newspaper circulation reached its peak in 1919. Thereafter, although the total number of papers sold has continued to rise slowly, the decrease in competing papers and competition from other media have produced a slow decline in circulation per household.

The article by R. B. Nixon traces this concentration of newspaper ownership. In recent years the total number of dailies in the United States has declined even though the number of cities being served has continued to rise. Within the cities there is less competition. About 97 per cent of all cities served by daily papers have no truly competitive choice; only a few large cities offer two or more independent dailies. Consolidation has been as much a local affair as a concerted build-up of newspaper empires. It is the result of economies of scale, i.e., the sharing of printing facilities, as well as the imperatives of advertising and the competition from radio and television. It should be noted that this concentration has not led to the develop-

[1]For a good but brief account of the origins and development of the press see Melvin L. DeFleur, *Theories of Mass Communication* (New York: McKay, 2nd ed. 1970). pp. 10–21.

ment of national newspapers with massive circulation, which are common in Europe, although the *New York Times* and the more specialized *Wall Street Journal* both are expanding in this direction. This lack of a national press is probably due less to transportation and technical difficulties than to the decentralized nature of American politics, which, together with the trade of localized advertisers, is often ignored by the more nationally oriented electronic media. But newspaper "groups," as Nixon's figures demonstrate, are again on the rise. Competition is no longer between rival newspapers but between the press and other media.

While the number of dailies has been declining, local weeklies have enjoyed a rapid growth in the suburbs. As D. R. Bowers indicates, this is the result of new offset printing methods and the separation of publishing and printing ownership. Another innovation in the newspaper business, the underground press, is claimed by T. Pepper to follow suburban patterns. These papers are not revolutionary but rather serve the specialized material needs of hippies and radical youth. They employ their own syndicated news services and are profit-making ventures.

The article by Chris Welles deals with the other half of the mass press, the magazine business.[2] In

[2]Other recent accounts of value include John Tebbel, "Magazines—New Changing, Growing," *Saturday Review*, (Feb. 8, 1969), pp. 55–57; *Business Week* (May 2, 1970), pp. 65–74; and *The Public Interest* (Summer, 1970).

1970 there were more than 750 consumer magazines on the market, and new entrants have been added in recent years: sixteen new magazines entered the field in 1968 alone, a year in which the top fifty magazines shared revenues in excess of one billion dollars. The largest are geared to and retain truly mass audiences. *Reader's Digest*, for example, had a circulation of 17.5 million in 1970, a large gain over its mid-1960's volume. *Life*, *Look*, and *Family Circle*, each with circulations of more than seven million, have not grown appreciably during this period. It is the large publication produced for the general public, such as the now defunct *Look* magazine, that has experienced the most difficulty in recent years. Their advertising prices are high—around $40,000 per page—and their revenues from readers, most of whom are subscribers, do not approach actual production costs. Subscribers of *Life*, for example, pay about twelve cents per copy, while its actual production cost is about forty-one cents. Advertisers with mass products have preferred to place their ads on television, which is cheaper and more effective. Smaller and more specialized magazines, however, led by *Playboy* and *Cosmopolitan*, and the hobby organs such as *Skiing* and *Yachting*, are able to "deliver" a concentrated group of consumers. They are therefore a good advertising buy for the non-mass producer, and their revenues reflect this. It seems, then, that magazines will take on a more specialized as opposed to mass character.

Reprinted from Gazette, XIV, no. 3 (1968), pp. 181–93. Used by permission of publisher and author.

Trends in U.S. Newspaper Ownership: Concentration with Competition

RAYMOND B. NIXON

ANYONE trying to understand recent trends in the concentration of ownership among daily newspapers in the United States is confronted by three major paradoxes:

1. Newspapers in 97% of the nation's 1,500 daily cities now enjoy a local "monopoly," and nearly half are owned by some group or national chain, yet competition among the mass media for the reader's time and the advertiser's dollar was never keener.

2. Certain policies of the Federal Government—even including some legal actions directed at local "monopolies"—actually seem to be encouraging still further concentration.

3. Despite the widely publicized deaths of several New York dailies and the economic woes of a few others in large metropolitan centers and very small cities, the newspaper industry as a whole was never more prosperous.

Indeed, a chief difference between concentration in the United States and elsewhere is that a recent spurt in the growth of national chains is not attributed by owners to rising costs and television competition, as it is in so many countries. On the contrary, it is clearly due to the unprecedented prosperity of local "monopoly" papers.

This does not mean that there are no storm signals ahead for the American press—far from it. Ten years ago a veteran Baltimore journalist, Gerald W. Johnson, predicted that unless publishers did a better job of living up to the responsibilities that a position of natural "monopoly" entails, there would be "political interference" with freedom of the press by 1968. The violent and often irrelevant criticisms voiced at recent Congressional hearings on proposed legislation to help "failing newspapers" have convinced some observers that Mr. Johnson's prediction is right on schedule.

Nevertheless, most U.S. publishers for several years have been basking in the glow of record-making profits, which have led in turn to the fabulous sums being offered by chain owners for newspapers in strong "monopoly" situations. When the Thomson organization of England and Canada in December 1967 paid $72,000,000 for a group of 12 small Ohio dailies (the largest financial deal in U.S. newspaper history), a newspaper trade journal remarked editorially: "Now the great American dream . . . is to work hard, buy or start up a paper, and then sell it to Lord Thomson." This may appear true for the moment, but if the British head of the fastest-growing U.S. chain carries out his announced intention of acquiring "at least 100" of the country's 1,749 dailies, there are signs that some of the dreamers may be in for a rude awakening.

THE HISTORICAL BACKGROUND

Ownership concentration is not a new phenomenon in U.S. journalism. Even Benjamin Franklin, who financed printers in going out to start newspapers, had a "chain" of sorts in Colonial days. A merger of two local papers took place as early as 1741, and the 1880 Census revealed the first known case of a morning and an evening paper under single owner-

TRENDS IN U.S. NEWSPAPER OWNERSHIP: CONCENTRATION WITH COMPETITION
Raymond B. Nixon

ship. It also was in 1880 that Edward W. Scripps laid the foundation for the first modern chain, the forerunner of the present Scripps-Howard group. Since that time the process of both local and national concentration has proceeded apace, following in the wake of far more sweeping mergers and consolidations in other forms of business and industry.

To understand the present situation, it is useful to recall the history of the American press in five periods, each identified by a label which seems to characterize the dominant trend for approximately 50 years. The dates are somewhat arbitrary, and the trends are by no means mutually exclusive, but they serve to remind us how much both the newspapers and the country have changed.

The first period (1733–1783) was that of the "fight for freedom." It begins with the founding of the New York *Weekly Journal* by John Peter Zenger, the central figure in the most celebrated free press trial of Colonial days; it ends with the winning of the War for American Independence. During this period a growing number of both newspapers and their readers were fighting for that freedom from external control which was essential before the press could perform its functions in a democracy. The tiny papers of political journalists like Sam Adams and Tom Paine were little more than propaganda leaflets. They did not have to be self-supporting.

From the beginnings of American independence in 1783 to the appearance of the first "penny papers" in 1833 was a period of "political party leadership." During these years such political leaders as Hamilton, Jefferson and Jackson, rather than the editors themselves, usually dictated the policies of official party newspapers. Such papers were subsidized in one way or another; their editors often were rewarded through appointment to nominal political office. Most newspapers were still too feeble to exist on the income from circulation and advertising alone.

Next (1833–1883), with the growth of the popular press, came a period of "personal editorial leadership." By responding to broader social needs and human interests, editors like James Gordon Bennett, Horace Greeley and Henry J. Raymond built up mass circulation for their "penny papers" and became great popular leaders in their own right. The American newspaper proved its ability to survive as an independent, self-supporting enterprise.

The fourth period (1883–1933) thus became one of "business office leadership." The year 1883 is easily remembered as a starting date, for this was when Joseph Pulitzer bought the New York *World*. Much more significant is the fact that this also was the approximate time when newspaper advertising first began to exceed circulation as a source of revenue. The same decade was marked by other momentous events: the beginnings of local combinations and national chains, as noted above, and a new emphasis upon objectivity in reporting, engendered by the telegraphic news agencies. The metropolitan daily was developing into a complex business enterprise, with the need for far greater capital investment and managerial ability than previously. Publishers like Adolph Ochs of the New York *Times* began to overshadow their editors.

While sound business leadership always will be essential to a press free from outside subsidy, it seems to this writer that the dominant trend of the fifth period, beginning with the advent of the "New Deal" in 1933, has been one of "growing social responsibility and inter-media competition." These two related tendencies emerged at this time because of the great depression, the rise of the welfare state with its accompanying economic regulations, and the increasing competition from new media, especially radio. Both tendencies were accelerated by the social, economic, technological and political developments following World War II, when television rapidly saturated the country.

Forced to compete with new media under vastly changed conditions, the U.S. daily newspaper has tended more and more to become a general vehicle of information and opinion designed to serve all groups within its circulation area—not a single

TRENDS IN U.S. NEWSPAPER OWNERSHIP: CONCENTRATION WITH COMPETITION
Raymond B. Nixon

party of faction. This new role has made many publishers and editors more conscious than ever of their broad obligations to the public, if for no other reason than to protect their investment. While one may agree with Gerald W. Johnson as to the need for more social responsibility, he also can point to signs of improvement.

THE GROWTH OF LOCAL "MONOPOLIES"

Table 1 shows the changing pattern of daily newspaper ownership since the 1880's, when the era of the predominantly commercial press began. Total circulation has gone up almost steadily to its present all-time high of 61,500,000, although the rate of growth has slowed down since the 1950's, due

partly to competition from television but also to the fact that there are fewer competing papers to buy. The number of general dailies reached its all-time peak of 2,202 in 1909–10, then declined for 25 years to a low of 1,744 in 1945. Since that time it has varied very little; the total of 1,749 dailies on January 1, 1968, was exactly the same as on January 1, 1946.

Throughout these same years, however, the number of cities with daily papers has continued to rise. It was 1,500 at the beginning of this year, it would be closer to 1,600 if we counted separately all the cities in the clusters served by the 89 "inter-city dailies."

The most significant part of Table I is to be found in the lines showing the emergence of local

TABLE 1

Trends in Ownership of English-Language Dailies of General Circulation and Content in the United States, 1880–1968*

	1880	1909-10	1920	1930	1940	1945	1961	1968
Circulation (thousands)	3,093	22,426	27,791	39,589	41,132	45,955	58,080	61,561
Total Dailies	850	2,202	2,042	1,942	1,878	1,744	1,763	1,749
Total Daily Cities	389	1,207	1,295	1,402	1,426	1,396	1,461	1,500
One-Daily Cities	149	509	716	1,002	1,092	1,107	1,222	1,284
% of Total	38.3	42.2	55.3	71.5	76.6	79.3	83.6	85.6
One-Combination Cities	1	9	27	112	149	161	160	150
Joint-Operation Cities					4	11	18	21
Total Non-Competitive	150	518	743	1,114	1,245	1,279	1,400	1,455
% of Total Cities	38.6	42.9	57.4	79.4	87.3	91.6	95.8	97.0
Cities with Two or More								
Competing Dailies	239	689	552	288	181	117	61	45
	1910	1923	1930	1940	1945	1961	1968	
Number of Groups and Chains	13	31	55	60	76	109	159	
Number of Group Papers	62	153	311	319	368	560	828	
Average Number per Group	4.7	4.9	5.6	5.3	4.8	5.1	5.2	
Number of Inter-City Dailies					20	68	89	

*Sources: Figures from 1945 to 1968 are from *Editor & Publisher International Year Book* for years covered, with minor corrections. Sources for earlier years are given in Raymond B. Nixon, "Trends in Daily Newspaper Ownership since 1945," *Journalism Quarterly*, 31:7 (Winter 1954).

Definitions: A "one-combination" city has a single morning paper and a single evening paper under the same ownership. A "joint-operation" city is one in which a morning and an evening paper combine their production and also usually their business operations, but retain separate ownership and editorial independence. An "inter-city" daily is the dominant local paper in two or more adjacent non-metropolitan cities. A "group" or "chain" consists of two or more papers in different cities under the same majority ownership or control.

TRENDS IN U.S. NEWSPAPER OWNERSHIP: CONCENTRATION WITH COMPETITION
Raymond B. Nixon

newspaper "monopolies." Whereas in 1880 only 38.3% of the daily cities had a single paper, and only one city had a morning-evening combination under single ownership, today the single-daily cities are 85.6% of the total. If the 171 cities with two dailies under a single ownership or in joint operating arrangements are added to the 1,284 single-daily cities, the number with a local "monopoly" (i.e., no locally competing dailies) rises to 1,455 or 97% of the total. In only three of the 45 competitive newspaper cities—New York, Boston and Washington—are there more than two separate daily ownerships.

The fact that locally competing newspapers virtually have disappeared from all except the largest cities has led even a former attorney for the Antitrust Subcommittee of the U.S. Senate to admit that there seems to be an "economic spectrum" which limits the number of papers the country can support, just as there is a physical spectrum which limits the number. of broadcasting stations. The pattern today is clearly for only one daily in cities up to approximately 150,000 population; a morning and an evening paper under single ownership or in joint operating arrangements in cities from 150,000 to 650,000; and two or more competing dailies only in cities of more than 650,000. The size of a community required to support a paper of any given frequency has been going up ever since the depression years.

Figure I is based upon records showing the number of new dailies started and the number of papers merged or suspended since 1930. Whereas there was a net loss of nearly 200 dailies in the depression and war years between 1930 and 1945, the number of losses between 1945 and 1968 was offset exactly by the number of new papers started. Nearly all these new dailies, however, have been in the faster-growing small cities and the suburbs; in fact, there has been no successful new general daily started in any non-suburban city of more than 200,000 population since 1941. Even that paper, the Chicago *Sun*, with a millionaire department-store owner behind it, had to merge with

another daily into the present *Sun-Times* before it became commercially profitable.

Many of the "starts" and "stops" recorded during these years were of weeklies which tried daily publication for a short time, then went back to a weekly basis, merged with another daily, or suspended altogether. Some merged with another paper in a neighbouring town and became part of an "inter-city daily," one which is the dominant local paper in two or more closely adjacent communities which have been "growing together" into a common retail market area.

While this study gives detailed information only for daily newspapers, there also are some 8,000 general newspapers of less than daily frequency in the United States, with a total circulation per issue of approximately 23,000,000. If one omits suburban weeklies and those published in cities which also have dailies, the proportion of "weekly towns" having only a single paper or a single publisher is approximately the same as the proportion of daily cities with a local "monopoly"; in 1959, for example, it was 94.8%. In some of the larger towns there are "twin weeklies"—two papers of different names, published on different days of the week by the same owner—corresponding to the morning-evening combinations in the daily field. Joint printing of several community weeklies or suburban papers in the same plant also has become a common practice.

Wherever feasible, both dailies and weeklies under a single ownership or joint operating arrangement tend to sell advertising in combination. This usually results in savings for the advertiser as well as in added profits for the publisher, since the same ad composition can be carried over from one paper to the other. In the 1950's the Antitrust Division of the Department of Justice tried to stop the use of the "forced combination" rate, but the U.S. Supreme Court held that the rate is not illegal unless there is clear evidence of monopolistic or predatory practices.

Underlying the trend toward local concentration in all countries, as the British Royal Commission on the Press has pointed out, is the basic principle of

TRENDS IN U.S. NEWSPAPER OWNERSHIP: CONCENTRATION WITH COMPETITION
Raymond B. Nixon

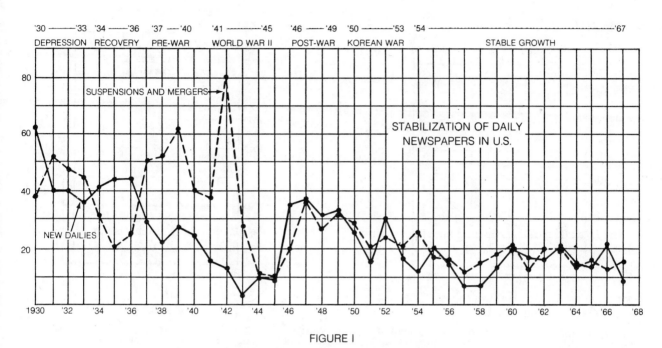

FIGURE I

Sources: Records of American Newspaper Publishers Association

the economy of large-scale operation. Once a newspaper is set into type and the plates are put on the press, the cost of production per copy goes down as circulation goes up. Thus, the newspaper or combination with a large circulation can provide better services and attract still more readers, while the paper with a smaller circulation finds itself in increasing difficulties. For this reason, most U.S. advertisers have come to prefer a single paper or a single-publisher combination, unless the city is large enough to support two distinctly different types of dailies, such as New York's *Times* and *Daily News*. Recent history also indicates that most American readers now prefer an "omnibus" paper, with a larger volume of news, features and advertising, to several smaller papers. A majority of the reading public, apparently, no longer expects nor wishes its local paper to take the initiative in political affairs.

The rise of inter-media competition. The prevalence of local newspaper "monopolies" would present a dismal picture, indeed, if newspapers in the United States were primarily political, or if broadcasting were a government monopoly, as it is in many other countries. But in a country where both the print and the broadcast media must depend upon the same audience and the same advertisers for support, one should look at competition among all the media.

Figures 2 and 3 show how the picture of local concentration and competition changes completely when independent radio and television stations are considered along with newspapers in the 1,500 daily cities. For while only 45 of these cities now have commercially competing local dailies, there are 1,298 daily cities with a total of 4,879 competing "media voices." By a "media voice" is meant any separate ownership of two or more newspapers or radio and television facilities, or any combination of

TRENDS IN U.S. NEWSPAPER OWNERSHIP: CONCENTRATION WITH COMPETITION
Raymond B. Nixon

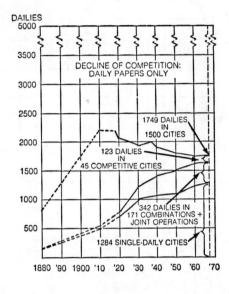

FIGURE 2

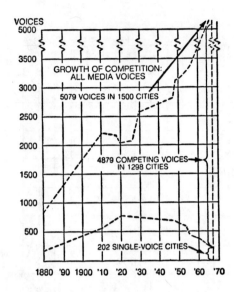

FIGURE 3

The sources on newspapers are the same for both figures as for Table I. In Figure 3, the numbers of independent radio and television stations from *Broadcasting Yearbook* are added to numbers of separate daily newspaper ownerships to obtain the total number of media voices as defined in the article.

these media. The emphasis thus is upon the number of separate owners in the field of local mass communication, rather than upon the number of newspapers or broadcasting stations alone.

The extent of inter-media competition is far greater than that indicated by these two charts. For one thing, most of the 202 "single-voice" cities shown by Figure 3 are suburban municipalities so close to a large central city that the absence of any "local" competition is completely meaningless. Many of these cities also have a weekly paper in competition with the single local daily or daily-broadcast combination. But in addition to the 1,500 daily newspaper cities represented by these graphs, there are 1,447 other U.S. communities that have a local radio or television station on the air daily. In other words, the total number of U.S. cities and towns with daily mass communication service at the local level is not 1,500, but 2,947. Obviously, inter-media competition has taken the place of inter-newspaper

competition alone. Likewise, the spread of radio and television has slowed down the establishment of newspapers, both dailies and weeklies.

While many broadcasting stations compete more in selling advertising than they do in bringing news and opinion to the public, most U.S. radio and television stations do subscribe to a telegraphic wire service and put the latest bulletins and news summaries on the air. Even this much news serves as a sword of Damocles over the head of any "monopoly" publisher who might be tempted to suppress or to distort news received from the same agency. The broadcasting of important political events and speeches undoubtedly has provided the public with a better check on the accuracy of the print media than was possible in an earlier era of more numerous but violently partisan newspapers. When the local weeklies, national news magazines and many new types of specialized publications also are brought into the picture, it is clear that Americans have access to a larger and more diversified volume of mass communication than ever before.

But why, it may be asked, has competition from the new media not brought financial distress to the American newspaper, as it apparently has to newspapers in so many other parts of the world? While the period of uninterrupted prosperity enjoyed by the country as a whole since 1960 is, of course, the underlying basic factor, there are three other differences between American newspapers and those elsewhere which must be taken into consideration.

First, radio and television in the United States, except for a relatively few educational stations, are privately owned and have been commercial competitors of newspapers from the beginnings of broadcasting. Thus, American papers have had longer to adjust their content and techniques to the new competition than have papers in those countries where advertising on the air is a more recent innovation, or perhaps still only a threat. (A newspaper or any other firm is restricted by government policy in the number of radio or TV stations it may own.)

Second, most American newspapers had become politically independent even before commercial radio became a serious competitor. Even in the 1920's a majority of the papers already had discarded their party labels, although it cannot be denied that their business-minded owners and publishers still tend normally to support the candidate of the more conservative party. But U.S. political parties no longer start or subsidize newspapers; they hire a public relations agency and utilize all the available mass media. As newspapers have become more objective in reporting the news, and fairer in presenting both sides of controversial issues, the need for a multiplicity of papers has tended to disappear, so far as the general public is concerned.

Third, the vast geographical area of the United States, with its wide diversity of regional interests and problems, has led to the development of newspapers that are primarily *local* in character. There are no really "national" U.S. dailies except the *Wall Street Journal* and the *Christian Science Monitor*, both

of which are highly specialized in their appeal. Consequently, while the local paper certainly cannot "monopolize" either news or advertising, it does have what economists call an "isolated market" or a "natural monopoly" for certain types of local information. No matter how much news, comment, entertainment and advertising of a general nature may be available over radio and television and in national publications, the reader still must turn to a local paper for detailed information about the place where he lives and works. Since more and more Americans now work in a central city but live in a suburban community, this gives both the large-city daily and the suburban daily or weekly distinctive functions to perform. Thus, the various media seem to supplement and complement each other even more than they compete.

Effect upon groups and chains. It is the success of local "monopoly" newspapers that has led to the recent upsurge in the growth of the newspaper "groups." And since starting a new newspaper in even a medium-sized city these days requires far more investment and risk than starting a new radio or television station, the single surviving paper or combination of papers in an economically sound community has come to have far greater value. A few years ago the value of a successful daily in a "monopoly" city usually was estimated at approximately $100 multiplied by the daily circulation, as against $30 multiplied by the circulation for a competitive daily. But the Thomson group broke all records in 1967 when it paid approximately $200 times their daily circulation for the 12 Brush-Moore dailies, all of which are "monopoly" papers.

While concentration of ownership has been increasing for many years, the tendency down to the late 1950's was upon local consolidations and the formation of small regional groups, with the principal owner living in close proximity to his papers. But by the 1960's, as Table 1 shows, the process of local concentration was virtually complete, and owners with funds to invest had to look farther afield. The recent tendency toward larger national

TRENDS IN U.S. NEWSPAPER OWNERSHIP: CONCENTRATION WITH COMPETITION

Raymond B. Nixon

chains may be intensified even more by the 1968 decision of the Supreme Court in an antitrust suit against the Los Angeles *Times*, forcing that firm to sell its morning-evening-Sunday combination in nearby San Bernardino.

Expansion is encouraged by policies of the Internal Revenue Service and decisions of the Tax Courts, which make it advantageous for business concerns to invest "accumulated earnings" in related enterprises, rather than to build up larger surpluses or to pay extra dividends. Some groups owned by a large number of heirs, like Brush-Moore, also have found it advantageous to sell to another newspaper organization through a tax-free exchange of stock, rather than in a cash transaction. All this is in addition to the fact that a successful newspaper chain has more "know-how" than an individual owner or newcomer to the field.

For these and other reasons, the total number of U.S. daily groups and chains has grown from a total of 13 with 62 papers in 1910 to 159 with 828 papers in May of 1968. The average size of groups, which declined during the 1940's, then remained fairly constant in the 1950's, also has started to climb. As shown by Table 1, it is now 5.2, as compared with 4.8 in 1945. (Data on the principal U.S. groups will be found in Table 2.)

In number of individual dailies, such relatively new groups as the Thomson U.S. chain (36 dailies), Gannett Newspapers (29), the Scripps League (28), Newhouse Newspapers (23) and Donrey Media (22) have pushed older and better known chains like Scripps-Howard (now only 17 dailies) and Hearst (now down to 8) out of the "top five." In both daily and seven-day circulation, however, the leader is still the Chicago *Tribune* group, which is confined to seven dailies in only three states, with the New York *Daily News* providing more than half total group circulation of 3,620,520. On a circulation basis, the other groups in the first five today are Newhouse, second; Scripps-Howard, third; Hearst, fourth; and Knight Newspapers, fifth.

Group and chain newspapers now control approximately 58% of the total daily circulation, 63% on

Sundays. But it should be noted that even the largest U.S. group today holds only 6% of the total daily circulation and 10% Sunday, as compared with the 13.6% daily and 24.2% Sunday of the Hearst chain at its height in 1935. The 36 papers of Thomson's U.S. chain, although they are the most numerous, have a total circulation of only 708,228, or a little more than 1% of the total for the country as a whole. No single U.S. group has ever held anything like the proportion of national circulation controlled by the larger chains in England, or by the Axel Springer organization in Germany.

When the writer made his first study of newspaper concentration in 1945, the decline of the older national chains led him to advance the hypothesis that there is a point in size—in the United States, at least—at which the economic advantages of group operation fail to compensate for the traditional opposition of Americans to absentee ownership. If the rapid growth of new groups like Thomson and Newhouse appears to indicate today that this principle no longer applies, it should be noted that all large U.S. chains now operate on the basis of giving the local publisher and editor almost complete autonomy, especially in matters of local editorial policy. It still seems quite probable to this writer that any absentee owner who tried to dictate local policy from afar, without regard to community needs and wishes, would encounter opposition that might lead to the kind of "political interference" that Gerald W. Johnson envisaged.

Only by continuing to perform a vital function for its readers and advertisers can any self-supporting newspaper—independent or chain-owned, competitive or "monopoly"—hope to prosper. If the relative calm that has accompanied the recent expansion of national chains means that U.S. citizens now accept their group-owned papers as responsible members of the local community, then we can expect the chains to expand even further. On the other hand, if the lack of more widespread opposition to local "monopolies" and chain ownership indicates that the U.S. public has come to look

TRENDS IN U.S. NEWSPAPER OWNERSHIP: CONCENTRATION WITH COMPETITION

Raymond B. Nixon

TABLE 2

Daily Newspaper Groups with 7-Day Circulation of One Million or More*

Name of Group	No. of Dailies	Weekday Circulation	Sunday Papers	Sunday Circulation	7-Day Circulation
1. Chicago Tribune Newspapers	7	3,627,916	5	4,959,453	26,337,375
2. Newhouse Newspapers	23	3,190,180	14	3,391,495	22,455,248
3. Scripps-Howard Newspapers (E. W. Scripps Co.)	17	2,504,466	7	1,841,753	16,788,344
4. Hearst Newspapers	8	2,080,647	7	2,712,635	14,850,223
5. Knight Newspapers	7	1,390,117	6	1,508,523	9,847,865
6. Gannett Newspapers	29	1,290,710	8	611,558	8,289,612
7. Cowles Newspapers	11	1,108,637	7	1,342,057	7,993,868
8. Ridder Publications	16	1,143,847	10	1,128,047	7,941,820
9. Times Mirror Company	3	964,702	2	1,222,059	7,006,908
10. Ochs Estate Newspapers	3	914,576	2	1,559,383	6,890,803
11. Field Enterprises, Inc.	4	1,015,071	1	717,814	6,794,942
12. James M. Cox Newspapers	7	861,403	3	780,564	5,941,637
13. Central Newspapers (Pulliam)	7	742,400	4	658,034	5,112,434
14. Robert McLean Newspapers	2	709,137	2	767,912	4,931,897
15. Thomson Newspapers	36	708,228	13	350,302	4,546,290
16. Kansas City Star Company	4	674,916	2	406,652	4,443,601
17. Copley Press	17	639,813	6	503,677	4,339,353
18. Harte-Hanks Newspapers	15	426,832	10	355,586	3,774,496
19. Booth Newspapers	9	534,373	6	434,350	3,640,588
20. Richmond Newspapers (Bryan)	4	471,741	2	379,934	3,210,380
21. Block Newspapers	5	501,963	1	183,093	3,183,073
22. Lee Newspapers	15	403,242	8	349,077	2,746,491
23. McClatchy Newspapers	3	337,993	3	395,924	2,433,882
24. Freedom Newspapers (Hoiles)	15	349,263	10	313,053	2,340,099
25. Federated Publications	9	281,296	6	237,681	1,925,457
26. Ingersoll Newspapers	8	284,936			1,705,648
27. Donrey Media Group (Reynolds)	22	240,937	20	237,141	1,590,080
28. Worrell Newspapers**	16	231,487	8	179,229	1,577,898
29. Perry Publications	15	243,756	9	189,597	1,572,712
30. Southern Newspapers (Walls)**	19	244,956	10	180,735	1,565,572
31. Scripps League Newspapers	28	241,355	8	95,289	1,552,519
32. Stauffer Publications	13	224,079	5	131,147	1,464,234
33. Speidel Newspapers	10	218,075	4	135,459	1,434,058
34. Ottaway Newspapers	8	206,524	2	76,608	1,315,752
35. Ogden Newspapers	9	167,970	2	91,870	1,000,083

*Seven-day circulation is the sum of the average number of copies sold on each weekday that the papers in the group are published, plus the circulation on Sunday if the paper has a Sunday edition.

**Worrell Newspapers and Southern Newspapers are joint owners of nine dailies and five Sunday papers. If the aggregate circulation for these papers is divided between the two groups, each group falls slightly below a million in seven-day circulation.

TRENDS IN U.S. NEWSPAPER OWNERSHIP: CONCENTRATION WITH COMPETITION
Raymond B. Nixon

upon newspapers as simply another form of commercial enterprise, and not an essential quasi-public institution, then new types of economic regulation may be expected. Indeed, the next period in the history of the U.S. press may be one of "increasing economic restrictions," and it may come well before 1983.

Reprinted from Journalism Quarterly *(Spring, 1969), pp. 43–46, 52. Used by permission of publisher and author.*

The Impact of Centralized Printing on the Community Press

DAVID R. BOWERS

THE tremendous growth of centralized printing and its effect on weekly newspapers, sometimes called the last bastion of a truly free and independent press,[1] has developed with little notice except by persons involved in it. Yet, it could be significant to communications in a mass society, especially at the grass roots level.

One important result of this phenomenon is that it permits someone with comparatively little capital to start a newspaper. "Perhaps," as a convention speaker declared, "newspapering has gone full circle from the fellow who came into town with a shirt tail full of type and a Washington hand press in years gone by to today's hotshot salesman with an IBM typewriter."

Community newspapers—and shoppers, many of which carry some news to increase reader traffic—are springing up over the country in heavily-populated urban neighborhoods, thriving suburban districts and mushrooming rural areas, founded by publishers who have less than $4,000 capital and in some cases less than $1,000.

Other discernible effects are:

The salvaging of marginal newspapers for many communities that otherwise would lose their only newspaper.

Encouragement of group or chain operation by enabling a central printing plant owner—or in some cases the owner of the paper without a plant—to start other newspapers.

Occasional cannibalization of newspapers by the central printing plant.

Increased competition in what were formerly one-newspaper communities.

Background for these developments has been the tremendous growth of photolithographic printing—popularly called "offset" and sometimes referred to as "cold type"—since World War II. Reason for the popularity is lower production costs. Expensive typesetting machines can be replaced by lower cost VariTypers or Justowriters or even electric typewriters, and quickly-trained, low-cost help can be hired to use these simplified keyboard machines.

A by-product is the printing of other newspapers or shoppers by an owner of photo-offset equipment. A reduction in his own costs plus generally speedier production of his own newspaper allow him to consider printing other publications. Theodore Peterson reported that by 1964 there were 1,100 plants printing two or more daily or weekly newspapers, totaling 2,900 newspapers,[2] and the trade press has reported additional ones in succeeding years. A survey conducted in 1968 by Fairchild Graphic Equipment indicated that 84% of newspaper and commercial printing plants using web offset presses manufactured by the company are printing other publications "on contract."[3]

The lower costs of photo-offset encourage the publisher of a new newspaper—and many existing papers—to seek production at the central plant rather than to tie up capital in expensive equipment. Omission of a press and other bulky equipment calls for less production space, resulting in

THE IMPACT OF CENTRALIZED PRINTING ON THE COMMUNITY PRESS
David R. Bowers

lower taxes (or rent) and upkeep.

It also permits the publisher of a weekly to bring his material to the central plant in either of two stages: camera-ready, where he or his staff produces the composition and makes the page paste-ups and the central printing plant has merely to make the plates and run them; or in rough form where the central plant does both composition and printing at relatively little cost.

Let us examine the effects previously mentioned. ► 1) *Newspapers — or shoppers — have become easier to start or acquire with comparatively little capital.*

Duane Dunham came out of military service in 1956 with $3,600 and established the Oak Creek (Wis.) *Pictorial*. Its ABC circulation today is 4,600 and its gross, $350,000.[4]

David D. Enersen started the McFarland (Wis.) *Community Life* in suburban Madison in 1966 with $500 capital plus an old IBM typewriter and a leased Filmotype to do his composition. Weekly income rose from $400 to $500 at the beginning to $1,200 to $1,300 in two years and continues to rise. Initially, Enersen and his wife operated the business on a part-time basis. The corporation now employs seven full-time and five part-time employees, is capitalized at $50,000.[5]

Dave McReynolds and two partners bought half-interest in the Stratford (Tex.) *Star* for $2,000 in 1962. He later acquired the entire property. This is in a rural area in the Panhandle in which irrigation has contributed to economic growth. A gross of $22,500 by the previous owner has been doubled in six years.[6]

Ned Curran talked a friend in 1966 into lending him the down payment for the Vienna (Va.) *Advertiser*, a shopper which a printer in poor health wanted to sell. He has increased circulation to 5,000 in this prosperous Washington suburb of 16,000.[7]

James A. Pratt bought the *Boone County Shopper* in Belvidere, Ill., in 1946 when it was six months old and ready to fold for $1,500. By 1961 he took in a full partner to help run the business, which now has an additional five full-time and four part-time employees.[8]

Paul A. Muse, editor-manager of the *Potomac News*, Dumfries, Va., reports his newspaper was started ten years ago with little capital and was printed elsewhere. It since has been reorganized into an operation of much larger scale and required a substantial capital commitment.[9]

All of these persons stress — and their comments are supported by central printing plant publishers — that endless hours of hard work by the owner, and frequently his wife, went into the success of these papers.

Louis A. Lerner, executive vice president of the Lerner Home Newspapers with headquarters in Chicago, asserts, "There is no question that today it is much simpler and easier to start a new newspaper without a great deal of capital at the front end for machinery and equipment. I think that this is a part of the newspaper revolution which is taking place."[10]

► 2) *A number of marginal newspapers have been salvaged for communities that otherwise would lose their only newspaper.*

Marion R. Krehbiel, Norton, Kan., dean of the nation's brokers in weekly and small daily newspapers, maintains "central offset has been and will be the salvation for a lot of 500 population towns that might otherwise lose their newspapers."[11]

Rigby Owen, owner of the Conroe (Tex.) *Courier*, which prints some 20 publications at its central offset plant, agrees that "the central plant is the answer for small town newspapers."[12]

Walter V. McKinney, third generation publisher of the 8,859-circulation semi-weekly Hillsboro (Ore.) *Argus*, adds that "The economy is forcing small newspapers to move toward the centralized printing plant."[13]

Carl A. Zielke, manager, Wisconsin Press Assn., reports that an elderly couple bought the Deerfield *Independent* and is running it out of loyalty to the community with the help of a central plant.[14]

In an article in *Quill* in 1963, Noel Duerden pointed out that with a central plant a weekly has better chance for survival because a publisher can concentrate on editing and business management to produce a better and more profitable newspaper. "Weeklies aren't Weaklies, anymore," he says.[15]

►3) *Group or chain operation of weekly newspapers is encouraged by enabling a central printing plant owner— or in some cases, the owner of the paper without a plant— to start other newspapers.*

Dunham of Oak Creek, Wis., mentioned earlier, started the Greendale *Village Life* and the Greenfield *Observer* in 1960. He has since added the *Tri-Town Hub* for Franklin-Hales Corners, *South Town Shopping Guide*, and Muskego Lakeland *News*.[16]

Enersen, of McFarland, Wis., started the Monona *Community Herald* in August, 1968, in a neighboring community.[17]

The previously-mentioned Conroe *Courier* management started papers in neighboring Huntsville and Cleveland, Tex.[18]

Robert G. Swan, owner of the Milwaukie (Ore.) *Review*, started the Gladstone (Ore.) *Review* in 1965.[19]

Typical of the growth in the large groups of weeklies is the Lerner Home Newspapers in Chicago. Lerner reports that in 1963 his operation had 23 newspapers. By September of 1968, it had 43 newspapers, covering a much wider area.[20]

Sun Newspapers in suburban Minneapolis and St. Paul publish 26 weekly newspapers.

Hicks-Deal Publications (nine) and Rogers-McDonald News Advertiser Group (seven) are central printing firms in the Los Angeles area which publish weekly newspapers. Perry Publications of West Palm Beach, Fla., publish both dailies and weeklies.

It should be noted that not all of these central printing plants are offset, although most are.

►4) *Occasional cannibalization of newspapers by the central printing plant.*

By its nature of printing newspapers for others, the central printing plant is in a position to absorb these publications when they come up for sale—or cannot pay their bills, in some cases.

One publisher, who must remain anonymous, quite frankly says he hopes to add papers which cannot pay their bills because he feels their failure is caused by their inefficient operation. He feels he

can make a number of them succeed through sound business methods.

Another publisher, who likewise will remain anonymous, reports that he bought a shopper in a neighboring community and eventually bought the town's newspaper and merged the two.

►5) *Increased competition in what were formerly one-newspaper communities.*

Press critics have cried out against diminishing competition and the resulting one-newspaper towns, as they are sometimes termed, as the phenomenon has grown since World War I. Central printing plants have made more feasible both competition in previous one-newspaper towns and the existence of competition in newly-developed areas.

Pratt, co-owner of the previously-mentioned *Boone County Shopper* in Belvidere, Ill., states frankly that "Our shopper was started to compete with a daily newspaper." Now in its 21st year of publication, the shopper has been accepted readily by the community, according to Pratt, because of dislike in certain quarters for the management of the daily.[21]

In far south Texas, Sam W. Burns competes against the local daily with his Harlingen *Press*, an offset weekly with supplementary shopper printed in an outside plant. Burns also started the Kenedy *Times* against the existing weekly in this south central Texas community of 4,301 in 1960.

Owen and his associates, of Conroe, Tex., started the Huntsville *Pictorial* which competed for some years against the existing weekly Huntsville *Item* in east Texas. Huntsville is a state college town of nearly 12,000.

In Vienna, Va., Curran notes he is competing against two area weeklies (also offset) as well as the three Washington dailies, a northern Virginia daily, and an aggressive area radio station.

While such competition can be healthy, it should be noted that it can also be arduous and frequently financially risky.

Edward M. Bauer Jr., publisher of the Half Moon Bay (Calif.) *Review*, reports that in 1964 a man and wife opposed his weekly with "one IBM typewriter and a contract with a central plant in

THE IMPACT OF CENTRALIZED PRINTING ON THE COMMUNITY PRESS
David R. Bowers

South San Francisco." The second paper failed after two years and Bauer estimates their losses in cash and time in the area of $28,000.[22]

Owen reports he and his associates had a total of $25,000 in his Huntsville venture over a period of six years before they got it on a paying basis.[23]

McReynolds reports that in the Texas Panhandle, offset papers and shoppers "come and go like weeds."[24]

Lloyd R. Pflederer, president of the Tazewell Publishing Co., a central plant in Morton, Ill., sees increasing costs, even in offset operation, playing a role in years to come. Five years ago, he says, he would have been enthusiastic about the possibilities but now "I am not at all enthused about the future of the small newspaper, and it being able to produce enough income to satisfy the requirements of a publisher in the present cost-of-living spiral."[25]

SUMMARY

▶ A researcher into this problem should be prepared to cope with some of the more obvious handicaps, particularly that of non-response from publishers of new newspapers. They are so busy trying to make their publications succeed editorially and financially, as well as trying to establish themselves personally in the community, that they have little time or inclination to answer queries.

It can be concluded that it is easier to start a weekly newspaper today because of the central printing plant. However, most respondents were of the opinion that the key to success is to find a community with potential growth in need of such a publication.

A number of respondents suggested that it might be better to take over an existing publication rather than go through the headaches of starting an enterprise. Larry Miller, general manager of the Kansas Press Assn., notes that Kansas laws prohibit a newspaper from obtaining legal advertisements until it has been in existence five years.[26]

Results of this study should counter claims that prohibitive costs today preclude all but the wealthy from publishing, which press critics feel is a severe blow to American democracy. This may be true in the daily newspaper field, but no longer applies to the weekly press.

Perhaps more significant, from the viewpoint of media economics and communication in a modern society, are two conflicting trends: The central printing plant encourages growth of group or chain ownership. On the other hand, it encourages the establishment of new newspapers in developing communities and increases competition in formerly one newspaper communities. These trends should be increasingly examined for their effects on grass roots communication.

[1]Bryce W. Rucker, *The First Freedom* (Carbondale, Ill.: Southern Illinois Press, 1968), p. 229.

[2]Address before the annual convention of the American Association of Agricultural College Editors, Athens, Ga., July 14, 1966, as reported in Rucker, *The First Freedom*, p. 33.

[3]*Editor & Publisher*, Nov. 9, 1968, p. 50.

[4]Duane Dunham (personal communication).

[5]David D. Enersen (personal communication).

[6]Dave McReynolds (personal communication).

[7]Ned Curran (personal communication).

[8]James A. Pratt (personal communication).

[9]Paul A. Muse (personal communication).

[10]Louis A. Lerner (personal communication).

[11]Marion R. Krehbiel (personal communication).

[12]Rigby Owen (personal communication).

[13]*Publishers' Auxiliary*, June 1, 1968, p. 16.

[14]Carl A. Zielke (personal communication).

[15]Noel Duerden, "Offset Revolution Takes Editor Out of Backshop," *The Quill*, September 1963, p. 16.

[16]Dunham, *op. cit.*

[17]Enersen, *op. cit.*

[18]Owen, *op. cit.*

[19]Walter V. McKinney, general manager, Hillsboro (Ore.) *Argus* (personal communication).

[20]Lerner, *op. cit.*

[21]Pratt, *op. cit.*

[22]Edward M. Bauer Jr. (personal communication).

[23]Owen, *op. cit.*

[24]McReynolds, *op. cit.*

[25]Lloyd R. Pflederer (personal communication).

[26]Larry Miller (personal communication).

Reprinted from The Nation *(April 29, 1968), pp. 569–72. Used by permission of publisher.*

The Underground Press: Growing Rich on the Hippie

THOMAS PEPPER

THE underground press has come of age. It is no longer underground and it isn't much of a press, but it does have fanfare—lots of it. In issue after issue in different cities around the country, underground editors proclaim that what they represent is the wave of the future, and that the future will be significantly better because of what they represent. As Allan Katzman, an editor of New York's *East Village Other*, told a correspondent for the ("establishment") *San Francisco Chronicle*, "America now finds itself split into two camps, two life cycles. A cultural evolution is taking place that will sweep the grey-haired masters into the garbage heap. Wisdom and time are on the side of youth." In similar vein, when *Open City* of Los Angeles announced a "national" edition last September, it explained in an editorial: "We feel that it is time that each of the groups now in revolt against an increasingly monolithic social system learns that it has much more in common with the other groups than it previously knew. Perhaps this way the separate, isolated rebellions which the Establishment finds comparatively easy to put down could be joined into one truly effective social and political uprising."

This self-generated excitement was made semiofficial last month when *Newsweek* and *The Wall Street Journal* ran survey stories. Both reported increasing circulation and increasing financial success for underground papers, and both elicited the customary hyperbolic quotes from the subjects of any such feature stories. Peter Werbe, coeditor of Detroit's *The Fifth Estate*, assured *Newsweek* readers that success would not spoil the underground press.

"I still view it as the first step in the guerrilla movement," the 27-year-old Werbe allowed. "Here we can begin to question the legitimacy of the System." Another underground editor, Marvin Garson, predicted: "It's going to get bigger all the time. There are going to be more and more papers that will give people coverage they're not getting—and will never get—from the daily papers."

Adding substance to such predictions is the appearance of at least two underground news agencies, roughly comparable to the Associated Press and United Press International of the regular world. One, the Underground Press Syndicate (UPS), is a kind of cooperative that permits some sixty papers to reprint one another's stories with a credit line attached. The other, Liberation News Service (LNS), sells its news articles, reviews and essays to subscribers for $180 a year. Based in Washington, LNS has recently advanced beyond the mails and introduced teletype machines.

Estimates of the number of underground papers and readers vary widely. *The Wall Street Journal* counted "more than 50," *Newsweek* "more than 150"; Marshall Bloom, an LNS executive, told *The New York Times* that nearly 200 underground papers had begun publication in the last two years. On the other hand, Bloom told *The Nation* that LNS services some 280 publications, of which 125 were "underground" in a general sense, some eighty were "peace" papers, and the rest were college papers not controlled by an administration. Readership estimates vary from 333,000 (by *The Wall Street Journal*) to 4.6 million (by Bloom). Right now, with

THE UNDERGROUND PRESS: GROWING RICH ON THE HIPPIE

Thomas Pepper

the whole underground movement in flux, no figure could be accurate for long.

What do these papers print, and what needs do they fulfill? Are they what they say they are? And are they affecting anyone, particularly their declared enemies, the established press and in turn established society?

In a real sense, the underground papers have brought home to everyone the fact that regular metropolitan dailies do not communicate with subcultures—those small, identifiable groups who remain interested in affairs too local even for a city paper. Instead, the metropolitan papers write for a mass audience, which to them means a middle-class audience, or at least an audience that is presumed to have middle-class mores. When big-city dailies do single out small, identifiable groups, they are careful not to upset existing social rankings. Whether in gossip columns, food recipes, features stories, or in the moral tone of editorials, local "out groups" have learned not to expect much from their city desks. There are exceptions but, as often as not, attempts to include such "out groups" are artificial, as in the "zone" editions that alter a few pages, or superficial, as in the coverage of sacraments like obituaries and high school sports.

The callousness of standardized news coverage has long been apparent to its victims—such groups as Bible Belt Southerners (who are pre-middle class), poor Negroes and unassimilated, ethnic white Northerners. Hence the vitality of ethnic radio stations which publicize the stories, the events, the songs and the concerns of America's subcultures, and which counterbalance the mass appeal of big papers by an exclusive appeal to special interests. The suburban newspapers—including all their drivel—fulfill an identical need for yet another subculture. By its success, the underground press has brought all these facts into the open, to a point where "intellectuals" are now aware of them, and to a point where an ordinary, predictable communications gap is transformed into big news—or as some people put it, into a sign of "sickness" in American society.

One should give credit where credit is due: By making both a financial and a cultural hit with their appeal to a rich and identifiable market, the underground papers have awakened virtually all concerned to a real deficiency in American newspaper journalism. But that is about all the underground press has done. It has certainly not improved the quality of journalism.

Indeed, the underground press has become a kind of suburban press all its own—a suburban press for the hippie and dropout set. The three basic commodities in today's underground newspaper—the advertising, the calendar of events and the artistic and political commentary—all have a parallel in the suburban press. Because the mores of the two audiences are different, the content of the ads, the calendars and the commentaries is different too; in the underground papers, the ads are vulgar, the calendars refer to love-ins rather than Little League, and the commentaries are critical and left wing rather than laudatory and conservative. But the difference between the underground and the suburban press is entirely one of content. The functions of both—to entertain and reinforce their audience—are the same. Suburban and underground editors give virtually the same justification for one-sided, sometimes polemical journalism—that the overwhelming influence of big-city dailies must be countered, and can be countered only if other voices are heard alone, crying in the wilderness with all their purity. Underground papers, like their suburban cousins, give readers what they want to read; they are a great new business, and far from representing a fundamental critique of American society, are actually full-fledged participants in it.

The formula for success in the journalistic underground was invented by *The Village Voice*, a tabloid with offices in Greenwich Village. Started in 1955, the *Voice* didn't turn a profit, according to a *Wall Street Journal* story, until 1963. Today, profit figures are withheld—probably because they are so large. Even before 1963, the secret to whatever appeal the *Voice* had was its technique of always outdoing the rest of the New York press: It stood to the left of the regular press politically, and to the imaginative side artistically. These were not difficult tasks, and there was an eager audience in those New Yorkers who—from a sense of duty or from a vested interest—feel permanently and gnawingly dissatisfied with American public life. With the demise of the New York *Herald Tribune*, the *Voice* has found it even easier to attract local readers who search for alternatives to reading only *The New York Times*. The *Voice*, a weekly, does not run news as such. It has sections devoted to reviews of music, movies, theatre, books and the press, and it regularly carries as filler material announcements that don't make the regular papers. In a typical issue, the *Voice* will run three or four long, personal, sometimes narcissistic commentaries on recent social or political events, with considerable emphasis on the abstract issues or moral principles thought to be relevant, and very little on the technical or bureaucratic aspects of fitting means to ends. The *Voice* prints a prodigious quantity of advertising, including retail shops, entertainment, books, off-beat fashions and classifieds. For the audience involved, the ads are informative and useful; they unquestionably pull well for the advertisers. Apart from everything else, the *Voice* is chic, as essential a piece of equipment to some New Yorkers as the *Trib* used to be to others.

The *Voice's* formula—always feed the reader something that outdoes the regular, local press—has now been copied throughout the country. The content may have changed—the *Voice* now seems conservative by comparison with some of the later entrants to the field—but the process and the significance remain the same. Like their innovative "enemies" in the business world, their avowed "enemies" in the established press, and their dominant ancestor, *The Village Voice*, today's underground papers are meeting previously latent consumer needs, catering uncritically to the tastes of their consumers, and prospering from a shrewd analysis of the contemporary leisure-time market. The Berkeley *Barb*, the *East Village Other*, and the Los Angeles *Free Press* led the way in classified ads, for example, by opening their columns to advertisers soliciting sex partners, nude models and drugs. The demand for similar papers has snowballed. In every case, the local appeal of ads and calendars is mixed with the national appeal of underground revolt. Helped along by low operating costs, permissive court decisions on pornography, and the fortunate coincidence that today's social rebels happen to be sons and daughters of relatively wealthy parents, the underground papers have flourished by making themselves useful to a select group of advertisers.

Local conditions do produce some substantive differences. In Los Angeles, a relatively new paper, the *Underground*, has attacked the *Free Press* for making an "'in' thing of sick sex and drugs." In North Carolina, the *Anvil* shuns vulgarity and tries, in a somewhat tortured way, to present serious political and economic analysis. But because of the overwhelming sameness in most underground papers, the best of them all probably wouldn't qualify as "underground" today. It is the Pittsburgh *Point*, a well-produced weekly, whose response to the modern world is more than an outraged scream. Its political reporting, while reflecting concern about war, race and moral principles, is also strikingly detached. In covering a conference on organizing the poor, for example, the *Point* managed to take some shots at the participants without feeling obliged to disagree with their overall aims. In other words, the *Point* noticed a nuance or two that its more frenzied counterparts could hardly afford to describe. After quoting speaker Nicholas Von Hoffmann complaining about "wasted oratory" in community organization, *Point* editor Charles C. Robb wrote: "Von Hoffmann wasted some oratory himself in a long, rambling talk that was half ad lib half read from scribbled notes." Later in the same article, Robb described one panelist as "the Negro grocer from Homewood who has become the loudest established black militant in the city." The *Point* also declared its preferences in last November's county election, but did not feel called upon to blame a conspiracy for their subsequent defeat.

THE UNDERGROUND PRESS: GROWING RICH ON THE HIPPIE
Thomas Pepper

Surprising as it might seem from the tone of the underground press, its writers are not the only people unhappy with the accomplishments of America's regular papers. There are plenty of critics — Irving Kristol, James Reston and McGeorge Bundy among them — who offer publishers both critiques and suggested reforms. And while the underground press may not realize it, the deficiencies of regular newspapers are only partly ideological. After all, the practices of the big-city papers, like those of the underground papers, make good economic sense. There is a limit to what can be done, and papers tend naturally to their most obvious, short-range tasks and stick naturally to traditional ways of doing things. Only the most ethically minded publishers seek quality for its own sake, whether in coverage of foreign affairs, city hall, or subcultures. And even among these publishers, an economic constraint will establish an outer limit to what is possible. Ironically, the most visible force for reform of big-city papers is neither the serious critics nor the underground critics but the new, slick city magazines. These magazines have demonstrated, by their own success, that the *nouveau riche* want and will buy more stimulating artistic commentary than is provided by the daily papers. Lately, the papers have been following suit.

The underground papers are not a quality press because they pander to their readers with a dexterity befitting the establishment papers they criticize so bitterly. In their own pages, instead of stimulating political and social discussion worthy of the society they say they seek, the underground papers offer nothing more than a stylized theory of protest. Indeed, by the definitions it now prescribes, the underground movement not only requires protest as an end in itself; it depends on protest. For without a dogged concentration on perpetual antagonism, some people might admit to improvements, "sell-out," and leave the movement. Then where would the underground papers be and what would they write about? This theme of "selling out" is a new and a hip variant of an old and inadequate form of social protest — one that was rejected both by the incremental reformers of civics-book America and by the professional revolutionaries of Russia, China and Africa, all of whom realized, sooner or later, that some positive program is needed to translate general goals into concrete benefits.

Instead of bringing much needed reforms to the established press, the underground papers have inspired their rich, fat, corporate enemies to enter the underground market themselves, and thus to cash in on yet another fad. This bears out the verdict of the London *Economist*, which wrote some nineteen months ago that "much of the new left's judgement of contemporary society is based on aesthetic rather than political or even moral criteria." It is helpful to separate the life style of the underground subculture from its claim to superior morality and from the specific political ideas buried beneath the psychedelic art work. One can then see that with an unholy mess like the Vietnamese War to provide a base for indignation, it has been all too easy for the movement to condemn everybody else. If things are less simple from now on — with equally moral politicans disagreeing over policies and judgments and hunches — the underground press may find that a tone of outrage, supplemented by ads for beads and uninhibited roommates, will not hold its profitable audience together.

Can Mass Magazines Survive?

CHRIS WELLES

Thomas R. Shepard, Jr., publisher of Look, *was running his finger down the table of contents of its next issue, due on the stands the following week. "My God!" he exclaimed. "Isn't that a dammed interesting thing. And this one. Look at this story. Howard Hughes! I predict it will be a real newsgetter." He looked up. "The power of* Look," *he said, "is that it spans the whole universe of interests. It is a platform for all Americans to turn to, to learn about the basic issues, the real gut issues of our day, race, the environment, the SST. . . . It is information and entertainment for the whole family."*

Garry Valk, publisher of Life, *stood by his desk holding up a copy of* Life *as if he were selling it on a busy corner. "Look at some of the stories we've covered," he said, pointing to the cover portrait of FBI chief J. Edgar Hoover. "Nobody else is doing the same kind of in-depth, investigative reporting. I don't know of any other magazine which is courageously covering the major issues of the day the way we do." He picked up several other copies from a stack on a table. "Look at this, Khrushchev. Red China." He displayed a half-dozen different issues. "If the American public is to tackle and solve the problems of our day, somebody has to tell them about it, and that's what we're doing."*

John Mack Carter, editor of Ladies' Home Journal, *one of the most successful women's magazines, glanced out his window in the direction of*
the Look *Building and the* Time & Life *Building, a few blocks away. "I'm sure the mass magazines can explain to you the importance of what they're doing, why it's very significant." he said. "But the question they must ask themselves is: Does anyone care? Does anyone really care? Do people need those magazines?" He looked down at a copy of the forthcoming issue of the* Journal *on his desk and patted it affectionately. "Our readers need this," he said. "I know it."*

Speculation on the future of large-circulation, large-size, general-interest magazines—principally *Life* and *Look*—has flourished for several years. While most people dismiss the self-styled soothsayers who regularly vie for the dubious honor of correctly predicting the exact date of terminal issues, there is general agreement that the mass magazines are "in trouble." Their trouble lies not so much with their readers—70 million adults are said to read each issue of *Life* or *Look*—but with their other constituency: advertisers.

Many magazines obtain most or all of their revenues from readers. But the mass magazines' traditional business strategy has been to lure large numbers of readers with costly promotional campaigns, cheap subscriptions, and low newsstand prices, and to offer them to advertisers at high page rates. According to a recent study by Oppenheimer & Co., advertisers pay about 70 per cent of the cost of publishing both *Life* and *Look*. The average *Life* reader, the study estimated, pays only about 12

CAN MASS MAGAZINES SURVIVE?
Chris Welles

cents for a magazine costing 41 cents to edit and print.

Advertisers, inevitably, possess a great deal of power. Their opinions, attitudes, and prejudices, however specious and illogical, are crucial to the two magazines' financial health. Since 1966, they have put less money into *Life* and *Look* every year: advertising pages in *Life* dropped from 3,300 to 2,043 last year, and revenues from $170 million to $132 million; at *Look* pages fell from 1,534 to 1,153, and revenues from $80 million to $63 million. Despite the recent economic upturn and an influx of cigarette advertising from TV, advertising revenues for both magazines are expected to drop again in 1971.

In search of reasons for advertiser disenchantment, I interviewed media specialists at more than a dozen major advertising agencies which advise hundreds of large corporations on placement of advertising. Predictably, all deny Madison Avenue is attempting to "kill" the mass magazines, as has been charged. As one media man puts it, "It would be ridiculous for us to willfully do anything to harm the health of these books. We want them to be around, so that we can have the option of using them when they're right for our clients." Almost no one mentions competition from TV, which heads most listings of the mass magazines' dilemmas; what almost all the media men do mention are the questions raised by John Mack Carter about the traditional role of the mass magazines.

"The real question about the mass magazines is their reason for being," says Philip Guarascio, associate media director for Benton & Bowles, which placed about $187 million worth of advertising in all media last year. "They're looking for an identity, some relevant editorial concept." "Both magazines are having a great deal of trouble defining their place in the world," adds Jules Fine, director of media for Ogilvy & Mather, which places $250 million in billings. Two decades ago, there was no question about their role. If someone wanted a graphic visual depiction and in-depth personal reportage of the major events of the day, *Life* and *Look* were virtually the only places to go. Today,

with variegated media proliferating everywhere, "they don't have their exclusivity anymore," says Guarascio.

The concepts of identity and reason for being are admittedly vague, but on Madison Avenue and in offices of major advertisers they are considered to be just as important for a magazine as "image" is for a politician. Just as it is difficult to quantify whether a man is a good political leader, it is difficult to establish whether a particular magazine makes an effective advertising medium. Madison Avenue is awash in what are called "the numbers"— voluminous analyses of interactions between the media and the public, who responds how to what. But most advertising men admit that unless differences between competing options are substantial, the relevant numbers are usually so contradictory or inconclusive that basing a decision solely on empirical evidence is impossible. Narrow choices tend to be made on the basis of beliefs, theories, notions, impressions, emotions, hunches, and intuitions. *Ex post facto*, numbers are then mobilized to lend the decisions weight and credibility. In this sort of environment, an elusive substance like identity can be paramount.

Garry Valk dismisses Madison Avenue's concern about the mass magazines' editorial purpose. "They think it should be like advertising copy," he says, "where you're told everything you want to know in a single line. But you just can't sit down and tell what *Life* does in one sentence. *Life* can't be pigeon-holed." "It's just a fad," adds Thomas Shepard. "It's some kind of kick that they're on."

The advertising world is about as free of fads as an average covey of teen-age girls, but its notions about *Life* and *Look* are based on widely held, long-standing precepts. The main one is that a magazine lacking a specific, well defined purpose is not really "needed" by readers and therefore is a relatively poor advertising vehicle. To understand this, it is necessary to examine another much broader theory which has gained acceptance far beyond Madison Avenue. It is the theory of the Dissolution of the Mass.

To a point in a society's development, the media become more and more national in scope and reach, attracting once regionally-confined advertisers eagerly seeking mass audiences. As the *Public Interest* pointed out in Summer, 1970, this trend seemed to reach an apogee in the 1950s and the early 1960s. Sociologists became deeply exercised about "mass culture," and social critics asserted that the growing monopolization of the mass media, as the *Public Interest* put it, "inevitably tended to homogenize and to debase culture, politics, and thought."

Whatever truth such fears contained has eroded steadily. Higher levels of affluence, education, and leisure time have permitted people to develop and exploit individual interests, tastes, and capabilities. This in turn has produced a growing fragmentation of the mass audience and the mass media. This trend appeared first in radio, where the national networks have all but disappeared, then in the movies, where releases for the mass have been supplanted by films for specialized groups, especially young people. In newspaper publishing, many big-city dailies have ceased publication, while small-town and suburban papers have thrived. In TV, the networks are losing their vitality and power, and the future appears to lie with the diversity inherent in cable TV and video cassettes. (Time, Inc., already has sold its radio and TV stations to concentrate on more advanced audio-visual pursuits, including CATV.) In magazines, *Collier's, Woman's Home Companion,* and the *Saturday Evening Post* have folded and other mass periodicals have been retrenching, while many specialty publications have been booming.

The prime movers in these upheavals in the magazine area have been not so much readers but advertisers; the *Post,* it is often pointed out, had millions of apparently loyal readers when it died. Advertisers have responded to the decline in mass tastes with an extensive proliferation of products, some entirely new, some differentiated versions of old products. Each of the products appeals to specific types of persons. Advertising agencies have directed research toward "demographics"—the specific characteristics of different media audiences.

Mass products did not disappear, of course. But when an advertiser wanted mass, he concentrated on prime-time TV, whose reach was believed to be not only cheaper than mass magazines but more effective: a message with sound and motion leaves a stronger impression than a relatively passive print ad. (The advertising cost per thousand persons reached via *Life* currently is about $7.71; via TV, about $3.60.) When he wanted "class" instead of mass, he targeted his appeal by concentrating dollars on more sharply focused TV programming, such as sports, specials, local shows, or local radio, specialty magazines, and other media with well defined, usually more affluent and educated audiences. Mass magazines were left mainly with liquor advertising, messages (insurance, corporate image) not considered especially amenable to televised images, ads containing coupons and slices of campaigns being promoted in all the media.

Despite these developments, *Life* and *Look* throughout the Sixties continued to believe that their most effective business strategy was to compete directly with prime-time TV by assembling larger and larger audiences. They continued their expensive circulation race and no one was very concerned about where the numbers came from as long as they kept coming. In 1963, *Look* triumphantly announced it had won—around the 7 million level, it had edged *Life* by a couple of hundred thousand; *Look* was now "Bigger than *Life.*" Smarting under this claim, *Life* made what is generally regarded as one of the most spectacular publishing mistakes of the decade: in 1968, to vault ahead of *Look,* it acquired a million and a half subscribers from the ailing *Saturday Evening Post,* and with grand flourishes announced a new circulation of 8.5 million and a new color page rate of $64,200—more than the cost of a minute of prime-time TV. Advertisers responded by running 13 per cent fewer ad pages in 1969.

Finally, in April of last year, *Look* withdrew from the "numbers game" by announcing a circulation cut from 7.7 million to 6.5 million. "*Look* is desperate," Lee Heffner, then *Life's* ad director, said in a memo to his staff. "If you have something people want, you get crowds. If you don't, forget it." *Look's* move, he added, represents an absence of a "sense

CAN MASS MAGAZINES SURVIVE?
Chris Welles

of commitment or responsibility to the reader." Six months later, *Life* began cutting its circulation to 7 million, and reduced color page rates to $54,000.

Gradually, both magazines have come to realize that their principal competitors are not prime-time TV shows, or even each other, but the various specialized media, particularly the specialized magazines. "Nobody really asks whether they are going to put their money in TV or *Life*," says James Tominy, director of media at LaRoche, McCaffrey & McCall. "First you usually analyze how much of your budget is going into TV and how much into print. Then you decide which publications get the business."

Life and *Look* used the circulation cuts to prune from their subscriber lists lower demography readers. Following the lead of other national magazines, they expanded their regional advertising editions based on zip codes and other data, and began investigating demographic "breakouts" of specific class groups of readers. Breakouts, though, are a problem for large-sized, large-circulation magazines with frequent deadlines. While the cost of breakouts is high, *Life* and *Look*, to remain reasonably competitive with smaller magazines, have had to keep their rates on regional editions relatively low. This reduces profitability to marginal levels. And the more *Life* and *Look* segment their national audience the more they risk luring regular advertisers away from their higher-profit national editions. *Look* has one demographic edition— "Top/Spot," with 1.2 million readers with an average income of $13,634—but *Life*, according to publisher Garry Valk, has no plans for a demographic breakout.

"If you want a more upscale demography," he says, "you can buy the specialty magazines. We can't do a demographic edition and effectively compete with them on a cost basis." Some media men suggest that if *Life* did move in this direction, it would come into even more direct competition with its sister magazines, *Time* and *Sports Illustrated*. *Time* now offers editions for businessmen, educators, doctors, and college students, and is said to be working on others.

Among all these somewhat bleak portents there has recently arisen one auspicious sign—albeit one manifested more in theoretical discussions than actual advertising purchases. That is, that the once axiomatic omnipotence of TV as the most effective mover of mass-distributed products is starting to be questioned. Media researchers have raised the issue of TV's growing "clutter"—an excessive number of rapid messages for viewers to comprehend or assimilate adequately—and, as more educated and more affluent segments of the population turn off TV and flee to print, its evolving image of a medium catering only to low-demography audiences.

By far the most potent talking point for the mass magazines' cause has been the now-famous General Foods survey. In a bold tactical thrust, the publishers of *Life*, *Look*, and *Reader's Digest* suggested to General Foods, one of the nation's largest package-goods advertisers, with 95 per cent of its budget in TV, a study of the relative effectiveness of TV and magazines in selling General Foods products. They offered to help finance it. General Foods agreed. "We knew we were taking our chances," says Thomas Shepard of *Look*, "but we felt that if the study came out in our favor an awful lot of people would pay attention." Sixteen months and $1.8 million later, the company announced that "magazines can provide our products with an effective selling vehicle—one that is generally comparable with television."

That conclusion, released last year, hardly sounds cataclysmic. Indeed, one can find many media experts who vehemently dispute its underlying data and dismiss its significance. "What the study did, though, was cause a controversy where no controversy existed before," says Jules Fine of Ogilvy & Mather. "It put an advertising agency which used to say TV was more effective, period, a little on the defensive. It forced people to evaluate alternate plans, to reexamine their points of view." Young "creative" types, long entranced by the expressive possibilities inherent in TV's qualities of sight, sound, and motion, were ordered to explore the potentialities of the less glamorous disciplines of print. Spurring everyone was the fact that General Foods had backed up its study by sharply increasing its advertising in *Life*, *Look*, and *Reader's Digest*.

Studies come and go on Madison Avenue, though. The TV networks have been laboring assiduously to destroy the General Foods findings, and they no doubt soon will produce a behemoth statistical compendium purporting to establish irrevocably, incontestably, TV's supremacy. No one at *Life* and *Look* seriously entertains the expectation that their magazines can recapture any major portion of the advertising lost long ago to TV. Their hope is acceptance by the big package-goods advertisers of the idea of a "media mix," with mass magazines used to reinforce TV appeals. In 1970, the four leading national advertisers—Procter & Gamble, General Foods, Bristol-Myers, and Colgate-Palmolive, all package goods manufacturers—spent $434 million in TV and only $45 million in magazines.

Whatever happens, the main focus of the discussion of mass magazines is no longer the "massness" of their audience. It has now become the massness of their editorial approach, which has undergone little basic change over the past two decades. Editors at *Life* and *Look* continue to relish what they believe to be their wide-open "franchise," their freedom to go anywhere, do anything that they think might make an interesting and exciting story. When they are asked to define the purpose of their magazines, they display somewhat pained expressions. It is as if a composer had been asked to explain what he "meant" by a piece of music. *Life* editor Thomas Griffith recently said he felt *Life* should concentrate on "the news and what we add to it, the human condition as it touches the reader's own life, and photojournalism." A framed poem on Thomas Shepard's wall includes such definitions of *Look*'s role as the representation of the "many faces of an urgent present."

Questioned about the advisability of a more precise formula, William B. Arthur, *Look*'s editor,

says, "I don't know how we'd go about setting up a formula. The world isn't a formula. Every day is different." The *Look* reader, he contends, is "a cross-section of the U.S.A." "It would be boring," adds managing editor Martin Goldman. "It would be no fun for us, and no fun for the reader. It just wouldn't work." One judges a good story idea, he goes on, by whether "it turns you on or off. If there's magic in it, you take it."

Neither magazine apparently sees much validity in the theory of the Dissolution of the Mass. Time, Inc., is presently testing four special-interest magazines. But previous experimentation with six special-interest inserts—Movie, Food, For Children, Your Money, Your Health, Travel—which would be bound into *Life* and then perhaps spun off as separate magazines, were abandoned. It also recently declined to back two detailed proposals for new magazines from top *Life* editors, who then decided to go ahead on their own. One, called *On the Sound*, is a recreational and conservation magazine for the Long Island Sound area, under editorial direction of former assistant managing editor Roy Rowan. It has published four issues and obtained considerable advertiser support. *Tomorrow*, a magazine on the environment organized by Lee Hall, editor of *Life*'s international editions, and Jeremy Main, an associate editor of *Fortune*, is still in the fund-raising stage.

"The entire demographic thrust of our nation," Thomas Shepard said in a recent speech, "is in the direction of a merging of interests, of the elimination of extremes at both ends and a massive gathering together toward the middle. . . . I see an especially bright future for the publications that bring various groups of Americans together in a climate of mutual interests and shared concerns."

The most financially successful magazines of the past ten years, however, have been designed to appeal to highly particularized intellectual, vocational, and avocational interests and are run by editors who know precisely what they are saying and to whom they are saying it. Helen Gurley Brown of *Cosmopolitan* month after month tells millions of "*Cosmopolitan* girls" how to catch and

CAN MASS MAGAZINES SURVIVE?
Chris Welles

keep a man. Clay Felker of *New York* week after week tells burgeoning numbers of upper-middle-class New Yorkers how to survive in their city. *Psychology Today, Playboy, Rolling Stone, Time, Newsweek,* even *TV Guide* and *Reader's Digest,* which both offer larger audiences on a per-issue basis than *Life* or *Look* (at a much lower cost which is more competitive with TV) — all of these publications, despite frequently wide-ranging editorial content, have a distinct identity and are sharply edited to appeal to particular groups of readers with particular interests. Each provides something — information, an approach, a philosophy, a format — which is distinctly its own.

Such an approach, in the view of Madison Avenue media specialists, gives a magazine two strong advantages in areas where TV is weakest: it creates a very specific type of audience, which provides advertisers with a clear sense of who is receiving their messages; and perhaps more important — particularly in an era of information overload — it establishes an "involvement" of readers with the magazine. It serves a clearly defined function which no other magazine is quite able to duplicate for them. They *need* it. This involvement, advertisers are certain, "rubs off" on their ads, which are better read and more readily believed and acted upon.

Life and *Look* are quick to point out that they also are distinctive. They mention the "extra dimension" they bring to the day's basic issues or the "why" they provide when everyone else is just telling "what." *Look* will talk about the news breaks their stories regularly receive on the wire services. *Life* will assert that "week after week, *Life* has the story nobody else gets. Or handles it in a way nobody else does." It will mention its exposés, its stories on the Mafia, its coverage of the Frazier-Ali fight by Norman Mailer and Frank Sinatra. They both will assert that they have so significantly upgraded their intellectual level they have become "class" instead of mass magazines.

Media experts at the agencies dismiss these arguments. Many individual *Life* and *Look* stories are superlative, the media men say, but the difference between the "extra dimension" provided on a

regular basis and what other media offer on the same issues is not distinctive enough to develop a real need for the magazines, to prompt readers to become involved with them. Media men also dispute the relevance of assertions of intellectual upgrading. "the better educated people become," says Philip Guarascio of Benton & Bowles, "and the more leisure time and money people have, the more discriminating they become in their media usage habits. A shotgun editorial approach just isn't worth that much to them."

The workings of the involvement philosophy are clearly illustrated in the long rivalry between *McCall's* and the *Ladies' Home Journal.* While the interests of men have become quite fractionalized, women have tended to remain a relatively homogeneous group. They also control most of the country's vast expenditures on food, drugs, and toiletries. This has permitted the major women's magazines, focused on the woman's role as a homemaker, successfully to maintain mass-sized audiences and at the same time provide advertisers with specificity and reader involvement.

The major attempt to break away from this pattern was made by Shana Alexander, a columnist for *Life* who in 1969 took over as editor of *McCall's,* generally regarded as the most sophisticated, if not the most profitable, of the women's magazines. Apparently infused by some of the ideas of women's liberation, she endeavored, with management's encouragement, to move *McCall's* away from "service" features and a singular preoccupation with the home to an investigation of the world's issues, about which she felt women were becoming more and more concerned. On Madison Avenue the reaction was alarm and rapid withdrawal of advertising. *McCall's* had begun to resemble *Life* and *Look.* Meanwhile, despite a highly publicized sit-in in his office by women's liberationists, John Mack Carter kept *Ladies' Home Journal* in traditional channels. Once nearly pushed out of business by *McCall's,* the *Journal* forged ahead.

Patricia Carbine, executive editor of *Look,* was brought in last fall to perform a rescue. She has turned the magazine back toward homemaking, but she has continued to offer carefully structured glimpses of the world beyond the home. Madison Avenue is skeptical that she can successfully involve both older conventional readers and younger more "liberated" ones. *McCall's*, which has reduced its page size and cut 1.1 million from its circulation, has suffered a further ad revenue drop for the first half of 1971, while the *Journal*—which recently ran a promotional ad entitled LIBERATION BEGINS AT HOME—was up 19 per cent in revenue.

Whatever the weight of all the sociological and psychological theorizing, there is no statistical proof of the alleged deficiency of reader involvement with and need for *Life* and *Look*. Apparent audience fragmentation notwithstanding, the two magazines retain a vast readership. Media researchers, consequently, are looking with intense interest at some forthcoming changes in the magazine business which may go a long way toward settling the matter. Over the next several years all magazines—but especially *Life* and *Look*, with their expensive formats —face severe cost increases. Paper prices are expected to double within five years; printing costs may go up 50 per cent within three years; and, unless the publishing lobby is more effective than it has been so far, postal rates for magazines will rise 142 per cent in five years.

Publishers are desperately seeking ways to save money—private magazine delivery methods even are under consideration—and increase revenues. A major increase in advertising rates for *Life* and *Look*, which already are marginally competitive, is out of the question. "The increases are going to be heavily skewed to the reader," says Garry Valk of *Life*. The magazine has already instituted a 25 to 30 per cent subscription renewal rate increase (phased in slowly, since only 5 to 6 per cent of the subscribers come up for renewals each month), and next year plans price-elasticity experiments with the subscribers in one selected state on the effects of an additional 25 to 30 per cent hike.

The big question is: will the reader pay? Faced with an annual bill from *Life* for $12 or $15 instead of $6 or less (the typical discount *Life* offers most of its readers), he may question seriously how much

the magazine means to him. Is it really necessary? Postal rates will also make it harder for circulation directors to keep prodding him into replying in the affirmative.

One of the advertising agencies' major questions about *Life* and *Look* then will be answered. "When you charge only 12 cents an issue to keep up circulation for something like *Life* or *Look*," says James Tominy of LaRoche, McCaffrey & McCall, "it raises questions about the vitality of the product. It doesn't indicate people care that much for it." If, as rates go up, reader renewal continues high, "need" will have been dramatically proved; broad, undefinable general interest will have been shown to be an effective editorial philosophy; and advertisers will have to reevaluate their assumptions. *Life* and *Look* might even find they can make subscriptions their chief revenue base, thus freeing themselves from subservience to the prejudices and whims of Madison Avenue.

If renewals are low, the effect could be extremely grave. One less-than-heartening omen is the steady decline in newsstand sales of the two magazines over the past two decades. *Life* now sells some 210,000 copies on the stands, compared to 2.5 million in 1947. *Look* has dropped from 1.4 million to 240,000. Advertisers watch newsstand sales on the theory that a reader making a conscious choice to buy an issue and pay the relatively high cover price is displaying a higher degree of need for and interest in the magazine than one who merely gets his regular copy in the mail. Significantly, 80 per cent of *Playboy's* circulation and 98 per cent of *Cosmopolitan's* is sold on the stands. *Playboy* costs $1 or more; *Cosmopolitan*, 75 cents. *Life* sells for 50 cents; *Look*, 35 cents. "In the long run," says Garry Valk, "it all comes down to the willingness of the readers to sustain the considerable price increases we put to them. They will decide whether Ralph Graves and his crew are producing a viable editorial service." He adds that present circulation levels are "not etched in granite" and that perhaps "the more you charge, the less units you may move."

Alternate methods of coping with cost increases might be reduction in the page size to that of *Time*,

CAN MASS MAGAZINES SURVIVE?
Chris Welles

a step taken recently by *Holiday*, *McCall's* (but not *Ladies' Home Journal*), and, as of this September, *Esquire*. A mere three-sixteenths' inch trim, begun last year, saves *Life* $500,000 annually. *Life* could also go biweekly, and both *Life* and *Look* could chop circulation further.

Any such changes, though, would almost certainly exacerbate perhaps the most delicate problem *Life* and *Look* must overcome on Madison Avenue: avoiding the smell of a loser.

Everyone in the industry knows that both magazines lost money last year and, like some other publications, have laid off dozens of staff members. Though a recent sale of properties to the New York *Times* has restored some stability to its balance sheet, Cowles Communications, *Look*'s owner, has lost money every year since 1967. Time, Inc., is financially healthier than Cowles, but its earnings have been dropping for four years. On the other hand, the cost of folding the magazines would be great. They carry more than $50 million in unfilled subscription liabilities and support huge corporate overhead plus such ancillary enterprises as book clubs. *Life* represents about a quarter of Time, Inc.'s revenues; *Look*, over a third of Cowles'.

The psychological blow to the two companies and their executives would be incalculable. Asked if he would fold *Life*, Roy Larson, chairman of Time, Inc.'s finance committee, responded, "I love all the magazines as I would my children." Gardner "Mike" Cowles, chairman of Cowles Communications, said not long ago, "My heart is in *Look* — it's my baby. I founded it thirty-three years ago. I'd sell everything to keep it going."

Despite all this, the possibility of death cannot be ruled out. "This industry is quick to castigate, to look for something to bury rather than to look for something to support," says Jules Fine of Ogilvy & Mather. "This is part cynicism, part a general maliciousness, part an attempt to avoid embarrassment over guessing wrong, part trying to be 'I told you so.' I mean, you don't have to use *Life* or *Look*. There are a lot of good substitutes. So instead of going into something with instability connected with it, where you have to stick your neck out, you tend to recommend something more reliable and safe."

As another media man points out, however, it would be an oversimplification to suggest that the fate of the magazines is entirely in the hands of Madison Avenue. "Right now," he says, "with the TV networks starting to fall apart, with all the better educated and affluent people running away from TV, it's a propitious time for the mass magazines. There are still a lot of talented people around at *Life* and *Look*. They can experiment with regional editions. Or demographic. I can't tell what they ought to be doing. But if they are going to just sit around and keep going the way they're going and wait until TV reorganizes itself, and CATV really comes in, and everybody has thirty or forty channels to choose from, or people start sending newspapers over TV sets, or whatever else is going to happen, they might just as well save themselves some money and close down tomorrow."

B. Radio

Radio was the first electronic medium to serve a mass public. Like the newspaper before it, its development had to await the development of technology and a person who recognized its potential. The first selection by Melvin DeFleur traces the development of radio from its take-off point set in motion by David Sarnoff. The early years of radio, which date only from the 1920's, have strongly influenced modern broadcasting and government policies towards it. Since the radio corporations extended their operations to television their early experiences with sound broadcasting decisively shaped the newer medium as well.

Broadcasting, as DeFleur notes, was a commercial undertaking from the outset, although the pattern of selling advertising was not established until the late twenties. The early interest was in selling receivers. Thus R.C.A. and Westinghouse operated stations to stimulate the sales of their own products. The early years, like those of newspapers previously, saw very rapid growth: the manufacture of receiving sets could not keep pace with demand and new stations, many organized into networks, were opened at a rapid pace. Indeed, too many stations operating on limited frequencies meant that signal interference became commonplace. The government, under pressure from dissatisfied listeners and outraged broadcasters, reluctantly stepped into the affairs of public broadcasting in 1927.

The Great Depression failed to slow the progress of radio in the thirties. By 1940 the number of sets in use averaged more than one per household, and this growth has been maintained with the development of cheap portable transistor sets. While the growth in sets has continued, the nature of broadcasting itself has changed radically from its nationally organized style of the thirties and forties, in which the names of its performers became household words, to a more diffuse role of providing background noise and local news. Radio now fulfills the entertainment and information needs that network television cannot offer.

The selection by William H. Honan discusses the new pluralistic broadcasting of today's radio, which parallels developments in magazines. Many stations are now programming exclusively for a specialized audience in terms of musical taste and age (which are closely related), ethnic origin, and political and religious persuasion. Fred Ferretti's article examines in detail one type of specialized radio, that serving the black community. Most of these stations, he notes, are owned by whites, so their profits are seldom returned to the black community. In addition, he argues, the stations are not meeting the basic demands of the Ghetto since—like most other radio stations—their public service broadcasting is meager. Thus, although audience appeal is diversified, most stations still operate on the same basic principle—that of generating private profits.

The Development of Radio

MELVIN L. DE FLEUR

A YOUNG radio engineer by the name of David Sarnoff had been rapidly advanced in the ranks of the American Marconi Company. He had achieved considerable public attention during the sinking of the ill-famed *Titanic* when she was ripped by an iceberg in mid-Atlantic. David Sarnoff remained at his telegraph key in a radio station in New York City decoding messages from the disaster scene. For three days and three nights he kept a horrified public apace of developments concerning the tragic incident. He was later moved up from this post to more important positions in the company. In 1916, Mr. Sarnoff sent a memorandum to his superiors. This now-famous memorandum in a sense did for radio what Benjamin Day did for the press almost a century earlier. It showed an economically profitable way by which radio could be used as a medium of mass communication for ordinary families. While the company did not immediately follow Mr. Sarnoff's advice, he successfully predicted the major outlines of radio as a mass medium (he wrote):

> I have in mind a plan of development which would make radio a "household utility" in the same sense as the piano or phonograph. The idea is to bring music into the house by wireless.
>
> While this has been tried in the past by wires, it has been a failure because wires do not lend themselves to this scheme. With radio, however, it would be entirely feasible. For example—a radio telephone transmitter having a range of say 25 to 50 miles can be installed at a fixed point where instrumental or vocal music or both are produced. . . . The receiver can be designed in the form of a simple "Radio Music Box" and arranged for several different wave lengths, which should be changeable with the throwing of a single switch or pressing of a single button.
>
> The "Radio Music Box" can be supplied with amplifying tubes and a loudspeaking telephone, all of which can be neatly mounted in one box. The box can be placed on a table in the parlor or living room, the switch set accordingly and the transmitted music received. . . .
>
> The same principle can be extended to numerous other fields as, for example, receiving lectures at home which can be made perfectly audible; also events of national importance can be simultaneously announced and received. Baseball scores can be transmitted in the air by the use of one set installed at the Polo Grounds. The same would be true of other cities. This proposition would be especially interesting to farmers and others living in outlying districts removed from the cities. By the purchase of a "Radio Music Box" they could enjoy concerts, lectures, music, recitals, etc. While I have indicated a few of the most probable fields of usefulness for such a device yet there are numerous other fields to which the principle can be extended.[1]

If Mr. Sarnoff had added the singing commercial and the soap opera, his description of radio as it would develop into a system of mass communication would have been almost perfect. Within ten years he was to see radio grow into a medium for household use, following almost to the letter the outline that he had dictated. David Sarnoff's suggested application of existing radio technology to this imaginative, new, and practical usage ranks as an insight with that of Marconi's idea of taking existing laboratory devices and using them as a wireless telegraph. Sarnoff himself played a major role in bringing about this transformation; he became in a short time the manager of a new corporation in the radio field and was able to help make his dream become a reality.

Feeble attempts to perpetuate governmental control over radio at the close of the Great War were crushed by outcries by private interests. Just as the federal government had allowed control of the telegraph to fall into the hands of private persons, it similarly handed over this important new medium of public communication to commercial interests. Radio was defined by this act as an *arena of business competition* as opposed to a public medium of communication to be operated by organizations of government. This decision was to have far-reaching effects and ramifications with which we live today. Other societies formulated different definitions concerning the control of broadcasting, and the systems of broadcasting that have developed in such countries as Great Britain, the Soviet Union, and others offer interesting contrasts with our own. That is not to say that they are better, only that they are very different due largely to historical reasons.

Once direct governmental control was eliminated, British and American commercial interests, which had prospered during the war, fought each other to gain control. The General Electric Company finally bought up the British shares of American Marconi and formed a new corporation with a patriotic name (apparently designed to dispel fears of foreign control). The new Radio Corporation of America (RCA) was able to consolidate a number of conflicting patent interests, and it gave control over wireless telegraphy and radio broadcasting in the United States to American stockholders. In 1919, David Sarnoff, who had forecast the "Radio Music Box," was appointed its first commercial manager.

COMMERCIAL BROADCASTING BEGINS

Shortly after World War I, the Westinghouse Company, a major American manufacturer of electrical equipment, attempted to move into the international wireless telegraph field. It was not particularly successful. This was due largely to the fact that its rival RCA owned most of the important patents. However, some of its directors were interested in the newer field of wireless telephony, and the company had done considerable research in this area. Dr. Frank Conrad was in charge of experiments with new and powerful transmitters of this type. In connection with this work, he not only built such a transmitter for experiments at the Westinghouse laboratory, but he constructed one at home over his garage so that he could continue his work in the evening. He licensed his home transmitter nearly a year later as station 8XK in April, 1920. He started to broadcast signals during the evening hours as he worked with his apparatus in attempts to improve its design. He soon found that people in the area were listening in on their amateur receiving sets. This proved to be a boon at first, because their letters, cards, and phone calls gave him some indication of the range and clarity of his transmitter. Before long, however, his circle of amateur radio listeners began to become a problem. To create a continuous sound, he had started to play the victrola over the air. His listeners began to demand particular songs and would even call him at odd hours to ask him to play a favorite record. Dr. Conrad solved the problem by regularizing his broadcasts, and with the cooperation of a local phonograph dealer, he was able to present continuous music for a two-hour period two evenings a week. The number of listeners grew rapidly, and his family enthusiastically joined in the fun to become the first "disc jockies."

All of this activity increased the demand for receiving sets in the area, and it became increasingly clear that there might be money to be made in the manufacture of such sets for home use. The commercial possibilities of this did not escape the attention of officials of the Westinghouse Company. They decided to build a larger transmitter in East Pittsburgh for the purpose of stimulating the sale of home receivers of their own make and the sale

THE DEVELOPMENT OF RADIO
Melvin L. DeFleur

of the components from which amateurs built such sets. It was in this way that Station KDKA, Pittsburgh, came into existence in the year 1920.

Although David Sarnoff had forecast the radio music box several years earlier, it was the decision of Harry P. Davis, vice-president of the Westinghouse Electric and Manufacturing Company, which concretely gave birth to commercial household radio. He decided that a regular transmitting station, operated by the manufacturer of receivers, would create enough interest in the sale of sets to justify the expense of operating the station. Although this financial basis for broadcasting has long since been replaced by the sale of air time for advertising, it was sufficiently practical at the time to get radio started as a mass medium.

To stimulate interest in the new station and, of course, to promote the sale of receiving sets, it was announced that the transmitter would broadcast the results of the 1920 Presidential election over the air. Bulletins were phoned to the station from a nearby newspaper, and the returns were broadcast during the evening of November 11 as they came in. An audience of between five hundred and a thousand people heard the word through the air that Warren G. Harding had been elected President of the United States. The event was a sensation; the dream of David Sarnoff had become a reality.

The Pittsburgh experiment was so successful that other stations were quickly launched. Transmitters began regular broadcasts in New York in 1921, followed by stations in Newark and other cities. Westinghouse soon had several competitors. The public's interest in radio had been growing. Its appetites for the new signals in the air had been whetted by the glamor and excitement of radio's brief history. The dramatic stories of rescues at sea, of daring flights over no-man's-land with radio telephones, and the struggles of giant corporations to gain control over wireless telegraphy had all contributed to this surging interest. When radio stations actually began to broadcast during regular periods with music and voices they could receive at home in their own cities, this latent interest suddenly

burst into a full blown craze. The public begin to clamor for radio. By 1922, the manufacture of home receivers was lagging hopelessly behind the receipt of orders. New stations were being built at a staggering pace. In the last half of 1921 licenses were issued for thirty-two new stations, but in the first half of 1922, this number had risen to 254! Although there were still many problems to work out concerning its financial base, its content, and its technical functioning, radio as a mass medium was off to a flying start.

THE EARLY DAYS OF RADIO AS A MASS MEDIUM; THE PROBLEMS OF INTERFERENCE AND FINANCE

One of the earliest problems which household radio encountered was brought on because of its own popularity. There is a limited spectrum of frequencies available that are suitable for broadcasting. In the beginning, no attempts were made by either government or private groups to regulate the frequencies transmitters in a given area would use. The Radio Act of 1912 did not specify frequencies for privately operated broadcast stations. The Secretary of Commerce, who licensed all new transmitters, had selected two frequencies, 750 kilocycles and 833 kilocycles. All stations were assigned one or the other. As the number of transmitters operating grew quickly, there developed an annoying number of instances where two stations were operating near enough to each other so that the program of one would be imposed upon the sound of the other. This type of interference could not easily be controlled. Many stations worked out gentlemen's agreements to divide up available time. There was no legal authority that could assign different positions on the radio band for every station to use and could rigorously enforce such regulations. Obviously, such a problem could be handled only by some form of governmental agency, but there was no adequate provision by Congress or by the states for such a controlling body. The Department of Commerce issued licenses to operate transmitters, but did little else. Because of the lack of control over this technical problem, confusion began to mount.

In the meantime, radio was advancing at a tremendous pace. In 1922, station WJZ in Newark successfully broadcast the World Series. Stations began to broadcast opera, concerts, news, dance music, lectures, church services, and a great variety of events. Voluntary experiments were tried by having nearby stations broadcast on wave lengths at least twenty meters different from each other as a means of avoiding overlap. In spite of efforts to combat interference, the problem continued to grow.

Successful experimentation with networks was tried, and it was found that several stations linked by wires could simultaneously broadcast the same program. The rush to build new transmitters continued, and by 1923 stations were to be found in most major cities across the nation.

But two major problems continued to plague the medium. The technical problem of interference was already badly out of hand, but there was also the problem of paying for the broadcasts. While the larger electrical manufacturers could afford to finance their stations out of their profits on the sale of sets, this was a limited expedient at best, and it was no help at all to the owners of stations who were not electrical manufacturers.

By the end of 1923, some of the initial enthusiasm for constructing radio transmitters began to sag as the hard financial facts had to be faced. There was simply no profit in broadcasting as such, and only those with other financial resources were in positions to continue in operation.

Now that a full year of nation-wide radio broadcasting had been completed the summer of 1923 afforded an opportunity to cast up the accounts, so to speak. This was indeed a disturbing experience, since the studio ledgers of every station disclosed entries almost entirely in the red ink. Fortunes had been squandered in the mad rush. . . . As early as December, 1922, the Department of Commerce reported the suspension of twenty stations for that month alone. With every succeeding month the casuality list had grown more appalling. Between March 19 and April 30, 1923, forty-two stations gave up their franchises. In the month of May there were 26 failures. June, 1923, saw fifty radio stations become silent. In July twenty-five franchises were surrendered. Thus in the period from March 19th to July 31st of this fateful year 143 radio stations went out of business.[2]

Unless some viable financial basis could be found, radio as a medium of communication to the American home was doomed.

But the public was not to be denied radio. The mid-1920's were years of prosperity for most Americans. The grim remembrances of the Great War were fading, and the nation was entering a period of industrial and financial growth. The new practice of installment buying was part of a great expansion of credit which was taking place in the entire economic structure. No one had any inkling of the eventual collapse that would begin in October of 1929. Installment buying made it easier for families of modest means to purchase consumer goods such as radio receivers. Radio listening was becoming increasingly popular, and pressure was being exerted on the Secretary of Commerce, Herbert Hoover, to do something about the interference problem. He did work out a system for assigning different wave lengths to various broadcasting stations, but the attempt to implement it was not completely successful. People who owned sets capable of picking up only one major frequency did not like the idea. Also, there was no actual way of enforcing the assignments, and some transmitters simply ignored the plan. On the other hand, many of the major stations, which were engaged in regular broadcasting, tried to follow the Secretary's assignments and did so with success.

The industry itself was exerting great pressure upon the Department of Commerce not only to regulate frequencies, but to limit the number of stations that could be licensed in a given area. The public, too, was becoming disenchanted with the cacophony that came out of their sets night after night. The problem of interference was getting

THE DEVELOPMENT OF RADIO
Melvin L. DeFleur

unbearable. Ancient spark transmitters used for marine broadcasts, Morse code amateurs, powerful stations which broadcast regularly, and local fly-by-night operators were all blasting each other over the air waves.

Four major conferences were held yearly (1922–1925) in Washington, D.C. to discuss the problems of broadcasting. The position of government was that it was up to the industry itself to clean up its own house. The newspapers had gotten along without government control. In fact they had fought it bitterly. The film industry was cleaning up its products. In a political system which stressed private initiative, it was felt by many government officials that federal control over broadcasting would be a dangerous precedent. In fact, Congress had repeatedly refused to consider bills on the subject. The only legislation in existence on radio was the old Radio Act of 1912, which was hopelessly out of date.

The problem was not an easy one to solve, even by government control. Since wireless telegraphy would also need regulation, the matter had international complications. In addition, there were the thousands of amateurs whose rights had to be protected. Not only were there more than 500 major stations operating on a regular basis, but there were approximately 1,400 small stations of very low wattage that operated when their owners had the urge. Yet, to pick up this jumble of signals, Americans spent 136 million dollars for receiving sets in 1923 alone.[3]

The Secretary of Commerce struggled valiantly to find a solution. He tried limiting the power and hours of operation of some stations so that they could share a given frequency. By 1925, every spot on the frequency band was occupied, some by several stations. The broadcast band could not conveniently be extended without severely infringing upon other important kinds of radio and wireless operations. There were 175 additional stations clamoring for licenses that could not be accommodated.

In 1926, this arbitrary control system collapsed. A federal court decided that the Secretary of Commerce had no legal basis to impose any restrictions on a station's power, hours of operation, or transmitting frequency. In that same year also, the Attorney General issued the opinion that the only existing legislation, the Radio Act of 1912, really did not provide a legal basis for any of the regulations he had been using. Mr. Hoover simply had to abandon the entire attempt in disgust, and he issued a public statement that urged radio stations to regulate themselves. They were unable to do so.

In the face of the utter chaos that followed, President Coolidge asked Congress to enact appropriate legislation to regulate broadcasting, including provisions for adequate enforcement. They did so in 1927. They first enunciated the important principal that *the air waves belong to the people*, and that they can be used by private individuals only with the formal permission of government on a short-term license basis. Licenses were to be granted or revoked when it was in the public interest, convenience, or necessity to do so. All licenses of existing stations were automatically revoked; and the industry had to start all over by applying formally for a franchise to operate and by providing adequate statements and explanations as to why it would be in the public interest for them to do so.

The Radio Act of 1927 was to be a temporary solution. After a seven-year period of observation, trial, and some readjustments, a new and more permanent set of statutes was written and a Federal Communications Commission (FCC) was established to enforce the provisions. The Federal Communications Act of 1934 has since become, with appropriate amendment from time to time, the principal regulating instrument for the broadcasting industry in the United States.

Meanwhile, the boisterous new industry continued to seek an adequate means of financial support. By the mid-1920's, broadcasters were still grappling with this problem. A committee of New York businessmen tried the experiment of soliciting funds directly from the listening audience for tne purpose of hiring high quality talent to perform over one of the larger stations in the area. While a trickle of funds came in, most listeners decided they would rather listen free to whatever happened to come their way than pay directly out of pocket to be assured of higher quality programs. This response typifies the feelings of the majority even today. It also explains in part why the public eventually accepted advertising messages as a means of financing broadcasting. They would rather put up with somewhat objectionable commercials than pay directly for their entertainment.

Other schemes were proposed. David Sarnoff felt that wealthy philanthropists should endow radio stations just as they did universities, hospitals, or libraries. Others suggested charging a license fee for operating a home receiver, the proceeds of which were to be divided among broadcasters. Many felt that the industry itself would solve the problem. The larger manufacturers of receiving sets were said to have an obligation to provide something to hear on their products. It was thought that this would eventually result in a small number of networks, each operated by a different manufacturer or group of manufacturers and that there would be few if any independent stations.

But while these debates were being carried on, advertising was quietly creeping in as a dependable source of revenue for radio broadcasts. In fact, as early as 1922, station WEAF had sold radio time for ten minute talks on behalf of a Long Island real estate company which was selling lots. Then major companies began to sponsor programs. A department store paid for an hour-long musical program. A tobacco company sponsored a radio variety show. A candy company presented two comedians. The public was much drawn to these, and audiences wanted more. At first, these sponsors made no direct advertising appeal for their products. They simply mentioned their name as sponsor or titled the program after the name of their product. This form of subtle advertising found little criticism. The general goal of sponsoring such a program was to create good will among the audience.

The Secretary of Commerce was dead set against open huckstering on radio. He said, "it is inconceivable that we should allow so great a possibility for service, for news, for entertainment, and for vital commercial purposes to be drowned in advertising chatter."[4] Many other voices were added to this view. Responsible officials in government, leaders of the industry, and many groups of listeners concurred.

But in our society, such an idealistic position was doomed from the outset. With listeners more interested in "free" entertainment than quality programming; with government playing only a technical role, primarily to keep frequencies unscrambled; with ownership of the media in the hands of profit-seeking companies and corporations the noble views of the Secretary of Commerce and his supporters were not consistent with the value system, the political structure, and the economic institution of the society within which the new medium was developing. The same socioeconomic forces that led newspapers to turn to selling space to advertisers so they could sell their products to a mass audience were to result in a parallel pattern for radio. The surrender to advertising was strongly resisted for some time, but inevitably it came. It was somewhat artificially held back briefly by the policies of the American Telephone and Telegraph Company, which controlled many patents, transmission lines, and radio equipment used by broadcasters. But even this opposition was relaxed, and the way was opened for the flood of commercial messages that are now so much a part of broadcasting in the United States.

At first, advertising was restrained and dignified. But soon it became increasingly direct and to the point. It would be incorrect to say the public welcomed advertising, but it is certainly true it welcomed what advertising revenues made possible.

THE DEVELOPMENT OF RADIO
Melvin L. DeFleur

The public was willing to hear the sponsor's pitch in order to be able to listen to his program. One reason for this was that programs were quickly designed to have great popular appeal. Money from advertising made it possible to hire effective talent. Individual comedians, singers, and bands soon developed large and enthusiastic followings. Weekly drama programs became popular. Programs for children were developed; sports broadcasts drew large audiences. A great variety of content was designed to capture the interest of different large components of the population.

By the end of the decade, the major problems of radio as a mass medium of communication were solved. The homeowner could buy a reasonably priced and reliable receiving set on time payments. The broadcaster received generous profits from selling his time to advertisers; sponsors sold products effectively over the air to a mass market; and talent with great popular appeal captured the nightly attention of the public. In the background, the new federal legislation had brought order out of chaos with respect to the interference problem. Only the ominous event of the [stock market] crash of 1929 threatened to muddy the picture. But as it turned out, this was to have little negative impact upon the growth of radio.

THE GOLDEN AGE OF RADIO

Radio flowered during the 1930's and the 1940's. These were very trying decades for the American society. The great depression and World War II were events that affected the destinies of every citizen, but they had little inhibiting effect on radio.

An overview of radio's growth in the American society can be obtained from Table 1, which shows the number of receiving sets in operation for selected years. By the end of the 1930's there was slightly more than one set per household in the United States. This remarkable growth in the use of radio receivers had occurred in spite of ten years of economic depression following the stock market collapse of '29. It should be emphasized for those who did not experience those tragic days that this was a period of great distress for American families. The pathos of an era when heads of families were unable to find employment and when there were few public agencies to turn to for relief cannot be adequately appreciated without having been personally involved. It was a time the people of the United States were gravely depressed in spirit as well as in an economic sense.

But in spite of the hardships of the times, radio seemed to thrive on the depression! Advertising revenues, instead of drying up, grew at an ever increasing pace. The number of radio sets owned by Americans about doubled every five years. Families who had reached the limit of their financial resources would scrape together enough money to have their radio receiver repaired if it broke down. They might have to let the furniture go back to the finance company or to stall the landlord for

TABLE 1
The Growth of Radio Set Ownership in the United States
(1922–1967)

Year	Total Number of Sets	Total Number of Households	Sets Per Household
1922	400,000	25,687,000	.016
1925	4,000,000	27,540,000	.145
1930	13,000,000	29,997,000	.433
1935	30,500,000	31,892,000	.956
1940	51,000,000	35,153,000	1.451
1945	56,000,000	37,503,000	1.493
1950	98,000,000	43,554,000	2.250
1955	135,000,000	47,788,000	2.825
1960	156,000,000	52,799,000	2.955
1965	227,000,000	57,251,000	3.965
1967	268,000,000	58,845,000	4.554

Sources: New York World Telegram Corporation, *The World Almanac, 1969* (New York, 1969), p. 62.

U.S. Bureau of Census, *Historical Statistics of the United States, Colonial Times to 1957* (Washington, D.C., 1960), Series A 242–244, p. 15.

U.S. Bureau of Census, *Current Population Reports: Population Characteristics*, Series P 20, No. 106 (January 9, 1961), p. 11; No. 119 (September 19, 1962), p. 4; No. 166 (August 4, 1967), p. 4.

Note: Figures after 1960 include Alaska and Hawaii.

the rent, but they hung grimly on to their radio sets.

Radio fit the needs of millions of hard-pressed people during that trying time. It had music to restore their sagging spirits, funny men to cheer them up and dramatic news to divert their attention from their personal problems. Amateur nights, evening dramas, soap operas, Western adventures, and variety shows were all followed avidly by loyal listeners night after night. On a summer night a person could walk down a street on the evening that a particularly popular comedian was on the air and hear the program uninterrupted through the open windows of every house he passed.

By the time the depression eased and the war was about to begin, radio was reaching every ear. In mid-1940, there were nearly one and a half sets per household in the United States. Radio had also become increasingly sophisticated in every sense. It was technically excellent. It was possible for direct broadcasts to be picked up and relayed to listeners in their homes from almost any point on the globe. News broadcasting had become a sophisticated art, and outstanding journalists had established themselves within this new medium. The press and radio had learned to live with each other after prolonged feuding, and radio had full access to the world's wire services.

During World War II, the radio industry made all of its resources available to the federal government. War information messages, domestic propaganda, the selling of war bonds, campaigns to reduce the civilian usage of important materials, and many other vital services were performed. It should be noted that the manufacture of home receiving sets was completely curtailed during the war years. Figure 1, the cumulative diffusion curve for radio sets, shows that from 1940 to 1945 no new sets were acquired by American households. Special attention should be called, however, to the sharp rise in sales during the following five-year period, when the cumulative diffusion curve recovered from the retardation of the war years and resumed its regular pattern of growth.

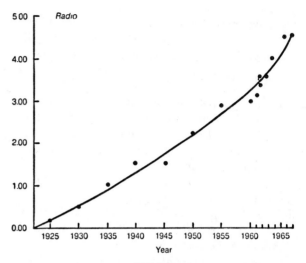

FIGURE 1

The Cumulative Diffusion Curve for Radio; Ownership of Receiving Sets Per Household in the United States (1922–1965)

Of greater sociological significance are the postwar years when radio was faced with vigorous competition from television. If radio had retained its original format and content, it would have remained a direct competitor of the newer medium which was apparently capable of gratifying the relevant needs of the mass audience in a more effective manner. At first, radio attempted to do this with the somewhat optimistic argument that over the years people had built up a deep loyalty to radio, which had served them so well, and they could not easily be lured away to a flashy new thing like television. The public turned out to be completely fickle, however, and as soon as families could afford television, they gleefully abandoned radio in favor of the tube. To put it in sociological terms, radio had been satisfying certain needs within the American society as a social system. However, when a more effective functional alternative became widely available, the earlier medium began to show signs of obsolescence.

Faced with the prospect of oblivion, radio was forced to find audience needs to satisfy that were

THE DEVELOPMENT OF RADIO
Melvin L. DeFleur

not being effectively served by television. It successfully found such needs, and radio remodeled itself along new lines. During the 30's, 40's, and even the early 50's, radio had successfully captured the attentions of the American family during the major evening hours, and they turned to their radio to listen to the country's most popular entertainers. As television grew, it took over these entertainers along with the family's evening time. Radio was displaced from the living room and had to be content with the bedroom, the kitchen, the automobile, and the beach. Transistor technology, which opened up a huge market for miniature sets, helped keep radio from the type of postwar decline that occurred with motion picture theaters as a result of television.

At present, radio seems to have found a workable formula. It caters to its audience during times when television is inappropriate. People listen when they wake up in the morning, while they are working, driving, playing, etc. But when evening comes and they settle down in their living rooms, the radio dial is turned off and the television set is warmed up. Radio remains as one of the most massive of our mass media in terms of the ownership of sets. Table 1 shows that Americans now own more than four sets per household. Figure 1 suggests that the curve of diffusion for radio has not yet begun to level off; it has by no means reached its peak. The trend toward miniaturization will probably continue and set ownership will soar even higher. Needless to say, the impressive number of sets owned by American families does not imply that they spend a corresponding amount of time in radio listening.

[1]Gleason L. Archer, *History of Radio to 1926* (New York: American Library Association, 1962), pp. 112–113.
[2]*Ibid.,* p. 312.
[3]Girard Chester, Garnet R. Garrison, and Edgar Willis, *Television and Radio*, 3rd ed. (New York: Appleton-Century-Crofts, 1963), p. 24.
[4]Alfred N. Goldsmith and Austin C. Lescarboura, *This Thing Called Broadcasting* (New York: Henry Holt and Company, Inc., 1930), p. 279.

Reprinted from The New York Times Magazine *(Dec. 3, 1967), pp. 56–76* © *1967 by The New York Times Company. Reprinted by permission.*

The New Sound of Radio

WILLIAM H. HONAN

RADIO station WEVD in New York City is looking for a Chinese disk jockey. Applicants should be acquainted with such personalities as Poon Sow Keng (the hottest rock 'n' roll singer today in Hong Kong), be able to report the time, news and temperature in easy-going Cantonese, and quote Confucius in the original. The resulting program may be of limited appeal—beneath the notice, one might guess, of a mass-media adman worth his double martini—and yet, it is chiefly this sort of specialization, or "fractionalization of the market," as they say in the trade, that accounts for the remarkable sonic boom reverberating from radio these days.

Right now, for example, there are more radios in the United States than people—262,700,000 at the last count. Forty-seven million sets were sold last year alone. Such profusion cannot be attributed merely to teen-agers buying transistor radios with which to annoy their parents—although that is a not inconsiderable factor. But parents are buying radios like hot cakes, too. They get them nowadays built into their tractors, hairdryers, Scotch bottles and even sunglasses. And the knobs on all these instruments are being clicked and twirled with astonishing frequency.

In fact—and this may be enough to make even Marshall McLuhan gulp with wonder—a recent Trendex survey conducted for the National Broadcasting Company found that more Americans now listen to radio in the course of an average week than watch TV. The audience for individual radio programs, of course, cannot compare with that of the most popular TV shows, but on a cumulative basis the figures indicate that 90.5 per cent of the adult population tunes in a radio sometime during the week as compared with 87 per cent who flick on television. That finding, the Trendex survey supervisor reported, "puts radio right back in the league with the other major media in terms of total audience dimensions."

The robustness of radio is also illustrated by the fact that the giant advertisers, most notably such bellwethers as the soap and automotive companies which shifted from radio to TV in the early nineteen-fifties, have once again become substantial radio time buyers. Colgate-Palmolive, for example, which was not even listed among the top 100 radio spot advertisers as recently as 1964 was 23rd on the list last year. Ford, General Motors and Chrysler were first, second and third, respectively, with a total expenditure last year of $56 million—up 17 per cent over the previous year and up 56 per cent over that of the year before.

The explanation for this renaissance of a medium which many condemned to a lingering death as recently as 10 years ago lies, to a great degree, with that sought-after Chinese disk jockey. For, once radio broadcasters began to face up to the fact that television had permanently taken their place as dispenser of general entertainment for the masses, they began experimenting with new formats and discovered that, collectively, they could capture their old audience piecemeal by directing strong appeals to specific fractions of the population.

THE NEW SOUND OF RADIO
William H. Honan

This discovery led to the development of all manner of limited-appeal programs, and the advancing trend is now doing away with even these one-hour or half-hour shows, since the stations themselves are beginning to take on the characteristics of a single, 24-hour program, narrowly addressed to a distinct slice of the population. Such broadcast parochialism is now revolutionizing the industry, with several stations almost every month dropping their old-style programing in preference for the new "continuous format."

Competition in a city like New York, where no fewer than 63 different AM and FM stations vie for attention, has naturally pushed specialization to an extreme, and some of the more popular formats appear to have been divided, subdivided and virtually pulled apart with tweezers in order that each station may find a niche (and presumably a distinct audience) it can call its own.

For example, WMCA, WABC, WJRZ, and WOR-FM are all what the casual listener might consider standard rock 'n' roll stations, but connoisseurs are aware that WMCA tries to add a local home-town flavor by using such disk jockeys as Joe O'Brien, who has a Yonkers accent; WABC seeks to impart an all-American tone to the proceedings with disk jockeys like Herb Oscar Anderson, who is from Minnesota and full of corn and good cheer; WJRZ restricts itself exclusively to that close relative of rock 'n' roll known as country-Western music; and WOR-FM lays stress on the subdivision known as folk rock, which may include such controversial ballads (which the other stations would never touch) as Phil Ochs's "I Ain't Marchin' Anymore" and Country Joe and the Fish's prickly L.B.J. put-on, "Super Bird."

Even in lesser cities than New York, however, format specialization has proceeded to a surprising degree. There are as many as 1,500 radio stations across the nation substantially if not exclusively devoted to country-Western music, according to the Country Music Association. And the all-talk or telephone-participation format is not only popular in New York City, where N.B.C.'s Brad Crandall and the insomniac Long John Nebel have large

followings, but Philadelphians like to hear themselves gabbing over the telephone with Jack McKinney over WCAU, and nearly everybody in Salina, Kan. (pop. 43,202) listens at one time or another to Mike Cooper on KLSI to catch the latest chatter about the local school merger and to hear Cooper adding his laconic "uh-huh" to a phoned-in beef about how all the rain in June loused up the local wheat crop.

Typical of the trend is a middle-sized city like Peoria, Ill., which now has as many as six radio stations, each with its own distinctive format. WIRL, Peoria's leading outlet, is a "top-40" or predominantly rock 'n' roll station. WXCL, the local N.B.C. affiliate, is devoted to country-Western music, WMBD, the C.B.S. affiliate, is strong on conversation and plays "middle-of-the-road" music (Frank Sinatra, Peggy Lee, Vic Damone). WMBD-FM specializes in "potted-palm" fare (schmaltzy renditions of the Warsaw Concerto, and the themes from "Intermezzo" and "Gone with the Wind").

WIVC-FM has female disk jockeys—or "program hostesses," as they are known in Peoria—and plays "adult" pop, jazz and classical music. Finally, WPEO, the Mutual affiliate, having recently tried and then dropped "top-40" and "middle-of-the-road" formats, became a virtually "all-talk" station in January of this year and then in September raided WXCL's country-Western disk jockey—Cal Shrum, an old Gene Autry sidekick—and is now trying to blend the recorded yodeling of assorted farmhands-turned-vocalists with its decidedly right-leaning cast of talkers, whose ranks include Fulton Lewis 3rd, the Rev. Carl McIntire and the suave pitchmen of H. L. Hunt's "Life Lines."

Such quick shifting from one format to another as practiced by WPEO is possible because the process is remarkably cheap. There is no retooling to be done, and usually disk jockeys who can handle one type of music can handle another as well. Subscriptions to the various record library services required to keep a radio station jangling with the latest tunes of whatever genre it chooses rarely run more than $300 or $400 a year. Furthermore, stations like WPEO—far from spending revenue when shifting to the seemingly expensive all-talk format—actually coin money in doing so. For every Fulton Lewis or Bill Stern whose tapes the station has to pay for, WPEO broadcasts several "Life Lines" or "20th-Century Reformation Hours" which are actually advertisements for which the station is handsomely compensated.

With specialization paying off in radio, a rise might be expected in new small stations throughout the country. Actually few new stations are being formed. As of Aug. 31, there were 4,145 AM and 1,712 FM stations—and these figures have held fairly steady for the last few years. It costs a minimum of $35,000 to start a station in a city the size of Fort Worth, Tex.—and this figure does not include promotion expenses, which are likely to be enormous.

But even that cost is not what stops people from starting new stations. The F.C.C. controls the issuance of new licenses very closely, since the radio band is now almost saturated, and thus even if an entrepreneur had the $35,000 to $100,000 to spend, he would have a tough time convincing the F.C.C. that Fort Worth, say, really needs a new radio station.

So far has format specialization progressed among radio stations throughout the United States today that local affiliates of the national networks have been ignoring network programing in preference for their own locally orginated material. In response to this trend, the A.B.C. radio network has recently announced that it plans to split up its piped fare into four separate subnetworks, each of which will cater to stations with distinctly different formats. There will be one subnetwork for stations with an all-talk or music-and-news format, another for "top-40" stations, one for those with more sophisticated FM formats and another for stations still using the old-style eclectic format. A.B.C.'s hope is that its subnetworks will be more congenial to highly specialized stations and will, in addition, make possible more than one A.B.C. affiliate in a given community.

There are, of course, other possible explanations besides specialization for the comeback of radio—

among them the portability and convenience of the new transistor sets, the fact that car radios have become virtually standard rather than optional equipment, the development of sophisticated techniques of audience measurement to demonstrate to advertisers the large, new, out-of-home listenership, and so forth. But the basic reason for the boom is that people are listening to the radio again because it is offering them something they want to hear and cannot find elsewhere.

Of New York City's bewildering array of radio stations, three picked more or less at random—WINS, WHOM and WBAI-FM—illustrate the latest types of specialization and to whom those new formats appeal.

In April 1965 WINS, a Westinghouse station, dramatically gave away its rock 'n' roll record library to Fordham University, kissed its disk jockeys goodby; hired 27 radio newsmen and began broadcasting news for 24 hours a day. Skeptics had said that the WINS anchor men would grow hoarse by early afternoon of the first day, and that if no worse disaster overtook the station, the babbling brook of news would simply run dry, and, on the first really slow day, WINS would be begging to get its records back from Fordham.

Neither of these eventualities came to pass. WINS provided enough anchor men so they could spell one another in half-hour shifts. And far from running out of news, a veritable geyser of gab was churned up by the stations 21 "airmen" covering New York City, by the squad of rewrite men who had access to all the major wire services and by correspondents of the Westinghouse communications network who were sending in "voice cuts" from such far-flung places as Madrid and Saigon.

As time went by, the WINS team of broadcasters developed an original and often rather exciting manner of news presentation, in which the process of news gathering is exposed to the listener in an unfolding drama. In a major news break, for example, the presentation begins with a high-pitched BEEP-BEEP-BEEP-BEEP which, according to high Westinghouse policy, may even interrupt a commercial (but never has). The beeping fades and the

THE NEW SOUND OF RADIO
William H. Honan

voice of the anchor man rises over it with: "Late word has just been received at the WINS newsroom that President Johnson and Premier Kosygin will meet tomorrow in the college town of Glassboro, N. J. Stay tuned for further details as they are received in the WINS newsroom."

Whatever was cut into is then resumed, but pretty soon "Jim McGiffert at the editor's desk," who has been madly pawing through a stack of reference books dumped in front of him, whisks the anchor man a "sidebar" about Glassboro— where it is, its population, principal industry, etc. The next morning, Sid Davis tells about the President's helicopter chugging up off the White House lawn; there is a quick switch to Doug Edelson at the Soviet Mission in New York describing the departure of Kosygin's limousine; then reports from Rod MacLeish, Paul Parker and Jim Gordon in Glassboro shouldering their way through the crowds and finally telling of the arrival of the dignitaries the moment they appear.

So impressed by this dramaturgy was Angus McDermid, the B.B.C.'s U.N. correspondent, that he was moved to do a special feature about WINS for the B.B.C., in which he commented enthusiastically: "I found myself waiting for the next thrilling installment. It was better than many a fictional radio series I can think of."

More jaundiced listeners, however, may note that all too often the instant news in these "thrilling installments" winds up having to be retracted or modified. For example, during the emergency session of the United Nations in the wake of the six-day war in the Middle East, WINS reported that a Mohawk Airlines jet bound for Washington, D.C., had crashed near Blossburg, Pa., and that many of the 34 passengers aboard were U.N. delegates. It was a thrilling installment, all right, but it later turned out to be an example of what Elmo Ellis of WSB, Atlanta, a sharp critic of broadcasting, once characterized as "rip-snorting, inaccurate news reports." No U.N. delegates had been on the flight.

WINS spokesmen argue that the Mohawk Airlines story was an unusual case. They add with

pride that WINS newsmen are not merely "rip-and-read" announcers who rip off the wire-service stories and blather them uncritically into the microphone, as do the "newsmen" at other stations they say they could name. The WINS newsmen, they say, have had analytical experience—four-fifths of them are former radio or TV station news directors—and normally they "don't jump." They did not jump on the air, for example, as did WQXR, with a rumor circulated by The Associated Press during the Newark rioting to the effect that Stokely Carmichael was leading a caravan of 33 cars into Newark. WINS newsmen were on their toes and knew Carmichael was in London at the time. And it was not a WINS man, they say, whom Newsweek pictured poking his stick microphone into the anguished face of a woman felled by a bullet on a Newark street; that, too, was "a man from another station we could name"—in this case, WMCA.

The all-news format for radio was originated not by WINS but by Gordon M. McLendon, the flamboyant Texas promoter who was also one of the first to use the "top-40" or "rock-around-the-clock" format. McLendon's station XTRA in Tijuana, Mexico, which broadcasts to Southern California, in 1961 became the first to go on an all-news bender, and was followed three years later by another McLendon property, WNUS in Chicago. (Philadelphia, Washington, Denver and St. Louis now have all-news stations, too.)

The original McLendon format, however, is substantially different from that of WINS. McLendon likens XTRA and WNUS to the weather- and time-dialing services of the telephone company, and believes that they will succeed to the degree that they strictly adhere to a "monotonous" recital of the headlines, eschewing all features and a commentary. The ultimate disaster for an all-news station, McLendon once remarked, would be for its listeners to tune in expecting to hear the latest bulletins and get instead a book review.

Disagreement is voiced by Charles F. Payne, the stocky, natty-looking general manager who now presides over WINS at its chic, midtown Park

Avenue headquarters. Also a Texan and by coincidence, the manager of two McLendon stations before he joined Westinghouse, Payne explains: "It's true, of course, that we cycle the headlines every 15 minutes, do a time check every 5, weather every 7 and so forth, so when you tune in you're never very far away from the bulletins. But in between we have special in-depth reports, a shopping feature, theater reviews, even editorials and sometimes a feature that continues in sections all day long—we call it a 'blitz'—on topics like the poor of New York, the overcrowded air corridors or the coming Broadway season. Furthermore, even the news bulletins are not 'monotonous.' They're changing all the time. Someone once said we're like a newspaper with 48 separate editions every day.

"The key to our format," Payne goes on, "is being informally informative. What we try to avoid is the old H. V. Kaltenborn pompousness. We want to create the image of the working newsman, the guy who's on the scene."

Although the sound of news would seem to have a universal appeal, WINS's most faithful listeners, according to a recent Politz survey, tend to be those New Yorkers with high incomes, college educations and relatively high-status jobs. Most listeners are between the ages of 25 and 64, teen-agers and senior citizens being conspicuously absent. When WINS first shifted to the all-news format, its audience, which has been accustomed to rock 'n' roll, fell off sharply. According to the latest surveys, however, the station has now more than doubled the size of its former audience—a success story which must have been read with interest across town at WCBS, which switched in August to an all-news format, too.

Another increasingly important specialization in contemporary radio is known as ethnic broadcasting, or, less euphemistically, as ghetto radio. There are now, for example, no fewer than three Negro stations broadcasting in New York City. WWRL, by far the most popular of these, anticipates that its annual revenue from advertising will rise above the $2-million mark this year, having practically quadrupled over the last four years.

WEVD, the formerly all-Yiddish station which now broadcasts in 13 different tongues, including Japanese and Norwegian, says that 1966 was "the best year ever" in its 40-year history. And The Wall Street Journal recently reported that because Pepsi-Cola was the first soft drink to advertise intensively on the local Spanish stations, Pepsi now outsells Coca-Cola two-to-one among New York's 1.5 million Spanish-speaking residents—a state of affairs that Coca-Cola is now trying to rectify by plugging away over "the Spanish Main," as the three stations between 1280 and 1480 kilocycles are known, with the jingle *Todo va mejor con Coke* ("Things go better with Coke").

Typical of the sound and format of ethnic broadcasting is that of WHOM, New York's foremost Spanish station, which is so hotbloodedly Latin that it has, quite literally, blown its fuse. The program responsible for this occasional boiling over—called *Debate Musical* ("Musical Debate")—is the top-rated Spanish disk-jockey show in New York and is hosted by Juan Rodriguez Diaz, a deceptively placid-looking Puerto Rican. On the program, which is broadcast live every weekday afternoon at 4, Diaz spins a couple of Spanish pop records and then urges his listeners to call in and "vote" for whichever one they liked best. He can stimulate as many as a thousand calls on a good afternoon, working himself into a frenzy as the votes mount up and bawling into the microphone in Spanish:

"The vote is even! It's even! We don't want any sleepy-heads here! No, you have to be *awake* to listen to *this* show! Call in! My friends! Call in! Look, if you don't call in right away, I'll fall down and break 14 ribs. I'll smash my head against the wall! If I don't get 400 calls right now, I'll break 44 ribs!"

Suddenly, the lights on all the studio telephones begin to flicker, indicating a shower of incoming calls. When this happens Diaz puts his hands to his temples, closes his eyes and shrieks with ecstasy: *Esto es treMENNNDO!* " WHOM's engineers, not one of whom understands Spanish, have learned to

THE NEW SOUND OF RADIO
William H. Honan

watch their volume-units meter with a hawk's eye when El Tremendo, as they call Diaz, gets lathered up and they "ride gain" on him with their volume controls like a destroyer captain in a gale. Nevertheless, on two consecutive days last summer, when Diaz was unloosing his "*Esto es treMENNNDO!*" he overloaded the station's 5,000-watt transmitter and blew out a high-voltage fuse, temporarily putting WHOM off the air.

That is overdoing it, perhaps, but the Latin sound and volatile temperament is all that WHOM has to sell, and the management evidently would rather err with too much than too little. "Language is our most important product," explains Ralph Costantino, WHOM's affable program director, who is himself of Italian extraction but survived the station's changeover in 1957 from Italian to Spanish broadcasting by virtue of his fluent Spanish. The dialect spoken over WHOM, he says, is Caribbean Spanish, interspersed with plenty of *ay benditos* and *Ave Marias!*, which are characteristic of the Puerto Rican and Cuban idiom one hears on East 125th Street.

So important is the sound of the Spanish language to the station's identity, in Costantino's opinion, that he has a rule of long standing that popular music, which constitutes from 65 per cent to 75 per cent of the station's programing, must be vocal rather than instrumental. Moreover, with the current unusual exception of The Monkeys and the Turtles, vocalists who sing in English are strictly *prohibido*. WHOM even snubbed Frank Sinatra's last big hit, "Strangers in the Night," and played instead Andy Russell's Spanish rendition "*Estraños en la Noche*," which had more tropical zing.

It is not only the disk jockeys and vocalists one hears over WHOM who radiate Latin excitement: newscasters do, too. Last summer, for example, one of WHOM's newsmen broke into a musical program almost hysterically shouting a news bulletin. Fortune Pope, the station's co-owner, who does not speak Spanish, happened to be listening and promptly called in to find out what in blazes was going on. "Has war been declared?" he asked. No, he was told, the news bulletin merely concerned a report

that Che Guevara was then rumored to have been seen somewhere in Venezuela.

"Our announcers become emotionally involved in the news when they read it," says Costantino. "It isn't that they aren't professional. It's just the Latin way. You should have heard them reporting the rioting in El Barrio the last week in July. It was . . . well, pretty loud."

Baseball games and soap opera—the latter still a great favorite with Spanish-speaking audiences—round out WHOM's regular fare, and they, too, are as popular as they are tempestuous. One of the most avidly followed "soaps" carried on WHOM is called "*Collar de Lagrimas*" ("Necklace of Tears"), and seems to consist chiefly of organ music and the sound of a woman sobbing, punctuated now and then by gunfire and commercials. (It also has an enormous audience in Cuba, and Fidel Castro will not permit Havana stations to broadcast it while he is making a speech.) The soaps are gradually giving way on WHOM, however, to the jiving sound of the *boogaloo* and *la nueva ola* (rock 'n' roll with a Latin beat), since the younger generation, according to the surveys, is now the dominant group in Spanish Harlem and it would rather twist and wriggle than sniffle and sigh.

So firm is the grip of the ethnic stations on their audiences that a recent Pulse survey shows the Spanish-speaking population, for example, listening to radio for an average of four hours a day, which is almost twice as much time as other Americans devote to the medium. This audience, according to surveys, is profoundly influenced by what it hears, whether commercials, news or comment.

It is particularly regrettable, then, that WHOM has an intellectual content of zero, and offers little that might be considered of geniune public service. (A notable exception among ethnic broadcasters is WLIB, the Harlem Negro station that last year won a Peabody Award—the highest honor in broadcasting—for a telephone-participation program that was believed to have served as a sort of social safety valve by permitting the frank airing of Negro grievances.) The rationale for the low level of programing by WHOM, according to Costantino, is that "most Puerto Ricans who have intellectual capacity are bilingual and thus get their stimulation from English-language sources" (which is a dodge), and that the station did in fact "give free air time to Spanish-speaking deputies of Mayor Lindsay and Cardinal Spellman to appeal for restraint during the summer rioting" (which is true enough, but surely the minimum in terms of social responsibility). A strong case can be made that ethnic radio stations like WHOM, which exploit commercially the linguistic handicap of their listeners, actually serve to perpetuate that handicap, and therefore ought to be charged with providing special counter-balancing educational services.

Another highly specialized area of radio broadcasting is occupied by the 350-odd licensed non-commercial stations in the United States which are affiliated with schools, churches, municipalities and foundations. A good many of these have undergone as much format refinement as any all-news or rock-around-the-clock station on the dial. Perhaps the best known of them in New York is WNYC, the city-owned station.

Other local noncommercial stations specializing in fine music and thoughtful discussions and lectures include Columbia University's WKCR-FM, Fordham University's WFUV-FM, the Riverside Church's WRVR-FM and the Pacifica Foundation's listener-sponsored WBAI-FM, which is the left-leaning "free-speech" station that was put off the air for 52 hours in September when its transmitter was wrecked by vandals. An articulate spokesman for WBAI is Larry Josephson, the hip disk jockey. Josephson, a rather corpulent, bearded, 28-year-old computer-programer by day, has for the last year and a half been conducting a far-out breakfast club for the station, irreverently called "In the Beginning," which is—in marked contrast to the usual fare at that hour—refreshingly grumpy, lusty and alienated.

Noncommercial stations have specialized just as have the commercial broadcasters, Josephson believes, not only because of the pressures of competition, which naturally affect them less, but in response to "the great diversity of life styles

today." Back in the thirties, he says, cultural unity give rise to relatively undiversified styles in the communication media. But today, in an era of cultural splintering, a great many people find themselves "disfranchised by the mass media" and they begin to seek new styles of experience elsewhere.

WBAI is attractive to at least some of these seekers—no one knows how many since its call letters have never appeared in a general audience survey—because it offers, according to Josephson, programs attuned to the new life styles, programs which are, in his words, "no longer sequential, but random, associative and parallel." Josephson cites as an example of such programing the breakfast club he convenes every weekday morning at 7 A.M. or whenever he gets around to arriving at the station (he is frequently late and sometimes never shows at all), and on which he is likely to say anything that pops into his head—it may be something fairly salacious or he may just indulge in a long spate of moaning and groaning.

Josephson points with admiration to his WBAI colleague, Bob Fass, the station's after-midnight disk jockey, who has lately been achieving remarkable effects by playing two records simultaneously—for example, pairing speeches by Timothy Leary and Lyndon B. Johnson about their respective visions; playing the voices of soldiers in a United States Army basic-training course along with a dog-training record, and so forth. Similar effects, Josephson says, were to be found in the dramatization of Christopher Morley's "The Trojan Horse," which juxtaposed cynicism and romanticism, and which the station broadcast, under the direction of Baird Searles, in a four-and-a-half hour spree on Oct. 8 and 9.

WBAI, like its commercial counterparts, Josephson says, has its very own sound. "Some people say it is the sound of boredom," he begins, adding: "To some extent that's true. Some say it's aggression—a kind of postured hipness. That's true, too. Some say it's amateurishness. Some call it humaneness, or love, or naturalness. It's all of that. Naturalness, especially. For example, when we're running

THE NEW SOUND OF RADIO
William H. Honan

behind time, we say so. When we make a mistake, we admit it. We don't try to come up with our radio-broadcast *persona grata* intact. When we read news, we try to read it like human beings. I hate WINS. They read everything in the same excited monotone. It isn't human.

A few weeks ago, Josephson took over WBAI's regular book-review program for half an hour, and what he said as well as the manner in which his material was presented pretty well illustrates the WBAI "sound" he was trying to describe.

To begin with, the program, which was scheduled to follow a commentary by a spokesman for the Socialist Labor party at 7 P.M., did not start until about 7:07. Then the announcer, who introduced the program as "Books to Buy, Borrow or Burn," tripped over a word, and neglected to say who the reviewer was going to be or to give the titles of the books to be discussed. The next voice was that of a newscaster announcing the beginning of World War II on a scratchy old record.

When it was finished, an obviously "live" voice came on the air and explained that the recording was from a broadcast by Edward R. Murrow from London. The live voice went on to say in a very intimate and unradiolike tone that Murrow was "the best broadcaster ever produced by this country." Murrow had also been an intelligent and effective foe of McCarthy, the voice said, but he should not be mistaken for a true liberal because he had condoned the execution of Julius and Ethel Rosenberg.

In any case, the voice continued, Murrow was great because he came through on the human level and he made you stop and think. A collection of Murrow's broadcasts, the voice added, had been published by Alfred A. Knopf Inc., in a book called "In Search of Light," which might well be read along with "Due to Circumstances Beyond Our Control" by Fred Friendly, who, as everybody knows, resigned from C.B.S. after the network refused to permit him to drop a rerun of "I Love Lucy" in order to carry the testimony of George F. Kennan before the Senate Foreign Relations Com-

mittee. Taken together, the voice commented, the two books reveal what is good and what is bad about broadcasting in America. "This is Larry Josephson," said the voice, and stopped.

There was a long pause—a *very* long pause—and then an old recording of Murrow's voice came on again, this time saying that he had just been with the first wave of U.S. troops to arrive at a concentration camp in central Germany called Buchenwald. His voice trembled perceptibly as he said: "Now let me tell this in the first person." Murrow then described the terrible scene in short, clipped language, remarking at one point: "Men tried to lift me to their shoulders. They could not. They were too weak." And later: "When I came in, they applauded. It sounded like the handclapping of babies."

After describing several other such scenes, Murrow said fervently: "I *pray you* to believe what I have reported about Buchenwald!" He closed by adding: "If I have offended you by this rather mild account of Buchenwald, I am not sorry."

Then the first voice, that of the WBAI announcer. came on once more to say that "Books To Buy, Borrow or Burn" was over, and, tripping over a word again, he introduced the next program, which was in French.

Will the specialized formats such as those represented by WINS, WHOM and WBAI continue to proliferate? Most radio spokesmen say yes. In fact Timebuyer, the trade magazine, recently declared that "everyone from career girls to bird watchers to traveling salesmen could well be the special province of a particular station." Others have suggested that an important area of specialization in the future will be politics—with radio stations not only backing candidates, as did WMCA in 1960 (endorsing John F. Kennedy for President), but identifying themselves as, for example, "the National Review of the air."

These notions may not be as far-fetched as they sound, what with stations like WNCN-FM in New York broadcasting programs of special interest to physicians, to which the general public is discouraged from listening, and like KADS in Los Angeles —another Gordon McLendon creation—which has become the first radio station in the country devoted exclusively to classified advertising.

Just as radio is now going through a fractionalization previously experienced by the printed media, so television will follow, industry spokesmen agree, especially once the U.H.F. stations begin to catch on. The interesting upshot of all this specialization may then be that the mass media, only recently condemned as purveyors of a bland, regularized sameness, may be counted in the near future as a vigorous force working for cultural diversity.

The level or quality of that diversity, of course, is another question, and that remains to be seen — perhaps to be overseen.

Reprinted from Columbia Journalism Review *(Summer, 1970), pp. 35–39.* ©. *Used by permission.*

The White Captivity of Black Radio

FRED FERRETTI

Among the dozens of changes of ownership in broadcast franchises last year were three involving William F. Buckley, Jr., columnist, TV host, and publisher of the *National Review*. With the Starr brothers of Omaha, Neb., he bought control of black-oriented radio stations WBOK New Orleans, WLOK Memphis, and KYOK Houston. Except for Buckley's notoriety, however, there was little unusual about the transactions. Of some 310 stations listed by the 1969 *Broadcasting Yearbook* as programming at least in part for blacks, all but sixteen were owned by whites—and no TV franchises in this country were owned by blacks. Nor was Buckley's three-station investment likely to be as unprofitable as *National Review* (which, like most magazines of comment and opinion, never is far from financial shoals): annual advertising billings on black-oriented radio stations are estimated at $35 million, and most earn profits ranging from comfortable to spectacular.

Unfortunately, most, too, are shameful caricatures of the public-service image suggested by requirements for a license to use public airwaves. A black disc jockey—paid far less than white counterparts on larger stations, and with less chance of advancement—may play an Aretha Franklin record, then in "down home" accents assert that the record undoubtedly "made your liver quiver and your knees freeze." Then he will segue into a frantic plug for a "Top Forty" rock number before playing the record—deafeningly. On the hour, news will consist of a piece of wire copy ripped from a teletype and read verbatim by the same disc jockey.

Required public service time will be filled mainly by pseudo-evangelist hours. And commercial sponsors will be sought willy-nilly, without sifting the the "dollar-down, dollar-a-week forever" entrepreneurs from the nondeceptive advertisers.

Not all black-oriented radio stations conform to this description, of course. Station WLIB in Harlem has won two Peabody Awards, most recently in April for a program called *Higher Horizons*, which attempts to provide students from disadvantaged backgrounds with information on how to enter colleges and how to finance their education. Other black-oriented stations also provide some noteworthy public service programs. Under pressure from citizen groups which have mounted challenges to broadcast franchises, more such programming improvements seem in the offing. But, on the whole, broadcasting stations oriented toward America's black citizenry remind one of nothing so much as Newton Minow's historic description of American commercial television—"a vast wasteland."

This is not merely because, as noted in a Race Relations Information Center study by Bernard E. Garnett earlier this year, "by and large 'soul' radio still is a black-oriented version of 'Top Forty' (also known as 'bubble gum') radio, which appeals mainly to white adolescents." (Most white-oriented radio, after all, is little more imaginative than that.) There are, as Garnett points out, these related factors:

Nearly a quarter-century after a radio station first geared its entire broadcasting format to black interests, there still is no nationwide black-oriented news network.

Blacks still comprise the vast minority in key executive positions at "soul" stations. Entertainment programming is based almost entirely on "Rhythm-n-Blues" or "rock" music, with little or no emphasis on black performances in jazz, "pop," folk, or other music modes.

Such circumstances never arose in the black press. For the black press, for all its problems, always has been owned largely by blacks. Because its main commodity was news and features, it had to provide at least minimal reporting and comment on community concerns; develop black management talent; and not only respond somewhat to the black community but at times provide critical leadership. Moreover, any black individual or organization could establish a newspaper or magazine if he could raise the money and find an audience, and publishers ranging from "establishment" commercial entrepreneurs to the Black Muslims and Black Panthers have done so [see "The Black Press in Transition," *Columbia Journalism Review*, Spring, 1970].

Broadcasting, however, requires not only capital but a license. Licenses are available only from the Federal Communications Commission. The FCC always has had an all-white membership and until recently almost never seriously questioned a license transfer or renewal application. Hence licenses for stations "serving" the black community could be transferred from white seller to white buyer with few questions asked, either about the relevance of programming to the black community or about the possible availability of a black owner.

Perhaps inevitably, then, in searching the list of some 7,350 commercial stations in *Broadcasting Yearbook*, one is extremely hard-pressed to find black-owned or black-managed stations. The Nashville-based Race Relations Information Center, in Garnett's report "How Soulful Is 'Soul' Radio?" lists only nine black-owned stations:

—KPRS, KANSAS CITY, MO., owned by Andrew Carter. Kansas City is 26 per cent black; KPRS ranks fifth in general audience ratings.

—WCHB AND WCHD-FM, DETROIT, owned by the Bell Broadcasting Company; president, Dr. Haley Bell, a black dentist. His two sons-in-law, Dr. Wendell Cox and Dr. Robert Bass, also dentists, are co-owners. Detroit's population is about 45 per cent black. WCHB is the first-ranked black outlet, and eighth-ranked generally.

—KWK, ST. LOUIS. Bell Broadcasting Company and Vickway Broadcasting Company, also black-dominated, both claim control; the courts and the FCC will eventually rule.

—WEBB, BALTIMORE; WJBE, KNOXVILLE, TENN.; and WRDW, AUGUSTA, GA., all owned by singer James Brown, thus making James Brown Broadcasting, Ltd., of New York, the country's only black-owned and operated radio chain. WJBE, bankrupt when Brown took it over, now ranks fourth in Knoxville, whose population is about 21 per cent black. WRDW is the top-rated black station in Augusta, which is about 50 per cent black, and second-ranked generally. No ranking is available on WEBB. Baltimore is about 25 per cent black.

—WHOV-FM, HAMPTON, VA., owned by the Hampton Institute Mass Media Arts Department.

—WSHA-FM, RALEIGH, N. C., owned by the Shaw University School of Communications.

The Center report notes that Atlanta's WERD, which for many years was the nation's only black-owned station, was bought by a white group in 1968. It remains black-programmed in Atlanta, a city 38 per cent black.

This roster of nine black-owned stations is augmented by seven others either entirely or partially black-owned, listed by *Advertising Age* last February 9. These are:

WGPR, DETROIT, whose chief owner is Dr. William V. Banks, a gynecologist. The outlet is ranked third in Detroit's black market and twelfth generally.

WMPP, CHICAGO HEIGHTS, ILL., owned by Charles J. Pinckard, a restaurant owner. It ranks fourth among Chicago's black-oriented stations.

WEUP, HUNTSVILLE, ALA., owned by Leroy Garrett. It is the only black station in a city which is 9 per cent black.

THE WHITE CAPTIVITY OF BLACK RADIO
Fred Ferretti

WTLC-FM, INDIANAPOLIS, IND., held since 1968 by Frank Lloyd. The station ranks first in the black market, third generally in a city which is 28 per cent black.

WORV, HATTIESBURG, MISS., owned by Vernon Floyd, just began broadcasting last Summer.

WWWS-FM, SAGINAW, MICH., even newer than WORV, is owned by Earl Clark, an engineer.

WVOE, CHADBOURN, N. C., is owned by Ebony Enterprises, principal owner Ralph Vaught, Jr. Chadbourn's population is about 20 per cent black.

The list is woefully meager. More distressing are the results of the Race Relations Information Center's survey of five white-owned-and-operated "soul" radio chains. The five are:

—ROLLINS, INC., BROADCASTING DIVISION, of Atlanta, which has four stations: WBEE, Chicago; WGEE, Indianapolis; WNJR, Newark; and WRAP, Norfolk, Va.

—ROUNSAVILLE RADIO STATIONS, Atlanta, with four stations: WCIN, Cincinnati; WLOU, Louisville, Ky.; WVOL, Nashville; and WYLD, New Orleans.

—SONDERLING BROADCASTING CORPORATION, of New York City, which has four stations: KDIA, Oakland; WDIA, Memphis; WOL, Washington, D. C. and WWRL, Woodside, N. Y.

—SPEIDEL BROADCASTERS, INC., Columbia, S. C., which has six stations: WHIH, Portsmouth, Va.; WOIC, Columbia; WPAL, Charleston, S. C.; WSOK, Savannah; WTMP, Tampa; and WYNN, Florence, S. C.

—UNITED BROADCASTING COMPANY of Washington, D. C., with four stations: WJMO, Cleveland; WFAN-TV, Washington; WOOK, Washington; and WSID, Balitmore. United began an all-black-programming TV experiment on WOOK-TV in Washington. The station, with youth dance parties, filmed gospel services, old movies, and talk shows, failed to attract viewers; its call letters then were changed to WFAN-TV, and the black-oriented programming was cut to about 60 per cent.

The RRIC survey of these five combines turned up these facts: in the twenty-two stations which make up the chains, there are eighty-four executive positions in station management and twenty-two news positions. Of these, blacks hold thirty executive positions and fourteen news jobs. But, the survey reported, many of these "executive" positions exist in name only. For example, on Speidel's WSOK, Charles Anthony, who does a disc jockey show, is listed as program director, news director, and public affairs director. He told the surveyors, "I wish I had the money to go with all my titles and responsibilities." WSOK also, it appears, has a sense of humor: along with its tapes sponsored by the NAACP and the Southern Christian Leadership Conference, it lists as public affairs broadcasts for its black audience fifteen-minute talks by Governor Lester Maddox and Senator Herman Talmadge. At Speidel's WYNN, Jack Singleton is listed as program director and news director, and United's WJMO has John Slade listed as station manager and news director.

Two years ago there reportedly was only one black station manager in radio, and there were so few black executives that a *Newsweek* study was prompted to observe that "on many stations only the disc jockeys and janitors are black." Generally speaking the news staffs on these stations are inadequate. In most instances they consist of one man. Often news "staffs" are parttime employees; news directors are disc jockeys who read wire copy. Public service activities generally seem to be of the support-your-community-fund variety; much of the on-the-air public service comes in packages from civil rights organizations.

Much of the news on black-oriented stations comes from the Mutual Broadcasting System, the American Contemporary Network (a division of American Broadcasting Company), United Press International Audio, or Metromedia News. But shows are pretaped and certainly not geared to local interests. There are, however, two organizations in New York—American Black Communications, Inc., and the Black Audio Network—that provide news and black-oriented features.

Barrie Beere, who runs American Black Communications, says that he has gotten the greatest response from a *Focus on Black* series of tapes done by Jackie Robinson, Ruby Dee, Ossie Davis, James Earl Jones, and Brock Peters. He has even sold these syndications to other than black-appeal stations, but says "by and large it has been our experience that the stations do not buy our service unless they can find themselves a sponsor to carry it." Jay Levy's Black Audio Network twice daily sends from New York phone feeds of several items, each 30 to 40 seconds long, designed to fit into standard news broadcast formats. The service, less than a year old, last Fall absorbed the Soul News Network after its founder and sole operator, Chris Cutter, had been unable to obtain regular sponsors or long-term station contracts.

There have been several other attempts at black-oriented networking. In the early 1950s Leonard Evans, founder of the black-oriented supplement *Tuesday*, launched the National Negro Network and built its client list to fifty stations—all but two owned by whites. But NNN was discontinued when white station owners began demanding, in Evans' words, "an unreasonably large share" of profits. After the assassination of Martin Luther King, Jr., black disc jockey Rudy Runnels at WIGO, Atlanta, was so deluged with phone calls asking for spot "feeds" that he organized a temporary national pool of reporters, including staff members of rival WAOK, Atlanta. Known as the American Freedom Network, the service provided coverage for some 200 stations. And two years ago, the American Broadcasting Company was known to have been contemplating an exclusive service for black-oriented stations, but it dropped the idea when, according to an ABC source, white-owned stations proved unwilling to yield profitable local commercial time for regular network feeds.

A few weeks ago in San Diego, Chuck Johnson, former general manager of XEGM, Tijuana, announced formation of a Black Video Syndication Network to service both radio and TV stations. TV programming is to include *Black '70* (patterned on NBC-TV's *Today*); a children's quiz program with ex-boxer Archie Moore as host; and several variety shows. At this writing radio network plans remain to be announced.

Efforts to create a news network for blacks are complicated by attitudes of many white owners of black stations. They claim that audiences want rhythm and blues and "soul," and all the rest is incidental. Alan Henry, vice president for operations of the Sonderling chain, insists, "As broadcasters, we don't dictate taste; our listeners do. 'Soul' music is what our listeners have shown they prefer, by and large, to other types. The reformists can like what they want, but the listeners dictate the programming." But Dr. S. F. Mack, associate communications director of the United Church of Christ, thinks differently. "The stations have fostered an atmosphere in which only the 'soul' format is successful. Consequently, too many blacks have gotten used to it, the way dope addicts get used to drugs."

Other authorities agree. William Wright, director of Unity House in Washington, D. C., and a force behind the Black United Front which is challenging the license of WMAL-TV, asks: "Do we need twenty-four hours of James Brown?" He answers: "No, we don't. If we're going to talk about freedom and self-determination, we need to hear our black heroes performing in other art forms. We need to talk about drug addiction, about slum landlords, about jobs, about education. But the white man gives us twenty-four hours of 'soul' because it pads his already stuffed pockets and keeps black people ignorant."

Citizen action already has been organized against several black-oriented stations. A coalition of citizen groups, for example, has complained to the FCC that Speidel's WOIC filed inaccurate data in its 1969 license application. The complaint contends that blacks received titles without pay or commensurate duties (News Director Parris Eley was alleged to be a disc jockey; Program Director Charles Derrick was said not to have the powers of that office). The station has denied the charges, and the FCC has scheduled a hearing. United's WOOK in Washington has been accused by a citizens' group

THE WHITE CAPTIVITY OF BLACK RADIO
Fred Ferretti

of broadcasting religious programs that offered illegal lottery numbers in the guise of scriptural references; an FCC hearing is scheduled. Rounsaville's WVOL has had a labor dispute pending in the courts since 1968. And *Variety* reported early this year on a four-city advertising boycott of United Broadcasting's properties by the Southern Christian Leadership Conference, plus a petition to the FCC opposing renewal of WJMO in Cleveland. The SCLC claims that policymaking blacks are virtually nonexistent at the station.

The most dramatic result thus far has been in Atlanta. There twenty black organizations, led by the local NAACP, have formed a coalition which won major concessions from twenty-two of twenty-eight stations—both black-oriented and general-audience. Included are agreements to hire and train more blacks, earmark executive positions for blacks, step up public service activities, and consult regularly on programming.

In the end, of course, the future of meaningful "soul" radio and of black-owned-and-operated stations will be only as bright or as swift to come as the increases in the number of blacks who can buy and know how to run radio stations. A singular worry at the moment is the "Pastore Bill," S.2004, introduced by Senator John Pastore. This, if passed —and it has not only a good deal of Congressional approval but also the hearty endorsement of the National Association of Broadcasters—would require the FCC to renew a currently held license without consideration of rival applications if the

Commission found that the licensee had served and presumably would continue to serve the public interest. Rival applicants would be considered only if the FCC decided against renewal. The Pastore Bill was followed by an FCC ruling under which license challengers would not be heard if current licensees substantially met the public interest.

With some justification, William R. Hudgins, president of Harlem's Freedom National Bank (the country's largest black bank), and other "soul" radio reformers fear that the Pastore Bill and/or the FCC ruling in effect would grant licenses in perpetuity, shutting off challenges—particularly black challenges—and thus barring black ownership of stations. Others believe that pressure on broadcasters—soul and otherwise—nonetheless will continue to mount, forcing either improvements or license denials. Those in this camp regard strides made in the Sixties as direct result of challenges, of monitoring, and of pressure.

One such believer is Del Shields, outspoken WLIB disc jockey in New York and the former executive director of the National Association of Television and Radio Announcers, whose members are primarily black disc jockeys. Says Shields: "No amount of legislation will make black people continue to accept the junk that's being offered them now. The Pastore Bill will be a severe cramp, but it will not be the end. As the pressure increases all over the country, white broadcasters either will have to improve their products, sell out to black interests, or be forced out."

C. TELEVISION

The United States was the first country to introduce television on a mass scale. By May, 1964, 92.8 per cent of all American households had at least one set. Of these, 18.2 per cent were multi-set households. There were an estimated 62,600,000 sets in use at that time.[1] The market for television sets is apparently close to saturation with new sets being sold primarily as replacements for earlier or defunct models. The demand for a second set in the household is almost certainly less pressing than it was for the first. The decline in television sales is reflected in recent production and sales figures. Small increases in monochrome set production in 1965 and 1968 and a continuing surplus of sets produced over sets sold in the United States are not indicators of domestic expansion but of an expanding export market. Domestic sales figures for recent years show a large drop in monochrome receiver sales and a steady increase in color set purchases, but there is an overall decline nevertheless. Due to the much higher unit price of the latter, however, dollar sales have probably continued to rise.[2]

By July, 1969, a little more than 32 per cent of American homes had color televisions, up from 28 per cent the previous year, 20 per cent in 1967, and 12 per cent in 1966: In mid-1969 there were an estimated 18.7 million homes equipped with color.[3] The proportion of these more expensive sets can safely be assumed to rise but primarily as replacements for old monochrome sets. Thus despite the introduction of color, the industry is no longer experiencing the bonanza expansion associated with a totally new product and virgin markets.

From the wide distribution of television sets it is clear that the potential audience for transmitting stations is very large. Although television developed earliest in the Northeast region of the country, by 1956 most of the United States consumer market was served, i.e., more than 60 percent of potential viewers in all regions. Large cities had the best coverage, but there was good coverage even in farm districts. Differences in the coverage of national markets stratified by income, education, family size, age of housewife, or age of children were very small.[4]

The television set in each household was on for an estimated average of five hours and forty six minutes per day in 1968, up four minutes from the previous year.[5] The time spent watching the medium is prodigious, but the annual increase is small

[1]*U.S. Bureau of the Census*, sample survey of 26,000 households, conducted in May, 1964. Quoted in tabular form by H. J. Skornia, *Television and Society* (New York: McGraw-Hill, 1965), p. 90.

[2]C. S. Aaronson, ed., *International T.V. Almanac* (New York: Quigley Publications, 1968 and 1970), pp. 22A, 24A.

[3]*Ibid.*, 1968, 1969, and 1970 editions, p. 26A.

[4]Leo Bogart, "The Growth of Television," Table 3 compiled from Market Research Corporation reports, in Wilbur E. Schramm, ed., *Mass Communications* (Urbana: University of Illinois Press, 1960), p. 108.

[5]The figures for 1965 and 1966 were 5 hours and 29 minutes and 5 hours and 32 minutes respectively. See *International T.V. Almanac*, 1968 and 1970 editions, both p. 26A. When asked how many hours they watched TV, national audience samples of individuals reported 2:17 hours in 1961, 2:38 in 1964, and 2:50 in January, 1971. See the Roper Organization, Inc., *An Extended View of Public Attitudes Toward Television and Other Mass Media, 1959–1971* (New York: Television Information Office, 1971), p. 5.

and unlikely to grow rapidly in the future. The viewing audience increases throughout the day: "From an early morning level of less than a half million households . . . [it] climbs to about 15 million households at mid-day. The audience almost doubles between 8 and 10 PM."[6] This summary statement apparently applied to the estimated average audience in the early months of 1967. Summer viewing rates are significantly lower, especially in the afternoon and evening. This is clear from the audiences in January-February 1967 and July-August 1966 since potential audiences had not changed radically. Morning, afternoon, and evening audiences for the winter months were 7.4, 17.1 and 30.4 million homes respectively. In the summer they were 6.0, 13.5 and 20.1 million.[7]

Television broadcasting in the U.S. has been overwhelmingly a commercial undertaking from the outset, although the airwaves are recognized by law, if not by the industry, to be public property. The Federal Communications Commission has been given a weak regulating authority over the medium's operators, which consists primarily in the power to grant or refuse licenses to transmitting stations. "Interference" by the FCC in commercial operations is strongly resisted by the corporations, and public sympathy usually goes to the local men of the "public" corporation rather than the government "intruders" from Washington. Indeed, it is the government as just another customer that usually must follow the dictates of the networks. A striking example of this is the treatment of politicians, who as legitimate representatives of the public should presumably have some right of access to the public air waves. They do, if they buy broadcasting time. Otherwise they must be interrupted by advertisements like everyone else.[8]

The triumph of commercial television was by no means inevitable. Governments in Europe, Canada, and Japan have managed to retain more regulatory powers, even though this often means that they must subsidize the medium. Britian and Germany, for example, both derive revenue for their support by imposing licensing fees on television receivers. Britain runs its own non-commercial network, while Germany limits advertising and prohibits the interruption of programs for commercial spots.

Public television in the U.S. is clearly no political match for commercial interests, and it lags behind its European counterparts. It is continuously short of capital and remains heavily dependent on private contributions. For many years NET (National Educational Television) was further handicapped by the "Educational" label that it carried. It has now been absorbed by PBS, the largest non-commercial network, and runs many cultural and general interest programs in addition to day-time school programming. Unlike their competitors, the public stations are openly expensive and require both tax money and contributions.[9] The financial burden of public broadcasting, of course, falls primarily on those who contribute voluntarily. The widely held belief that commercial television broadcasting is free while public broadcasting is a luxury or liability is encouraged by the major networks. For example, they are opposed to "Pay TV" because they claim it would constitute the selling of public

---

[6]*International T.V. Almanac*, 1968, p. 26A.

[7]*International T.V. Almanac*, 1968, p. 26A. The 1970 *Almanac* lists January-February 1968 audiences as 9.3, 19.1 and 29.0 million homes for the same viewing periods. This indicates audience gains in the morning and afternoon over previous years but a loss of prime time evening viewers.

[8]The Head of State, of course, is an exception. Thus President Nixon has been a prolific user of pre-empted television time.

[9]The recently founded Corporation for Public Broadcasting is grossly underfinanced. The original Carnegie Corporation commission recommended funding of at least $100 million per year, a sum about the equivalent of clandestine CIA payments to its overseas radio stations. The administration's requested appropriation in 1968 was $4.5 million. See Erik Barnouw, *The Image Empire* (New York: Oxford University Press, 1970), pp. 193–5, 339. Subsequent appropriations have risen to $23 million in fiscal 1970 and $35 million projected for 1971 and for 1972.

property, and deny the right of the individual owner to tune-in free.

Skornia has argued that commercial broadcasts are in fact by no means free to the consumer. There are, he says,

many channels through which funds are secured from the citizen to pay for broadcast service. They are indirect, and they may or may not be too high. They are, however, very real. They include what he pays for receiving equipment, installation, upkeep, and electricity or batteries; [that] part of the television-advertising products goes to pay for television time and talent costs and various other expenses. . . . [10]

The receiver costs would presumably have to be borne under any system. Most of the broadcasters' expenses are met directly by advertising fees, but these, claims Skornia, are passed on to the consumer in the form of higher prices. The standard apologia for advertising—that it increases market size, which leads to subsequent economics of scale in production, distribution, and marketing, and hence lower consumer costs—is rejected by Skornia as a myth. He finds no instances of price reduction after any successful advertising drive. Good advertising means good profits for the manufacturer, advertising agency, television networks and stations. The latter, it may be noted, do not re-allocate the bulk of their surpluses to provide better public service, nor do they cut back on commercial spot sales. They do what any rational corporation does to benefit itself—they diversify and expand.

The networks program ostensibly "what the public wants." But it is unclear who constitutes the "public," although to commercial spokesmen it is apparently the biggest minority at any given time. Nor is it readily apparent how the desires of the public, however defined, are made known. Many program decisions obviously are made initially by the networks and their sponsors. The audience is consulted, and then extremely haphazardly, only after the program is aired. The networks thus

constitute a far from perfect public forum for two-way communication.

Commercial television organizations broadcasted from 662 stations (499 VHF, 163 UHF) in 1969 compared to 637 the previous year, 611 and 587 stations in 1967 and 1966, and 569 in 1965.[11] There remains a limited station expansion, most of which can be attributed to new UHF transmitters (7 new VHF and 44 UHF stations were added between 1967 and 1969). The revenues for networks and stations have similarly increased every year since 1947, growing from to $2.20 billion in 1966 to $2.52 billion in 1968. The early growth rates of more than 100 per cent per year, however, are now a thing of the past. Income before federal taxes has also risen steadily, from more than $311 million in 1962 to almost $493 million in 1966 and $495 million in 1968. A disproportionate share of this income was taken by the three largest companies: In 1968 the three networks earned $56.4 million, their fifteen owned and operated stations a further $122.4 million, while the remaining $316.0 million was distributed among the 622 independently owned stations.[12] Revenues to the networks came primarily from the sale of advertising time and programs to their owned and affiliated stations. The shares of individual networks in this revenue between 1965 and 1967 show that CBS is still the dominant network corporation at home.[13]

The major networks are not autonomous entrepreneurial establishments in any real sense. NBC

---

[10]Skornia, *op. cit.*, p. 90.

[11]All statistics in this paragraph are from the *International T.V. Almanac*, 1968, 1969, 1970 editions, pp. 20A-26A in each.

[12]In 1966, network earnings and those of their stations were $78.7 million and $108.1 million, respectively. The other 593 stations shared $306.1 million between them. See *International T.V. Almanac*, 1968 edition, pp. 20A, 22A.

[13]Computed from data in 1968 and 1970 *Almanacs*.

Per Cent of Total Network Revenue

	1965	1966	1967
ABC	27%	28%	27.5%
CBS	39%	39%	39.0%
NBC	34%	33%	33.5%

is a subsidiary of RCA as are Hertz, Commercial Credit Co., Random House, Sunbury and Dunbar Music, and Defense Electronic Products; while CBS's "family" is reported to include Holt, Rinehart & Winston, Creative Playthings, Baily Films, and the New York Yankees baseball team. ABC-TV and its international divisions are part of the greater ABC-Paramount organization which is in turn linked to Gulf Western. An earlier merger of ABC with International Telephone and Telegraph Corporation (ITT) proposed in December, 1965, was forbidden by the United States Department of Justice early in 1968. Even so, it is apparent that all the networks have commercial links or interests that extend far beyond public broadcasting.

The networks actively promote the ideology of free commercial television, programming for mass markets, time priority for advertising, and resistance to regulation. Alan Thomas has pointed out that each television viewer has three distinct roles: As *audience* he wants to be entertained and to indulge himself; as *market* he is open for a sale; but as *public* he rationally dictates what he needs for his own good. In Canada, Thomas explains, the

> . . . public strongly supports the Canadian type of broadcasting, although as audience many of the same people may watch television programs from United States stations along Canada's borders. The Canadian Public is very Canadian. The Canadian Audience and Market are essentially American—very much like the people of the United States in the same roles.[14]

United States television at home, with minor exceptions, serves audience and market.

[14]Alan Thomas, *Audience, Market, Public: An Evaluation of Canadian Broadcasting*, Occasional Paper No. 7 (University of British Columbia, Department of University Extension), April, 1960, cited in Skornia, *op. cit.*, p. 122.

The first selection on television, an article by Hyman H. Goldin, outlines the part played by the networks in television broadcasting. He describes their affiliation arrangements and their position as middlemen between program producers and transmitting stations. The big three clearly dominate television in the U.S. and take a disproportionate share of profits. Their domination may eventually be weakened in the future by new innovations—notably the growing use of satellites and the expansion of cable television.

Several media critics, including Harry Skornia, studied the owners and higher executives of the networks and concluded that they are overwhelmingly oriented toward business. These critics blame the economic imperatives which guide the networks for the banality of TV programming. These criticisms are examined by Robert Eck, who concludes that bad programming is not due to ignorant or sinister managers, pollsters, sponsors, or advertisers; rather, it results from the commercial nature of the broadcasting enterprise itself. Paul Klein's argument which follows generally agrees with Eck but places a share of the blame on the passiveness of audiences.

The selections by Sir William Haley and Mel Wax both deal with news programming. Haley shows how commercialism influences broadcast journalism. Newscasters have been promoted as entertainment stars and the news in general is treated as just one more program in which to set advertisements. Such failure to take the information function of the news seriously, he warns, poses a dangerous threat to democracy. Wax describes the highly successful news activities of a public TV station in San Francisco with which he is intimately involved. He demonstrates that the mass public will watch quality news presented by expert reporters without the usual news gimmickry, if given the chance.

Reprinted from Atlantic *(July, 1969), pp. 87–89. Copyright © 1969, by The Atlantic Monthly Company, Bostin, Mass. Reprinted with permission.*

The Television Overlords

HYMAN H. GOLDIN

AT THE apex of the television structure are the network overlords, CBS, NBC, and ABC. These three networks dominate television as General Motors, Ford, and Chrysler control the fortunes of the automobile industry. For the American public, television is network television: the program it watches on the screen typically bears a network stamp. For the owner of the local station, whether baron or serf, the prime source of economic affluence is affiliation with a network. Next to the FCC license, his most treasured asset is the network contract. In the national television power game the local station is a pawn, or at best a knight.

For example, NBC, in unity with its parent, RCA, decided in the mid-1950s to upgrade the size of the markets in which it owned stations. This plan served both the manufacturing interests of RCA and the broadcast interests of NBC. Inconveniently, Westinghouse, a rival in the equipment field, owned an NBC-affiliated station in Philadelphia, close to a central RCA complex. Westinghouse was told that if it wished to continue its affiliations with NBC, it must transfer its ownership of the Philadelphia station to the network and accept in its place the NBC station in Cleveland, a $3 million cash settlement, and a less desirable market. After an agonizing internal struggle, Westinghouse succumbed. The FCC, which had conducted a thorough investigation disclosing the coercive tactics, shrugged its shoulders and concluded that if Westinghouse, a giant in its own right, "agreed," the FCC had no choice but to approve the transfer. Subsequently

the Justice Department and the federal courts invalidated the transfer and the FCC ultimately required that NBC return to Cleveland, and Westinghouse regained its station in Philadelphia. Westinghouse, it should be noted, is the largest of the non-network multiple owners.

While there is now and then private grousing among affiliates, direct confrontation on general policy by an individual or group of affiliates, when it occurs, is kept within definite bounds. The areas in which there is occasional dissent have to do with network compensation payments, the amount of commercial time adjacent to or within a network program permitted the affiliates, and sexy programs.

The national media market in which television is pre-eminent is a network domain. The networks create a national audience for advertisers. Each network produces or selects a program schedule for nationwide distribution; each selects for affiliation approximately 200 local stations in as many cities, reaching into practically every television household; each rents interconnection facilities from the Telephone Company to transmit simultaneously to each affiliate the programs and advertising messages which originate largely in Hollywood and New York; each network determines the time at which such programs will be broadcast locally; and finally, each network contracts with national advertisers through advertising agencies to defray the program and time costs and supply the advertising "plugs," and these monies the network shares—

THE TELEVISION OVERLORDS
Hyman H. Goldin

unevenly—with its affiliates.

Except for news, public affairs, and sports, the overwhelming proportion of network programs are not produced by the networks, but the networks acquire rights from program packagers, TV film companies, and feature-film distributors. These suppliers engage in intensive competition to persuade the three overlords to look favorably upon their works—pilot programs and story lines into which they have sunk tens and hundreds of thousands of dollars—and to bless them with network acceptance. Not surprisingly, allegations of abuse abound.

The tangible result of this complex of technical and economic arrangements is that for a single Wednesday hour, 9 P.M. to 10 P.M., advertisers pay the networks roughly $950,000 for a total of 18 minutes of advertising participations (6 minutes per network). Payments by advertisers for the network participations are not publicly disclosed, but the trade publications occasionally disclose so-called price lists used by networks in negotiations with advertising agencies. In addition to the network commercials, "nonprogram" matter includes promotional announcements, credits, public service spots (for example, the anti-cigarette ads), and commercial spots inserted locally by each affiliated station.

Advertisers compete for this opportunity because they are assured that over 32 million television homes (out of an industry estimate of 57.5 million TV homes) are tuned to the network programs during the hour—and to the accompanying commercial messages.

The overwhelming proportion of potential viewers in the other 25 million TV households are not using their sets because the family members are not at home, are engaged in other activities, or are not interested in any of the programs televised. Only a small percentage of the public during prime time tunes to the non-network programs beamed by unaffiliated stations (usually in the score of major metropolises where there are more stations than networks).

The networks play a dual role in the system: they not only control network program production or selection and network distribution, but through their owned stations in the larger markets control network program exhibition for some 25 to 30 percent of all TV homes. In the three most important centers—New York, Los Angeles, and Chicago—only the networks themselves through their owned stations broadcast network programs.

Two financial yardsticks of network dominance are their shares of industry revenues and profits. Of the $2.275 billion television revenues recorded for 1967, 53 percent ($1.216 billion) went to the three network overlords, including their 15 owned stations. The remainder was shared by 604 other TV stations. Similarly, of the industry's profits, only slightly less than 40 percent ($160 million) went to the three network organizations.

Among the overlords, CBS and NBC are more equal than ABC. The Big Two lead in ratings, fulltime affiliates, and profits. Financial figures for the industry are published annually by the FCC, but without disclosing individual network or station expense. However, a highly regarded and generally accurate trade-press newsletter (*Television Digest*) has published this "secret" information. The figures for 1967 revealed that ABC lost $17 million on its network operations, and received only 8 percent of the combined network and owned-station profits as contrasted with CBS's 48 percent and NBC's 44 percent.

The [following] figures do not include revenues that networks gross from other television activities. For example, after programs have exhausted their network runs, high-rated series (for example, *Perry Mason, The Flintstones, Gilligan's Island, The Munsters, I Love Lucy, The Twilight Zone, Route 66*) are sold market-by-market to any station that will pay the price (affiliated or not) as "syndicated" programs. The networks also sell their series to television authorities in other countries, and because costs have been recovered from domestic sales, they are competitive with lower-budgeted foreign productions. Not only do the networks dominate the U.S.

Network Operations: 1967			
	CBS	NBC	ABC
	(millions of dollars)		
Network revenues	$362	$327	$264
(before federal income taxes)			
Network profits	42	31	(17)
Owned-station revenues	95	95	73
Owned-station profits	35	40	29
(before federal income taxes)			
Combined network and	77	71	12
owned-station profits			
Percentage share of network	48%	44%	8%
and owned-station profits			

(*Television Digest*, vol. 8, no. 19, May 6, 1968, p. 1.)

television program market, they are also an important source of popular American TV programming on world television.

The network system creates rich rewards not only for the overlords but for the constituent affiliated stations. Indeed the mutual interest of the networks and the affiliated stations in the system explains the vitality and durability of the network institution both economically and politically. A station can plug into a network line and receive a daily stream of programs having broad appeal to its public. Of course each station also includes in its daily schedule programs which it produces or acquires from non-network sources: notably news, weather, and sports, films produced for TV (distributed by independent syndicators as well as by networks), and feature films.

The network pays the affiliate somewhat less than 30 percent of the gross charges for broadcasting the program. In addition, the station is permitted by the network to sell a prescribed amount of commercial time within and adjacent to the network programs, the proceeds from which it does not share with the network. In a large market a single 20-second "adjacency" will bring $1000 to $1500, because the network program has created a mass audience for the station. It is no wonder that when a station sells for $20 million or more, the tangible

property may be valued only at $2 million whereas the primary asset is the network contract. Several of the media barons, including Westinghouse, Time Inc., and Corinthian, have sought to persuade the Internal Revenue Service, the tax courts, and the federal judiciary that the network contracts should be eligible for amortization, thus reducing the annual tax obligations of stations they bought.

Only in the largest markets do unaffiliated stations — and usually only one such independent station per market — reap the fullness of the television bounty.

From the early days of broadcasting, the power of the network "chains" has troubled Congress, the FCC, and the Justice Department as well as disaffected elements within the industry. Various network investigations and hearings have led to restrictions: a network organization may not own or operate more than one network; it may not option the time of its affiliates; it may not contract for more than a two-year term; it may not control the rates charged by affiliates for non-network times; and it may not prevent an affiliate from contracting with more than one network. And, of course, it may not own and operate more than seven AM radio stations, seven FM radio stations, and seven television stations of which no more than five may be VHF stations. These and other network rules and regulations have corrected the grosser abuses of network power.

But network dominance persists. It persists because network service is integral to the nation's broadcast service and has been so recognized by Congress and the FCC. It persists because network service enjoys overwhelming public acceptance. A network commands talent and resources immeasurably greater than those available to any single station or groups of stations.

Networks are the source of *Laugh-In, Bonanza, Mission Impossible, Mayberry RFD, FBI, Bewitched,* the Bob Hope specials; of coverage of professional and college football, the World Series, the Olympics, political conventions, presidential campaigns, presidential messages, the daily news, space flights,

THE TELEVISION OVERLORDS
Hyman H. Goldin

United Nations debates, congressional hearings, and unscheduled "special events." Much of this would not otherwise be available with anything like the immediacy and thoroughness that network economics makes possible.

Earlier, the same three networks, CBS, NBC, and ABC, dominated radio. Ultimately their control was undermined, not by governmental actions, but by changing technology. Popular recordings gave stations an alternative and competitive program service. Concurrently, the superior television medium captured the night-time audiences, the prime target of network advertisers.

If networking in television is changed in the future, the cause will be technology and not governmental intervention. A prevalent myth is that if networks were licensed or directly regulated by the FCC, they would become significantly more responsive to the public interest. The truth is that most network practices are within the purview of existing FCC authority. This is particularly true because each TV network owns stations which are licensed. In some areas, the network acts "as if" it were licensed by the FCC. For example, a complaint of unfairness lodged against a network program need not be pursued with each of the 200 affiliated stations that may have aired the program but with the network that originated it.

Technological changes in the offing could alter the present network system. For example, when a satellite-to-home service becomes economically feasible, network overlords could reach the public directly without the assistance of local affiliates. This would undermine most of the television barons and, at least initially, further strengthen the power and profitability of the networks. However, if enough channels were available for satellite-to-home broadcasting, or if by governmental decree use of the available channels were required to be leased on a common-carrier basis (or even rationed), other national program suppliers could compete with the networks. Conceivably, the networks could slip from being overlords to being merely greater barons than any current counterpart.

Alternatively, if all homes were connected by cable—as is technically feasible and not impossible economically within the next two decades—the networks could rent national channels and reach directly into all homes. Such a system would open a larger number of other communications channels to competing program suppliers.

In the long run, television audiences could become as fragmented as radio audiences, and TV network dominance would wane.

Challenges are also posed by the advent of subscription television and the introduction of the EVR (electronic video recording). Neither is an immediate threat to the networks. Furthermore, if subscription television should prove popular, the networks have made explicit that nothing would prevent their entry into that field; while the EVR, the visual counterpart of the stereo record, is an invention of CBS.

More likely during the next five years is the appearance of a fourth network to compete with, and share the profits with, the other three. As experience in radio suggests, this will be a change without a difference.

The Real Masters of Television

ROBERT ECK

As THE television network librarians begin to tally and rack this season's last cans of film and tape, it is possible to predict with sad certainty what next year will bring.

Except for more old movies, next year's commercial television will be the same as this has been. The same green tendrils of hope will grow into the same weedy crop of formula-written, formula-directed shows, ranging from pseudo-Westerns through cast-iron fantasies, to what *Variety* once called hix pix. This prediction is also valid for 1968, and the year after that, and the year after that, ad infinitum.

Why can't commercial television be improved? After all, its diseases seem to be no mystery. Everyone knows it is infested by evil advertising men who befoul the programs with their greedy touch. Their dupes, the sponsors, are for the most part a group of well-meaning, affluent bumblers — misguided souls who need instruction in cultural responsibility from you, me, Goodman Ace, and David Susskind. The networks they deal with are stupid bureaucracies, dominated by frightened vice-presidents, natural enemies of everything that is fresh and intelligent. To make matters worse, all three idiot species are being bamboozled by a fourth: the audience researcher, a charlatan who has persuaded them he can take a continuous count of the nation's many millions of television viewers, either by telephoning the homes or bugging the sets of a thousand or two families whose identities are shrouded in mystery. By contrast to these fools

and villains, there are a few exemplary sponsors who, out of the sheer goodness of their enlightened hearts, pay for the programs you and I like. And waiting in the wings is a benevolent government, needing only stronger prompting to move onstage and straighten out the mess.

If these familiar figures of cocktail-party folklore even came close to representing the actualities of commercial television, there might be some hope for improvement. But they do not. They are a collection of wishes, falsehoods, and semi-truths, embodied in explanatory myths. As we shall see, it is not because of these myths but because of the more complex realities underlying them that commercial television is as amenable to reform as the adult Bengal tiger.

THE MYTH OF THE EVIL ADMAN'S INFLUENCE

While it has become fashionable among intellectual liberals to lay the sins of our materialism at the doorstep of the advertising agent, today's television programming is one sin he can rightly disclaim. He has virtually nothing to say about it. There was a time when he was a grand panjandrum of programming, but that was thirty years ago, in the heyday of radio, when advertising agencies literally produced the programs their clients sponsored. In 1940, for example, A. D. Lasker, the head of Pepsodent's advertising agency, could decide whether Bob Hope, popular star of Pepsodent's radio show, would get the thousand-dollar weekly

THE REAL MASTERS OF TELEVISION
Robert Eck

raise he was asking for. In 1967, Johnny Carson, popular star of *The Tonight Show*, who earns over $200,000 a year, need not even say hello to an advertising agent.

Although the business patterns of radio carried over into the early days of television, by the mid-1950s the television networks succeeded in taking away from the advertising men the controls they had historically exercised over program material. In this, the networks had no choice. Not only were television shows far more difficult to produce than radio shows, but television itself was rapidly growing into a business far more vast and risky—a business in which the profits (and the eventual existence) of a network depended not on its ability to cozen sponsors but to deliver measurable audience. Programming—the means of doing this—could not be left in the hands of outsiders, semi-professionals, men to whom entertainment was only a sideline.

For the same reasons, production of television shows shifted from Chicago and New York to the foothills of the Santa Monica mountains. The moviemakers out there were not only the most expert producers of mass entertainment but also the most efficient. The money put into a live production is gone the moment the floodlights die. but films can be sold and resold, again and again, both here and abroad. A filmed TV series can be profitable even if it loses money on its first run.

Nowadays, the networks make a practice of inviting advertisers and their agencies to preview the prototype films of such series (the pilots), but that's about as far as it goes. Admen do not put programs on the air, don't materially change them once they're on, and don't take them off.

THE MYTH OF THE
AUDIENCE-COUNTING CHARLATANS

Nothing about television has been the subject of so much childish pique and wishful thinking as the rating services which undertake to measure television audiences. Inside the business, they are hated and feared, because their tabulations can make a

man a potential millionaire or a failure in a matter of weeks. Outside, they are distrusted by many egocentric citizens who refuse to believe that the viewing habits of a small group of strangers could possibly reflect their own and, by the same token, the nation's. These are the people who, in the words of a disgusted research director, "think you have to drink the whole quart of milk to discover it is sour."

The plain truth about audience counting is that nobody in his right mind would spend millions out of a private, corporate, political, or charitable purse to propel images into an uncharted void. Even the BBC uses random samples of its audience for guidance. And while random sampling can always be attacked because it only approaches perfection, so can a literal head-count. The more heads that must be counted, the more chances there are for human error in interviewing and arithmetic. This is why the Bureau of the Census sometimes prefers random sampling to a total count.

The standard, though far from the only audience sample in the television business is that of the Nielsen Audimeter survey, which measures audience continuously by means of a recording device attached to television sets in some 1,400 homes. There are a few drawbacks to this ingenious system. First, it assumes that whenever a set is turned on, so are its owners, which is usually, but not always, true. Second, families who are *not* keenly interested in television generally refuse to let the Nielsen people install Audimeters in their sets. Third, not all Audimeter recordings reach Nielsen headquarters in Evanston, Illinois, in time for inclusion in the tabulations. Fourth, the Nielsen sample has an admitted statistical error of three points.

Of course, the networks, the advertisers, the agencies, all of whom employ statistical experts, are fully aware of the weaknesses of the Nielsen figures; but they also know that these figures are considerably better than none at all, so they use them in a fairly uninhibited fashion.

The two most important aspects of this use seem to have escaped public notice:

(1) Both the men who run the networks and the men who run the companies that use network advertising know that everyone uses the same audience figures and that, therefore, their competitors are subject to the same errors and inadequacies as are they. For competitive business purposes, the inadequacies of the ratings tend to wash out over a period of time, just as would the inadequacies of a short deck in a poker game.

(2) The audience count is not a popularity contest or even primarily a guide to the judgment of network executives. It is part of a financial measurement.

For each dollar a businessman spends, he wants a comparative measure of what it has bought. In the case of advertising audience, his measure is cost per thousand people reached. He started using this measure long before network television, or even network radio, existed. To find which of several newspapers or magazines gave him the most for his money, he divided the cost of putting an ad in each of them by the number of thousands of people who bought copies. Now he does the same for television, dividing the cost of a minute commercial (about $40,000 in prime evening time) by the number of thousands of viewers who were tuned in.

"How much do I pay for every thousand people my commercial reaches—a dollar-and-a-half, a dollar-seventy-five, two dollars, two-twenty-five?" It is on the answer to this question that television shows succeed or fail, far more than on the gross figures of the Nielsen or Trendex ratings. The BBC, of course, would never use it audience figures in this way, but the BBC has no stockholders and requires no profits.

THE MYTH OF THE BUMBLING, UNENLIGHTENED SPONSORS

A shocking thing has happened to most old-fashioned television sponsors. They have disappeared. In their place is a heartless scheme called a scatter plan. Except in moments of extreme frustration, nobody in the business ever wanted a sponsor to vanish. A few years ago, in fact, the networks would only sell the commercial use of a weekly show to a regular weekly sponsor or, at most, to two alternating sponsors. However, the supply of companies with enough advertising money to buy television time this way is limited. NBC and CBS, then the undisputed leaders of the field, were able to attract such large advertisers without undue difficulty. But it was a different matter for ABC. Lacking the programming, the audience, and the stations to get all the large sponsors it needed, ABC began selling off its unsponsored time *à la carte*, offering smaller advertisers the chance to buy a minute here and a minute there.

What began as pure expedient has since grown to be the dominant trade practice, transformed into the scatter plan, a sophisticated purchasing device that permits the advertiser to purposefully scatter his commercials among different shows on the same network. Most television advertisers, including the biggest, are delighted with the scatter plan because it permits them to reach a wider number of viewers; it offers them more likelihood of reaching the kind of viewers they want to reach; it lets them suit their expenditures to the season (as the barrage before Christmas or June graduation indicates); and it averages their risks. Sponsored shows may turn out to be unwatched turkeys; scatter plans do not.

That's why probably three-quarters of all national television—amounting to around a billion dollars annually—is now paid for by scatter plans. It's not unusual for Procter & Gamble, one of the country's three or four heaviest television advertisers, to have commercials for its products on thirty to forty shows. A booming pharmaceutical firms such as Miles Laboratories may have commercials on half that number.

A scatter plan is born when an advertising agency tells the networks that one of its clients is in the market for television time, and describes the nature of the desired audience. If a client is a breakfast-food maker, he will usually want a family audience, which he can get by scattering his commercials among such early evening shows as *Lassie*, *Daktari*,

THE REAL MASTERS OF TELEVISION
Robert Eck

The Andy Griffith Show, and *Lost in Space.* If he makes floor wax, he will pick daytime shows that appeal more to women than to children. The businesses that make stickum for false teeth and mine gold out of tired blood want to talk to older people, which means they prefer such shows as *Candid Camera, What's My Line?,* and *The Lawrence Welk Show.*

The scatter plans submitted by the networks are almost never bought before being subjected to a process of juggling and horse trading: "Look, the way it is now, the price is all wrong. A dollar-fifty-four a thousand. And you've given us four minutes on *Make a Bet,* which we all know is a dog. Tell you what, though, we'll take two of those four minutes on *Make a Bet,* if you'll give us the other two minutes on a *Lucy* re-run." If the suggested changes are made and the plan bought, a housewife in Houston will see a new commercial while watching a re-run of *I Love Lucy.* She will never know or care that somewhere up North, an agency man is telling his client, "On the basis of the Nielsens, we are getting daytime women for a dollar-forty-seven a thousand," and that she is a .147-cent daytime woman.

For all his arrogant foibles, the old-time sponsor usually took a proprietary pride in his show. It was more apt to be a manifestation of his vanity than an accurate reflection of the show's intrinsic worth, but it did exist and it could be appealed to. It has been replaced by the depersonalized processes of an audience market, in which viewers by the millions are counted, sorted, graded, and sold to specification at so much a thousand head. There is not much to be gained by writing a letter of praise — or disgust — to a scatter plan.

THE MYTH OF THE EXEMPLARY, ENLIGHTENED SPONSORS

Most of the fast-vanishing breed of real sponsors remaining on television are distinguished by their benignity. They sponsor fine programs and regularly receive Good Boy Medals in the form of various trophies, plaques, and journalistic commendations, accompanied by the wistfully spoken hope that other advertisers will take the hint and become good boys, too.

This, alas, will never be. The good sponsor is a rare bird not only in its sponsoring habits but also in its generally peculiar business characteristics. Unlike the bulk of television advertisers, the sponsor of the *Bell Telephone Hour* is a huge natural monopoly whose profits will not be even slightly affected by the way it uses television. The *Hallmark Hall of Fame* is the darling of one of the last of the old school of owner-managers, a rough-hewn multimillionaire named Joyce Hall, who can do pretty much what he likes. What he likes is to sponsor inoffensive plays of proven worth, elegantly produced. The extent to which this has helped Hallmark sales will never be known since greeting-card sales do not respond to television advertising in the directly traceable way sales of many household products do.

Other "cultural" sponsors are often companies with small advertising budgets who use the opportunity afforded by public-affairs or cultural uplift shows to buy television time cheap. Prior to each season, the networks plan for and underwrite the costs of a number of thoughtful pieces of reportage and a few well-intended dramatic shows, knowing even as they do it, that low audience forecasts will make it necessary to sell them off to commercial sponsors at a loss.

A startling insight into the strange economies of such programs is provided by the case of the Arthur Miller play, *Death of a Salesman,* one of the most impressive shows of 1966. It was produced by David Susskind and sponsored by Xerox Corporation, a company that in May 1966, received a trustees' award from the Academy of Television Arts and Sciences for its contributions to the betterment of television programming. However, Susskind was not paid to produce *Salesman* by this exemplary sponsor, but by CBS, in whose vaults the completed tape reposed for some months while CBS vainly sought sponsors—and while the asking price kept dropping. When Xerox at last bought the telecast of the play, they got it for what can be described in today's market as a song. The financial realities behind *Death of a Salesman* are:

Production cost (with no profit for the network)	$580,000
Network time charges	300,000
Total cost to CBS	$880,000
Price to Xerox	250,000
Net loss to CBS	$630,000

In other words, the real sponsor of *Death of a Salesman* was the network, which cut its losses by selling the ostensible sponsorship to Xerox, a company whose enormous profits and lack of need for broad television audience eminently quality it for the role of patron of the arts.*

As time goes by, we shall probably see fewer rather than more good sponsors in television. In the case of the authentically benevolent sponsors, the by-guess-and-by-God judgment of old-line management will give way to the facts-and-figures quantification of Harvard Business School graduates. The rest of the good sponsors are dependent on the willingness of the networks to produce and sell good shows at fire-sale prices. Since the networks' recent profits have been phenomenal, we can assume their current willingness to absorb losses for the sake of prestige is about as high as it is ever going to be. Any reverses in profit will probably be reflected by the departure of some of those good sponsors who are only good when the network helps them be.

THE MYTH OF THE STUPID BUREAUCRATIC NETWORKS AND THEIR FRIGHTENED VICE-PRESIDENTS

"Television is a triumph of equipment over people and the minds that control it are so small you could put them in the navel of a flea and still have room beside them for a network vice-president's heart."

When Fred Allen said that in 1952, he was suffering from an illusion still shared by millions who assume from the nature of most television programming that the networks are in the communications and entertainment business.

They are not.

It is true they deal in communications and entertainment. It is true that millions of words are annually printed to describe television programming. It is also true that from time to time, a network president will strike a Belasco pose. But the fact is that, unlike a Belasco, a Merrick, or a Bing, he collects no subscriptions and has no box office. He gets every cent of his money from advertisers. The network he operates is a gigantic, electronic medicine wagon with a Hollywood cast, whose entire reason for being lies in its ability to gather millions of men, women, and children to see and hear the advertiser's pitch.

The networks' business is the audience-delivery business, and if their vice-presidents are frightened men, they have good reason to be. They are involved in a unique and frightening enterprise. Their customer, the typical television advertiser, is a maker of package goods. His products (soda pop, soap, prepared foods, etc.) cost little, are bought often, and are used in every home. His audience requirements are limitless and unrelated to cultural or socioeconomic levels. He wants as much audience as he can get as cheap as he can get it.

This customer's principal audience supplier, the network, knows that for its part, the more scatter-plan audience it can deliver per dollar of production and telecasting charges, the lower the advertiser's true cost will be, the more he will tend to use the network for his advertising, and the more money the network will make. What this has led to is unparalleled in the history of publication, radio, theater, or motion pictures—a quest for audience which, carried to its logical end, is impossible and absurd. The mechanical rabbit each network is

THE REAL MASTERS OF TELEVISION
Robert Eck

chasing is no less than total share of total audience: all the television viewers in the United States. No network will ever catch the rabbit, but they cannot stop themselves from trying.

The consequences of the chase revealed themselves drastically for the first time during the 1959–60 season, a year that gave the lie to the irreparable optimists who thought, and still may think, that television, properly used, can slowly lift the tastes of the masses, shaw by shaw, until 25 million American families commonly spend evenings of Shakespeare in their living rooms.

In 1959, NBC and CBS were sufficiently rich and successful to try to inaugurate a process of cultural uplift and were, in fact, presenting a fairly wide spectrum of regular programming which ranged from *Playhouse 90* to the equally well-rehearsed *$64,000 Question*. ABC, unfortunately, was poor, insecure, and ambitious. In the fall of 1959, under the guidance of a shrewd, personable sales executive, Oliver Treyz, ABC launched a group of new shows distinguished by stylized violence and unstylized gore. Its many new cops-and-robbers shows included the renowned *Untouchables* series, as well as *Hawaiian Eye* and *The Dectectives*, while five new Westerns brought its total number of Westerns to a total of ten a week.

This move was righteously criticized in press and pulpit but, in terms of the multitudes of viewers it could deliver to advertisers, the 1959–60 season proved the turning point in the fortunes of ABC. As an audience-delivery system, it suddenly moved up from a low third place to a close second, forcing NBC and CBS to compromise their programming standards so rapidly and completely that by spring of 1961, Ollie Treyz had what must have been the extreme pleasure of salting his competitor's wounds. In a speech delivered in April of that year, he accused NBC and CBS of slavishly copying ABC's grand new program ideas and coolly suggested they stick to their own lasts.

Of course they weren't about to follow Treyz's advice. He had taught them a lesson of the most unforgettable kind: an expensive one. In the audience-delivery business, you do not have the luxury of setting either your standards or those of your audience. Instead, they are set for you by the relative success of your competitors.

Since then, the pursuit of total audience has been conducted with tactics not always successful but usually pragmatic and cunning. In general, the networks have learned how to deftly mass-produce the predictable novelties and uncomplicated heroes, clowns, and villains that have always delighted the mass of humanity. There is nothing new about Tarzan, who joined the NBC program lineup in 1966. He made a fortune for his creator, Edgar Rice Burroughs, fifty years ago, probably because in fashioning him Burroughs hit on a simple heroic archetype of great antiquity. Tarzan's essential character (such as it is) bears a striking resemblance to that of Enkidu, the nature-boy of the five-thousand-year-old Sumerian story of Gilgamesh. In the words of the epic, Enkidu is "the strongest in the world, he is like an immortal from heaven. He ranges over the hills with the wild beasts and eats grass . . . He fills in the pits which I dig and tears up my traps set for the game; he helps beasts escape and now they slip through my fingers." Zane Grey, Gene Porter, Conan Doyle, and most of the other turn-of-the-century popular novelists could have been highly successful television writers. Moreover, if you bother to examine such popular home entertainment devices of the 'thirties as *The Saturday Evening Post* and *Collier's*, you will find a blueprint for most of today's nighttime programming in the form of serial episodes built around a few continuing characters: the Mr. Glencannon sea stories, the Ephraim Tutt law stories, the Perry Mason and Nero Wolfe detective stories. Westerns were an editorial habit. Other program materials can be traced to the once-popular, now vanished, pulp magazines that specialized in war, Western, crime, and science fiction.

In the circumstances, it is inaccurate to complain that the audience-delivery systems are subverting the popular taste. What they are doing is accommodating it better than it has ever been accommodated before. A prime example is the TV version of the Western. Western films have been a foolproof staple of the entertainment field ever since Blace Tracey silently gunned down Silk Miller in *Hell's Hinges*, fifty years ago, because they can be filmed with cost-cutting speed and almost invariably make money. So it is hardly surprising to find a lot of television time given over to the horse opera. What comes as a slight shock is to realize that many of television's so-called Westerns—including the most popular—aren't real Western at all. From time to time, a posse may still pursue the villains up the draw, a stage may be held up, there may be gunfights; but for the most part television's Western heroes are concerned with Human Problems. The badman is as frequently reformed as killed. Often he is completely missing from the script.

For purposes of audience delivery, the trouble with the authentic Western is that its appeal is restricted to grown men and small boys; so a bastard form has begun to replace it, the sagebrush soap opera: Marshal Dillon of *Gunsmoke* is Dodge City's resident sociologist and Ben Cartwright, the patriarch of *Bonanza*, is kindly, wise, old Father Barbour in chaps. Underneath the outward semblance of the violent morality play that men and boys find relieving and pleasurable, the sagebrush soap opera presents the emotionally manipulative, self-conscious interplay of communal and family personalities women enjoy. The hero may, in fact, be an entire family, because the show is intended to attract entire families.

The immense popularity of *Bonanza*, champion of this new breed, testifies to the fact that the constant attempt to deliver larger audiences has made American commercial television the most awesome mechanism of mass entertainment ever devised. Week in and week out, *Bonanza* draws audiences far larger than the total population of most European countries. A number of other shows draw almost as strongly; and during the prime evening hours, the average number of viewers attracted by the combined offerings of the three networks can be estimated at around 70 million.

That is quite a house.

To suggest in the face of such monumental achievement that the networks have failed is to spit into the wind. In their own terms, at least, they have been a resounding success. Today, as they settle into their mature business practice, we can confidently expect them to continue chasing the uncatchable rabbit with the sharpened skills and elastic agility born of bitter but rewarding experience. Theirs is an infinite pursuit which has in it small room for cultural dabblings.

THE MYTH OF THE BENEVOLENT GOVERNMENTAL POWER

During his tenure as crusading chairman of the Federal Communications Commission, Newton Minow, with strong support from the press, managed to badger the networks into carrying slightly more public-service programming. He also managed to convey to the public the impression that the federal government was capable of improving the quality of commercial television.

That is mostly a false impression. Not only is the power to regulate program content specifically denied the Commission under section 326 of the Federal Communications Act; it is doubtful that any such power could exist because of the practical difficulties that lie in the way of defining it. To put up a stop sign at a traffic intersection, and require everyone to come to a full stop before crossing, is a perfectly workable arrangement. But to put up a sign saying "good judgment," and to pass a law requiring everyone to use good judgment before crossing, verges on nonsense. Yet the problem of defining good judgment at an intersection is trivial beside the problem of defining good judgment in the construction of the 7,000 hours of programming each station broadcasts in the course of a year.

What the government can do—and has done very little—is encourage alternatives to commercial network television. With Minow cheering it on, Congress did pass a law requiring that all new TV sets be capable of receiving ultra-high-frequency

THE REAL MASTERS OF TELEVISION
Robert Eck

signals. This was done in order to stimulate estab-lishment of UHF stations, but whether these will ever provide an attractive alternative to the net-works remains to be seen. The two UHF stations in my area fill their time with ancient, sub-B movies, sportscasts, travelogues, old BBC programs, and the Manion Forum.

The FCC could, but probably will not, improve educational television by approving the Ford Foundation plan to form a nonprofit corporation to manage the forthcoming domestic communications satellite. This plan would give educational television its first national hookup free, plus a badly needed $30 million a year out of the satellite's commercial revenues.

Again, by encouraging that fifteen-year-old orphan, pay-TV, the FCC might help create a desirable alternative to present commercial pro-gramming. A year ago, after studying the 1965 petition of Zenith Radio Corporation—which, with RKO General, has been running a long-term pay-TV experiment in Hartford, Connecticut—the Commission declared itself ready to authorize national pay-TV, subject to comment from those affected by it. At this writing, it had not acted, but favorable action was expected.

The common denominator of these alternatives is that all of them—UHF, satellite communications, pay-TV—are products of advances in a sophisticated and rapidly accelerating technology. This technology itself eventually may supply the most flexible and practical alternative to commercial television in the form of a simple, low-cost video recorder-player for home use. There now exists a small recorder which uses ordinary quarter-inch audio tape to record and play back both color and black-and-white television programs. Invented by Marvin Camras of the Illinois Institute of Technology's Research Institute, it is capable of recording or playing two hours of unbroken material and could be made to sell for less than $300. In essence, the video re-corder (and someday there will be even easier and cheaper forms of it) is an alternative not only to commercial television, but also to pay-TV, for wide-spread ownership of recorders would result in a video recording industry and in the sale, rental, and library loan of recorded television programs of much the same general range as today's audio recordings. The effective differences between com-mercial television, pay-TV, and video recording can be put this way: no matter how much you might like to see a special television production of *Der Freischütz*, you are not likely to see it on commercial television. In the improbable event that it does appear, it will do so just once, on a Saturday or Sunday afternoon, and it will be thoroughly frac-tured by commercials. Your chances of seeing it on pay-TV would probably not be a great deal better. If it should be programmed, there would be no commercials, but you would have to watch it on one of the few days it was being presented. With video recorders and recordings, your chances of see *Der Freischütz* would be quite good. You could rent it without any commercials and watch it any time of the day you pleased.

Unfortunately, however, this agreeable prospect lies some distance in the future—by five, ten, or fifteen years. Right now, the large electronics firms are too busy making color sets for the multitudinous majority who dote on commercial television to worry about making recorders for the minority who do not.

And until video recording or some other alterna-tive is realized, we will continue to be stuck with commercial television, which will continue to grind its repetitive, skillful, profitable way. Television reviewers will angrily scold, instructively praise, and loudly hope. Television producers will brag about hairbreadth advances over mediocrity. Television executives will count their cultural contributions and discuss their frequently magnificent public-information programs. Do not be deceived. Critics and defenders alike are symbiotically linked to the great audience-delivery systems. Those systems are married to cost-per-thousand, compelled to the pursuit of total audience, and—with factories in Hollywood, main offices in New York, gala intro-ductory promotions each fall, and franchised dealers throughout the country—are among America's biggest and most successful mass-production businesses.

Ask NBC to give you just two unbroken hours of fine, honest repertory one evening a week for thirty-nine weeks.

If they will, General Motors will build you an Aston Martin.

*The critical and popular success of this televised Miller play doubtless encouraged Xerox to sponsor Miller's *The Crucible*, now scheduled for showing May 4. That same success has probably also encouraged CBS to insist that this time Xerox shoulder a larger share of the cost.

Reprinted from "The Men Who Run TV Aren't That Stupid . . . ," New York (January 25, 1971), pp. 20, 21, 29. Used by permission of author and publisher.

The Television Audience and Program Mediocrity

PAUL KLEIN

For nearly twenty years I have been watching people watch television. In my time as a specialist in audience measurement at one of the networks, thousands of ideas for new shows have been kicked around, hundreds of pilot scripts have been shot, several dozen new stars and series have come and gone, and a relative handful of programs have survived more than a few seasons. I have brooded about why some programs get, and why so many more fail to get, an audience of commercially acceptable size. I have reached several conclusions. One of them is that when it comes to television, a lot of you otherwise nice people out there are compulsive liars.

You lie to your friends. "I don't watch television much except for the news, maybe a movie, and an occasional special or sports show," you keep telling them. And you lie to yourselves. "I think I'll watch a little TV tonight," you say to yourself. You don't say, "I think I'll watch a little TV tonight *just like I did last night*," because you cannot admit, even to yourself, the nature and extent of your addiction to TV. Watching television seems to be in our day what sex was in the age of Queen Victoria—a filthy little habit best not spoken of.

Make no mistake, though, you *are* hooked, chained or otherwise enslaved by your vice. No one can say whether television programming is better or worse this year than it ever was. But the audience out there in prime time, between 7:30 and 11 at night, is as big as ever. This year, in fact, it is a little bigger because of:

☐ an increase in color-TV penetration; you are buying more expensive receivers so that you can hate the damned thing in living color;

☐ an increase in community-antenna subscribers; you are signing up for CATV service so that you can get a wider choice of hateful images and see them more clearly in the bargain;

☐ an increase in multi-set homes; you are buying second, third, and even fourth TV sets so that several members of the same family can be bored by different programs simultaneously;

☐ a decrease in competition from other media; the increase in clear, colorful video pictures has denied other vehicles for advertising—magazines, for example—their uniqueness.

This year, as a result, 36 million homes—75 million people—are watching TV in prime time at any given moment, and the three networks command over 91 per cent of this huge audience. (Independent and educational channels get the rest.) The bigger a network's share of this audience, the more it can charge for the time it sells to advertisers. The rating points which express share of audience are, in effect, the only way the networks have yet figured out to price their merchandise, which is *your* time and attention.

The single most important thing to know about the American television audience is its amazingly constant size. At any given moment in prime time most of the week it stays at about 36 million sets, whether the network shows at a given hour are strong, weak, so-so, or one of each. It's not the same person in each home watching through the evening. It isn't even the same 36 million homes. The precise composition of the audience is changing every half-hour. The point of nearly every strategy and tactic a network can devise is to get the largest possible share of that audience in each half-hour.

Why does the audience remain so constant even though you say you don't care that much for what's on? After contemplating this curious behavior over the years, I have worked out a theory. I call it the Theory of the Least Objectionable Program. Theory, hell. A few explainable exceptions aside, it has the reliability of natural law. According to my theory, you don't watch particular programs. *You watch television.* The medium. The tube. You turn on the set because it is there—*you can't resist*—and you then settle down to watch that program among all those offered at a given time which can be endured with the least amount of pain and suffering.

You view television irrespective of the content of the program watched. And because the programs are designed to appeal to the greatest number of people—rich and poor, smart and stupid, tall and short, wild and tame—you're probably watching something that is not your taste. Nevertheless, you take what is fed to you because you are compelled to exercise the medium. The result, after a night's viewing, is guilt. That's why you lie to yourself and your friends. You keep thinking you should have been reading, or something.

The dynamics of LOP are observable elsewhere. In politics, for example, it is called choosing the lesser of two (or, lately, three) evils. The League of Women Voters demands that you vote, dammit. The act of voting—irrespective of the content voted for—is held to be essential to the preservation of democracy. If you don't vote, you are warned, the lesser evil you voted for last time may disenfranchise you.

LOP is the same demand, only it is a demand we make of ourselves. The alternative to submitting to LOP is to turn the damned set off and find something else to do. Fat chance. Television viewing, like nail-biting, is something you will stop tomorrow.

The thing I like about my theory is that it explains several phenomena that are otherwise inexplicable. In an age that prizes novelty, LOP explains why some new and even likable faces vanish so quickly and why some old ones hang in there. It explains why New York's taste frequently differs, radically, from national preferences.

Most importantly, LOP explains why some interesting programs die and some stupid programs seem to thrive. Place a weak show against weaker competition, LOP teaches us, and it inevitably looks good; it may even look like a hit—get huge ratings and a quality audience if the time period it fills has that audience. Place a strong show against a stronger show and, never mind whether it is far superior to a dozen other shows on the air in other time slots, it will look like a bomb.

The theory of LOP has a corollary that derives directly from it. Since one man's Green Acres is another man's Slough of Despond, you may confidently bet the family jewels that, regardless of quality, the winner in a given time period will be the network that is *counter-programming* that slot. Just as Buckley counter-programmed Ottinger and Goodell and won, a weak *old* folks' show will beat two *young* folks' shows because all the old folks will gather before "their" show while the two youngies must share their audience.

A very old law has also become more and more useful in figuring out program popularity. I didn't discover this one. Sir Isaac Newton did. I mean his First Law of Motion, the one that says that a body at rest tends to stay at rest. Once a viewer chooses his LOP, he may have to fiddle with a lot of knobs should he decide to switch channels, especially if it's an older color set. So, because a viewer in a chair tends to stay in his chair, an LOP renders great service to the program following it. It can become, in the trade's argot, a strong lead-in.

THE TELEVISION AUDIENCE AND PROGRAM MEDIOCRITY
Paul Klein

Incredible as it may seem, then, despite the money, creative juices, and intelligence that often go into a quality network program, the payoff is really determined by 75 million different thresholds of pain plus the law of inertia.

The best network programmers understand this. They are not stupid. They like most of the stuff they put on about as much as you do. But they also know that a program doesn't have to be "good." It only has to be less objectionable than whatever the hell the other guys throw against it.

For the October-December period of the 1970–71 season, the National Broadcasting Company—my old outfit—had a very slight lead over the Columbia Broadcasting System in their perennial battle for the largest share of the prime-time audience. On the basis of the latest Nielsen data, NBC is getting 32 per cent of the available audience, CBS 31 per cent. The third network, the American Broadcasting Company's, is running third, with a 29 share, but ABC is doing interesting things.

Next month, network salesmen will start selling time for the new season starting next September. They will have their hands full. Like the rest of us, programmers and advertisers try to read the future by analyzing the past, and so the outlines of next season are already visible. . . .

Next season the scheduling of prime-time programs will be a whole new ballgame. The Federal Communications Commission has decided to allow the networks only three hours of prime-time programming. (They had been allowed three and a half hours.) The jockeying for position under the new rule has already begun. However simple it sounds, the decision greatly complicates the networks' lives.

NBC was first to announce which three-hour period it would program. It chose 8 to 11 p.m., thereby returning the 7:30-to-8 p.m. slot to its affiliates to program themselves. I think the decision pleased the stations. They'll undoubtedly find it easier to program 7:30 p.m. than 10:30 p.m.

CBS digested the NBC announcement and then announced that it would program 7:30 to 10:30 p.m., giving its affiliates the 10:30-to-11 p.m. period to program themselves. This, CBS told Variety, would give CBS a huge audience lead at 7:30 to 8 p.m., some of which it will keep all night long. Some will remember that ABC started to raise hell with the ratings of CBS and NBC back in the late fifties by programming action-adventure at 7:30 to 8 p.m. At the time, CBS and NBC had been programming network news strips.

CBS' logic is only half right, I think. If ABC goes the same way as CBS, NBC will get huge audiences at 10:30 to 11 p.m. This audience will lead into the late-night shows on all NBC-owned local stations. In New York, for example, this would mean that NBC's news show on Channel 4 would, for the foreseeable future, enjoy very much higher ratings than its competition on CBS' Channel 2 and ABC's Channel 7. This, in turn, would give a huge advantage to Johnny Carson over Merv Griffin (or his replacement) and Dick Cavett (or his replacement). The combination of a strong 10:30-to-11-p.m. half-hour with its naturally good demographics plus the strength accruing to both the local news show and the Tonight Show make NBC's 8-to-11-p.m. move a sound one—but, again, only if ABC goes along with CBS at 7:30. If ABC goes at 8 p.m., CBS' lead at 7:30 p.m. may be too great to bear.

A lot also depends on the local programming plugged in at 7:30 p.m. Despite the FCC's interest in opening up prime time for many more program producers, the public may end up with significantly less program choice. An NBC station, for instance, may end up carrying one half-hour program "stripped" across five nights instead of five separate programs on the five nights. We are entering the Let's Make a Deal era of prime-time programming. Cheap strip programming, if it can get the audience, is a better economic move for local stations than good films. The quiz/game show is just that kind of programming. And since the FCC has ordered that, beginning in 1972, the top 50 markets must play, in prime time, only original programming (no Dragnet repeats), these stations must go the strip route.

But I think many stations will choose to expand their news coverage. I think it would make sound

THE TELEVISION AUDIENCE AND PROGRAM MEDIOCRITY
Paul Klein

economic sense in the long run. News, well done, with an adequate staff, builds a local program with strong local interest that is more salable to advertisers than bimodal stripped games. In the short run, though, news is risky. If NBC affiliates play news at 7:30 p.m., CBS stations playing network bimodals such as *Family Affair* will get huge ratings. It is imperative, therefore, that more people in the business learn about the lingering irrelevancies of ratings.

Ratings have not always had a stultifying effect on TV programming. When television started, those who acquired sets first tended to live in the larger marketing areas, and they tended to be people who had the dough to pay for a 10-inch Dumont. Given the high correlation between money and education, these early TV viewers tended to be high up on various socio-economic scales, and the programs that appealed to them tended to be the more sophisticated visual fare. That's how the so-called "golden-age" of TV (live drama and all that) was possible.

But in the mid-fifties, set ownership proliferated furiously, entering small towns and rural areas. Mindless situation comedies and the Western suddenly became the dominant program types as viewers with decidedly different tastes became the majority audience. They were not a real majority in terms of the population as a whole, but they did the majority of the viewing.

This is all to say that the period after the golden age—the family age—led to rules which executives lived by (sit-com will always beat dramas, for example) which *were* valid and are now increasingly irrelevant. Just how irrelevant they have become has been obscured, however, because by now everyone is addicted to TV.

But people's willingness to settle for the least objectionable program available has made the advertisers who want them *less* secure, not more so. The young-adult and upper-income audiences are a fickle bunch, and programming by the old rules is an increasingly costly and, I believe, ultimately, self-defeating game. Time will tell.

These uncertainties notwithstanding, the three-hour rule is a boon to the networks—at least a temporary one. With cigarettes gone, there will not be enough advertising dollars around to buy all the available time even at distress prices. The forced cutback to three hours of network programming amounts to a forced reduction in inventory. The cut, eliminating one-seventh of all available time, nearly equals the time previously bought up by cigarette dollars. Of course, the cut *adds* inventory to the local stations, which had been sharing in the networks's tobacco revenues. They will now have to pay for their own programming and scrounge around for ad dollars, some of which will inevitably be monies that used to go to the networks. In effect, then, the networks will have a considerable lower gross next season—with a lower profit, if they have any profit at all.

CBS has broken the "minute" dam, going to 30 seconds as the basic unit of sale. There used to be three minutes of time to sell in a prime-time half-hour. Now, there are six 30-second units to sell. This will open up prime-time to small-budget advertisers. In fact, some daytime advertisers will graduate to night time, creating some problems for daytime sales. But you will see a lot more USO, United Fund and other public-service advertisements on all networks until the inventory is reduced.

Whatever else next year's schedule turns out to be, it *will* be

—different from any previous network schedule, because of the three-hour rule;

—tougher to sell in the 30-second era than ever before;

—more irrelevant in terms of homes ratings, as the 30-second buyers take advantage of their ability to buy the right audience profile for the product being advertised.

In the long run, though, all this may lead to better TV for the addicts among us—that is, just about all of us—because the lowest-priced programming will end up being *reality* programming—news and public-affairs documentaries, and such—which, after all, the networks are uniquely equipped to do well.

Reprinted from Columbia Journalism Review *(Spring, 1970)* ©, *pp. 7–11. Used by permission of author and publisher.*

Where TV News Fails

SIR WILLIAM HALEY

In 1944, when victory in World War II was clearly in sight, the British Broadcasting Corporation arranged a Commonwealth Broadcasting Conference in London to discuss postwar service. When the war had begun in 1939 the BBC, which had started the first television service in the world, had had to shut the service down. As most of those at the conference had never seen TV, we opened the transmitter for one afternoon and showed them transmissions on closed circuit. A discussion followed about how TV was likely to develop. I said that I thought its main long-term service would be in news. As communications developed—we could not foresee satellites but we were sure that some sort of relays would eventually span the globe—every country would have visual access to every other country's happenings. The TV screen, wherever it might be, would be a window on the world. (It was, I think, the first time that metaphor was used for the TV screen.) And I forecast that for the completely natural use of this service flat TV receivers would have to be designed so that, like windows, they could be fitted flush into the walls of every home (and, while this is not yet a practical possibility, it will come).

There are three points to this story. The first is the youth—one might say infancy—of TV even in 1970; less than twenty-six years ago well over 99.99 per cent of all those now viewing throughout the world had never seen TV. The second point is the incredible scientific and technical strides the new invention has made in that short time; as I write

this the BBC is on the eve of receiving in England its first color program direct from Australia. The third—and by far the most important—point is that although the closed circuit showing resulted in some discussion of this conception of international news by television, there was none at all of the problems it would create. The point can be made even stronger. Although many of those present at the conference had been responsible for handling radio news for up to twenty years, no one foresaw that the televising of news would bring problems exclusively its own.

One can make excuses. We were still at war. The 1936–39 TV programs were a novelty and not an integrated service. Before the war the BBC's news had not acquired the importance, authority, philosophy, and stature that came during it. In 1944 we had neither the time nor the men to engage in deep thinking about the principles of televising news. Even if we had thought about them the problems could not have been foreseen. They could emerge only in practice. And what emerged in the early days was not final. Not only did the resources of TV change and evolve; the news itself changed and evolved. Neither the BBC nor the American networks nor other countries' television organizations faced as recently as 1960 the deep and confusing issues that they are having to wrestle with in 1970.

One of the problems my immediate colleagues and I did recognize as soon as we restarted TV in 1946 was that it was not possible to put the BBC's famous *Nine O'clock News* before the cameras and just leave it at that. It is perhaps necessary to explain that the 9 p.m. news, the BBC's main news program throughout the war, became a national and, to some extent, an international institution. Inside the United Kingdom it achieved such authority that, no matter what the British newspapers might report, people did not accept it until they had heard it on the 9 o'clock news. The BBC's news bulletins were also the main lifeline to occupied Europe and a major factor in the Resistance.

This authority of the BBC's news did not depend solely on its accuracy. Just as important to the millions who listened was its sense of news values. The length and placing of each item were objectively and professionally considered. Even the serious British newspapers would compare their main news page stories with the selection in the 9 o'clock news. They would go their own way, but they wished to study their judgment alongside that of the BBC's.

It was quickly found that preserving this judgment in TV news was a seemingly impossible task. Visual news values are in almost inverse ratio to real news values. What is most exciting to see is generally the least important to know about. To start a TV news program with an item of the seriousness and length it would be given in radio news would in all likelihood result in losing the viewer's attention. He would do something else until the news was over.

The BBC was not prepared to have two standards of news values for its programs—one for radio and the other for TV. So in the first years after the war the BBC had no televised news. It merely read the 9 o'clock radio news in the TV program without any attempt to add visual material. Later, TV news programs were started. Much professional skill has been brought to bear on the problem of visual values and real news values, and some progress has been made, but the problem is still far from solved.

I think it has been solved even less in the United States. Sixteen months of American viewing left me with the conviction that the truth has not yet been realized that even supposedly exciting events by their recurring similarity lose all interest. By and large, fires, floods, sinking ships, railway and car smashups, even earthquakes have little originality. They all look the same on the TV screen. The same is now true of demonstrations. There is little significant visual difference between them, whether they be in the United States, in Britain, in France, Italy, Germany, or Japan. Yet they go on being shown because they represent action. They assume a bogus interest. In fact they bore the viewer. Worst of all, they waste scarce and valuable time that could have been given to items that really matter.

It is sometimes argued that this time-wasting is not serious because American TV stations give so much more time to news than the British and stations of other nations do. This is a fallacy. Once stories are not tautly edited and lose proportion and significance, the whole idea of news loses significance for the viewer. And the loss of significance is not made up by deep treatment of important and serious news items in documentaries. What documentaries I saw during my stay in the United States convinced me that the BBC is far ahead of the networks in this field. American TV documentaries have not the skill at getting at essentials, and the deep probing into them, that British documentaries have. All too often the longer they go on the more superficial they become. This is possibly one reason for the present reluctance of American TV stations and sponsors to sink money and time into news documentaries. Whatever the reason, the lack of enthusiasm for news documentaries struck me as one of the most serious developments in the tidal wave of TV that has swamped the American public's time and attention. It can have grave consequences for American democracy—unless the news stories are restructured or a corrective is provided in some other way.

These are elementary facts. It has been necessary to start with them because they are fundamental. They are as much at issue today as they were when TV was restarted twenty-four years ago. In some ways they are more so. The journalist has not been able to withstand the engineer. More and more

WHERE TV NEWS FAILS
Sir William Haley

technical resources and devices have been offered him. They have mastered him, and not he them. The outcome is even more crucial now that satellite communication is becoming common. Because the satellite relay does stand to open up the whole of the free world, because its cost is high, and because no conceivable distance—not even that from the moon to the earth—is any longer a bar to immediacy, both significance and journalistic judgment are in danger of suffering greater blows than ever before.

For some time now the immense engineering resources available to TV reporters and correspondents have highlighted the ordinariness and inanity of much of what those resources are employed to transmit. The old metaphor of using a sledgehammer to crack a nut can all too often be modernized into "using a satellite to relay a television correspondent." It is not the correspondent's fault. He is as much a victim as the viewer. The urge to show things as they have happened or, better still while they are happening leaves no time for the old journalistic skills. Air travel and the international telephone similarly in some way hamper the newspaper correspondent. Men are flown half across the world to a trouble spot they have never seen before and are expected to send back measured dispatches within twenty-four hours of their arrival. Even then the newspaperman has some little time to think and write. The TV camera team must move in at once. It gets wherever it can as quickly as it can, the correspondent being left with the job of conveying the idea that what the viewer is seeing is the whole—or at least representative of the whole—of whatever is being covered. It can be neither.

The occasional roundups are even worse. They purport to be a summing-up, a considered general judgment. Hardly a situation in the world today can be thus treated properly with the resources and the time the TV correspondent has at his disposal. The camera is always pressing upon him. So is the editor at home, anxious to use the satellite—not only to televise him but other correspondents as

well. The more commonplace the use of the satellite becomes, the more will station prestige (and eventually correspondent prestige) demand that everyone shall use it. The cost being so high, each use will be only a fraction of what it ought to be— if it is to be used at all. Thus there will flash on the home screens of Britons, Americans, Frenchmen, Italians, Germans, and others a succession of *obiter dicta* from men who are forced to do an inadequate job and who look as if they knew they were doing it.

For in yet another way the pressures on the TV journalist are greater than those on his newspaper brother. Not only is he expected to do twice as much twice as fast in a tenth of the space; he has the added load of having to be seen for much of the time he is doing it. This personalizes the news, making it more difficult than ever to form a true opinion of its objective value. It also debases the role of the journalist by making him, consciously or unconsciously, and at the very best to some infinitesimal degree, an actor.

That being so, it seems to me TV reporting from one country to another should not be left solely in the hands of the regular correspondent. The more important the events being covered, the more vital it is that journalists of the country where the news is originating should be used to complement the TV network's or station's own man. *And both men should be given time to do a thorough, responsible job.*

The existence of the TV international relay and of the satellite ought to make TV news editors and managers reconsider the whole scope and role of television journalism. (One of the major weaknesses of TV journalism in some countries is that both editors and managers have a say in the matter.) The old patterns were never very good; these new inventions make them completely outworn. Instead of using the new aids for yet more variegated and more heterogeneous news stories, the journalists of this new television age should scrap present methods and use the new devices to increase the depth of treatment of the news that has significance and really matters. The faster communications become, and the more widely their net is thrown, the greater is the need to eschew any immediacy that has to be paid for by perfunctoriness. TV news should be more than a peep show. People may be titillated by the latest incident, whether it matters or not, being flashed to them in a split-second across thousands of miles. That is not journalism. It often is not news.

What is news? Some of us discussed this at one of the Columbia-duPont Broadcast Survey luncheons last year. Someone asked what had been the greatest TV newscast of the year. The Apollo's pictures of the first man landing on the moon were suggested. Stress was laid on the many hours the program had lasted and the world excitement at the event. I objected that it had not been news. It was a show—admittedly a most historic and spectacular show—but a show nonetheless. News is not a happening. It is what journalists make of it. It is the sifting, reporting, and evaluating of what has happened. In the case of the moon landings this was done subsequently. It was not done by the Apollo camera automatically sending to earth the pictures of the first men treading the lunar surface. This may seem to be a fine distinction. I believe it to be a fundamental one. And it is precisely because I do not believe that TV newsmen are making this distinction that I think TV news has so far missed its purpose.

This would not matter so much if newspaper readership in the United States and Britain was still on the increase. When TV started I forecast that its inability to deal with news adequately would give newspapers a second chance—in Britain at any rate. To some extent it has done so. But the opening of the whole world to news, the speed with which it is now communicated to newspapers, radio, and TV, the multiplicity of seemingly insoluble national and international dilemmas, have led to a flight from the news by those who, if a nation is to be healthy, should most be following it. Added to this is the increasing specialization in all kinds of activity. Here, too, results which used to take months, if not years, to circulate internationally

now do so in days. It has all become too much of a load for many of those who have the world's work to do. A growing number of business and professional men and women now need only the publication that gives them the specialized information they need; for the news as a whole they depend on the nightly TV news broadcast.

This habit is, I think, more common in the United States than in Britain. In both countries the economic forces attacking newspapers are the same. Geography makes the consequences different. In the United Kingdom 54 million people live in an area slightly smaller than that of Wyoming. In spite of casualties it is therefore still possible to have eight national newspapers, with varying coverage of national and international news, able to get onto any British breakfast table. The vast continent that is the United States makes national newspapers well nigh impractical. Casualties among American newspapers have left the overwhelming majority of cities with only one newspaper. Often its coverage of national and international news is not such as to make it obligatory reading. In addition, the vastness of the United States precludes there being many single focal points of news interest.

Americans have nowhere near the same interest in the proceedings of Congress as the British have in daily reports of the meetings of the House of Commons. The uncertainty of the General Election date keeps British politics continuously alive to some degree. The various sections of the nation are conscious of their abiding or changing political loyalties, and have papers to cater to them. Among the serious newspapers there is the *Daily Telegraph* to meet the needs of the Right, the *Guardian* those of the Left, and the *Times* those of the center. The popular newspapers also have identifiable stances. And the fact that all these papers circulate through the whole of the kingdom gives the British press a place and a voice that has not yet suffered much from TV.

British newspapers also do a better job than TV in reporting on the arts, law, science, local government, and the whole range of subjects which tradi-

WHERE TV NEWS FAILS
Sir William Haley

tionally make the best complete newspapers. On neither side of the Atlantic so far has TV news sought to give a regular service in these news areas. Here, too, geography may make it more difficult for American TV to deal adequately with this responsibility. But the need is there; it must be met.

While geography can modify the consequences of scientific, economic, industrial, and social progress, it cannot quarantine them absolutely. Their effect on different countries is mainly a matter of time and degree. The most widespread problem of journalism today—of TV journalism more than of newspaper journalism—is the problem of every avocation. It is the problem of men and women everywhere. Mankind is failing to cope with the vastly increased speed of its communications. Jet travel—soon it will be supersonic—leads statesmen in time of crisis to fly to see each other before they have had time to consider what they are going to say when they get there. The greater the emer-

gency, the less time they take to assess it. Businessmen start negotiations at the end of long flights when they are in no condition to do so. (Some large business organizations now recognize this and impose a forty-eight-hour assimilating period on their executives.)

News arrives in such proliferation and at such a rate that before it can be digested and judged it is overtaken by the next day's flood. Correspondents and reporters are mentally breathless. Refuge is sought in generalization. Speculation takes the place of judgment. Today's big news may prove to be tomorrow's trivia.

It is perhaps too much to ask television journalists to be the pioneers in reversing a trend that is bedeviling all mankind. But as their influence grows so does their responsibility. And that responsibility is to make the gadgets—even the satellites—their servants and not their masters, and to remember what is the true function of a journalist.

Reprinted from The Nation *(April 13, 1970), pp. 433–35. Used by permission of publisher.*

TV News: Wrong Mix

MEL WAX

THE real problems of television news are not those cited by the Vice President, by those network presidents who responded to his Des Moines TV speech with such self-righteous indignation, nor even — troublesome though they may be — censorship, monopoly control, liberal bias, conservative bias, the Eastern establishment, or the fairness doctrine. The faults are deeper than that; they are embedded in the fundamental premises of television newscasting, its roots in radio and its evolution as radio with pictures.

Neither television, nor radio, offer much incentive for good reporting. Without good reporting, a high quality news program is not possible. Observe your local telecaster with a critical eye. The chances are that that handsome talking head hasn't covered a story all day, or even written the headlines he's mouthing. He speaks distinctly, if monotonously. He probably doesn't sport a beard or long hair. Nor is he bald. He wears a necktie and a conventional suit — nothing flashy. He smiles, but he seldom laughs. He leads into deodorant commercials with the same authority he gives a battlefront report. He's plastic. And he's not a reporter; he's a performer.

Indeed, despite the complaint of Chet Huntley, among others, that it is demeaning for newsmen to be members of a union of "singers, actors, jugglers, announcers, entertainers and comedians," your local TV news anchor man probably belongs to AFTRA — the American Federation of Television and Radio Artists — which also represents the jokesters and songsters.

Under most contracts, the men who write the TV news are paid according to the number of stories they can cram on the air, not the quality of their work. An energetic performer can score with three, or four, or more stories a night, at $25 to $100 per item aired. What's the sense of digging into a complicated story for three or four days, when it will earn the same fee as a quickie?

Robert McNeil, former NBC-TV newsman, says:

In several ways, the money involved acts as a disincentive to reporters. Young men rising in the industry desire to be commentators in the studio, not reporters on the beat. To be taken out of reporting and given a program is considered success; if the program is taken away, that is failure. Moreover, a man cannot easily combine a daily in-studio commitment with the work of a reporter. If he tried, by being absent from the program to do some extended reporting, he loses fees.

The most successful broadcasting journalists are thus largely prevented from going out of the office to do reporting, assuming they are trained journalists and want to go out. Many, especially at the local station level, are not journalists, and do not relish reporting.

At the national level, a sprinkling of able, sensitive reporters try valiantly to overcome the built-in inhibitions of the TV news format. They rarely succeed on the nightly newscast. Good reporting sometimes appears on the air when the traditional newscast format is junked, and reporters are given the range of CBS's *60 Minutes*, or even a full-scale documentary. Some of the best television reporting was done on the now defunct Public Broadcast

TV NEWS: WRONG MIX
Mel Wax

Laboratory. Its documentaries on the Kansas City police and on the Pentagon were outstanding.

There is great television coverage of moon shots. There is some remarkably good reporting at political conventions and some bad reporting too. Such events as a Presidential assassination, or the coronation of a queen, have enjoyed perceptive and thorough reporting. Sports reporting is of very high quality, a happy blend of the qualified specialist reporter and the new technology.

But the mix doesn't occur often on newscasts. Even the sports reporter is then generally restricted to a dreary recital of scores, with graphics, plus film of the winning touchdown. The present format—the anchor man; the bubbly weather girl or man, writing on a transparent weather map; the sports reporter—must go. It serves no useful purpose. The anchor man should be replaced by honest-to-God reporters. Television should take a lesson from newspapers, and begin training and hiring reporters for special fields of competence—in education, urban affairs, race relations, science, ecology, politics.

If television is to inform the 50 million viewers who watch the tube for news every night, it must provide much more than headline bulletins and dramatic film of fires, accidents and shootings. It must make an effort to tell not only what happened but why it happened and what it means. Most television newsmen now provide little more than a thirty-second film interview. In thirty seconds, or forty-five seconds, or even in a minute, a reporter can't do much in the way of interpretive reporting, even if he has the necessary skills.

On commercial television the goal is ratings—the size of the audience a sponsor can buy—and it applies to news as well as to *Ed Sullivan* and *Laugh-In*. For the news director, this translates into a directive to keep news brief, punchy, lively, "interesting." A vice president for news for a major network once explained that television news will never carry a report on the national budget because it's too complicated, it isn't visual, and who cares. . . .

The national budget is important. It should be both reported and analyzed on television newscasts, as it is in the better newspapers. The technology of the medium is not what makes news. If it's news in the printed press, it's news in the visual press. Or it should be. In most major cities where there are three or four VHF stations, you can flick the dial from one news program to another and find the same stories, often offered in the same sequence. They even present commercials in the same time breaks, and reserve the same spots for sports, weather and the daily features. On any channel you will find the same predictable press conferences, the same "visually exciting" events, the same non-news. A local television news program that regularly carries "enterprise stories"—ones that aren't offered to them on a silver platter—is as rare as snow in August.

Two years ago, in San Francisco, there was a newspaper strike. On Channel 9, the education station, we had no regular news operation—news is expensive and beyond the financial ability of most public television. But because we were concerned that commercial television would be unable to fill the news gap, KQED moved into the news business. [See "TV's First Real Paper" by Michael Harris, *The Nation*, March 18, 1968.]

We hired good reporters from the struck papers, the *Chronicle* and the *Examiner*. We put them "up front" where reporters belong. They covered the news and they told about it on the air. Film and still pictures were used, but sparingly. We had a tiny budget, and print reporters are nervous about visuals. For the ten weeks the strike lasted, we were on the air every night for an hour, and sometimes two hours. The local commercial station, by their own admission, were blanked. We beat them consistently with news. We attracted an enormous audience—so heavy that restaurants complained that nobody came to eat between 7 and 8 P.M. We demonstrated, conclusively, that there is a place for a good reporter on a television news program.

When the strike ended, KQED received a grant from the Ford Foundation for some $748,000 to try the same reporting format for a year, on an experimental basis. The challenge was to attract the same caliber of reporter, the same large audience, to produce a quality news product when the newspapers were available. And, in so doing, we hoped to discover a more effective way to present news on television.

We put together what is perhaps the best team of reporters for any local television news program in the United States—eleven of them, plus a political cartoonist. Most made the switch from newspapers, but one had news magazine experience, and a few had even worked on television and/or radio. But the criterion for selecting them was their competence as reporters, not their handsome faces. Some have beards, some are balding, some are not handsome, some are young, and some are older. All are good reporters.

Most of the staff have specialties—in science, racial problems, urban affairs, politics, transportation. On Mondays we call in a lawyer to report on the day's U.S. Supreme Court decisions—not just what they are, but what they mean. We employ specialists in other areas when the need arises. We also discuss the news on the air among ourselves, or with guests ranging the political spectrum from Jerry Rubin to John D. Rockefeller III.

With a larger budget, and more confidence, we use more film—not thirty-second stand-ups but

films that tell a story better than we can with words, or better than we can with words alone. The basic credo of television news is that television is a visual medium: therefore everything must be visual. Nonsense. Visuals make sense sometimes; sometimes they are meaningless.

Newsroom is now the most popular program on Channel 9, and it's the liveliest and, perhaps, the most controversial television program in the San Francisco Bay Area. Among other things, it has had an effect on the quality of reporting on commercial stations. The Ford grant has been renewed for a second year. *Newsrooms* are spreading to other public television stations—Pittsburgh, Dallas, Washington, D.C.—with Ford Foundation support. Fred Friendly, the former CBS-TV news executive and now television adviser to McGeorge Bundy, president of the Ford Foundation, has dreams of a national *Newsroom* for public television.

What also tickles me—as one who spent most of his career as a newspaper man—is that, for the first time in San Francisco, both the *Examiner* and *Chronicle* are monitoring our news programs. They lift three to five news stories a week from us—rather than the other way around.

There is no reason why television news programs must be bad. There is little wrong with them that good reporters can't cure.

D. The U.S. Mass Media System

The individual operation of the media in the United States has been examined in the preceding sections. The task here is to draw an overview of media as a whole, that is, to account for the ways in which they relate to and influence each other.

Despite the government's attempt to regulate the electronic media and its incursion into educational public broadcasting, the U.S. system is overwhelmingly a commercial business enterprise. Profit motives and economic imperatives are therefore foremost, and these demand an emphasis on mass entertainment rather than the maximum spread of public information or the nurture of artistic creativity.

Harry Skornia has pointed out that because broadcasting is a business operation it must serve its stockholders first and then the public.[1] This also presumably applies to newspapers and mass circulation magazines. Because of ownership patterns broadcasting is also antagonistic to labor organizations. Thus when labor news is presented it is usually unsympathetic to labor as opposed to stockholder interests. The major broadcasters, in addition to their dependence on corporate advertising, are linked directly to the economy. This is especially clear if the parent company is tied to the "military-industrial complex" by holding companies seeking defense contracts or is engaged in overseas activities. In such cases, despite seemingly autonomous

news staffing, the conflict of interest in reporting military and foreign news is evident. Such conflicts lead beyond mere broadcasting to an examination of the role of corporations *vis-a-vis* the public in our society. Broadcasting corporations, like corporations in general, are inherently undemocratic and, claims Skornia, avoid collective responsibility. What Skornia has in mind is the way in which the corporation manufactures a positive image or externalizes responsibility. Thus in recent off-shore oil spills, oil companies have received credit for their clean-up effort, despite the fact that some of the spills resulted from their criminal negligence for which they have been condemned and fined. In the second method of shifting responsibility, auto accidents become solely the fault of drivers, and industrial effluents become what one recent advertisement for eye drops has called "eye pollution."

The selections here do not deal specifically with the implications of commercial control since these are dealt with at length elsewhere in this volume. Instead they focus on the financial empires that cut across the media themselves and anchor the mass media firmly within the overall matrix of big business in the United States.

Johnson's article basically agrees with Skornia's views summarized above, but his attention is primarily on cross-media mergers and corporate ties. He deals at length with the proposed merger of ITT and ABC—which failed—and notes that total corporate domination can be avoided only by con-

[1] See his *Television and Society*, especially pp. 17–38.

tinuous and successful efforts to keep ownership diversified.

The selection from *Atlantic* which follows consciously picks up on Johnson's work and illustrates the way in which the media fit into the general economy.[2] In the first section, five types of media baronies are outlined. These are local monopolies in which all of a city's media are controlled by the

[2]The Commissioner's work reprinted here is a revised version of his article referred to by the *Atlantic* staff writers.

same enterprise; regional concentrations; multiple-ownership, for example, newspaper chains; multi-media ownership; and conglomerates, that is, linkages with non-media corporations. The second part provides an atlas of some of the larger media empires insofar as these can be determined from public sources. These include the multi-media holdings of Time, Cowles, Post, Gannett, New-house, Hearst, Scripps-Howard, and similar media chains. With such factual information the characteristic commercial nature of the mass media in the United States becomes readily apparent.

Reprinted from How to Talk Back to Your Television Set (New York: Bantam Books, 1970), pp. 39–69, by permission of author and Atlantic-Little, Brown and Co. Copyright © 1967, 1968, 1969, and 1970 by Little, Brown and Company.

The Media Barons and the Public Interest

NICHOLAS JOHNSON

BEFORE I came to the Federal Communications Commission my concerns about the ownership of broadcasting and publishing in America were about like those of any other generally educated person.

Most television programming from the three networks struck me as bland at best. I had taken courses dealing with propaganda and "thought control," bemoaned (while being entertained by) *Time* magazine's "slanted" reporting, understood that Hearst had something to do with the Spanish-American War, and was impressed with President Eisenhower's concern about "the military-industrial complex." The changing ownership of the old-line book publishers and the disappearance of some of our major newspapers made me vaguely uneasy. I was philosophically wedded to the fundamental importance of "the marketplace of ideas" in a free society, and a year as law clerk to my idol, Supreme Court Justice Hugo L. Black, had done nothing to weaken that commitment.

But I didn't take much time to be reflective about the current significance of such matters. It all seemed beyond my ability to influence in any meaningful way. Then, in July 1966, I became a member of the FCC. Here my interest in the marketplace of ideas could no longer remain a casual article of personal faith. The commitment was an implicit part of the oath I took on assuming the office of Commissioner, and, I quickly learned, an everyday responsibility.

Threats to the free exchange of information and opinion in this country can come from various sources, many of them outside the power of the FCC to affect. Publishers and reporters are not alike in their ability, education, tolerance of diversity, and sense of responsibility. The hidden or overt pressures of advertisers have long been with us.

But one aspect of the problem is clearly within the purview of the FCC—the impact of *ownership* upon the content of the mass media. It is also a part of the responsibility of the Antitrust Division of the Justice Department. It has been the subject of congressional hearings. There are a number of significant trends in the ownership of the media worth examining—local and regional monopolies, growing concentration of control of the most profitable and powerful television stations in the major markets, broadcasting-publishing combines, and so forth. But let's begin with a look at the significance of media ownership by "conglomerate corporations"—holding companies that own, in addition to publishing and broadcasting enterprises, other major industrial corporations.

During my first month at the FCC I studied the cases and attended the meetings, but purposefully did not participate in voting on any items. One of the agenda items at the July 20 Commissioners' meeting proposed two draft letters addressed to the presidents of International Telephone and Telegraph and the American Broadcasting Company, ITT and ABC, Messrs. Harold Geneen and Leonard Goldenson. We were asking them to supply "a statement specifying in further detail the manner in which the financial resources of ITT will enable ABC to improve its program services and thereby better serve the public interest." This friendly inquiry was my first introduction to the proposed ITT-ABC merger, and the Commission majority's attitudes about it. It was to be a case that would occupy much of my attention over the next few months.

There wasn't much discussion of the letters that morning, but I read carefully the separate statements filed with them by my two responsible and experienced colleagues, Commissioners Robert T. Bartley and Kenneth A. Cox, men for whom I was already feeling a respect that was to grow over the following months.

Commissioner Bartley, a former broadcaster with the deep and earthy wisdom one would expect in a Texas-born relative of the late Speaker Sam Rayburn, wrote a long and thoughtful statement. He warned of "the probable far-reaching political, social and economic consequences for the public interest of the increasing control of broadcast facilities and broadcast service by large conglomerate corporations such as the applicants." Commissioner Cox, former lawyer, law professor, counsel to the Senate Commerce Committee, and chief of the FCC's Broadcast Bureau, characterized the proposed merger as "perhaps the most important in the agency's history." He said the issues were "so significant and far-reaching that we should proceed immediately to designate the matter for hearing."

Their concerns were well grounded in broadcasting's history and in the national debate preceding the 1934 Communications Act, we were appointed to enforce. Precisely what Congress intended the FCC to do was not specified at that time or since. But no one has ever doubted Congress's great concern lest the ownership of broadcasting properties be permitted to fall into a few hands or to assume monopoly proportions.

The 1934 Act was preceded by the 1927 Radio Act and a series of industry Radio Conferences in the early 1920's. The conferences were called by then Secretary of Commerce Herbert C. Hoover. Hoover expressed concern lest control over broadcasting "come under the arbitrary power of any person or group of persons." During the congressional debates on the 1927 Acts a leading Congressman, noting that "publicity is the most powerful weapon that can be wielded in a republic," warned of the domination of broadcasting by "a single selfish group." Should that happen, he said, "then woe be to those who dare to differ with them." The requirement that licenses not be transferred without Commission approval was intended, according to a sponsoring Senator, "to prevent the concentration of broadcast facilities by a few." Thirty years later, in 1956, Senate Commerce Committee Chairman Warren G. Magnuson was still warning the Commission that it "should be on guard against the intrusion of big business and absentee ownership."

These concerns of Congress and my colleagues were to take on fuller meaning as the ITT-ABC case unfolded, a case which eventually turned into an FCC *cause célèbre*. It also demonstrated the enormity of the responsibility vested in this relatively small and little-known Commission, by virtue of its power to grant or withhold membership in the broadcast industry. On a personal level, the case shook into me the realization, for the first time in my life, of the dreadful significance of the ownership structure of the mass media in America.

THE ITT-ABC MERGER CASE

ITT is a sprawling international conglomerate of 433 separate boards of directors that derives about 60 percent of its income from its significant holdings in at least forty foreign countries. It is the ninth largest industrial corporation in the world in size of work force. In addition to its sale of electronic equipment to foreign governments, and operation of foreign countries' telephone systems, roughly half of its domestic income comes from U.S. Government defense and space contracts. But it is also in the business of consumer finance, life insurance, investment funds, small loan companies, car rentals (ITT Avis, Inc.), and book publishing.

This description of ITT's anatomy is taken (as is

THE MEDIA BARONS AND THE PUBLIC INTEREST
Nicholas Johnson

much of this ITT-ABC discussion) from opinions written by myself and Commissioners Bartley and Cox. We objected, vigorously, to the four-man majority's decision to approve the merger. So did some Senators and Congressmen, the Department of Justice, the Commission's own staff, the American Civil Liberties Union, a number of independent individuals and witnesses, and a belated but eventually insistent chorus of newspaper and magazine editorialists.

What did we find so ominous about the take-over of this radio and television network by a highly successful conglomerate organization?

In 1966, ABC owned 399 theaters in 34 states, 5 VHF television stations, 6 AM and 6 FM stations (all in the top 10 broadcasting markets), and, of course, one of the 3 major television networks and one of the 4 major radio networks in the world. Its 137 primary television network affiliates could reach 93 percent of the then 50 million television homes in the United States, and its radio network affiliates could reach 97 percent of the then 55 million homes with radio receivers. ABC had interests in, and affiliations with, stations in 25 other nations, known as the "Worldvision Group." These, together with ABC Films, made the parent corporation perhaps the world's largest distributor of filmed shows for theaters and television stations throughout this country and abroad. ABC was heavily involved in the record production and distribution business, and other subsidiaries published three farm papers.

The merger would have placed this accumulation of mass media, and one of the largest purveyors of news and opinion in America, under the control of one of the largest conglomerate corporations in the world. What's wrong with that? Potentially a number of things. For now, consider simply that the integrity of the news judgment of ABC might be affected by the economic interests of ITT—that ITT might simply view ABC's programming as a part of ITT's public relations, advertising, or political activities. This seemed to us a real threat in 1966, notwithstanding the character of the manage-ment of both companies, and their protestations that no possibility of abuse existed. By 1967 the potential threat had become reality.

ITT's continuing concern with political economic developments in foreign countries as a result of its far-flung economic interests was fully documented in the hearing. It showed, as one might expect, ITT's recurrent concern with internal affairs in most major countries of the world, including rate problems, tax problems, and problems with nationalization and reimbursement, to say nothing of ordinary commercial dealing. Its involvement with the United States government, in addition to defense contracts, included the Agency for International Development's insurance of 5.8 percent of all ITT assets.

Testimony was offered on the fascinating story of intrigue surrounding "Operation Deep Freeze" (an underwater cable). It turned out that ITT officials, using high-level government contracts in England and Canada, had brought off a bit of profitable international diplomacy unknown to the United States State Department or the FCC, possibly in violation of law. Further inquiry revealed that officers and directors of ITT's subsidiaries included two members of the British House of Lords, one in the French National Assembly, a former premier of Belgium, and several ministers of foreign governments and officials of government-owned companies.

As it seemed to Commissioners Bartley and Cox, and to me, when we dissented from the Commission's approval of the merger in June, 1967, a company whose daily activities require it to manipulate governments at the highest levels would face unending temptation to manipulate ABC news. Any public official, or officer of a large corporation, is necessarily clearly concerned with the appearance of some news stories, the absence of others, and the tone and character of all affecting his personal interests. That's what public relations firms and press secretaries are all about. We concluded, "We simply cannot find that the public interest of the American citizenry is served by turning over a

THE MEDIA BARONS AND THE PUBLIC INTEREST
Nicholas Johnson

major network to an international enterprise whose fortunes are tied to its political relations with the foreign officials whose actions it will be called upon to interpret to the world."

Even the highest degree of subjective integrity on the part of chief ITT officials could not insure integrity in ABC's operations. To do an honest and impartial job of reporting the news is difficult enough for the most independent and conscientious of newsmen. Eric Sevareid has said of putting on a news program at a network relatively free of conglomerate control: "The ultimate sensation is the feeling of being bitten to death by ducks." And ABC newsmen could not help knowing that ITT had sensitive business relations in various foreign countries and at the highest levels of our government, and that reporting on any number of industries and economic developments would touch the interests of ITT. The mere awareness of these interests would make it impossible for those news officials, no matter how conscientious, to report news and develop documentaries objectively, in the way that they would do if ABC remained unaffiliated with ITT. They would advance within the news organization, or be fired, or become officers of ABC — perhaps even of ITT — or not, and no newsman would be able to erase from his mind the idea that his chances of doing so might be affected by his treatment of issues on which ITT is sensitive.

In 1967 CBS was reportedly involved, almost Hearst-like, in a nightmarish planned armed invasion of Haiti. It was an exclusive, and would have made a very dramatic start-to-finish documentary but for the inglorious end: U.S. Customs wouldn't let them leave the United States. Imagine ITT, with its extensive interests in the Caribbean, engaged in such undertakings.

The likelihood of at least some compromising of ABC's integrity seemed inherent in the structure of the proposed new organization. What were the *probabilities* that these potentials for abuse would be exercised? We were soon to see the answer in the bizarre proceedings right before our eyes.

During the April 1967 hearings, while this very issue was being debated, the *Wall Street Journal* broke a story by Fred Zimmerman that ITT was going to extraordinary lengths to obtain favorable press coverage of those very hearings. Eventually three reporters were summoned before the examiner to relate for the official record the incidents that were described in the *Journal*'s exposé.

An AP and a UPI reporter testified to several phone calls to their homes by ITT public relations men, variously asking them to change their stories and make inquiries for ITT with regard to stories by other reporters, and to use their influence as members of the press to obtain for ITT confidential information from the Department of Justice regarding its intentions. Even more serious were several encounters between ITT officials and *New York Times* reporter Eileen Shanahan.

On one of these occasions ITT's senior vice president in charge of public relations went to the reporter's office. After criticizing her dispatches to the *Times* about the case in a tone which she described as "accusatory and certainly nasty," he asked whether she had been following the price of ABC and ITT stock. When she indicated that she had not, he asked if she didn't feel she had a "responsibility to the shareholders who might lose money as a result of what she wrote." She replied "My responsibility is to find out the truth and print it."

He then asked if she was aware that I (as an FCC Commissioner) was working with a prominent Senator on legislation that would forbid any newspaper from owning any broadcast property. (The *New York Times* owns station WQXR in New York.) In point of fact, the Senator and I had never met, let alone collaborated, as was subsequently made clear in public statements. But the ITT senior vice president, according to the *Times* reporter, felt that this false information was something she "ought to pass on to [her] . . . publisher before [she wrote] . . . anything further" about the case. The obvious implication of this remark, she felt, was that since the *Times* owns a radio station, it would want to consider its economic interests in deciding what

THE MEDIA BARONS AND THE PUBLIC INTEREST
Nicholas Johnson

to publish about broadcasting in its newspaper.

To me, this conduct, in which at least three ITT officials, including a senior vice president, were involved, was a deeply unsettling experience. It demonstrated an abrasive self-righteousness in dealing with the press, insensitivity to its independence and integrity, a willingness to spread false stories in furtherance of self-interest, contempt for government officials as well as the press, and an assumption that even as prestigious a news medium as the *New York Times* would, as a matter of course, want to present the news so as to serve best its own economic interests (as well as the economic interests of other large business corporations).

But for the brazen activities of ITT in this very proceeding, it would never have occurred to the three of us who dissented to suggest that the most probable threat to the integrity of ABC news could come from *overt* actions or written policy statements. After the hearing it was obvious that that was clearly possible. But even then we believed that the most substantial threat came from a far more subtle, almost unconscious, process: that the questionable story idea, or news coverage, would never even be proposed—whether for reasons of fear, insecurity, cynicism, realism, or unconscious avoidance.

CONCENTRATION OF CONTROL OVER THE MEDIA

Since the ITT-ABC case left the Commission I have not ceased to be troubled by the issues it raised—in many ways more serious (and certainly more prevalent) for wholly domestic corporations. Eventually the merger was aborted by ITT on New Year's Day of 1968, while the Justice Department's appeal of the Commission's action was pending before the U.S. Court of Appeals. However, I ponder what the consequences might have been if ITT's apparent cynicism toward journalistic integrity had actually been able to harness the enormous social and propaganda power of a national television network to the service of a politically sensitive corporate

conglomerate. More important, I have become concerned about the extent to which such forces *already* play upon important media of mass communication. Perhaps such attitudes are masked by more finesse than that displayed in the ITT-ABC case. Perhaps they are even embedded in the kind of sincere good intentions which caused former Defense Secretary (and former General Motors president) Charles Wilson to equate the interests of his company with those of the country.

I do not believe that most owners and managers of the mass media in the United States lack a sense of responsibility or lack tolerance for a diversity of views. I do not believe there is a small group of men who gather for breakfast every morning and decide what they will make the American people believe that day. Emotion often outruns the evidence of those who argue a conspiracy theory of propagandists' manipulation of the masses.

On the other hand, one reason evidence is so hard to come by is that the media tend to give less publicity to their own abuses than, say, to those of politicians. The media operate as a check upon other institutional power centers in our country. There is, however, no check upon the media. Just as it is a mistake to overstate the existence and potential for abuse, so, in my judgment, is it a mistake to ignore the evidence that does exist.

In 1949, for example, it was reported that officials of the Trujillo regime in the Dominican Republic had paid $750,000 to officers of the Mutual Radio Network to gain favorable propaganda disguised as news. (Ownership of the Mutual Radio Network changed hands once again a few years later without any review whatsoever by the FCC of old or new owners. The FCC does not regulate networks, only stations, and Mutual owns none.) RCA was once charged with using an NBC station to serve unfairly its broader corporate interests, including the coverage of RCA activities as "news," which other newsmen considered unnewsworthy. There was speculation that after RCA acquired Random House, considerable pressure was put on the book publishing house's president,

Bennett Cerf, to cease his Sunday evening service as a panelist on CBS's *What's My Line?* The Commission has occasionally found that individual stations have violated the "fairness doctrine" in advocating causes serving the station's economic self-interest, such as pay television.

Virtually every issue of the *Columbia Journalism Review* reports instances of such abuses by the print media. It has described a railroad-owned newspaper that refused to report railroad wrecks, a newspaper in debt to the Teamsters Union which gave exceedingly favorable coverage to Jimmy Hoffa, the repeated influence of the DuPont interests in the editorial functions of the Wilmington papers which it owned, and Anaconda Copper's use of its company-owned newspapers to support political candidates favorable to the company.

Edward P. Morgan left ABC to become the commentator on the short-lived Ford Foundation-funded Public Broadcasting Laboratory. (He has since returned to ABC.) Mr. Morgan has always been straightforward, and he used his final news broadcast before going to PBL to be reflective about broadcasting itself. "Let's face it," he said. "We in this trade use this power more frequently to fix a traffic ticket or get a ticket to a ball game than to keep the doors of an open society open and swinging. . . . The freest and most profitable press in the world, every major facet of it, not only ducks but pulls its punches to save a supermarket of commercialism or shield an ugly prejudice and is putting the life of the republic in jeopardy thereby."

Economic self-interest *does* influence the content of the media, and as the media tend to fall into the control of corporate conglomerates, the areas of information and opinion affecting those economic interests become dangerously wide-ranging. What *is* happening to the ownership of American media today? What dangers does it pose? Taking a look at the structure of the media in the United States, I am not put at ease by what I see.

Most American communities have far less "dissemination of informaion from diverse and antagonistic sources" (to quote a famous description by the Supreme Court of the basic aim of the First Amendment) than is available nationally. Of the 1500 cities with daily newspapers, 96 percent are served by single-owner monopolies. Outside the top 50 to 200 markets there is a substantial dropping off in the number of competing radio and television signals. The FCC prohibits a single owner from controlling two AM radio, or two television, stations with overlapping signals. But it has only recently expressed any concern over common ownership of an AM radio station and an FM radio station and a television station in the same market. Indeed, such ownership is the rule rather than the exception and probably exists in your community. In more than 70 communities *all* media outlets are owned by a single newspaper-radio complex, and more than 90 communities are dominated by newspaper-television joint ownerships. Most stations are today acquired by purchase. And the FCC has, in part because of congressional pressure, rarely disapproved a purchase of a station by a newspaper.

There are few statewide or regional "monopolies"—although some situations come close. But in a majority of our states—the least populous—there are few enough newspapers and television stations to begin with, and they are usually under the control of a small group. And most politicians find today, as Congress warned in 1926, "woe be to those who dare to differ with them." Most of our politics is still state and local in scope. And increasingly, in many states and local communities, Congressmen and state and local officials are compelled to regard that handful of media owners (many of whom are out-of-state), rather than the electorate itself, as their effective constituency. Moreover, many mass media owners have a significant impact in more than one state. One case that came before the FCC, for example, involved an owner with AM-FM-TV combinations in Las Vegas and Reno, Nevada, along with four newspapers in that state, seven newspapers in Oklahoma, and two stations and two newspapers in Arkansas. Another involved ownership of ten stations in North Carolina and adjoining southern Virginia. You may never have

THE MEDIA BARONS AND THE PUBLIC INTEREST
Nicholas Johnson

heard of these owners, but I imagine the elected officials of their states return their phone calls promptly.

The principal national sources of news are the wire services, AP and UPI, and the broadcast networks. Each of the wire services serves on the order of 1200 newspapers and 3000 radio and television stations. Most local newspapers and radio stations offer little more than wire service copy as far as national and international news is concerned. To that extent one can take little heart for "diversity" from the oft-proffered statistics on proliferating radio stations (now over 6000) and the remaining daily newspapers (1700). The networks, though themselves heavily reliant upon the wire services to find out what's worth filming, are another potent force.

The weekly newsmagazine field is dominated by *Time, Newsweek,* and *U.S. News & World Report.* (The first two also control substantial broadcast, newspaper, and book or publishing outlets. *Time* is also in movies [MGM] and is hungry for three or four newspapers.) Thus, even though there are thousands of general and specialized periodicals and program sources with significant national or regional impact, and certainly no "monopoly" exists, it is still possible for a single individual or corporation to have vast national influence.

What we sometimes fail to realize, moreover, is the political significance of the fact that we have become a nation of cities. Nearly half of the American people live in the six largest states: California, New York, Illinois, Pennsylvania, Texas, and Ohio. Those states, in turn, are substantially influenced (if not politically dominated) by their major population-industrial-financial-media centers, such as Los Angeles, New York City, Chicago, and Philadelphia—the nation's four largest metropolitan areas. Thus, to have a major newspaper or television station influence in *one* of these cities is to have significant national power. And the number of interests with influence in *more* than one of these markets is startling.

Most of the top fifty television markets (which

serve approximately 75 percent of the nation's television homes) have three competing commercial VHF (very high frequency) television stations. There are about 150 such VHF commercial stations in these markets. Less than 10 percent are today owned by entities that do not own other media interests. In 30 of the 50 markets at least one of the stations is owned by a major newspaper published in that market—a total of one-third of these 150 stations. (In Dallas-Fort Worth *each* of the network affiliates is owned by a local newspaper, and the fourth, an unaffiliated station, is owned by Oklahoma newspapers.) Moreover, half of the newspaper-owned stations are controlled by seven groups—groups that also publish magazines as popular and diverse as *Time, Newsweek, Look, Parade, Harper's, TV Guide, Family Circle, Vogue, Good Housekeeping,* and *Popular Mechanics.* Twelve parties own more than one-third of all the major-market stations.

In addition to the vast national impact of their affiliates the three television networks each *own* VHF stations in all of the top three markets—New York, Los Angeles, and Chicago—and each has two more in other cities in the top ten. RKO and Metromedia each own stations in both New York City and Los Angeles. Metromedia also owns stations in Washington, D.C., and California's other major city, San Francisco—as well as Philadelphia, Baltimore, Cleveland, Kansas City, and Oakland. RKO also owns stations in Boston, San Francisco, Washington, Memphis, Hartford, and Windsor, Ontario—as well as the regional Yankee Network. Westinghouse owns stations in New York, Chicago, Philadelphia *and* Pittsburgh, Pennsylvania, Boston, San Francisco, Baltimore, and Fort Wayne. These are but a few examples of today's media barons.

There are many implications of their power. Groups of stations are able to bargain with networks, advertisers, and talent in ways that put lesser stations at substantial economic disadvantage. Group ownership means, by definition, that few stations in major markets will be locally owned. (The FCC recently approved the transfer of the last available station in San Francisco to the absentee ownership of Metromedia. The only commercial station locally owned today is controlled by the San Francisco *Chronicle*.) But the basic point is simply that the national political power involved in ownership of a group of major VHF television stations in, say, New York, Los Angeles, Philadelphia, and Washington, D.C., is greater than a democracy should unthinkingly repose in one man or corporation.

CONGLOMERATE CORPORATIONS

For a variety of reasons, an increasing number of communications media are turning up on the organization charts of conglomerate companies. And the incredible profits generated by broadcast stations in the major markets (television broadcasters *average* a 90 to 100 percent return on tangible investment annually) have given FCC licensees, particularly owners of multiple television stations like the networks, Metromedia, Storer Broadcasting, and others, the extra capital with which to buy the New York Yankees (CBS), Random House (RCA), or Northeast Airlines (Storer). Established or up-and-coming conglomerates regard communications acquisitions as prestigious, profitable, and often a useful or even a necessary complement to present operations and projected exploitation of technological change.

The national problem of conglomerate ownership of communications media was well illustrated by the ITT-ABC case. But the conglomerate problem need not involve something as large as ITT-ABC or RCA-NBC. Among the national group owners of television stations are General Tire (RKO), Avco, Westinghouse, Rust Craft, Chris Craft, Kaiser, and Kerr-McGee. The problem of *local* conglomerates was forcefully posed for the FCC in another case early in 1968. Howard Hughes, through Hughes Tool Company, wanted to acquire one of Las Vegas's three major television stations. He had recently acquired $125 million worth of Las Vegas real estate, including hotels, gambling

casinos, and an airport. These investments supplemented 27,000 acres previously acquired. The Commission majority blithely approved the television acquisition without a hearing, overlooking FCC precedents which suggested that a closer examination was in order. In each of these instances the potential threat is similar to that in the ITT-ABC case—that personal economic interests may dominate or bias otherwise independent media.

CONCENTRATION AND TECHNOLOGICAL CHANGE

The problem posed by conglomerate acquisitions of communications outlets is given a special but very important twist by the pendency of sweeping technological changes which have already begun to unsettle the structure of the industry.

President Johnson appointed a distinguished task force to evaluate our national communications policy and chart a course for realization of these technological promises in a manner consistent with the public interest. (Unfortunately its report ignored questions of media ownership structure or media responsibility.) Private interests have already begun to implement their own plans on how to deal with the revolution in communications technology.

General Sarnoff of RCA has hailed the appearance of "the knowledge industry"—corporate casserole dishes blending radio and television stations, networks, and programming; films, movie houses, and record companies; newspaper, magazine, and book publishing; advertising agencies; sports or other entertainment companies; and teaching machines and other profitable appurtenances of the $50 billion plus "education biz."

And everybody's in "cable television"—networks, book publishers, newspapers. Cable television is a system for building the best TV antenna in town and then wiring it into everybody's television set for a fee. It improves signal quality, increases the number of channels, and has proved popular. But the new technology is such that it has broadcasters and newspaper publishers worried. For the same

THE MEDIA BARONS AND THE PUBLIC INTEREST
Nicholas Johnson

cable that can bring off-the-air television into the home can also bring programming from the cable operator's studio, or an "electronic newspaper" printed in the home by a facsimile process. Books can be delivered (between libraries, or to the home) over "television" by using the station's signal during an invisible pause. So everybody's hedging their bets—including the telephone company. Indeed, about all the vested interests can agree upon is that none of them want us to have direct, satellite-to-home radio and television. But at this point it is not at all clear who will have his hand on the switch that controls what comes to the American people over their "telephone wire" a few years hence.

WHAT IS TO BE DONE?

It would be foolish to expect any extensive restructuring of the media in the United States, even if it were considered desirable. Technological change can bring change in structure, but it is as likely to be change to even greater concentration as to wider diversity. In the short run at least, economics seems to render essentially intractable such problems as local monopolies in daily newspapers, or the small number of outlets for national news through wire services, newsmagazines, and the television networks. Indeed, to a certain extent the very high technical quality of the performance rendered by these news-gathering organizations is aided by their concentration of resources into large units and the financial cushions of oligopoly profits.

Nevertheless, it seems clear to me that the risks of concentration are grave.

Chairman Philip Hart of the Senate Antitrust and Monopoly Subcommittee remarked by way of introduction to his antitrust subcommittee's recent hearings about the newspaper industry, "The products of newspapers, opinion and information, are essential to the kind of society that we undertake to make successful here." If we are serious about the kind of society we have undertaken, it is clear to me that we simply must not tolerate concentration of

media ownership—except where concentration creates actual countervailing social benefits. These benefit cannot be merely speculative. They must be identifiable, demonstrable, and genuinely weighty enough to offset the dangers inherent in concentration.

This guideline is a simple prescription. The problem is to design and build machinery to fit it. And to keep the machinery from rusting and rotting. And to replace it when it becomes obsolete.

America does have available governmental machinery which is capable of scotching undue accumulations of power over the mass media, at least in theory and to some extent in practice. The Department of Justice has authority under the antitrust laws to break up combination which "restrain trade" or which "tend to lessen competition." These laws apply to the media as they do to any other industry.

But the antitrust laws simply do not get to where the problems are. They grant authority to block concentration only when it threatens *economic* competition in a particular economic *market*. Generally, in the case of the media, the relevant market is the market for advertising. Unfortunately, relatively vigorous advertising competition can be maintained in situations where competition in the marketplace of ideas is severely threatened. In such cases, the Justice Department has little inclination to act.

Look at the Chicago *Tribune*'s purchase of that city's most popular and most successful FM radio station. The *Tribune* already controlled two Chicago newspapers, one (clear channel) AM radio station, and the city's only independent VHF television station. It controls numerous broadcast, CATV, and newspaper interests outside Chicago (in terms of circulation, the nation's largest newspaper chain). But, after an investigation, the Anti-trust Division let this combination go through. The FM may be a needless addition to the *Tribune*'s already impressive battery of influential media; it could well produce an unsound level of concentration in the production and supply of what Chicagoans see, read, and hear about affairs in their community, in the nation, and in the world. But it did not threaten the level of competition for advertising money in any identifiable advertising market. So, it was felt, the acquisition was not the business of the Justice Department. Initially the FCC found no concentration problems in this acquisition and approved it. However a Chicago citizens group persuaded the U.S. Court of Appeals that the FCC had not fulfilled its responsibilities, and the court remanded the case to the Commission. Ultimately, the *Tribune* and the FCC threw in the sponge, and the FM station was given to educational interests in Chicago.

Only the FCC is directly empowered to keep media ownership patterns compatible with a democracy's need for diversified sources of opinion and information.

In earlier times, the Commission took this responsibility very seriously. In 1941, the FCC ordered NBC to divest itself of one of its two radio networks (which then became ABC), barring any single network from affiliating with more than one outlet in a given city. (The Commission has recently waived this prohibition for, ironically, ABC's four new national radio networks.) In 1941 the Commission also established its power to set absolute limits on the total number of broadcast licenses any individual may hold, and to limit the number of stations any individual can operate in a particular service area.

The American people are indebted to the much maligned FCC for establishing these rules. Imagine, for example, what the structure of political power in this country might look like if two or three companies owned substantially all of the broadcast media in our major cities.

But since the New Deal generation left the command posts of the FCC, this agency has lost much of its zeal for combating concentration. Atrophy has reached so advanced a state that the public has of late witnessed the bizarre spectacle of the Justice Department, with its relatively narrow mandate, intervening in FCC proceedings, such as ITT-ABC, to create court cases with names like

The United States vs. The FCC.

This history is an unhappy one on the whole. It forces one to question whether government can ever realistically be expected to sustain a vigilant posture over an industry which controls the very access of government officials themselves to the electorate.

I fear that we have already reached the point in this country where the media, our greatest check on other accumulations of power, may themselves be beyond the reach of any other institution: the Congress, the President, or the Federal Communications Commission, not to mention governors, mayors, state legislators, and city councilmen. Congressional hearings are begun and then quietly dropped. Whenever the FCC stirs fitfully as if in wakefulness, the broadcasting industry scurries up the Hill for a congressional bludgeon. And the fact that roughly 60 percent of all campaign expenses go to radio and television time gives but a glimmer of the power of broadcasting in the lives of Senators and Congressmen.

However, the picture at this moment has its more hopeful aspect. There does seem to be an exceptional flurry of official concern. Even the FCC has a rulemaking proceeding underway that could limit the number of broadcasting stations a single licensee could own in the same market. The Department of Justice, having broken into the communications field via its dramatic intervention before the FCC in the ITT-ABC merger case, has also been pressing a campaign to force the dissolution of joint operating agreements between separately owned newspapers in individual cities, and opposed an application for broadcasting properties by newspaper interests in Beaumont, Texas. It has been scrutinizing cross-media combinations linking broadcasting, newspaper, and cable television outlets. On Capitol Hill, Senator Phil Hart's Antitrust and Monopoly Subcommittee and Chairman Harley Staggers' House Interstate and Foreign Commerce Committee have both summoned the Federal Communications Commission to appear before them in recent months, to acquaint the Commission with the

THE MEDIA BARONS AND THE PUBLIC INTEREST
Nicholas Johnson

committees' concern about FCC-approved increases in broadcast holdings by single individuals and companies, and about cross-ownership of newspapers, CATV systems, and broadcast stations. Representatives John Dingell, John Moss, and Richard Ottinger have introduced legislation which would proscribe network ownership of any non-broadcast interests. Senator McIntyre has introduced legislation to bust up some of the worst local concentrations.

Twenty years ago Robert M. Hutchins, then chancellor of the University of Chicago, was named chairman of the "Commission on Freedom of the Press." It produced a thoughtful report, full of recommendations largely applicable today—including "the establishment of a new and independent [nongovernmental] agency to appraise and report annually upon the performance of the press," and urged "that the members of the press engage in vigorous mutual criticism." Its proposals are once again being dusted off and reread.

What is needed now, more than anything else, is to keep this flurry of interest alive, and to channel it toward constructive reforms. What this means, in practical fact, is that concern for media concentration must find an institutional home.

The Department of Justice has already illustrated the value of participation by an external institution in FCC decision-making. The developing concept of a special consumers' representative offers a potentially broader base for similar action.

But the proper place to lodge continuing responsibility for promoting diversity in the mass media is neither the FCC nor the Justice Department nor a congressional committee. The initiative must come from private sources. Plucky Nader-like crusaders such as John Banzhaf (who single-handedly induced the FCC to apply the "fairness" doctrine to cigarette commercials) have shown how responsive government can be to the skillful and vigorous efforts of even a lone individual. But there are more adequately staffed and funded private organizations which could play a more effective role in policy formation than a single individual. Even the FCC,

where the public interest gets entirely too little representation from private sources, has felt the impact of the United Church of Christ and the Citizens Communication Center with their interest in the influence of broadcasting on race relations and in the programming responsibility of licensees, and of the American Civil Liberties Union, which submitted a brief in the ITT-ABC case.

Ideally, however, the resources for a sustained attack on concentration might be centered in a single institution, equipped to look after this cause with the kind of determination and intelligence that the Ford Foundation and the Carnegie Corporation, for example, have brought to bear in behalf of the cause of public broadcasting and domestic satellites. The law schools and their law reviews, as an institution, have performed well in this way for the courts, but have virtually abdicated responsibility for the agencies.

Such an organization could devote itself to research as well as representation. For at present any public body like the FCC, which has to make determinations about acceptable levels of media concentration, has to do so largely on the basis of hunch. In addition, private interest in problems of concentration would encourage the Justice Department to sustain its present vigilance in this area. It could stimulate renewed vigilance on the part of the FCC, through participation in Commission proceedings. And it could consider whether new legislation might be appropriate to reach the problem of newspaper-magazine-book publishing combinations.

Legislation does not, however, appear to be the desire of Vice President Agnew, and others in the Nixon Administration, who have been quite critical of the content of the mass media and have even referred to the problems of concentration of control (of those stations and newspapers critical of the President). They have taken little interest in even-handed reforms applicable to all media owners. Indeed, the President's "Director of Communications," Herbert Klein, has indicated his opposition to Senator McIntyre's bill. When the Assistant

Attorney General for Antitrust, Richard McLaren, opposed the newspaper-industry backed monopoly authorization bill ("the failing newspaper act"), he was reversed by the White House, and the Department of Commerce was directed to testify in favor of the bill. When the trade press reported that six of the seven Commissioners were opposed to the broadcast license automatic renewal bill (S. 2004, introduced by Senator Pastore and others), President Nixon appointed to the Commission two new Commissioners favorable to the legislation – and the Commission ultimately adopted as a "policy statement" most of the provisions of the legislation.

If changes are to be made (or now dormant standards are to be enforced) the most pressing political question is whether to apply the standards prospectively only, or to require divestiture. It is highly unlikely, to say the least, that legislation requiring massive divestiture of multiple station ownership, or newspaper ownership of stations, would ever pass through Congress. Given the number of station sales every year, however, even prospective standards could have some impact over ten years or so.

In general, I would urge the minimal standard that no accumulation of media should be permitted without a specific and convincing showing of a continuing countervailing social benefit. For no one has a higher calling in an increasingly complex free society bent on self-government than he who informs and moves the people. Personal prejudice, ignorance, social pressure, and advertiser pressure are in large measure inevitable. But a nation that depends upon the rational dialogue of an informed electorate simply cannot take any unnecessary risk of polluting the stream of information and opinion that sustains it. At the very least, the burden of proving the social utility of doing otherwise should be upon him who seeks the power and profit which will result.

During the past year or so, we have seen a heartening stimulation of the national awareness of the problems and implications of mass media ownership. The FCC dusted off its ten-year-old

proceeding on network ownership and control of programming, and received an unprecedented musical presentation during this hearing from one of the most creative men in television, Mason Williams – who subsequently published it as *The Mason Williams FCC Rapport.* The importance of networks is clear – in 1968 the three networks and the fifteen stations they *own* earned more than one-half of the total television industry revenues. More than 90 percent of the most profitable stations were affiliates which depend almost exclusively upon the networks for their programming.

The Department of Justice has continued the interest it demonstrated in the ABC-ITT case. It challenged the common newspaper-broadcasting-cable ownership in Cheyenne, Wyoming – ultimately set for hearing by the FCC. Reportedly it was opposition from the Antitrust Division that deterred the announced mergers between Westinghouse and MCA, Inc. and between Metromedia and Transamerica. The Department filed pointed comments with the FCC concerning the relationships between telephone companies and cable television service. It secured a consent decree divestiture of a television-newspaper combine in Rockford, Illinois – which, incidentally, the Commission had tacitly approved a short time before by renewing the station's license. The Department filed comments in an FCC rulemaking suggesting that review of newspaper ownership of broadcast stations and their possible divestiture be considered. It seems unfortunate if not ludicrous that the Department's Antitrust Division, already understaffed and overworked, has had to prod the FCC in its own supposed area of expertise.

As a result of this prodding, however, the FCC has made some tentative and hesitant moves. An inquiry was opened into conglomerate ownership of broadcast properties. Hearings were ordered to explore concentration questions in San Francisco, Minneapolis and Wichita, Kansas. (The parties in Wichita later terminated their merger agreement rather than go through an evidentiary hearing.) The Commission preferred a competing applicant over the former newspaper licensee (the Boston *Herald-Traveler*) in the *Boston Channel 5* case. But conglomerate acquisitions continue to be approved without hearing, and the general inquiry languishes as forces inside and outside the Commission oppose its progress. The Commission has refused, by a three-to-three vote, to review the renewal of the Mormon Church's holdings in Salt Lake City. In fact, the very day the conglomerate inquiry was announced the Commission approved further acquisitions by three major conglomerates, including a major defense contractor and the Mormon Church.

Even these feeble efforts produced an industry backlash of substantial proportions. The *Boston Channel 5* decision was probably the principal impetus to the broadcasting industry's push for legislation limiting the role of public groups who might raise ownership objections at license renewal time. S. 2004 was introduced by 22 Senators and 118 Congressmen during 1969. The FCC had already cut back to thirty days the time during which public groups could make their views known. Then the FCC adopted its policy statement immunizing from competitive challenge any licensee who can show he has "substantially served" his community. The meaning of those words has yet to be determined; but the policy statement so effectively adopted the intent of the protectionist S. 2004 that further Congressional proceedings are unlikely. At this writing the FCC had two new Nixon appointees with the prospect of a Republican majority by July 1, 1970. A number of potential FCC actions which could improve present media concentration patterns stand in the wings. The record of President Nixon's FCC has yet to be written.

Whatever may be the outcome, the wave of renewed interest in the impact of ownership on the role of the media in our society is healthy. All will gain from intelligent inquiry by Congress, the Executive, the regulatory Commissions—and especially the academic community, the American people generally, and the media themselves. For, as the Supreme Court has noted, nothing is more important in a free society than "the widest possible dissemination of information from diverse and antagonistic sources." And if we are unwilling to discuss *this* issue fully today we may find ourselves discussing none that matter very much tomorrow.

The American Media Baronies

ATLANTIC STAFF WRITERS

IT IS, or should be, of more than casual concern who owns any city's newspaper, radio, and television facilities. In more cities than most people have realized, a significant proportion of these communications outlets are owned by one man or one company; or a major paper or broadcast facility, or perhaps both, are subsidiaries of a large national business, often one with its own other interests to serve. Ownership of media for fun, profit, and significant power is increasingly characterized by Very Big Business.

Last year, the *Atlantic* published an article by Federal Communications Commissioner Nicholas Johnson ("The Media Barons and the Public Interest," June, 1968) warning of the dangers of diminished competition in "the marketplace of ideas," and examining the "impact of *ownership* upon the control of media." As previously promised, we present the *Atlantic's* atlas of the men, families, and combines who dominate the newspapers, radio, TV, and other media in this country, and trace some of the developments in slowly awakening Washington since Commissioner Johnson's article appeared.

The problem of who owns what facilities for telling us what is going on, and what to think about it, takes a variety of forms. Broadly, there are five types of baronies. However, one baron may be an example of more than one sort of communication power. What follows is a description of each type, with examples. Guides to these and other baronial holdings [are then outlined in detail]. Strange as it may seem, there is no single government agency in Washington which has made it its business to assemble all of the data on the reaches of this country's most powerful communicators in usable form. Only now, and still on an *ad hoc* basis, has there begun to be even any serious interest in the question.

THE LOCAL MONOPOLY

One owner may dominate a city's media. For example, one man, Donald W. Reynolds, owns Fort Smith, Arkansas's, two newspapers and its only television station. Reynolds is also an example of one man having great impact on entire regions (see page 94) through concentrated ownership of newspapers and/or broadcast properties in Arkansas and Oklahoma and Nevada. In Niles, Michigan, the Plym family owns the only daily newspaper, the only AM radio station, and the only FM station. There is no local television outlet. According to the information supplied by the FCC to the Senate Antitrust and Monopoly Subcommittee, as of late 1967 there were seventy-three communities where one person or company owned or controlled all of the local newspaper and broadcast outlets.

REGIONAL CONCENTRATION

There are a striking number of areas of the country where one media baron may not have a

THE AMERICAN MEDIA BARONIES
Atlantic Staff Writers

pure monopoly, but can have an equivalent impact through his preponderant interests. A branch of the Booth family, for instance, owns a string of newspapers in Michigan and contiguous areas, as well as an important interest in the company which owns and operates the Detroit *News* and the NBC TV and radio outlets in that city. Another branch owns several radio and CATV interests in the same region. There are separate companies involved, and the Booth family contends that they are controlled by separate and unfriendly branches of the family tree, and the FCC has accepted this rationale, but not unanimously. The owner of major news facilities in the most important city of a given state usually speaks to the state as a whole, and can constitute an enormous power in the state's affairs. The Mormon Church may be the most extraordinary example of regional power. Through an affiliate, the Bonneville International, the Church of the Latter Day Saints not only has extensive broadcast interests of its own but has negotiated a set of alliances with other Salt Lake City media owners, giving the combined group a mighty voice throughout the mountain states of the West. (The Mormons' interests are not at all confined to broadcasting. They are also reported to have holdings in a beet sugar company, a Salt Lake City department store, two Salt Lake City hotels, life and fire insurance companies, a bookstore, some six hundred farms, a real estate management company, a trucking company, sugar and pineapple plantations, three large Canadian ranches, forty mills, factories, and salvage stores, and substantial land in Florida.)

Relieved of the burdens of running the country, Lyndon B. Johnson has now had time to devote more attention to the family broadcasting collection, accumulated during Mr. Johnson's years in politics. (It was always argued that Lady Bird was the brains behind the whole thing.) The Johnsons own an AM and FM radio station and a TV station in Austin, as well as half a cable television company in that city. They also own 29 percent of a Waco, Texas, AM radio and TV station, which in turn owns a majority of the stock of a number of other radio and television stations in Texas. The former President's media baronial appetites are said to be whetted, not sated.

MULTIPLE OWNERSHIP

Anyone who owns more than one of a given kind of medium is, at least, an absentee owner, and at most, a national power. Gannett, Ridder, and Newhouse may not be household words everywhere in the nation, but they are in political circles in Washington, and of course in the many cities throughout the country where each owns frequently the only newspaper. Flourishing publishers are often considered by Presidents to be the sorts of people who ought to be the United States ambassadors abroad. This has been more true recently of Republicans than Democrats; John F. Kennedy showed more affinity for lowly journalists in ambassadorial posts. But mighty publishers have substantial access to the White House. Mr. Nixon recently appointed Walter Annenberg to the American Embassy in London. Annenberg is the owner of two Philadelphia newspapers, and television stations in Philadelphia, Altoona-Johnstown, and Lancaster-Lebanon, Pennsylvania; Binghamton, New York; Hartford-New Haven, Connecticut; and Fresno, California. He also is the proprietor of such variegated magazine properties as *Seventeen*, *TV Guide*, and the *Morning Telegraph*, a racing daily. Queried on whether Mr. Annenberg had to divest himself of his communications holdings now that he was an official servant of the State Department, a Department spokesman said that there were no rules requiring such action and was surprised that the question should even arise.

The "Big Six" — NBC, CBS, ABC, RKO, Westinghouse, and Metromedia — are the most striking examples of multiple broadcasting power. Each of the networks, beyond their vast national impact through their hundreds of affiliated stations, owns television stations in several major cities, including the three most important television markets, New York, Los Angeles, and Chicago. There are, as Commissioner Johnson pointed out, "many implications of their power. Groups of stations are able to bargain with networks, advertisers, and talent in ways that put lesser stations at substantial economic disadvantage. Group ownership means, by definition, that few stations in major markets will be locally owned. . . . But the basic point is simply that the national political power involved in ownership of a group of major VHF television stations in, say, New York, Los Angeles, Philadelphia, and Washington, D.C., is greater than a democracy should unthinkingly repose in one man or corporation."

MULTIMEDIA OWNERSHIP

Men or companies which have collected more than one kind of communications outlet—broadcasting and newspapers and/or magazines—can show up in different sorts of baronies: one with a local monopoly; one with regional concentration; a large company with great competitive advantages and a variety of interests to be served, the public interest being of unknown rank. RCA, for example, is a single company containing subsidiary companies which own a book-publishing company (Random House), radio stations, television stations, a radio and TV network (NBC), a record company, and a major manufacturer of television sets. Time Inc., the Washington *Post-Newsweek* complex, and the Cowles Communications and the Minneapolis Star and Tribune Company are all large and powerful publishing-broadcasting enterprises.

CBS is one of the more dazzling multimedia owners. Besides its network operations, it owns television stations in five major cities, a record company, musical-instrument manufacturing companies, a book-publishing house (Holt, Rinehart and Winston), educational film producers, CATV systems, Creative Playthings toys, and the New York Yankees.

CONGLOMERATES

RCA and CBS, of course, can also be termed conglomerates.

Conglomeration is a two-way street, and just as a number of communications media owners have used their enormous earnings to branch into other unrelated businesses, so have unrelated businesses increasingly eyed broadcasting properties as a means to enhanced power and earnings. (TV stations, on the average, earn nearly 100 percent return on tangible investment.) The worry here, as was brought out in the controversy over ITT's now abandoned attempt to wed ABC, is that there will be almost irresistible pressure and incentive to use the communications subsidiary to promote the corporate interests of the holding company. A conglomerate can be a community affair. Howard Hughes, aside from his other business interests, constitutes a conglomerate in Las Vegas alone: he owns land, hotels, casinos, an airport; and then acquired a television station there. (Having been warded off in his attempt in 1968 to purchase ABC, Hughes did acquire Sports Network, Inc., a significant occasional sports broadcasting network. The widespread assumption is that Hughes plans to build it into a rival television network. This is, by the way, an example of the frying-pan—fire syndrome of media ownership. While critics of the networks' power would welcome a rival, Hughes is not their idea of Lochinvar. On those rare occasions when a baron's holdings are challenged, it is frequently by another baron.) . . .

A BARONY ATLAS

When Lord Thomson, the Canadian-born doyen of British press magnates, acquired the rights to television in Scotland several years ago, he proclaimed that he now possessed "a license to print money." The same can be said of the communications industry in America today. With a very few exceptions, newspapers in this country have never been so prosperous. "It's like stealing," one contented newspaper publisher remarked to us recently. "And the more monopolistic newspapers get, the healthier they have become economically." There ought to be some happy consequences for the public as a result of this trend; there is at least

THE AMERICAN MEDIA BARONIES
Atlantic Staff Writers

the possibility. New York media broker and consultant Vincent J. Manno argues, "Group ownerships invariably have the financial stability to maintain editorial independence of the printed word, and thereby enjoy the potential to serve the general community."

Broadcasting is different. Though the public "owns" the airwaves, a small number of persons who hold the federal government's franchises to broadcast reap heavy profits from the money advertisers pour into TV and radio broadcasting (some $3.2 billion last year). All but the UHF channels and, of course, the educational TV stations, are automatic moneymakers, and small radio stations that rent the air with inanities send their owners well-laden to the banks.

It is no wonder that such operations, with their almost certain profits plus their prestige and their immense power to inform or misinform or omit to inform, are among the most desirable, most sought after properties in the world of business. In setting out to assemble a modest *Atlantic* Atlas of some of the more important of the individuals and some lesser-known communications combines, we found who owns what, where? to be only a part of the question. More difficult, it became apparent, was the question, who owns what, when?

The whirlwind velocity with which the larger combines recombine and split, enter and break off engagements, couple, reproduce offspring, contrive advantageous liaisons between progeny and distant cousins, and otherwise besport themselves in what sometimes seems like a corporate bacchanalia, has made it difficult for us to keep pace with all of it long enough to get it down on paper. A recent issue of the breathlessly phrased Gallagher Report suggests the timber of media-baron mating calls:

Time-Life Broadcast Marches On. President Wes Pullen plans to increase subsidiary's $22 million revenues via expansion of tv production facilities. Sets up production centers in Grand Rapids, Denver, San Diego, Indianapolis. Wants to sell second Time-Life Nature series to networks, educational films, tv commercials, special events (a la Indianapolis 500 race coverage for Goodyear Tire & Rubber). Company to capitalize on 11-million-foot backlog of March of Time film. Re-edit for production of historical documentaries. Wes has 14 CATV outlets threatened by multi-media ban. Manhattan Cable Television makes slow progress —has mere 10% of estimated 300,000 potential homes. Pullen lost out to Post-Newsweek Stations chairman Larry Israel in race to acquire Miami ABC-TV affiliate WLBW.

It is all pretty hectic—and heady—stuff. When we began assembling the Atlas, we were able to draw on obvious sources for details about the "public" companies. Officers of a few of the privately owned baronies, like John Cowles, Jr., of Minneapolis, were helpful in providing data. But for persons engaged in the craft of informing, most media barons are surprisingly uncommunicative about the size, extent, and income of their suzerainties.

The *Atlantic* tested various methods of ascertaining such facts—our researchers have consulted the source books (*Editor and Publisher, Standard & Poor's* Indexes, *Television Factbook*), authorities in the field, and finally, the companies themselves. No two sets of findings matched. Telephone calls to staff personnel produced quite different details and statistics from personal letters to heads of corporations. The media baronies are so big, so fluid, so upwardly, inwardly, outwardly mobile that they themselves don't seem to know how big they are on a given day. It must be stated, accordingly, that the information presented here is current and complete as of the time we went to press only insofar as the media barons' own Domesday Books are current and complete.

LEGEND

 Newspaper   Magazine   Radio   Television   X CATV   Book Publisher

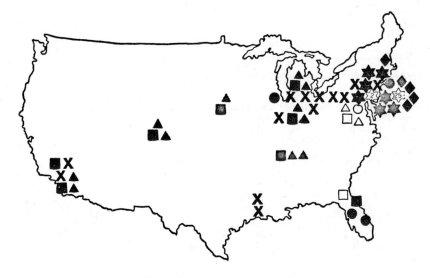

Time Inc. (black)

Almost everyone has heard of *Time*, the weekly newsmagazine, and of *Life*, *Fortune*, and, perhaps, *Sports Illustrated*, published by the same company. But not everyone knows that Time Inc. is also a major broadcaster (with a large quota of TV and radio stations in lucrative markets), a purveyor of teaching machines, a book publisher, owner of thirteen CATV systems (including one that serves the lower half of Manhattan), a big shareholder in MGM, a papermaker, owner of some 600,000 acres of timberland, and a part owner of media in South America, West Germany, Hong Kong, and Australia. Life, a $160-million-a-year enterprise, has been regrouping of late to extend its lease on life as a mass magazine in the age of TV—not an easy thing to do. For the first quarter of 1969, Time Inc. reported a loss of $300,000 (less than the combined salaries of its chairman of the board and president), and the stock tumbled from an Olympian 100 into the 60s. But the outfit is rich and diversified. Last year's revenues: $567,811,000. Recently it bought thirty-two neighborhood newspapers in the Chicago area, is looking for more newspapers to buy, is thinking about starting new magazines on food and TV. Where it all will end knows Mammon.

Cowles Communications, Inc. (gray)

Look magazine is the big moneymaker for Cowles Communications— it accounted for 61 percent of the company's total revenues last year. But Cowles Communications is also into other magazines (*Family Circle*, *Venture*), business and trade publications, newspapers,* broadcasting (in Des Moines, Memphis, and Orlando, Florida), books, foreign publications, and a three-dimensional printing process, and some of these efforts at diversification—notably the young Suffolk (Long Island) *Sun* and the XOGRAPH three-dimensional printing process—operate in the red. Cowles's revenue last year was $164,959,000, but it came out with a net loss of $972,000 (down from 1967's net loss of $3,478,000).

If anything happened to *Look*, Cowles Communications would be in trouble. According to Cowles Communications' annual report,

"because of increased costs, [*Look's*] profit in 1968 was less than in 1967. The Magazine had only a slight gain in advertising revenue. . . ." But the report pooh-poohs some "typical" stockholder questions ("how does the demise of the *Saturday Evening Post* affect *Look* and the magazine industry?") with uplifting statistics and commentary: "In the last five years, advertising in the leading consumer magazines measured by the Publishers Information Bureau has climbed over 28% to a dollar total of $1,196,055,761. In the same period, circulation for these magazines increased by approximately 19%. . . . The *Post* was in ill health, not the magazine business. . . ." Cowles Communications is headed by Gardner ("Mike") Cowles; it is the only one of the three Cowles baronies to be held publicly. (For the others, see the section on Minneapolis and Des Moines below.)

*Not shown here is an Ocala, Florida, newspaper and printing operation, the remnants of the Perry newspaper group. In April, Cowles agreed "in principle" to pay Perry an estimated $4.8 million worth of Cowles common stock for the properties.

Washington Post—Newsweek (black outline)

The Post Company, owner of the capital's leading paper, the Washington *Post* (daily circulation: 479,644), and *Newsweek* (worldwide circulation: 2,571,480), is a streamlined instrument of national influence. Its chiefs, the late Eugene Meyer, the late Philip Graham, and the former's daughter and latter's widow, Katherine Meyer Graham, have built their empire with an emphasis on quality rather than quantity. They have not, however, neglected to acquire milch cows which keep the farm profitable; the Post Company owns the CBS outlets in Washington, D.C.—WTOP-TV and WTOP-AM and FM, and the Jacksonville, Florida, CBS television outlet as well.

There are other pursuits: Newsweek, Inc. publishes *Art News*. The Post Company and the (Los Angeles) Times-Mirror Company operate a successful news syndicate; the Post Company is one of the three owners of the International *Herald Tribune* in Paris (these two interests are not shown on this map). The company's current figure for "consolidated revenue" is "in excess of $100 million." The *Post* aspires to reach, and if possible, pass, the New York *Times* in prestige. *Newsweek* has been bothering stomach linings at Time Inc., and Mrs. Graham, very much the boss-lady, gets invited to all the best parties—Nixon's as well as Capote's.

THE AMERICAN MEDIA BARONIES
Atlantic Staff Writers

Gannett

As the Gannett Company puts it in their 1968 annual report, "A major advantage enjoyed by the Company over all but the very largest single newspapers lies in corporate size sufficient to maintain production staffs able to evaluate new production methods. . . ." He who is big need never be small. Gannett now owns thirty dailies and nine broadcasting stations (soon to be eight) in six states, growing out of Frank Gannett's chain of upstate New York newspapers founded in 1906 (shown here, with a few surrounding properties). Recent expansion has been consummated with gusto: Gannett bought the nine Macy chain papers in New York's Westchester and Rockland counties in 1964; Cape Kennedy, Florida, area newspapers and radio stations in 1965 and 1966; a group of Illinois newspapers in 1967; and early this year the San Bernardino, California, *Sun* papers (the seller was the Los Angeles *Times*; price: $17,700,000). The *Wall Street Journal* reports that Gannett has agreed to pay an estimated $15 million in cash and securities for two Pensacola, Florida, papers in the old Perry chain. Total

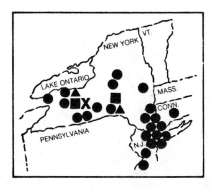

daily circulation for Gannett's papers: 1,315,663. 1968 revenues were $123,738,688; net income was $8,624,451. Competently edited, generally with a Rotary-Kiwanis conservative bent, the Gannett chain is today run by Paul Miller, once Washington Bureau Chief of Associated Press.

The Minneapolis Star and Tribune *(gray)*, the Des Moines Register *(black outline)*, Ridder *(black)*

To state the links and the distinctions between the several enterprises controlled by members of the Cowles family is not to say what they mean. For the record, Cowles Communications (see above) is to be distinguished from the Des Moines Register and Tribune Company, and both are to be distinguished from the Minneapolis Star and Tribune Company. In fact, Gardner Cowles, chairman of the board of Cowles Communications (which owns the CBS radio-TV outlets in Des Moines), is president of the Des Moines Register and Tribune Company; his brother, John Cowles, Sr., is chairman of the boards of both the Des Moines Register and Minneapolis Star and Tribune Companies, and the latter's son, John Cowles, Jr., president of the Minneapolis Star and Tribune Company, is a member of the board of directors of the Des Moines Register and Tribune Company. As John Cowles, Jr., puts it,

> Because the Des Moines Register and Tribune Company and the Gardner Cowles Foundation, Inc. (of Des Moines, my Grandparents' charitable foundation) each owns more than one percent

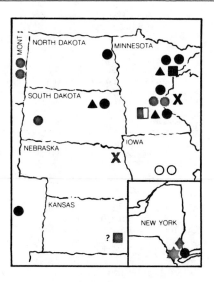

of the stock of Cowles Communications, Inc., and of Minneapolis Star and Tribune Company, the FCC apparently considers the New York, Des Moines and Minneapolis companies to comprise a single "group" of interests. This FCC definition is perhaps responsible for the erroneous public impression that the three companies are managed by some single, over-all,

holding company or trust. Except for the overlap, however, of my Uncle Mike [Gardner Cowles], my Father and me with respect to Des Moines Register and Tribune Company, the editorial and business managements of the three companies are separate and unrelated.

The Des Moines company publishes the morning Des Moines *Register* and evening *Tribune* and a Sunday paper. Though financial statements are not made public, the annual revenues can be estimated at over $25 million.

But up in Minneapolis, things are more complicated. The Minneapolis Star and Tribune Company (annual revenues: over $50 million) owns *Harper's* magazine in New York (through a wholly owned subsidiary, Harper's Magazine Inc.), newspapers in Montana and South Dakota, a CATV system in Nebraska, a television station in Kansas (which the company is trying to sell to Gaylord of Oklahoma; see below), as well as the Minneapolis morning and evening newspapers. What is currently concerning the FCC is the question of "concentration" arising from the fact that the Minneapolis Star and Tribune Company owns 47 percent of the operator of Minneapolis-St. Paul's CBS radio and television outlets; the controlling 53 percent is in turn owned by the publisher of two St. Paul newspapers, namely the Ridder family's Northwest Publications, Inc. through a company called Mid-Continent Radio-Television, Inc. (which in turn is partly owned by another company called MTC Properties, Inc., which in turn is a non-

Cowles stockholder [14.7 percent] in the Minneapolis Star and Tribune Company. Phew.)

The Ridder family has other broadcast and newspaper interests from the Midwest to the Rockies, publishes sixteen papers in Cali-

fornia and the *Journal of Commerce* in New York. The Ridder people did not respond to our request for a ball-park figure on company's dollar volume; an informed guess at the Ridder interests' worth is $100 to $150 million.

Newhouse

Samuel I. Newhouse is nothing if not acquisitive. His empire of twenty-plus dailies has undergone electrification (television and radio properties, some of them in cities where Newhouse also owns major newspapers [Portland, Oregon; St. Louis, Missouri; Syracuse, New York; and Birmingham, Alabama] and a collection of nine CATV systems) and beautification: *Vogue, Glamour, Mademoiselle,* and *House & Garden* lead Newhouse's magazine chain. Syracuse is the traditional seat of the Newhouse barony, but his influence is national, if not too frequently exercised. (As is the case with many of the larger groups, the chain's endorsement of LBJ in the 1964 election was a rare show of unified editorial policy.) Long green,

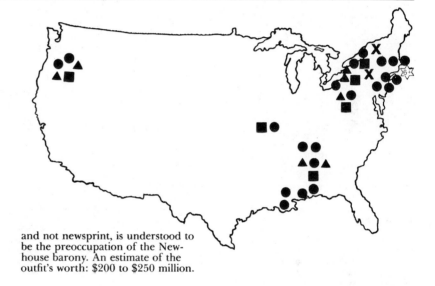

and not newsprint, is understood to be the preoccupation of the Newhouse barony. An estimate of the outfit's worth: $200 to $250 million.

Bonneville International, affiliated with the Mormon Church *(gray)*; Kearns-Tribune *(black outline)*; and Glassman-Hatch *(black)*

Three Salt Lake City baronies which are engaged in a variety of joint enterprises dominate the state of Utah with their newspaper, broadcast, and cable television interests, and dominate as well the microwave systems which connect cable TV and broadcasting outlets all over the Rocky Mountain states. The group owns important broadcast properties in neighboring states, and Bonneville, the Mormon Church affiliate, also has an estimated $20 million (just under 5 percent) interest in the Los Angeles *Times.* God is very much alive, and on the air (but not in Salt Lake City, tax-exempt). Here are some guesses about the three outfits' value: Bonneville: $60 to $75 million Glassman-Hatch: $15 to $18 million. Kearns-Tribune: $12 to $15 million.

THE AMERICAN MEDIA BARONIES
Atlantic Staff Writers

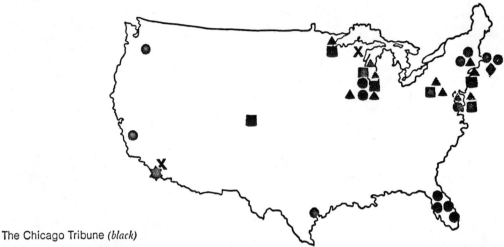

The Chicago Tribune (*black*)

A mighty fortress is the Chicago *Tribune*, a bulwark of *ancien régime* conservatism never yielding. Colonel McCormick, creator of "The World's Greatest Newspaper," is gone, but the men who command his caissons go rolling along. If the *Tribune* weren't the circulation leader in Chicago and surrounding suburbs (805,924 daily), and if the New York *Daily News* (which the Tribune Company now controls) weren't the nations' largest circulation paper (2,102,655 daily), television and radio properties in these top markets would help; the Tribune Company owns them anyway. An afternoon Chicago paper, *Chicago Today* (née Chicago's *American*), broadcast interests in Minnesota, Colorado, and Connecticut, CATV systems in Michigan and California, and newspapers in Florida constitute the Tribune Company's outer barricades. The Tribune Company is worth something in the $250 million range, say men in the business. One assessment of its 1968 gross sales: $300 million.

Hearst (*gray*)

No longer the mammoth of the journalistic jungle of earlier days, the Hearst Corporation is still an important owner of newspapers, magazines at home (*Harper's Bazaar, Good Housekeeping, Cosmopolitan, Town & Country, House Beautiful, Popular Mechanics*) and abroad, radio and television properties, and a newspaper feature syndicate. One center of Hearst power is Baltimore, where it owns the evening *News-American* and the NBC radio and TV affiliates. Total daily circulation for eight newspapers: 1,851,012. William Randolph Hearst, Jr., doesn't like to talk about money, but our research suggests that the corporation is worth $250 million; one estimate of Hearst's gross sales figure for 1968: $400 million.

Gaylord (*black*)

At ninety-six, E. K. Gaylord is a proto-typical regional press lord. His Oklahoma Publishing Company owns the state's most influential and profitable newspaper and TV properties (as well as television stations in Texas, Wisconsin, and Florida), and is wont to employ them as weapons of war against legislation he dislikes (the Great Society's Model Cities program) and politicians he opposes (Oklahoma's liberal former senator Mike Monroney).

Don Reynolds (*gray*)

Don Reynolds' headquarters are in Arkansas, where he owns newspa-pers, radio and television outlets; his Donrey Media Group spreads westward and follows patterns of regional concentration: ten newspapers in Oklahoma, radio-television combinations in Laredo, Texas, and (not shown here) Reno and Las Vegas, Nevada, and a scattering of newspapers in California, Washington, Nevada, and Hawaii. Invoking limits on what publishers call "the people's right to know," Reynolds and Gaylord are closemouthed about their fortunes. Some insiders' guesses about the worth of the two baronies: Reynolds, $30 to $35 million; Gaylord, $60 million. Last year, we were reliably told, Gaylord grossed about $33 million.

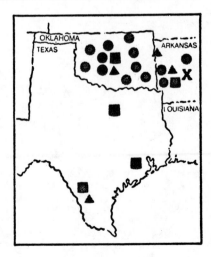

The Los Angeles Times

The Chandler family is one of the most formidable institutions in Southern California, and their Los Angeles *Times* is the most powerful paper in the West (daily circulation: way ahead of all competition in California at 958,124, and rising), and not at all shy about exercising its considerable (generally Republican) influence. It is also, perhaps, the most improved American newspaper of recent decades. That would satisfy most publishers, but the Times-Mirror Company's interests have spread eastward and northward to include a trail of book publishers (including one important one, NAL-World), *Popular Science* magazine, joint ownership of the L.A. *Times*-Washington *Post* News Service, and a forest-products operation which yields the *Times* the paper it's printed on. Times-Mirror's 1968 net income from operations, or revenues of $353 million: $24,197,000.

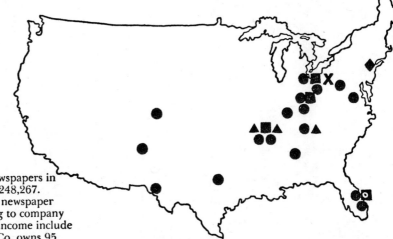

Scripps-Howard

Scripps-Howard's chain of sixteen daily newspapers in major cities now reaches a circulation of 2,248,267. "Annual revenue from all sources" for the newspaper company "exceeds $250 million," according to company president Jack R. Howard. Sources of the income include United Press International (E. W. Scripps Co. owns 95 percent), news syndicates, and the *World Almanac*. In the cities of Cincinnati, Cleveland, and Memphis, where the E. W. Scripps Company has a predominant position in newspaper ownership, its publicly owned kinsman, the Scripps-Howard Broadcasting Company, owns television properties.

Scripps-Howard Broadcasting's annual report for 1968 noted a year of "turmoil, tensions and taxes"—an apparent reference both to national and to industry unrest—but was able to report net operating revenues for the year of $22 million and net income of $4.9 million. Jack Howard cited as one source of trouble "an accelerating trend of actions and proposals by the FCC which would change long-standing historical patterns of ownership in the broadcasting industry to promote affirmatively a wider diversification of control" of the mass media. He advised stockholders, "We are hopeful that industry efforts to reverse this trend will be successful, but we feel that our stockholders should be aware of the situation." There are clouds in medialand.

MEDIA REGULATORS: CONGRESS AND THE FEDERAL COMMUNICATIONS COMMISSION

Part II

INTRODUCTION

The mass media are regulated by a wide variety of government agencies. The basic guidelines have been produced by the executive branch of government and congressional legislation. On a day-to-day basis the Justice Department and the Federal Trade Commission have been involved with enforcing regulatory laws, but the most important agency in such matters is the Federal Communications Commission, which is specifically charged by the government with the task of regulating the electronic media. It has the authority to license stations, suggest broadcasting regulations to the United States Congress and President, and prosecute stations and networks for alleged violations of existing laws. The private industry, however, apparently has the upper hand in many of the disputes that are crucial to its operation. Due in part to its public image as the donor of "free" services and its powerful control of communications media themselves, it has successfully portrayed the FCC as an "intruding" organization that works against the public interest.

The weakness of the FCC relative to the private television industry could be attributed to collusion between the regulator and regulated as indicated by the interlocking of elite personnel. It is true, for example, that a retired commissioner is admirably suited for lucrative posts in the private industries that he had regulated during his FCC tenure. As with other government officers, such changes in

employment are not unprecedented. A few commissioners sometimes may have relaxed controls to keep open future employment channels, but such conflict of interest is difficult to prove and clearly does not apply to such outspoken commissioners as Nicholas Johnson, whose continuous attack on the networks scarcely endears him to the industry's leaders. The cause of the Commission's weakness, therefore, is probably not due to the doubtful integrity of commissioners but to the more basic structural defects of its organization.

The FCC has a phenomenally wide range of duties which include a plethora of responsibilities, many of which are only vaguely defined, in the nation's sophisticated and expanding communications channels.[1] These range from space satellites, to telegraph and telephone use, to the protection of individual privacy in new wire connected computer systems; and from all public and private broadcasting to the licensing of pocket paging devices. There are currently more than 7200 public radio and TV stations in operation.[2] The Commission is responsi-

[1]The following two paragraphs are based on information given in Federal Communications Commission, *The F.C.C. in Fiscal 1968 — A Summary of Activities* (Washington, D. C., F.C.C., 1968)
[2]In addition to this there were 1.7 million private stations operating in 1968. These are licensed by the FCC as "Safety and Special Radio Services." They include police, military, aircraft, industrial, and marine transmitters.

ble for the application of the Fairness Doctrine, i.e., the rules relating to advertising, political campaigning, and personal attack in each of these stations. In fiscal year 1968, which may be taken as an indicator of current activity, the Commission also prepared and held hearings on proposals to establish subscription television and to limit newswire contracts with broadcasters, in addition to fulfilling its more basic task of investigating a large number of cases of alleged programming and license violations. In most of these investigations it issued warnings to the offenders. Two licenses were revoked—the Commissioners' primary sanction—and 167 stations were given revocation warnings, but only a small fraction of stations—35 of the 7200—were actually subjected to field investigations.[3]

The Commission had to fulfill these multiple tasks with a staff that averaged 1470 employees and a budget of $19.17 million. This hardly indicated the dominance of "Big Government" in mass communications. Thus, for example, the commercial television companies (whose income was more than 20 times the total FCC appropriation) could therefore easily out-staff, out-spend, and generally out-flank the Commission on any matter in which regulation might be for the public interest but which would also greatly inconvenience the corporations. Despite the good intentions of the FCC, its overall structural weakness—resulting from its small budget and staff together with its poorly defined authority—is such that commercial broadcasting and the emerging new forms of communication in fact go virtually unregulated.

The interplay between the government and the electronic media—the press is largely self-regulating—during 1968 was outlined by the DuPont-Columbia survey team.[4] Their report deals in some detail with the year's docket of litigation before

Congress and the FCC, several parts of which—for example, the challenges to station licenses on the basis of conflict of interest—helped make 1968 a rather disturbing year for the broadcasting establishment. Because of the latter's overwhelming lobbying power in Washington, the authors concluded with a weak plea for them to exercise enlightened self-interest. The futility of such pleas was pointed out by Robert Eck in the previous section.

In the first selection on regulation, Elizabeth B. Drew takes up the performance of the FCC in more detail. She argues in support of the structural weakness hypothesis suggested above and ultimately calls for Presidential initiative to reform the Commission. In the article which follows, Commissioner Nicholas Johnson vents some of his grievances. After outlining the Commission's official duties he documents the failure of the FCC to undertake them. The task that he sees before the Commission is one of continuously attempting to create and maintain competitive operation of the broadcast media. He would also like to ensure their democratic use by actively including the public in the FCC's activities. This would enhance decentralized regulation, which, he argues, would also be beneficial. His hope for the future of politics and the wise use of the media rests with the public.

The remaining selections deal specifically with some of the issues raised in the preceding articles. First, Mullally examines the costs and benefits of the Fairness Doctrine. The new powers of the FCC to enforce "fairness" and preclude personal attacks probably will not prevent the networks from dealing with their normal range of controversial issues, but the activities of the more scurrilous local stations might be curbed more effectively. Ruth Lieban's work which follows, however, indicates how slowly the wheels of change turn. There was

---

[3]This excludes the inspections of field engineers. They made 12,000 inspections of radio stations in fiscal 1968, 1500 of these in the "Broadcast Services." They found more violations of regulations than the total number of inspections.

[4]See "Government and Broadcast Journalism" in Marvin Barrett, ed., *Survey of Broadcast Journalism 1968–1969.* (New York; Grosset and Dunlap, 1969), pp. 29–49.

nothing heavenly about the Paradise, California radio station that she describes: Programming was cheap, local citizens were subject to violent verbal assault over the air waves, and ultra-conservative political views generally were to the fore on any issue. In this case, however, sustained citizen protests ultimately prevailed. The last article, by Daniel Henninger, deals with action taken to regulate advertisers using the mass media. The Federal Trade Commission handles this task, and, like the FCC, its actions are usually slow and often indecisive.

Is the FCC Dead?

ELIZABETH BRENNER DREW

THERE are scattered about Washington a number of relics of the 1930s, including some government agencies. They stand as antiquated responses to the challenges of another era. They go about their business with thirty-year-old machinery while the space age streaks by them. In some cases this is harmless enough. But with new communications technology exploding all about, the obsolescence of the Federal Communications Commission is not to be taken lightly.

The idea was that an independent federal agency would regulate the use of the publicly owned airwaves in the public interest, and assure an economic and efficient communications system. Yet the FCC botched the development of AM and FM radio, of VHF and UHF television, of allocating radio channels for other services; and it is now spreading confusion in the new field of community antenna television. It has been immobilized over pay-TV for fourteen years. To this day, there is no coherent FCC policy on minimal performance standards for broadcasting.

Disappointing as this record is, it could be lived with, as other policy failures are tolerated, if that were all there was to it. What worries close observers is that this same agency is now confronting a new set of developments undreamed of when it was established—of nations communicating within and between each other via satellites, of communication through a laser beam, of computers taking over from telephones and wire services, of ingenious electronic methods of invading privacy, of saturation of the electromagnetic spectrum while tech-

nological breakthroughs await its use, of mergers within the industry with unforeseen consequences. The evidence is that it cannot handle the job. What the consequences will be of permitting it to continue to try is anybody's guess.

Newton Minow, who took a turn not long ago as chairman of the FCC, described it after his resignation as "a quixotic world of undefined terms, private pressures and tools unsuited to the work."

In regulating broadcasting, for instance, the Commission is to "encourage the larger and more effective use of radio in the public interest." What the Commission has made of these instructions is only one example of how the FCC chronically resolves the dilemma of nurturing the private and protecting the public interests. Over the years the majority of FCC commissioners have escaped the broadcasting conundrum by wrapping themselves in Section 326 of the Communications Act of 1934, which proscribes censorship. While it is a long way from censoring to requiring minimal quality programming, they make the trip with no difficulty.

The Commission's power over broadcasting stems from its responsibility for allocating space in the publicly owned electromagnetic spectrum. The spectrum is like a mammoth rainbow divided into "bands," or groups of frequencies, which are allocated for use by a particular type of radio service— the AM and FM bands for radio, VHF and UHF bands for television, or other bands for private uses. A company seeking to operate a radio or television broadcasting station applies to the FCC for the use of a particular frequency, or channel, during certain hours over a given radius. The applicant pays homage to the principles of serving the community by providing public affairs broadcasts and quality services; and if he is more persuasive than fellow applicants for the same channel, in exchange for a $75 to $100 fee he is granted a lucrative broadcast license.

In 1965 the television broadcasting industry had a net income of $447.9 million, nearly triple that of ten years ago; the radio broadcasting industry had a net income of $81 million, nearly double that of 1955. It has been estimated that some TV stations earn over $10 million a year. But the FCC has long agreed with the industry that to suggest measurable obligations to the public is to interfere with "free enterprise" and "freedom of speech." Edward R. Murrow once remarked: "I can find nothing in the Bill of Rights or the Communications Act which says that [networks and stations] must increase their net profits each year, lest the Republic collapse." On the other hand, the current FCC chairman, Rosel Hyde [since replaced by Dean Burch—ed.], typifies the traditional FCC stance: "The law forbids *me* from interfering with programming, even if it doesn't forbid some other commissioners." The argument goes on, even though the proponents of minimal standards have long since lost.

The Commission grants and renews licenses to use the airwaves for some five million transmitters —radio, television, marine, police, fire, industrial, transportation, amateur, citizens, and common carrier. Each year it processes some 800,000 license and renewal applications. The 7000-odd commercial radio and television licenses must be renewed every three years. When any station wants to increase its power or move its antenna, the FCC must consider the request. While it says that it cannot spare the manpower to check on whether broadcasters actually perform as promised in their license applications, the Commission vigilantly tracks down shrimp fishermen who use dirty words over their radios. The 1966 annual report tells us that it "closed down 40 unlicensed broadcast operations, the latter mostly by juveniles," and investigated "over 500

cases of troublesome radiation from faulty garage door openers."

To handle all of this, plus regulating AT&T, a $35 billion industry, and the other common carriers, such as ITT and Western Union, plus facing the issues raised by new developments in the fast-changing communications industry, the Commission has a staff of 1500 and a budget of $17 million. This is slightly more than one third of the budget of the Bureau of Commercial Fisheries.

There are seven commissioners, more than on any other major regulatory agency except the Interstate Commerce Commission, each serving seven years. The commissioners are appointed by the President, who also designates the chairman, and are confirmed by the Senate.

The Commission's problems are deeper than the personalities of seven men at any given time. Partly they are the problems of any bureaucracy—of frozen-in personnel, of overproceduralized methods, of indecision. Partly they are the problems of any commission—of getting a majority in sustained agreement on complex issues, of each of the commissioners asserting prerogatives and independence, of the difficulty for the staff to proceed on any assumption of what the Commission's view is, of staff and commissioners making alliances and playing off one against the other. One staff member told me how a certain FCC commissioner is considered to be inclined to the most recent view he has heard, so various staff members vie to be the last to phone him before a Commission meeting. The turnover in Commission membership exacerbates the problem of policy continuity and even simple administration of the agency. More than one FCC commissioner has complained recently of the difficulty of securing paper clips.

Partly, the FCC's problems are those shared by all of the regulatory agencies. John Kenneth Galbraith has written that "regulatory bodies, like the people who comprise them, have a marked life cycle. In youth they are vigorous, aggressive, evangelistic, and even intolerant. Later they mellow, and in old age—after a matter of ten or fifteen years—they

IS THE FCC DEAD?
Elizabeth Brenner Drew

become, with some exceptions, either an arm of the industry they are regulating or senile." Supreme Court Justice William O. Douglas, who once headed the Securities and Exchange Commission, has suggested that every regulatory agency be abolished every ten years. Nobody loves them. For instance, the FCC occupies two dingy, labyrinthine floors in the Post Office Department, with the spillover staff lodged over a grocery store on 12th Street. While other agencies have limousines, FCC commissioners ride around in the mail-delivery station wagon; when all seven are being transported, the most junior rides in a jump seat facing out the back.

Presidents pay fitful attention to the regulatory agencies and have frequently used them as dumping grounds for burned-out politicians or difficult characters who must be given a job. Presidents Kennedy and Johnson put up admirable but incomplete resistance to this tradition. Congress insists that they are an "arm of Congress," keeps them weak through meager budgets, and frequently jumps on them when they make a move or badgers them for not moving. Early in the Kennedy Administration, regulatory agency chairmen met informally to share their sorrows; they called their group, appropriately, "The Tightrope Club."

On the whole, however, the more politically powerful is the industry to be regulated, the more likely are congressmen to frown at regulation, and there are few groups more powerful than the broadcasters. A broadcaster's friendship can mean life or death for a member of Congress; his station may treat the congressman's every utterance as newsworthy, or give aid and comfort to the enemy. Nevertheless, the FCC has been all too prone to bend before the real and imagined and anticipated pressures from Congress. It tends, even more than other agencies, to confuse the demands of a few congressmen for the will of Congress. At times it retreats further than the opponents require.

For years, for example, the Commission had a vague policy that too many commercials were too many, but it never stipulated how many were too many. In 1963 it proposed to adopt as a rule the limits contained in the National Association of Broadcasters' Code: that commercials should take up no more than eighteen minutes out of an hour of radio time, and sixteen minutes out of an hour of television time. The FCC would enforce a rule to which the broadcasters in a burst of public spirit had "voluntarily" subscribed. If the NAB caught an offender, he lost his Seal of Good Practice; if the FCC caught him, he might be fined $1000 a day. Industry codes are a time-honored tactic for heading off government regulation; and although the FCC would not have been expected seriously to enforce the industry's standards, many stations did not want it even to entertain the idea of regulating commercial time. The House Interstate and Foreign Commerce Committee, then heavily weighted by congressmen inclined to industry's viewpoint held a hearing and issued a report condemning the Commission's proposal. Shortly thereafter, the FCC formally backed off, but to underscore the point, the House voted 317 to 43 not to permit it to adopt the rule anyway.

Since the Senate did not act on the House resolution, it did not have the force of law. In light of the lopsided House vote, it would have been understandable for the Commission to drop the commercial issue for the time being. But the FCC kept marching backward. The Commission had been asking radio stations that were members of the NAB code to explain their reasons if they ran more than the code's limit of eighteen minutes of commercials in an hour. Stations that did not belong to the code were queried only if they ran more than twenty minutes. The NAB complained to the FCC that it had established a double standard, which was encouraging members to drop out of the code. In response, last fall the FCC changed its policy and asked all stations if they planned more time for commercials than permitted under the NAB code, and if so, why. However, Chairman Hyde, according to *Broadcasting* magazine, quickly reassured broadcasters that the FCC would not be inflexible. It quoted him as saying the Commission would still "stress the idea that responsibility in this matter is more properly the concern of the licensee."

Subsequently, *Broadcasting* reported that "word got around that the FCC was accepting explanations from a good many licensees who reported they were exceeding the code's limitations on commercials." In desperation, the NAB early this year eased the already generous code rules in order to be as lenient toward its members as the government agency supposedly regulating them.

There are a number of broadcasting pressure groups—the networks, FM broadcasters, "Daytimers," advertisers, and so on—which form ad hoc coalitions, depending on the issues at hand. That they do as well as they do is less a testimonial to their professionalism than to the fact that there is hardly ever anyone on the other side. Even "public-spirited" newspapers, often owned by station owners as well, may applaud calls for better programming, but when an issue such as commercials arises, they are either silent or pro-industry.

Each year, the commissioners dutifully attend the NAB's convention in Chicago (except in a presidential inaugural year, when the broadcasters go to Washington), visiting the hospitality suites and learning to understand the industry's problems. Then they return to Washington to regulate it. The key pressure on the Commission, however, works more quietly. "It works subtly, almost silently," says a former commissioner, "like the water on the stone. If you want to be reappointed, you do not want to earn the enmity of AT&T, a network, a multiple-station owner. These are really the insidious pressures. We spend too much time reading the trade press, and care too much what they say about us."

If a commissioner does not want to stick around the agency, likely as not he ends up with the industry. If one were to include law practices, it is probable that 90 percent of the commissioners who leave the FCC take jobs involving the industry.

Occasionally, as in the late fifties, there are out-and-out scandals involving the FCC, but it seldom comes to that. The industries that deal regularly with the Commission learn to be decorous. In more than one sense. Commissioners' desks are littered with little plastic gewgaws, pieces of cable, models of satellites, many of them personally inscribed. One commissioner approvingly explained to me that when he lunches at an AT&T headquarters "they never serve pâté de foie gras, or strawberries out of season."

Many an FCC staff member also has departed for the more lucrative pasture on the other side of the FCC, but as a general rule the staff is not as soft on industry as the commissioners are. Some of the highest-level staff inevitably reflect the commissioners' views, but as a general rule it is the staff which wants to act, punish, or investigate, and the Commission which demurs. . . .

The most common explanation put forward for the Commission's chronic failure of foresight is that it is too busy with its day-to-day problems. It is therefore fair game to examine how well the Commission does what it does do. (It should be said here that in my many visits to the Commission offices I detected no signs of frenzied labor, or of long hours.) For all of its burdens, the Commission meets only one day a week, and frequently disposes of its business by lunchtime. Each Wednesday morning, the Commissioners mount the semicircle dais in their meeting room and deliberate whether Broadcaster X may move his antenna tower, or Broadcaster Y may go from 250 watts to 500 watts. A Commission meeting apparently resembles nothing so much as a Mad Tea Party, with comissioners dozing and bickering and catching at straws.

Earlier this year, for example, the Commission deliberated whether an unpopulated mountain is a "community" and somberly concluded that it was not. On another occasion the staff brought before the Commission the request of a group of Delaware educators for a small closed-circuit television system. The staff suggested that since the rules involved were so many and so complex, the Com-

IS THE FCC DEAD?
Elizabeth Brenner Drew

mission should waive the lot of them. John Gardner once remarked that "the last act of a dying organization is to get out a new and enlarged edition of the rule book."

While some problems before the Commission take years to resolve, it can act with surprising dispatch, as it did in the case of the merger of ABC and ITT. The proposed merger would be the largest in the history of broadcasting; the two companies have a combined revenue of over $2 billion annually. ABC and ITT applied for FCC approval of the merger on March 31, 1966. During the summer, because Commissioner Bartley was pushing for a full evidentiary hearing, the Commission scheduled a one-day meeting in which principals of the two companies would tell the commissioners why they wanted to merge. Questioning by Bartley, Cox, and Johnson extended the "hearing" into two days, September 19 and 20. Meanwhile, Hyde had been writing to the Justice Department's Antitrust Division, asking if it saw any problems. The Division finally responded with a five-page single-spaced letter from Assistant Attorney General Donald F. Turner stating that Justice was "not presently contemplating an action under the antitrust laws" but laying out "the possibilities of adverse effects [which] are significant enough . . . that they deserve full and serious consideration by the Commission." Turner's letter arrived after 6 P.M. on December 20. The following morning the Commission approved the merger.

The principal reason given for approval was the one advanced by the applicants: that ABC needed additional revenues, which ITT could provide, to make it more competitive with the other networks. Bartley, Cox, and Johnson dissented. Bartley charged that the Commission had "rushed into an approval of the merger" without considering "fundamental questions of highest importance." Johnson said he was "simply stunned and bewildered." He pointed out that ABC was already a profitable venture, and that ITT had made no commitment of funds to ABC. He and Bartley

worried about the effects on ABC's news and public-affairs programming of ITT's extensive overseas holdings, and about the economic effects on the broadcasting industry of having one major broadcaster part of a huge conglomerate corporation.

Justice petitioned the FCC to reopen the case, charging that the FCC had violated the law by holding such a brief hearing, that it had failed to examine "crucial facts." The Department later produced evidence that funds would not actually be passing from ITT to ABC, but that ITT was looking upon ABC as a source of funds—$100 million over the next five years. The FCC's own staff subsequently agreed with Justice on this key point, and the Commission reluctantly reopened the case. It declared that in the light of "the public interest in a prompt settlement of the present uncertainty, we think that expedition is required." A new decision was expected as early as June.

The Commission can also show dispatch in renewing license applications. When a broadcaster applies for a license, he makes specific pledges about the amount of time he will devote to public-affairs programming and local service. It is explained that the Commission does not have the manpower to monitor stations to see if in fact these pledges are carried out, but that his program practices will be closely examined when he files for his triennial license renewal. Minow and Henry instituted a renewal application form designed to draw more information about actual programming practices, but this information appears to be of little moment to the Commission. Earlier this year, Cox and Johnson dissented from the routine renewal of a group of 206 licenses when the applications showed that 2 proposed no news programming whatsoever, 7 proposed no public-affairs programming, 23 proposed less than one percent of their time to be devoted to public affairs, and 88 proposed no other type of public-service programming. "It seems to me," said Cox, that stations "are downgrading their commitments . . . because they feel the majority of the Commission won't do anything about it." Cox charged that the Commission was making "a farce of the whole reporting and reviewing process."

Theoretically, the Commission sought to reduce its agenda by developing a set of standards for licensees and permitting the Broadcast Bureau itself to grant and renew licenses if they meet those standards. "Frankly," conceded one commissioner, "I couldn't tell you what the standards are now. The staff sort of figures out our current policy from what we did in the last two months." Though there is a great deal of talk about delegating, the Commission is too suspicious of the staff and the staff is too perplexed about Commission policy for it to happen much. One of the penalties of all this is a serious backlog of contested applications, and for the wrong reasons. There are some cases of competing applications for licenses, or appeals from a Commission decision, which have been before the Commission for ten or twenty years.

Minow believes that the station-by-station license and renewal procedure, conceived in the days before networks, amounts to swatting gnats. Henry came to believe that it would make more sense to establish minimal requirements and then give licenses away by lottery. The broadcasters, typically confusing a privilege with a right, say that station licenses ought to be granted permanently, subject to revocation for cause. It is possible that they suggest this in knowledge of the Commission's record of revoking licenses: 1 in 1961, 5 in 1962, 4 in 1963, 4 in 1964, 0 in 1965, and 2 in 1966. The record of renewals refused is not much more extensive: 16 in the last 5 years. Hyde's solution is to renew licenses for five- instead of three-year periods ("with maturity goes responsibility").

When Congress in 1962 created the hybrid Communications Satellite Corporation—part owned by the common carriers, most AT&T, and part a public corporation—to operate an international satellite, it left a number of issues unresolved. Should Comsat compete with the common carriers, or should it be a common carriers' carrier? The Commission chose the latter course, thus guarding against severe competition for the carriers. Who should operate the lucrative ground stations, Comsat, the carriers, or someone else? The Commission "temporarily" permitted Comsat to operate the first ones and told Comsat and the carriers to get together and carve up the rest. This is an odd way to proceed on such an important matter, but by thus splitting the baby, nobody got too hurt. Except perhaps the baby, but it is too early for the layman to know that.

Also left unresolved by Congress was the enormously important and complex question of who is to operate a domestic satellite system, or systems, and for what purposes. What kind of domestic system, or systems, should there be, available for what kinds of uses, by whom, and how competitive? Should the common carriers continue to be protected from the competition of new technology? Who will benefit—or will anyone—from the costs saved by communicating by satellite? Technically, some of the issues are before the Commission in the form of the Ford Foundation's proposal for a satellite system for television, with the money saved when the commercial networks switch from conventional to satellite communications to be turned over to public television. Comsat, now an aggressive creature itself, countered by urging the FCC to permit it to operate a general-purpose domestic system, arguing that that is what Congress intended, that technology is ready and time is wasting. (Whether technology is ready is debated by the experts.) The satellite issues are so fundamental, the competing interests so great—the networks, AT&T, which earns $50 million a year from carrying television signals, the nation's largest foundation, Comsat—and the stakes are so large that it is possible that Congress and the White House will make the decisions. (The separate issue of public television raised by the Ford and Carnegie Foundations is already before Congress.) That might be just as well. I asked Chairman Hyde how many FCC employees were studying the issues raised by Ford. "Only one full-time person," he replied.

The Commerce Department, ordinarily not a very melodramatic place, completed a study not

IS THE FCC DEAD?
Elizabeth Brenner Drew

long ago of what it called the "silent crisis"—the shortage of spectrum space—and recommended a special group with an initial budget of $11 million, eventually $50 million, to handle the problem. The FCC, in a major leap forward, will devote $300,000 to research on spectrum allocation this year. The questions involved are complicated and important: what are the relative social, economic, even political implications of allocating more or less space to the various users—from doctors' beepers to police cars to television stations to communications satellites? Should traditional users, such as oil companies and ham radio operators, be displaced in favor of new technologies such as pocket telephones? The popularity of a children's walkie-talkie toy last Christmas caused something of a crisis for the FCC. What should be done about this? Or is it perhaps time to rearrange the allocations among private spectrum users? The FCC still proceeds, according to a system established some twenty years ago, to grant a certain band across the country to each type of private user, although the need for the forestry band is minimal in New York City, and there is even less demand for the taxicab band in the Gulf of Mexico.

Is cable television, which reduces the use of spectrum space, something that ought to be encouraged on those grounds, regardless of the discomfort to established television interests? Does it suggest methods of bringing other services, such as facsimile, data, or shopping, into the home? What does it mean that within five years about half of all information transmitted will be between computers, and how can the competing interests between, say, AT&T and IBM, be resolved, preferably with the public getting its share of the benefits? The FCC has begun a study of the computer issue, but no special staff has been assigned to it.

Chairman Hyde explains that the acute staff shortage is ameliorated by the fact that "we get a lot of valuable help from various industry groups." Hyde said that the industry groups give information and advice, and that a representative of the FCC sits in their meetings to prevent collusion.

But collusion is not the only danger, nor is it likely to be eradicated by the FCC representative. Many government agencies set up business advisory committees as a way of getting advice and keeping peace; but there can be a problem when a limited staff is dependent upon the industry to the point where the industry can dominate the agency's policies. Presumably Congress did not set up regulatory agencies with the intent of having the agencies turn to the industry to inquire how it should be regulated.

There is thus a great deal of evidence that it is time to redefine and re-evaluate the FCC's mission. It is time to dust off "the public interest" and re-examine where it comes in. It is not all that new to suggest that the FCC should be revised. The law journals are full of suggestions for changing the FCC, and the literature is a nitpicker's delight. Most of it is in terms of establishing more clear-cut procedures on behalf of the applicants. But the FCC's problems are beyond nitpicking, and of importance to more than the clients. A thorough re-evaluation would suggest a number of new combinations, ranging from tinkering with the existing institution, to transferring some of its functions elsewhere, to starting afresh. There are some basic principles on which thoughtful critics agree: somewhere there must be an agency with sufficient funds for research, in house or contracted out, that can keep the government abreast of communications developments. There must be sophisticated analysis of the interrelated communications issues which are now approached in a haphazard *ad hoc* manner.

It is all too easy to call for a reorganization of an agency which does not seem to be coping, for reorganization for its own sake means next to nothing without a redefinition of purpose and without sufficient resources in both staff and funds to carry it out. Yet there have been many worthy suggestions for structural changes: almost all observers of the FCC feel that seven commissioners is at least two too many (Henry thinks it is four too many, and Minow concluded it was six too many);

no one disputes that the machinery must be streamlined. But none of this will matter unless the FCC,
or whatever agency emerges, is invested with the
mission and prestige which the issues before it demand, and which in turn will attract, and hold,
good men. It would be naïve to suggest that such
an agency could operate, or its leaders could be
chosen, without regard to the political context,
but it is not too much to ask that it be more independent of it.

One close observer has suggested that the issues
are so important that the agency should be as
prestigious as a U.S. Court of Appeals, and the
appointments to it taken as seriously. Perhaps
commissioners should serve for longer terms. Certainly the agency might be less composed of men
who use it as a sinecure or springboard. The FCC
cannot be expected to work a self-transformation.
That leaves Congress and the White House, and
this sort of reform is not likely to start in Congress.

Reprinted from Columbia Journalism Review *(Winter, 1969–70), pp. 28–33.* ©. *Used by permission of the author.*

What the FCC Must Do

NICHOLAS JOHNSON

Virtually every country in the world treats broadcasting as an activity possessed of unique public responsibilities. In many countries—Scandinavia among them—all stations are owned and programmed by an agency of government or a public corporation. Other nations have recently supplemented their public broadcasting facilities with the competition of privately owned, commercial stations—subject to government regulation. Japan is an example. When England supplemented its world-famous BBC with a commercial "independent television service" the new stations continued to be publicly owned. They are merely programmed, during portions of the week, by various programming companies licensed for fixed terms by the Independent Television Authority (ITA). (Unlike the FCC, the ITA has been quite freely encouraging competition by refusing to renew some companies' authority.)

During the debates on the Radio Act of 1927 and the Communications Act of 1934, Senators and Congressmen repeatedly expressed their awareness of the potential economic and political power of this industry, its great opportunity and responsibility, and the need for a close public check upon it. As early as November, 1927, Secretary of Commerce Herbert Hoover urged at the Fourth National Radio Conference that each applicant for a broadcast license be required to prove "that there is something more than naked commercial selfishness in his purpose. . . . [W]e should not freeze the present users of wave lengths permanently in their favored position, irrespective of their service."

In 1927 and 1934 Congress purposefully provided that an FCC license would be only "for the use . . but not the ownership" of the assigned frequency. A six-month license term was originally specified. Later, as the industry gained political power, this term was extended to one year and then to three years. (Recently the industry has been urging a *five*-year term!)

After the original term the FCC must make *an affirmative finding*, every three years, that a renewal of the license will serve the public interest; it is not, like a license to practice law, something that lasts for life unless revoked. The FCC may refuse to renew, and grant the license to another party. Thus the licensee's relationship to the Government is very much like that of a highway contractor—he is free to bid against others for an extension of the profitable relationship, but he is not entitled to an additional term as a right. As Judge Warren Burger said for the U.S. Court of Appeals, "after nearly five decades of operation the broadcast industry does not seem to have grasped the simple fact that a broadcast license is a public trust subject to termination for breach of duty."

For a variety of reasons, the system simply hasn't worked as intended. As in so many other instances of "regulation" of an industry, the FCC has permitted irresponsibility to run rampant—under its imprimatur and protection. Lest there be any doubt the drubbing the public has taken under its leadership, consider these cases:

—The FCC once decided that a radio station proposing thirty-three minutes of commercials per hour would be serving the public interest. *(Accomack-North Hampton Broadcasting Co., 1967.)*

—It permitted the wholesale transfer of construction permits from one licensee to another, prompting the Special Investigations Subcommittee of the House Interstate and Foreign Commerce Committee to conclude in 1969: "The Commission apparently confused its role as guardian of the public interest with that of guardian of the private interest."

—The FCC approved a license transfer application for a station that quite candidly conceded it proposed to program no news and no public affairs at all. *(Herman C. Hall, 1968.)*

—When presented with charges that a Southern station was engaged in racist programming, the FCC first refused to let the complainants participate in the case, then found that the station's performance entitled it to a license renewal. *(Lamar Life Broadcasting Co., [WLBT], 1965; 1968.)* Even technical violations get little attention. Recently the Commission refused to consider revoking the license of a station whose owner, it was charged, had ordered his engineer to make fraudulent entries in the station's log book, operated with an improperly licensed engineer, and whose three stations had amassed eighty-seven other technical violations over a three-year period.

Violations of the most elementary principles of good business practice don't arouse the Commission to action. Recently the FCC examined the record of a station guilty of bilking advertisers out of $6,000 in fraudulent transactions. The local Better Business Bureau had complained. The station was already on a one-year "probationary" license status for similar offenses earlier. The result? The majority had no difficulty finding the station had "minimally met the public interest standard," and it therefore renewed the license. *(Star Stations of Indiana, Inc. [WIFE], 1969.)*

Every industry requires *some* minimal standards—in this instance, of programming, advertising, ownership patterns, technical performance, and business practices. The FCC is not providing them.

Nor is the industry doing any better with "self regulation." The New York Code manager of the National Association of Broadcasters Code of Good Practice, Warren Braren, recently resigned rather than continue to work with an organization so little concerned about its own standards. When the Eisenhower Commission on violence addressed the matter of the industry's "self regulation" of violence, it concluded, "The television industry has consistently argued that its standards for the portrayal of violence and its machinery for enforcement of these standards are adequate to protect the public interest. We do not agree."

If FCC regulation hasn't worked, and industry self-regulation is even weaker, what alternatives are there?

There are two principles to which we are deeply committed in America: competition and democracy. Institutions spring up from time to time that deviate from these principles, but we eventually bring them into conformity. And if we cannot create pure "competition" or "democracy" in a situation we try to simulate them; to make the institutions work *as if* competition and popular control were a check upon them. So it has been with broadcasting.

We want the American people to have "the best"—the best cameras, copying machines, television programming. Every businessman takes a risk of losing his position in the market. A multi-million-dollar plant can become worthless overnight. Bankruptcy rates are high. Those are risks the American people, and their government, are willing to take; those are risks the American businessman is willing to exchange for the opportunity to make great profits. When the Polaroid camera came on the market, no one concerned himself about providing protection to conventional camera makers and their "right" to continue in business. No one thought of requiring Xerox first to prove that conventional copying machines were not serving the public interest, before displacing other manufacturers' positions in the market. What we do as a people, in effect, is to subject the products

WHAT THE FCC MUST DO
Nicholas Johnson

offered for sale to a "comparative hearing"; the one that wins is rewarded with handsome profits, the one that loses may suffer losses in the millions.

This kind of pure competition cannot work in TV programming. There are only a limited number of available frequencies; the demand exceeds the supply. There is no way that the new programming idea can find its way into the marketplace. Our typically American solution has been to try to simulate that market process. Congress has provided that no one has a "right" to have his station license extended beyond its original term, that competing applications can be filed, that they must be considered by the people's representatives (the FCC), that programming proposals will be compared, and that the people will thus be assured "the best" in television programming as in other areas of their lives.

To select "the best" is a pragmatic approach. The best may not be very good. It may be an unexpected deviation from our previous standards. But standards tend, by their nature, to be minimal and conventional. One of the beauties of competition is that it is innovative. You cannot "predict" a Polaroid, a Xerox, or a transistor; but you want a system that makes them available to the people when they come along. It is impossible to define the "perfect note." But it is possible for us to determine which of two notes is the higher. That is what the FCC must do when comparing programming proposals.

Not only does competition lead to innovation from newcomers to an industry; it also offers a spur to improve performance on the part of those already in the business. The broadcasters have complained that unless competing applications are curtailed, those in the business will have to cut back on investment in programming. In fact, the broadcasters' response to competitive challenges has not been to cut back upon programming; they have responded to competition like any other industry. *Variety* reports:

The recent wave of license challenges . . . has without question raised the level of program aspira-

tion in most major markets, and particularly in those where the jump applications were filed. There is on the whole discernably more local involvement, more community affairs and educational programming, more news and discussion and more showcasing of minority talent since the license challenges than there were before.

This is healthy; it's American: it benefits everyone.

The argument is made by some broadcasters that they cannot fight "blue sky" promises from a fly-by-night applicant for their license. Of course, this could be a theoretical problem. But the FCC has had more than forty years' experience in evaluating programming proposals—and the financial and professional ability of applicants to deliver on them. Its record is pretty good. It can be expected to continue to be biased in favor of the existing operator, and to take a very realistic look at competing proposals. Moreover, the incumbent operator is in the very best position to reply to impractical proposals. He may have tried some of them, and can explain why they didn't work. The "blue sky" objection to competing applications simply cannot withstand close analysis.

The benefits of competition are not limited to comparative evaluation of programming proposals. Ownership is also a legitimate consideration. In many communities the FCC has permitted the owner of the only AM station to acquire the only FM because there were no competing applications for the FM. The public is better off, the majority has reasoned, with the additional service run by a monopolist than without it at all. If there is only one man in town who wants to run the morning and evening newspaper, TV station, and AM-FM radio stations, there's not much the FCC can do about it short of shutting down some of these facilities. When a potential new operator comes along there is.

Nor is competitive ownership limited to considering the number of commercial operators. Blacks, who now own less than ten of the 7,500 operating stations and none of the nation's TV stations, believe themselves even further excluded from participation in the ownership of the most valuable stations by the "Pastore Bill." It is no solution to argue that minority groups should be satisfied with access to ownership of the most undesirable properties—those which at best promise short-term losses and a minimal possibility for long-run viability. Nor can we expect that blacks will be able in the near future to acquire the most desirable properties by bidding in the virtually free market for broadcast licenses. This bill will cut off the only avenue to responsible minority participation in the ownership and operation of broadcast stations. And "minority groups" change. That's why ownership should remain as flexible ten years from now as today. Mexican-Americans and the American Indians are beginning to get organized. Senior citizens, the young (a major portion of the radio audience), and the new-found "Middle America" are also "minority groups."

There are other alternatives to station ownership by white businessmen. Congress and the FCC have provided a great deal of encouragement to the competition known as "educational broadcasting." Hopefully, we both intend to provide it even more support. But many communities are now without VHF educational TV stations, or AM educational radio stations. Should competing applications for these facilities from public broadcasting stations be forever prohibited in these communities? There are now audience-supported radio stations in the area of New York, Los Angeles, San Francisco, Houston, Seattle, and St. Louis. These stations provide a noncommercial service so valued by the audience that it is willing to sustain the programming with voluntary contributions. This is yet another pattern of alternative ownership and competition.

What if a community group offered to operate a local commercial station on a nonprofit basis, plowing the money from commercials back into programming and other broadcast-related activities? Should the community be denied this service? Should consideration of this "competing application" be refused until the FCC has first found that one of the local stations is not serving the public

interest (or, in Chairman Burch's proposed language, that it is not "substantially . . . attuned to meeting the needs and interests of its area")?

The practical advantages of competition aside, there is even some question as to whether the "Pastore Bill" is Constitutional. The First Amendment flatly bars Congress from enacting laws abridging the freedoms of speech and the press. If Congress were to state that only one, two, or three persons would be permitted to operate newspapers in any one community, such a law would clearly violate the Constitution. And if Congress were to state that no more than three named persons could use "soap boxes" to speak in a public park at a time, such a law would also violate the Constitution. Free speech is not truly "free" if one is forced to speak in a closet. The First Amendment sanctions, not just "speech," but "effective speech" [*Edwards v. South Carolina, 1963; Saia v. New York, 1948*]; the effectiveness of this speech depends on the existence and nature of an appropriate forum. There is no more appropriate "public forum" today than the radio and television media. It does no good to say that citizens have the rights of free speech and press, and then deny them access to the most important methods of communication to modern man: the broadcast media.

So much for "competition." The other basic principle is "democracy," or as the redundant expression has it, "participatory democracy." Our country is caught up in a wave of citizen and consumer participation. We have suddenly become aware of just how unrepresentative and unresponsive our major institutions are. We are reforming our national party structure and procedures. Citizen panels are being established to review complaints against the police, and to participate in local educational policy. Increasing amounts of education, leisure time, and disposable income are creating an exponential growth in the number of people who want, and know how to get, "a piece of the action."

Broadcasting cannot expect to be immune. During the 1968 Presidential campaign each candidate made participatory democracy a part of his program. President Nixon talked of listening posts to hear directly from the people; George Wallace urged the return of more power from Washington to local communities; Robert Kennedy spoke of "participatory democracy"; and Eugene McCarthy, of "the new politics." Hubert Humphrey used similar rhetoric. The challenge is to devise systems that leave the people as much opportunity as possible for participating in the decisions that affect their lives. In a densely populated, highly industrialized nation there will be a need for a great many national decisions.

In broadcasting, we must arrive at some national plan for the allocation of TV channels across the country. But who operates those stations, and what they program, need not be determined nationally. There is a balance between popular control and federal regulation. When we can devise ways meaningfully to involve the public in the regulatory process we thereby reduce the need for government-initiated regulation.

What can we do? FCC Commissioner Kenneth Cox and I have set forth our modest efforts at programming evaluation and standards in opinions dealing with renewals in Oklahoma, New York, and the Washington, D.C., area. These studies—especially the latter two—represent an effort to rank stations by common criteria. It is an effort to stimulate competition, or the comparative hearing process. It provides a means whereby the Commission could, if it so chose, undertake a more thorough review of the performance of those stations that rank in the bottom 25 per cent or 10 per cent. So far, as Professor Louis L. Jaffe has noted, "The Commission has not seen its way clear even to respond on the merits" to this suggestion.

Congressman John Moss of the House Interstate and Foreign Commerce Committee has urged that public renewal hearings be held in the communities where the stations are located. Local hearings might prove impractical for all communities, but encompassing the top hundred markets would require less than three additional hearings a month for FCC examiners.

There are other ways of telling the public of its rights in the license renewal process. Full-page ads and repeated, intelligible radio and TV announcements could be used—instead of the present small-print legal notices and rare and perfunctory broadcast announcements. The FCC could provide the same kind of information and assistance to public groups interested in the renewal process that it now provides broadcasters when its top staff travels about, speaking, answering questions, and distributing literature and helpful hints to licensees about to fill out renewal forms. Most important, if public participation is to work effectively, Congress and the Commission must recognize the tremendous handicap in financial and professional resources that any public group confronts when competing against a well established broadcaster. There must be some economic incentive for the protesting group. The possibility of competing applications, with the ultimate reward of obtaining the license, is such an incentive —and another reason why competing applications should not be discouraged.

The law has often recognized the need for such incentives. Treble damages are awarded in some antitrust cases, as an incentive to private policing rather than the alternative of more government action. Statutes provide the award of attorneys' fees in some instances. Other agencies—like the National Labor Relations Board or the Neighborhood Legal Services Project of the Office of Economic Opportunity—provide lawyers directly to complaining parties.

There are 7,500 stations in this country. All the licenses in a given state come up for renewal at the same time. With three-year terms, this means roughly 2,500 a year. Even if the FCC were to take away two or three licenses a year—something it has yet to do during its forty-two-year history— we would still be providing rubber stamp renewals to 99.9 per cent of the stations. Professor Jaffe has posed the question "whether a communication industry financed by private capital can be run on a three-year basis." Given an industrywide average 100 per cent rate of return annually on depreciated tangible investment, and a 99.9 per cent (or better) probability of license renewal, I would agree with Professor Jaffe that "once the question is asked it appears to be almost rhetorical." The really outstanding broadcaster has little to fear. He knows the people of his community and they know him. He heads off legitimate complaints before they become serious. He seeks out representatives from all segments of his audience, including potential protestors, even before they look for him. He knows such an approach is good, audience-building business—as well as public service. Any group seriously looking for a license to challenge is going to go after the station with the worst record in town, not his station.

Further, there is no reason why the FCC need hold long, useless, harassing hearings. Administrative practice is flexible enough to permit the FCC to draft hearing issues tightly, and to use informal pre-hearing procedures, to dispose of the frivolous cases quickly. (In fact, the most innovative current development has been the negotiated "settlements" in Texarkana and Rochester between outraged citizens and local broadcasters; renewal hearings were contemplated, then dropped, in exchange for concessions.)

Finally, if anyone in or out of the industry is seriously interested in helping to draft standards for the comparative evaluation of stations' license renewal, their contribution will be most welcome. In our renewal opinions, Commissioner Cox and

I have called on the academic community to devote some of its intellectual resources to this problem. So far there has been no response.

It is significant, I believe, that the FCC is officially on record as opposing the "Pastore Bill." Its members feel deeply enough about it to have presented an unusual number of personally prepared statements. Some believe the present procedure—if made to work—is best. Others have attempted to fashion compromise positions that give away less than the bill. None, however, on the old Commission, offered the bill their enthusiastic support. Only one Commissioner does so now, in a most summary and general statement.

The issue before us ought to be stated starkly. It is, quite simply, who is to retain the potential to rule America. We know, if we are honest with ourselves, which segments of the economic and social structure have the loudest voices in the decision-making process in Washington. But the *potential* for popular check remains. It remains, however, only so long as the people can obtain education and information, only so long as they can communicate with each other, only so long as they can retain potential control over the mass media of this country. So long as we preserve the people's *potential* to rule—their *potential* opportunity to participate in the operation of their mass media—there is some hope, however small, that some future generation—perhaps the next—will use this potential to rebuild America.

Reprinted from "The Fairness Doctrine: Benefits and Costs," Public Opinion Quarterly *(Winter, 1969–70), pp. 577–82. Used by permission of publisher and author.*

The Fairness Doctrine: Benefits and Costs

DONALD MULLALLY

T HAS become fashionable in Washington to examine government programs in terms of "cost effectiveness," which is, roughly speaking, an analysis of the immediate and long-range costs of a particular program balanced against hypothesized immediate and long-range benefits, particularly when compared with alternatives. Because it is almost axiomatic in the legal sense that every piece of legislation or regulation has its cost, it is particularly appropriate to apply the notion of cost effectiveness to the decisions of regulatory agencies in such fields as transportation, finance, and communications. A case in point is the fairness doctrine.

The fairness doctrine is not new; it has its roots in the speeches of Herbert Hoover and in decisions of the Federal Radio Commission as early as 1929.[1] In essence, the fairness doctrine requires that when a broadcaster allows his facilities to be used for the presentation of one side of a controversial issue, he must see that other (contrasting) viewpoints are presented as well. This so-called general fairness doctrine was formally promulgated by the Federal Communications Commission in 1948 in its *Report on Editorializing by Broadcast Licensees.*[2] The fairness doctrine remained a matter of general policy, applied on a case-by-case basis, until the summer of 1967 when the Commission adopted as *rule* certain provisions of the doctrine which have become the subject of extensive litigation; the issues were decided just six months ago by the United States Supreme Court in a unanimous decision, and the Commission's new rules were thereby upheld. It is

the purpose of this article to examine those new rules from the standpoint of cost effectiveness.

The rule adopted by the Commission on July 5, 1967, required that in the case of an "attack" on the "honesty, character, integrity, or like personal qualities of a person or group" during the presentation of views on a controversial issue of public importance, the broadcaster (licensee) is required to give notice to the person attacked not later than one week following the attack, to provide a tape, script, or summary of the attack, and to offer time for a response over the station's facilities. In the event that the broadcaster editorially endorses or opposes a candidate, a tape or script must be provided to attacked or unendorsed candidates within 24 hours after the editorial is broadcast. If the editorial is aired within 72 hours prior to an election, the notice and script must be provided prior to the broadcast. This was the gist of the rule adopted by the FCC in July 1967.[3] Later, under pressure from broadcasters and others, the FCC twice amended the rule.[4] To understand these amendments, it is important to distinguish between the so-called general fairness doctrine and the personal attack rule. The general fairness doctrine is the simple requirement that contrasting views be presented. The personal attack rules are those rules adopted in the summer of 1967, requiring notice, presentation of a script or tape, and the offer of reply time to specific persons or groups. As finally amended, the *personal attack rules* would not apply to attacks upon foreign groups or foreign public

THE FAIRNESS DOCTRINE: BENEFITS AND COSTS
Donald Mullally

figures, to attacks made by bona fide political candidates or their spokesmen or associates, or (perhaps most importantly) to bona fide newscasts, bona fide news interviews, on-the-spot coverage of a news event, *or to commentary or analysis contained within these programs.* But, and this is especially important, commentary within a news program (such as Eric Sevareid's commentary within the Walter Cronkite CBS Evening News program) *is still subject to the general fairness doctrine.*

What does this complicated regulation mean in practice? If, for example, Eric Sevareid should on the CBS Evening News program give an opinion concerning the activities of the Students for a Democratic Society at a particular academic institution, CBS would be obligated under the general fairness doctrine to present contrasting views. But even if attacked directly, the SDS would have no right of reply because the commentary or analysis came within the context of a news program. On the other hand, if Mr. Sevareid were to do a documentary, and therein criticized the SDS, the personal attack rules would come into play. CBS would have to allow the SDS to defend any attack made upon its honesty, character, integrity, or similar qualities. The important distinction is that the personal attack rules do not apply to comments made in the context of a news broadcast, but will apply to a documentary or special; the general fairness doctrine continues to apply to the former situation. I strongly suspect that the implications of these rules have not been fully comprehended by many groups, both political and nonpolitical.

What benefits are expected to accrue from this rule of the Commission? Regulation of broadcasting in this country proceeds from the apparently sound principle that because broadcasters use a valuable frequency belonging to the public, they are therefore trustees for the public, and should serve the public interest. It has been the Commission's position that it is in the public interest to have an informed body politic—a public which has had presented to it the various shades of opinion on controversial issues of public importance. The fairness doctrine exists to insure that broadcasters will not abuse their public trust by presenting only one viewpoint.

There can be no doubt that *unfairness* has at times been a problem. One clear-cut case in recent years is that of WGCB, a station in the quiet town of Red Lion, Pennsylvania, run by a Bible Presbyterian minister. WGCB carried a program in November, 1964, called "Christian Crusade." During this program the Reverend Billy James Hargis, a minister of conservative bent, attacked Fred J. Cook, author of an anti-Goldwater book, stating (among other things) that Cook had previously made false charges against public officials, had worked for the "left-wing publication *The Nation*, one of the most scurrilous publications of the left which has championed many communist causes over the years," and had written the book to "smear and destroy Barry Goldwater."[5]

Cook wrote to the station asking for time to reply. The station sent him its rate card, explaining that the Hargis program had been paid for at commercial rates. Cook refused to pay for the right to reply, and was upheld in his position by both the FCC and the U.S. Court of Appeals for the District of Columbia, which held the fairness doctrine to be constitutional.[6] In the absence of this principle, it might have been possible for a well-funded pressure group to attack an individual (not just a political candidate) and place him in the position of having to buy expensive radio or TV time to recover his reputation.

In several cases in the not-too-distant past, stations have editorially endorsed (or opposed) candidates shortly before an election. This has on occasion given incalculable advantage to the endorsed candidate, while precluding the possibility of reply by unendorsed or "attacked" candidates. This sort of problem would also be remedied by the recently approved rules.

The Commission, until it adopted fairness rules, had few remedies. It could, for example, direct compliance; it could grant short-term renewals only; finally, it could revoke the station's license

THE FAIRNESS DOCTRINE: BENEFITS AND COSTS
Donald Mullally

on the grounds that it was not operating in the public interest. With the adoption of the new fairness rules and their sanction by the U.S. Supreme Court, the FCC can now impose "forfeitures" or fines on stations that violate the rules. The Commission has always considered license revocation a very drastic step, and has hesitated to use it in isolated cases of unfairness. In fact, until the summer of 1969 not one license had *ever* been revoked for violation of the fairness doctrine.[7] Presumably the Commission will now have a more effective, or at least a more flexible, remedy.

In short, those who have supported the fairness doctrine, and particularly those who have supported the new personal attack rules, believe that the rules will prevent objectionable unfairness by both private individuals and station licensees. Furthermore, it is hoped that the rules will give the public greater access to all sides of important controversial issues and political questions. These benefits seem to be realistic and substantial, but there are costs, as broadcasters attest. It is at this point that we must ask whether we can afford the benefits of fairness, or whether, like many commercial products, we cannot afford to be without them.

Some of the most highly regarded programs on television today are "public affairs programs"—programs which, by their very nature, deal with controversial issues of public importance. These broadcasts deal with questions of public policy, with the conduct of governmental affairs, with the actions of political figures, and with the comments of public figures on the course of contemporary history. We have come to enjoy documentaries dealing with such subjects as hunger in America, the radical activities of such groups as SDS, ferment in the churches, and a host of other subjects. We watch stimulating comments by erudite and informed observers of the world situation, and decry the fact that such programs are in such short supply. Will the fairness rules have an inhibitory effect on these programs—and if they

do, is it necessarily bad? Perhaps just as important a question is the one raised by the entire broadcast industry: Do these new fairness rules (and even the general fairness doctrine) restrict the constitutional rights of broadcasters—rights of free speech long enjoyed by the print media?

Worried about the implications of the newly adopted personal attack rules, the Radio-Television News Directors' Association, the Columbia Broadcasting System, and the National Broadcasting Company joined forces in an attempt to have the fairness doctrine (or, at the least, the new rules) declared unconstitutional by the courts. These groups were initially successful, and the U. S. Court of Appeals in the Seventh Circuit upheld their position when the case came to trial last spring. Their argument was appealing: broadcasters, afraid of triggering the fairness doctrine's requirements of free reply time, burdened by the requirements of giving notice, and hampered by the difficulty of clearing time not only for a documentary or a special but for the reply to that program on all of the stations coast to coast, would merely throw up their hands and restrict themselves to the bland, the insipid, and the uncontroversial. Moreover, the burden might not fall on the networks, but upon individual stations ill equipped to handle the reams of correspondence, the mailing of tapes and scripts, and the conflicting claims of groups eager to reply locally to a view expressed on a network program. Indeed, said the broadcasters, the end result of all this confusion might well be an order from network executives and from local program directors that controversial issues simply be avoided. This would indeed be an awesome cost to pay for the fairness doctrine.[8]

When the case reached the Supreme Court, the FCC was upheld. Mr. Justice White, speaking for the entire Supreme Court (except for Mr. Justice Douglas, who did not take part in the case), dissected the constitutional arguments with some care. He noted particularly that (1) the dire consequences predicted are at best speculative;

stations and networks have in the past done a rather good job of living up to a standard of responsible fairness while presenting controversial issues with some regularity; (2) network executives themselves have stated that they will not be intimidated by the FCC's rules and regulations; (3) there are certain differences between the electronic media and the print media which make different standards appropriate.[9]

While it is beyond the scope of this article to examine the first-amendment issues with regard to the print media and the electronic media, two facts are indisputable: (1) we *are* restricting the freedom of the broadcaster when we burden him with an obligation triggered by his statement or the statement he allows to be broadcast; (2) if we do not place this burden upon him, we allow the broadcaster himself to restrict the freedom of others to express their opinions, and on an entirely arbitary basis.

In analyzing the costs and the benefits of this particular bit of regulation, we should not lose sight of the fact that the general fairness doctrine has been around for many years. I suspect that the major impact of the new rules will be felt by those few irresponsible stations that have escaped the FCC's overwhelming power in the past merely because license revocation is so drastic. The new rules give the FCC effective sanctions that can be applied at the time of the violation, rather than at license renewal time.

---

[1]*Great Lakes Broadcasting Co.*, 3 F.R.C. Ann. Rep. 32, 33 (1929), reversed on other grounds 37 F. 2d 993, cert. dismissed 281 U. S. 706 (1930).

[2]Federal Communications Commission, *Report on Editorializing by Broadcast Licensees*, 13 F.C.C. 1246 (1949).

[3]Federal Communications Commission, Docket No. 16574, 10 RR 2d 1901, amended 10 RR 2d 1904, amended 32 Fed. Reg. 11531, 10 RR 2d 1911.

[4]*Ibid.*

[5]*Red Lion Broadcasting Co. v. Federal Communications Commission*, 381 F. 2d 908 (1967), 10 RR 2d 2001, affirmed 395 U. S. 367, 37 LW 4509 (June 1969).

[6]Following affirmation of the lower-court decision by the United States Supreme Court, WGCB—in June of 1969—offered Mr. Cook free time for a reply to the program of November, 1964. Mr. Cook declined the offer, stating that he felt it would be unwise to reopen the entire affair at this late date. *Broadcasting*, Vol. 77, No. 1, 1969, p. 9.

[7]One case, that of WLBT, Jackson, Miss., is still in litigation. The station was accused of cutting off civil rights stories which originated on network news programs, among other things. In one of his last decisions as a judge of the Court of Appeals for the District of Columbia, Mr. Justice Warren E. Burger (now of the United States Supreme Court) ordered the station off the air. See 38 LW 2002 (1969), reporting *United Church of Christ v. FCC.*

[8]*Radio & Television News Directors Association v. FCC*, 400 F. 2d 1002, reversed 395 U. S. 367, 37 LW 4509 (June 1969).

[9]*Ibid.*

Reprinted from The Alfred I. DuPont Survey of Broadcast Journalism 1968–1969 *(New York: Grosset & Dunlap, 1969), pp. 112–21.*
Copyright © 1969 by The Trustees of Columbia University in the City of New York.

The Public Airwaves and Trouble in Paradise

RUTH LIEBAN

KEWQ, the only radio station in Paradise, California (population approximately 8,000) was scheduled for renewal of its license October 3, 1968. Prior to this, the FCC had received many complaints about the station from listeners, in small part about syndicated programs, but mainly about a phone-in program called "Opinion Please." In its application for renewal, KEWQ filled out the necessary forms, giving present and proposed programming and commercial information. On August 29, 1968, it stated it was on the air 92 hours a week with a program format of talk, 10 percent; religious, 40 percent; miscellaneous, 43 percent. In its proposed format (talk, 40 percent; religious, 17 percent; miscellaneous, 43 percent), it vouched that "time will be made available for programs relating to public issues of importance. . . . In case of controversial issues, effort will be made to broadcast both sides of a controversy." (It was already aware of the letters that had been filed with the FCC.)

Present and proposed programming broke down as follows [in the second column].

It was further proposed that programs would be religious and musical, would furnish telephone opinions, talk features, special guests, and a medical radio network feature from the University of California.

In the past, of the 92 broadcast hours, 5 hours and 57 minutes had been devoted to commercials,

PROGRAM TYPE	PRESENT		PROPOSED	
	Hours*	Percent of Total	Hours*	Percent of Total
News	17	18.9	14	14
Public Affairs†	13	14.3	14	14.7
Other, exclusive of sports and entertainment	17	19	22	22.5

*Minutes not included.

†Many hours are available without charge to various groups, including discussion of public issues with public participation through the use of Beeper telephone.

or 6.5 percent. In the future, it was proposed that a maximum of 20 percent be devoted to commercial time.

It was further stated that William Ledbetter was in charge of all decisions regarding programming—a significant name in view of the complaints received.

The earliest correspondence found in the file was from Doran Tregarthen, then superintendent of schools in Paradise, in September 1967. To quote from the letter, apparently referring to the open-mike "Opinion Please" program, "I am informed that one caller stated, 'We got the Jew out of the Recreation District and now we are going to get Tregarthen.' I wish to know if I can secure a recording of any comment that is critical of me, and

THE PUBLIC AIRWAVES AND TROUBLE IN PARADISE
Ruth Lieban

if I can secure, free of charge, time to reply. . . ."

An official of the FCC replied on September 11 that there was no requirement that a station keep tapes or transcripts of *all* broadcasts, only those involving personal attack. The letter ended, "We cannot ascertain if a personal attack was made on you." The Fairness Doctrine Primer issued in 1964 was enclosed. Doran Tregarthen is no longer superintendent of schools in Paradise, but had to seek employment in another town.

On September 22, 1967, Senator George Murphy sent a brief note to the FCC, drawing attention to an enclosed letter from Mrs. John Hanford of Paradise, who had written to him complaining of the vicious personal attacks made by KEWQ over the air. On October 22, Mr. William G. Ray, the head of the FCC's Complaints and Compliances Division, answered that he had been unable to ascertain if the station had violated any personal attack regulation, and enclosed the July 1, 1964 Fairness Doctrine Primer.

By December of that year, a small group of citizens was apparently up in arms and wrote to the FCC that nine of them had volunteered to listen to the station on a systematic basis for a two-week period. Their findings indicated that the station met the needs of only a narrow segment of the community, and that the requirements of the Fairness Doctrine were not being met. Too much time was being devoted to religious programs (190 minutes a week) and call-ins (200 minutes). Only 225 minutes were given over to news.

Mrs. Archie McDonald, chairman of the group, listed a number of station annoyances. The station consistently ran the Paul Harvey, John Birch, and Stuart McBirnie syndicated programs. It carried six or seven religious programs daily—but only those of the fundamentalist belief. The president of the local college, Dr. Robert Hill, had been attacked on the air, without receiving notification of the attack.

Negroes per se were attacked regularly on the station. In the summer of 1967, word was spread by KEWQ callers that a "nigger" was coming to town (none live in Paradise). Actually, a Negro was in town participating by invitation in a grassroots civic survey. However, "Sheriff's cars were posted at the two main entrances to town to stop an expected Negro invasion," wrote Mrs. McDonald.

In January and February 1967, the station apparently had put on a drive soliciting some written testimony in its behalf. Letters, which were duplicated over and over again and placed in the record, came in praising the station, from "us older folk who do not care for rock and roll and such." "Also enjoy your 'Opinion Please' and listen every day." A few other letters from established organizations thanked the station for giving them free time for fund drives and public notices.

Here the matter lay, until the station was forced to post a notice in the local newspaper that it filed for a renewal of its license. Once more, a group of concerned citizens wrote to the FCC protesting the unsatisfactory performance of the station. In September 1968 the letters started to come in. A. B. Everts complained of the number of syndicated programs the station carried: "Life Line" (Hunt); "Bible Institute of the Air" (Burpo); "Voices of Americanism" (McBirnie); etc. The call-in program was the "most disgusting." He cited what was happening to a proposal to vote for incorporation of the city in the November election. Callers on "Opinion Please" were urging the listeners to withdraw their funds from a local bank, because the manager, a man by the name of Harris, supported and was made chairman of the incorporation committee. It had also been suggested that listeners write the headquarters of the bank, complaining of Harris's activities.

Mrs. Grace Hodgkins, who had formed the committee, wrote that she was very embarrassed by phone-ins suggesting that "Hodgkins disease" was spreading. Mrs. A. B. Johnson deplored the "hate-filled comments on 'Opinion Please'" and protested that the news was edited to suit the station's purposes. James Flood was another of the fourteen

THE PUBLIC AIRWAVES AND TROUBLE IN PARADISE
Ruth Lieban

who wrote opposing license renewal. He mentioned attacks on the school curriculum and aspersions on the mental health program.

A legal petition was filed with the FCC by the Paradise Citizens for Civic Responsibility. The group was said to be composed of eighty or ninety apolitical persons, representing a cross-section of the community, whose objective was to combat all forms of extremism, far left or far right. The petition, dated November 25, 1968, protested granting a renewal of license, charging that KEWQ represented far-right extremism. The following items were listed:

1. KEWQ claimed to have consulted such community organizations as the Paradise Recreation District and the Paradise Unified School District, which in fact never were consulted.

2. The petitioners were entitled to receive from KEWQ fair presentation of all matters affecting them as citizens (both local and national), without slant, distortion, or prejudicial programming. The station also had the obligation to make facilities available to the public.

3. The Fairness Doctrine had been violated by call-in programs wherein citizens were afforded time (often prime) to express political and personal views without adequate time afforded for the opposing points of view. The last three years, the station had encouraged right-wing extremists to take over the station to the exclusion of any other group.

4. The petitioners submitted monitored tapes which revealed vicious attacks on community organizations and persons by the phone-in show. Rarely did the station broadcast calls from those attacked. No victim was given notice of smears, or allowed air time to defend himself, contrary to Fairness Doctrine regulations.

5. In effect, the station attempted to persuade members of the audience to adopt a particular ideology and to aid in the destruction of responsible elements of the community which it purported to serve.

6. According to FCC regulations, the station was obliged to consult with representative groups and leaders. KEWQ consulted only with right-wingers. For example, the station made claim to have consulted:

ORGANIZATION	COMMENT BY PETITIONER
Paradise Unified School District	Never did
Paradise Recreation District	Never did
Paradise Christian School	
Sierra Christian School	Right-wing
Christian Business Men's Association	Right-wing
Butte County Supervisors	Consulted only two right-wing members
American Legion	
Sierra Christian Academy	

Not consulted were fourteen groups such as the P.T.A., the Chamber of Commerce, the Ministerial Association, etc.

7. The programs were not in the public interest. The public was insulated from objective viewpoints of national problems, trends and news.

The petition requested a hearing on the above matters before renewal and, pending a decision, the granting of only a temporary license.

Exhibit A consisted of a list of the officers and committee members—businessmen, school administrators, members of the League of Women Voters, a dentist, etc.

Exhibit B contained a list of thirteen persons and groups attacked, from the League of Women Voters (seven times) to the Americans for Democratic Action, the American Civil Liberties Union, the United Nations, Robert Kennedy, Martin Luther King, Earl Warren, and "a vicious personal attack on Judy Conley, Former Vice-Mayor of Chico, California."

In response to the petition, William Ledbetter, president of the Butte Broadcasting Company, wrote, apologizing for the delay (February 3, 1969), which was caused by the illness of his vice-president. The following charges, he said, were in error:

1. He had letters on file from the Paradise Recreation and Park District "praising the station's positive, definite influence." The chairman of the Unified School District had written, ". . . real breath of fresh air to be able to listen to as informative and inspiring a radio station as KEWQ."

2. The allegations were false concerning "Opinion Please," since two phone lines were used for the call-ins and callers were taken in turn. Furthermore, in the event of an attack, as in the case of the Institute for American Democracy, KEWQ had made time available for IAD's reply. The Birch Society had been attacked and given opportunity to reply. In the case of the National Council of Churches, it had never answered the offer for time. "We have aired *all* religious programs." The station also ran a daily Jewish program, which was "terminated for lack of response." Though there are no Negroes in Paradise, "we are opposed to racial prejudice . . . and try to air well-known black religious leaders." A weekly one-hour program produced by the University of California at Berkeley was also carried.

3. "Opinion Please" had no bias. In over two years, five moderators ran the show, with widely divergent points of view.

4. The supposed attacks under the Fairness Doctrine were vague and ambiguous, without date and text. Attacks were implied rather than stated. Some agencies supposedly attacked have actually praised the station in letters.

5. The station *did* consult many community leaders.

6. In answer to complaints about adequate news coverage, "we have A.P. and use ABC Information Radio Network. Now we feel with a daytime only station, A.P. and ABC are too much news . . . in conflict with a number of our morning religious broadcasts."

7. As for Joyce Cameron, one of the petitioners, her husband was advertising manager for a competitor, KPAY Chico.

8. To claims of unbalanced programs: In July 1968, Sam Hart, black leader, had three hours of programs. "Now we have Tom Skinner, black, on a weekly, free show for 30 minutes."

9. Listeners had objected to the University of California program on sex, but the program was continued. (Note: When applying for a renewal, KEWQ had referred to this program as "medical.")

10. The "Opinion Please" show had been cancelled. Callers admitted to taping the calls, and tried to insult the moderator into expressing his views, contrary to the rules of the Fairness Doctrine. In future, "we intend to cover controversial issues on programs not involving audience participation."

11. KEWQ ended its reply: "We ask the petitioners to supply us with specific suggestions as to the needs of the community, and specific programs to meet those needs which have been overlooked. We further agree to make a reasonable amount of time available to the community without charge."

Ledbetter enclosed letters, "unsolicited from community contacts, secured as a result of operation in the public interest." The letters, thanking the station for aid with bazaars, fund drives, and so on, came from the Boy Scouts, Salvation Army, Camp Fire Girls, First Church of Christ, 4-H Club, Day Care Center, and Fire Department, and also commented at times on "enjoyment of good Christian music." The station submitted a total of eighteen letters written during the three-year span.

Meanwhile, FCC's William Ray had written to Mrs. Hodgkins, January 23, 1969, defining the Fairness Doctrine and Section 315. "Material in possession of the Commission does not appear to justify a conclusion that the station has failed to comply with the Fairness Doctrine. However . . . you have the opportunity to reply with factual details within 20 days." (The station had taken from November 25 to February 3 to answer the petitioners.) This appears to have been an FCC form letter and was apparently sent to all who had written in to protest the renewal of KEWQ's license back in September and October 1968.

THE PUBLIC AIRWAVES AND TROUBLE IN PARADISE
Ruth Lieban

Answers were sent back, for the third time in some cases. On February 10, Mrs. Grace Hodgkins replied that the station had endorsed Wallace, Rafferty, and Dunaway (for Congress). Ledbetter had read newspaper editorials supporting his candidates, and muttered "Hogwash" when ABC news came on disagreeing with his view. She produced tapes of Ledbetter from June 1968: "We've lost the world to Communism right in the public schools. . . . Where do we go to? . . . Rhodesia is about the last place to go where there is any freedom. . . . Congressmen and Senators no longer represent the people . . . The Supreme Court is breaking down the laws . . ." Attacks on Earl Warren, the League of Women Voters, and the United Nations, as well as support for right-wing local school supervisors, were substantiated.

A. B. Everts responded on February 9, with perhaps the most damning indictment of the station's claim that it had reflected the community as a whole. KEWQ had taken a "call-in" poll just before the November election. Everts compared the results of the poll and the actual vote in Paradise.

CANDIDATE	KEWQ CALL-IN VOTE	ACTUAL PARADISE VOTE
Nixon	22%	56%
H. H. Humphrey	2%	30%
Wallace	76%	12%
Cranston	2%	36%
Rafferty	98%	64%
Dunaway	93%	53%
H. Johnson	2%	45%

Everts noted that whenever Ledbetter had acted as moderator of "Opinion Please," the program always "got out of hand." He produced the following quotations from Ledbetter on the air: *October 23* — "I don't think he [Vice President Hubert Humphrey] is going crazy. He's there already." *September 19* — "The YMCA and YWCA are anything but Christian." *September 23* — "Biz Johnson [a local politician] is buying votes with our money. . . . If we take away their money, we can do away with the professors at the University of California."

October 21 — "Let's exchange the League of Women Voters for the crew of the Pueblo." Everts quoted another caller to the effect that "many teachers here are Marxists."

On January 27, Mrs. A. B. Johnson wrote to the FCC to say that the KEWQ reply was laughable, that their supporting letters were all from extreme rightists, that most of their daytime hours were taken up with "Opinion Please," except for the McIntire and McBirnie programs. The so-called Jewish Program had as a speaker a Jew who lashed out at Orthodox and Reformed Jews, and also at all liberals. The Negroes Ledbetter had put on the air were hired by FACT or the John Birch Society.

Mr. and Mrs. H. Pease reported on February 6 that a new Saturday afternoon call-in program had gone on KEWQ, "Are You Listening, Uncle Sam?", criticizing the federal government.

On February 7, Mrs. Archie McDonald replied to Ray's letter to her: "I have stopped listening to the station from sheer agony. . . . I trust your agency will attempt an on-the-scene investigation of current program practices."

On February 10, the manager of the Paradise Chamber of Commerce, Margot Johnson, sent the FCC a disclaimer that it had had any constructive contact with the station. In fact, the station had refused to follow up on the Chamber's suggestion that the station assist in making a community survey. A letter of February 7 revealed that the station had broadcast "many unkind things about Negroes." Letters of February 10 claimed that "the station does not represent younger, more progressive individuals in the community." Another person wrote that her house had been attacked by young hoodlums after she had spoken on the station in defense of a proposed new textbook, *Land of the Free*, for the school system. They "disparage, threaten, and drive off the air those with more liberal views," she wrote. "They call any opposition Communists and threaten to drive them out of town."

On March 3, the complete file of the attack on the IAD and its reply was sent to the FCC by the

IAD. Finally, six of the original complainants gave up and made no further reply to the FCC letter of January 23.

On February 6 the station petitioned to deny the request that a hearing be held on the license renewal in Paradise. Some months passed while the FCC pondered the situation. In the meantime the station continued as though the license had been renewed as of October 3, 1968.

Then something must have happened. A letter, dated July 5, 1969, came from the Paradise Citizens for Civic Responsibility, asking that the FCC withdraw the petition of November 25, 1968. Since November, the letter began, "substantial changes have taken place." Although areas of concern still existed, the organization was no longer in opposition to the renewal of the station's license.

Three days later, a letter from KEWQ explained this surprising about-face. William Ledbetter had resigned from the station, and moved to another state. KEWQ was arranging the sale of his and his wife's interests to two other stockholders in the station. The letter gave notice that a community survey would be conducted to ascertain local needs, and an amended application filed.

On June 9, in his opinion in the two cases before the Supreme Court involving the Fairness Doctrine, Justice Byron White wrote:

> It does not violate the First Amendment to treat licensees given the privilege of using scarce radio frequencies as proxies for the entire community, obligated to give suitable time and attention to matters of great public concern. To condition the granting or renewal of licenses on a willingness to present representative community views on controversial issues is consistent with the ends and purposes of those constitutional provisions forbidding the abridgment of freedom of speech and freedom of the press. Congress need not stand idly by and permit those with licenses to ignore the problems which beset the people or to exclude from the airways anything but their own views of fundamental questions.

License renewal for KEWQ is still pending. But in light of new developments, it would seem that the principle embodied in Justice White's opinion may yet prevail for the only broadcast station in Paradise. The outlook for KEWQ and the Paradise Citizens for Civic Responsibility appears to have brightened.

Reprinted from The New Republic *(May 2, 1970), pp. 17–19. Reprinted by permission of* The New Republic, © *1970. Harrison-Blaine of New Jersey, Inc.*

The One-Eyed Slicker

DANIEL HENNINGER

For a decade Geritol's TV medicine man, Ted Mack, has been telling drowsy viewers that Geritol would bring them back to life. And the Federal Trade Commission has been telling Geritol, in formal complaints and cease and desist orders, that its claims were deceptive and to discontinue the misleading commercials. Geritol persisted. Last week the Justice Department filed a $1 million suit against Geritol ($500 thousand against manufacturer J. B. Williams and $500 thousand against the Parkson Advertising Agency) for failing to comply with the Commission's directives.

Geritol's pitch for its life-giving tonic is a direct descendant of the frontier medicine show of a century ago. After a sword swallower, fire eater, banjo player or singing girl had gathered the curious, a "slicker" sold Jo-He Magnetic Oil (a 75-cent, three-ounce bottle cured colds, piles, ague, rheumatism, scald head, cancer and croup) or Indian Sagwa or Wizard Oil. When he had most of the town on Wizard oil, he moved on. Other slickers dealt in fruit trees, sold with pretty-pictured catalogs but which arrived from back East half dead; or lightning rods—installation for $53 and an "inspector" to come by shortly with a $20 rebate.

A century later the salesman, now a corporation, partnered with television to make available: extra dry deodorants, enzyme detergents (12 brands), hair sprays, nose sprays, laxatives, sleeping pills, smoking cures, anything. A 60-tablet bottle of Bufferin costs 88 cents, but enough of it is sold to make worthwhile the $9.25 million *Advertising Age*

says Bristol-Myers spent on 882 Bufferin commercials in 1968. Television promotion does not come cheaply—60 seconds on network TV cost $40–60 thousand. Television commands that price because it guarantees a nightly audience of 125 million people. In a minute or less the advertiser tries to convince these millions that his product is *different* from the rest, faster working, longer lasting, better looking, etc. The medicine show lives.

Last year Dristan told allergy sufferers, "Do anything you darn well please without worryin' about hayfever miseries," and, "Now I can even chew on ragweed!" With considerably less verve Allerest said ". . . you can enjoy life the way regular people do if you take Allerest." The Federal Trade Commission filed complaints against Allerest and Dristan on the grounds that neither completely prevents or relieves allergy symptoms as their commercials implied. (The FTC holds that a commercial's deception turns not on its literalness but on the impression it gives viewers.) Both signed consent agreements and discontinued the ads. A commercial for Contac nasal spray squirted Contac and a competitor onto rice paper. Contac's bigger puddle proved it put "more decongestant where the sinus congestion is." The implication, the FTC said, was that Contac could better penetrate mucous membrane to relieve congestion, which it cannot do. Menley-James replied they were simply showing that Contac produces 40 percent more spray through the bottle's bigger hole. Vicks promoted Sinex nasal spray last year with a demonstration in which two men with congested noses lean over a breathing apparatus made of two vertical tubes in the middle of which is some cotton. One man squeezes Sinex into the bottom of his tube, looks up and says, "I can feel it." The other man, using the competition, says nothing got through the cotton in his tube. The voiceover comments that the vapors in Sinex are powerful enough to penetrate congestion. The Commission challenged the impression that Sinex passed through cotton and nasal mucous to effect instant free breathing. In it consent agreement Vicks denied any intention to demonstrate that Sinex penetrated the cotton.

When STP oil treatment made its television debut, its commercials featured Andy Granatelli, the racing buff, who told how well STP worked in his racers. The FTC compelled Granatelli to make clear in future ads that he is president of STP, Inc. Several years ago Colgate-Palmolive demonstrated Rapid Shave's beard-softening ability by spreading it on sandpaper, then shaving the sandpaper clean. An FTC investigation disclosed that that would have required soaking the sandpaper for over an hour, and in fact, the on-camera demonstration was performed with sand spread over glass. A recent Commission action against Colgate-Palmolive indicates how a technically honest commercial can mislead. A sandwich was wrapped in C-P's Baggie; another was wrapped in a competitor's plastic bag. They were submerged in water, bag X filled with water but Baggie did not: proof that Baggies keep food fresher. The FTC said the demonstration was valid but the conclusion was not—with normal use the competitor's bag keeps anything as fresh as does the amphibious Baggie. In another commercial, the remarkable clarity of Libbey-Owens-Ford auto glass was traced to the fact that the car's windows were rolled down. LOF said it was raining the day of filming.

One person who cares that TV commercials bilk consumers of millions annually is a law professor John Banzhaf III. Banzhaf organized four George Washington University law students into a group called TUBE (Termination of Unfair Broadcasting Excesses). Watching TV the students compiled a small but representative list of televised deception. (TUBE's list would be longer had they been able to read the ad copy on file at the FTC, but the Commission says the copy for the televised commercials is confidential.)

TUBE found that children are easy marks for phonied-up commercials. During the Saturday morning cartoon and toy orgy a boy might see this ad for Johnny Lightning racing cars—Announcer: "Here come the 1970 Johnny Lightning *Challengers!* New triple threat three engine dragster . . . the *speed* hungry spoiler . . . the *bug* bomb . . . the *powerful* smuggler . . . the *sand* stormer . . . the *explosive* TNT . . . they are beautiful and they are *fast!*" A small group of boys are staring at toy cars racing around a track. Backgrounds blur, the camera zooms in, cars fill the screen, leap into the air and are caught in slow motion and stop action. Little girls as well have been known to tire quickly of expensive dolls that don't dance and run like the ones on television. Like the running Barbie doll that suddenly becomes human—"Wow! She's real like me!" cries a thrilled little girl. Deception in these ads might be arguable because kids don't pay for toys and Dad knows he's been shilled when he buys them.

TUBE alleges many commercials for enzyme detergents are misleading (named were Ajax, Drive, Fab, Axion, Oxydol and Gain). A typical enzyme ad for Procter and Gamble's Gain says "We're at the San Pedro Wharf where the fish bloodstains put on this apron are a day old. Look! Set in, locked in bloodstains." Seconds later P & G's man produces a spotless apron. "Look! Set in, locked in bloodstains virtually Gone, Gone, Gone! . . . Everything is unbe*liev*ably clean with the unbe*liev*able detergent—Gain! What TUBE found hard to believe was the impression that one need only pop his clothes and some enzymes into a washer to work the miracle. In fact, says TUBE (and Consumers' Union), enzyme detergents require presoaking, often overnight, and are only effective on protein-base stains. Last winter Listerine mouthwash was

THE ONE-EYED SLICKER
Daniel Henninger

touted as a weapon in the "cold" war: "This cold season, fight back with Listerine antiseptic." Whatever Listerine does, it doesn't prevent colds. Banzhaf believes that advertisers should have to indicate the damage their products may cause and cites as example some whitening toothpastes that contain abrasives harmful to tooth enamel. Arthur Godfrey moved in this direction when he told Colgate-Palmolive that he would no longer do commercials for Axion, a presoaker, unless allowed to say that phosphates in Axion were a water pollutant. C-P consented. Now Godfrey appears (less frequently) by a river in the Everglades and says that pollution is a serious problem, that Axion, like all detergents, pollutes water but until government and industry come up with a solution, stick with Axion.

One thing hyperbolic ad minds may do freely is "puff." Puffing is saying one's product is the best tasting, quietest, cleanest, smoothest, whitest, brightest and so on. The puffing principle evolved in the early days of television when it was thought that viewers would see, smell, listen, taste and feel for themselves. Over the years, though, some advertisers have puffed their products beyond this simple test: one detergent gets clothes "whiter than white"; another goes "all the way beyond white!" "The reason the laws allows this," says John Banzhaf "is that it can't think of any way around it. The courts can't get involved in tasting and things like that." A new ad genre is the spontaneous, man-on-the-street testimonial, a child of TV news interviews. In a Shell gasoline commercial, an actor posing as a gas station attendant berates a customer for using Shell, but the customer defends Shell gasoline like a Kuwaitian sheik. For this commercial, and others of its type, it may be necessary to film hundreds of people to capture the right offhand response. All this soft-core fraud gets on television because no one can or wants to stop it. The three major networks have Standards and Practices departments which are supposed to screen out deceptive ads before they appear. The only requirement for the job is that one be able to see. Warren Braren, former head of the New York office of the National Association of Broadcasters' Advertising Code, says "the network editors have no legal or scientific training and they don't have any scientific authorities to turn to for opinions. For example you may have a case in which an editor's mother uses a particular laxative; it's fine for her, and on that basis he'll approve the claim. Or an editor may get substantiating reports on comparative claims for auto tires. The editor doesn't have the expertise to determine the validity of these tests, so he may discuss it with someone else in the department. The networks take these tests on face value and hope that nobody asks any questions." Another individual in the ad-regulation business says the editors are overworked and that pulling a deceptive ad isn't worth the grief: "NBC looks over maybe 2000 ads a month handled by six or seven editors at a national level, not spot and local stuff. If it's in preproduction or script form and not blatant, they may let it go for lack of time. Or an ad may get by because it comes in as a final film already locked into a schedule. If the editor blows the whistle on a multi-million dollar project, the agency's lawers rush in saying if you don't take our schedule we'll switch to another network. It may go up to the vice president in charge of sales, pressure is put on and they accept the schedule. It's the facts of life."

Occasionally the networks pass on questionable ads to the Advertising Code at the NAB, the industry's self-regulatory agency. The Code has a Medical and Science Advisory Panel which serves on a limited, non-fee basis. When its opinion is sought, say Braren, "the outcome is often beneficial to the cause of truth in advertising." Last year the Code staff asked for some money to put several specialists on retainer. The NAB denied the money. Also denied was a request for a few thousand dollars to research problem areas like drugs, detergents and toothpastes. "Self-regulation," says Braren, "is thought of as a means of keeping the government off the broadcaster's back." The government, the FTC, really doesn't cause the broadcasters much backache. About 75 percent of the complaints the FTC files against TV advertisers are settled by consent agreements in which the company answers a cease and desist order by promising not to continue the specific, offending commercial. There is no fine or sanction so consent agreements don't carry much punch. Despite Geritol's frequent contributions to the FTC consent file, it appears regularly on Huntley-Brinkley and Walter Cronkite. And consent agreements have no effect on similar claims by other manufacturers. Ignoring Geritol's run-ins with the FTC, Sterling Drug (Bayer aspirin) last year introduced Super Ionized Yeast for iron anemia deficiency ("Chances are you may have the Gray Sickness"). Sterling's consent agreement reads like a photocopy of the Geritol file. Most other FTC complaints are settled through lengthy litigation during which the commercial still may appear.

The Commission now is in a court fight with Bristol-Myers and the outcome may numb the entire analgesics industry which annually spends $125 million advertising aspirin and has yearly sales to retailers of over $400 million. About ten years ago, the FTC issued a complaint against Bristol-Myers' Bufferin and Excedrin. During the heyday of the hard-sell commercial, Bufferin's housewife burned clothes while ironing, her baby spilled milk and another child fell off his tricycle. "Tension! Tension! Tension!" echoed a voice with each disaster. The housewife took two Bufferin, which works "twice as fast as aspirin," and relieves "tension headache." An Excedrin ad in this vein claimed that Excedrin was 50 percent stronger than aspirin, reduced swelling tissue, relieved tension and was an antidepressant. (Since then Excedrin has somehow gotten stronger and slightly confusing. David Janssen, who as a doctor in the "Fugitive" was for three years the most believable man in America, says "Two Excedrin contains twice as much pain reliever as *four* of the best selling aspirin.") The FTC said their studies showed none of these claims to be true, and for similar reasons filed complaints against Anacin, Bayer and St. Joseph's aspirin. Shortly, the Commission dismissed the complaints, which would have produced endless litigation, in favor of rules to regulate the entire industry. The proposed rules would forbid the aspirin people from making any of the above claims unless they proved they had used nonprescriptive analgesics within legal limits to produce a more effective pain reliever (a difficult trick because the federal Food and Drug Administration has determined the types and amount of analgesic they may use). The rules also proscribe any efficacy or safety claim "which contradicts, or in any manner exceeds, the warnings, statements or directions" on the product's label, which specific were it applied to all TV commercials would do away with many of them.

The analgesics industry in the person of Bristol-Myers is challenging in court the Commission's authority to make such rules. The rules themselves will be contested at Commission hearings for which the manufacturers will produce house physicians to support their claims. Should the rules become final, the admen will work with the not very compelling fact that "aspirin is aspirin."

Troubling as these rules may be for the future of aspirin, they get at only part of the deception problem. For one thing it is never announced that last night's commercial demonstration was a hoax and will no longer be seen because the manufacturer signed a consent agreement. Few can forget the Colgate toothpaste commercials in which "Gardol's protective shield" saved the announcer from baseballs, golf balls and coconuts. Fewer still may recall the FTC proceeding that concluded that Colgate with Gardol didn't completely prevent cavities by creating a "protective shield" or anything else. And unlike the dissatisfied farmer of a century ago, you can't beat your money out of them. Senator Philip Hart has introduced a bill to give consumers more effective recourse than indignation. Hart's amendment to the FTC act would enable anyone to use a final cease and desist order as prima facie evidence of deception and would permit class actions, making it possible to sue a company over a product that sells for about a dollar, but that has sales of several hundred thousand dollars. Speaking before the American Advertising Federation earlier this year,

THE ONE-EYED SLICKER
Daniel Henninger

President Nixon's national affairs counsellor Bryce Harlow characterized bills like Hart's as the work of "far-out consumer advocates." He urged the admen to support the President's Consumer Protection Act which permits fewer class actions. TUBE would dispense with the FTC altogether and has petitioned the FCC to suspend the license of any station airing deceptive commercials. For now reform of the advertisers, broadcasters and regulators isn't much more than a thought.

ADVERTISING:
THE MEDIA
SUPPORT SYSTEM

Part III

PART III   ADVERTISING: THE MEDIA SUPPORT SYSTEM

INTRODUCTION

Many people have expressed uneasiness about the adver-
tising enterprise in our time. To put the matter abruptly,
the advertising industry is a crude attempt to extend the
principles of automation to every aspect of society. Ideally,
advertising aims at the goal of a programmed harmony
among all human impulses and aspirations and endeavors.
Using handicraft methods, it stretches out toward the
ultimate electronic goal of a collective consciousness.

H. Marshall McLuhan[1]

The far reaching, overall effect and the aims of
advertising suggested by McLuhan may be valid
topics for exploration. But advertising's importance
to the mass media is not subject to any doubt, for
the advertising industry is the vital means for the
media's support. Newspapers and magazines could
not be marketed at existing prices, nor could commercial radio and television be broadcast without
their massive advertising revenues. We have already
seen how changes in medium preference affected
magazines and how the switch to cable television
may change network revenues. In return for current levels of financial sponsorship considerable
time and space are devoted to advertising. Television advertisements may run as high as eighteen
minutes per hour, while news magazines devote
about 30 per cent of their space to their sponsors.
Large circulation newspapers (e.g., *New York Times*)
use about 40 per cent of their space for advertis-

ing, while smaller local papers may be as much as
60 per cent advertising, excluding classified ads.
This is about three or four times more space than
they usually devote to international, national, and
local news combined.

The advertising industry is a sizable part of the
economy in the United States. In 1966, for example,
the total expenditure on advertising amounted to
$16.6 billion, which was 2.6 per cent of the national
income. Newspapers and magazines received the
greatest share of this figure, almost 42 per cent,
radio's share was 6 per cent, while television obtained 17 per cent.[2] In 1968, total volume had
risen to over $18 billion with the media share of
this revenue remaining about the same.[3] The United
States has the world's largest total volume and the
highest outlays per person.[4]

The advertising agency is one of the most curious
enterprises in the economy and perhaps one of the
most competitive. Since its main product is ideas,
it requires very little capital investment. Indeed, an
agency can be started by a single individual with
little more than a typewriter, a desk and access to
photographic and drawing equipment. If the
would-be ad-man is creative enough to hold down
a few good contracts, he is in business. In this way

[1]*Understanding Media* (New York: McGraw-Hill, 1964),
p. 227.

[2]International Advertising Association, *Advertising In-*
vestments Around the World Eighth IAA Biennial Report,
(New York, I.A.A. 1967), n.p.

[3]*Ibid.*, Ninth IAA Biennial Report, (New York, A.I.I.
1970), p. 31.

[4]*Ibid.*, p. 9.

agencies can go from virtually nothing to multi-million dollar operations in a few years. Conversely, even the largest agencies can never be fully secure since their clients can easily switch agencies and may do so every few years as a matter of policy. Some corporations will then give a new, spectacularly successful agency their business.

Nonetheless, there are tried and tested giants at the top which are big enough to survive the loss of a few clients, even major ones. J. Walter Thompson, Young and Rubicam, and McCann-Erikson had domestic billings of $436, $356 and $246 million respectively in 1970. Like most of the top agencies, they have extensive operations overseas. Thus for the big three, approximately 35%, 38%, and 21% of their total billings respectively for 1966 were in foreign markets. By 1970, the proportions of overseas trade had increased to 43%, 55%, and 32% respectively.[5] Together with many leading advertisers, they are becoming increasingly international concerns. Such agencies clearly have sufficient economic strength to be a powerful influence on the media industries (and society in general) if they chose to exercise their potential.

The type of advertisement placed in each of the media varies considerably due to the different types of audience they reach. Thus newspaper advertising consists primarily of local plugs for retail stores, while magazines and television enjoy the bigger product-oriented contracts, including the public relations pitches made on behalf of the major corporations (e.g. steel and power companies) which are not directly selling anything.

Advertising revenues for television derive primarily from personal and household consumer goods (see table below). Between 1966 and 1968 there were some noticeable increases in product category expenditures, among which cosmetics and laundry products grew the most rapidly. Confections, dental, and household paper products showed

---

[5]Figures in this paragraph were reported in *Advertising Age*, February 26, 1968, p. 48, and February 22, 1971, p. 26.

declines. Overall, personal and household-cleaning products increased their share of total expenditures relative to the proportion spent for food and drink and all other products.

The conclusion suggested by the table is that eating, drinking, smoking, and cleaning are the main activities TV advertisements promote—together they constituted 75.6 per cent of all expenditures in 1966, and 77.6 per cent in 1970—all of which are rather commonplace activities to be so heavily urged in the new "electronic" age through its most advanced medium. Of course, everyone needs to do them and the market is truly a mass one for these products, so advertising is justified. On the other hand, people can be expected to fulfill their basic needs without the urgings of advertising, although perhaps a few would be less well-scrubbed and over-fed. Competition is strong among the producers of these goods, but they compete with each other through advertising rather than price. Some corporations, such as those manufacturing detergents, carry this to the extreme by promoting their own rival products against each other. The standard rationale for advertising—that it disseminates useful product information and therefore stimulates the market—is not an accurate description in the case of such products.

The first selection in this section deals with the information aspect of advertising. A. Q. Mobray laments the fact that advertisements seldom give accurate information about their products. The consumer is never informed whether the product is safe, will work, or how long it will last. Mobray points to the need for product standards and accurate information of the type that manufacturers themselves demand when they buy component materials and equipment. Consumer groups, however, must first combat outright deception. Pressuring producers to adopt fair labelling standards is a small step which must be followed by other actions to eventually increase the truthful content of advertising. But the FTC moves slowly on false claims, as Henninger's article in the previous section demonstrates. It will probably be a long time before

Estimated TV Advertising Expenditures in the U.S. by Product, 1966 and 1968
(Rounded millions of dollars)

	1966	*1968*
Food, Drink, etc.	$1279 (49.2%)	$1309 (46.4%)
Ale, beer & wine	101	85
Confections, soft drinks	166	138
Drug Products	243	259
Food & grocery	516	573
Pet products	40	47
Tobacco & supplies	213	208
Cleaning: Personal & Household	687 (26.4%)	880 (31.2%)
Cosmetics, toiletries	295	400
Dental products	112	104
Household cleaners, etc.	90	100
Laundry products	147	249
Household paper products	42	28
All other products	635 (24.4%)	634 (22.5%)
Automotive	160	199
Gasoline & lubricants	67	85
Total	$2601 (100%)	$2824 (100.1%)

Source: Grouped from expenditures by product as listed in C. S. Aaronson, ed., *International T.V. Almanac* (New York: Quigley Publications, 1970), pp. 24A, 26A.

pseudo-information such as "whiter than white" or claims that cola X "has a lot to give," while "things go better with Y" drop out of the ad-man's lexicon.

The next three articles deal with some of the indirect effects of advertising. Herbert E. Krugman investigates the effect of what Stan Freburg has called the "Normandy Beach" technique—the constant repetition of the advertising "message" until it finally gets through to the audience. Such repetition, it is claimed, may lead to a complex type of unconscious learning rather than an outright change of attitude. W. M. Weilbacher interprets another extensive consumer response survey which indicates that advertising agents in fact do not know how the effects of repetition change over time. Advertisers perhaps know less than we think they do. This theme is developed on a more theoretical level by William A. Yoell. He finds that many of the psychological underpinnings of the advertising industry are out of date or misapplied.

Much more knowledge of consumer behavior is necessary before the success of a campaign can be predicted. If we are to avoid the type of manipulation foreseen by McLuhan, we can only hope that his advice to advertisers that they become more sophisticated and scientific goes unheeded.

The final selection by George A. Kirstein subtly deals with the overall effect of advertising on our society by imagining what would happen if a total moratorium on advertising were imposed. (Attempts have recently been made to ban all advertising on children's TV programs, so perhaps this article will not remain entirely fictional.) Papers and magazines would immediately become much more expensive, and broadcasting would have to rapidly convert to a subscription pattern. But product information would be considerably improved—sales of *Consumer Reports* would sky-rocket—books would suddenly become more valued, and the landscape and airwaves more aesthetic and better suited to an advanced civilization. The economy, meanwhile, would not collapse as the advertisers rationale would lead us to predict. His dream, however, is not likely to come true. For a total ban on advertising would require not only the self-conscious action of a well organized majority of consumers but their ability to outflank the powerful media interests which would be destroyed in the process. For advertising control is a matter of high finance and power not of the public interest.

Reprinted from The Nation *(September 15, 1969), pp. 245–48. Used by permission of publisher.*

What Consumers Need: Show Biz or Hard Facts

A. Q. MOWBRAY

THE state of the U.S. market place is nowhere better illustrated than in a television commercial now going the rounds for Oxydol. The scene is a modern, cheerfully appointed home laundry. A young man is being instructed in the mysteries of detergent quality by a bright young housewife. What, he asks, is so good about Oxydol? "It's those green things." she tells him, pointing to the flecks of green bleach in the pile of detergent she has poured into his outstretched hand. "But how well does it work?" he persists, all male innocence and gawk. "Stick your head in the basket," she leers, nodding toward the washing machine, "and you'll find out."

For fumbling young man read typical consumer. For impertinent housewife read U.S. manufacturer. And for "green things" read all the advertising puffery and nonsense that manufacturers substitute for hard information when touting their wares. How well does it work? The most adroit young minds in our society are hired to devise slick phrases with which to brush off such questions. Instead of giving hard answers, detergent manufacturers give you a choice between the credibility of Eddie Albert and Arthur Godfrey.

What the consumer needs in order to make rational choices among competing products is standards for those products—standards of performance, standards of durability, standards of safety. How well does it work? How long will it last? Is it safe? The paucity of standards for consumer products is at the heart of most of the consumer questions that have found their way to Washington during the past several years. Much of our annual highway carnage has been attributed to a need for safety standards for automobile design. Truth in packaging is unattainable without either standard net contents or standard unit price statements. Truth in lending is now being achieved through standard methods of stating the cost of borrowing. Wholesale meat can be provided only through sanitation and inspection standards. And so on.

Where the public health and safety are concerned, there seems to be a growing realization that the government, and especially the federal government, can no longer rely on the spotty and often ineffectual efforts of manufacturers to build safety into their products. Recent hearings of the National Commission on Product Safety are filled with testimony on eyeglass frames that burst into flame; fragile glass in storm doors that shatters and kills small children on impact; cribs that strangle infants, toys that stab them, floor grates that burn them; and ungrounded electrical appliances that electrocute their parents. Few who have seen this testimony deny that there is vast room for improvement in this field. In this complex technological world it is unreasonable to hope that all man-made hazards can be eliminated, but it seems clear that they can be greatly reduced. It is equally clear that the federal government must, at the very minimum, serve as the stimulus to industry in a sweeping program to improve

WHAT CONSUMERS NEED: SHOW BIZ OR HARD FACTS
A. Q. Mowbray

the safety of its products. The commission will be making recommendations next year on how the government should fulfill its responsibility. These recommendations are awaited with great interest by industry and consumers alike.

There is hope, then, that answers will soon be forthcoming to the question, Is it safe? But that leaves untouched the two remaining consumer questions: How well does it work? How long will it last? In the areas of performance and durability, the role of the government is not nearly so well defined, and the role of standards is not nearly so well understood by consumers.

When a manufacturer buys the materials that he uses in making his products, he refers to standards. He gives the materials supplier a standard specification spelling out the performance characteristics the material must have, and he also stipulates the standard test methods that will be used to sample and test the material to insure compliance with the standard specification. When General Motors buys material from U.S. Steel, it does not rely on assurances from the steel company that the shipment will be "new and improved" with twice the active ingredient of shabby old Brand X. GM says in very hardheaded terms that the steel must meet certain specifications as to strength, hardness, ductility, corrosion resistance, or whatever property is of interest, and it must pass certain standard tests to prove it.

The interesting and little understood aspect of this transaction is that both the standard specification and standard test method were agreed upon long before it took place. They were developed by representatives of the producer (U.S. Steel), the consumer (General Motors), and most other buyers and sellers of steel in the country, working voluntarily in a committee of an organization called the American Society for Testing Materials, a nonprofit society organized just for this purpose: to develop the standards without which commerce in the materials of manufacturing and construction would be all but impossible.

This is the *modus operandi* of the so-called voluntary standardization system that grew up in this country at the turn of the century. The emphasis is on voluntary because the work of developing the standards is contributed voluntarily by industry, and also because use of the standards, once developed, is wholly voluntary. There is no compulsion by government either to develop or to use the standards. The main point, however, is that such compulsion is entirely unnecessary. The commercial transaction is between two industries, each of which recognizes the need for the standard, and each of which can summon the technological expertise needed to comprehend the problem, to develop the solution, and to defend its interests in arriving at a balanced consensus. The process of developing the standard, as well as the act of buying and selling, involves a confrontation between equals, and the result is a balanced standard and a fair transaction.

When we turn to the consumer market place, we find a completely different ball game. The producer (General Motors) and the consumer (you or I) no longer deal as equals. The result is that standards for performance and durability of automobiles are all but nonexistent, and the consumer is adrift in a sea of non- and misinformation. Choices must be made on the basis of advertising claims, rumors, subliminal appeals to sexual prowess, and a vacant stare under the hood.

Compared with the orderly processes of the industrial market place, the consumer market place is a scene of anarchy. Organizations such as Consumers Union do a creditable job of attempting to provide information about products that will enable the consumer to make a rational choice. But such efforts by a private organization are necessarily limited by the support that can be generated among enlightened consumers, as well as by a lack of consumer product standards. The plea now from consumer advocates is for a nationwide, systematic program to develop standards for consumer products. There seems little doubt that this plea will eventually be answered. The key question is, will such a program be organized by industry, by government or by a cooperative effort of the two?

Foot-dragging among manufacturers is widespread. Some still cling to the ostrich principle. The problem doesn't really exist, they maintain — manufacturers flood consumers with information about their products. This yammering for consumer standards comes from a few vocal gadflies and malcontents, and if ignored it will eventually go away. The ranks of these hard-core *caveat emptor* types are being thinned by the encroachment of reality, but some die hard.

Other manufacturers resort to the too-many-variables ploy. The argument goes about as follows: When a new toaster, say, is carried home by the typical housewife, it is impossible to predict how she will use it, or abuse it, and therefore it is obviously impossible for the manufacturer to give her any hard assurances about how it will perform or how long it will last. Consumers are too unpredictable, service conditions too widely changeable, for the manufacturer to devise any test to simulate actual use. One of Betty Furness' favorite lines during her last months in office was to ask manufacturers why they couldn't tell her how long her washing machine was likely to last. Upon hearing this, the manufacturers would smile patronizingly and exchange words of pity over this poor woman who obviously had no concept of the very complex nature of simulated service testing, reliability, quality control and other highly technical matters.

What Miss Furness meant, of course, and what consumers all over the country would like to be told, is *how long* a representative sample of that model of toaster or washing machine performed in a standard test that was fairly designed to simulate average use. Everyone understands the variable nature of consumer use, but if all competing toasters are subjected to the same standard test, certainly the results would be helpful in comparing similar products and deciding which one to acquire with one's hard-earned cash.

When U.S. Steel sells a piece of steel to General Motors, no guarantee can be given as to how well that particular product will bear up under the conditions of manufacture in a given GM process. What U.S. Steel *can* say, however, is that similar pieces of steel performed in a given way when subjected to tests designed to simulate that process, or designed to measure properties critical to that process. Similarly, we do not ask General Motors to tell us how long our Chevrolet will run before the brakes need to be relined, because General Motors cannot possibly know our driving habits. We *would* like to know how long a similar model bore up in a standard road test.

But automobile manufacturers prefer to hire glittering young ladies to simper at us from our television screens while they run silken fingers along shining fenders and croon love songs to the deep-pile interiors. This is the third source of difficulty: many manufacturers prefer to compete on the basis of show biz rather than hard facts, on the theory that a few million bucks spent on high-power persuasion yields a lot more mileage than the same money invested in product quality. If it is a competitive market place, the competition is in advertising copy and television talent. Where no measure of quality exists, there can be no competition in quality.

Some manufacturers defend the *status quo* by pointing out that the consumer will be fooled only once, and if he is dissatisfied he will change brands. But in the absence of information about product performance, reliability or durability, how can the disgruntled buyer know that the change will be for the better? And more to the point, why should it be necessary for him to be fooled even once? Why should he not be given comparative information about competing brands so that he can make a rational choice in the first place?

An increasing number of Congressmen are asking these questions. Some believe that this shopping-information gap must be filled by an agency of the federal government. Sen. Philip A. Hart (D., Mich.), for example, has introduced a bill that would establish a National Consumer

WHAT CONSUMERS NEED: SHOW BIZ OR HARD FACTS
A. Q. Mowbray

Service Foundation "to receive, assemble, evaluate, act upon, and disseminate information helpful to consumers of the United States in performing their economic function more efficiently." One of the tasks of the foundation would be to "formulate and publish standards for specific consumer products or categories of such products which will facilitate the determination of values by consumers." Senator Hart envisions a kind of super Consumers Union, linked to a huge computer system and making its vast store of information available to the shopper at the point of sale. The consumer would merely slip a quarter in a slot and out would come all the data on all competing brands.

A large and growing number of responsible manufacturers—no doubt motivated in part at least by the "threat" of government action—are attempting to persuade industry leaders that the voluntary standardization system, which has worked so well in providing the thousands of standards by which industrial products are bought and sold, must be brought to bear on the vast unsolved problem of standards for consumer products. The arguments in favor of doing this are very persuasive.

Standards development requires an enormously complex organization, foolproof procedures, and a great variety of technical skills. All these already exist in the private sector. In the technical society mentioned earlier, for example, the American Society for Testing Materials, there are more than 100 standing committees developing and perfecting standards year in and year out for thousands of materials and products used by industry. These committees are manned by the nation's foremost technical experts—the engineers and scientists in the companies engaged in producing and buying these materials and products. For an organization such as this to take on the job of developing standards for consumer products would be but a simple expansion of scope. Further, the entire operation is supported and financed by industry— no public funds are required.

On the other hand, for the government to take on the job would require the creation of an agency to duplicate this enormous reservoir of technical skills and knowledge. Such an agency would have to include technical people with expertise on every consumer product in the market place. The prospect is staggering. Even if such an organization could be created, it would be difficult for it to maintain its expertise at the needed level. In today's fast-moving technologies, this can be done most effectively as a member of the producer organization.

Most observers of the standards scene, both in and out of government, agree that this is a job that can be done most efficiently and effectively in the private sector. The voluntary system has worked well in providing industrial standards; we should find a way for it to work equally well in providing consumer standards. There are two major differences that must be accounted for, however, before this can be possible.

The first of these is the matter of consumer representation on the standards writing team. If it is an industrial standard, the consumer is an industry, and there is no problem. In the case of the steel purchase cited earlier, the consumer is General Motors Corporation, quite a formidable voice on any team. In this situation, the producer industries and consumer industries come together on an equal footing, and the chances for a consensus reflecting both points of view are excellent.

If it is a consumer standard, however, who is to voice the wishes of the consumer? Consumers are unorganized and lack the financial resources and pool of technically competent manpower necessary to engage in standards development on a par with representatives of the manufacturing industries. It has been suggested that the government fill this need, not by sending representatives from government agencies to man the committees but by contracting with competent technical consulting firms to represent the consumer interest on committees developing consumer product standards.

The second major difference between industrial

and consumer standards is the matter of incentive. Given their "druthers," manufacturers on the whole would prefer that there be no standards for consumer products. They pay fervent lip service to the virtues of competition, but they are much more comfortable without it.

The present incentive that is moving some manufacturers gingerly to examine the need for consumer standards is the "consumerist" movement, now in full cry, and its attendant cloud, no bigger than a housewife's hand, that threatens to grow into the thunderhead of government domination of our nation's system of standards development. This threat must either materialize or disappear for the tension cannot be maintained indefinitely. If it materializes, the ball game is over. If it disappears, the government must then find a way to provide a permanent, effective incentive to the private sector to develop the standards so sorely needed by our nation's consumers.

The issue is joined. No bands play, no troops march. The struggle goes on quietly in Congressional staff offices, industry board rooms, and the committees of standards writing groups. Despite the lack of noise and the almost total lack of public understanding of the question, the outcome will have incalculable economic consequences for industry and consumers. The free enterprise system faces a major trial. If it fails to measure up, we will all be the losers.

Reprinted from Public Opinion Quarterly *(Fall, 1965), pp. 349–56. Used by permission of publisher and author.*

The Impact of Television Advertising: Learning Without Involvement

HERBERT E. KRUGMAN

AMONG the wonders of the twentieth century has been the ability of the mass media repeatedly to expose audiences numbered in millions to campaigns of coordinated messages. In the post—World War I years it was assumed that exposure equaled persuasion and that media content therefore was the all-important object of study or censure. Now we believe that the powers of the mass media are limited. No one has done more to bring about a counterbalancing perspective than ex-AAPOR president Joseph Klapper, with his well-known book *The Effects of Mass Media*,[1] and the new AAPOR president Raymond Bauer, with such articles as "The Limits of Persuasion."[2]

It has been acknowledged, however, that this more carefully delimited view of mass media influence is based upon analysis of largely noncommercial cases and data. We have all wondered how many of these limitations apply also to the world of commerce, specifically advertising. These limitations will be discussed here as they apply to television advertising only, since the other media include stimuli and responses of a different psychological nature, which play a perhaps different role in the steps leading to a purchasing decision.

The tendency is to say that the accepted limitations of mass media do apply, that advertising's use of the television medium has limited impact. We tend to feel this way, I think, because (1) we rarely feel converted or greatly persuaded by a particular TV campaign, and (2) so much of TV advertising content is trivial and sometimes even silly. Nevertheless, trivia have their own special qualities, and some of these may be important to our understanding of the commercial *or* the noncommercial use and impact of mass media.

To begin, let us go back to Neil Borden's classic Harvard Business School evaluation of the economic effects of advertising.[3] Published in 1942, it concluded that advertising (1) accelerates growing demand or retards falling demand, i.e. it quickens the pulse of the market, and (2) encourages price rigidity but increases quality and choice of products. The study warned, however, that companies had been led to overlook price strategies and the elasticity of consumer demand. This was borne out after World War II by the rise of the discounters!

The end of World War II also brought mass television and an increased barrage of advertising messages. How much could the public take? Not only were early TV commercials often irritating, but one wondered whether all the competition would not end in a great big buzzing confusion. Apparently not! Trend studies of advertising penetration have shown that the public is able to "hold in memory," as we would say of a computer, a very large number of TV campaign themes correctly related to brands. The fact that huge sums and energies were expended to achieve retention of these many little bits of information should not deter us from acknowledging the success of the overall effort.

It is true that in some categories of products the

sharpness of brand differentiation is slipping, as advertising themes and appeals grow more similar. Here the data look, as one colleague put it, "mushy." In such categories the product is well on its way toward becoming a commodity; even while brand advertising continues, the real competition is more and more one of price and distribution. But prices, too, are advertised, although in different media, and recalled.

What is lacking in the required "evaluation" of TV advertising is any significant body of research specifically relating advertising to attitudes, and these in turn to purchasing behavior or sales. That is, we have had in mind a model of the correct and effective influence process which has not yet been verified. This is the bugaboo that has been the hope and the despair of research people within the industry. Always there looms that famous pie in the sky: If the client will put up enough money, if he will be understanding enough to cooperate in blacking out certain cities or areas to permit a controlled experiment, if the cities or areas under study will be correctly matched, if the panels of consumers to be studied will not melt away in later not-at-homes, refusals, or changes of residence, if the sales data will be "clean" enough to serve as adequate criteria—*then surely* one can truly assess the impact of a particular ad campaign! Some advertisers, too, are learning to ask about this type of evaluation, while the advertising agencies are ambivalent and unsure of their strength.

This seems to be where we are today. The economic impact of TV advertising is substantial and documented. Its messages have been learned by the public. Only the lack of specific case histories relating advertising to attitudes to sales keeps researchers from concluding that the commercial use of the medium is a success. We are faced then with the odd situation of knowing that advertising works but being unable to say much about why.

Perhaps our model of the influence process is wrong. Perhaps it is incompletely understood. Back in 1959 Herbert Zielske, in "The Remembering and Forgetting of Advertising," demonstrated that

advertising will be quickly forgotten if not continuously exposed.[4] Why such need for constant reinforcement? Why so easy-in and easy-out of short-term memory? One answer is that much of advertising content is learned as meaningless nonsense material. Therefore, let us ask about the nature of such learning.

An important distinction between the learning of sense and nonsense was laid down by Ebbinghaus in 1902 when he identified the greater effects of order of presentation of stimuli on the learning of nonsense material. He demonstrated a U curve of recall, with first and last items in a series best remembered, thus giving rise also to the principles of primacy and recency.[5]

In 1957, many years later, Carl Hovland reported that in studying persuasion he found the effects of primacy and recency greater when dealing with material of lesser ego-involvement. He wrote, "Order of presentation is a more significant factor in influencing opinions for subjects with relatively weak desires for understanding, than for those with high 'cognitive needs'."[6] It seems, therefore, that the nonsensical à la Ebbinghaus and the unimportant à la Hovland work alike.

At the 1962 AAPOR meetings I had the pleasure of reading a paper on some applications of learning theory to copy testing. Here it was reported that the spontaneous recall of TV commercials presented four in a row formed a distinct U curve. In the same paper a re-analysis of increment scores of fifty-seven commercials tested in a three-position series by the Schwerin television testing method also showed a distinct U curve, despite the earlier contentions of the Schwerin organization. That real advertising materials presented in so short a series could produce distinct U curves seemed to confirm that the learning of advertising was similar to the learning of the nonsensical or the unimportant.[7]

What is common to the learning of the nonsensical and the unimportant is lack of involvement. We seem to be saying, then, that much of the impact of television advertising is in the form of learning without involvement, or what Hartley calls "un-

THE IMPACT OF TELEVISION ADVERTISING: LEARNING WITHOUT INVOLVEMENT
Herbert E. Krugman

anchored learning."[8] If this is so, is it a source of weakness or of strength to the advertising industry? Is it good or bad for our society? What are the implications for research on advertising effectiveness?

Let us consider some qualities of sensory perception with and without involvement. Last October I participated along with Ray Bauer, Elihu Katz, and Nat Maccoby in a Gould House seminar sponsored by the Foundation for Research on Human Behavior. Maccoby reported some studies conducted with Leon Festinger in which fraternity members learned a TV message better when hearing the audio and watching unrelated video than when they watched the speaker giving them the message directly, i.e. video *and* audio together.[9] Apparently, the distraction of watching something unrelated to the audio message lowered whatever resistance there might have been to the message.

As Maccoby put it, "Comprehension equals persuasion": Any disagreement with any message must come after some real interval, however minute. Bauer proposed a restatement of this point as "Perception precedes perceptual defense," to which Maccoby agreed. The initial development of this view goes back before World War II to the psychologist W. E. Guthrie.[10] It receives more recent support from British research on perception and communication, specifically that of D. E. Broadbent, who has noted the usefulness of defining perception as "immediate memory."[11]

The historical importance of the Maccoby view, however, is that it takes us almost all the way back to our older view of the potent propaganda content of World War I, that exposure to mass media content is persuasive per se! What is implied here is that in cases of involvement with mass media content perceptual defense is very briefly postponed, while in cases of noninvolvement perceptual defense may be absent.

Does this suggest that if television bombards us with enough trivia about a product we may be persuaded to believe it? On the contrary, it suggests

that persuasion as such, i.e. overcoming a resistant attitude, is not involved at all and that it is a mistake to look for it in our personal lives as a test of television's advertising impact. Instead, as trivia are repeatedly learned and repeatedly forgotten and then repeatedly learned a little more, it is probable that two things will happen: (1) more simply, that so-called "overlearning" will move some information out of short-term and into long-term memory systems, and (2) more complexly, that we will permit significant alterations in the *structure* of our perception of a brand or product, but in ways which may fall short of persuasion or of attitude change. One way we may do this is by shifting the relative salience of attributes suggested to us by advertising as we organize our perception of brands and products.

Thanks to Sherif we have long used the term "frame of reference," and Osgood in particular has impressed us with the fact that the meaning of an object may be perceived along many separate dimensions. Let us say that a number of frames of reference are available as the primary anchor for the percept in question. We may then alter the psychological salience of these frames or dimensions and shift a product seen primarily as "reliable" to one seen primarily as "modern."[12] The product is still seen as reliable and perhaps no *less* reliable than before, but this quality no longer provides the primary perceptual emphasis. Similarly, the product was perhaps previously seen as modern, and perhaps no *more* modern now — yet exposure to new or repeated messages may give modernity the primary role in the organization of the percept.

There is no reason to believe that such shifts are completely limited to trivia. In fact, when Hartley first introduced the concept of psychological salience, he illustrated it with a suggestion that Hitler did not so much increase anti-Semitic attitudes in Germany as bring already existing anti-Semitic attitudes into more prominent use for defining the everyday world.[13] This, of course, increased the probability of anti-Semitic behavior. While the shift in salience does not tell the whole

THE IMPACT OF TELEVISION ADVERTISING: LEARNING WITHOUT INVOLVEMENT

Herbert E. Krugman

story, it seems to be one of the dynamics operating in response to massive repetition. Although a rather simple dynamic, it may be a major one when there is no cause for resistance, or when uninvolved consumers do not provide their own perceptual emphases or anchors.

It may be painful to reject as incomplete a model of the influence process of television advertising that requires changes in attitude *prior to* changes in behavior. It may be difficult to see how the viewer of television can go from perceptual impact directly to behavioral impact, unless *the full perceptual impact is delayed.* This would not mean going into unexplored areas. Sociologists have met "sleeper effects" before, and some psychologists have long asserted that the effects of "latent" learning are only or most noticeable at the point of reward. In this case, it would be at the behavioral level involved in product purchases rather than at some intervening point along the way. That is, the purchase situation is the catalyst that reassembles or brings out all the potentials for shifts in salience that have accumulated up to that point. The product or package is then suddenly seen in a new, "somehow different" light although nothing verbalizable may have changed *up to that point.* What we ordinarily call "change of attitude" may then occur after some real interval, however minute. Such change of attitude after product purchase is *not,* as has sometimes been said, in "rationalization" of the purchase but is an emergent response aspect of the previously changed perception. We would perhaps see it more often if products always lived up to expectations and did not sometimes create negative interference with the emerging response.

I have tried to say that the public lets down its guard to the repetitive commercial use of the television medium and that it easily changes its ways of perceiving products and brands and its purchasing behavior without thinking very much about it at the time of TV exposure or at any time prior to purchase, and without up to then changing verbalized attitudes. This adds up, I think, to an under-

standable success story for advertising's use of the television medium. Furthermore, this success seems to be based on a left-handed kind of public trust that sees no great importance in the matter.

But now I wonder about those so-called "limits of effectiveness" of the noncommercial use of the mass media. I wonder if we were not overusing attitudes and attitude changes as our primary criterion of effectiveness? In looking for behavioral changes, did we sometimes despair too soon simply because we did not find earlier attitude changes? I wonder if we projected our own attitudes and values too much onto the audiences studied and assumed that they, too, would treat information about such matters as the United Nations as serious and involving? I wonder also how many of those public-spirited campaigns ever asked their audiences to *do* something, i.e. asked for the kind of concrete behavior that at some point triggers whatever real potentials may have developed for an attitude change to begin or perhaps to complete its work.

I would like to suggest, therefore, that the distinction between the commercial and the noncommercial use of the mass media, as well as the distinction between "commercial" and "academic" research, has blinded us to the existence of two entirely different ways of experiencing and being influenced by mass media. One way is characterized by lack of personal involvement, which, while perhaps more common in response to commercial subject matter, is by no means limited to it. The second is characterized by a high degree of personal involvement. By this we do *not* mean attention, interest, or excitement but the number of conscious "bridging experiences," connections, or personal references per minute that the viewer makes between his own life and the stimulus. This may vary from none to many.

The significance of conditions of low or high involvement is not that one is better than the other, but that the processes of communication impact are different. That is, there is a difference in the change

THE IMPACT OF TELEVISION ADVERTISING: LEARNING WITHOUT INVOLVEMENT
Herbert E. Krugman

processes that are at work. Thus, with low involvement one might look for gradual shifts in perceptual structure, aided by repetition, activated by behavioral-choice situations, and *followed* at some time by attitude change. With high involvement one would look for the classic, more dramatic, and more familiar conflict of ideas at the level of conscious opinion and attitude that precedes changes in overt behavior.

I think now we can appreciate again why Madison Avenue may be of little use in the Cold War or even in a medium-hot presidentail campaign. The more common skills of Madison Avenue concern the change processes associated with low involvement, while the very different skills required for high-involvement campaigns are usually found elsewhere. However, although Madison Avenue generally seems to know its limitations, the advertising researchers tend to be less clear about theirs. For example, from New York to Los Angeles researchers in television advertising are daily exacting "attitude change" or "persuasion" scores from captive audiences, these scores based on questionnaires and methods which, though plausible, have no demonstrated predictive validity. The plausibility of these methods rests on the presence of a more or less explicit model of communication effectiveness. Unfortunately, the model in use is the familiar one that assumes high involvement. Perhaps it is the questionnaires and the research procedures themselves that are responsible for creating what high involvement is present, which would not otherwise exist. The wiser or more cautious researchers meanwhile retreat to the possibilities of impersonal exactness in controlled field experiments and behavioral criteria. What has been left out, unfortunately, is the development of a low-involvement model, and the pre-test measures based on such a model. The further development of this model is an important next step, not only for the perhaps trivial world of television advertising but for the better understanding of all those areas of public opinion and education which, socially important as they may be, may simply not be very involving to significant segments of the audience.

In time we may come to understand the effectiveness of mass media primarily in terms of the *consistency* with which a given campaign, commercial or noncommercial, employs talent and research sensitively attuned to the real level of audience involvement. In time, also, we may come to understand that behavior, that is, verbal behavior and overt behavior, is always consistent provided we do not impose premature and narrowly conceived rules as to which must precede, or where, when, and how it must be measured.[14]

---

[1]Joseph Klapper, *The Effects of Mass Media*, Glencoe, Ill., Free Press, 1960.

[2]Raymond Bauer, "The Limits of Persuasion," *Harvard Business Review*, September-October, 1958, pp. 105–110.

[3]Neil Borden, *The Economic Effects of Advertising*, Chicago, Irwin, 1942.

[4]H. A. Zielske, "The Remembering and Forgetting of Advertising," *Journal of Marketing*, January 1959, pp. 239–243.

[5]H. Ebbinghaus, *Grundzuge der Psychologie*, Leipzig, Germany, Veit, 1902.

[6]C. T. Hovland *et al.*, *The Order of Presentation in Persuasion*, New Haven, Yale University Press, 1957, p. 136.

[7]H. E. Krugman, "An Application of Learning Theory to TV Copy Testing," *Public Opinion Quarterly*, Vol. 26, 1962, pp. 626–634.

[8]This is the title of a working manuscript distributed privately by E. L. Harley in 1964, which concerns his experimentation with new methods of health education in the Philippine Islands.

[9]L. Festinger and N. Maccoby, "On Resistance to Persuasive Communications," *Journal of Abnormal and Social Psychology*, Vol. 68, No. 4, 1964, pp. 359–366.

[10]E. R. Guthrie, *The Psychology of Learning*, New York, Harper, 1935, p. 26.

[11]D. E. Broadbent, *Perception and Communication*, London, Pergamon Press, 1958, Chap. 9.

[12]Psychological salience was first discussed in this manner by E. L. Hartley, *Problems in Prejudice*, New York, Kings Crown Press, 1946, pp. 107–115.

[13]*Ibid.*, p. 97.

[14]The consistency of verbal and overt behavior has also

163

been reasserted by Hovland, who attributes pseudo-differences to those *research designs* which carelessly compare results of laboratory experiments with results of field surveys (C. I. Hovland, "Reconciling Conflicting Results Derived from Experimental and Survey Studies of Attitude Change," *American Psychologist*, Vol. 14, 1959, pp. 8–17); by Campbell, who attributes pseudo-differences to the fact that verbal and overt behaviors have different situational thresholds (D. T. Cambell, "Social Attitudes and Other Acquired Behavioral Dispositions," in S. Koch, ed., *Psychology: A Study of a Science*, Vol. 6, McGraw-Hill, 1963, pp. 94–172); and by Rokeach, who attributes pseudo-differences to the fact that overt behavior is the result of interaction between *two* sets of attitudes, one toward the object and one toward the situation, and that most research leaves one of the two attitudes unstudied (M. Rokeach, "Attitude Change and Behavior Change," paper presented at the annual conference of the World Association for Public Opinion Research, Dublin, Ireland, Sept. 9, 1965).

Reprinted from Public Opinion Quarterly *(Summer, 1970), pp. 216–23. Used by permission of publisher and author.*

What Happens to Advertisements When They Grow Up?

W. M. WEILBACHER

THE American Association of Advertising Agencies sponsored a major study of consumer response to advertising in 1963 and 1964. The major findings of that study were well publicized in 1964 and 1965 and a thorough description and analysis of the study was published in 1968 by the Harvard Business School under the general authorship of Raymond A. Bauer and Stephen A. Greyser of Harvard, with the collaboration of Donald L. Kanter and W. M. Weibacher. This book was entitled *Advertising in America: The Consumer View.*[1]

The research procedure was a mixture of the conventional and the unusual. The respondents first expressed their attitudes about advertising as an institution. Next, with the help of a hand counter and diary, they counted advertisements from four media (TV, radio, newspapers, and magazines) which engaged their attention as they went about their daily routine. From the advertisements that engaged their attention (caused them to depress the counter), the respondents were asked to identify and describe those that were *informative* or *annoying* or *offensive* or *enjoyable*. These four categories were defined broadly for our respondents: pilot work indicated that the four concepts, as defined, covered a high fraction of consumer response; and that no other categories would significantly expand the coverage of these four.

Out of this twofold procedure a mass of information about attitudes toward advertising was developed. In addition, detailed records on some 9,325 advertisements which were of particular import to our respondents, either positively or negatively, were also developed.

Here are the major findings from this work:

1. Advertising is not a central issue in the day-to-day life of consumers: they are more immediately concerned with other things.

2. A great many of the physical opportunities that consumers have for exposure to advertising pass them by. In fact, the data show, using a particular set of measurement procedures, that consumer attention is engaged by about 80 advertisements each day. Looking at it from the consumer's point of view, this is really quite a generous allotment of time to advertising from among all the activities which engage and involve him.

3. When an advertisement does engage the consumer's attention, it is very likely not to strike him as offensive or annoying, but it is not very likely to strike him as informative or enjoyable, either. Only about 16 per cent of the advertisements that consciously engage the consumer's attention are found by him, on a given day, to be informative or enjoyable or annoying or offensive. The bulk of these are, however, informative or enjoyable.

4. There are no product categories or brands which produce *consistently* offensive or annoying advertising: advertising which offends some, entertains others; advertising which annoys some, informs others.

5. When a consumer categorizes an advertisement as *enjoyable*, he is likely to do so because of the creative elements or because it provides an

opportunity for personal identification with the advertising situation.

Advertisements are categorized by respondents as *informative* because they teach the respondents something about the product; or because they created a "you are there" feeling of involvement with the product in use; or because they seemed particularly truthful and, therefore, informative.

6. Advertisements are categorized by respondents as *annoying* because they contradict what the consumer has experienced with, or knows about, the product. Advertising treatment is also grounds for annoyance. Advertising with irritating elements or advertising that is repeated too frequently or advertising that talks down to the consumer can annoy him.

Advertisements *offend* because they contradict consumer's knowledge of, or experience with, the product. But they also offend because of consumer's moral reservations about the product class, or its potential effect upon children. Again, advertising treatment, repetition and condescension can lead to consumer offense.

7. Consumers apparently failed to categorize the bulk of the advertisements which engaged their attention primarily because they lack personal interest in or involvement with the product category, or because of the sameness and lack of distinction of the advertisements themselves.

Do these findings give us new insight into how the advertising process works, or what contributes to advertising effectiveness? What are the implications of these general findings for the creator of advertising and for the copy researcher?

These findings do seem to suggest some rather novel hypotheses about the solution of advertising problems, and new ways of thinking about what advertising effectiveness and efficiency may be. The study generates these new insights because it concentrates on the consumer as he is exposed to and responds during the whole life cycle of individual advertisements. But before going into these different perspectives, it will be productive to consider the way current copy research tends to channel the thinking of the advertising student and practitioner.

Copy research on a mocked-up advertisement or on a finished advertisement concentrates on what effect that advertisement—as a single discrete entity—has upon consumers. The researcher hypothesizes that a successful advertisement will have particular effects upon the consumer who is exposed to it. He exposes the consumer to the advertisement and measures these hypothesized effects: what he remembers; or whether his attitudes change, and how; or whether his pupil dilates or contracts; or whether he wants a year's supply of the product more now than before; or whether he is more likely to say he will buy the product as a result of seeing the advertising; or whatever.

But in his preoccupation with these response patterns, which he hypothesizes to reflect at least a fraction of the potential advertising effect, the researcher has lost very substantial sight of how the consumer responds to an advertisement when he happens to come upon it as a part of his daily perceptual experience.

At least three kinds of factors affect the consumer's response to an advertisement in such a real-life setting. First is the content of the advertisement itself. Second are various characteristics of the individual consumer: his sex, his age, his intelligence, his affluence, his consumption style, his innate predisposition to buy particular classes of goods, his feelings about advertising, the way in which he has learned or trained himself to defend his senses and perception from mass communication assault, whether he is alert and inquiring or dull and sickly, and so on and so on. The third and final factor affecting the consumer's response to an advertisement is *his past history of exposure to the same advertisement or advertisements that are so similar as to be perceptually equivalent.*

Copy research procedures are attuned to advertisement content and probably screen out or randomize some of the second class of factors. But they are indifferent to most of the second

WHAT HAPPENS TO ADVERTISEMENTS WHEN THEY GROW UP?
W. M. Weilbacher

class of factors and generally ignore the third factor completely. Yet these unaccounted-for factors may well be the dominant elements mediating consumer response to advertisements.

Advertising professionals tend to think about the consumer's past history of exposure to the same advertisement in terms of "wear out." Wear out seems to mean, in its common usage, that advertisement effectiveness gradually decays or wanes. At some point in time, it is believed, an advertisement loses its sharp cutting edge. When this point is reached, the old advertisement is retired in favor of another. The determination of this point in time is largely a judgmental matter. There is little general knowledge about this process: the one point that "wear out" studies using contemporary copy research procedures makes is that decay apparently varies from advertisement to advertisement. Such studies, when they exist, generally show a fairly slow onset of decay.

However, evidence seems to be accumulating from laboratory studies that conventional copy research studies of wear out may have underestimated the speed and seriously distorted our understanding of the nature of this decay process. For example, Herbert E. Krugman observes:

> Therefore, we introduce another question about the work of communication. We have already proposed the question, "How much work is there to be done?" and and answered by saying that there was a finite and measurable amount of work to be done. Now we propose to ask, "How will we know when the work is done, i.e. completed?" The proposed answer follows: when the stimulus has lost excitement, when the response has returned to rest or to some form of plateau. . . .
> I previously cited an eye movement study in which the range of respondent differences in average number of cells scanned for three trials was 5.5, 3.6 and 1.8. This would imply general completion by a fourth trial. Now if we look at pupil (i.e. pupillometer) data where we have three or more exposures, we find this sort of thing on some samples of 25 respondents each: that average response may go up dramatically on second

exposure and down dramatically on third, may go up on second exposure and then plateau, may go up slightly on second exposure and up slightly on third, and may also go down on second exposure and stay down. What I should like to emphasize is two-fold: first, that there were no cases of dramatic increase followed by dramatic increase, and second, that in two-thirds to three-fourths of the cases the third response was down, i.e., lower than the second response.[2]

And Robert C. Grass has written:

> All of these considerations suggest that it may be extremely important to create *continued* attention to an advertising campaign if it is desired to maintain communication values at their maximum. How continuous attention can be generated is a matter for the advertising experts, but certainly one general implication is that it might be wise to base a campaign on many different advertisements.[3]

The Bauer and Greyser study is germane to this inquiry because it does provide a first approximation of how consumers respond, after natural exposure, to advertisements over the advertisement's whole life. This first approximation comes as a result of consumer confrontation with individual advertisements as a part of his daily perceptual routine. The measurement does not proceed, as do conventional copy research procedures, from an assumption about how advertisements should work if they are to be effective, but permits the consumer to serve as a reporter of his own exposures. Perhaps the measurement was distorted and crude and even somewhat artificial; most first measurements of anything are. But the procedure permitted consumers to select 9,325 advertisements that they considered *informative* or *enjoyable* or *annoying* or *offensive*. About 50,000 other advertisements were not so selected even though they did engage the consumer's attention. What kind of process have we tapped here? Why did these consumer reactions occur?

Is it not probable that each advertisement has a life cycle all its own, and that its impact, interest, and effect vary over its life? When an advertisement is fresh and new, it must have close to maximum opportunity to entertain and inform. Fresh information, in or out of an appealing context, can become stale fairly quickly. A gentle and amusing exposition loses its charm after repeated exposure. I suspect, for example, that the information that Crest has ADA approval has been assimilated into the available knowledge of those consumers that care. Perhaps an early Crest commercial, proclaiming this fact, would seem informative to some if repeated today, but I doubt that this unit of information is really very new. And I wonder if a Bert and Harry Piel beer commercial would entertain viewers much anymore.

It is probable that the Bauer and Greyser study reported the minimum number of consumer reactions to advertisements as enjoyable and informative: those advertisements that were fresh and new to the respondents, that had not been repeated enough to have gone beyond the point of consumer information or entertainment. In our desire to simplify and differentiate our communications, advertising creative people have deliberately and undoubtedly minimized the amount of work that an advertisement has to do, exactly as Herbert E. Krugman has suggested. Thus, the informativeness and entertainment of a particular advertising communication may be, at best, transitory and short lived.

At the other end of the scale, the study probably achieved a maximum measure of annoyance and offense. If an advertisement annoys or offends a particular consumer inherently, then it will annoy or offend him whenever he is exposed. Other advertisements may become annoying or offensive after a series of exposures. It may take more exposures to pass this threshold with some people than with others. But once an advertisement has crossed the threshold of annoyance or offense, it will continue to annoy or offend until it is removed from public view. Thus, annoyance and offense in advertising is inherently cumulative.

In between the quicksilver state, for the individual advertisement, of entertainment/informativeness, and the cumulatively reinforcing state, for the individual advertisement, of annoyance/offensiveness, there may be a kind of limbo: in this limbo exist the advertisements to which consumers will not respond. Some of this lack of response will spring from inherent consumer characteristics: the consumer does not consume the brand in question for product or price or packaging or distribution or other marketing reasons; the consumer can't afford the product; the consumer will not consume the product for moral or health reasons; the consumer prefers to consume a complementary type of product; the consumer distrusts advertisements; the consumer does not permit any advertisements to penetrate his defenses; or whatever. But some of this lack of response will be for reasons for which the creators of advertising are professionally responsible — because of advertising failure. It is not clear, in this context, what all the grounds for such advertising failure may be, but at least two of them are quite obvious:

1. Creative work may simply not be good enough to engage the attention of consumers. Creative work may be good enough to cause attention engagement, but not good enough to inform or entertain. After all, even in conventional copy testing, even among product prospects, there are people who do *not* recall the advertisement or whose attitudes don't change after exposure, or whose pupils contract rather than dilate, and so forth.

2. And, of course, advertisements may perform well on first exposure but pass into limbo sometime later because their information and/or entertainment content becomes stale to the consumer. Such advertisements may produce no response at all — that is, may pass into limbo — for a good long time *before* they begin to annoy or offend. The lack of knowledge about consumer knowledge, attitudes, perceptual mechanisms, physiological processes, that work together to force advertisements into this limbo is clear.

WHAT HAPPENS TO ADVERTISEMENTS WHEN THEY GROW UP?

W. M. Weilbacher

The point is that we know almost nothing about what happens to advertisements when they grow up. How important is such knowledge likely to be? Assume for just a moment that the hypothesis of advertisement life cycle that I have sketched is correct and that the effective life of most advertisements is relatively short; that is, that many advertisements pass into limbo, or beyond, relatively shortly after their performance has been assessed in copy testing, when, because they are fresh and new, they have maximum opportunity to evoke a consumer's response.

Here are the kinds of conclusions one might draw if this life cycle model were confirmed:

1. *It is important to proliferate messages.* Regardless of whether or not the wear out of individual advertisements and commercials can be gauged, it is important continuously to refresh the creative work, lest some of it pass into consumer limbo. In this formulation, the individual advertisement is not perceived as an enduring work of art, but rather as a vehicle of communication that is doomed to ultimate ineffectiveness as surely as the butterfly is doomed to death.

2. *It may be important to consciously proliferate message content, insofar as product characteristics will permit it.* Just as advertisers have learned to segment markets, perhaps they will have to learn to segment messages to stimulate the individual response characteristics within a market. Instead of loading all the details into the body copy, why not create individual advertisements about them? Why must, for example, there be a central campaign theme if there is more than one thing that can be said about the product? Perhaps a lot of products are simply not that full of characteristics, but perhaps many of them have been shackled with endless repetition of a single theme that has long since passed into consumer limbo.

3. And how about the usage of media? Instead of running one advertisement in sixteen books with high duplication, why not run four *different* advertisements in a single issue of four magazines? Or sixteen advertisements in a single issue of one mass magazine? Or sixteen *different* messages in sixteen different selective magazines? How valuable is repetition, after all? Is there not a deadly distinction to be made between frequency and repetition? To reach a single consumer with several different messages, each challenging his attention, is one thing. To reach a single consumer with the same message time after time may be the road to limbo, boredom, and rejection.

No argument is made here for or against such changes in the approach to the solution of advertising problems. This is simply an interpretation of the Bauer and Greyser study which could lead to such conclusions if the interpretation were confirmed. It suggests a series of questions on which research is needed and it suggests the fallibility of any copy research procedure or decision system that ignores what happens to advertisements when they grow up and live with total consumers by whom advertising is occasionally encountered and perceived as life itself unfolds.

This study may have inadvertently drawn aside a curtain. It suggests that the advertising researcher should try to generalize about the consumer as a consumer of advertising. He should try to find out what consumer processes shape the life of advertisements in time. He should discover the mechanics of consumer perceptual defenses as they are applied and adapted to advertising messages. He must become concerned with the life cycle of advertisements: with their productive life, progressive decay, and inevitable death in the world of consumers.

[1] Division of Research, Harvard Graduate School of Business, Boston, 1968.

[2] Herbert E. Krugman, "Processes Underlying Exposure to Advertising," *Proceedings of the 14th Annual Conference, Advertising Research Foundation*, New York, 1968, pp. 18, 19.

[3] Robert C. Grass, "Satiation Effects of Advertising," *Proceedings of the 14th Annual Conference, Advertising Research Foundation*, New York, 1968, pp. 27–28.

Reprinted from Marketing/Communications *(August, 1970), pp. 42–44. Used by permission of publisher and author.*

The Abuse of Psychology by Marketing Men

WILLIAM A. YOELL

New products are introduced to the consumer market. Their development and introduction has been preceded by months, perhaps years, of market research, including the application of psychological techniques to determine consumer motivations as well as concepts, attitudes and perceptions. Psychological techniques were applied to determine how to present and market the products and what types of consumers were most likely to buy the products. The products fail. Why?

Psychological studies reveal that an established product with declining sales requires a change of "image." Additional psychological studies are conducted to reveal what the corporate or product "image" should be. Sales continue to decline; the "image" of the company does not change. Why?

The answer lies in the misuse and abuse of psychological techniques.

The first mental testing movement began with the development of the first intelligence test by Binet-Simon (1905). It was developed from the purely practical goal of discovering an objective method of assessing the intellectual level of French children. Since then, hundreds of tests have been devised to assess various facets of an individual's characteristics; to determine what kind of person he is; how he can be expected to behave and perform; what his unconscious motivations are—whether this be in his role as consumer, employer or citizen.

The abuse and misuse of psychological techniques has become an albatross around the neck of business. Techniques are borrowed from the psychological clinic, the analyst's couch, from the theories that have failed in the area in which they were developed and applied; theories and techniques that have never passed the acid test of empirical proof, but which have been repeatedly disproved. Business has never bothered to investigate the background and development of these theories and techniques— their limitations, their legitimate purpose and function.

Forgotten in this stampede to analyze consumers, products, companies was the fact that few, if any, psychological theories have ever been proved. In fact most have been contradicted; most are pure theory without any semblance of proof. This is true particularly of the Freudian, Gestalt, Adlerian and Jungian schools of psychological thought, and these men were the first to admit there was little scientific evidence or empirical proof for their ideas and theories.

No one has yet proved that psychological techniques designed to uncover causes of irrational behavior, emotional or psychotic behavior, traumatic experiences, personality defects, neuroses can and do determine why consumers buy automobiles, floor waxes; why their attitude is what it is toward a particular company.

Generally, business utilizes two basic groups of psychological techniques. The first group includes psychological performance tests, all of which have their roots in Freudian psycho-analytic techniques and theory. The subject is required to do something: answer questions, solve problems, draw

THE ABUSE OF PSYCHOLOGY BY MARKETING MEN
William A. Yoell

pictures, interpret pictures or ink blots, make up stories. Group or focus discussion sessions are part of this first group—five to ten people participating in a discussion on a particular topic—an outgrowth of the psycho-analytic theory of group therapy.

The second kind involves the application of devices such as the tachistoscope, galvanometer, eye blink measuring devices. These measure such things as nerve impulses, muscle twitches, skin conductance, the theory being that when presented with statements, words, if they have significance for the individual, these will show up in physiological reactions. Business utilizes them to determine how the public feels about a company; whether a product, an advertising campaign is liked, preferred; which package is preferred.

Most techniques have their basis in Freudian theory and in introspection. These techniques are pre-scientific, lacking experimentation and producing data that are impossible to distinguish from empirical fact. These include rating scales, personality inventories, projective techniques. For instance, psycho-analytic theory holds that by attributing his own consciously unacceptable motives and attitudes to others, or to objects, the individual is able to avoid seeing them as belonging to himself. There has never been any proof of this theory. In fact, Freud specifically stated the projections are onto the analyst—not other people, and certainly not to root beer, deodorants or political candidates.

It is also part of psycho-analytic theory that the attribution of traits are projections by people who repress their sexual, aggressive, oral, anal motives and that the projective techniques uncover these. But if this were so, there is no evidence that these techniques apply to toothpaste, breakfast cereal, companies. Moreover, in the clinic no one projective technique is used, but a battery of them to determine if a person is a repressive type, uses defense mechanisms, is anxious, has castration anxieties. When these techniques are used by business, no more than a single test is applied. More importantly, these tests depend upon introspection, upon the self-analysis of the individual. If scientists depended upon introspection, color blindness would still be undiscovered.

The nature of the stimulus that causes a particular response can only be obtained by analyzing current and past behavior—not by having people probe their own minds.

One projective technique is the Manifest Anxiety Scale, which consists of presenting the individual with statements and asking him to select the one which in his opinion is true, false, doubtful, or some such variation. For instance, "I am sometimes troubled by what people think of me." "People who drink beer love life and are happy-go-lucky" (agree, agree strongly, disagree).

This technique was never designed to determine motives or attitudes toward beer or toward anything else, but to determine to what extent anxieties interfered with or inhibited learning.

The Thematic Apperception Test is another such example, (referred to as TAT in psychological circles). This involves presenting individuals with a picture that is vague, indistinct. The individual is asked to tell what he thinks is happening.

This test was designed to assess the individual differences in imagery achievement and their effect on learning. The originator of this technique concluded he was uncertain as to whether or not his tests measured anything. Yet, this TAT technique is used to measure and determine the attitudes and motivations of consumers.

The results from projective techniques have given rise to such absurdities as "products and companies have personalities." Personality requires behavior to express itself and inanimate objects do not behave.

It does not seem logical that the 6,500 items on the super market shelf transmit personality to the shopper, or have personality infused into them by the shopper.

Businessmen paraphrase the results of projective and other psychological techniques with such generalities as "people buy emotionally." It is questionable if they observed consumers in the act of buying or measured the blood pressure, heart and pulse rate before and after and during purchase. It is doubtful that consumers buy a bottle of soda pop, a can of soup, a package of frozen peas with love, hate, anger, greed, awe, fear, terror, jealousy, lust, rage.

Another projective technique is the focus interview which consists of a moderator and a dozen or so individuals who have come together to freely discuss a particular subject—a household product, a company, advertisements, a new package. This technique, borrowed from the group therapy sessions of Freud, is never used in isolation in the clinic—it is preceded by many tests. To name a few: the Worcester Scale of Social Attainment Test, the Blacky or Iowa picture test, the Stroop test, the measurement of the Zeigarnick effect. If such pre-tests are not given, and they are not in the business world, then all that results is a response that might strike a chord in the analyst's mind, that is no more significant than personal judgment.

What we must be careful of in group interviewing is the fact that private and public attitudes are different. There is the trite but true example of people in a small community exhibiting one attitude toward card playing or drinking for public scrutiny, and another set of attitudes in the privacy of their own homes.

A group discussion was designed to determine attitudes toward traditional food preferences and through this, attempt to increase consumption of these meats which were generally rejected—kidneys, sweetbreads, etc. Women indicated whether they intended to use these meats and the response was unanimously "yes." Follow-up studies revealed only 3% did. Public opinion differs from private. There are so many imponderables. For instance, smaller groups inhibit ideas; ideas are increased when groups are larger. Change the analyst, change one member of the group and the statements change.

Eye blink and pupil dilation devices are used by business on the theory that if a subject is presented with a statement, a package, a situation, a word or a phrase, the name of a company, a product, the eye blink or pupil dilation will measure and indicate positive or negative reactions, depending upon the number of eye blinks or the contraction of the pupil in a specified period of time. These techniques were designed and used only to determine how the eye or vision functions.

Eye movements do not measure interest, degree of liking, disliking. They establish only visual continuities. As measures of company, product, advertisement, product interest, they are meaningless.

There is a difference between description and cause. This is what psychological techniques used by business fail to differentiate with the line of questioning. The various factors from group interviewing or rating scales are factored out through factor analysis. But the factors might be fictional. In factor analysis, the factors extracted depend on the particular items which are included in the original rating scale. You get out what you put in. As Vernon said in regard to personality trait analysis: "Factors can only cover those facets of personality (product) which are presented in the test battery and hence the universality is limited by the comprehensiveness of personality (product) traits." He says further: "The subjects' attitudes distort the ratings and since subjective measures of conduct are not yet developed, none of the factorizations yet made has disclosed the real elements of personality (product)."

When we know the history of consumers, how they adjust to situations, the nature of the situations to which they have been exposed, when we have a history of their use, we know the factors which are vital and then can predict what will happen.

Reprinted from The Nation (*June 1, 1964*), *pp. 555–57. Used by permission of publisher.*

The Day the Ads Stopped

GEORGE G. KIRSTEIN

THE day the advertising stopped began just like any other day — the sun came up, the milk was delivered and people started for work. I noticed the first difference when I went out on the porch to pick up *The New York Times*. The newsdealer had advised me that the paper would now cost 50¢ a day so I was prepared for the new price beneath the weather forecast, but the paper was thinner than a Saturday edition in summer. I hefted it thoughtfully, and reflected that there really was no alternative to taking the *Times*. The *News* had suspended publication the day before the advertising stopped with a final gallant editorial blast at the Supreme Court which had declared the advertising prohibition constitutional. The *Herald Tribune* was continuing to publish, also at 50¢, but almost no one was taking both papers and I preferred the *Times*.

As I glanced past the big headlines chronicling the foreign news, my eye was caught by a smaller bank:

1 KILLED, 1 INJURED IN
ELEVATOR ACCIDENT AT MACY'S.

The story was rather routine; a child had somehow gotten into the elevator pit and his mother had tried to rescue him. The elevator had descended, killing the woman, but fortunately had stopped before crushing the child. It was not so much the story as its locale that drew my attention. I realized that this was the first time in a full, rich life that I had ever read a newspaper account of an accident in a department store. I had suspected that these mis-

fortunes befell stores, as they do all business institutions, but this was my first confirmation.

There were other noticeable changes in the *Times*. Accounts of traffic accidents now actually gave the manufacturers' names of the vehicles involved as, "A Cadillac driven by Harvey Gilmore demolished a Volkswagen operated by. . . ." The feature column on "Advertising" which used to tell what agencies had lost what accounts and what assistant vice president had been elevated was missing. As a matter of fact, the whole newspaper, but particularly the Financial Section, exhibited a dearth of "news" stories which could not possibly interest anyone but the persons mentioned. Apparently, without major expenditures for advertising, the promotion of Gimbels' stocking buyer to assistant merchandise manager was not quite as "newsworthy" as it had been only yesterday. Movies and plays were listed in their familiar spot, as were descriptions of available apartments in what used to be the classified section. The women's page was largely a catalogue of special offerings in department and food stores, but no comparative prices were given and all adjectives were omitted. One could no longer discover from reading the *Times*, or any other paper, who had been named Miss National Car Care Queen or who had won the Miss Rheingold contest.

Driving to work, I observed workmen removing the billboards. The grass and trees behind the wall of signs were beginning to reappear. The ragged posters were being ripped from their familiar locations on the walls of warehouses and stores, and

THE DAY THE ADS STOPPED
George G. Kirstein

the natural ugliness of these structures was once more apparent without the augmenting tawdriness of last year's political posters or last week's neighborhood movie schedules.

I turned on the car radio to the subscription FM station to which I had sent my $10 dues. The music came over the air without interruption, and after awhile a news announcer gave an uninterrupted version of current events and the weather outlook. No one yet knew which radio stations would be able to continue broadcasting. It depended on the loyalty with which their listeners continued to send in their subscription dues. However, their prospects were better than fair, for everyone realized that, since all merchandise which had previously been advertised would cost considerably less on the store counter, people would have funds available to pay for the news they read or the music or other programs they listened to. The absence of the familiar commercials, the jingles, the songs and the endless repetition of the nonsense which had routinely offended our ears led me to consider some of these savings. My wife's lipsticks would now cost half as much as previously; the famous brand soaps were selling at 25 per cent below yesterday's prices; razor blades were 10 per cent cheaper; and other appliances and merchandise which had previously been nationally advertised were reduced by an average of 5 per cent. The hallowed myth that retail prices did not reflect the additional cost of huge advertising campaigns was exploded once and for all. Certainly these savings should add up to enough for me to pay for what I listened to on my favorite radio station or read in the newspaper of my choice.

After parking my car, I passed the familiar newsstand between the garage and the office. "*Life* $1," the printed sign said. "*Time* and *Newsweek*, 75¢." Next to these announcements was a crayon-scrawled message! "*Consumer Reports* sold out. Bigger shipment next week." I stopped to chat with the newsie. "The mags like *Consumer Reports* that tell the truth about products are selling like crazy," he told me. "*Reader's Digest* is running a merchandise analysis section next month." I asked about the weekly

journals of opinion. He said, "Well now they are half the price of the news magazines—*The Nation* and *The New Republic* prices have not gone up, you know, but I don't think that will help them much. After all, a lot of magazines are going to begin printing that exposé-type stuff. Besides, people are buying books now. Look!" He pointed across the street to the paperback bookstore where a crowd was milling around as though a fire sale were in progress.

I walked over to the bookstore and found no special event going on. But books represented much better value than magazines or newspapers, now that the latter were no longer subsidized by advertisements, and the public was snapping up the volumes.

Sitting in my office, I reviewed the events and the extraordinary political coalition that had been responsible for passing the advertising prohibition law through Congress by a close margin. The women, of course, had been the spearhead of the drive. Not since the Anti-Saloon-League days and the militant woman-suffrage movement at the beginning of the century had women organized so militantly or expended energy more tirelessly in pursuit of their objective. Their slogans were geared to two main themes which reflected their major grievances. The first slogan, "Stop making our kids killers," was geared mainly to the anti-television campaign. The sadism, killing and assorted violence which filled the TV screens over all channels from early morning to late at night had finally so outraged mothers' groups, PTAs and other organizations concerned with the country's youth that a massive parents' movement was mobilized.

The thrust of the women's drive was embodied in their effective two-word motto, "Stop lying." Women's organizations all over the country established committees to study all advertisements. For the first time in history, these common messages were analyzed in detail. The results were published in anti-advertising advertisements, by chain letter and by mouth. The results were devastating. No dog-food manufacturer could claim that pets loved

THE DAY THE ADS STOPPED
George G. Kirstein

his product without having the women demand, "How in the name of truth do you know? Did you interview the dogs?" No shampoo or cosmetic preparation could use the customary blandishments without having the women produce some witch who had used the particular product and who had lost her hair, developed acne or had her fingernails curl back.

Women led the attack, but the intellectuals soon joined them, and the clergy followed a little later. The intellectuals based their campaign largely on the argument that the English language was losing its usefulness, that word meanings were being so corrupted that it was almost impossible to teach youth to read to any purpose. One example commonly cited was the debasement of the superlative "greatest." The word had come to mean anything that didn't break down; viz., "the greatest lawn mower ever," interpreted realistically, was an instrument that, with luck, would cut grass for one summer. The clergy's campaign was geared simply to the proposition that it was impossible to teach people the virtues of truth when half-truths and lies were the commonly accepted fare of readers and viewers alike.

Opposition to the anti-advertising law was impressive, and at the beginning it looked as if all the big guns were arrayed against the women. Spokesmen for big business contended throughout the campaign that elimination of advertising meant elimination of jobs. The fallacy of this argument was soon exposed when all realized that it was not men's jobs but simply machine running time that was involved. By this decade of the century, the cybernetic revolution had developed to a point where very few men were involved in any of the production or distribution processes. No one could feel much sympathy for the poor machines and their companion computers because they would be running only four hours daily instead of six.

Some merchants tried to blunt the "stop lying" slogan by telling the absolute truth. One San Francisco store advertised:

2,000 overcoats—only $12 Let's face it—our buyer goofed! These coats are dogs or you couldn't possibly buy them at this price. We're losing our shirt on this sale and the buyer has been fired. But, at least, many of these coats will keep you warm.

The trouble with this technique was that it backfired in favor of the women. The few true ads, by contrast, drew attention to the vast volume of exaggeration, misrepresentation and outright lies that were printed as usual. The advertising industry published thirteen different editions of its "Advertisers Code" in the years preceding the law's passage, but few could detect any difference from the days when no code at all existed.

The press, of course, was the strongest opponent and loudest voice against the advertising prohibition. Its argument was largely legalistic, based on the First Amendment to the Constitution, for the publishers had decided at the outset of their defense not to emphasize the fact that if advertising stopped, readers would actually have to pay for what they read, rather than have America's largest corporations pay for the education and edification of the public. However, the words "Free Press" came to have a double meaning—both an unhampered press and a press that charged only a nominal fee for the publications.

The constitutional argument was really resolved in that final speech on the floor of the Senate before a gallery-packed audience, by Senator Thorndike of Idaho. His memorable ovation, certainly among the greatest in the Senate's distinguished history, concluded:

And so, Mr. President, the opponents of this measure [the advertising prohibition] claim that the founders of this republic, our glorious forefathers, in their august wisdom, forbade the Congress to interfere with the freedom of the press to conduct itself in any way it found profitable. But I say to you, that the framers of our Constitution intended to protect the public by permitting the press, without fear or favor, to examine all of the institutions of our democracy. Our forefathers planned a press free to criticize, free to analyze, free to dissent. They did not plan a subsidized press, a conformist press, a prostitute press.

The applause was thunderous and the bill squeaked through the Senate by four votes. Three years later, the Supreme Court upheld Senator Thorndike's interpretation. That was two days ago, and today the advertising stopped.

All morning I worked in the office, and just before noon I went uptown for lunch. The subway cars were as drab as ever and seemed a little less bright because of the absence of the familiar posters. However in one car the Camera Club of the Technical Trades High School had "hung" a show of New York City photographs chosen from student submissions. In another car, the posters on one side carried Session I of a course in Spanish for English-speaking riders, while the opposite side featured the same course in English for those speaking Spanish. This program was sponsored by the Board of Education which had subcontracted the administration of it to the Berlitz school. A poster in both languages in the middle of the car explained that the lessons would proceed on a weekly basis and that by sending $1 to the Board of Education, review sheets and periodic tests would be available upon request.

On Madison Avenue, the shopping crowds were milling around as usual, but there was a noticeable absence of preoccupied and hatless young men hurrying along the street. The retirement plan that the advertising industry had worked out through the insurance companies was fairly generous, and the majority of key personnel that had been laid off when the agencies closed were relieved not to have to make the long trek from Westport or the nearer suburbs each day. Some of the copywriters who had been talking about it since their youth were now really going to write that novel.

Others had set up shop as public relations counselors, but the outlook for their craft was not bright. Without the club of advertising, city editors looked over mimeographed press releases with a new distaste, and it is even rumored that on some newspapers the orders had come down to throw out all such "handouts" without exception. On the magazines, the old struggle between the editorial staff and the advertising sales staff for dominance had finally been resolved by the elimination of the latter. There were even some skeptics who believed that public relations counseling would become a lost art, like hand basket weaving. So most former advertising copywriters planned to potter about in their gardens, cure their ulcers and give up drinking. They were not so many. It was a surprise to most people to learn that the advertising industry, which had had such a profound effect on the country's habits and moral attitudes, directly employed fewer than 100,000 people.

Outside 383 Madison Avenue, moving vans were unloading scientific equipment and laboratory accessories into the space vacated by Batten, Barton, Durstine & Osborn. The ethical drug industry had evolved a plan, in the three-year interim between the passage of the advertising prohibition and the Supreme Court's validation of it, to test all new drugs at a central impartial laboratory. Computers and other of the latest information-gathering machinery were massed in the space vacated by this large advertising agency to correlate the results of drug tests which were being conducted in hospitals, clinics, laboratories and doctors' offices throughout the world.

The Ford Foundation had given one of its richest grants, nearly three-quarters of a billion dollars, to the establishment of this Central Testing Bureau. The American Medical Association had finally agreed, under considerable public pressure, to take primary responsibility for its administration. It was pointed out to the doctors that when the drug companies could no longer make their individual claims through advertisements in the AMA bulletin or the medical society publications, a new and more reliable method of disseminating information would be required. At the outset, the AMA had joined

THE DAY THE ADS STOPPED
George G. Kirstein

the drug companies in fighting bitterly against the prohibition, but the doctors now took considerable pride in their centralized research and correlation facilities. The AMA bulletin, once swollen to the bulk of a small city's telephone directory, was now only as thick as a summer issue of *Newsweek*. Doctors no longer would find their mail boxes stuffed with throw-away material and sample pills; but they would receive the weekly scientific report from Central Testing Bureau as to the efficacy of and experience with all new preparations.

Late in the afternoon, I began to hear the first complaints about the way the new law worked. One of the men came in and picked up a folder of paper matches lying on my desk. "I'm swiping these; they're not giving them out any more, you know." Someone else who had been watching TV said that the two channels assigned to the government under a setup like that of the B.B.C., were boring. One channel showed the ball game, but the other had been limited to a short session of the Senate debating the farm bill, and a one-hour view of the UN Security Council taking up the latest African crisis. My informant told me the Yanks had won 8 to 0, and the Senate and the UN weren't worth watching. I reminded him that when the channel that was to be supervised by the American Academy of Arts and Sciences got on the air, as well as the one to be managed by a committee of the local universities, things might improve. "Cheer up," I told him, "At least it's better than the Westerns and the hair rinses."

Oh, there were some complaints, all right, and I suppose there were some unhappy people. But personally I thought the day the advertising stopped was the best day America had had since the last war ended.

THE IMPACT ON THE AUDIENCE: THE SOCIAL PSYCHOLOGY OF MASS COMMUNICATIONS

Part IV

PART IV   THE IMPACT ON THE AUDIENCE: THE SOCIAL PSYCHOLOGY OF
MASS COMMUNICATIONS

INTRODUCTION

The study of mass communications has been overwhelmingly concerned with social psychology, with the ways in which the media influence their audience. In Parts V and VI which follow we will take up some of the more controversial issues of media effects, the way they shape the overall cultural climate of society, their implications for crime and violence, and their political uses. The task here is to outline the better established knowledge that has been obtained from the empirical findings of several decades of research. The first section deals with the basic communication process and information flow and with the capabilities of messages to change opinions and behavior of their audience.

Ⓐ. Communication Process and Flow

The opening selection by Schramm outlines the basic chain of communication. Information held by the sender is "coded," that is, an idea is put into words, print, or film. This message is then sent out as a "signal." If it is received by an audience, it is "decoded" by them, and interpreted again as an idea. Only then is the information received. At every link in this chain the intended message of the sender can be distorted. The intended meaning may not be conveyed in the coding process, the signal may be faulty and consequently not received, the decoder may infer meanings other than those intended, and finally the message may be rejected by the receiver. Schramm outlines the conditions under which such breakdowns can be avoided. In mass communications the sender is an organization, while the receivers are individuals. Unlike face-to-face communication there is no real feedback by which the receiver in turn becomes the sender. The communicator therefore has no immediate cues to indicate whether his message has been received as intended.

The sender in Schramm's communication scheme must sift his information before he codes a message. He selects from all the information available to him only those elements that he wants to convey. If he is a newspaperman or TV newsman he will probably rely on a wire service for his information. The content of the wire he receives is a product of several editorial stages. The field reporter is selective in what he reports, and then regional and national wire editors decide which news items to pass on.

Any person who serves this information-editing function may be called a "Gate Keeper." White's article examines in detail the way that one of these men, a newspaper wire editor, goes about his task. His decisions, it is argued, were highly subjective; that is, they reflected his own values and prejudices rather than those of his audience or the intrinsic "newsworthiness" of the items he selected. This subjectivity no doubt affects all "Gate Keepers" to a degree.

At the other end of the communication chain mass media messages often do not go directly to the target audience. Instead there is what has been termed a "two-step flow" of information. The message transmitted by the mass media is picked up by "opinion leaders" who pass it on to the mass population. This idea has generated considerable interest among communication researchers. The article by Allen is in this tradition. Allen shows that knowledge of public affairs was greater for those in his sample who talked about the news rather than those who merely absorbed it from the media. Thus interpersonal contacts probably reinforced mass-directed messages. Other researchers, however, have set out to test the two-step flow hypothesis and found it less convincing than expected.[1]

[1]See for example Verling C. Troldahl, "A Field Test of a Modified 'Two-step Flow of Communication' Model," *Public Opinion Quarterly*, (Winter, 1966–7), pp. 609–623, and Bradley S. Greenberg, "Person-to-person Communication in the Diffusion of News Events," *Journalism Quarterly*, (Autumn, 1964), pp. 489–494.

People today may well be turning more than ever before to the media rather than other individuals, not only for technical information but for news on political and social issues as well.

Wales, Rarick, and Davis are similarly concerned with the receiver end of the communications chain.

Their small study indicates that decoders have a tendency to exaggerate the message actually transmitted. The remaining articles deal with the manner in which these messages are received by the audience and the subsequent effects on its beliefs and behavior.

Reprinted from The Process and Effects of Mass Communication *(Urbana: University of Illinois Press, 1955), pp. 3–10, 13–17. Used by permission of publisher.*

How Communication Works

WILBUR SCHRAMM

THE PROCESS

IT WILL be easier to see how mass communication works if we first look at the communication process in general.

Communication comes from the Latin *communis*, common. When we communicate we are trying to establish a "commonness" with someone. That is, we are trying to share information, an idea, or an attitude. At this moment I am trying to communicate to you the idea that the essence of communication is getting the receiver and the sender "tuned" together for a particular message. At this same moment, someone somewhere is excitedly phoning the fire department that the house is on fire. Somewhere else a young man in a parked automobile is trying to convey the understanding that he is moon-eyed because he loves the young lady. Somewhere else a newspaper is trying to persuade its readers to believe as it does about the Republican Party. All these are forms of communication, and the process in each case is essentially the same.

Communication always requires at least three elements—the source, the message, and the destination. A *source* may be an individual (speaking, writing, drawing, gesturing) or a communication organization (like a newspaper, publishing house, television station or motion picture studio). The *message* may be in the form of ink on paper, sound waves in the air, impulses in an electric current, a wave of the hand, a flag in the air, or any other signal capable of being interpreted meaningfully. The *destination* may be an *individual* listening, watching, or reading; or a member of a *group*, such

as a discussion group, a lecture audience, a football crowd, or a mob; or an individual member of the particular group we call the *mass audience*, such as the reader of a newspaper or a viewer of television.

Now what happens when the source tries to build up this "commonness" with his intended receiver? First, the source encodes his message. That is, he takes the information or feeling he wants to share and puts it into a form that can be transmitted. The "pictures in our heads" can't be transmitted until they are coded. When they are coded into spoken words, they can be transmitted easily and effectively, but they can't travel very far unless radio carries them. If they are coded into written words, they go more slowly than spoken words, but they go farther and last longer. Indeed, some messages long out-live their senders—the *Iliad*, for instance; the Gettysburg address; Chartres cathedral. Once coded and sent, a message is quite free of its sender, and what it does is beyond the power of the sender to change. Every writer feels a sense of helplessness when he finally commits his story or his poem to print; you doubtless feel the same way when you mail an important letter. Will it reach the right person? Will he understand it as you intend him to? Will he respond as you want him to? For in order to complete the act of communication the message must be decoded. And there is good reason, as we shall see, for the sender to wonder whether his receiver will really be in tune with him, whether the message will be interpreted without distortion, whether the "picture in the head" of the receiver will bear any resemblance to that in the head of the sender.

We are talking about something very like a radio or telephone circuit. In fact, it is perfectly possible to draw a picture of the human communication system that way:

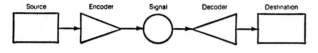

Figure 1-1.

Substitute "microphone" for encoder, and "earphone" for decoder and you are talking about electronic communication. Consider that the "source" and "encoder" are one person, "decoder" and "destination" are another, and the signal is language, and you are talking about human communication.

Now it is perfectly possible by looking at those diagrams to predict how such a system will work. For one thing, such a system can be no stronger than its weakest link. In engineering terms, there may be filtering or distortion at any stage. In human terms, if the source does not have adequate or clear information; if the message is not encoded fully, accurately, effectively in transmittible signs; if these are not transmitted fast enough and accurately enough, despite interference and competition, to the desired receiver; if the message is not decoded in a pattern that corresponds to the encoding; and finally, if the destination is unable to handle the decoded message so as to produce the desired response—then, obviously, the system is working at less than top efficiency. When we realize that *all* these steps must be accomplished with relatively high efficiency if any communication is to be successful, the everyday act of explaining something to a stranger, or writing a letter, seems a minor miracle.

A system like this will have a maximum capacity for handling information and this will depend on the separate capacities of each unit on the chain— for example, the capacity of the channel (how fast can one talk?) or the capacity of the encoder (can your student understand something explained

quickly?). If the coding is good (for example, no unnecessary words) the capacity of the channel can be approached, but it can never be exceeded. You can readily see that one of the great skills of communication will lie in knowing how near capacity to operate a channel.

This is partly determined for us by the nature of the language. English, like every other language, has its sequences of words and sounds governed by certain probabilities. If it were organized so that no set of probabilities governed the likelihood that certain words would follow certain other words (for example, that a noun would follow an adjective, or that "States" or "Nations" would follow "United") then we would have nonsense. As a matter of fact, we can calculate the relative amount of freedom open to us in writing any language. For English, the freedom is about 50 per cent. (Incidentally, this is about the required amount of freedom to enable us to construct interesting crossword puzzles. Shannon has estimated that if we had about 70 per cent freedom, we could construct three-dimensional crossword puzzles. If we had only 20 per cent, crossword puzzle making would not be worth while.)

So much for language *redundancy*, as communication theorists call it, meaning the percentage of the message which is not open to free choice. But there is also the communicator's redundancy, and this is an important aspect of constructing a message. For if we think our audience may have a hard time understanding the message, we can deliberately introduce more redundancy; we can repeat (just as the radio operator on a ship may send "SOS" over and over again to make sure it is heard and decoded), or we can give examples and analogies. In other words, we always have to choose between transmitting more information in a given time, or transmitting less and repeating more in the hope of being better understood. And as you know, it is often a delicate choice, because too slow a rate will bore an audience, whereas too fast a rate may confuse them.

Perhaps the most important thing about such a

system is one we have been talking about all too glibly—the fact that receiver and sender must be in tune. This is clear enough in the case of a radio transmitter and receiver, but somewhat more complicated when it means that a human receiver must be able to understand a human sender.

Let us redraw our diagram in very simple form, like this:

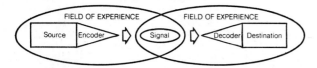

Figure 1-2.

Think of those circles as the accumulated experience of the two individuals trying to communicate. The source can encode, and the destination can decode, only in terms of the experience each has had. If we have never learned any Russian, we can neither code nor decode in that language. If an African tribesman has never seen or heard of an airplane, he can only decode the sight of a plane in terms of whatever experience he has had. The plane may seem to him to be a bird, and the aviator a god borne on wings. If the circles have a large area in common, then communication is easy. If the circles do not meet—if there has been no common experience—then communication is impossible. If the circles have only a small area in common—that is, if the experiences of source and destination have been strikingly unlike—then it is going to be very difficult to get an intended meaning across from one to the other. This is the difficulty we face when a non-science-trained person tries to read Einstein, or when we try to communicate with another culture much different from ours.

The source, then, tries to encode in such a way as to make it easy for the destination to tune in the message—to relate it to parts of his experience which are much like those of the source. What does he have to work with?

Messages are made up of signs. A sign is a signal that stands for something in experience. The word "dog" is a sign that stands for our generalized experience with dogs. The word would be meaningless to a person who came from a dog-less island and had never read of or heard of a dog. But most of us have learned that word by association, just as we learn most signs. Someone called our attention to an animal, and said "dog." When we learned the word, it produced in us much the same response as the object it stood for. That is, when we heard "dog" we could recall the appearance of dogs, their sound, their feel, perhaps their smell. But there is an important difference between the sign and the object: the sign always represents the object at a reduced level of cues. By this we mean simply that the sign will not call forth all the responses that the object itself will call forth. This sign "dog," for example, will probably not call forth in us the same wariness or attention a strange dog might attract if it wandered into our presence. This is the price we pay for portability in language. We have a sign system that we can use in place of the less portable originals (for example, Margaret Mitchell could re-create the burning of Atlanta in a novel, and a photograph could transport world-wide the appearance of a bursting atomic bomb), but our sign system is merely a kind of shorthand. The coder has to be able to write the shorthand, the decoder to read it. And no two persons have learned exactly the same system. For example, a person who has known only Arctic huskies will not have learned exactly the same meaning for the shorthand sign "dog" as will a person who comes from a city where he has known only pekes and poms.

We have come now to a point where we need to tinker a little more with our diagram of the communication process. It is obvious that each person in the communication process is both an encoder and a decoder. He receives and transmits. He must be able to write readable shorthand, and to read other people's shorthand. Therefore, it is possible to describe either sender or receiver in a human system thus:

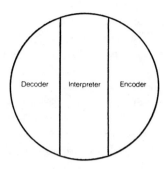

Figure 1-3.

What happens when a signal comes to you? Remember that it comes in the form of a sign. If you have learned the sign, you have learned certain responses with it. We can call these mediatory responses, because they mediate what happens to the message in your nervous system. These responses are the *meaning* the sign has for you. They are learned from experience, as we said, but they are affected by the state of your organism at the moment. For example, if you are hungry, a picture of a steak may not arouse exactly the same response in you as when you are overfed.

But subject to these effects, the mediatory responses will then determine what you do about the sign. For you have learned other sets of reactions connected to the mediatory responses. A sign that means a certain thing to you will start certain other processes in your nerves and muscles. A sign that means "fire," for example, will certainly trigger off some activity in you. A sign that means you are in danger may start the process in your nerves and muscles that makes you say "help!" In other words, the meaning that results from your decoding of a sign will start you *en*coding. Exactly *what* you encode will depend on your choice of the responses available in the situation and connected with the meaning.

Whether this encoding actually results in some overt communication or action depends partly on the barriers in the way. You may think it better to keep silent. And if an action does occur, the nature

of the action will also depend on the avenues for action available to you and the barriers in your way. The code of your group may not sanction the action you want to take. The meaning of a sign may make you want to hit the person who has said it, but he may be too big, or you may be in the wrong social situation. You may merely ignore him, or "look murder at him," or say something nasty about him to someone else.

But whatever the exact result, this is the process in which you are constantly engaged. You are constantly decoding signs from your environment, interpreting these signs, and encoding something as a result. In fact, it is misleading to think of the communication process as starting somewhere and ending somewhere. It is really endless. We are little switchboard centers handling and rerouting the great endless current of communication. We can accurately think of communication as passing through us—changed, to be sure, by our interpretations, our habits, our abilities and capabilities, but the input still being reflected in the output.

We need now to add another element to our description of the communication process. Consider what happens in a conversation between two people. One is constantly communicating back to the other, thus:

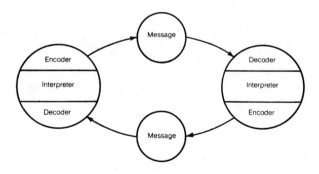

Figure 1-4.

The return process is called *feedback*, and plays a very important part in communication because it tells us how our messages are being interpreted. Does the hearer say, "Yes, yes, that's right," as we try to persuade him? Does he nod his head in agreement? Does a puzzled frown appear on his forehead? Does he look away as though he were losing interest? All these are feedback. So is a letter to the editor of a newspaper, protesting an editorial. So is an answer to a letter. So is the applause of a lecture audience. An experienced communicator is attentive to feedback, and constantly modifies his messages in light of what he observes in or hears from his audience.

At least one other example of feedback, also, is familiar to all of us. We get feedback from our own messages. That is, we hear our own voices and can correct mispronounciations. We see the words we have written on paper, and can correct misspellings or change the style. When we do that, here is what is happening:

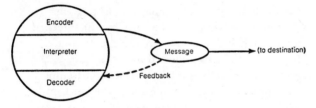

Figure 1-5.

It is clear that in any kind of communication we rarely send out messages in a single channel, and this is the final element we must add to our account of the communication process. When you speak to me, the sound waves from your voice are the primary message. But there are others: the expression on your face, your gestures, the relation of a given message to past messages. Even the primary message conveys information on several levels. It gives me words to decode. It emphasizes certain words above others. It presents the words in a pattern of intonation and timing which contribute to the total meaning. The quality of your voice (deep, high, shrill, rasping, rich, thin, loud, soft) itself carries information about you and what you are saying.

This multiple channel situation exists even in printed mass communication, where the channels are perhaps most restricted. Meaning is conveyed, not only by the words in a news item, but also by the size of the headline, the position on the page and the page in the paper, the association with pictures, the use of boldface and other typographical devices. All these tell us something about the item. Thus we can visualize the typical channel of communication, not as a simple telegraph circuit, in which current does or does not flow, but rather as a sort of coaxial cable in which many signals flow in parallel from source toward the destination.

These parallel relationships are complex, but you can see their general pattern. A communicator can emphasize a point by adding as many parallel messages as he feels are deserved. If he is communicating by speaking, he can stress a word, pause just before it, say it with a rising inflection, gesture while he says it, look earnestly at his audience. Or he can keep all the signals parallel—except *one*. He can speak solemnly, but wink, as Lowell Thomas sometimes does. He can stress a word in a way that makes it mean something else—for example, "That's a *fine* job you did!" And by so doing he conveys secondary meanings of sarcasm or humor or doubt.

The same thing can be done with printed prose, with broadcast, with television or films. The secondary channels of the sight-sound media are especially rich. I am reminded of a skillful but deadly job done entirely with secondary channels on a certain political candidate. A sidewalk interview program was filmed to run in local theaters. Ostensibly it was a completely impartial program. An equal number of followers of each candidate were interviewed—first, one who favored Candidate A, then one who favored Candidate B, and so on. They were asked exactly the same questions, and said about the same things, although on opposite sides of the political fence, of course. But there was one interesting difference. Whereas the supporters of Candidate A were ordinary folks, not outstandingly attractive or impressive, the followers of Candidate B who were chosen to be interviewed invariably had something slightly wrong with them. They looked wild-eyed, or they stuttered, or they wore unpressed suits. The extra meaning was communicated. Need I say which candidate won?

But this is the process by which communication works, whether it is mass communication, or communication in a group, or communication between individuals. . . .

HOW COMMUNICATION HAS AN EFFECT

The chief reason we study this process is to learn something about how it achieves effects. We want to know what a given kind of communication does to people. Given a certain message content, we should like to be able to predict what effect that content will have on its receivers.

Every time we insert an advertisement in a newspaper, put up a sign, explain something to a class, scold a child, write a letter, or put our political candidate on radio or television, we are making a prediction about the effect communication will have. I am predicting now that what I am writing will help you understand the common everyday miracle of communication. Perhaps I am wrong. Certainly many political parties have been proved wrong in their predictions about the effects of their candidates' radio speeches. Some ads sell goods; others don't. Some class teaching "goes over"; some does not. For it is apparent to you, from what you have read so far, that there is no such thing as a simple and easily predictable relationship between message content and effect.

Nevertheless, it is possible to describe simply what might be called the conditions of success in communication—by which we mean the conditions that must be fulfilled if the message is to arouse its intended response. Let us set them down here briefly, and then talk about them:

1. The message must be so designed and delivered as to gain the attention of the intended destination.

2. The message must employ signs which refer to experience common to source and destination, so as to "get the meaning across."

3. The message must arouse personality needs in the destination and suggest some ways to meet those needs.

4. The message must suggest a way to meet those needs which is appropriate to the group situation in which the destination finds himself at the time when he is moved to make the desired response.

You can see, by looking at these requirements, why the expert communicator usually begins by finding out as much as he can about his intended destination, and why "know your audience" is the first rule of practical mass communication. For it is important to know the right timing for a message, the kind of language one must use to be understood, the attitudes and values one must appeal to in order to be effective, and the group standards in which the desired action will have to take place. This is relatively easy in face-to-face communication, more difficult in mass communication. In either case, it is necessary.

Let us talk about these four requirements.

1. *The message must be so designed and delivered as to gain the attention of the intended destination.* This is not so easy as it sounds. For one thing, the message must be made available. There will be no communication if we don't talk loud enough to be heard, or if our letter is not delivered, or if we smile at the right person when she isn't looking. And even if the message is available, it may not be selected. Each of us has available far more communication than we can possibly accept or decode. We therefore scan our environment in much the same way as we scan newspaper headlines or read a table of contents. We choose messages according to our impression of their general characteristics—whether they fit our needs and interests. We choose usually on the basis of an impression we get from one cue in the message, which may be a headline, a name in a radio news story, a picture, a patch of color, or a sound. If that cue does not appeal to us, we may never open our senses to the message. In different situations, of course, we choose differently among these cues. For example, if you are speaking to me at a time when I am relaxed and unbusy, or when I am waiting for the kind of message you have (for instance, that my friends have come to take me

HOW COMMUNICATION WORKS
Wilbur Schramm

fishing), then you are more likely to get good attention than if you address me when noise blots out what you say, or when all my attention is given to some competing message, or when I am too sleepy to pay attention, or when I am thinking about something else and have simply "tuned out." (How many times have you finished speaking and realized that your intended receiver had simply not heard a word you said?) The designing of a message for attention, then, involves timing, and placing, and equipping it with cues which will appeal to the receiver's interests.

2. *The message must employ signs which refer to experience common to both source and destination, in order to "get the meaning across."* We have already talked about this problem of getting the receiver in tune with the sender. Let us add now that as our experience with environment grows, we tend to classify and catalog experience in terms of how it relates to other experience and to our needs and interests. As we grow older that catalog system grows harder and firmer. It tends to reject messages that do not fit its structure, or distort them so that they do fit. It will reject Einstein, perhaps, because it feels it can't understand him. If an airplane is a completely new experience, but a bird is not, it may, as we have said, interpret the plane as a large, noisy bird. If it is Republican it will tend to reject Democratic radio speeches or to recall only the parts that can be made into pro-Republican arguments; this is one of the things we have found out about voting behavior. Therefore, in designing a message we have to be sure not only that we speak the "same language" as the receiver, and that we don't "write over his head," but also that we don't conflict too directly with the way he sees and catalogs the world. There are some circumstances, true, in which it works well to conflict directly, but for the most part these are the circumstances in which our understandings and attitudes are not yet firm or fixed, and they are relatively few and far between. In communicating, as in flying an airplane, the rule is that when a stiff wind is blowing, one doesn't land cross-wind unless he has to.

3. *The message must arouse personality needs in the destination and suggest some way to meet those needs.* We take action because of need and toward goals. In certain simple situations, the action response is quite automatic. When our nerves signal "pain-heat-finger" we jerk our fingers back from the hot pan. When our optic nerve signals "red traffic light" we stop the car. In more complicated situations we usually have more freedom of choice, and we choose the action which, in the given situation, will come closest to meeting our needs or goals. The first requisite of an effective message, therefore (as every advertising man knows), is that it relate itself to one of our personality needs—the needs for security, status, belongingness, understanding, freedom from constraint, love, freedom from anxiety, and so forth. It must arouse a drive. It must make the individual feel a need or a tension which he can satisfy by action. Then the message can try to control the resulting action by suggesting what action to take. Thus an advertisement usually tells you to buy, what, and where. Propaganda to enemy troops usually suggests a specific action, such as surrender, subversion, or malingering. The suggested action, of course, is not always the one taken. If an easier, cheaper, or otherwise more acceptable action leading to the same goal is seen, that will probably be selected instead. For instance, it may be that the receiver is not the kind of person to take vigorous action, even though that seems called for. The person's values may inhibit him from doing what is suggested. Or his group role and membership may control what action he takes, and it is this control we must talk about now.

4. *The message must suggest a way to meet those needs which is appropriate to the group situation in which the destination finds himself at the time when he is moved to make the desired response.* We live in groups. We get our first education in the primary group of our family. We learn most of our standards and values from groups. We learn roles in groups, because those roles give us the most orderly and satisfying routine of life. We make most of our communication responses in groups. And if communication is

going to bring about change in our behavior, the first place we look for approval of this new behavior is to the group. We are scarcely aware of the great importance our group involvements have for us, or of the loyalties we develop toward our several groups and institutions, until our place in the group or the group itself is threatened. But yet if our groups do not sanction the response we are inclined to make to communication, then we are very unlikely to make it. On the other hand, if our group strongly approves of a certain kind of action, that is the one we are likely to select out of several otherwise even choices.

You can see how this works in practical situations. The Jewish culture does not approve the eating of pork; the Indian culture does not approve the slaughter of cows, and the eating of beef. Therefore, it is highly unlikely that even the most eloquent advertisement will persuade an orthodox Jewish family to go contrary to their group sanctions, and buy pork; or an orthodox Hindu family, to buy beef. Or take the very simple communication situation of a young man and a young woman in a parked automobile. The young man communicates the idea that he wants a kiss. There isn't much likelihood of his not gaining attention for that communication or of its not being understood. But how the young woman responds will depend on a number of factors, partly individual, partly group. Does she want to be kissed at that moment? Does she want to be kissed by that young man? Is the situation at the moment—a moon, soft music from the radio, a convertible?—conducive to the response the young man wants? But then, how about the group customs under which the girl lives? If this is a first date, is it "done" to kiss a boy on a first date? Is petting condoned in the case of a girl her age? What has she learned from her parents and her friends about these things? Of course, she won't knowingly have a little debate with herself such as we have suggested here, but all these elements and more will enter into the decision as to whether she tilts up her chin or says, "No, Jerry. Let's go home."

There are two things we can say with confidence about predicting communication effects. One is that a message is much more likely to succeed if it fits the patterns of understandings, attitudes, values and goals that a receiver has; or at least if it starts with this pattern and tries to reshape it slightly. Communication research men call this latter process "canalizing," meaning that the sender provides a channel to direct the already existing motives in the receiver. Advertising men and propagandists say it more bluntly; they say that a communicator must "start where the audience is." You can see why this is. Our personalities—our patterns of habits, attitudes, drives, values, and so forth—grow very slowly but firmly. I have elsewhere compared the process to the slow, sure, ponderous growth of a stalagmite on a cave floor. The stalagmite builds up from the calcareous residue of the water dripping on it from the cave roof. Each drop leaves only a tiny residue, and it is very seldom that we can detect the residue of any single drop, or that any single drop will make a fundamental change in the shape or appearance of the stalagmite. Yet together all these drops do build the stalagmite, and over the years it changes considerably in size and somewhat in shape. This is the way our environment drips into us, drop by drop, each drop leaving a little residue, each tending to follow the existing pattern. This personality pattern we are talking about is, of course, an active thing—not passive, like the stalagmite—but still the similarity is there. When we introduce one drop of communication into a person where millions of drops have already fallen and left their residue, we can hardly expect to reshape the personality fundamentally by that one drop. If we are communicating to a child, it is easier, because the situation is not so firmly fixed. If we are communicating in an area where ideas and values are not yet determined—if our drop of communication falls where not many have fallen before—then we may be able to see a change as a result of our communication.

But in general we must admit that the best thing we can do is to build on what already exists. If we

HOW COMMUNICATION WORKS
Wilbur Schramm

take advantage of the existing pattern of understanding, drives, and attitudes to gain acceptance for our message, then we may hope to divert the pattern slightly in the direction we want to move it. Let's go back to elections again for an example. It is very hard to change the minds of convinced Republicans or Democrats through communication, or even to get them to listen to the arguments of the opposing party. On the other hand, it is possible to start with a Republican or Democratic viewpoint and slightly modify the existing party viewpoints in one way or other. If this process goes on for long enough, it may even be possible to get confirmed party-men to reverse their voting pattern. This is what the Republicans were trying to do in the 1952 election by stressing "the mess in Washington," "time for a change," "the mistakes in Korea," and "the threat of Communism," and apparently they were successful in getting some ordinarily Democratic votes. But in 1952, as in every campaign, the real objectives of the campaigning were the new voters and the undecided voters.

The second thing we can say with confidence about communication effects is that they are resultants of a number of forces, of which the communicator can really control only one. The sender, that is, can shape his message and can decide when and where to introduce it. But the message is only one of at least four important elements that determine what response occurs. The other three are the situation in which the communication is received and in which the response, if any, must occur; the personality state of the receiver; and his group relationships and standards. This is why it is so dangerous to try to predict exactly what will be the effect of any message except the simplest one in the simplest situation.

Let us take an example. In Korea, in the first year of the war there, I was interviewing a North Korean prisoner of war who had recently surrendered with one of our surrender leaflets on his person. It looked like an open and shut case: the man had picked up the leaflet, thought it over, and decided to surrender. But I was interviewing him anyway, trying to see just how the leaflet had its effect. This is what he told me.

He said that when he picked up the leaflet, it actually made him fight harder. It rather irritated him, and he didn't like the idea of having to surrender. He wasn't exactly a warlike man; he had been a clerk, and was quiet and rather slow; but the message actually aroused a lot of aggression in him. Then the situation deteriorated. His division was hit hard and thrown back, and he lost contact with the command post. He had no food, except what he could find in the fields, and little ammunition. What was left of his company was isolated by itself in a rocky valley. Even then, he said, the morale was good, and there was no talk of surrendering. As a matter of fact, he said, the others would have shot him if he had tried to surrender. But then a couple of our planes spotted them, shot up their hideout, and dropped some napalm. When it was over, he found himself alone, a half mile from where he had been, with half his jacket burned off, and no sign of any of his company. A couple of hours later some of our tanks came along. And only then did the leaflet have an effect. He remembered it had told him to surrender with his hands up, and he did so.

In other words, the communication had no effect (even had an opposite effect from the one intended) so long as the situation, the personality, and the group norms were not favorable. When the situation deteriorated, the group influence was removed, and the personality aggression was burned up, then finally the message had an effect. I tell you this story hoping it will teach you what it taught me: that it is dangerous to assume any simple and direct relationship between a message and its effect without knowing all the other elements in the process.

Reprinted from Journalism Quarterly *(Fall, 1950), pp. 383–90. Used by permission.*

The "Gate Keeper": A Case Study in the Selection of News

DAVID MANNING WHITE

IT WAS the late Kurt Lewin, truly one of the great social scientists of our time, who applied the term "gate keeper" to a phenomenon which is of considerable importance to students of mass communications. In his last article,[1] before his untimely death, Dr. Lewin pointed out that the traveling of a news item through certain communication channels was dependent on the fact that certain areas within the channels functioned as "gates." Carrying the analogy further, Lewin said that gate sections are governed either by impartial rules or by "gate keepers," and in the latter case an individual or group is "in power" for making the decision between "in" or "out."

To understand the functioning of the "gate," Lewin said, was equivalent to understanding the factors which determine the decisions of the "gate keepers," and he rightly suggested that the first diagnostic task is the finding of the actual "gate keepers."

The purpose of this study is to examine closely the way one of the "gate keepers" in the complex channels of communication operates his "gate."

Wilbur Schramm made an observation central to this whole study when he wrote that "no aspect of communication is so impressive as the enormous number of choices and discards which have to be made between the formation of the symbol in the mind of the communicator, and the appearance of a related symbol in the mind of the receiver."[2] To illustrate this in terms of a news story let us consider, for example, a Senate hearing on a proposed bill for federal aid to education.

At the hearing there will be reporters from the various press associations, Washington correspondents of large newspapers which maintain staffs in the capital, as well as reporters for local newspapers. All of these form the first "gate" in the process of communication. They have to make the initial judgment as to whether a story is "important" or not. One has only to read the Washington stories from two newspapers whose general editorial attitudes differ widely on such an issue as federal aid to education to realize from the beginning of the process the "gate keepers" are playing an important role. The appearance of the story in the Chicago *Tribune* and the Chicago *Sun-Times* might well show some differences in treatment. It is apparent that even the actual physical event of the Senate hearing (which we might call the *criterion event*) is reported by two reporters in two different perceptual frameworks and that the two men bring to the "story" different sets of experience, attitudes and expectations.

Thus a story is transmitted from one "gate keeper" after another in the chain of communications. From reporter to rewrite man, through bureau chief to "state" file editors at various press association offices, the process of choosing and discarding is continuously taking place. And finally we come to our last "gate keeper," the one to whom we turn for the purpose of our case study. This is the man who is usually known as the wire editor on the non-metropolitan newspaper. He has charge of the selection of national and international news which will appear on the

THE "GATE KEEPER": A CASE STUDY IN THE SELECTION OF NEWS
David Manning White

front and "jump" pages of his newspaper, and usually he makes up these pages.

Our "gate keeper" is a man in his middle 40s, who after approximately 25 years' experience as a journalist (both as reporter and copy-editor) is now the wire editor of a morning newspaper of approximately 30,000 circulation in a highly industrialized mid-west city of 100,000. It is his job to select from the avalanche of wire copy daily provided by the Associated Press, United Press and International News Service what 30,000 families will read on the front page of their morning newspapers. He also copy-edits and writes the headlines for these stories. His job is similar to that which newspapermen throughout the country hold in hundreds of non-metropolitan newspapers.[3] And in many respects he is the most important "gate keeper" of all, for if he rejects a story the work of all those who preceded him in reporting and transmitting the story is negated. It is understood, of course, that the story could have "ended" (insofar as its subsequent transmission is concerned) at any of the previous "gates." But assuming the story has progressed through all the "gates," it is obvious that this wire editor is faced with an extremely complicated set of decisions to make regarding the limited number of stories he can use.

Our purpose in this study was to determine some preliminary ideas as to why this particular wire editor selected or rejected the news stories filed by the three press associations (and transmitted by the "gate keeper" above him in Chicago) and thereby gain some diagnostic notions about the general role of the "gate keeper" in the areas of mass communications.

To this end we received the full cooperation of "Mr. Gates," the above-mentioned wire-editor. The problem of finding out what Mr. Gates selected from the mass of incoming wire copy was not difficult, for it appeared on the front and "jump" pages of his newspaper each morning. Actually, we were far more concerned with the copy that did not get into the paper. So for the week of February 6 through 13, 1949, Mr. Gates saved every piece of wire copy that came to his desk. Instead of throwing the dispatch into the waste basket once he had decided not to use it, he put it into a large box next to his desk. Then at one o'clock when his pages were made up and his night's work through, Mr. Gates went through every piece of copy in the "reject" box and wrote on it the reason why he had initially rejected it, assuming that he could recall the reason. In the cases where no ascertainable reason had occurred to him he made no notations on the copy. Although this meant that Mr. Gates had to spend between an hour-and-a-half and two hours each night at this rather tedious phase of the project, he was perfectly willing to do this throughout the entire week.

When Mr. Gates had turned over the raw material of his choices for the week period, we tried to analyze his performance in terms of

---

TABLE 1

Amounts of Press Association News Mr. Gates Received and Used During Seven-Day Period

Category	Wire Copy Received Col. In.*	% of Total	Wire Copy Used Col. In.*	% of Total
Crime	527	4.4%	41	3.2%
Disaster	405	3.4	44	3.4
Political				
State	565	4.7	88	6.8
National	1722	14.5	205	15.8
Human Interest	4171	35.0	301	23.2
International				
Political	1804	15.1	176	13.6
Economic	405	3.4	59	4.5
War	480	4.0	72	5.6
Labor	650	5.5	71	5.5
National				
Farm	301	2.5	78	6.0
Economic	294	2.5	43	3.3
Education	381	3.2	56	4.3
Science	205	1.7	63	4.9
Total	11,910	99.9	1297	100.1

*Counting five lines of wire copy as one column inch.

THE "GATE KEEPER": A CASE STUDY IN THE SELECTION OF NEWS
David Manning White

certain basic questions which presented themselves. These questions are applicable not only to this particular "gate keeper," but with modifications to all of the "gate keepers" in the communications process. Thus, after determining what wire news came in during the week in terms of total column inches and categories, we measured the amount of wire news that appeared in the papers for that period.

Assuming that five lines of wire copy are equivalent to a column inch in a newspaper, Mr. Gates received approximately 12,400 inches of press association news from the AP, UP and INS during the week. Of this he used 1297 column inches of wire news, or about *one-tenth*, in the seven issues we

measured. Table 1 shows a breakdown by categories of the wire news received and used during the week.

It is only when we study the reasons given by Mr. Gates for rejecting almost nine-tenths of the wire copy (in his search for the one-tenth for which he has space) that we begin to understand how highly subjective, how reliant upon value-judgments based on the "gate keeper's" own set of experiences, attitudes and expectations the communication of "news" really is. In this particular case the 56 wordings given may be divided into two main categories: (1) rejecting the incident as worthy of being reported, and (2) selecting from many reports of the same event. (See Table 2.)

TABLE 2

Reasons for Rejection of Press Association News Given by Mr. Gates During Seven-Day Period

Reason		Number of Times Given
Rejecting incident as worthy of reporting		423
Not interesting (61); no interest here (43)	104	
Dull writing (51); too vague (26); drags too much (3)	80	
No good (31); slop (18); B. S. (18)	67	
Too much already on subject (54); used up (4); passed—dragging out*; too much of this; goes on all the time; dying out	62	
Trivial (29); would ignore (21); no need for this; wasted space; not too important; not too hot; not too worthy	55	
Never use this (16); never use (7)	23	
Propaganda (16); he's too red; sour grapes	18	
Wouldn't use (11); don't care for suicide stories; too suggestive; out of good taste	14	
Selecting from reports of the same event		910
Would use if space (221); no space (168); good—if space (154); late—used up (61); too late—no space (34); no space—used other press service; would use partially if space.	640	
Passed for later story (61); waiting for later information (48); waiting on this (33); waiting for this to hatch (17); would let drop a day or two (11); outcome will be used—not this; waiting for later day progress	172	
Too far away (24); out of area (16)	40	
Too regional (36)	36	
Used another press service: Better story (11); shorter (6); this is late; lead more interesting; meatier	20	
Bannered yesterday	1	
I missed this one	1	

*In this and other cases where no number follows the reason, that reason was given only once.

THE "GATE KEEPER": A CASE STUDY IN THE SELECTION OF NEWS
David Manning White

Thus we find him rejecting one piece of wire copy with the notation, "He's too Red." Another story is categorically marked "Never use this." The story dealt with the Townsend Plan, and because this "gate keeper" feels that the merits of the Townsend Plan are highly dubious, the chances of wire news about the Plan appearing in the paper are negligible. Eighteen pieces of copy were marked "B. S."; 16 were marked "Propaganda." One interesting notation on a story said "Don't care for suicides." Thus we see that many of the reasons which Mr. Gates gives for the rejection of the stories fall into the category of highly subjective value-judgments.

The second category gives us an important clue as to the difficulty of making choices of one piece of copy over another. No less than 168 times, Mr. Gates makes the notation "No space." In short, the story (in his eyes) has merit and interest, he has no "personal" objections to it, but space is at a premium. It is significant to observe that the later in the evening the stories came in, the higher was the proportion of the "no space" or "would use" type of notation. As the evening progresses the wire editor's pages become more and more filled up. A story that has a good chance of getting on the front page at 7:30 or 8 o'clock in the evening may not be worth the precious remaining space at 11 o'clock. The notation "Would use" is made 221 times, and a similar one "Good—if space" is made 154 times. Other reasons which fall into the mechanical category are "Used INS—shorter" or "Used UP—this is late." Even in this category, though, we find subjective value-judgments such as "Used AP—better story" or "Used INS—lead more interesting."

Now that we have some preliminary knowledge of the manner in which Mr. Gates selects or rejects news for his front and "jump" pages, it might be interesting to examine his performance for a specific day. In Table 3 the amount of type of news which appeared on the front and "jump" pages edited by Gates for February 9, 1949 is presented. Table 4 shows the total number of

TABLE 3

Column Inches Devoted to Content Categories in February 9, 1949, Issue*

Category		Front Page and Jump
Local		3.50
Crime		5.00
Disaster		9.75
Political		41.25
Local	9.75	
State	19.50	
National	12.00	
Human Interest		43.75**
International		23.00
Political	11.50	
Economic	11.50	
War	.—	
National		24.25
Labor	19.25	
Farm	.—	
Economic	5.00	
Education		.—
Science		6.00***

*Banner not included.
**About one-half of this amount were Cardinal Mindzenty stories, which, because of the human appeal, were classed as Human Interest.
***Three column picture not included.

dispatches (classified as to type of story) received but not used.

During this particular week the Cardinal Mindzenty trial was receiving wide play from newspapers throughout the land and the press associations were filing many stories covering all phases of the case. So in making a comparison of the dispatches received and the stories which appeared it should not be surprising to note that Human Interest news was used most. Yet even in his treatment of the Mindzenty case, Mr. Gates used highly subjective reasons in his selection of stories. Particularly interesting in this connection is his remark on an Associated Press story which he rejected with the comment *Would pass, propaganda itself.*" The story dealt with a statement by Samuel Cardinal Stritch, who said, "It is very unfortunate that our news agencies are

THE "GATE KEEPER": A CASE STUDY IN THE SELECTION OF NEWS

David Manning White

TABLE 4

Number of Pieces of Press Association Releases Received But Not Used, February 9, 1949

Category	Received before Front Page Was Made Up	Received after Front Page Was Made Up	Total Received For Day
Local	3		3
Crime	32	1	33
Disaster	15		15
Political			22
Local	1	2	
State	10	2	
National	6	1	
Human Interest	65	14	79
International			46
Political	19	5	
Economic	9	1	
War	10	2	
National			37
Farm	2		
Labor	13	1	
Economic	17	4	
Education	3	2	5
Science	5	2	7
Total for Day	210	37	247

not giving their sources of information in their day-by-day reports on the trial of Cardinal Mindzenty. It should be made clear that restrictions have been made on the few American correspondents who have been present at the trial." It is obvious that Mr. Gates resented the implication by Cardinal Stritch that the press associates were not doing all they could to tell the Mindzenty story. The comment which Mr. Gates put on a United Press story dealing with Cardinal Stritch's statement, "No space — pure propaganda," illustrates his sensitivity on this particular point. And when the story came to his attention for the third time that evening as an International News Service dispatch he again rejected it, this time with the statement "Would pass." Perhaps his feeling of anger against the story had cooled by this time, but Mr. Gates still considered the story worthless.

Political news enjoyed the second largest play. Here we begin to have an indication of preference, as political news ranked only fifth in the "dispatches received" department. Political news seems to be a favorite with Mr. Gates, for even if we subtract the almost ten inches given to a local political story it ranks second in play.

While a total of 33 crime stories was received, only five column inches of crime appeared on the front and "jump" pages of Mr. Gates' paper. The obvious conclusion is that crime news, as such, does not appeal to this wire editor. But it should be noted that no "big" crime stories broke that day.

As one examines the whole week's performance of Mr. Gates, as manifested in the stories he chose, certain broad patterns become apparent. What do we know, for example, about the kinds of

THE "GATE KEEPER": A CASE STUDY IN THE SELECTION OF NEWS
David Manning White

stories that he selected in preference to others from the same category? What tests of subject matter and way-of-writing did Mr Gates seem to apply? In almost every case where he had some choice between competing press association stories Mr. Gates preferred the "conservative." I use this expression not only in terms of its political connotations, but also in terms of the style of writing. Sensationalism and insinuation seemed to be avoided consistently.

As to the way-of-writing that he preferred, Mr. Gates showed an obvious dislike for stories that had too many figures and statistics. In almost every case where one news agency supplied a story filled with figures and statistics and the competing agency's story was an easier going, more interpretative than statistical type of story, the latter appeared in the paper. An indication of his standards for writing is seen in Table 1, where 26 stories were rejected as being "too vague," 51 rejected for "dull writing" and 61 for being "not interesting."

Another question that should be considered in this study (and subsequent ones) is: Does the category really enter into the choice? That is, does the wire editor try to choose a certain amount of crime news, human interest news, etc.? Are there some other divisions of subject matter or form which he chooses in this manner, such as a certain number of one-paragraph stories?

Insofar as this "gate keeper" is representative of wire editors as a whole, it does not appear that there is any conscious choice of news by categories. During this particular week under examination an emphasis on the Human Interest type of story was seen mainly because of the large news appeal of the Cardinal Mindzenty story. It would be most interesting and valuable to ascertain how a wire editor determines what one issue or type of story is "the" story of the week. Many times that decision is made by "gate keepers" above him, or by "gate keepers" in competing media. Can a wire editor refuse to play a story "up" when his counterpart in the local radio station is playing it

to the hilt? Likewise, can a wire editor play down a story when he sees competing papers from nearby metropolitan areas coming into his city and playing up the story? These factors undoubtedly have something to do in determining the wire editor's opinion as to what he should give the reading public the next morning. This brings up the rather obvious conclusion that theoretically all of the wire editor's standards of taste should refer back to an audience who must be served and pleased.

Subsequent to Mr. Gates' participation in the project to determine the "reasons" for selecting or rejecting wire stories during a week, he was asked to consider at length four questions which we submitted. His answers to these questions tell us much about Mr. Gates, particularly if they are collated with the "spot" reasons which came under the pressure of a working night.

Question 1: "Does the category of news affect your choice of news stories?"

The category of news definitely enters into my choice of stories. A crime story will carry a warning as will an accident story. Human interest stories provoke sympathy and could set examples of conduct. Economic news is informative for some readers and over the heads of others. I make no attempt to hold a rigid balance in these selections but do strive for variety. The category of news suggests groups that should be interested in a particular story, that is, teachers, laborers, professional people, etc. Wire service reports can't keep a strictly balanced diet and for this reason we could not attempt it. For the most part, the same thinking applies in the selection of shorts, although some are admittedly filler material.

Question 2: "Do you feel that you have any prejudices which may affect your choice of news stories?"

I nave few prejudices, built-in or otherwise, and there is little I can do about them. I dislike Truman's economics, daylight saving time and warm beer, but I go ahead using stories on them and other matters if I feel there is

THE "GATE KEEPER": A CASE STUDY IN THE SELECTION OF NEWS

David Manning White

nothing more important to give space to. I am also prejudiced against a publicity-seeking minority with headquarters in Rome, and I don't help them a lot. As far as preferences are concerned, I go for human interest stories in a big way. My other preferences are for stories well-wrapped up and tailored to suit our needs (or ones slanted to conform to our editorial policies).

Question 3: "What is your concept of the audience for whom you select stories and what sort of person do you conceive the average person to be?"

Our readers are looked upon as people with average intelligence and with a variety of interests and abilities. I am aware of the fact we have readers with above average intelligence (there are four colleges in our area) and that there are many with far less education. Anyway, I see them as human and with some common interests. I believe they are all entitled to news that pleases them (stories involving their thinking and activity) and news that informs them of what is going on in the world.

Question 4: "Do you have specific tests of subject matter or way of writing that help you determine the selection of any particular news story?"

The only tests of subject matter or way of writing I am aware of when making a selecton involve clarity, conciseness and angle. I mentioned earlier that certain stories are selected for their warning, moral or lesson, but I am not inclined to list these reasons as any test of subject matter or way of writing. The clarity trio is almost a constant yardstick in judging a story, especially when I often have three of a kind, AP, UP and INS. Length of a story is another factor (or test) in a selection. The

long winded one is usually discarded unless it can be cut to fill satisfactorily.

It is a well known fact in individual psychology that people tend to perceive as true only those happenings which fit into their own beliefs concerning what is likely to happen. It begins to appear (if Mr. Gates is a fair representative of his class) that in his position as "gate keeper" the newspaper editor sees to it (even though he may never be consciously aware of it) that the community shall hear as a fact only those events which the newsman, as the representative of his culture, believes to be true.

This is the case study of one "gate keeper," but one, who like several hundred of his fellow "gate keepers," plays a most important role as the terminal "gate" in the complex process of communication. Through studying his overt reasons for rejecting news stories from the press associations we see how highly subjective, how based on the "gate keeper's" own set of experiences, attitudes and expectations the communication of "news" really is.

[1]Lewin, Kurt, *Channels of Group Life*, Human Relations, Vol. 1, No. 2, p. 145.

[2]Schramm, Wilbur, *Mass Communications*, U. of Illinois Press, Urbana, 1949, p. 289.

[3]By far the majority of the approximately 1,780 daily newspapers in this country are in the smaller cities not on the main trunk wires of the press associations. Their reliance on the single wire "state" operations which emanate from the larger cities thus places great responsibility in the hands of the wire editor. [This was written in 1950; the national wire is now more common. – Ed.]

Reprinted from Journalism Quarterly *(Autumn, 1969), pp. 492–98. Used by permission. Author's note: William Erbe designed and administered the survey and made these data available. The author cautions, however, that any errors in the analysis or interpretation are solely his own.*

Social Relations and the Two-Step Flow: A Defense of the Tradition

IRVING L. ALLEN

KATZ and Lazarsfeld described the roles of social relations in the diffusion of ideas from the mass media to the terminal audience and generalized that social relations function in two ways to diffuse communications through social structures: first, as channels through which communications are relayed, and second, as sources of social pressures and social support that influence the decision-making process.[1] These social sanctions also determine, in part, selective exposure, perception and retention of media content and thus the amount and quality of personal influence and information that is transmitted. The two-step flow hypothesis states that messages are received from the mass media by opinion leaders who pass them along by word-of-mouth to the terminal audience.

It is not completely clear to what extent the hypothesis was intended to describe, or did in fact describe, the diffusion of substantial news content or information, as distinct from interpersonal influence concerning the news. It is widely assumed, however, that the hypothesis also described the flow of mass-communicated information through networks of interpersonal relations.[2] There is little, if any, convincing empirical evidence of a substantial effect of ordinary interpersonal relations on the diffusion of mass-communicated information, except in the special case of the diffusion of major news events. The news-diffusion studies, however, do not answer the question of how many persons who first heard the news by word-of-mouth would have heard the news subsequently upon their first

casual or customary contact with the ubiquitous mass media and therefore cannot be considered the test of how person-to-person diffusion of information generally supplements direct exposure to the media.[3] It remains problematic whether usual day-to-day information about public affairs is collected from, or as a result of, ordinary social encounters, once persons have had an opportunity to select or reject communications from the mass media.

Several studies have associated public-affairs information levels with "gregariousness" and "social participation," which were variously defined, and suggested that the socially active are, therefore, more likely to receive or to pass on information by word-of-mouth.[4] But gregariousness in all its forms is associated with a host of other variables, many of which also are associated with information levels. Few, if any, researchers have elaborated an analysis far enough to determine if social participation is *independently* related to the possession of information. One result of this ambiguous situation is that this traditional interpretation of the two-step flow hypothesis has been called into question.

Among the various reformulations and reinterpretations of the two-step flow hypothesis, two are pertinent to this problem. First, the importance of opinion leaders—those persons who admit on surveys that they frequently give or are sought out for their opinions—in the diffusion of substantive message content has been questioned. Troldahl and Van Dam, for example, concluded that such opinion

SOCIAL RELATIONS AND THE TWO-STEP FLOW: A DEFENSE OF THE TRADITION

Irving L. Allen

leaders "may not be doing much to pass mass-media content and influence to persons in the less active segment of the population," and that opinion givers and opinion askers are about equally informed and talk mainly to one another.[5] A more fluid concept of the opinion leader in the information diffusion process as anyone who is asked to, or chooses to, transmit a communication by word-of-mouth, regardless of whether it is informational or influential in content and regardless of the consistency of this role from one social encounter to another, would likely reestablish the function of the role.[6]

Second, the amount and type of message content diffused by opinion leaders has been questioned. Deutschmann and Danielson suggested that only a small proportion of message content is passed on by word-of-mouth, and that it is likely to be supplementary rather than initial informaton about the news.[7] Troldahl sharpened this criticism by suggesting that there is a one-step flow of *initial* information and a two-step flow of influence on beliefs, attitudes and behavior.[8] However, the bits and items of information that constitute an individual's collection of information is the cumulative product of supplementary, as well as initial, information. As certain events, issues and series of related events and issues receive sustained coverage by the mass media, an easy distinction between initial and supplementary information becomes more difficult.

Other evidence, however, supports the traditional interpretation of the hypothesis. A 1963 Roper poll, for example reported that 4% of adult Americans said they got *most* of their news by talking to other people.[9] It is likely that a much larger proportion gets *some* of their news by talking to others and that supplementary information on specific news events is also relayed over and above this amount. Robinson moreover reported that well over half of the respondents in a Detroit survey gave a personal source, as opposed to media sources, as most important in their knowledge of a current foreign-affairs issue, and concludes that "the evidence definitely points

to the crucial importance of face-to-face communication *and* printed media in spreading and interpreting foreign-affairs information."[10]

Information about public affairs flows freely in interpersonal encounters insofar as individuals associate in informal groups with others having similar interests and goals, especially friends, acquaintances and intimates.[11] Sustained, familiar, and easy interaction among persons with similar interests is conducive to the exchange of mass media experiences, ideas and information, especially when the message or information is perceived to be relevant or of interest to another. Lane noted that most informal political discussions are about politically important people and concrete elements of politics rather than issues and the more abstract elements of politics, and usually about domestic rather than foreign affairs.[12] An increment of awareness of bits of information and news inevitably results from these many everyday encounters and conversations about mass-media experiences. Information flow, therefore, may be facilitated or retarded by people being more or less in contact with the networks of interpersonal relations. The amount of social participation denotes the number of opportunities for information to flow between persons. The general hypothesis of this study is that some increment, probably a relatively small one, of general public-affairs information possessed by individuals is directly and independently related to the amount of interpersonal relations.

The hypothesis assumes a causal model in which social relations are antecedent to an increment of information. The flow of information and exertion of social pressures are not observed directly or reconstructed *ex post facto* from respondents' testimonies but are *attributed* to various social encounters. The amount of social relations is an *indirect* index to the likelihood that the relaying and sanctioning functions are operating to increase the level of information in the theoretically proposed ways. One could argue, on the contrary, that persons gather virtually all their information from

SOCIAL RELATIONS AND THE TWO-STEP FLOW: A DEFENSE OF THE TRADITION
Irving L. Allen

the mass media and that the interest in public affairs reflected by this media monitoring leads to higher rates of social interaction in order to gratify interests in public affairs.[13] The preponderance of theory and research evidence, however, weighs toward the antecedence of social relations to the possession of information.

THE RESEARCH DESIGN

The data are from sample surveys conducted in 1962 in three small Iowa urban communities.[14] The three communities differed widely in socioeconomic characteristics and were chosen to represent roughly a variety of small towns and cities in the Midwest. Households were selected in a two-stage stratified-area probability sample design. One adult respondent was randomly chosen in each sample household. The three samples were combined (N=625) and analyzed in the aggregate.

Respondents were administered a simple name-awareness test on which they could express knowledge and assessments of nine persons and seven organizations that were contemporaneously prominent and, in most cases, controversial in national political affairs. Each name-item had been featured recently and prominently in the mass media, including the most frequently read local newspaper. Sixty-six or over 10% of the respondents professed some "knowledge" of a bogus item, the name of a fictitious organization included in the list. These respondents were dropped from the sample because there was considerable evidence that as a group they gave invalid responses to other items as well, and their exclusion does not bias the representativeness of the remaining samples (N=559).[15]

The dependent variable is an unweighted 12-item test or index of one kind of public-affairs information.[16] The items had been in the news long enough for the audience to have ample opportunity to attend, select and retain information from either relations or the mass media or both. Each of the 559 respondents was assigned

an integral score on a range of scores from zero to twelve, according to the number of items of which he was aware. The Spearman-Brown split-half reliability coefficient is .82. In the data presentation, the test is divided into tertiles of "low" (0 to 4 items), "medium" (5 to 7 items), and "high" (8 to 12 items).

The independent variable, the number and variety of informal encounters, is measured by asking respondents a series of questions about how often they made visits and how often they received visits for each of four categories of ordinary social contacts: relatives and in-laws, neighbors, work and business friends and a residual category of "other friends" not included in the first three. Each of the eight questions contains six categories of visiting frequency to which scores were assigned ranging from zero for "never" to five points for "once a day or more." Each of the eight questions was equally weighted and the scores summed into a single index by which each respondent was scored on a range from 0 to 40 points. In the data presentation, the distribution of scores is divided into tertiles of "low" (13 or fewer points), "medium" (14 to 19 points), and "high" (20 or more points).

THE FINDINGS

At the outset one must take account of the fact that some persons *never* discuss public affairs in their social encounters and are therefore irrelevant to the hypothesis. Respondents were asked, "*When you get together with your friends would you say that you discuss public issues like government regulations of business, labor unions, taxes, farm programs or foreign affairs?*" The respondents' replies were recorded in terms of "frequently," "occasionally" or "never." If informal social contacts are causally related to the possession of information, then the number of social relations will be directly related to information possessed for persons who discuss public affairs but not for persons who never discuss public affairs.

Table 1 shows that an association of $d=.110$ (not presented in tabular form) between informal social relations and the possession of information is slightly increased in the contingents to $d=.134$ for respondents who discuss public affairs and decreased to $d=.076$ for respondents who never discuss them.[17] This negative association is small and probably spurious, although the small number of cases in the subset precludes a conclusive analysis. It cannot be concluded that the number of informal relations is independently related to the possession of information for respondents who discuss public affairs until controls are introduced for other variables that may be associated both with the possession of information *and* informal relations.

Individual predispositions to be well-informed about public affairs, which are related to personal and background traits, are indexed by combining three variables—education, occupational prestige and sex—into a single index of an individual's predisposition to possess information, regardless of why or how he collects the information. In a separate analysis of these data, each of the three traits in this index was observed to be indepen-

dently related to the information test, roughly to the extent they are weighted in this index. Each respondent received from one to five points corresponding to five levels of education (eighth grade or less, some high school, high school graduate, some college, college graduate).

In addition, each male respondent received one point, and each respondent received one additional point if he or she was in the top tertile on the prestige of their present occupation, according to Duncan's "NORC Transform" score.[18] The distribution of scores ranging from one to seven points is divided into tertiles of "low" (1–2 points), "medium" (3–4 points), and "high" (5–7 points). The tertiles are divided such that, if a respondent receives the two additional points both for being male and for having high prestige, it will place him one and only one tertile higher than that in which he would have fallen had he received points only for education. One additional point may or may not place a respondent in a higher adjacent tertile, depending on the points received for education.

Although not presented in tabular form, the direct association between scores on the seven-point Index of Individual Predisposition to Possess Information and the tertiles of test scores is very high ($d=.587$) and perfectly monotonic. The validity of the index, therefore, is demonstrable as indirect correlative validity, and assumed to be sufficiently valid and discriminating to adequately control for individuals' predispositions to collect public-affairs information from any source. If the observed association between informal relations and the possession of information obtains only because both are related to demographic traits of respondents, of which three of the most important are controlled by the predisposition index, then any "spurious" association would be substantially reduced or disappear in the partial contingency tables. The association between the Informal Social Relations Index and the Predisposition Index for those who discuss public affairs is $d=-.026$ in a 3×3 table, calculated

TABLE 1

Public Affairs Information
by Informal Social Relations and Discussion

Informal Relations	Possession of Information (%)			N
	High	Medium	Low	
	Discusses Public Affairs			
High	40	42	18	(132)
Medium	38	43	19	(165)
Low	24	44	32	(117)
	$d=.134, p=.002$[a]			
	Does Not Discuss Public Affairs			
High	10	27	63	(30)
Medium	7	36	58	(45)
Low	15	32	53	(47)
	$d=-.076, p=.337$[b]			

[a]One-tailed test
[b]Two-tailed test

SOCIAL RELATIONS AND THE TWO-STEP FLOW: A DEFENSE OF THE TRADITION
Irving L. Allen

with informal relations as the dependent variable. Therefore, virtually none of any relationship observed between informal relations and the possession of information among discussants can be accounted for by their mutual relationship to the predisposition index.

Table 2 shows that the direct associations between informal relations and the possession of information remain strong, perhaps even increasing a little at the medium and low predisposition levels, where they are also perfectly monotonic. The coefficient of $d=.074$ at the high predisposition level is reduced relative to the coefficient of $d=.134$ in Table 1, but this may reflect nothing more than the acute attenuation of cell frequencies at the low-information level. But even here a 13% point difference remains between respondents with high information. The persistence of the associations in the partial contingents moreover is not an artifact of grouping scores on the predisposition index for a similar pattern of differences obtains among respondents with each of the seven scores on the predisposition index.

DISCUSSION

The data give encouraging support to the traditional interpretation of the two-step flow hypothesis that social relations are directly and independently related to an increment of public-affairs information possessed by individuals. The causal direction in the proposed model is not completely verified by these cross-sectional data. Theory and previous research strongly suggest the antecedence of social relations to information but do not preclude the possibility of some mutual determination between social encounters and gathering information. One of the motivations of individuals to monitor public-affairs content in

TABLE 2

Public-Affairs Information Among Discussants by Informal Social Relations and Individual Predisposition to Possess Information

Informal Relations	Possession of Information (%)			N
	High	Medium	Low	
	High Predisposition			
High	57	38	5	(42)
Medium	63	35	2	(57)
Low	44	54	2	(41)
	$d = .074, p = .154^a$			
	Medium Predisposition			
High	37	47	15	(60)
Medium	26	51	22	(76)
Low	17	47	36	(36)
	$d = .176, p = .005^a$			
	Low Predisposition			
High	23	37	40	(30)
Medium	19	38	44	(32)
Low	10	31	59	(39)
	$d = .157, p = .039^a$			

[a]One-tailed test

the media is to gather information that is socially useful. If one is inclined to seek out social encounters to use this information in interaction with others, then it is also likely that these encounters, in turn, create pressures to gather new and additional information from the media. In either image of the process, social relations, whether they result from or result in gathering information from the media, are an important and little understood factor in the news diffusion process. In any event, these data suggest that it is yet too soon to abandon the idea that opinion leadership and interpersonal relations are important in the two-step flow of news.

[1]Elihu Katz and Paul F. Lazarsfeld, *Personal Influence* (Glencoe, Illnois: The Free Press, 1955), Part I, esp. pp. 44–5, 82–3; and Elihu Katz, "The Two-Step Flow of Communication: An Up-to-Date Report on an Hypothesis," *Public Opinion Quarterly*, 21:61–78 (Spring 1957).

[2]See, e.g., Ralph O. Nafziger, Warren C. Engstrom and Malcolm S. McLean, Jr., "The Mass Media and an Informed Public," *Public Opinion Quarterly*, 15:105–14 (Spring 1951); Gordon K. Hirabayshi and M. Fathalla El Khatib, "Communication and Political Awareness in the

Villages of Egypt," *Public Opinion Quarterly*, 22:357–63 (Fall 1958); Alfred O. Hero, *Opinion Leaders in American Communities: Studies in Citizen Participation in International Relations*, Vol. VI (Boston: World Peace Foundation, 1959), p. 27 *et passim;* James E. Brinton and L. Norman McKown, "Effects of Newspaper Reading on Knowledge and Attitudes," *Journalism Quarterly*, 38:187–95 (Spring 1961).

[3]Irving L. Allen and J. David Colfax, "The Diffusion of News of LBJ's March 31 Announcement," *Journalism Quarterly*, 45:321–4 (Summer 1968).

[4]E.g., Nafziger, Engstrom and McLean, *op. cit.;* Brinton and McKown, *op. cit.;* and Harold Mendelsohn, "Broadcast vs. Personal Sources of Information in Emergent Public Crises: The Presidential Assassination," *Journal of Broadcasting*, 8:147–56 (Spring 1964).

[5]Verling C. Troldahl and Robert Van Dam, "Face-to-Face Communication About Major Topics in the News," *Public Opinion Quarterly*, 29:626–34 (Winter 1965–66).

[6]Everett M. Rogers, *Diffusion of Innovation* (New York: Free Press, 1962), pp. 226–7, argues that opinion leadership is a continuous variable, most people having at least some of the quality.

[7]Paul J. Deutschmann and Wayne A. Danielson, "Diffusion of Knowledge of the Major News Story," *Journalism Quarterly*, 37:345–55 (Summer 1960); and Paul J. Deutschmann, "Viewing, Conversation and Voting Intentions," in Sidney Kraus, ed., *The Great Debates* (Bloomington, Ind.: Indiana University Press, 1962), pp. 232–52.

[8]Verling C. Troldahl, "A Field Test of a Modified 'Two-Step Flow of Communication' Model," *Public Opinion Quarterly*, 30:609–23 (Winter 1966–67).

[9]Elmo Roper and Associates, *New Trends in the Public's Measure of Television and Other Media* (New York: Television Information Office, 1964), p. 2. Martin Kreisberg, "Dark Areas of Ignorance," in Lester Markel, ed., *Public Opinion and Foreign Policy* (New York: Harper and Bros., 1949), pp. 49–64, cites unidentified national poll data, presumably from the 1940s, that show about 10% of respondents said they got most of their public-affairs information by word-of-mouth.

[10]John P. Robinson, *Public Information About World Affairs* (Ann Arbor, Mich.: Survey Research Center, 1967), p. 39.

[11]Hero, *op. cit.*, p. 58, e.g., cites some 15 studies of value homophily in social groups and political discussion. Robinson, *op. cit.*, p. 38, e.g., notes that persons are more apt to discuss foreign affairs with co-workers, friends, neighbors and immediate family.

[12]Robert E. Lane, *Political Life* (New York: Free Press, 1959), pp. 86–92.

[13]Troldahl and Van Dam, *op. cit.;* Brinton and McKown, *op. cit.*, also suggest that knowledge about a public issue leads to greater primary group interaction about the subject; Robinson, *op. cit.*, pp. 35–8, discusses the difficulty of determining the direction of cause between political conversation and the possession of information.

[14]For a complete description of the sample design and estimates of its representativeness, see William Erbe, "Social Involvement and Political Activity: A Replication and Elaboration," *American Sociological Review*, 29:198–215 (April 1964).

[15]For an analysis of this procedure, full question wording, and a detailed description of how the questions were asked, see: Irving L. Allen, "Detecting Respondents Who Fake and Confuse Information About Question Areas on Surveys," *Journal of Applied Psychology*, 50:523–8 (December 1966).

[16]The items are: Senator Barry Goldwater, Dr. Martin Luther King, Senator Joseph McCarthy, Walter Reuther, Dr. Fred Schwarz, Robert Welch, American Civil Liberties Union, Americans for Democratic Action, Congress of Racial Equality, John Birch Society, National Association for the Advancement of Colored People, United World Federalists.

[17]Robert H. Somers, "A New Asymmetric Measure of Association for Ordinal Variables," *American Sociological Review*, 27:799–811 (December 1962).

[18]Albert J. Reiss, Jr., *Occupations and Social Status* (New York: Free Press of Glencoe, 1961), Ch. 6 and Appendix B. Unemployed, disabled and retired persons are given the scores for their last full-time occupations. Housewives are given the score for the occupation of the family breadwinner, as are other dependents.

Reprinted from Journalism Quarterly *(Summer, 1963) pp. 339–42. Used by permission of publisher.*

Message Exaggeration by the Receiver

MAX WALES, GALEN RARICK AND HAL DAVIS

MUCH discussion—and some research—has been devoted to the problem of message distortion by the communicator, whether he be newspaper reporter, advertising copywriter or broadcaster. Interest has often centered on distortion in the direction of exaggeration or sensationalism, and discussion usually revolves around the biases, predispositions and motives of the communicator.

As early as 1870, a critic wrote that

If we could only have newspapers which simply professed to give the news, we might begin to get some glimmering of truth from them. . . . Distortion of perspective is what some of the gentlemen who conduct the daily press seem to consider their charter of success.[1]

As recently as the spring of 1962, Greenberg and Tannenbaum reported that communicator accuracy is related to cognitive stress. That is, when journalism students had to write stories about a faculty committee report, they made more errors when the report was contrary to their biases and predispositions than they did when the report supported them. Furthermore, substantively the message distortion was in the direction of supporting the communicators.[2]

These are but two of the many articles in which communicator errors have been examined or decried. On the other hand, relatively few observers have concerned themselves with the possibility that the message may tend to suffer the same sort of distortion from the receiver as it does from the sender, i.e., the extent and direction of distortion are dependent upon the needs and predispositions of the communicator *and* the audience.

In other words, most of the literature on the mass media dealing with message exaggeration has examined *what encoders do to messages*; it is suggested here that it should also be helpful to examine *what decoders do to messages*.

Hastorf and Cantril,[3] Cooper and Jahoda,[4] and Hyman and Sheatsley[5] have provided data on perceptual processes which support this line of reasoning. Hastorf and Cantril found that college students err in their perception of a football game film in keeping with their biases. Cooper and Jahoda found that prejudiced people tend to react to anti-prejudice propaganda by evading the message or by distorting it to make it consistent with, or at least not contrary to, their prejudices. Hyman and Sheatsley present evidence in support of their theory that a person's perception and memory of messages are often dependent upon his wishes, motives and attitudes.

It follows then that in developing a hypothesis concerning message distortion by the receiver, one should take into account the needs and predispositions of audiences.

Studies of media consumption have frequently shown that a majority of people spend a great deal of time attending to fantasy or escapist fare. Klapper devoted an entire chapter to the research literature concerning audience consumption of and addiction to what he called "escapism."[6]

The evidence presented by Klapper seems to indicate that one reason people attend to such fare is that they need drama and excitement in their lives. That is, they are predisposed to "escape" from dull, frustrating circumstances. Consequently, it is postulated in this study that one way a person can fulfill the need for drama and excitement is to invest the messages he receives with these qualities by exaggerating their contents.

An experiment was designed to test the following hypothesis:

More people will exaggerate messages they receive than will minimize them.

If this hypothesis is correct, it means that when people recall the content of a communication, they will not make random errors. Instead, more of them will commit errors in the direction of exaggeration than in the direction of minimization. It should be noted that this hypothesis does not predict the frequency or proportion of error but rather stipulates the predominant direction of error when it occurs.

THE STUDY DESIGN

The subjects for this experiment were 39 sophomores and juniors attending a college course in advertising. An "after-only" design was utilized.

At the beginning of the experiment, the subjects were told merely that it was desired that they read "some copy." The regular instructor was absent, and the students had been informed that they were to have a guest lecturer. Each student was given three pieces of copy to read, with the order of presentation being systematically rotated. One piece of copy was a fictitious news release from the university concerning recommendations that the academic requirements of the university be made more rigorous. The other two were advertisements. one for a certain type of kitchen sink and the other for an Oriental air line.

Immediately after the subjects had read the copy, they were given a multiple-choice recall test.

There were five questions about the news release, two about the kitchen sink advertisement, and one about the air line copy. The ordering of these questions was systematically rotated.

Three possible answers were provided for each question, and the subject was asked to check the correct ones. Only one answer for each question was correct, i.e., repeated a statement of fact from the copy. Another answer exaggerated that statement, and the third minimized it. The order of these three possible answers was also systematically rotated throughout the test. Following are the findings and analysis of the study.

FINDINGS AND ANALYSIS

On the recall test, 254 (81.7%) of the 311 responses were correct. (One of the 39 subjects failed to respond to one of the eight items.) Since this test was given immediately after the copy was read, it is not surprising that so many of the answers were correct. However, the question remains: When errors were made, did more subjects exaggerate the message than minimized it?

A net score was computed for each subject by assigning a value of 0 to a correct answer, -1 to a minimization, and $+1$ to an exaggeration. This meant that the possible range of net scores was from -8 to $+8$. However, the obtained range, as shown in Table 1, was from -2 to $+4$.

Out of a total of 57 error responses, 41 were exaggerations and only 16 were minimizations. Nine of the subjects made no errors, and four others made "balanced" errors, i.e., there was a minimization for each exaggeration. Consequently,

TABLE 1

*Distribution of Net Scores on
Recall Test for All 39 Subjects*

Net Score	-2	-1	0	$+1$	$+2$	$+3$	$+4$
Frequency	2	4	13	11	6	2	1

MESSAGE EXAGGERATION BY THE RECEIVER
Max Wales, Galen Rarick and Hal Davis

26 subjects committed net error in one direction or the other. Of these, 20 had net positive (exaggeration) scores, while only six had net negative (minimization) scores.

If people are as likely to minimize as they are to exaggerate messages received, one would predict that out of the 26 scores which were not zero, 13 would be positive and 13 would be negative. Consequently, a Chi Square test was employed to see if the obtained distribution differed significantly from these figures. Obviously, the difference is in the hypothesized direction. The Chi Square value of 7.54 with one degree of freedom is significant at well beyond the .005 level by one-tailed test. So, in this experiment, when the receivers of messages made recall errors, there was a highly significant tendency to exaggerate rather than minimize.

There is the possibility, of course, that the bias was in the measuring instrument rather than in the subjects. That is, it may be that the multiple-choice items were such that it was "psychologically easier" to make an exaggerated error than it was to make a minimized one. However, the experimenters attempted to make the two error alternatives to each item equally plausible, and it is suggested that a more definite answer to this question could be provided by added research.

Such studies might also attempt to answer such questions as: What are the educational, sociological, and psychological characteristics of people who tend to exaggerate messages received as contrasted to those of people who tend to minimize them and to those of people who tend to do neither? Are people more likely to exaggerate messages which are threatening or potentially punishing to them than they are to exaggerate messages which are comforting or potentially rewarding? Can certain techniques of writing be employed to reduce greatly the exaggeration of a message by a receiver?

SUMMARY AND DISCUSSION

Many observers have concerned themselves with the problem of exaggeration by the communicator. Relatively few, however, have considered the matter of exaggeration of a message by the receiver. There is much research evidence that many people are addicted to escapist or fantasy fare in the mass media. Consequently, it was inferred that there is a need for drama or excitement, and that this predisposition will tend to lead to exaggeration when errors are made in the recall of a message.

In this experiment, students read some copy and were immediately given a multiple-choice recall test. It was found that significantly more students committed error in the direction of exaggeration than committed error in the direction of minimization even though most of the responses were correct.

It can be inferred from the results of this experiment that in the communication process, the tendency toward exaggeration may be as much a part of decoding as it is a part of encoding. It is suggested that research might make it possible to specify the type of personality most likely to exaggerate and the conditions under which exaggeration is most likely to occur.

For the journalist, there are implications that in addition to trying to avoid making exaggerated statements, he should attempt to find ways of writing that will reduce exaggeration by his audience. Perhaps the skillful use of intentional redundancy would be one of them.

[1] A. G. Sedgewick, editorial in the *Nation*, 10:54 (Jan. 27, 1870).

[2] Bradley S. Greenberg and Persy H. Tannenbaum, "Communicator Performance under Cognitive Stress," *Journalism Quarterly*, 39:169–78 (Spring 1962).

[3] A. H. Hastorf and H. Cantril, "They Saw a Game: A Case Study," *Journal of Abnormal and Social Psychology*, 49:129–34 (1954).

[4] E. Cooper and M. Jahoda, "The Evasion of Propaganda," *Journal of Psychology*, 23:15–25 (1947).

[5] H. Hyman and P. Sheatsley, "Some Reasons Why Information Campaigns Fail," *Public Opinion Quarterly*, 11:412–23 (1947).

[6] J. T. Klapper, *The Effects of Mass Communication* (Glencoe, Ill.: Free Press, 1960), Chapter VII, "The Effects of Escapist Media Material."

B. Persuasion, Opinion Change, and Audience Behavior

Gerhart D. Wiebe attempts to explain why the audience for thoroughly banal television programs continues to be very large. He claims that such programs serve the psychological needs of the audience. They do not make intellectually demanding appeals to change nor present unfamiliar subject matter which would require concentrated attention. The programs are geared to existing values and sentiments. The effect of such media content, however, is probably less innocuous than Wiebe infers. There is considerable hidden bias, albeit of a conservative nature, in even the tamest program.[1]

The article by Leon Festinger which follows deals with the relation of opinion to behavior change. He notes that researchers often have been overly concerned with opinion change and have merely assumed that behavior is consequently modified. Actual results when both opinion and behavior change are measured are less convincing. It appears that a new opinion may often be insufficiently internalized to modify behavior—thus the espousal of "correct" opinions on race may not change the actual behavior of whites towards minority peoples. Subsequent behavior may in fact be more strongly opposed to the new opinion than before. Thus Festinger discusses an experiment in which sub-

jects were given instructions on dental hygiene. Those who received the strongest appeal showed the largest change in attitude, but the smallest change in subsequent behavior. (This in part validates what Wiebe claimed about media appeal.) The strong message may be convincing at first, but rejected later if it doesn't fit the recipient's existing cognitive structure. In addition, notes Festinger, a new attitude must be reinforced by external support.

Carter, Pyszka, and Guerrero give evidence that runs contrary to Wiebe's findings and Festinger's seminal theory of cognitive dissonance. They found in three experiments that their subjects did not necessarily avoid material that was contrary to their existing attitudes, even if such selective exposure was normally the case. Audiences, it seems, will seek out adverse information to help formulate new values: We are not dealing with a mass of entirely closed minds. Bauer's article, which concludes this section, investigates this autonomy of audiences. He summarizes many of the findings of communications research and detects two conflicting traditions: a *social model*, which stresses media exploitation of a preponderantly passive audience, and a *scientific model*, which emphasized the transactional nature of communications. He prefers the latter view of communications. Evidence for the former, however, can scarcely be denied. A synthesis of the two, then, should be on the agenda for future research.

[1]For an extremely well documented exposé of such bias see Robert Cirino, *Don't Blame the People* (Los Angeles: Diversity Press, 1971). Part of this work is reprinted in the next section of this volume.

...om Public Opinion Quarterly *(Winter, 1969–70), pp. 523–36. Used by permission of the publisher and author. Originally ...as an address to the World Assembly of the World Association for Christian Broadcasting, in Oslo, Norway on June 25, 1968.*

Two Psychological Factors in Media Audience Behavior

GERHART D. WIEBE

THE central problem to be explored here may be introduced by reference to two familiar observations. The first is that the broadcast media in the United States generate huge audiences. The second is that the content of very popular programs is generally regarded by members of the intellectual community as being light, superficial, trivial, and in some cases as vulgar and even harmful.

The remarkable size of audiences is regularly documented by the rating services and the caliber of program content is deplored by critics and scholars with comparable regularity. The situation is documented and deplored, but it is not explained. The implications for broadcasters devoted to education, the arts, and religion are serious and perplexing. The media seem to open the way to intellectual, cultural, and spiritual refinement for the millions, but the millions elude the proferred enlightenment, preferring the light, the superficial, the trivial.

The problem is familiar. So also are several prescriptions for improvement. It is frequently argued that tastes would improve if people were exposed to programs of high caliber. But the record is discouraging. Consider, for example, the thirty-three-year history of Sunday afternoon concerts by the New York Philharmonic Orchestra, broadcast by the Columbia Broadcasting System without commercial sponsorship for twenty-six of those years. Despite vigorous promotion, good scheduling (unchanged for twenty-one years), and excellent production, the audience for these concerts did not grow. Its ratings remained with some variation at about a third of those of numerous standard mystery series, and at about a fifth of the highly popular Lux Radio Theater.[1] Similar examples can be cited in other content areas. Opportunity is apparently not enough.

A second proposal for improving public taste would restrict program offerings to those of high intellectual, moral, and artistic quality long enough so that discriminating taste would become habitual and normative among the public. This proposal, like the earlier one, finds rough going in the light of experience. After some twenty years of programing in England controlled exclusively by the BBC, commercial television came to England. With it came some commercial entertainment series from the United States, which, according to the present hypothesis, should have found a very chilly reception. But that isn't what happened.

The appetite in the United States for light diversion on television is perhaps most thoroughly and authoritatively documented in the late Dr. Steiner's book, *The People Look at Television.*[2] Steiner studied both attitudes toward television and actual viewing behavior by the same respondents. He found that people verbalized more interest in fine programing than their viewing behavior demonstrated. And further, that although the college-educated respondents differed in their program preferences from the less well educated in expected ways, the degree of difference was remarkably small. For example, during periods when cultural entertainment, public information programing, and light entertainment were available simultaneously,

TWO PSYCHOLOGICAL FACTORS IN MEDIA AUDIENCE BEHAVIOR
Gerhart D. Wiebe

a random distribution of the audience would allocate 33 per cent to each type. Since light entertainment predominates most of the time, the simultaneous availability of the three types constitutes an unusual opportunity for those with discriminating tastes to tune in quality programing. Still, even during these periods, 40 per cent of those with college education chose the light entertainment.[3] In general, there is a tendency toward an inverse relationship between audience size and the cultural merit of the program.

This observation is not peculiar to our time, nor is it confined to the broadcast media. With the introduction of printing in the fifteenth century the treasures of learning, which had been severely restricted, were henceforth as widely available as was literacy. But instead of grasping the unprecedented opportunities for enlightenment, the public appetite, from the first decades of printing, was for the light, the superficial, the trivial, and, it may be added, for the scandalous, the seditious, and the vulgar. H. A. Innis, in *Empire and Communication*, quotes a seventeenth-century observation that "The slightest pamphlet is nowadays more vendable than the works of learnedest men." This pattern even appears to predate the press. A pre-Gutenberg example appears in the relation of the wandering minstrel to the public appetite for messages that offend refined taste. This intriguing parallel remains to be explored on another occasion.

I share the concern expressed by musicians, scientists, poets, dramatists, educators, theologians, critics, and others of comparable intellectual accomplishment regarding the apparent waste, the loss of opportunity in the general preference for the trivial. But I no longer believe that what has been called "the taste for trash" can be remedied by scholarly exhortation or by attempting to teach good taste or by increasing budgets for cultural offerings. The best hope of understanding this problem, and then perhaps improving the situation in some degree, seems to lie in posing the hypothesis that the observed behavior has positive psychological utility. If this utility can be identified, then

perhaps, as we learn to understand it, we may be able to apply this knowledge to the general welfare. In pursuing this path I have set aside observations on the media themselves, turning instead to patterns of psychological and sociological behavior that are independent of the media.

Two such patterns will be discussed. Both appear to contribute to a theoretical understanding of media audience behavior. The first is the apparent difficulty with which humans acquire *the concept of the other*. By "the other," I mean simply a person other than oneself.

RELUCTANCE TO COPE WITH OTHER

We begin with findings relating to infant egocentrism. The term egocentrism is used here, not in the pejorative sense of selfishness or conceit, but simply in nonvalued reference to preoccupation with self. The psychologist Piaget has contributed much to our understanding of infant egocentrism. His ingenious experiments indicate that for the infant, when an object at which he is looking is screened from view, it is not just hidden. For the infant, it apparently ceases to exist.[4] A learning process precedes the child's recognition that objects and persons actually occupy space and exist as permanent and substantial entities.

The child's early preoccupation is in the discovery and maintenance of self. His success in this early learning obviously depends on the solicitude of the mother or her substitute, but the relationship is not reciprocal. The human infant levies demands on the outside, and apparently perceives the objects and persons that make up the outside as ephemera among which he seeks need satisfaction – primarily nourishment and comfort. Human young do not mature without elaborate care. The dependence of the maturation process on consistent and solicitous care is dramatically documented in the work of the psychoanalyst Dr. Rene Spitz.[5] I believe, however, that developmental psychologists have tended, until recently, to underemphasize the unilateral, taking orientation of the young child's interaction with the outside.

TWO PSYCHOLOGICAL FACTORS IN MEDIA AUDIENCE BEHAVIOR
Gerhart D. Wiebe

The traditional concept of the mother-child relationship during the first year as one of reciprocal love must be re-examined. Findings suggest that in the normal process of maturation during the first year a child cannot be said to perceive another person as an individual autonomous other. Spitz has recently reported experiments showing that the treasured smiling response, observed at about six months, is elicited equally well by mother or stranger, male or female, old or young, even by a person in a mask so long as the face presented to the baby is animated, and is presented head on.[6]

The critical period of the infant's dependence on solicitous care by a specific individual during the last part of the first year appears to be largely a need for stimulation and nourishment in accustomed ways as the child practices his early and precarious attempts to cope with the insubstantial outside.

Moving along in time, we come to a series of findings on six-year-olds reported by Piaget. He observed and then studied what he called egocentric language among six-year-olds. He divides egocentric speech into three subgroups—repetition, monologue, and collective monologue. The point in common among these three categories is that the speech is not addressed to anyone. Although the presence of others sometimes seems to serve as a general sort of stimulus, the child during egocentric speech apparently does not actually address other persons. He seems rather to "talk past them."

Piaget found that something over a third of the speech of the six-year-olds he studied fell into this category of egocentric language.[7] Thus, even in groups of six-year-olds, where language would seem so obviously to be a tool of interaction, much behavior contradicts this expectation, and consciousness of the other is only inconsistently observed.

More recently the work of Dr. Melvin H. Feffer,[8] proceeding from that of Piaget, indicates that the ability to assume different social perspectives is only gradually developed, that it is correlated with chronological age, and that its measurement, still far from precise, may well turn out to be an important index to psychological maturation.

These findings from developmental psychology document the relatively slow emergence of the concept of *the other* in contrast with the precocious development observed in what might be called the unilateral achievement of self-expression and need gratification.

Such concepts as sharing, mutuality, reciprocal relationships, empathy, service, interaction, all of these positively valued concepts, endlessly stressed in the process of socialization, turn out, on examination, to refer to rather sophisticated, psychologically demanding processes which call for a well-developed sense of *the other*. They are essentially *social* processes which require the surrender or at least the inhibiting of the early deep-seated pattern of egocentrism.

How does this late-developing sense of *the other* relate to media behavior? The relationship seems quite direct when it is recalled that the media, by definition, remove *the other*. The media present printed symbols or sounds or images, but never persons. The media reinstate the opportunity to enjoy the early pattern of taking without deference to the reciprocal needs of the giver. The media offer immediate need gratification without "paying the piper." They provide the sense of experience without the accommodation required in true participation. One may weep or laugh or hate or fear and escape the necessity of acknowledging the physical existence and the reciprocal demands of those others who arouse the emotion. The media allow the audience member to resume the infantile posture observed by Piaget in which, when the stimulus is removed, it ceases to exist. Reality, on the other hand, is beset with people and things that resist, react, encroach, demand. Small wonder, then, if, when people are weary and frustrated and crowded, they embrace the media where people and things are ephemera—as they once were for each of us. It is characteristic of popular media content that it maximizes immediate need gratification, minimizes intellectual effort, and excuses the

TWO PSYCHOLOGICAL FACTORS IN MEDIA AUDIENCE BEHAVIOR
Gerhart D. Wiebe

audience member from acknowledging a substantial other.

But the point appears to have reference to broadcasters as well as to audiences. Broadcasters tend to consider their mission accomplished when their message is released. The sequel is seldom investigated except by commercial broadcasters, who are disciplined by the buying responses of those others out there. Perhaps this deep-seated reluctance to cope with the other influences behavior on both the sending and the receiving sides of the media.

It is often said, that the media bring people into contact with each other. We must be more literal. The media transport only symbols. They do not bring people together. On the contrary, the media stand between people. The media may *invite* subsequent interaction, but they do not and cannot provide it.

This is the first idea that seems to merit careful study. Facility in personal interaction comes late in the developmental sequence. The phenomenon of talking past people rather than with them is familiar. Interpersonal frictions plague adult life. The fact that media messages provide the illusion of interaction together with immunity from *the other* seems to relate a basic psychological factor to media audience behavior.

THREE ASPECTS OF SOCIALIZATION

The second point relates to the process of socialization, and particularly to the individual's resistance to this process.

Socialization has been defined by the Hartleys as "the process by which an individual becomes a member of a given social group."[9] The identity of the "actor" and the "acted-upon" in this process is clear. The group requires; the individual adjusts. But each human being has inherent tendencies, innate patterns, which would direct growth in ways different from those that actually occur if this growth were uninfluenced by the requirements of the group.

It follows that the socializing process does not simply mold inert stuff. It is rather the modifying and changing of a dynamic system, deflecting it from the course it would otherwise follow. Socialization is alteration of forces in motion, and when one alters the direction of forces in motion, he encounters resistance. This resistance to socialization is familiar, but it has received rather little attention from social psychologists except as an inconvenience that must be handled in order to proceed with the essential business of qualifying the individual for group membership.

The typical example of socialization is the parent training the child. The child's changing toward normative behavior is seen as the essential content of socialization. Seen from the child's point of view, however, the process of socialization is a series of defeats and compromises in which what he wants to do must bow to what he is required to do. In a good parent-child relationship, the child's sacrifice is in some degree compensated by praise and other rewards.[10] Even so, however, viewed by the child, the process is coercive. Impulse is inhibited. Spontaneity is modified. The individual must adapt to the group prescription.

It would be remarkable indeed if all of this compromising, substituting, bending, changing, giving up to which the growing human is subjected during socialization did not generate a deep and persistent pattern of counteraction. Behavior that fits this expectation is, of course, familiar. In addition to their outright opposition to prescribed behavior, the young retreat and restore themselves somewhat through secret retaliation against authority figures. In solitude and with peers, in both manifest and symbolic behavior, in their play and their fantasy, children assuage the discomforts of the socializing process and find some degree of psychic face-saving that makes the losing battle tolerable.

From the child's point of view, socialization can be seen as consisting of three sorts of behavior. The first includes learning, refinement, improvement in the direction of prescribed behavior. The second includes the relatively stable, acceptable, everyday

TWO PSYCHOLOGICAL FACTORS IN MEDIA AUDIENCE BEHAVIOR
Gerhart D. Wiebe

behavior at one's achieved level of socialization. The third includes the retaliatory, assuaging, indemnifying counterstrokes just discussed. These three phases of socialization may be referred to as *directive*, *maintenance*, and *restorative*. For convenience these labels will be used as if they referred to discrete categories. Actually I see them as zones in a continuum.

The process of socialization is inconceivable without communication. Professor Merton calls communication the instrument of social process. If we view socialization in terms of the messages involved, we find the *directive*, *maintenance*, and *restorative* aspects of socialization clearly identifiable in corresponding categories of messages.

Directive messages come from authority figures. They command, exhort, instruct, persuade, urge in the direction of learning, of new understandings that represent progress in the estimation of authority figures. Directive messages call for substantial and conscious intellectual effort on the part of the learner.

Maintenance messages include all the everyday messages sent and received in the customary business of living. They call for relatively little conscious intellectual effort.

Restorative messages, including individual fantasies, are those with which the individual refreshes himself from the strain of adapting, the weariness of conforming. They provide an interim for the reasserting of impulse. The child, seemingly with perverse precociousness, articulates his restorative messages as he screams, complains, jeers, taunts, defies, says forbidden words, and gleefully plays out cruel and destructive fantasies.

The socializing process is concentrated in childhood and youth, but it continues in adult society. Many elements of media audience behavior seem to fit into a coherent pattern if they are viewed as responsive to *directive*, *maintenance*, and *restorative* messages in the context of adult socialization.

In beginning this exploration we must differentiate between the purpose a message is meant to perform by the sender, and the purpose it actually performs for the receiver. Communicators tend to speak primarily in terms of the sender's intention. But much of the following discussion is couched in terms of the receiver's reaction. Certainly the two points of view cannot be assumed to be identical. We will frequently refer to a message that is intended as *directive*, but received as *maintenance*, or one that is intended as *maintenance* but is received as *restorative*.

DIRECTIVE MEDIA MESSAGES

Directive messages call for learning, for changed behavior, new differentiations, refined perceptions. Such responses require the expenditure of intellectual effort on the part of the neophyte. In childhood, these changes customarily take place, whether in home, church, or school, in a disciplined face-to-face relationship. This pattern appears to extend beyond childhood. If a person can read and has access to a good library, the prerequisites for a college education would appear to be present. But professors who command the respect of their students continue to be required. The printed Bible has not made the church obsolete nor has it reduced the role of the clergy. Granting the existence of the exceptional few with unusually high motivation, it seems to be true that the large majority of people do not move to higher spiritual or artistic or intellectual levels except within the disciplined context of a face-to-face pupil-teacher relationship.

The media do not provide this relationship. Certainly they can supplement and enrich the learning process. But I find no evidence that by themselves they will bring about substantial learning among the rank and file of a society—presumably because most people will not expend the required intellectual effort in the absence of an authority figure. This generalization finds strong support in Dr. Wilbur Schramm's book, *The New Media*, published in 1967.[11] In this survey of education by radio and television in many nations, Dr. Schramm reviews 23 projects. He reports many reasons for failure or success. But in no instance does he report success

TWO PSYCHOLOGICAL FACTORS IN MEDIA AUDIENCE BEHAVIOR
Gerhart D. Wiebe

in the absence of a face-to-face relationship between the learner and a teacher, monitor, parent, or comparable authority figure.

Once an individual has achieved a unit of learning within such a structural situation, he may voluntarily enter the audience for broadcasts featuring these recently acquired concepts and insights, but he then experiences such programs as *maintenance* rather than *directive* messages.

MAINTENANCE MEDIA MESSAGES

Who, then, among the general public, tunes in media messages intended to educate, to elevate, to present substantial new insights, to refine? Even though such programs do not command very large audiences, people do tune them in. The answer, in substantial degree, seems to lie in the familiar observation that the large majority of those who tune in religious programs are already religious. Most of those who tune in a science series already understand science at about the level presented in the series. I believe Dr. Paul Lazarsfeld first documented this pattern of media audience behavior years ago when he found that the audience for a radio series entitled "Americans All, Immigrants All," changed significantly from program to program with each nationality group tending to tune in the program about itself, but being less faithful in listening to the programs about other nationality groups where more learning would have been achieved. *Thus, given a range of choice, media audiences, through a self-selecting process, tend to turn messages intended to be directive into maintenance messages.*

Stated differently, given a permissive situation with available alternatives, people avoid the intellectual effort required in a true learning situation, preferring messages that review or embellish or elaborate what they already know. This, in essence, is what *maintenance* messages do. News programs will serve as the prototype of media *maintenance* messages. They are intended to extend or update the audience member's information about the world he already knows, and they seem, in general, to

perform that function. They do not call for disciplined intellectual effort.

There is a second way in which messages intended as *directive* are transformed into a *maintenance* function. Child psychologists have long known that children, exposed to programs intended for adults, perceive what they are ready to perceive, but miss many points that seem quite obvious to adults. I hypothesize that this same pattern persists in adult audiences so that in listening to a news program, or to a political speech, or to a sermon, people hear what they can comfortably accommodate in the context of their present knowledge, and very little more.

When do media messages move audience members to subsequent action? The answer, in terms of the present hypothesis, must be sought in a combination of at least three factors. First, in the existing readiness, the present predisposition among audience members to react. Secondly, in the social provisions for facilitating such action, and third, in the appeal of the message. Media messages themselves are only one of at least three factors. Seen in this way, the limitations as well as the power of media messages become less obscure. By way of illustration, consider the general experience in the United States regarding advertising on the one hand and sermons about brotherhood on the other. Successful advertising, if my observations are correct, succeeds not by the power of the medium and the message alone. Its success depends on these elements in combination with at least two other factors, namely a favorable predisposition among the audience and a retail establishment that facilitates the completion of the requested behavior. Sermons on brotherhood, on the other hand, though they have been numerous, and often eloquent, as in the case of the late Dr. King, bring very little positive change in behavior. Why? Our hypothesis suggests that audience members are not favorably disposed toward changing accustomed ways, and further, that social and institutional arrangements tend to impede rather than to facilitate changed behavior in this area.

TWO PSYCHOLOGICAL FACTORS IN MEDIA AUDIENCE BEHAVIOR
Gerhart D. Wiebe

RESTORATIVE MEDIA MESSAGES

What of the *restorative* category? The adult counterpart of youthful protest and retaliation against authority figures appears spontaneously, and apparently inevitably, as an antidote for the strictures of organized living. Mimicry, caricature, pantomime, satire, gossip, ribald ballads, malicious rhymes, broad humor, scandalous drama, such messages as these were popular before the days of Gutenberg. They have appeared persistently through history and have withstood the most harsh attempts at suppression. Their counterparts in media content fit our expectations for *restorative* messages and lend strong support to the hypothesis that the *restorative* aspect of socialization is served copiously, though of course not exclusively, by the kinds of media content that seem so deplorable to those with discriminating taste.

Restorative media messages feature crime, violence, disrespect for authority, sudden and unearned wealth, sexual indiscretion, freedom from social restraints. The themes of these most popular media messages seem to make up a composite reciprocal of the values stressed in adult socialization.

Because the very essence of restorative messages is their token retaliation against the establishment, the likely effect of well-intentioned attempts by proponents of high standards to "improve" popular *restorative* content is clear. Let's take out the violence, we say, and substitute a theme of cooperative problem solving. The *restorative* essence is removed and directive content is substituted. The psychological utility of the message is altered and its popularity is correspondingly reduced.

It was observed earlier that messages intended as *directive* are often received as *maintenance*. There is a similar mechanism that appears regarding the *maintenance* and *restorative* categories. News messages, for example, are supposed to inform the audience about happenings of significance so that audience members will be better able to maintain a clear view of the world in which they live. But if we examine the contents of news programs or of newspapers, it is

hard to escape the conclusion that other criteria have also gotten into the picture. Crime, scandal, sports, accidents, fires, comics—such categories as these receive more attention than would seem to be justified by their true importance in shaping our concept of the reality in which we live. I believe their prominence can be better understood by seeing them as *restorative* messages in a *maintenance* format.

The *restorative* mechanism hypothesized here has as perhaps its chief merit the characteristic of releasing hostility in small amounts. Seen in quantitative terms, it follows that if an individual or members of a subgroup or indeed of a whole society perceive themselves as oppressed or frustrated in nearly intolerable ways, the restorative mechanism may not suffice to provide the required relief. In such cases, messages intended as *restorative* may trigger overt retaliatory behavior in grossly antisocial forms. The pattern suggested here is familiar in its childhood version, where, among inhibited children, fun often escalates into fighting.

Throughout history, authority figures, and particularly those in autocratic hierarchies, have kept anxious watch on popular satire, comedy, songs, rhymes, stories, dramas, festivals. There is always the question whether retaliation against the establishment will remain token, and so restorative, or whether it will override social restraints. The answer is appropriately sought, less in analysis of message content than in the psychological condition of audience members. Perhaps one measure of a society's health is the degree to which it can tolerate the restorative mechanism without risking escalation into action that threatens some segment of the social structure.

Should a society regulate the amount of restorative content to which adults have access? In childhood the amount of make-believe, petty sadism, and noisy play is limited by authority figures. But in adulthood, given a permissive situation and available alternatives among media offerings, no comparable institutionalized regulation exists. Whether such regulation should exist is a matter of momentous significance, but it is beyond the scope of the present discussion.

The two mechanisms discussed here interact with each other and, no doubt, with many other factors too. In concluding, I will attempt to relate *reluctance to cope with the other* successively with *directive, maintenance,* and *restorative* messages, and to do this with reference to the current and crucial problem of race relations in the United States.

RELUCTANCE TO COPE WITH THE OTHER AND DIRECTIVE MESSAGES

We have observed that *directive* media messages, that is messages intended to bring about substantial learning, do not generally succeed unless linked with a structured, face-to-face, teacher-pupil relationship. This observation applies to the teaching of content that does not call for changes in interpersonal behavior, such as mathematics or the understanding of serious music. If, in addition to the intellectual work required, the lesson also requires greater refinement and discipline in interpersonal relationships, reluctance to cope with the other intervenes to further reduce the chances of success.

If Dr. Martin Luther King had expected whites who heard his broadcast messages substantially to increase their understanding of Christianity and also reflect this understanding in their behavior toward blacks, he would have been unrealistic according to the present hypotheses. But apparently he had no such expectations. He did not stay in the broadcasting studio. Even though he had no special liking for the hurley-burley of the pavements, he carried his mission into face-to-face interaction, and it is there that changed behavior was accomplished.

The present formulation appears to accommodate the remarkable and tragic fact that in a nation where Christianity has been the dominant religion for three centuries, and where few living adults have not heard Dr. King and others of like mind via the media, behavior patterns toward blacks have not changed substantially except as such behavior has been compelled by law or in physical confrontations.

RELUCTANCE TO COPE WITH THE OTHER AND MAINTENANCE MESSAGES

We have mentioned two ways in which messages intended as *directive* are transformed into *maintenance* messages at the receiving end. Although I do not have specific data to prove it, it seems highly likely that both mechanisms have been used with regard to media messages on civil rights. First, the media audiences for civil rights leaders, I speculate, have included a much larger proportion of those already favorable to the civil rights campaign than of those who oppose it. Second, among those who favor the civil rights campaign, such exhortations as those of Dr. King have been selectively perceived so that, for example, northern audience members could sincerely agree that blacks should be served in southern restaurants while still feeling no need to take specific steps in breaking through established patterns of discriminatory housing in their own northern neighborhoods.

Maintenance messages provide additional information that extends, updates and elaborates one's view of reality at approximately his achieved level of socialization. The media perform this function in the United States with remarkable success. By doing so, audience members with a predisposition or readiness to behave in a given manner may be notified of a new or improved social situation in which such behavior is facilitated. Thus the announcement of a civil rights protest demonstration, according to our hypothesis, will activate that small proportion of audience members who have reached the conviction that they must participate in such an activity, and the probably somewhat larger number of those who like to go as spectators to see what happens while avoiding the personal commitment of actual participation. The very large majority,

TWO PSYCHOLOGICAL FACTORS IN MEDIA AUDIENCE BEHAVIOR
Gerhart D. Wiebe

however, receive the news, perceive it in a manner consonant with their existing view of things, and then continue behaving very much as they ordinarily do.

RELUCTANCE TO COPE WITH THE OTHER AND RESTORATIVE MESSAGES

The function of the *restorative* mechanism is to provide token retaliation against authority figures. It reverses deference lines so that the acted-upon becomes the actor. In order to insure victory in these forays of the weak against the strong, *restorative* messages typically involve symbolism, metaphor, fantasy. Institutionalized ceremonies, often featuring costumes and masks, provide occasions in many societies where the weak are guaranteed immunity in acts that would bring stern punishment in everyday life. Either by social or by individual devices, the *restorative* mechanism evades the danger of a forthright test of power with established authority figures. The *restorative* mechanism thus accommodates reluctance to cope with the other.

We have hypothesized a tendency on the part of media audience members to transform messages intended as *directive* or *maintenance* into *restorative* messages if content lends itself to such transformation. This opportunity is certainly present in the case of speeches, documentaries, and televised news reports on the civil rights campaign. In one way or another, these messages say "we are oppressed and we appeal for justice." But the white audience member, preoccupied with his own frustrations, can easily perceive such a message as symbolic reference to his own problems, and treat such reports of social reality as if they were drama. Black audience members, on the other hand, many of whom carry nearly explosive accumulations of resentment, are more likely to experience such messages in a personal and literal rather than metaphorical sense, and in some cases are stimulated to gross antisocial behavior.

CONCLUSION

Two psychological patterns that contribute to the understanding of media audience behavior have been discussed. These patterns have not been projected as a comprehensive theory. It is presumed that additional factors remain to be explored. It is suggested, however, that the factors discussed here go far toward providing a substantial psychological rationale for the gap between the persistent hopes of intellectuals on the one hand and persistent mass audience behavior on the other.

Several implications for operating policy seem to follow, and these will now be made explicit.

1. The media cater to a natural reluctance to cope with the other. This is most true precisely in those instances where the coping is expensive, bothersome, time-consuming, or fraught with trouble. Recourse to media messages as substitutes for faulty primary interpersonal relationships is suspect. It is likely to be an evasion, and an unsuccessful one. Examples are use of media messages for the substantial improvement of child-rearing, education, the inculcation of interpersonal values, the healing of intergroup conflict. This does not deny the high value of media messages in all of these instances as supplement, enrichment, reinforcement. It does reaffirm the primary importance of face-to-face relationships.

2. The permissiveness and the phenomenal solitude that generally characterize the reception of media messages maximize the opportunity and the likelihood that they will be selected and perceived in ways that minister to intrapersonal impulse gratification. Media messages intended to change, elevate, refine overt interpersonal behavior will seldom succeed except where they resonate a favorable predisposition in the receiver, and guide him to face-to-face arrangements that facilitate the desired behavior.

[1]These proportions have been confirmed by an industry researcher. The enormous size of broadcast audiences is illustrated by the estimate that the Philharmonic, with its relatively low ratings, still reached approximately 1,500,000

homes on an ordinary Sunday afternoon.

[2]New York, Knopf, 1963, esp. ch. 6.

[3]*Ibid.*, p. 201.

[4]Jean Piaget, *The Construction of Reality in the Child*, New York, Basic Books, 1954, pp. 20–40.

[5]Rene Spitz, *The First Year of Life*, New York, International Universities Press, 1965, chs. 14, 15, 16.

[6]Spitz, *op. cit.*, p. 86.

[7]Jean Piaget, *The Language and Thought of the Child*, London, The Humanities Press, 1952, ch. 1.

[8]*Journal of Personality*, Vol. 28, 1960, pp. 383–396.

[9]Eugene L. and Ruth E. Hartley, *Fundamentals of Social Psychology*, New York, Knopf, 1952, p. 202.

[10]The zestful and loving relationship in which learning is mutually delightful to parent and child, teacher and student, receives short shrift here, not because its desirability is undervalued but because no substantial counterpart appears in media audience behavior. It does not help to explain the reality we seek to understand. Perhaps even in home, school, and church it is more talked about than achieved.

[11]Unesco, International Institute for Educational Planning, 1967.

Reprinted from Public Opinion Quarterly *(Fall, 1964), pp. 404–17. Used by permission of the publisher and author. This article was the author's presidential address for the Division of Personality and Social Psychology at the meetings of the American Psychological Association in September 1963.*

Behavioral Support for Opinion Change

LEON FESTINGER

THE last three decades have seen a steady and impressive growth in our knowledge concerning attitudes and opinions—how they are formed, how they are changed, and their relations to one another. For example, we now know a good deal about the effects on opinion change of varying the structure of a persuasive communication—whether it is one-sided or two-sided, whether it is fear-arousing or not, whether pro arguments precede or follow con arguments, and whether it is attributed to trustworthy or untrustworthy sources. Phenomena such as sleeper effects, immunization to counter-propaganda, assimilation and contrast effects, are beginning to be understood. We have also learned a great deal about attitude and opinion change in small face-to-face groups, about the relationship between personality variables and opinion change, about factors affecting resistance to persuasive communications, and so on. I do not intend to review seriously all this work. Anyone who wants to has only to start looking for the names of Hovland, Janis, Kelley, McGuire, Newcomb, Katz, Peak, Kelman—there are many others but these would do for a start.

There is, however, one important gap in our knowledge about attitude and opinion change—a gap that is doubly peculiar when seen in relation to the strong behavioral emphasis in psychology in the United States. I first realized the existence of this gap on reading a manuscript by Arthur R. Cohen. Let me read to you the paragraph that startled me. Cohen's manuscript focuses on the ". . . ways in which persuasive communicators and

members of one's social group come to influence the attitudes of the individual." In his concluding remarks he says:

> Probably the most important and long-range research problem in the sphere of attitude theory has to do with the implications of attitude change for subsequent behavior. In general, most of the researchers whose work we have examined make the widespread psychological assumption that since attitudes are evaluative predispositions, they have consequences for the way people act toward others, for the programs they actually carry out and the manner in which they perform these programs. Thus attitudes are always seen to be a precursor to behavior, a determinant of what behaviors the individual will actually go about doing in his daily affairs. However, though most psychologists assume such a state of affairs, very little work on attitude change has explicitly dealt with the behavior that may follow upon a change in attitudes. Most researchers in this field are content to demonstrate that there are factors which affect attitude change and that these factors are open to orderly exploration, without actually carrying through to the point where they examine the links between changed attitudes and changes in learning, performance, perception and interaction. Until a good deal more experimental investigation demonstrates that attitude change has implications for subsequent behavior, we cannot be certain that our change procedures do anything more than cause cognitive realignments, or even, perhaps, that the attitude concept has any critical significance whatever for psychology.[1]

I was, at first reading, slightly skeptical about the assertion that there is a dearth of studies relating attitude or opinion change to behavior. Although I could not think of any offhand, it seemed reasonable that many of them would be scattered through the journals. Consequently, I started looking for such studies and asked others if they knew of any. After prolonged search, with the help of many others, I succeeded in locating only three relevant studies, one of which is of dubious relevance and one of which required re-analysis of data. The absence of research, and of theoretical thinking, about the effect of attitude change on subsequent behavior is indeed astonishing.

Before telling you about these three studies I would like to make sure that the problem is clear. I am not raising the question of whether or not attitudes are found to relate to relevant behavior. Let us accept the conclusion that they are related, at least to some extent, although even here relatively few studies in the literature address themselves to this question. A fairly recent study by De Fleur and Westie provides a good example of the kind of relationship between existing attitudes and relevant overt behavior that may be found under controlled conditions with good measurement.[2]

The investigators obtained measures of attitudes toward Negroes from 250 college students. The particular attitude measure employed was apparently reliable, test-retest measures over a five-week interval yielding a correlation of +.96. They selected, from these 250 students, 23 who had scored in the upper quartile and 23 who had scored in the lower quartile, matching the two groups on a number of other variables. These two extreme groups were then compared on a rather clever measure of overt behavior with respect to Negroes. A situation was constructed in which it was believable to ask each of them to sign an authorization permitting use of a photograph of himself sitting with a Negro. The subject was free not to permit the photograph to be taken at all, or, if he signed the authorization, to permit any of a number of possible uses of the photograph ranging from very limited use in laboratory experiments to, at the other extreme, use in a nationwide publicity campaign. The signing

of the authorization was real, and may be regarded as an instance of overt commitment. As the authors say: "In American society, the affixing of one's signature to a document is a particularly significant act. The signing of checks, contracts, agreements, and the like is clearly understood to indicate a binding obligation on the part of the signer to abide by the provisions of the document."

What, then, is the relationship found between the measure of general attitudes toward Negroes and the behavioral measure? Table 1 presents a summary of the data. Clearly, there is a relationship between the attitude and the behavior. Those who are prejudiced are less willing to have the photograph taken and widely used. True, it is a relatively small relationship, although highly significant statistically. The smallness of the relationship is emphasized when we recall that we are comparing extreme groups. But nevertheless, it is comforting to know that a relation does exist. One can understand the smallness of the relationship by realizing that overt behavior is affected by many other variables in addition to one's own private attitude.

But data such as this do not answer the question we wish to raise here. The fact that existing attitudes relate to overt behavior does not tell us whether or not an attitude *change* brought about by exposure to a persuasive communication will be reflected in a *change* in subsequent behavior. To answer this question we need studies in which, after people have been exposed to a persuasive communication, a measure of attitude or opinion is obtained on the basis of which attitude change can be assessed. Such studies must also, some time

---

TABLE 1

Relationship between Race Attitudes and Level of Signed Agreement to be Photographed with Negro

Signed Level of Agreement	Prejudiced Group	Unprejudiced Group
Below mean	18	9
Above mean	5	14

BEHAVIORAL SUPPORT FOR OPINION CHANGE
Leon Festinger

later, provide an indication of behavior change relevant to the opinion or attitude, so that one can see whether the cognitive change had any effect on subsequent behavior. We may even be content with studies in which overt behavior is not actually observed. If the subjects are asked questions about what they actually did, this may suffice.

As I mentioned before, we were able to locate only three studies reasonably close to meeting these requirements. One of these, the data from which I re-analyzed, was part of a larger series of studies conducted by Maccoby et al.[3] These investigators selected a sample of mothers whose only child was between three and twelve months old. Each of these mothers was interviewed and was asked, among other questions, at what age she believed toilet training of the child should begin. Three weeks later, each of these women was again interviewed. This time, however, two different procedures were followed. Half the mothers, selected at random, were designated as a control group and were simply re-interviewed. In this second interview they were again asked the age at which they thought toilet training of the child should begin. The other half of the sample, the experimental group, were first exposed to a persuasive communication and then re-interviewed with the same interview used in the control group. The persuasive communication was a specially prepared, illustrated pamphlet entitled "When to Toilet Train Your Child." Each mother in the experimental group was handed this pamphlet and asked to read it, then and there, while the interviewer waited. The pamphlet argued strongly for starting toilet training at the age of twenty-four months. The re-interview occurred immediately after the mother had read the pamphlet. Thus, a comparison of the results of the two groups on the first and second interviews indicated how successful the pamphlet was in changing their opinion concerning when toilet training should start.

In order to assess the persistence of the change in opinion brought about by the pamphlet, both groups of mothers were again interviewed about six months later and were again asked at what age they thought toilet training should begin. Finally, and most importantly for our present concern, about a year after the initial interviews, on the asumption that most of the mothers would have started toilet training already, they were interviewed again and asked at *what age they had actually started.* This last may certainly be regarded as a simple, and probably truthful, report of their actual behavior. Consequently, one can look at the relationship between attitude change and behavior.

In any study in which people are interviewed and re-interviewed over a period of a year, there is an inevitable attrition. Some mother left the area, others simply could not be reached for one or another interview, and the like. Actually, in this study the drop-out rate was remarkably small. About 80 per cent of the initial sample was actually interviewed all four times, 45 mothers in the experimental group and 47 mothers in the control group. At the time of the fourth interview 34 mothers in each of the two groups had begun toilet training their child and, consequently, it is only for these 68 mothers that we have a measure of actual behavior. The other 24 mothers (11 in the experimental group and 13 in the control group) who had not yet started toilet training by the time of the last interview were asked when they intended to start. Although for these we cannot say that we have a measure of actual behavior, we will present the results for them also.

TABLE 2

Attitude Change and Behavior of Mothers Who Had Started with Respect to Toilet Training
(data in months)

	Control (N = 34)	Experimental (N = 34)
Immediate opinion change (Interview 2 — Interview 1)	−0.2	+2.3
Delayed opinion change (Interview 3 — Interview 1)	+0.8	+1.6
Effect of opinion change on behavior (Interview 4 — Interview 1)	+2.0	+1.2

First, however, let us look at the data presented in Table 2 for those who had started toilet training. The data are rather startling to contemplate — although perhaps not too startling. It is clear that the persuasive communication was quite effective in immediately changing the opinions of the mothers in the experimental group. The change, on the average, was to advocate toilet training 2.3 months later than on the initial interview. The control group did not change materially — actually moving slightly in the direction of advocating earlier toilet training.

Six months later the change was still maintained, although somewhat reduced in magnitude. The experimental group still advocated that toilet training begin 1.6 months later than they had on the initial interview. The control group, however, also now advocated somewhat later toilet training. Nevertheless, there was still a clear difference between the two groups.

When we examine when these mothers actually started to toilet train their child, however, we are met with a surprise. There is, if anything, a reverse relationship between attitude change and behavior. The mothers in the experimental group actually started toilet training 1.2 months later on the average than they had initially advocated. But the mothers in the control group, who had never been subjected to any experimental persuasive communication to change their opinion, started toilet training 2.0 months later than their initial opinion would have indicated. Apparently, in the usual American home, as the child gets older, events conspire to delay toilet training somewhat beyond what the mothers think is probably desirable. But the opinion change in the experimental group clearly did not carry over to affect behavior.

We can also see evidence of the same thing in the data for those mothers who had not as yet started to toilet train their children at the time of the fourth interview. These are presented in Table 3. Here again it is clear that the persuasive communication had a strong immediate effect on the opinions of the mothers in the experimental group and that, six months later, this effect had been maintained.

The difference between the control and the experimental groups was almost as large after six months as it was immediately after the persuasive communication. It is also clear that events conspired to make these mothers delay the actual onset of toilet training and conspired equally for both groups. The changed opinion had no effect on the actual behavior of these mothers. The difference between their initial opinion and their intention at the time of the fourth interview was high because these data are for a selected group who had not yet started to toilet train their children. The important thing, however, is that there was no difference between the experimental and control groups.

Another way to look at the data is as follows. Both Table 2 and Table 3 show that the persuasive communicaton was effective for the experimental group and that the impact of the persuasive communication was still present six months later. If this opinion change had had any effect on behavior, we would expect that, by the time of the fourth interview, a larger percentage of the mothers in the control group would have already started to toilet train their children. More of the mothers in the experimental group, having become convinced that toilet training should start later, would *not* yet have started. Actually, the difference was negligible and slightly in the reverse direction. Thirty-four out of 45 mothers in the experimental group and 34 out of 47 mothers in the control group had already

---

TABLE 3

Attitude Change and Intentions of Mothers Who Had Not Started with Respect to Toilet Training
(data in months)

	Control (N = 13)	Experimental (N = 11)
Immediate opinion change (Interview 2 — Interview 1)	−1.2	+2.2
Delayed opinion change (Interview 3 — Interview 1)	+0.3	+3.0
Effect of opinion change on intention (Interview 4 — Interview 1)	+5.1	+5.2

BEHAVIORAL SUPPORT FOR OPINION CHANGE
Leon Festinger

started toilet training by the time of the fourth interview. All in all, we can detect no effect on behavior of a clear and persistent change in opinion brought about by a persuasive communication.

Let us proceed to examine another relevant study. This study, reported by Fleishman, Harris, and Burtt, attempted to measure the effects of a two-week training course for foremen in industry.[4] This training course stressed principles of human relations in dealing with subordinates. Clearly, we are not faced here with the impact of one short persuasive communication but rather with a series of such communications extending over a two-week period. These persuasive communications took the form of lectures and group discussions, assisted by visual aids and role playing. For our purposes here, we may, perhaps, safely regard this two-week training session as a concerted attempt to persuade the foremen that mutual trust, warmth, and consideration for the other person are important aspects of effective leadership. (Before anyone misinterprets what I have said, let me hasten to add that undoubtedly other things went on during the two weeks. I have simply abstracted the aspect of the training session that resembles a persuasive communication.)

Given such a prolonged exposure to such a heavy dose of persuasion, we can well imagine that the opinions of the trainees would change from before to after the two-week session. The investigators attempted to measure any such opinion change in the following way. Before the training session and on its last day, the foremen were given a questionnaire measuring their opinions concerning leadership on the part of foremen. The major dimension on the questionnaire of interest to us here is one the authors label "consideration," made up of questions on such things as friendship, mutual trust, and warmth between the leader and his group. As one would expect, the investigators found a clear, appreciable, and significant change on this dimension from before to after the training session. The two weeks of persuasion were effective and the foremen now

thought that the dimension of "consideration" was more important than they had previously believed.

This study is relevant for our present purposes because the investigators proceeded to obtain a subsequent on-the-job behavioral measure relevant to the dimension of "consideration." They compared the behavior of those foremen who had attended the training session with a comparable group of foremen who had not. The results are rather surprising. In general, there were no very consistent differences in behavior between the group of foremen who had, and the group who had not, been exposed to the two-week training session. This, in itself, is worrisome. Significant opinion change brought about as a result of a two-week exposure to a series of persuasive communications shows no relationship to behavior. But the results are actually even more surprising than this. The investigators divided their group of "trained" foremen into subgroups according to how recently they had completed the training course. After all, it might be reasoned that the effect of the training disappears with time. If so, one should at least be able to observe an effect on behavior among those who had most recently completed their two-week training course. The results show that the "most recently trained sub-group" was actually *lower* in consideration *behavior* than the group that had never been exposed to any training—had never been exposed to the impact of the persuasive communications. Once more we see the hint of a slightly inverse relationship between attitude change and behavior.

We will now proceed to examine the only other study we were able to find bearing on the question of the relation between opinion change and behavior. This is the well known study by Janis and Feshbach on the effects of fear-arousing communications.[5] Because the authors of this study did not interpret their data as bearing on this question, we will have to put a different interpretation on their experiment in order to make it relevant. Perhaps this different interpretation is not justifiable. But since so few published studies could be found that bear on our problem at all, I will proceed with the reinterpretation.

Of four groups of high school students used in the experiment, one, the control group, was not exposed to the relevant persuasive communication. The other three groups each heard an illustrated lecture about proper care of teeth and gums that attempted to persuade them that it was important to care for the teeth properly in order to avoid unpleasant consequences. The lectures each of the three groups heard differed in their emphasis on the painful consequences of improper oral hygiene. In the words of the authors:

> One of the main characteristics of the *Strong* appeal was the use of personalized threat-references explicitly directed to the audience, i.e., statements to the effect that "this can happen to you." The *Moderate* appeal, on the other hand, described the dangerous consequences of improper oral hygiene in a more factual way using impersonal language. In the *Minimal* appeal, the limited discussion of unfavorable consequences also used a purely factual style.

One might expect that the more emphasis put upon the importance of proper oral hygiene, and the more personal the importance is made, the more effective the communication would be in making the listener feel that proper oral hygiene is something to be concerned about. Thus, we might expect that the Strong appeal would be most effective, and the Minimal appeal least effective, in persuading people to be concerned about proper oral hygiene. One week before hearing the lecture, and immediately after hearing the lecture, all the subjects were asked two questions about how concerned or worried they were about the possibility of developing diseased gums and decayed teeth. The authors interpret these questions as indicating the degree of emotionality aroused by the persuasive communication, but, for the sake of our re-interpretation, let us look at the answers as reflecting opinion change. After all, the communications attempted to concern the listeners about these things. Let us see how well they succeeded. The data are shown in Table 4.

As one might expect, the persuasive communications were all effective to some extent — they all succeeded in creating more change in concern about oral hygiene than appeared in the control group. Within the experimental conditions we find that the Strong appeal was, plausibly, most effective. The Moderate and Minimal appeals seem to have been about equally effective.

The three persuasive communications, in addition to attempting to persuade the listeners of the importance of oral hygiene, also attempted to persuade them about the proper way to brush one's teeth and the characteristics of a "proper" type of toothbrush. Here, however, the three communications were equal. Before and after measures were obtained concerning the beliefs in the desirability of the recommended characteristics of a toothbrush. On these issues, where the communications did not differ, the authors state, ". . . all three experimental groups, as compared with the Control group, showed a significant change in the direction of accepting the conclusions presented in the communication. Among the three experimental groups, there were no significant differences with respect to net changes."

TABLE 4
Percentage Who Felt "Somewhat" or "Very" Worried about Decayed Teeth and Diseased Gums

	Before	After
Strong appeal (N = 50)	34	76
Moderate appeal (N = 50)	24	50
Minimal appeal (N = 50)	22	46
Control group (N = 50)	30	38

BEHAVIORAL SUPPORT FOR OPINION CHANGE
Leon Festinger

In other words, the three experimental groups were equally persuaded about the proper procedures to use in caring for the gums and teeth, but the Strong appeal group was made to feel these procedures were more important. If there were a simple, straightforward relationship between opinion or attitude change and behavior, one would expect the control group to change their behavior least (or not at all) and the Strong appeal group to change their behavior most.

On the initial questionnaire, given one week before the students heard the persuasive communications, five questions asked them to describe the way they were currently brushing their teeth—in other words, asked them to report their behavior. A week after having been exposed to the persuasive communications they were again asked these same five questions, covering aspects of tooth brushing that were stressed in the persuasive communications as the proper way to brush one's teeth. The answers were scored in terms of whether the student did or did not use the recommended practice. Since these questions asked the students about what they actually did when they brushed their teeth, perhaps it is legitimate to regard their answers as truthful reports concerning their actual behavior. This may or may not be a valid interpretation of their responses, but, assuming that it is, let us see what the relationship is between attitude change and their reported behavior. Table 5 presents the data on the percentage of subjects in each group who changed in the direction of increased use of the practices recommended in the persuasive communication.

It is clear from even a cursory glance at the data that the results do not represent a simple relation between attitude change and behavior. It is true that those who heard any of the persuasive communications reported more change in their behavior than the control group. This, however, may simply reflect the fact that subjects in the experimental conditions learned the proper terminology and what is approved. The interesting

TABLE 5

Percentage Who Changed Toward Increased Use of Recommended Dental Practices

	Per Cent Who Changed
Strong appeal	28
Moderate appeal	44
Minimal appeal	50
Control group	22

comparison is among the experimental groups. Within the experimental conditions, the relation between behavior and the degree to which students were made to feel concerned about oral hygiene was actually in the reverse direction from what one would expect from any simple relationship between attitude change and behavior.

The authors offer as an explanation for the inverse relationship the hypothesis that the Strong appeal created strong fear and, hence, subjects exposed to this communication were motivated to avoid thinking about it. Perhaps this is the correct explanation, although little evidence is presented in the study to support the assertion that strong fear was aroused in the Strong appeal condition. And it is certainly not clear why people who are more concerned about something are not more likely to take action. If we think of the results of this study together with the results of the previous studies I described (and let me stress again that these are the only three studies I have been able to find that are at all relevant to the issue at hand), it seems clear that we cannot glibly assume a relationship between attitude change and behavior. Indeed, it seems that the absence of research in this area is a glaring omission and that the whole problem needs thinking through.

Let us, for the sake of the present discussion, put aside the possibility that responses to a questionnaire after having been exposed to a persuasive communication may reflect nothing more than "lip service"; that is, the person's real opinions and attitudes may not have changed at all but his responses may simply reflect a desire not to appear unreasonable in the eyes of the experimenter. This kind of thing may affect responses to questionnaires to some extent, but it seems unreasonable to imagine that it is a dominant effect or that it could account for differences among experimental conditions. Undoubtedly, to a major extent, a person's answers to a questionnaire reflect how he really feels about the issue at that moment. Then why should one not observe a clear relationship with behavior?

I would like to suggest one possible reason for a complex relationship between attitude or opinion change and behavior. I have no data to support this suggestion, but perhaps it may offer some conceptual basis for future research that will clarify the problem. I want to suggest that when opinions or attitudes are changed through the momentary impact of a persuasive communication, this change, all by itself, is inherently unstable and will disappear or remain isolated unless an environmental or behavioral change can be brought about to support and maintain it.

To illustrate and amplify this suggestion, let us imagine a person who held the unlikely opinion that giving speeches was a productive and worthwhile thing to do. Undoubtedly, such an opinion would have been developed over many years on the basis of his own experience, what other people say about it, and also his own needs and motives. For example, he has observed that many people engage in the practice of giving speeches and from this it seems clear that it must have some desirable aspects. He has even read that at A.P.A. conventions papers are held to short periods of time because so many people (more than can be accommodated) want to make speeches. Surely, giving a speech must be a good thing to do. What is more, he has observed that many people actually go to listen to such speeches—a fact that certainly supports his opinion.

There is even more to the "reality" basis he has for this opinion. Once when he gave a speech,

two people came up to him afterward and told him how wonderful they thought it was. What better evidence could he have that it was indeed worthwhile to engage in this activity? Furthermore, no one ever came up to him to tell him it was a waste of time. In addition, he found that he got quite a bit of personal satisfaction out of having all those people listening to what he said. All in all, the opinion became rather well established. There was considerable evidence to support it, none to contradict it, and it was a pleasant opinion to hold.

Needless to say, such a well-established opinion would affect the person's behavior. This does not mean that at every possible opportunity he would give a speech, but rather that he would be more likely to do so than someone who did not hold the opinion that such speeches were very worthwhile. It would not be a perfect relationship, since many other factors would affect his behavior, for example, the availability of time and whether or not he really had anything to say. But, by and large, one would observe a positive relationship.

Let us now imagine that the following unhappy incident occurs in the life of this contented speechmaker. One day, shortly before he is to leave town to go to some distant place to deliver a speech, he happens to engage in conversation with a few of his friends. One of them, on learning about the imminent trip, raises the question as to why it is necessary or valuable to do this kind of thing. After all, the monetary cost and the time spent are rather large. What does an audience get out of a personally delivered speech that they couldn't get just as well out of reading it?

Let us imagine the highly unlikely event that, in the ensuing discussion, no one is able to come up with a good answer to this question and so a real impact is made on the speechmaker's opinion. If one were to give this person a questionnaire at this moment, one would discover that a change in his opinion had been brought about. He would feel less certain that it was a good thing to do. But what are the implications for the future of this

BEHAVIORAL SUPPORT FOR OPINION CHANGE
Leon Festinger

change in his opinion? After this friendly but unsettling discussion, our speechmaker returns to the same environment that produced his opinion initially, and, we can consequently assume, there will be pressures to return to his former opinion. Pressures, indeed, that he has not felt in a long time. Furthermore, he is about to leave to make a speech and he goes ahead with what he is already committed to doing. This obviously further helps to restore his former opinion. The world he encounters remains the same, his experiences remain the same, and so his opinion will tend to revert. His behavior will remain the same or perhaps even intensify in an effort to restore his former opinion. The exact content of his opinion may indeed have changed somewhat and become more differentiated. He may buttress his original opinion by the notion that many people will listen to a speech who would not read it and that it is important to communicate to many people; he may persuade himself that the personal contact is in some unspecified way very important; he may even tell himself that a practice so widespread must be good even if he, at the moment, cannot see its good aspects clearly.

It is my present contention that, in order to produce a stable behavior change following opinion change, an environmental change must also be produced which, representing reality, will support the new opinion and the new behavior. Otherwise, the same factors that produced the initial opinion and the behavior will continue to operate to nullify the effect of the opinion change.

Thus far we have speculated mainly about some possible reasons for the *absence* of a relationship between opinion change following a persuasive communication and resulting behavior. We have not grappled with the perplexing question raised by the persistent hint of a slightly inverse

relationship (if three times may be called persistent). I must confess that I have no very good or interesting speculations to offer here. Let me also emphasize that the data certainly do not warrant assuming that such an inverse relationship really does exist: they do no more than raise a possible suspicion. If this inverse relation is found not to exist, there is, of course, nothing to explain. If, however, it does exist, we must find some explanation for it.

What I want to stress is that we have been quietly and placidly ignoring a very vital problem. We have essentially persuaded ourselves that we can simply assume that there is, of course, a relationship between attitude change and subsequent behavior and, since this relationship is obvious, why should we labor to overcome the considerable technical difficulties of investigating it? But the few relevant studies certainly show that this "obvious" relationship probably does not exist and that, indeed, some nonobvious relationships may exist. The problem needs concerted investigation.

[1] Arthur R. Cohen, *Attitude Change and Social Influence*, New York, Basic Books, in press.

[2] M. L. De Fleur and F. R. Westie, "Verbal Attitudes and Overt Act: An Experiment on the Salience of Attitudes," *American Sociological Review*, Vol. 23, 1958, pp. 667–673.

[3] N. Maccoby, A. K. Romney, J. S. Adams, and Eleanor E. Maccoby, *"Critical Periods" in Seeking and Accepting Information*, Paris-Stanford Studies in Communication, Stanford, Calif., Institute for Communication Research, 1962.

[4] E. Fleishmann, E. Harris, and H. Burtt, *Leadership and Supervision in Industry: An Evaluation of a Supervisory Training Program*, Columbus, Ohio State University, Bureau of Educational Research, 1955.

[5] I. Janis and S. Feshbach, "Effects of Fear-arousing Communications," *Journal of Abnormal and Social Psychology*, Vol. 48, 1953, pp. 78–92.

Reprinted from Journalism Quarterly *(Spring, 1969), pp. 37–42. Used by permission of the publisher.*

Dissonance and Exposure to Aversive Information

RICHARD F. CARTER, RONALD H. PYSZKA AND JOSE L. GUERRERO

WHEN Festinger first introduced his theory of cognitive dissonance, it showed promise of great utility to communication researchers:[1] It grew out of a study of communication processes; it postulated a concept, cognitive dissonance, of broad generality in human behavior; it hypothesized that communication behavior was an important means of coping with dissonance when it occurred.

The generality was achieved in part by the postulate that dissonance was both a perceived cognitive discrepancy between two relevant elements *and a homeostatic motive state.* Dissonance, then, was viewed as an aversive stimulus, to be reduced by one or another mode.

Because social interaction is a primary source of cognitive elements, it was expected that exposure to information in the dissonance condition would be consistent with this postulate. That is, the individual experiencing dissonance would avoid any information which was further productive of dissonance.

Since then, the theory has been subject to critical review on this point. Freedman and Sears have summarized the evidence relative to the hypothesis and found the avoidance hypothesis to be poorly supported by the research findings.[2]

What support they found was in favor of another hypothesis about communication behavior—that the individual experiencing dissonance would expose himself to information consonant with his values.

They suggested that there might be contingent conditions that affected the way experimental subjects were behaving. They suspected that utility of the information was involved. This is a very reasonable view, because the word (information) itself suggests utility.

In recent years, Festinger and his associates have restricted the generality of the dissonance concept, and thereby minimized the contingency of utility. They have postulated that the decision which produces the dissonance must have implications for subsequent behavior—i.e., the individual must be committed.[3] Thus the individual would be expected to show consistency of values in exposure to information because there would be minimal utility in attending to value assertions favorable to an alternative that has been foreclosed to behavior.[4]

The restriction had the added feature of insuring that a motive state was in fact present, and that the motive state was directly related to the values held for the alternatives in the decision situation (i.e., degree of dissonance is seen as proportional to the importance of the alternatives).

In the above discussion, we referred to two hypotheses—one of avoidance and one of exposure to consonant information. This distinction was not made explicit by Festinger. And the research based on this theory has neglected the distinction completely. Typically, experimental subjects have been offered a choice of information, some consonant with a previous decision and some dissonant (i.e., not consonant).

Yet the distinction needs to be made. The avoidance hypothesis refers to dissonance pro-

DISSONANCE AND EXPOSURE TO AVERSIVE INFORMATION
Richard F. Carter, Ronald H. Pyszka and Jose L. Guerrero

ducing information; the consonance hypothesis refers to dissonance reducing information. They can be seen as two parts of one hypothesis only if the homeostatic motive postulate holds.

The motive postulate allows one to argue the case of complementary hypotheses because the *value assertions* of proffered information relative to the chosen alternative determine whether dissonance is being produced or reduced. Negative assertions about a chosen alternative or positive assertions about an unchosen alternative increase dissonance in this view while positive assertions about a chosen alternative and negative assertions about an unchosen alternative decrease dissonance.

The individual in a dissonance condition, then, is considered as having the rather simple task of electing more or less dissonance. His preference is taken to be obvious, given the homeostatic motive postulate.

But the motive postulate has the effect of equating nonconsonant information, in a situation offering a choice of information, with dissonance producing information. The whole point of the utility contingency is that this is not the case. Some—if not a good deal—of such nonconsonant information may not be dissonance producing, and not avoided.

If avoidance is to occur, it should be pointed out, it should occur without reference to a choice of proffered information, some consonant and some nonconsonant. The latter is a test of selective exposure, and assumes that avoidance is half of selective exposure. But avoidance ought to be observable with respect to only nonconsonant information (i.e., without a choice).

Further, avoidance should occur more often when the nonconsonant information is more aversive—i.e., more dissonance producing in view of the motive postulate. It is to a test of the avoidance hypothesis *per se* that we now turn.

Three recent studies furnish evidence on the validity of the avoidance hypothesis and on the viability of the motive postulate.[5]

STUDY NO. 1

To find avoidance in response to dissonance, it was deemed necessary to concentrate on making the proffered information as threatening as possible. Thus it would be more aversive information and there would be more motivation to avoid it.

In this first study, by Pyszka, no attempt was made to vary the aversiveness of the information. What was attempted was to make the information more aversive than previous studies had succeeded in doing.

For this reason, the proffered information did not focus on the negative aspects of the chosen alternative but rather on the negative aspects of the individual making the choice. Given that avoidance is conceived as a defense employed to protect the individual, it was reasoned that it should be more likely to occur in the face of an attack on the individual himself.

(Prior studies of dissonance and avoidance necessarily assume that the individual identifies with the chosen alternative and thus defends it. This assumption was not made here.)

Three conditions were induced, one lacking dissonance and two with dissonance.[6] Subjects were students enrolled in an introductory marketing course in the School of Business at the University of Wisconsin. The experiment was disguised as an outside reading assignment in the course.

Subjects were told that they would have to read one of two articles for that assignment. Several days before the subjects were to choose between the articles, the experimental conditions were induced. They were to be applicable only for those students who were originally favorable to liberal credit policies.[7]

In one condition, subjects were asked to state their views on liberal credit—as in previous studies of dissonance with commitment. In another condition, only a basis for such preference was given (through the presentation of a fictitious poll result which stated that young people—college students in particular—were the most enthusiastic supporters

DISSONANCE AND EXPOSURE TO AVERSIVE INFORMATION
Richard F. Carter, Ronald H. Pyszka and Jose L. Guerrero

TABLE 1

Article Choice by Dissonance Induction Condition and Identification with Liberal Credit

		Choice of Article:	
Condition	Identification[A] (Perceived Threat)	Liberal Credit	Convenience Packaging
1 (Control)	a. No (N = 6)	3	3
	b. Yes (N = 6)	3	3
2 (Dissonance, without commitment)	a. No (N = 9)	4	5
	b. Yes (N = 15)	11	4
3 (Dissonance, with commitment)	a. No (N = 4)	3	1
	b. Yes (N = 18)	13	5

[A]Identification with liberal credit was a necessary condition for dissonance to occur. It can be seen that identification was more frequent in the non-control conditions and highest when commitment was expressed by the subjects.

of liberal credit). In the control condition (no dissonance), neither induction was made.

The inductions were made in quiz sections of the class. The class as a whole was told that another topic, convenience packaging, was very much at the forefront of marketing today.[8]

At the time the subjects were to choose between the two articles, summaries were presented. Both were *ad hominem*. They attacked persons in favor of liberal credit and convenience packaging, respectively, both directly and indirectly—as members of a reference group (i.e., students).

The subjects' selections served as the measure of avoidance. In addition, subjects were questioned to ascertain whether identification with liberal credit had occurred (i.e., if a threat had been perceived) and if the summaries were perceived as credible.

Table 1 shows the relative selection of the article on liberal credit for those who were initially favorable to liberal credit (and who perceived the summaries to be credible) by the three experimental conditions. It can be seen that the effect of increasing the aversiveness of the information did not evoke more avoidance in the dissonance conditions; the opposite occurred (see conditions 2b and 3b).[9]

We had not succeeded in observing increased avoidance with what we thought was a more aversive information stimulus. When asked, subjects said they felt challenged to read the article on liberal credit.[10] This would seem to indicate that the stimulus was strong enough, but that the response of avoidance was not appropriate.

STUDY NO. 2

The second study, by Guerrero, was carried out as a consumer survey of women's preferences among cars. Subjects were wives of university graduate students.

Of the 38 subjects, half were asked to indicate their interest in reading an article critical of their choice and the other half their interest in reading an article critical of persons making such a choice.

These questions were put for six aspects of the car-buying decision: the brand actually purchased; a brand considered but not purchased; a brand not considered for purchase; the attribute (feature) considered most important in a car by the respondent; an attribute considered but not most important; and, an attribute not considered important.[11]

DISSONANCE AND EXPOSURE TO AVERSIVE INFORMATION
Richard F. Carter, Ronald H. Pyszka and Jose L. Guerrero

TABLE 2

Interest Ratings for Aversive Information by Degree of Relevance and Aspect of Decision

Degree of Relevance/ Aspect of Decision	Aversive Information: Attack on Choice	Aversive Information: Attack on Individual Making Choice
1 High Relevance:		
a. Chosen Brand	5.47	5.42
b. Chosen Attribute	4.89	5.00
2 Moderate Relevance:		
a. Considered Brand	5.10	5.10
b. Considered Attribute	4.15	3.73
3 No Relevance:		
a. Brand Not Considered	2.89	3.52
b. Attribute Not Considered	3.81	3.57
	(N = 19)	(N = 19)

Interest in reading these articles was assessed on a seven-point scale. Lower interest ratings were taken to indicate greater likelihood of avoidance.

Table 2 shows the difference for interest ratings in each of the six conditions. Where the brand or attribute was highly relevant, we again see that attacking the individual himself for making a choice is not more likely to produce avoidance behavior to proffered aversive information.

There was some indication of avoidance with respect to aversive information about less relevant attributes — but not less relevant brands. If the apparent avoidance was due to the lesser relevance of the aversive information to the decision, then avoidance should have been observed for brands as well.

It should be noted that the large difference in any condition (3a, Brand Not Considered) indicates less avoidance with an attack on the individual himself rather than on the choice.

STUDY NO. 3

One further approach to the problem was undertaken in the study by Carter. He gave each experimental subject both an attack on the choice and on himself — separately — for a more sensitive comparison of the difference in avoidance.

Subjects were 64 junior high school students who had participated in an experiment designed to arouse fear levels with regard to dental hygiene. Dissonance was induced for these students and they were asked to indicate their interest in reading each of two reports: the first concerning "the cost, in manhours lost to society, of neglected dental health procedures" (attack on choice — i.e., to neglect dental hygiene); and, the second concerning "teenagers" as the group most likely to neglect the proper dental health procedures (attack on individual).

Table 3 shows subjects' interest ratings on a seven-point scale of interest for three different levels of fear arousal.[13] At each level, it can be seen that the attack on the individual (as a member of the student peer group) leads to less avoidance.[14]

As in the Guerrero study, relevance (here inferred from degree of fear arousal) plays a very important part in determining likelihood of avoidance.

DISCUSSION

The senior author has criticized in an earlier paper the validity of the motive postulate for the concept of dissonance.[15] It was argued that dissonance

DISSONANCE AND EXPOSURE TO AVERSIVE INFORMATION
Richard F. Carter, Ronald H. Pyszka and Jose L. Guerrero

TABLE 3

Interest Ratings for Aversive Information by Degree of Fear Arousal

| | Aversive Information: | |
| | Attack on | Attack on Individual |
Degree of Fear Arousal	*Choice*	*Making Choice*
High (N = 32)	3.91	4.38
Moderate (N = 18)	2.94	4.00
Low (N = 14)	2.71	3.71

should be formulated simply as a perceived cognitive discrepancy.

In this alternative view, avoidance—or any other reduction mode—would have to be a learned response to the kind of situation in which dissonance occurred. The dissonance *per se* would only be a signal that some response be made.

No inference would be made, then, that the dissonant state included any motive aspect relative to the values associated with objects chosen or not chosen. It could not be assumed that responses would be "supportive" of the value position implicit in the chosen alternative. The only expectation is that the responses be relative to the fact that a cognitive discrepancy has been perceived.

That there is an acknowledged repertoire of reduction modes for dissonance states is consistent with this view. The notion that dissonance is a motive state as well implies that there be some similarity among the reduction modes (e.g., as exemplified in the "supportive" view) but the response repertoire is considered to include leaving the field and—under extreme conditions—nonsupportive behavior. Thus the repertoire itself is more consistent with the notion of dissonance being a cognitive signal.

The general thrust of recent theoretical analyses of the role of mass media in affecting individual behavior has emphasized the supportive implications.[16] Exposure to mass media content has been seen as a supportive response. The individual is viewed as selecting that content which is supportive of his values, with the corollary that any effect of the exposure is primarily reinforcing of those values.

Exception to this point of view was taken by the senior author in a previous article.[17] And more recently, Sears and Freedman have also questioned the validity of the selective exposure hypothesis—although not rejecting the corollary.[18]

The supportive view focuses on the *expressive* function of the individual's communication behavior. But communication behavior has the additional function of value *formulation*. In this second function, one can not readily accept, *a priori*, the notion that aversive information is to be avoided. And any theoretical view of cognitive processes should be skeptical of a postulate which constrains us from observing formulative functions of communication behavior.

If, as the senior author suggested earlier, we postulate simply that a functionally autonomous motive (e.g., need for orientation) exists, then some response to a cognitive discrepancy can be expected. Additional aspects of motive, such as those related to situational importance, can then be viewed in their interaction with the cognitive state of dissonance. Thus, for example, the notion of "degree of dissonance" can be seen to represent the interaction of a cognitive state (perceived discrepancy) and of a motive state (perceived importance of situation).[19]

[1]Leon Festinger, *A Theory of Cognitive Dissonance* (Evanston, Ill.: Row, Peterson, 1957).

[2]Jonathan L. Freedman and David O. Sears, "Selective Exposure," in Leonard Berkowitz, ed., *Advances in Experimental Social Psychology*, Vol. 2 (New York: Academic Press, 1965), pp. 57–97.

DISSONANCE AND EXPOSURE TO AVERSIVE INFORMATION

Richard F. Carter, Ronald H. Pyszka and Jose L. Guerrero

[3]The restriction was first suggested by Brehm and Cohen, then adopted by Festinger. See: Jack W. Brehm and Arthur R. Cohen, *Explorations in Cognitive Dissonance* (New York: Wiley, 1962); Leon Festinger, "The Theory of Cognitive Dissonance," in (Wilbur Schramm, ed.): *The Science of Human Communication* (New York: Basic Books, 1963), pp. 17–27; Leon Festinger *et al.*, *Conflict, Decision, and Dissonance* (Stanford, Calif.: Stanford University Press, 1964).

[4]Festinger *et al*, *ibid.*, p. 156. They do not go so far as to say that commitment is irrevocable, however. (If they did, they would reduce the scope of the theory to rationalization.)

[5]Three papers given at the 1967 convention of the Association for Education in Journalism, Boulder, Colorado: Richard F. Carter, "Cognitive Discrepancies and Avoidance"; Ronald H. Pyszka, "The Avoidance of Threatening Information," and Jose L. Guerrero, "Avoidance, Relevance and Exposure to Discrepant Information."

[6]Two dissonance conditions were induced in order to see if the presumed necessary condition of commitment is in fact necessary. The evidence (Table 1) suggests it is not. The state of identification needed for perceiving information to be aversive was achieved in both experimental conditions.

[7]Unfortunately, only about a third of the class did have such an opinion, severely reducing the number of subjects in the experimental conditions.

[8]Subjects in the control group were given a similar reference to liberal credit.

[9]Comparing the non-dissonance conditions (1a, 1b, 2a and 3a) with the dissonance conditions, a chi square of 2.64 is obtained, which yields: $p = .11$.

[10]The question specifically asked about a perceived challenge. Among the subjects choosing liberal credit, those in the dissonance condition were more likely to say they felt challenged.

[11]Subjects had been asked earlier in the interview about their most recent car purchase in order to determine appropriate brand names and attributes to be used in these questions.

[12]The three-way interaction (relevance × focus of attack × brand) vs. attribute is significant to the .001 level. The two-way interaction, relevance × focus of attack, is not significant. A better explanation of the three-way interaction must be based on the brand vs. attribute distinction, which is also significant in the two-way interaction with relevance. Guerrero's study was designed primarily to show that such an interaction would occur. Focus of attack was expected to be a factor without interaction, if at all.

[13]The measure of fear level was taken as part of the earlier experiment.

[14]The main effect of focus of attack is significant at the .001 level.

[15]Richard F. Carter, "Cognitive Discrepancies and Communication Behavior," paper read at 1966 convention of Association for Education in Journalism, Iowa City, Iowa.

[16]See, for example: Joseph T. Klapper, *The Effects of Mass Communication* (Glencoe, Ill.: Free Press, 1960); Bernard Berelson and Gary A. Steiner, *Human Behavior* (New York: Harcourt Brace and World, 1964).

[17]Richard F. Carter, "Communication and Affective Relations," *Journalism Quarterly*, 42:203–12 (Spring, 1965).

[18]David O. Sears and Jonathan L. Freedman, "Selective Exposure to Information: A Critical Review," *Public Opinion Quarterly*, 31:194–213 (Summer, 1967). These authors suggest the selectivity is not so evident in the exposure *per se* as in the evaluation made of the content given exposure.

[19]Carter, 1966, *op. cit.*

Reprinted from American Psychologist *(May, 1964), pp. 319–28. Copyright 1964 by the American Psychological Association and reproduced by permission.*

The Obstinate Audience

RAYMOND A. BAUER

Not long ago, Henry Murray (1962), in an address entitled, "The Personality and Career of Satan," gibed at psychologists for undertaking Satan's task of shattering man's faith in his own potentialities:

> Man is a computer, an animal, or an infant. His destiny is completely determined by genes, instincts, accidents, early conditioning and reinforcements, cultural and social forces. Love is a secondary drive based on hunger and oral sensations or a reaction formation to an innate underlying hate. . . . If we psychologists were all the time, consciously or unconsciously, intending out of malice to reduce the concept of human nature to its lowest common denominators . . . then we might have to admit that to this extent the Satanic spirit was alive within us [p. 53].

Isidor Chein (1962), too, sides with the humanist against the scientist in psychology.

> Among psychologists whose careers are devoted to the advancement of the science, the prevailing image of Man is that of an impotent reactor. . . . He is implicitly viewed as robot . . . .
> The opening sentence of *Ethical Standards of Psychologists* is that, "the psychologist is committed to a belief in the dignity and worth of the individual human being." . . .
> But what kind of dignity can we attribute to a robot [p. 3]?

The issue is not, however, whether the *findings* of social science do and should have an influence on how we run our lives and think about ourselves, an influence to a certain extent inevitable and, to some, desirable. The real issue is whether our social model of man—the model we use for running society—and our scientific model or models—the ones we use for running our subjects—should be identical. That the general answer should be identical. That the general answer should be "No," I learned when working on my doctoral thesis (Bauer, 1952), which was a chronology of Soviet attempts to keep the social and scientific models of man in line with each other, for I became soberly aware then of the delicacy and complexity of the relationship of the social and the scientific models of man.

I shall here discuss the relationship of these two models in the area of social communication. I shall set up two stereotypes. First, the social model of communication: The model held by the general public, and by social scientists when they talk about advertising, and somebody else's propaganda, is one of the exploitation of man by man. It is a model of one-way influence: The communicator *does* something to the audience, while to the communicator is generally attributed considerable latitude and power to do what he pleases to the audience. This model is reflected—at its worst—in such popular phrases as "brainwashing," "hidden persuasion," and "subliminal advertising."

The second stereotype—the model which *ought* to be inferred from the data of research—is of communication as a transactional process in which two parties each expect to give and take from the deal approximately equitable values. This, although it *ought* to be the scientific model, is far from

THE OBSTINATE AUDIENCE
Raymond A. Bauer

generally accepted as such, a state of affairs on which W. Philips Davison (1959) makes the comment:

> The communicator's audience is not a passive recipient—it cannot be regarded as a lump of clay to be molded by the master propagandist. Rather, the audience is made up of individuals who demand something from the communications to which they are exposed, and who select those that are likely to be useful to them. In other words, they must get something from the manipulator if he is to get something from them. A bargain is involved. Sometimes, it is true, the manipulator is able to lead his audience into a bad bargain by emphasizing one need at the expense of another or by representing a change in the significant environment as greater than it actually has been. But audiences, too, can drive a hard bargain. Many communicators who have been widely disregarded or misunderstood know that to their cost [p. 360].

Davison does not contend that all the exchanges are equitable, but that the inequities may be on either side. He only implies that neither the audience nor the communicator would enter into this exchange unless each party expected to "get his money's worth," at least most of the time. After all, Davison is not speaking as a social philosopher nor as an apologist for the industry, but as an experienced researcher trying to make sense out of the accumulated evidence.

Whether fortunately or unfortunately, social criticism has long been associated with the study of communication. The latter was largely stimulated by the succession of exposés of propaganda following World War I, particularly of the munitions-makers' lobby and of the extensive propaganda of the public utilities. There was also social concern over the new media, the movies and radio, and the increasingly monopolistic control of newspapers. Propaganda analysis, which is what research communication was called in those days, was occupied with three inquiries: the structure of the media (who owns and controls them, and what affects what gets into them); content analysis (what was said and printed); and propaganda

techniques (which are the devil's devices to influence people). In this period, *effects* for the most part were not studied: They were taken for granted. Out of this tradition evolved Laswell's (Smith, Laswell, & Casey, 1946) formulation of the process of communication that is the most familiar one to this day: "Who says what, through what channels [media] of communication, to whom [with] what . . . results [p. 121]." This apparently self-evident formulation has one monumental built-in assumption: that the initiative is exclusively with the communicator, the effects being exclusively on the audience.

While the stimulus and the model of research on communication were developing out of the analysis of propaganda, survey research, relatively independently, was evolving its technology in the commercial world of market research and audience and leadership measurement. As is well known, Crossley, Gallup, and Roper each tried their hands at predicting the 1936 presidential election and whipped the defending champion, the *Literary Digest*. By 1940, Lazarsfeld was ready to try out the new technology on the old model with a full-scale panel study of the effects of the mass media on voting in a national election, having tested his strategy in the New Jersey gubernatorial race in 1938.

The results of this study, again, are well known. Virtually nobody in the panel changed his intention, and most of the few who did so attributed it to personal influence (Lazarsfeld, Berelson, & Gaudet, 1948). The mass media had had their big chance—and struck out. Negative results had been reached before but none which had been demonstrated by such solid research. A number of equally dramatic failures to detect effects of campaigns carried on in the mass media followed, and by the end of the decade Hyman and Sheatsley (1947) were attempting to explain why. No one could take the effects of communication for granted.

As a matter of fact a considerable number of the sociologists studying communication grew discouraged with inquiring into the immediate effects of the mass media, and went looking for "opinion leaders," "influentials," the "web of influence," and so on. At the same time, a few here and there began doing something we now call "functional studies." They were curious to know how the audience was behaving.

In the meantime, at just about the time that the students of the effect of communication in a natural setting were beginning to wonder if communication ever had effects, experimental studies were burgeoning under essentially laboratory conditions. Experiments had been conducted before, but the tradition of experimenting on the effects of communication was vastly enhanced by the War Department's Information and Education Division, and after the war by Hovland and his associates at Yale (Hovland, Lumsdaine, & Sheffield, 1949). The Yale group's output, and that of colleagues and students of Kurt Lewin, account for a very high proportion of the experimental work on the subject in the past 2 decades.

The experimenters generally had no trouble conveying information or changing attitudes. Of course nobody stopped to record very explicitly the main finding of all the experiments: that communication, given a reasonably large audience, varies in its impact. It affects some one way, some in the opposite way, and some not at all. But nevertheless the experimenters got results.

By the end of the 'fifties it was quite clear that the two streams of investigation needed reconciling, and Carl Hovland (1959) did so. More recently, pursuing the same theme, I stated Hovland's major point as being that the audience exercises much more initiative outside the laboratory than it does in the experimental situation (Bauer, 1962). The audience selects what it will attend to. Since people generally listen to and read things they are interested in, these usually are topics on which they have a good deal of information and fixed opinions. Hence the very people most likely to attend to a message are those most difficult to change; those who can be converted do not look or listen. A variety of studies attribute to this circum-

stance alone: the fact that actual campaigns have often produced no measurable results, while quite marked effects could be produced in a laboratory.

Two favorite problems of the laboratory experimenters take on quite a different aspect when considered in a natural setting. One is the question of the order of presentation of arguments. Is it an advantage to have your argument stated first (the so-called law of primacy) or stated last (the so-called law of recency)? In a laboratory the answer is complex but it may be quite simple in a natural situation: He who presents his argument first may convert the audience and they in turn may exercise their oft-exercised prerogative of not listening to the opposing case. Hence to have the first word rather than the last could be decisive in the real world, but for a reason which may seem irrelevant to the relative merits of primacy versus recency.

Of course, another important variable is the credibility of the source. By creating an impression of the credibility of the stooge or experimenter in the laboratory, it is often possible to convert a person to a position far removed from his original one. But in real life, the audience usually does its own evaluation of sources, and at a certain point sometimes arrives at a result quite the opposite of that reached experimentally. If the audience is confronted with a communicator trying to convert it to a position opposed to its own, it is likely to see him as "biased," and the like, and come away further strengthened in its own convictions.

It was quite clear from Hovland's piece, and should have been even earlier, that the characteristic behavior of the audience in its natural habitat is such as to bring about crucial modifications of the results seen in the laboratory. In general, these modifications are strongly in the direction of suppressing effect.

In a sense, Joseph Klapper's 1960 book, *The Effects of Mass Communication*, marks the end of an era. Twenty years earlier, a social scientist would have taken effects for granted and specified the devices the propagandist employed to achieve them. But Klapper (1960) makes statements like these:

THE OBSTINATE AUDIENCE

Raymond A. Bauer

"[my position] is in essence a shift *away* from the tendency to regard mass communication as a necessary and sufficient cause of audience effects, toward a view of the media as influences, working amid other influences, in a total situation [p. 5]." He sees communications as operating through mediating factors—group membership, selective exposure, defense mechanisms—"such that they typically render mass communication a contributory agent, but not the sole cause in a process of reinforcing the existing conditions. (Regardless of the condition in question . . . the media are more likely to reinforce [it] than to change) [p. 8]." Change takes place, according to Klapper, in those rare circumstances when mediating forces are inoperative, when they are occasionally mobilized to facilitate change, or in certain residual situations. He reviews the literature on the effect of variation in content, mode of presentation, media, and so on, but rather than taking effects for granted, he searches for the exceptional case in which the mass media change rather than fortify and entrench.

Klapper recommends what he calls the "phenomenalistic" and others have called the functional approach. The study of communication has traditionally (although not exclusively) been conducted from the point of view of the *effects intended by the communicator*. From this perspective, the disparity between actual and intended results has often been puzzling. The answer has come increasingly to be seen in entering the phenomenal world of the audience and studying the functions which communication serves. The failure in research to this point has been that the audience has not been given full status in the exchange: The intentions of its members have not been given the same attention as those of the communicator.

Some will argue that these generalizations do not hold true of advertising. They do. But until now no one has undertaken to match the effects of communication in various areas according to comparable criteria and against realistic expectation.

Actually much more is expected of the campaigns with which academic psychologists are associated than is expected of commercial promotion. For example, a paper on governmental informational campaigns concluded with these words (Seidenfeld, 1961): "while people are willing to walk into a drugstore and buy low calorie preparations and contraceptives, they are not very anxious to take shots for protection against polio or attend a clinic dealing with sexual hygiene." By the author's own figures, 60% of the public had had one or more polio shots and 25% had had the full course of four. According to his expectations, and probably ours, these were hardly satisfactory accomplishments.

Yet, what about the highly advertised product, low in calories, with which he was comparing polio inoculations? Presumably he had heard that it was a smashing commercial success, or had seen some dollar volume figure on gross sales. Actually, it was being bought by 4% of the market—and 60% and even 25% are larger figures than 4%. Our unacknowledged expectations must be reckoned with.

These differences in expectation and criteria produce much confusion, usually on the side of convincing people that commercial campaigns are more successful than others. Yet, consistently successful commercial promotions convert only a very small percentage of people to action. No one cigarette now commands more than 14% of the cigarette market, but an increase of 1% is worth $60,000,000 in sales. This means influencing possibly .5% of all adults, and 1% of cigarette smokers. This also means that a successful commercial campaign can alienate many more than it wins, and still be highly profitable.

Equally misleading is the frequent reference to percentage increase on some small base. This device has been a particular favorite of both the promoters and the critics of motivation research: One party does it to sell its services, the other purportedly to warn the public; both exaggerate the effect. Thus, for example, the boast, "a 300% increase in market share," means that the product increased; but it may easily be from 1% of the market to 3%. Or we may have a 500% gain in preference for "the new package" over the old one. That there is that much consensus in the esthetic judgment of the American public is a matter of interest, but it tells nothing about the magnitude of consequences on any criterion in which we are interested. I have made some computations on the famous Kate Smith war-bond marathon, which elicited $39 million in pledges. Kate Smith moved apparently to a maximum of 4% of her audience to pledge to buy bonds; the more realistic figure may be 2%! In the commercial world this is a rather small effect as judged by some expectations, but yet an effect which often adds up to millions of dollars.

But commercial promotions often do not pay their way. The word is currently being circulated that a mammoth corporation and a mammoth advertising agency have completed a well-designed experiment that proves the corporation has apparently wasted millions of dollars on promoting its corporate image. Some studies have shown that an increase in expenditures for advertising has, under controlled experimental conditions, produced a decrease in sales.

The truth is now out: that our social model of the process of communication is morally asymmetrical; it is concerned almost exclusively with inequities to the advantage of the initiators, the manipulators. From the social point of view this may be all to the good. The answer to the question whether our social and scientific models should be identical is that there is no reason why we should be equally concerned with inequities in either direction; most of us consider it more important to protect the weak from the powerful, than vice versa. However, no matter how firmly committed to a morally asymmetrical social model, investigators should note that inequities fall in either direction and in unknown proportions.

The combination of this asymmetry and the varying expectations and criteria mentioned earlier fortifies the model of a one-way exploitative process of communication. And it is probably further reinforced by the experimental design in which the subject is seen as *reacting* to conditions established by the experimenter. We forget the cartoon in which one rat says to another: "Boy, have I got this guy trained! Every time I push this bar he gives me a pellet of food." We all, it seems, believe that *we* train the *rats*. And while the meaning of "initiative" in an experimental situation may be semantically complicated, the experimenter is usually seen there as *acting* and the subjects as *reacting*. At the very least and to all appearances, the experimental design tends to entrench the model of influence flowing in one direction.

The tide is, in fact, turning, although as a matter of fact, it is difficult to say whether the final granting of initiative to the audience, which seems to be imminent, is a "turn" or a logical extension of the research work of the past 25 or 30 years. Obviously Davison and Klapper and others, such as the Rileys, Dexter and White, Charles Wright, and Talcott Parsons, regard their position as the logical conclusion of what has gone before rather than a drastic inversion. So-called "functional" studies are increasing in volume, and appear now to be a matter of principle. In any event, Dexter and White (in press), the editors of the forthcoming reader whose tentative title is *People, Society, and Mass Communication*, are firmly committed to this point of view and have organized the book upon it.

Traditionally, the name "functional studies" has been applied to any work concerned with a range of consequences wider than or different from those intended by the communicator. Two early classics, both done in the 'forties, are studies of listening to daytime radio serials: one by Herta Herzog (1944), and the other by Warner and Henry (1948). They established that women used the radio serials as models for their behavior in real life. In the late 'forties, Berelson (1949) studied how people reacted to not having newspapers during a strike, work which Kimball (1959) replicated in the newspaper strike of 1948. The variety of functions the newspapers proved to serve is amazing, including the furnishing of raw material for conversation. "The radio is no substitute for the newspaper.

THE OBSTINATE AUDIENCE
Raymond A. Bauer

I like to make intelligent conversation [Kimball, 1959, p. 395]." There was also research on the adult following of comics (Bogart, 1955), children's use of TV (Maccoby, 1954), and the reading of *Mad* magazine (Winick, 1962).

From a cursory glimpse, one concludes that early functional studies suffered from a tendency to focus on the deviant. Or, put another way, functional or motivational analysis (motivation research can be regarded as a subdivision of functional analysis) was ordinarily evoked only when the stereotyped model of economic rational man broke down. The findings advanced scientific knowledge but did little to improve the image of man in the eyes of those committed to a narrow concept of economic rationality. We may well argue that the social scientists' model of man is in reality broader, more scientifically based, and even more compassionate; but the public may not think so.

Thus, the early functional studies added to knowledge of the process of communication by including effects intended by the audience. There is a question, however, as to what they did to the social model of the process. Certainly the work of motivation research was written up in such a way as to confirm the exploitative model. But more recent functional studies focus on ordinary aspects of communication, and present the audience in a more common, prosaic, and, therefore, more sensible light.

Meanwhile, new trends have been developing in psychological research on communication. Until about a decade ago, the failure of experimental subjects to change their opinions was regarded as a residual phenomenon. Little systematic or sympathetic attention was paid to the persistence of opinion. The considerable volume of recent research using what the Maccobys (Maccoby & Maccoby, 1961) call a homeostatic model is dominated by theories based on the psychology of cognition, Heider's balance theory, Festinger's dissonance theory, Osgood and Tannenbaum's congruity theory, and Newcomb's strain for symmetry. While the proponents of each theory insist on adequate

grounds on their distinctiveness, all agree that man acts so as to restore equilibrium in his system of belief. In any event, homeostatic studies do finally accord some initiative to the audience. Specifically, they reveal individuals as deliberately seeking out information on persons either to reinforce shaken convictions or consolidate those recently acquired. Festinger, for example, is interested in the reduction of dissonance following upon decisions—which means he views people as reacting to their own actions as well as to the actions of others. This influx of new ideas and new research is a valuable and welcome addition to both the theory and practice of social communication.

Restoring cognitive equilibrium is, however, only one of the tasks for which man seeks and uses information. Furthermore, the homeostatic theories, while according initiative to the audience, make it peculiarly defensive. They do little to counteract the notion of a one-way flow of influence—although it must be conceded that a scientific model is under no moral obligation to correct the defects, if any, of the social model.

Much is gained by looking upon the behavior of the audience as full-blown problem solving. Such a viewpoint requires the assumption that people have more problems to solve than simply relating to other people and reducing their psychic tension, among them being the allocation and conservation of resources.

The mass media have long been criticized because they facilitate escape from the responsibilities of the real world. But Katz and Foulkes (1962) point out that if man is to cope adequately with his environment, he must on occasion retreat to gather strength. Hence, escape per se is not a bad thing: It is socially approved to say, "Be quiet! Daddy is sleeping," although not yet approved to say, "Be quiet! Daddy is drinking." They take a generally irresponsibly handled problem of social criticism and convert it into one of the allocation and conservation of resources. It would take close calculation to decide whether an hour spent drinking beer in front of the TV set would, for a given individual, result in a net increase or decrease in his coping effectively with the environment. Yet, while the data they require are manifestly unattainable, their very way of posing the problem raises the level of discourse.

The necessity for taking explicit cognizance of the audience's intention was forced on us when we were studying Soviet refugees. We knew that virtually every Soviet citizen was regularly exposed to meetings at which were conveyed a certain amount of news, the party line on various issues, and general political agitation and indoctrination. In free discussion our respondents complained endlessly of the meetings so we knew they were there. But when we asked them, "From what sources did you draw most of your information about what was happening?" only 19% specified them, in contrast to 87% citing newspapers, 50% citing radio, and another 50% word of mouth (Inkeles & Bauer, 1959, p. 163). Gradually the obvious dawned on us; our respondents were telling us where they learned what *they* wanted to know, not where they learned what the regime wanted them to know.

A similar perplexity arose with respect to the use of word-of-mouth sources of information. It was the least anti-Soviet of our respondents who claimed to make most use of this unofficial fountain of information. Rereading the interviews, and further analysis, unraveled the puzzle. It was the people most involved in the regime, at least in the upper social groups, who were using word-of-mouth sources the better to understand the official media, and the better to do their jobs (Inkeles and Bauer, 1959, p. 161)! As a result we had to conduct analysis on two levels, one where we took into account the intentions of the regime, the other, the intentions of the citizen. Thus, viewed from the vantage point of the regime's intention, the widespread dependence upon word of mouth was a failure in communication. From the point of view of the citizen and what he wanted, his own behavior made eminent sense.

At the next stage, we benefited from the looseness of our methods, the importance of the people we were studying, and from highly imaginative colleagues from other disciplines. We were studying the processes of decision, communication, and the like, in the business and political community. As we studied "influence" by wandering around and getting acquainted with the parties of both camps, and kept track of what was going on, the notion of a one-way flow became preposterous. A Congressman, for example, would snort: "Hell, pressure groups? I have to roust 'em off their fat rears to get them to come up here." It also became clear that men in influential positions did a great deal to determine what sort of communication was directed toward them (Bauer, Pool, & Dexter, 1963). At this juncture, Ithiel de Sola Pool crystallized the proposition that the audience in effect influences the communicator by the role it forces on him. This idea became the organizing hypothesis behind the Zimmerman and Bauer (1956—this experiment was replicated by Schramm & Danielson) demonstration that individuals process new information as a function of their perceived relationship to future audiences. Specifically, they are less likely to remember information that would conflict with the audience's views than they are to remember information to which the audience would be hospitable.

The final crystallization of my present views began several years ago when a decision theorist and I together reviewed the studies by motivation researchers of the marketing of ethical drugs to doctors. Surprisingly, I found the level of motivation discussed in these reports quite trivial, but the reports provided perceptive cognitive maps of the physician's world and the way he went about handling risk. The now well-known studies of the adoption of drugs by Coleman, Menzel, and Katz (1959) contributed data consistent with the following point: Physicians become increasingly selective in their choice of information as risk increases either because of the newness of the drug or difficulty in assessing its effects. Thereupon, a group of Harvard Business School students (in an unpublished manuscript) established by a question-

THE OBSTINATE AUDIENCE
Raymond A. Bauer

naire survey that as the seriousness of the disease increased, physicians were increasingly likely to prefer professional to commercial sources of information.

Parenthetically with respect to the Coleman, Menzel, and Katz (1959) studies whose data I said are "consistent with" the notion of risk handling: I am convinced that this way of thinking is wholly compatible to the authors. Yet their presentation is sufficiently dominated by the prevailing view of "social influence" as a matter of personal compliance that one cannot be entirely sure just where they do stand.

Why doesn't the physician always prefer professional to commercial sources of information? The physician is a busy man whose scarcest resources are time and energy, two things which commercial sources of information, on the whole, seem to help him conserve. Even so, he is selective. Let us assume two components in the choice of source of information: social compliance and the reduction of risk. Consider, then, that the doctor may be influenced by his liking either for the drug company's salesman who visits his office, or for the company itself. We may assume that, of these two components of influence, social compliance will be more associated with his sentiments toward the salesman and risk reduction with the company's reputation.

In a study conducted with the Schering Corporation (Bauer, 1961), I found that in the case of relatively riskless drugs, the correlation of preference for drugs with preference for salesman and for company was about equal. However, with more hazardous drugs—and with large numbers of subjects—preference for the company carried twice the weight of preference for the salesmen: The physicians selected the source closest associated with reduction of risk.

In the latest and fullest development of this point of view, Cox (1962) asked approximately 300 middle-class housewives to evaluate the relative merits of "two brands" of nylon stockings (Brand N & Brand R) as to over-all merits and

as to each of 18 attributes. After each rating the subject was asked to indicate how confident she was in making it. The subjects then listened to a tape-recorded interview with a supposed salesgirl who stated that Brand R was better as to 6 attributes, whereupon they were asked to judge the stockings again and to evaluate the salesgirl and their confidence in rating her. Finally, they completed a questionnaire which included three batteries of questions on personality, one of which was a measure of self-confidence.

The findings of interest here bear upon personality and persuasibility. Male subjects low in generalized self-confidence are generally the more persuasible. Females are more persuasible in general but on the whole this is not correlated with self-confidence or self-esteem.

The reigning hypotheses on the relationship of self-confidence to persuasibility have been based either on the concept of ego defense (Cohen, 1959) or social approval (Janis, 1954), and Cox chose to add *perceived self-confidence in accomplishing a task*. He was dealing, then, with two measures of self-confidence: generalized self-confidence, presumably an attribute of "personality"; and specific self-confidence, that is, perceived confidence in judging stockings.

It has been suggested that the reason that in women personality has not been found correlated with persuasibility is that the issues used in experiments have not been important to them. And importance may account for the strong relationship Cox found when he gave them the task of rating stockings. That he was testing middle-class housewives may be why the relationship was curvilinear. (That is to say, his subjects may have covered a wider range of self-confidence that might be found in the usual experimental groups.) Women with *medium* scores on the test of self-confidence were the most likely to alter their rating of the stockings in the direction recommended by the salesgirl; those scoring *either* high or low were less likely to accept her suggestion. As a matter of fact, countersuggestibility apparently crept in among the women low in self-confidence; those who rated lowest were almost three times as likely as the others to change in the *opposite* direction. Since these findings were replicated in three independent samples, ranging from 62 to 144 subjects, there is little reason to question them for this type of person and situation. The differences were both significant and big.

The curvilinear relationship was not anticipated, and any explanation must, of course, be ad hoc. One might be that, faced with the difficult task of judging between two identical stockings and the salesgirl's flat assertion that one was better than the other, the women tacitly had to ask themselves two questions: Do I need help? Am I secure enough to accept help? Accordingly, the subjects most likely to accept the salesgirl's suggestion would be those with little enough self-confidence to want help, but still with enough to accept it. As an explanation, this is at least consistent with the curvilinear data and with the apparent counter-suggestibility of the subjects with little self-confidence.

This explanation, however, should not apply to individuals confident of their ability to perform the task. And this turned out to be the case. Among the subjects confident they could perform the *specific* task, generalized self-confidence played little or no role. The usual notions of social compliance and ego defense were virtually entirely overriden by the subject's confidence in her handling of the task—a conclusion which is supported, no matter how the data are combined.

My intention in telling this is to present a promising experiment in regarding the audience as being involved in problem solving. As already suggested, theories of social communication are caught between two contrasting models of human behavior. One we may call the "influence" model: One person does something to another. We have partially escaped from the simplest version of it, and now regard the audience as influenced only in part, and in the other part solving problems of ego defense or of interpersonal relations.

Meanwhile, there is the always endemic model of economic rationality which in one or another of its forms sees man as maximizing some tangible value. This latter, very simple problem-solving model we spontaneously use when we *judge* behavior, particularly with respect to whether it is rational or sensible or dignified. Thus ironically, we use the influence model, or the modified influence model, to explain why people do what they do, but we use the economist's problem-solving model for evaluating the behavior. There is scarcely a surer way of making people look foolish!

There is no reason why the two models should not be seen as complementary rather than antagonistic. But the fusion has not taken place to any conspicuous degree in the mainstream of research, as can be seen most clearly in literature on informal communication and personal influence. There are two major traditions from which this literature has developed (Rogers, 1962): One, that of the heartland of social communication, stresses social compliance and/or social conformity. The other tradition, that of rural sociology, is concerned with how farmers acquire knowledge useful in their day-to-day problems. While the two have in certain respects become intermeshed after some decades of isolation, overtones of social compliance and conformity persist in the social-psychological literature. There is little reference to problem solving.

The students of one of my colleagues who had read a standard treatment of the role of reference groups in buying behavior discussed it entirely without reference to the fact that the consumers might want to eat the food they bought!

The virtue of Cox's data is that they enable us to relate the problem-solving dimensions of behavior to social relationships and ego defensive. It is interesting that—in this study—the more "psychological" processes come into play only at the point at which felt self-confidence in accomplishing the task falls below a critical point. Thus, tendency to accept the suggestions of the alleged salesgirl in Cox's experiment must be seen as a function of

THE OBSTINATE AUDIENCE
Raymond A. Bauer

both ability to deal with the task and personality.

The difficulty of the task may either fortify or suppress the more "social-psychological" processes, depending on the specific circumstances. Thus, study of drug preference shows that as the task gets easier, the individual can indulge in the luxury of concurring with someone whom he likes, whereas when risk is great he has to concentrate on the risk-reducing potentialities of the source of information.

Thus the full-blown, problem-solving interpretation of the behavior of an audience in no sense rules out the problems with which students of communication have recently concerned themselves: ego defense and social adjustment. As a matter of fact, such problems seem explorable in a more profitable fashion if, simultaneously, attention is paid to the more overt tasks for which people use information. Yet, while there has been a consistent drift toward granting the audience more initiative, it cannot be said that the general literature on communication yet accords it a full range of intentions.

Of course, the audience is not wholly a free agent: It must select from what is offered. But even here, the audience has influence, since it is generally offered an array of communications to which it is believed it will be receptive. The process of social communication and of the flow of influence in general must be regarded as a transaction. "Transactionism," which has had a variety of meanings in psychology, is used here in the sense of an exchange of values between two or more parties; each gives in order to get.

The argument for using the transactional model for *scientific* purposes is that it opens the door more fully to exploring the intention and behavior of members of the audience and encourages inquiry into the influence of the audience on the communicator by specifically treating the process as a two-way passage. In addition to the influence of the audience on the communicator, there seems little doubt that

influence also operates in the "reverse" direction. But the persistence of the one-way model of influence discourages the investigation of both directions of relationship. With amusing adroitness some writers have assimilated the original experiment of Zimmerman and Bauer to established concepts such as reference groups, thereby ignoring what we thought was the clear implication of a two-way flow of influence.

At our present state of knowledge there is much to be said for the transactional model's pragmatic effect on research, but at the same time it is the most plausible description of the process of communication as we know it. Yet there seems to be a tendency to assume that words such as "transaction," "reciprocity," and the like imply exact equality in each exchange, measured out precisely according to the value system and judgment of the observer. This is nonsense. Obviously there are inequities, and they will persist, whether we use our own value systems as observers or if we have perfect knowledge of the people we observe.

The rough balance of exchange is sufficiently equitable in the long run to keep *most* individuals in our society engaged in the transactional relations of communication and influence. But some "alienated" people absent themselves from the network of communication as do, also, many businessmen who have doubts about the money they spend on advertising. The alienation is by no means peculiar to one end of the chain of communication or influence.

This point of view may be taken as a defense of certain social institutions such as advertising and the mass media. There is a limited range of charges against which *impotence* may indeed be considered a defense. Once more, ironically, both the communicator and the critic have a vested interest in the exploitative model. From the point of view of the communicator, it is reassuring that he will receive *at least* a fair return for his efforts; to the critic, the exploitative model gratifies the sense of moral indignation.

BAUER, R. A. *The new man in Soviet psychology.* Cambridge: Harvard Univer. Press, 1952.

BAUER, R. A. "Risk handling in drug adoption: The role of company preference." *Publ. Opin. Quart.,* 1961, 25, 546–559.

BAUER, R. A. "The initiative of the audience." Paper read at New England Psychological Association, Boston, November, 1962.

BAUER, R. A., POOL, I. DE SOLA, & DEXTER, L. A. *American business and public policy.* New York: Atherton Press, 1963.

BERELSON, B. "What missing the newspaper means." In P. F. Lazarsfeld & F. N. Stanton (Eds.), *Communications research, 1948–1949.* New York: Harper, 1949. Pp. 111–129.

BOGART, L. "Adult talk about newspaper comics." *Amer. J. Sociol.,* 1955, 61, 26–30.

CHEIN, I. "The image of man." *J. soc. Issues,* 1962, 18, 36–54.

COHEN, A. R. "Some implications of self-esteem for social influence." In C. I. Hovland & I. L. Janis (Eds.), *Personality and persuasibility.* New Haven: Yale Univer. Press, 1959. Pp. 102–120.

COLEMAN, J., MENZEL, H., & KATZ, E. "Social processes in physicians' adoption of a new drug." *J. chron. Dis.,* 1959, 9, 1–19.

COX, D. F. "Information and uncertainty: Their effects on consumers' product evaluations." Unpublished doctoral dissertation; Harvard University, Graduate School of Business Administration, 1962.

DAVISON, W. P. "On the effects of communication." *Publ. Opin. Quart.,* 1959, 23, 343–360.

DEXTER, L. A., & WHITE, D. M. (Eds.) *People, society and mass communication.* (Tentative title) Glencoe, Ill.: Free Press, in press.

HERZOG, HERTA. "What do we really know about daytime serial listeners?" In P. F. Lazarsfeld & F. N. Stanton (Eds.), *Radio research, 1942–1943.* New York: Duell, Sloan & Pearce, 1944. Pp. 3–33.

HOVLAND, C. I. "Reconciling conflicting results derived from experimental survey studies of attitude change." *Amer. Psychologist,* 1959, 14, 8–17.

HOVLAND, C. I., LUMSDAINE, A. A., & SHEFFIELD, F. D. *Experiments in mass communication.* Princeton: Princeton Univer. Press, 1949.

HYMAN, H. H., & SHEATSLEY, P. B. "Some reasons why information campaigns fail." *Publ. Opin. Quart.,* 1947, 11, 412–423.

INKELES, A., & BAUER, R. A. *The Soviet citizen.* Cambridge: Harvard Univer. Press, 1959.

JANIS, I. L. "Personality correlates of susceptibility to persuasion." *J. Pers.,* 1954, 22, 504–518.

KATZ, E., & FOULKES, D. "On the use of the mass media for 'escape.'" *Publ. Opin. Quart.,* 1962, 26, 377–388.

KIMBALL, P. "People without papers." *Publ. Opin. Quart.,* 1959, 23, 389–398.

KLAPPER, J. *The effects of mass communication.* Glencoe, Ill.: Free Press, 1960.

LAZARSFELD, P. F., BERELSON, B., & GAUDET, HAZEL. *The people's choice.* New York: Columbia Univer. Press, 1948.

MACCOBY, ELEANOR E. "Why do children watch T.V.?" *Publ. Opin. Quart.,* 1954, 18, 239–244.

MACCOBY, N., & MACCOBY, ELEANOR E. "Homeostatic theory in attitude change." *Publ. Opin. Quart.,* 1961, 25, 535–545.

MURRAY, H. A. "The personality and career of Satan." *J. soc. Issues,* 1962, 18, 1–35.

ROGERS, E. M. *Diffusion of innovations.* Glencoe, Ill.: Free Press, 1962.

SEIDENFELD, M. A. "Consumer psychology in public service and government." In R. W. Seaton (Chm.), Consumer psychology: The growth of a movement. Symposium presented at American Psychological Association, New York, September 1961.

SMITH, B. L., LASWELL, H. D., & CASEY, R. D. *Propaganda, communication and public opinion.* Princeton: Princeton Univer. Press, 1946.

WARNER, W. L., & HENRY, W. E. "The radio daytime serial: A symbolic analysis." *Genet. Psychol. Monogr.,* 1948, 37, 3–71.

WINICK, C. "Teenagers, satire and Mad." *Merrill-Palmer Quart.,* 1962, 8, 183–203.

ZIMMERMAN, CLAIRE, & BAUER, R. A. "The effects of an audience on what is remembered." *Publ. Opin. Quart.,* 1956, 20, 238–248.

MASS MEDIA, MASS SOCIETY, AND MASS CULTURE

Part V

INTRODUCTION

During the last two centuries many changes have taken place in Western societies, changes which many social scientists claim have produced a qualitatively unique form of organization. This is often referred to as mass society. With the democratic revolutions in America and France at the end of the 18th century, men—and later women—came to be viewed increasingly as political equals. The industrial revolution which followed completed the pulverization of the old aristocratic order in Europe and the nascent one in the United States. Although industrialization shattered the economic basis of the old middle class, advanced industry did not lead to a simple division of society into impoverished workers and rich owners as Karl Marx had predicted. Instead, a wide range of skills were needed, so many, in fact, that class divisions were no longer clearly visible.

The industrial order created a society in which numerous specialized occupations were needed, none of which unequivocally could provide a social identity. Belonging to a nation or state became more important and meaningful than identification through work, for one could no longer be simply an aristocrat or a peasant. In this sense society became more of a mass. Industrialization also gave rise to an explosive growth of cities, and cheap transportation between them facilitated the establishment of national rather than local markets. Regional differences became less significant, and the new urban man, with his standardized, mass-produced possessions and uniform environment, became more like his fellow citizens than ever before. Bigness, standardization, the sheer concentration of numbers, and equality between men are the characteristics of mass society.

The mass media are themselves a product of this mass society, as earlier sections have shown. For they, too, produce a standard product for their audiences. It is often argued that the development of mass society leads to a homogenization of culture—the arts, values, and overall style of life for the population—in part due to the media's impact. Proponents of this view of the media claim that the media constantly need material for their mass audiences. To fill their pages and airwaves they borrow and popularize work meant for more refined tastes. A record album entitled "Beethoven's Greatest Hits" comes readily to mind. Artists themselves are tempted by the lucrative popular market, and artistic standards are undermined. The criteria of excellence becomes: "If it sells, it's good."

Of course, this uniformity of culture is a matter of degree. Audiences themselves are not entirely homogeneous, for distinct social groupings do still exist, e.g., ethnic groupings, youth, and college educated "high-brows." These groups often attract their own specialized media. But the historical drift nevertheless seems to be toward cultural uniformity.

The following selections take up some of the features of mass media impact. The first four articles deal with the shaping of life styles. These are followed by a consideration of propaganda, and its ability to impart uniform opinions to the masses. Finally there is an examination of the work of H. Marshall McLuhan and his claim that the media, especially radio and television, have a revolutionary effect on society.

A. The Shaping of Life Styles

The theme of mass society and culture is taken up by Aubrey Smith, himself a television "insider." He warns that television is a "great leveler" which draws material from all other media and breaks down cultural uniqueness. He argues that it should be a "window on culture" by showing us the infinite diversity of man and art. To do so, it must cater to individuals rather than abstract masses. Randall Jarrell has noted that the media world is for many people the *real* world—news is only believed after it has been reported by the press.[1] The media world is oriented toward the present and future, stresses glamour and youth— which makes the everyday world appear dull—and urges instant consumption of a never-ending string of consumer goods. In this way they fashion materialistic values and aspirations that dominate our lives and conversations and corrupt or isolate the serious artists in our midst. Loring Mandel, who is himself a serious artist, writes in his article

[1]Randall Jarrell, "A Sad Heart at the Supermarket" in Norman Jacobs, ed., *Culture for the Millions* (Princeton: Van Nostrand, 1961), pp. 97–110.

about the frustrations of working within the system. Television, he claims, distorts reality by attempting to offend neither the public nor the sponsors. Commercial control, he argues, brews pollution. Smith, however, gives evidence that society in turn influences the media. Thus, standards for language and the treatment of sexual matters are changing slowly.

The article by Bradley Greenberg and Brenda Dervin implies that we must moderate our views on the pervasiveness of the media. Their surveys show that the tastes and amount of media exposure of the poor is different from the rest of the population. In many ways the poor are much more homogeneous than the general population, for they watch more television and the most popular programs, while exhibiting less exposure to such specialized media as magazines and newspapers. The media habits of the poor, both black and white, do not vary very much, so different tastes and exposure, at least as far as could be determined here, were due more to class, i.e., income levels and occupations, than to race.

Reprinted from American Scholar *(Spring 1966), pp. 303–9. Used by permission of the author.*

Television: Window on Culture or Reflection in the Glass?

AUBREY SINGER

BEFORE I begin, let me explain where I stand. I am not an academic. I am a practicing television executive producer and manager. I believe with Leo Rosten that the media, especially television, are enterprises not I. Q. tests. They feed on inventiveness, not analytic discipline. They require creative skills and nonstandardized competences. It is from this standpoint that I write.

Television is something by our times, out of our times, for our times. It reflects the virtues and faults of our times.

Its electronic principles were conceived by the prophets of technology about the same time that practical radio was being demonstrated, that Einstein was laying the basis for the exploitation of matter, that concepts of anthropology were shifting to concepts of sociology.

Television was conceived at the end of the century when man's curiosity was optimistic, charitable and untarnished, when man still believed in God, in man, in laissez-faire economy and in the rigidity and essential firmness of the world around him. Although this world was changing with increasing pace, Marlowe's lovely lines written in the last half of the sixteenth century fit the vision of man and the ambitious aspirations of the times.

> Nature that fram'd us of four elements,
> Warring within our breasts for regiment,
> Doth teach us all to have aspiring minds

> Our souls, whose faculties can comprehend
> The wondrous architecture of the world:

> And measure every wand'ring planet's course,
> Still climbing after knowledge infinite,
> And always moving as the restless spheres,
> Will us to wear ourselves and never rest,
> Until we reach the ripest fruit of all,
> That perfect bliss and sole felicity,
> The sweet fruition of an earthly crown.

There it is, the reconciliation with environment to reach felicity through knowledge.

But in the fifty years from the turn of the century, in the fifty years that television has grown from an idea to fulfilled reality, man has changed and his ideas have changed his environment. Earth, air, fire and water lost their place as observed and simple absolutes two hundred years ago. It has taken this time for a new idea, the equivalence of space, time, energy and mass, to become their substitute.

Those old four fundamental elements, those archetypes of our environment, today are held in low respect. Earth is consumed for minerals, moved by the mountain, shaped, bored into, synthesized. Air is flown over and above, liquified, solidified, split into constituent gases; its climate is altered, its heat and cold ignored. Fire is made small before the power of the nucleus: man can imitate the sun. Aqualung, bathyscaphes and permeable membranes are letting us return to our beginnings, to the sea that was the womb of life.

TELEVISION: WINDOW ON CULTURE OR REFLECTION IN THE GLASS?
Aubrey Singer

In fifty years man has not merely come to control environment at will. His familiarity and dominance now hold it in contempt. After all, when an astronaut can fly through space, when a picture can be transmitted around a planet or from another planet, when a jet can fly from London to New York in a few hours (and all this was developed within the last two decades), it is not surprising that man should have suffered an implosion of his horizons. Our personal and terrestrial worlds are no longer large enough— the immediate world has given way to the desperately desired imminence of the future world. "Give us this day our glimpse of tomorrow."

But when we look at tomorrow we have lost our vision of Utopia. Consciously people are led to believe the promised future is here. Unconsciously they suspect the vision of new bright lands has vanished forever. Along with our vision of Utopia we are losing our capacity for anger and indignation with what we see going on around us.

In his book *The Dehumanization of Art*, Ortega y Gasset says in a memorable passage: "A fundamental revision of man's attitude towards life is apt to find its first expression in artistic creation and scientific theory. The fine texture of both these matters renders them susceptible to the slightest breeze of the spiritual trade winds."

Architects, designers, composers, scientists and writers are being buffeted by the spiritual hurricane which is shaking our times. Compare the words of Marlowe's sturdy vision which I quoted earlier with E. E. Cummings' poem written with a profound sense of anxiety sometime in the 1940's.

What if a much of a which of a wind
gives the truth to summer's lie;
bloodies with dizzying leaves the sun
and yanks immortal stars awry?
Blow king to beggar and queen to seem
(blow friend to fiend: blow space to time)
—when skies are hanged and oceans drowned,
the single secret will still be man

The belief in the human spirit remains but is surrounded with a deep unease, perhaps inspired by those zephyrs of the first half of the century— relativity and quantum mechanics, psychiatry and sulphonamide, and the new knowledge of the impermanence of the universe. None of this gives a static vision—it speaks of the new relationships and resonances with which the human psyche has to reconcile itself.

And the last verse, in a spasm of buffeted prophecy, foresees our twenty post-war years and the new revolutions that were to come:

what if a dawn of a doom of a dream
bites this universe in two,
peels forever out of his grave
and sprinkles nowhere with me and you?
Blow soon to never and never to twice
(blow life to isn't: blow death to was)
—all nothing's only our hugest home;
the most who die, the more we live

There's the spiritual jet stream for you. There's U.235 and plutonium, A-bombs and H-bombs and amino acids, computers and all the paraphernalia of our moments caught in a poet's glimpse at the start of our epoch.

The poem hints too at the new changes in quality produced by the changes in quantity and the organization of quantity. It hints at mass culture in all its impact, at cinemas, national newspapers, radio and paperbacks and television and tape recordings, at punched cards and computer codes. It hopes against hope that man himself will come through all this and retain his identity.

But it's too late, for surely the point about our present-day condition lies in the Marxist tag, "A change in quantity brings a change in quality." Philosophically debatable perhaps, but tenable when one looks at the changes our new techniques have wrought in modern urban society. The change in the number of man has produced a change in the quality of man. Somehow, compressed and crowded urban man is losing his

TELEVISION: WINDOW ON CULTURE OR REFLECTION IN THE GLASS?

Aubrey Singer

individuality and becoming a cell in a larger organism.

In fact, for man to survive (and he needs nothing less than a lost Utopia really to achieve survival) he is being forced to accept (albeit and surprisingly rather willingly) a degree of organization that can lead to nothing less than insectivization. The dull routines and social customs of mankind are amenable to statistical measurement and indeed organization is now planned to facilitate this measurement. Within this framework the in-dividual turns in on himself and frenetically tries to assert his individuality and, up to a point, the more he tries to do this the more he is a subject for statistical study. From the world of things man is moving to the world of probabilities.

Television is of all this, the twentieth-century born and bred product of our society. By our times, out of our times, for our times. Its electronic principles may be fifty years old but the persuasive networked home entertainment we know today began twenty years ago in 1945. Then there were perhaps a hundred thousand sets in the world. Now there are about one hundred and fifty million. Then it covered a few urban areas in experimental form. Now it is possible to ring the northern hemisphere.

Theoretically a picture could originate in Tokyo, be sent across to Vladivostok, thence to Moscow, through Europe to Britain, across the Atlantic by satellite, across America by landline, across the Pacific by satellite and back to Tokyo. Puck said he'd put a girdle round the earth in forty minutes — that old Shakespearean square! Television can girdle the earth in about a fifth of a second, and it's no longer a miracle. Along with our contempt for spatial environment has come a loss of wonder. *Sic transit gloria imago mundi* — thus passes the glory of the image of the world, and man looks around and wonders who devalued his psyche.

Those who sense this loss react strongly; for instance, television has become the chopping block for the liberals. While in the 1930's they

indulged in political or social activity, now their attentions and frustrations are turned on the mass media, with special emphasis on television. If juvenile delinquency increases — blame television; if there is any decline in moral standards — blame television; if man feels cheated in any way by this society he has created, then blame is turned on television.

In one aspect, and alas its most common aspect, television as practiced today is just one of the many windows through which we observe, transmit and reflect our valuation of society to each other. If indeed there has been a change in the quality of life, if indeed our times have belittled our stature, the television medium in this aspect only responds to and reflects the social climate. It has little to do with the initial creation of a spiritual trade wind. It is only a sort of air conditioner that processes and gets this wind into homes more quickly.

There is, however, another aspect of television. There are times when television acts in its own right, when it evaluates the new Renaissance in its own terms, when it uses its power of communi-cation not merely to convey other people's images but rather to create out of its potentialities its own genuine statements. This is the television at which we in television have got to aim. When we do we can claim equal responsibility with those who create the values of society. With architects, authors, scientists, designers, film-makers, with all those who create and communicate original work.

If we avoid enlisting in the creative spearhead, then television abandons itself to the role of reflector. If we in television do not have the courage to speak our own mind — utter our own statements — then there are plenty who will buy our time from us, for communication, like nature, abhors a vacuum.

If television chooses to take the side of the creative talent, it joins with those trying to reach a new relationship with the shifting face of society and the fading importance of environment. It will react to the different visions of how this might

TELEVISION: WINDOW ON CULTURE OR REFLECTION IN THE GLASS?
Aubrey Singer

be achieved. For the poet: "The single secret is still man." For the composer: It can be as escapist as romanticism or as brittle and "switched on" as the new sound. For the artist: Let a Francis Bacon painting speak for itself. For the architect: Let me quote from a recent publication: "We are concerned not with architecture or town planning but with the creation of environment for every scale of human association." (Saadrach Woods, 1963.)

Perhaps the architect speaks his mind most openly. At least he admits he wants to tailor the cosmos. He might be accused of the sin of pride but he latches on to the important truth that man must continually strive to live in a homeostatic relationship with society as well as environment. For it is this aspect of feedback, and control by feedback, that has become more important to our creative thinkers than the old indefinable frozen moment when things were still against a sharp background.

This is the new relationship in which television must share, the new relationship of man to his world, of man to art, the newfound relationship of man to mind. Recently in a B.B.C. program we asked a psychiatrist to define mind:

Interviewer: If the mind can influence the body to make a father experience the discomforts of pregnancy, how do you define mind, Professor Trethowan?

Professor Trethowan: Well, that's very difficult. Mind: mind is a function of the brain, it's a function of the sensory organs which feed it, it's a function of the motor organs which give it expressions. Mind, I think, is communication. Communication between man and his environment, communication between man and himself, communication between man and man. Mind is feeling and knowing. Knowing comes from the barrier of consciousness and mingles with the other contents of the deeper parts of the mind, is reflected back again like sound from the ocean floor where it breaks consciousness and modifies knowing once again. What we see here is mind as a continuous oscillating, fluctuating process, it's a cybernetic process, there's a feedback between man and his environment, a feedback between the inner man and the outer man.

These new thoughts, these new relationships and resonances are what concern us today. Perhaps we've not lost our vision of Utopia. Perhaps it's changing. As man changes. Perhaps what we're all a party to is a struggle between man and mankind: the point of evolutionary decision between Homo sapiens and (dare I coin the word) Homo cyberneticus.

If television is to play its part in helping man define his role then on its part society must know what to expect from this electronic window — whether merely to expect a reflection from the glass or whether to expect a good view of the cultural countryside.

What is the role of television? It's difficult to define. At its most ordinary it acts as an extension of vision. It relays routine information, routine entertainment, routine education, into the drawing rooms of the audience. At its best it bestows insight. It heightens perception, reveals new relationships and brings with it a new view of our daily lives.

Television is rapidly becoming one of the main contributors to the stream of information that makes up the feedback from the world to man. In taking over, ruthlessly and with compulsion, television processes other media and tends to drown them out. Before the electronic age there was a time when the channels of information, painting, music, literature, were held in balance and did not draw on each other very much. Mass communications, especially television in its routine moments, now draws relentlessly from all other media, from films, from literature, from graphic design, from theater, from events. In doing so — both because of its limitations and because of the frequency and thoroughness with which it does so — television is tending to act as a great leveler, a sort of tomato ketchup on a feast of culture.

If this is so then all the more do we have to

TELEVISION: WINDOW ON CULTURE OR REFLECTION IN THE GLASS?
Aubrey Singer

be wary of the ubiquitous images of television. Those images are aggressively sociable and the medium that carries them technically complex; because of their easy acceptability and the facility with which they reach us in our homes these images become more credible, more important, than the reality they represent. Television supersedes reality and this new reality, this electronic picture, is a pale and transient thing compared with some of the images lying around our cultural supermarket. For instance, have you ever seen a TV picture that was really beautiful in the same way that some photographs are outstandingly so? In TV there is little or nothing that is pictorially beautiful. I suppose it has something to do with the size of screen, lack of definition and transient nature of the medium.

No, television is at its best when it's not trying to ape other media and achieve goals outside its limitations. Television is at its best in raw direct communication between people with things to say. Television favors the articulate and scorns the dumb. In television, unlike the movies, a word is worth ten thousand pictures. Television's real discovery has been the extrovert personality, the bridging of distance and, above all, the immediacy of the happening.

While there are advantages and disadvantages inherent in television itself, the mere business of operating the medium carries its own share of mixed blessings.

At the moment there are several limitations in the number of frequencies available to television operators. This of course means that under present legislation here and in Britain there is a limit to **competition**.

Making these channels available to the largest audience entails large financial outlay on capital equipment and high operating costs. Nevertheless it has been discovered on both sides of the Atlantic that television is amenable to the same management principles as any other mass distribution process. These principles require that the largest

potential audience for a given type of program be reached at the lowest cost. Television by any present criterion of efficiency is too expensive to exist in a vacuum.

The managers of TV running their enterprises on a basis of profit or cost effectiveness are well aware of these problems. However, as they shuffle their programs on the chessboards of their schedules, they are aware that in the eyes of their critics the competitive search for audience, the rate at which television swallows material, and the sheer amount of air time to be filled tends to make them play down to lesser cultural levels, supporting complacency rather than satisfying aspiration.

Obviously there is a large measure of truth in the criticism. Alas, the more so on your side of the Atlantic than on mine. But these problems are worldwide—television's costly and complex technical facilities tend to lead to a homogeneity of product on the one hand and on the other have far outstripped our knowledge of the audience.

We know some things about our audience. In most cases we consider it to be very large. For instance, in Britain certain of our television shows can command an audience of up to forty percent of the adult population of the United Kingdom, that is, about twenty-two million people. This is the mass audience the advertisers and professional managers of television are interested in.

On the other hand the audience is very intimate and very small—the family circle grouped around the television set. This is the audience that the television producer should be interested in. For television is an intimate dialogue, a two-way interacting variable between producer and receptor: "a continuous, oscillating, fluctuating process, it's a cybernetic process, there's a feedback between man and his environment, a feedback between the inner man and the outer man." Forgive me for again quoting that definition of mind but that's what television should be about, and I suspect that in the case of a successful program

TELEVISION: WINDOW ON CULTURE OR REFLECTION IN THE GLASS?
Aubrey Singer

"the oscillating processes" at both ends of the system produce an intellectual resonance in audience and also in producer.

To take an analogy from another area, this small intimate audience is the fundamental particle of which the mass audience is composed. Like the fundamental particles of physics it is subject to indeterminancy. That is, if you try to experiment with it the mere act of experimentation alters the nature of the experimental subject and therefore renders the experiment valueless.

The prime arts work at this quantum level. Composers, authors, painters don't try to gratify an audience. They try to communicate. If they communicate to a large number of those quanta of society so be it, but it is not their prime purpose in life. And it is working in this area of uncertainty and unpredictability, of having to rely on intuition rather than knowledge, that distinguishes the artist from the craftsman.

But for the manager with a large competitive stake in television this is a most unsatisfactory state of affairs. He can't afford failure and therefore he invokes mathematical statistics, for while the individual is unpredictable, the mass is only too subject to measurement.

Consider a scene that for me is even more important than those old visual clichés, the A-bomb explosion at Alamagordo or the rockets shooting up from Cape Kennedy: the grounds of Naworth Castle in England. It was under a rock overhang on those grounds in the year 1889 that Francis Galton first formulated the idea of mathematical correlation: an idea that made it possible to represent by a system of numbers the degree of relationship or of partial causality between the different variables of our ever-changing universe.

That picture should be the icon hung in the office of every television manager, for by using the techniques based on Galton's flash of intuition he can with some degree of safety ensure a mass audience for his product. And not merely this. The fabricators of his product have made it so bland that it suits all palates, for the ultimate discovery is that the television he has made to please a national mass audience will, with adjustment of language, gratify an international audience and travel with ease from country to country.

In view of the fact, this odd thought occurs to me. C. G. Jung proposed the idea of a collective unconscious. I wonder if the spread of television is not more than playing its share in the formation of a collective conscious. As people for the first time really see each other on the screen, on one hand they might get an idea of each other's humanity, but on the other the process whereby man becomes a cell in an organism inevitably will be speeded up.

Throughout this paper I have stressed that television is something created by our times for our times. We live in an age where the information about the world is increasing exponentially. We live in an age where man is graduating from machines that amplify his energy and assist his muscles, to machines that amplify his mental capacity and assist his intellect in the control of his surroundings.

Television is something new and persuasive, one of the two media that can keep pace with the times. Perhaps the formation of this collective conscious is just the first step in the new directions that man is taking.

Recently in one of our programs we did a story on trends in science fiction, interviewing many authors. Since this genre had already predicted flights to the moon and telecommunication satellites as far back as 1910, we asked these writers what areas concerned them at this moment. Their answer was robots! And they saw man building parts of his robots into himself.

Clearly they see the emergence of "Homo cyberneticus." The new trend, this spiritual trade wind, is already discernible. Western man is desperately trying to come to grips with the machine. He sees his individuality being submerged in a tabulated mass, his ideas being catalogued

TELEVISION: WINDOW ON CULTURE OR REFLECTION IN THE GLASS?

Aubrey Singer

in a memory store, his actions being predicted in the banks of calculating transistors. This trend explains the popularity of television shows that depict man in a dominant friendly or understandable relationship with a machine: "The Man From U.N.C.L.E.," "Dr. Who" (the Daleks), the James Bond stories. It also explains pop art, op art, recent sculpture and science fiction.

Unlike other intellectual revolutions, in which the thinking only slowly percolated through the strata of society, this revolution is likely to go quickly. Television has already started the work of feedback and information with unrivaled rapidity. But in operating at the predictable mass level, in so consciously attempting to please, the medium is throwing away opportunities, all too often wasting its potential in internal rivalry, failing to attract the best talent and thus not providing the motivations expected of any leader.

This situation grew out of the beginning of radio, for this first precursor of television started in an atmosphere of hotly debated political compromise. In the United States it was decided that it should remain in the hands of private enterprise, in Britain it was thought too big to be dominated by advertisers, and so we started the B.B.C., whose independence was assured by the unwritten checks and balances in our own constitutional process. Since that time under your antitrust laws you've had to break up one network. We in Britain decided that monopoly was stifling and brought in a second television system, this one based on advertising.

Systems that have grown out of compromise are not necessarily the answer. They are too big, too heavily involved in getting audiences in order to prove their efficiency and justify their capitalization. Yet can any other system provide the amount of high standard continuous entertainment, information and education in such a widespread manner?

Why has nobody attempted to undertake a design study of a television system in present-day terms? I don't know what such a study would produce but the specification outlining the parameters of the design might be as follows:

"Mankind needs a system of television communication so designed and controlled that communication can occur between all levels of our audience and all levels of the culture represented by that audience. The audience should be able to select from any of these levels when and as it wishes. In order to achieve this, ways should be explored to ensure that the costs of television apparatus and production come down, thus reducing the operator's need for large audiences and enabling him to design programs for the unit rather than the mass."

The rub of the design problem would be to prevent such a system from becoming an Orwellian nightmare, for such a window on culture would be a two-way affair in which the image might well increase its transcendence over reality. Television receivers would become communicators; not only would they receive local network and international programs, but by means of wave guides (to provide the channels) and small cameras and cheap video recorders they would become a link between the viewer and his personal world, between the home, the library, the bank, the office, the shops and, of course, the Government.

To design such a machine is problem enough, but to design a system (no! let's call it a medium) not merely for social communication but also capable of responding to the whole range of values and spiritual needs is problem indeed. It is the very heart of the design challenge and of our present dilemma. For the paradox is surely this:

On the one hand mankind needs a large "machine" element in order to integrate with the new cybernetic culture so eagerly awaited. These machines, mechanical, mathematical and social, are utterly essential if mankind is to come to grips with and accept his new environmental surrogates, the equivalence of space, time, energy and mass.

TELEVISION: WINDOW ON CULTURE OR REFLECTION IN THE GLASS?
Aubrey Singer

On the other hand, man—the individual man—recognizes that in using these machines and adapting himself to their techniques, he must assume their attributes. This is the moment of terrible truth, for in gaining "the sweet fruition of an earthly crown," the individual risks submerging his humanity and becoming a digit in a socio-cybernetic system.

As a television man I know where I stand. I believe that it is not the job of mass communication to pander to mankind. Rather we should use our ubiquity to seek out and service the individual.

I believe that television, given the opportunities, can be more than of our times, out of our times and for our times. I believe it can be ahead of our times, providing crucial leadership, fostering man's awareness of his position, providing the feedback that enables us to utilize the full spectrum of our total vision. It will be and should be an open window on our culture, helping to ensure that "the single secret will still be man."

Reprinted from New York Times *(March 25, 1970).* © *1970 by The New York Times Company. Reprinted by permission*

Television Pollutes Us All

LORING MANDEL

TELEVISION is an ecological problem. It is. Like many other industrial, social political contributors, television has made life too toxic. It's a polluter, and has done much more than its owners and managers believe to produce the lethal atmosphere we're dangling in.

These are speculations that keep rising to the surface when I face the telecast of a play I have written. Given my belief that our present television programming is a national disaster, and given that I have made my living as a supplier of some of that programming, it should be easy to understand from where these speculations arise. It may be ungenerous to commit them to print. It may even be imprudent (or, in this case, imprudential). But here is the argument.

Oil corporations blacken our beaches and our skies and have cooperated with some of our largest corporate complexes — aviation, military, construction, transportation — to make a substantial part of the world uninhabitable for many forms of life, including ours. Americans, convinced, that brightness and whiteness are even closer to Godliness than good old cleanliness was, have produced a race of phosphor-bearing detergents and towel-fluffers that has incalculably altered the natural balance (from which we evolved). Our rivers and lakes are sinkholes. Man may be a temporary matter, but suds are forever.

Mass transportation has produced a sooty sulfurous fog which hangs like a shroud over cities and suburbs, easily seen from the jet window as a writer shuttles from coast to coast, making his contribution.

Americans consume power as if it were really as clean and odorless as a copper wire, while the power companies hurl tons of ashes into the air every hour to produce their thing. Blessed with the fruit of the no-deposit-no-return-zip-top-indestructible-sharp-edged container, we have produced parks that are uninhabitable and battlefield beaches (where the waves of oil roll in like some lugubrious surf).

And television feeds us poison ivy lying to us about what life is really like, what people are really like. Communication between people is increasingly out of sync. Television has lied to us about ourselves, and because it shovels information at us in such quantities so relentlessly and with such impact, we believe it instead of believing our own guts. We find it harder to understand each other. We find it harder to understand ourselves.

Of course, it's pollution.

TVstations meet their commitments to the public with perhaps 15 to 20 per cent of their programming. (I am lumping in network and local output, news and public service programs, educational stations, and I think the estimate is probably generous.) In the New York viewing area, of an output of probably more than 700 hours of TV each week — figuring here on my scratchpad — only 140 hours a week are given over to windows through which we can view the real world, while 560 hours a week are given over

TELEVISION POLLUTES US ALL
Loring Mandel

to painted doors by which we can shut it out, escape from it.

We have many bright, good, progressive network managers who might concede that the opinion-forming power of their news and public affairs programming is substantial, but they will deny, and deny, that their entertainment programming has its impact as well. Since all (or almost all) opinion-related material has been carefully excised from entertainment programming, the networks maintain that the impact is neutral.

There is no neutral information. Everything bears its comment, and has its impact. Even the absence of meaning conveys meaning.

Entertainment programming, film or tape, series or special, comedy or action-adventure, tells us certain things. That America is traditionally anti-intellectual. A lie. That the Good Man is the Man Who Ultimately Goes Along. A lie. That beneficence is inherent in business. A lie. That love is good, sex is better, and that passion doesn't exist. That any means are justifiable. That passivity is wise. That intensity is a spectator sport. That people bleed only from the corner of the mouth, and that instant regeneration of human tissue is a fact of violence. And by the purposeful omission of material that is relevant to our contemporary situation the entertainment programers make reality more foreign to us. By expressing simplistic solutions to all problems, they rob us of the tools of decision. The truth is not in them.

This, of course, is simplistic too. Who says what the Truth is? It's a little different for each of us. But if there is some existential truth, surely it will show up even in honest diversity. At least it's a goal to aim for. Yet I must tell you, I have never heard of any advertising agency (and they, perhaps more than networks, control what you see on television) which accepted Truth as a reason for doing anything (or not doing it). Sales, Client Image, Projected Audience Appeal, these are the watchwords. I have spoken to network program developers and know that Truth is not considered a productive standard for material. It is not

policy. Instead, policy means Fantasy, Enchantment, Escape, Unreality. And the power of the Groin.

And yet here I am with a show going on. A drama that juxtaposes certain events in the life of a man, a doctor—the loss of his office, the deterioration of a world in which he had been functional. How the events of the story contribute to the doctor's future is the underlying quest of the drama. I have aimed for truth, not simply verisimilitude, and so have most of those who collaborated in the production.

I have been able to write toward the truth, or its essence, because I deal in an obsolete form, the TV drama, where it is not quite so necessary to succumb to the dicta of mass audience programming. Not quite. Almost every writer I know who contributes to this tiny niche in the TV schedule aims high. None of us has to go to story editors with, "I envision this fabulously rich man who gives away a million dollars to some deserving person every week," or, "We take this white girl who happens to have black skin . . ."

Yet, since Agnew, the possible arenas for drama have become fewer. Under attack from many elements of an exacerbated society, networks are being led back by their advertisers into safe havens. Really sensitive subject matter is undesirable, and in many ways there is less freedom today than 10 years ago. I wonder if my 1967 drama for "CBS Playhouse," "Do Not Go Gentle Into That Good Night," which dealt in part with homes for the elderly, could be done today. Just to ask the question is a measure of what has happened. But what does it matter in the general pattern of programming? A small fleck in a wide fabric. Of the many thousands of viewing hours a year, the little obsolete art form of the television drama fills only 12 or 14.

Environmental pollution, that's what it's all about.

And why not? Regardless of what we wish it to be, television is just another industry with another product. When Jack Gould said ten years ago, "The thing I object to is that the world of commerce is using the resources of the theater, of all our culture, for sales purposes," he might as well have been objecting to the 24-hour day. That being true, where we're at is no surprise. As long as people buy the products and services that waste our minds and ecology, pollution pays. When broadcasters say they're giving the public what it wants, they're probably right. But so is Con Ed. So is Detroit. So is Procter and Gamble. So is the Pentagon. And we're dying.

Norbert Weiner, the man whose legacy includes a major share of the modern computer, understood this process and identified it as "The traditional American philosophy of progress." And the great-grandchildren of his computers are now being used to pre-test the sales potential of ideas before they are allowed (or disallowed) exposure on "Free TV."

The Government can do nothing, nor does it want to. Senator Pastore, for all his concern about sex and violence, has proposed a law affecting TV station licenses that will (if much independent comment can be trusted) only consolidate more power in the hands of those who have it now. The Administration has attacked informed news analysis, when critical. FCC Commissioners are largely management-oriented. Television reporters are being forced to work for the Attorney General. Those politicians in Congress who depend on television exposure to maintain their public identities are not about to bite the hand, nor do they nibble. And advocates of censorship who find much to offend them on the tube are largely offended by the truth they see, not the lies.

Even in my small area, there are obstacles once a story and script are accepted. One may find his work altered by knowing or unknowing hands: by directors; by star-sized actors whose only goal is to play Christ no matter what the part is written to be and who will castrate director, writer, script, everyone, to have it their way; by critics who are wedded to ideas of the well-made play form and will not find any merit in originality unless it is labeled as Experimental or comes from another country, and/or those critics who maintain a rigorously Shavian standard for drama specials and quite a different one for the weekly inundation of crap that pours from the set. Television pollutes us all.

Perhaps television should be forced into a limited profit structure, like many utilities, so that it would not have to compete for the advertising dollar at the expense of its potential. I am certain, however, that as long as 80 per cent—or even 50 per cent—of its programming is stridently anti-intellectual, misleading about the inner life of human beings, false about the nature and quality of life, television is fostering the disintegration of our society. It reinforces the polarizing of this country, bears some share of responsibility for our persecution of independent youth, for political hucksterism, for our hanging judge in Chicago, for police in L.A. who draws guns on traffic violators, for our agonizingly agnewized contempt for the value of protest, of dissent, or opinion, of thought, even of civilized discourse. We are lost in Kansas City with the roadmap from Nashville, and we're going mad from irrelevance!

It's in the air. It's pollution.

President Nixon's speechwriter says ". . . recognition of the truth that wealth and happiness are not the same thing requires us to measure success or failure by new criteria." I'm with him there. Isn't there some way we can turn television into a part of real life rather than a destroyer, so that it can serve the needs of people before the needs of commerce?

Probably not.

Reprinted from Columbia Journalism Review *(Spring, 1968), pp. 19–23.* ©. *Used by permission of author and publisher.*

Is Anything Unprintable?

LEE H. SMITH

WHEN Michael McClure's play, *The Beard*, opened in New York last fall, the daily reviews were unanimous on two points. They didn't like the play very much and they didn't want to talk about it very much. The reason for the latter seems clear. The play, a fanciful sex duel between Jean Harlow and Billy the Kid, not only contained a good deal of verbal obscenity, it also ended in one of the most startling scenes ever staged. *The New York Times* described that finale as "a highly publicized sexual act" (referring, somewhat cryptically, to the notoriety the play had received in San Francisco). The *Daily News* called it "an unorthodox sex act." The *New York Post* glided over it as "a sexual act that can't be described in a family newspaper." What the reviews couldn't say—or wouldn't say—was what the fuss was all about: an act of cunnilingus.

For better or for worse, American society has become increasingly concerned with its sex life and more and more eager to talk about it in public. The taboos against strong language and references to sex are vanishing with such staggering speed that it is often hard to remember what last year's taboos were. Two years ago, the movie *Who's Afraid of Virginia Woolf?* created a stir when Richard Burton said "hump the hostess." Today, the film *In Cold Blood* uses much earthier language and no one bothers to mention it. Norman Mailer was an iconoclast when he wrote the verb "fug" in *The Naked and The Dead.* In his latest novel, *Why Are We In Vietnam?*, he uses much more

explicit obscenities much more often and hardly anyone is surprised.

Candor is not restricted to the arts. Women hem their skirts well above their knees and trot off to cocktail parties where "The Pill" has replaced breastfeeding versus bottlefeeding as the favorite topic of conversation. Homosexuals have emerged from the shadows to parade in front of the White House and the Pentagon to demand equality, including the right to serve in the armed forces. August state legislatures openly debate the pros and cons of relaxing the laws for abortion—a word that used to be anathema almost everywhere. Schools across the country are beginning to feel the pressure to provide sex education, even for grammar school pupils.

The sexual revolution is real enough. For responsible newspapers, magazines, and radio and television stations that presents a problem: How can they report the revolution without compromising their standards? Some publications, of course, have a vested interest in cheering the revolution on. Magazines such as *Playboy* and its female counterpart, *Cosmopolitan*, often seem to be leading the way. But many more editors seem to be thoroughly confused. They want to keep up with what's happening but they aren't quite certain how to do it. More and more editors are faced with the problem of separating what is pertinent from what is simply prurient and trying to define the line between good reporting and bad taste. Some publications have been extremely bold, others far too reticent. And surprisingly, television—usually thought of as the meekest of the media—may be on its way to establishing a standard that accepts progress and yet maintains good taste; it may help the so-called "family" publications decide what can be said and what cannot.

Government censorship doesn't offer much guidance. The Supreme Court in recent years has decided it will allow just about anything short of what it considers hard-core pornography or (in the case of Ralph Ginzburg's conviction) hard-sell titillation—boundaries most editors have no intention of approaching. A few publications are exploring and exploiting that frontier, most recently the growing band of underground newspapers scattered in hippie enclaves from New York's East Village to San Francisco's Haight Ashbury district. The *East Village Other*, one of the most successful undergrounders, recently displayed, for example, a somewhat fuzzy photograph of what appeared to be an act of homosexual fellatio. And in the classified pages anyone can put his sexual appetites on the block. One ad in the same issue ran: "Attention!!! Dominant male wishes to meet docile female, gay or straight. We will have a whipping good time." As a result of such frankness, the Brooklyn District Attorney's office seized 1,000 copies of the paper and the editors of *EVO* are going to have to defend their candor in court.

The older *Village Voice*, which straddles the underground and the Establishment, draws the line at peddling perversion in its classifieds. "If you allow those," says editor Daniel Wolf, "suddenly you discover you're running an adjunct to Bellevue." But by most standards the *Voice* is unabashedly frank. "We have always been more open than most papers," observes Wolf. The *Voice* has used the common four-letter words freely for years. Lately the *Voice* has started running front-on photographs of nudes, collected by *Voice* photographers making the rounds of Greenwich Village dances and art shows. "We

didn't sit around and discuss it," says Wolf. "We had the pictures and we just said 'what the hell' and shoved them in."

At other publications such decisions are momentous, even when an editor knows he is reaching a limited, sophisticated, and well-educated audience. Robert Manning, editor of *The Atlantic*, recalls pondering over a reportorial piece on Harlem in which the writer quoted a young boy sticking his head out of the window and shouting, "Fuck you, white cop." Says Manning: "I looked at it, stared at it, and finally decided the only way to convey the full gut of it was to use it. The idea that a Negro boy of four, five, or six was already conditioned to that extent seemed to me to be something worth conveying. Dots would have undercut the impact."

Manning declines to allow four-letter words in fiction, but Willie Morris, editor of *Harper's*, says he will permit four-letter words in fiction or non-fiction when they are used by established authors. "This is something we would never do lightly," says Morris, "but times have changed. American readers are now infinitely more sophisticated than at any other time and they even demand more of the language than at any other time." Morris turned over the entire March issue of the magazine to Norman Mailer—an act that would make most editors shudder—for his journalistic report. "The Steps of the Pentagon." The report is witty, moving, and, in part, scatological.

Intellectual monthlies such as *Harper's* and *The Atlantic* can proceed rather boldly without worrying about offending large groups of readers. Candor becomes a real problem for general circulation newspapers and magazines that reach mass audiences. Advertising departments are particularly nervous. They diligently "ink in" clothes on unclad starlets in movie ads and edit out the explicit language underneath. When the Yugoslav film *Love Affair—Or The Case of the Missing Switchboard Operator* opened in New York in February the *Times* and the *Post* were sent an ad displaying a nude woman lying face down on

IS ANYTHING UNPRINTABLE?
Lee H. Smith

a bed. Both newspapers "draped" a towel over her and the *Post* added a brassiere as well. This coverup seemed reasonable enough. The ad was nothing but a cheap come-on.

Often, however, advertising departments are over-zealous. When the Yale University School of Drama opened its season last fall, the school routinely sent out an ad that listed the plays, including John Ford's seventeenth-century tragedy *'Tis Pity She's A Whore*. The *New Haven Register* reformed the lady somewhat and changed the title to *'Tis Pity She's Bad*. The *Hartford Courant* turned her into a mystery woman by truncating the title to read *'Tis Pity She's*. Donald Spargo, advertising director for the *Register*, explained that the wording of the ad was read to him over the phone and that if he had realized it was a title, he probably wouldn't have touched it. But Sidney Kaplan, advertising manager for the *Courant*, stood fast. "We just didn't run it, period," he snapped. "We try to run a clean newspaper."

The *New York Times Book Review* recently became alarmed that a deluge of ads for marriage manuals and other non-fiction works dealing with sex was giving the book review a bad image. As a result, the *Times* decided to close the *Review*, probably the country's major display case for publishers, to all non-fiction sex books—the important as well as the trivial and the titillating.

Editors are similarly fearful that the wrong word or picture is going to bring them reprisals from their readership. Over the past twenty years or so they have been slowly and cautiously scratching out such euphemisms as "social disease," "illegal operation," and "assault" and penciling in the more specific "syphilis," "abortion," and "rape." In some cases they have moved boldly. *Newsweek* magazine put a partly nude Jane Fonda on its cover in November to illustrate its special report on "The Permissive Society." *Life* magazine ran an excerpt from *The Naked Ape* in which British zoologist Desmond Morris examines man as a primate. The first paragraph of the excerpt included the sentence: "He [man] is proud that he has the biggest brain of all the primates but

attempts to conceal the fact that he also has the biggest penis, preferring to accord this honor falsely to the mighty gorilla." (That same observation was to cause a considerable amount of trouble for other publications later.)

Some newspapers have been equally outspoken. Unfortunately, one of the best of them is now dead: the *New York Herald Tribune*. When Dr. William H. Masters and Mrs. Virginia Johnson published *Human Sexual Response*, a physiological study of the sexual act, in 1966, the *Herald Tribune* science editor, Earl Ubell, was unabashed in his summary and consequently helped dispel some disturbing myths about sexual performance. In paraphasing the book's conclusions Ubell included such paragraphs as: "Neither the size of the male sex organ, the penis, nor that of its corresponding anatomical part in the female, the clitoris, has any relation to the adequacy of the man or woman as a sex partner."

The *New York Times* was more reticent, for which the *Times* is now apologetic. "I think we were wrong," says *Times* managing editor E. Clifton Daniel. "This was a serious work and it would have been perfectly acceptable to quote words such as penis and clitoris."

The *Times* has become more candid recently and such sensitive topics as homosexuality are reported liberally. And in its recent series on the drug-obsessed society the *Times* quoted a girl who said she took amphetamines to prolong her sexual activities. "I once stayed in bed for three days with a man," the girl was quoted as saying, "taking pills to keep going and smoking pot to enjoy myself." Still, the *Times* proceeds cautiously. When theater critic Clive Barnes reviewed *The Beard* he first wrote the word "cunnilingus." Metropolitan news editor Arthur Gelb asked him to take the word out: "It wasn't a big argument but at this time I just don't think we should use it. That might not be the case a month from now."

Other newspapers, perhaps a majority, are much more conservative. A former reporter on one of the largest papers in upstate New York says her movie reviews were consistently bowdlerized. In discussing *A Guide for the Married Man* she tried to convey the tone of the film by referring to "bouncing bosoms and fannies." The phrase was softened to read "flouncing females." In outlining the plot of *The Family Way* she said of the young bride: "After six weeks of marriage she was still a virgin." The desk changed it to read: "The marriage was not consummated"—a throwback to 1953 when the word "virgin" made *The Moon Is Blue* a "dirty" movie.

Usually, such editing is carried out quietly. But this January two of the nation's most influential publications—*The Chicago Tribune* and *The Washington Post*—were caught editing in public. The two papers decided to recall some 1.7 million copies of *Book World*, the Sunday book review supplement they have published jointly since last September, when they spotted a page-one review they found offensive.

Peter Farb, a New Yorker who writes science books for laymen, reviewed Morris's *The Naked Ape* and paraphrased some of the book's conclusions, including: "The human male and not the gorilla possesses the largest penis of all primates; the human's preferred face-to-face mating is due to the frontal position of sexual signaling devices."

In New York, *Book World's* editor, Byron Dobell, a former managing editor of *Esquire* magazine, approved the review and dispatched it to be printed for the *Post* in Philadelphia and to Chicago to be printed for the *Tribune*. *Tribune* editor W. D. Maxwell and publisher J. Howard Wood picked up copies from an early press run and apparently carried them off to the *Tribune* board of directors' meeting in Fort Lauderdale, Florida. Five days before the book review was scheduled to appear, Maxwell put in an urgent call to Thomas Furlong, managing editor in charge of features. Maxwell's order was to kill the review. Some 3,000 copies had already been sent to bookstores, libraries, and publishers, but the *Tribune* managed to collect more than a million copies that had been sent to distributors or were still in the plant. The page-one review was killed and a review that was scheduled to have run the following week was substituted. (Estimates

of the cost of the kill ranged from $30,000 to $100,000.) The *Post* did not kill the review but did strike out the lines referring to penis from its 500,000 copies. (The *Post* had been much bolder in 1966 when it ran Ubell's review of *Human Sexual Response*.)

The *Tribune's* kill seemed to be consistent with Maxwell's policy. The story goes that in 1961 he was given a copy of *The Carpetbaggers* by a well-meaning friend who thought it was a Reconstruction novel. Maxwell was so shocked that he ordered the book eliminated from the *Tribune's* best-seller list and, to exclude similar works, he changed the name of the section to "Among the Best-Sellers." *Tribune* readers were thus "protected" from a significant—if depressing—scrap of sociology: The American public buys a lot of trash.

Because it does so much of its editing in public—"bleeping out" of offensive words—television often seems to be the most cautious of the media. But lately the bleeps have been fading and television has been growing much bolder. Five years ago, David Susskind invited a group of panelists that included *Playboy* editor and publisher Hugh Hefner and psychologst Dr. Albert Ellis to discuss "The Sexual Revolution in America." The show was taped but Bennett Korn, then a vice president of WNEW, refused to let it go on the air. Last year Susskind taped an even more delicate discussion, "Homosexuality: Perversion or Sickness?", with two psychiatrists and Dick Leitsch, president of the homosexual Mattachine Society. The show was broadcast to thirty cities across the country without objection from station managements.

Earl Ubell, who is now science editor for WCBS-TV, believes that he has been just as frank on television as he was on the *Herald Tribune* and that his only restraint is to make certain he delivers his information on sex soberly with no hint of a snicker or a raised eyebrow. And recently, Johnny Carson demonstrated that even a mass audience of network viewers will accept a serious discussion of sex. Carson interviewed Desmond Morris on *The Tonight Show* and needled *The Chicago Tribune*. "You talked about his [man's] penis," Carson said to Morris.

IS ANYTHING UNPRINTABLE?
Lee H. Smith

"And they took that out of the paper in Chicago, because it would offend people . . . And I don't understand it, in this day and age, that you could not use that in a family newspaper." No bleep. No outraged phone calls to local television stations. Ernest Lee Jahncke Jr., NBC's vice president for standards and practices, explains why the network didn't bleep the reference. "This wasn't a lot of quipping and kidding around," he says. "It was a serious discussion, an adult discussion."

Television seems to be developing an "adult" standard for coping with the problem of sexual candor. Newspapers and many magazines persist in feeling inhibited by "family" standards. Even *The Wall Street Journal* — hardly a publication one passes on to the children — falls back on this excuse. When Edmund Fuller reviewed Mailer's *Why Are We in Vietnam?* for the *Journal* last fall he said: "Whether or not this newspaper is a family one depends, we suppose, on the family. But it is enough of one that we are restricted from offering you a slice of this pungent literary haggis for your own revulsion."

The premise that mass publications must be edited for "families" always seems to ignore the fact that families are growing up. Also, it begs the question of why publications should be edited for the most innocent reader. Most readers (if Marshall McLuhan is right, all readers) are adults and want to be written as adults. Furthermore, the "family" standard is an unprofessional one that isn't applied to other areas of coverage. Any correspondent who filed from Saigon that he is witnessing a war that can't be talked about in a family newspaper would be hastily recalled.

This does not mean that editors should discard good taste and indulge themselves in titillation and gratuitous obscentiy. On the contrary, it means that they should use good taste as a standard — their own good taste — and not waste their time trying to anticipate the most hysterical reaction of the most sensitive reader. The story of the candid society is too big to be ignored and from all indications it will run for a long time.

Reprinted from Public Opinion Quarterly *(Summer, 1970), pp. 224–35. Used by permission.*

Mass Communication Among the Urban Poor

BRADLEY S. GREENBERG AND BRENDA DERVIN

DESPITE the considerable attention now focused on poverty, there is a dearth of information about the communication behavior of the poor, particularly their mass media behavior.[1] The Kerner Commission report[2] and other authoritative sources[3] on poverty have emphasized that the poor live in a subculture, suggesting that the behaviors, attitudes, and feelings of the poor are different from those of the rest of society. Yet, in one important class of behaviors and attitudes — those dealing with the media by which the majority society can communicate with the poverty subculture — empirical data are minimal.

Prior research yielded two working hypotheses. The first was to expect considerable difference between low-income and general population adults in their media behavior. The classic media use studies and the few studies that specifically compared the poor with the general population have agreed, for example, that the poor use more TV and less print media than the general population.[4] The second hypothesis, less well supported by the literature, was to expect considerable similarity between low-income blacks and low-income whites. Considerable research suggests that the poor live in a subculture that makes them much alike no matter what their race or ethnic origin.[5] Herzog, for example, has argued that socio-economic status is a stronger variable than race in relation to family patterns and life styles.

METHOD AND PROCEDURES

Low-income sample. A low-income sample was obtained through a three-stage process. First, three 20-block areas within urban Lansing were identified by local OEO personnel as having the highest concentrations of low-income residents. Next, 10 blocks were randomly sampled within each of the three areas. A starting point for interviewing was selected randomly for each block. The third sampling stage was done in the field. Interviewers began knocking on doors at the random starting point, moving counterclockwise until they had completed 10 interviews on the designated block. Only English-speaking persons at least 18 years of age were interviewed.

The half-hour questionnaire[6] was personally administered by trained interviewers during a three-week period from February 16 to March 14, 1967. Interviewers averaged one refusal for every two interviews obtained. A low-income sample of 312 respondents was obtained — 131 blacks, 150 whites, and 31 Spanish-origin respondents, who were not used in this analysis.

Of the low-income sample, 61 per cent had 11 years of education or less, compared with 18 per cent for the general population sample. Only 10 per cent of the low-income sample reported jobs which fit white-collar descriptions, compared with 67 per cent of the general population sample.[7]

MASS COMMUNICATION AMONG THE URBAN POOR
Bradley S. Greenberg and Brenda Dervin

Low-income blacks were younger than low-income whites; had larger households, more children, and were more likely to have more adults living in the household. They had more people in the household holding jobs, they had lower occupational prestige; and they were more likely to be unemployed or on welfare. They had lived in the city fewer years and were, for the most part, originally from the South. These differences would all be expected on the basis of previous research.[8] No difference in current weekly income was found for these two subgroups.

General population sample. A shorter version of the same questionnaire was administered by phone to a systematic probability sample of 285 numbers drawn from the 1967 Lansing phone book. The survey was done April 18–20, 1967, by eight experienced female interviewers, making at least three callbacks to each number. Of the 285 sampled numbers, 206 interviews (72 per cent) were completed. Fifteen per cent refused; 8 per cent could not be reached because they were always busy or no one answered; and in 5 per cent of the cases the phone had been disconnected or was not residential; or no one could speak English or was over 18 years of age.

The questionnaires used with both samples tapped four central areas of mass communication behavior: media ownership, media use, media content preferences, and media attitudes. The statistical significance of comparisons was tested by chi-square.

MEDIA OWNERSHIP

The initial task was to determine what media were regularly available. Table 1 reports the availability of TV sets, radios, daily newspapers, phonographs, and phonograph records for both the low-income and general population samples, and the black and white low-income subsamples.

In comparing the low-income sample with the general population, two findings stand out. First, the low-income respondents were as likely as general population respondents to own at least one TV set — 97 per cent of both samples do. Second, the general population adults were significantly more likely to have all *other* types of media available. In juxtaposition, these two findings suggest the relative importance of TV within the media environment of the poor.

The consistency of these significant differences, however, cloaks another finding. While the general population was more likely to have more media available, the low-income population was certainly not media-poor. Only 3 per cent of the low-income sample reported not owning a TV set, 7 per cent did not have at least one radio, 25 per cent did not have a newspaper delivered, 23 per cent did not own a phonograph, and 22 per cent had no phonograph records. Thus, while the general population had comparatively more media available, a majority of the low-income respondents were affluent in terms of the media available to them.

Fewer media ownership differences existed between the low-income black and white respondents. Low-income whites were no more likely than low-income blacks to own a TV or a color TV set, or more radios. Low-income whites were more likely to have a newspaper delivered, but interestingly enough the phonograph ownership pattern was reversed. Low-income blacks (84 per cent) were significantly more likely than whites (71 per cent) to own one or more phonographs, and to own more phonograph records. This latter difference was accounted for mainly because 29 per cent of the whites owned no records at all, compared with only 13 per cent of the blacks.

TELEVISION USE AND CONTENT PREFERENCES

Table 2 reports the amount of television viewing for each group and the regular viewing of 12 top-rated TV shows. The most striking difference

TABLE 1

Media Ownership

| | | | | Low-Income | | |
Media	Low Income (N = 281)	General Population (N = 206)	p	White (N = 150)	Black (N = 131)	p
No. of working TV sets						
0	3%	3%	n.s.	3%	2%	n.s.
1	63	58		66	60	
2 or more	34	39		31	38	
Color TV						
Don't own	91	78	<.001	91	91	n.s.
Do own	9	22		9	9	
No. of radio sets						
0	7	0	<.001	6	8	n.s.
1	31	17		30	32	
2	29	26		30	27	
3 or more	33	57		34	32	
Newspaper delivered daily						
No	25	14	<.01	20	31	<.05
Yes	75	86		80	69	
Phonographs						
0	23	14	<.02	29	16	<.01
1 or more	77	86		71	84	
No. of phono records						
0	22	17	<.05	29	13	<.01
1–49	27	21		23	31	
50–99	18	28		17	20	
100 or more	32	34		31	35	

between the low-income and the general population samples is the very large difference in viewing time. Forty-one per cent of the general population sample reported that they had not watched TV the previous day, compared with 24 per cent of the low-income sample. Only 17 per cent of the general population reported viewing 4 or more hours the previous day, compared with 53 per cent of the low-income sample.

The mean number of hours viewed for the general population was 2.0, compared with 5.2 for the low-income sample. With 16 hours considered as a waking day, the low-income adults spent, on the average, almost one-third of that day viewing TV in comparison with one-eighth for the general population. In fact, more than one-fourth of the low-income respondents spent more than one-half of their day watching TV.

An over-all measure of the number of 12 top-rated TV shows viewed regularly agrees with the general TV viewing time results, with the low-income sample watching a significantly greater number of these shows. Separate comparisons for each of the 12 top shows indicate that on 8 of the

MASS COMMUNICATION AMONG THE URBAN POOR

Bradley S. Greenberg and Brenda Dervin

TABLE 2

Television Usage and Content Preferences

Viewing and Preference	Low Income (N = 281)	General Population (N = 206)	p	Low-Income White (N = 150)	Low-Income Black (N = 131)	p
Hours viewed yesterday						
0	24%	41%	<.001	23%	25%	n.s.
¼–3¾	23	42		25	20	
4–7¾	26	12		29	24	
8 or more	27	5		23	31	
No. of 12 top TV shows[a] watched regularly						
0–4	31	58	<.001	33	28	n.s.
5–6	18	20		21	15	(<.10)
7–8	27	15		29	26	
9–12	23	7		17	30	

[a] The 12 TV shows listed were among the top-rated shows in the nation for the period October 1966–January 1967. Since TV ratings vary greatly depending on any given week's TV fare, four different weeks of TV ratings were used in compiling this list—the Arbitron ratings for 1/18/67 and 10/23/66 and the Nielson ratings for 12/18/66 and 11/5/66. Specials and movies were deleted. Of the shows remaining, any show which was ranked in the top 12 on two or more of the rating lists was included. Source for rating lists was *Broadcasting Magazine*. The 12 shows included: Beverly Hillbillies, Andy Griffith, Green Acres, Bonanza, Daktari, Ed Sullivan, Lucy, Red Skelton, Jackie Gleason, Walt Disney, Lawrence Welk, and Bewitched.

12, the low-income adults were significantly more likely (all at $p < .001$) to be regular viewers.

More important, however, is the relative popularity of the 12 shows in each sample. The rank order correlation between the two samples was .03, indicating that the favorite shows of the low-income adults were not the favorites of the general population.

We also analyzed the daily viewing patterns of the two samples. The low-income adults started their viewing earlier, continued their viewing at a higher level throughout the day, and ended their viewing later. The largest differences occurred in the morning and afternoon, when the general population viewing remained stable at around 4 to 10 per cent while that of the low-income sample ranged from 14 to 36 per cent. Indeed, the peak afternoon viewing for the low-income sample was not very

different from their peak evening viewing (48 per cent).

Between the white and black low-income subsamples there were no consistent differences. Blacks were not significantly more likely than whites to watch more television, although the mean differences (5.7 *vs.* 4.8 hours a day) indicates such a trend. Nor were the two subsamples different in the number of top TV shows they watched regularly.

This lack of differences carries over into the content of viewing, also. For 6 of the 12 top TV shows at that time, the proportion of black respondents viewing regularly equaled the proportion of whites. The pattern of differences on the remaining shows was not interpretable. More interesting, however, is that when the proportion of viewers watching a show regularly was converted to ranks, the rank order correlation was .72 ($p < .01$), indicating substantial similarity of preferences. This result is even more striking when compared to the correlation of .03 obtained between the low-income sample and the general population sample.

The emerging pattern suggests that low-income blacks and whites were quite like each other in their TV behavior, and collectively quite different from the general population.

NEWSPAPER USE AND CONTENT PREFERENCES

Again, there was greater difference in newspaper usage between the low-income and general population respondents than between the low-income blacks and whites. Fewer low-income respondents reported reading a newspaper every day (65 per cent *vs.* 77 per cent); and fewer reported reading all of the newspaper regularly (17 per cent compared with 39 per cent).

Although the two income samples were not significantly different in terms of the number of newspaper sections they reported reading regularly, they differed in terms of the content and popularity of particular sections read. The general population sample was significantly more likely to read the front page (60 per cent *vs.* 41 per cent), the comics (25 per cent *vs.* 12 per cent), and sports (30 per cent *vs.* 19 per cent). The low-income sample was significantly more likely to report reading "head-lines" (22 per cent *vs.* 12 per cent) and classified ads (12 per cent *vs.* 4 per cent). The rank-order correlation between the two samples was .23, not significant. This difference in newspaper section popularity between the two samples coincides with the difference in their preferences for television shows.

The only variable showing a significant difference between the two low-income groups was the portion of the newspaper read regularly. Among white respondents, 23 per cent reported regularly reading "all" the paper; among blacks, that figure was 10 per cent. This general lack of difference between the low-income subsamples was sustained in an analysis of the content of their newspaper reading. When the proportions of regular readers for the 13 sections were converted to ranks, the correlation between the two groups was .74 ($p < .01$). For blacks and whites combined, the three major reading categories were the front page (41 per cent), the headlines (22 per cent), and the sports news (19 per cent).

USE OF OTHER MEDIA

The use of radio, magazines, movies, and phonographs is reported in Table 3. The general population sample tended ($p < .10$) to use radio more than the low-income sample. As would be expected from their greater use of newspapers, they also read magazines more frequently. Over-all movie attendance was infrequent—70 per cent or more of both samples had last attended a movie a month or more ago. Nevertheless, the general population sample indicated significantly more recent attendance.

With phonograph use, as with television, the low-income sample reported significantly greater time expenditure. Fifty-nine per cent of the low-income adults had spent at least some time on phonograph use, compared with 23 per cent of the general population. This finding is even more intriguing in light of the significantly greater ownership of both phonographs and phonograph records by the general population. The significant difference in phonograph use was maintained when non-owners were excluded from the analysis.

Again, media use differences disappeared when low-income whites were compared with low-income blacks. Only for time spent on phonograph use were the two samples different—71 per cent of the blacks reported spending some time on phonograph use on the previous day, compared with 46 per cent of the whites.

MEDIA ATTITUDES

The low-income sample was consistently more favorable toward television on all media attitude

MASS COMMUNICATION AMONG THE URBAN POOR
Bradley S. Greenberg and Brenda Dervin

TABLE 3

Usage of Other Media

Media	Low Income (N = 281)	General Population (N = 206)	p	Low-Income White (N = 150)	Low-Income Black (N = 131)	p
Hours radio listening yesterday						
0	39%	30%	n.s.	40%	37%	n.s.
1/4–3/4	11	17	(<.10)	14	8	
1–1 3/4	19	24		19	19	
2–3 3/4	16	12		13	19	
4 or more	15	17		13	18	
When last read magazine						
Never	16	10	<.01	19	13	n.s.
More than week ago	17	7		13	21	
Week ago	12	14		14	11	
Few day ago	16	16		15	17	
Today or yesterday	38	53		38	38	
When last attended movie						
0–3 weeks ago	14	30	<.001	12	16	n.s.
4 or more weeks ago	86	70		88	84	
Hours spent on phonograph use yesterday						
0	41	76	<.001	54	29	<.001
Less than 1	41	9		33	48	
1 or more	18	14		13	23	

measures in Table 4. In terms of medium preferred for world news, for example, two-thirds of the low-income adults cited television in comparison with one-third of the general population. For local news, the low-income sample cited TV more frequently than the general population sample. For the low-income sample, radio was the most frequently cited medium for local news, followed by television, newspapers and people. In contrast, the general population sample indicated newspapers as their most preferred medium for local news, followed by radio, television, and people.

This general pattern of attitudes was supported by three items asking respondents to choose which medium they would believe in the case of conflicting reports. Consistently, the low-income sample chose television over newspapers and over radio, and radio over newspapers ($p < .001$ for all three comparisons). This same pattern existed in the general population sample, but was less strong.

When the low-income sample was divided into white and black subsamples, many of these attitude differences disappeared. Low-income respondents overwhelmingly preferred TV for world news, and

MASS COMMUNICATION AMONG THE URBAN POOR

Bradley S. Greenberg and Brenda Dervin

TABLE 4

Media Attitudes

Attitude	Low Income (N = 281)	General Population (N = 206)	p	Low-Income White (N = 150)	Low-Income Black (N = 131)	p
Medium preferred for world news						
Television	69%	38%	<.001	68%	68%	n.s.
Radio	16	28		13	21	(<.10)
Newspapers	15	34		19	11	
Medium preferred for local news						
Television	30	21	<.001	33	27	<.01
Radio	34	31		34	32	
Newspapers	22	41		26	19	
People	14	7		7	22	

there was no difference between them by race.

The lack of attitudinal difference between blacks and whites was maintained for the items which asked respondents to choose the more credible of two media. For one media attitude item, however, there was a clearly significant difference between low-income blacks and whites. Table 4 shows that whites gave almost equal preference to TV, radio, and newspapers, and low preference to people (7 per cent) as the preferred source for local news. A much higher percentage (22 per cent) of blacks cited people as their preferred medium for local news.

DISCUSSION

These findings support our two working hypotheses reasonably well. The low-income sample was, indeed, considerably different from the general population sample, while low-income blacks were considerably like low-income whites in terms of these mass communication behaviors.

Differences found where none were expected between low-income whites and blacks provide speculative opportunities. The whites used newspapers more and the blacks used phonographs more. Perhaps, since white low-income respondents have at least their race in common with the majority society, the newspaper is a more useful source of information to them. The black poor do not have even this similarity and, therefore, must locate more specialized sources for materials particularly relevant to them. Their increased use of phonographs may be a way for them to get more black music, soul and gospel music, for example, than they can find on television or radio. This reasoning is further supported by the blacks' more frequent citation of "people" as a source for local news. If the majority media—television, radio, newspapers—do not report on news within the black ghetto, then other sources must be found for this information.

Such speculation requires further support. In particular, a thorough study of the interpersonal communication behavior of the poor seems in order, as well as a study of which sources—people and media—serve which functions for low-income persons. We also need to know much more about the communication exchanges between the majority culture and the poverty subculture.

MASS COMMUNICATION AMONG THE URBAN POOR
Bradley S. Greenberg and Brenda Dervin

[1] While no one study provides a comprehensive picture of the media behavior of the poor, several studies have looked at aspects of the question. These studies break down generally into three types: (a) studies focusing on poor respondents in general (Lewis Donohew and B. K. Singh, "Poverty 'Types' and Their Sources of Information about New Practices," paper presented before the International Communication Division, Association for Education in Journalism, Boulder, Colorado, August 1967; Leslie W. Sargent and Guido H. Stempel III, "Poverty, Alienation, and Mass Media Use," *Journalism Quarterly*, Vol. 45, 1968, pp. 324–326); (b) studies focusing on black respondents only (T. H. Allen, "Mass Media Use Patterns and Functions in a Negro Ghetto," master's thesis, University of West Virginia, 1967; Jack Lyle, "The Negro and the News Media," in Jack Lyle, *The News in Megalopolis*, San Francisco, Chandler Press, 1967, pp. 163–182); and (c) studies comparing black and white respondents (James W. Carey, "Variations in Negro/White Television Preferences," *Journal of Broadcasting*, Vol. 10, 1966, pp. 199–211; Maxwell E. McCombs, "Negro Use of Television and Newspapers for Political Information, 1952–1964," *Journal of Broadcasting*, Vol. 12, 1968, pp. 261–266; A. M. Barban and W. F. Grunbaum, "A Factor Analytic Study of Negro and White Responses to Advertising Stimuli," *Journal of Applied Psychology*, Vol. 49, 1965, pp. 274–279; Walter M. Gerson, "Mass Media Socialization Behavior: Negro-White Differences," *Social Forces*, Vol. 45, 1966, pp. 40–50).

[2] *Report of the National Advisory Commission on Civil Disorder*, New York, Bantam Books, 1968.

[3] See, for example, Elizabeth Herzog, "Some Assumptions about the Poor," *The Social Service Review*, Vol. 38, 1963, pp. 389–402; Lola M. Irelan and Arthur Besner, "Low-Income Outlook on Life," *Welfare in Review*, Vol. 3, No. 9, September 1965, pp. 13–19; Oscar Lewis, "The Culture of Poverty," *Scientific American*, Vol. 215, No. 4, October 1966, pp. 19–25.

[4] See, for example, Allen, *op. cit.*, Sargent and Stempel III, *op. cit.*; and these classic media studies: Merrill Samuelson,

Richard F. Carter, and Lee Ruggels, "Education, Available Time, and the Use of the Mass Media," *Journalism Quarterly*, Vol. 40, 1963, pp. 491–496; and Bruce H. Westley and Werner J. Severin, "Some Correlates of Media Credibility," *Journalism Quarterly*, Vol. 41, Summer 1964, pp. 325–335.

[5] See, particularly, Leonard Broom and Norval D. Glenn, "Negro-White Differences in Reported Attitudes and Behavior," *Sociology and Social Research*, Vol. 50, 1966, pp. 187–200; Albert K. Cohen and Harold M. Hodge, Jr., "Characteristics of the Lower Blue-Collar Class," *Journal of Social Problems*, Vol. 10, Spring 1963, pp. 103–134; Lenore Epstein, "Some Effects of Low Income on Children and Their Families," *Social Security Bulletin*, Vol. 24, February 1961, pp. 12–17; Gerson, *op. cit.*; Herzog, *op. cit.*; Suzanne Keller, "The Social World of the Urban Slum Child: Some Early Findings," *American Journal of Orthopsychiatry*, Vol. 33, 1963, pp. 823–831.

[6] Complete sets of marginal data from this study are available from the authors in mimeographed form. Readers may also obtain a copy of the study questionnaire from the authors.

[7] Statistical presentation of the demographic comparisons of low-income respondents with general population respondents, low-income whites with low-income blacks, and general population respondents with census data are included in Bradley S. Greenberg and Brenda Dervin, *Report #5, Project CUP: Mass Communication among the Urban Poor*, Department of Communication, Michigan State University, March 1969, mimeo. A forthcoming book (Bradley Greenberg and Brenda Dervin, *The Use of the Mass Media by the Urban Poor*), to be published by Praeger in 1970, includes the study reported here.

[8] A number of studies suggest that those characteristics which delineate poverty will be even more characteristic of low-income blacks than of low-income whites. For example, see Arthur Besner, "Economic Deprivation and Family Patterns," *Welfare in Review*, Vol. 3, No. 9, 1965, pp. 20–28; Epstein, *op. cit.*, Herzog, *op. cit.*, Keller, *op. cit.*

B. Propaganda and the Mass Media

The age of mass media has coincided historically with a vast increase in the use and importance of propaganda. This is by no means accidental. The mass media are inevitably the voices of a select number of people who control the key means of persuasion in society. In modern societies people are expected to have opinions on a wide range of topics and therefore have a strong need for propaganda. As Jacques Ellul has noted:

> The public will accept news if it is arranged in a comprehensive system, and if it does not speak only to the intelligence but to the "heart." This means, precisely, that the public wants propaganda, and if the State does not wish to leave it to a party, which will provide explanations for everything (i.e. the truth), it must itself make propaganda. Thus, the democratic state, even if it does not want to, becomes a propagandist state because of the need to dispense information.[1]

Because there are often discrepancies between the government's interpretation of events and that offered by the mass media, neither of which may be compatible with public opinion, the U.S. is internally vulnerable to credibility gaps. This, of course, is normal in a democracy but as Ellul has pointed out, competition in the Cold War—clearly a propaganda contest—demands a united voice from the country, which is the antithesis of democracy.

The selection by Terence Qualter included here outlines the main techniques of propaganda. Like

Ellul, his definition of the term goes beyond that of most laymen who tend to see propaganda as persuasive lies told by some person or organization they don't like, (e.g., communist propaganda, Republican propaganda for Democrats, and vice versa). To him, propaganda is any message that "works on the minds of other men, seeking to influence their attitudes and thereby their actions." Thus propaganda may be political, commercial (i.e., advertising), or religious, etc; good, evil, or neutral. Those who know the techniques, it should be noted, in fact readily switch from one type of persuasion to another, thus justifying the utility of this broad definition. For example, skilled advertisers may handle not only consumer goods but religious revivals[2], political campaigns, and the type of national "image making" (i.e., propaganda) directed at foreign countries.

Terence Qualter outlines several basic propaganda techniques, which include mass appeal, mental contact, optimum media mix, counter-propaganda, emotional transferal, and the psychological principles of persuasion dealt with in Part IV. He distinguishes between the types of propaganda used by radio, television, and the press and outlines the imperatives of each.

The article by Herbert Schiller which follows closely examines the propagandistic uses of the media in industrial societies, which he claims lead to a form of mind management. This theme is

[1] Jacques Ellul, *Propaganda*, translated by Konrad Kellen and Jean Lerner (New York: Knopf, 1966), p. 250.

[2] See for example Robert L. Shayon, "Packaging Jesus," *Saturday Review*, March 13, 1971.

skillfully tied in with social and cultural changes taking place in the rich nations. Commercial message skills are being applied more and more to political management, a topic which will be taken up in Part VI. Finally, Robert Cirino investigates in detail propaganda in the American media. The media, he claims, are inherently conservative and represent the views of the establishment. In the book from which his piece was excerpted, Cirino has amassed considerable evidence supporting this position. But, as he points out, unlike their treatment of left viewpoints, the media do not label their own bias as propaganda. Thus we are seldom aware of the status quo viewpoint of our own press.

Reprinted from Propaganda and Psychological Warfare *(New York; Random House, 1962), pp. 70–80, 83–86, 89–93. Copyright ©*
1962 by Random House, Inc. Reprinted by permission of the publisher.

The Techniques of Propaganda

TERENCE H. QUALTER

T HE propagandist works on the minds of other men, seeking to influence their attitudes and thereby their actions. The measure of his success is the apparent willingness with which they do the things he wants them to do, whether it be to vote for his party, to accept with good grace a higher price for food, to make sacrifices now for victory later, or to take the pledge.

No matter what the object of his campaign, the propagandist will almost certainly come up against a certain amount of opposition. Indeed the only reason why the particular skills of the propagandist are called for is because such opposition exists. There is no need for propaganda to encourage people to do what they were determined to do anyway, although some propagandists have enormously enhanced their own prestige and the reputation of their profession for infallibility by making a great deal of noise and display at the rear of a popular movement which they afterwards claim to have inspired and led. The propagandist's aims may be frustrated and opposed by various obstacles. There is, first of all, the competition of rival propagandists that, as well as providing direct counter-propaganda, can in some circumstances so condition public opinion that no form of propaganda is able to produce automatic response. Again, propaganda can achieve only limited success against strongly entrenched attitudes or against basic human instincts. For instance, it is easier to arouse hysterical hatred and fear of an enemy in time of war than to inculcate a spirit of universal brotherly love in time of peace. A third source of difficulty for the propa-

gandist lies in the danger or the hardship of a proposed activity. This is met variously in campaigns ranging from the appeal to fight and perhaps to die for one's country, to the annual request to "Give to the Community Chest." Finally there is what might be called the "inertia of public opinion," what Mosca had described as the "conservatism" of the masses, which makes it so much easier to strenthen allegiance to an existing faith than to win converts to a new faith. Skilled party propagandists, who have long recognized this, concentrate on making sure that their own supporters turn out to vote and concern themselves less with winning over the opposition. Writing at the turn of the century, Ostrogorski described such popular election tactics as special parades, bands, noise and spectacle, "political" picnics, barbecues and dances, and the display of emblems, flags, and stickers with the comment (substantiated by modern research) that, while all these things won few new votes for the party, they roused enthusiasm and awakened the apathetic who were already aligned with the party.[1]

To get his message across, despite all obstacles, the propagandist needs a number of very special talents. He must first of all be a skilled psychologist with a deep understanding of the complexities of the human mind and its motivations. Throughout history certain men have had an intuitive grasp of psychological principles. But propaganda on a large, systematic scale had to wait until the development of modern experimental psychology gave rise to a science with a substantial body of data and a means of training people in its use.

THE TECHNIQUES OF PROPAGANDA
Terence H. Qualter

The propagandist must address a particular group in a particular time and place. If he is to succeed in influencing that group, he must know how it is composed; he must be aware of the nature and strength of existing attitudes to the subject of his campaign; and he must also know enough history and sociology to understand how these attitudes came into being. The larger the group, the more complicated are the motives which guide it. When one reaches a group as large as the nation, one has to appeal to many sides of human nature even to the extent of being contradictory. . . .

One of the first stages in a propaganda campaign is to determine the rational or non-rational content of the message. A non-rational appeal allows even greater range of choice for it can be focused on a wide variety of emotions and instincts common to the whole human race—fear, self-preservation, aggressiveness, love, gregariousness, and so on—and it may also be directed at those racial characteristics, historical traditions and cultural features peculiar to any one nation at any one period of history.

Another common technique of propaganda is to transfer the emotional attitudes aroused by one situation over to another which may in itself have been incapable of arousing any significant response at all. That is to say, for example, a propagandist for the cause of Nordic superiority might use the record of Japanese barbarisms in the Pacific War to arouse the anger and hatred of his audience against those responsible for them. He might then attempt to transfer those emotional reactions to other Japanese living peaceful and inoffensive lives on the Pacific Coast of America. There might be no logical connection justifying any such transfer, but experience has shown that once an emotional attitude is aroused it will tend to embrace other situations introduced at the same time. The emotional transfer can also operate not only from person to person, but from person to thing and back again. The nation's flag can become a symbol of the nation's history and can evoke the pride and courage originally inspired by the record of great deeds. In turn, the respect for the flag can be transferred to the one who carries it, or to those responsible for its safekeeping. An awareness of the force of this kind of transfer and the ability to stimulate it is one of the major weapons in the propagandist's armory.[2]

The propagandist will not succeed unless he can make full mental contact with his audience, speaking a language they will understand and displaying some kind of emotional sympathy with their attitudes. The fanatical extremist does not usually make a good propagandist because of his failure to appreciate that others can, with equal sincerity and good will, hold opposing views. This is the weakness of much Communist propaganda originating in or inspired by Moscow. It is couched in the pedantic terminology of those who see in Marxism the culmination of political wisdom and in all other faiths nothing more than criminal folly. It is full of such phrases as "Capitalist lackeys," "Fascist hyenas," "bourgeois decadence" and the like, phrases which strike no responsive chord from the working class in the Western democracies.

The failure to communicate is something more than failure to use the correct local idiom. It involves the whole manner of presenting propaganda. The selection of such details as the color and texture of paper, the layout, the use and style of illustration, the type face, binding, and format in general must be guided by the customs of those for whom it is intended.[3]

So far [we have] . . . been concerned with the material content of the propaganda message, with such things as the text of a pamphlet, the script of a speech or film, the situation portrayed in a drawing or cartoon, the wording of a banner, or the symbolism of a flag or uniform. Discussions of propaganda material involve considerations of truth and falsehood, emotional or rational forms of expression, and questions of fact or opinion. Having once determined this material the propagandist must then see that it reaches his audience. The techniques of communication by which the propagandist transmits his material to an audience can be conveniently termed the "instruments of propaganda" and these can in turn be classified as "primary" and "secondary" instruments.

The primary instruments, which are the actual forms in which the propaganda material is presented, demonstrate the propagandist's amazing versatility and ingenuity. Propagandists have used for their primary instruments: speeches, rumors, telephone messages, rallies and demonstrations (including exhibitions of violence), marches, uniforms and costumes with badges, buttons and armbands, flags and banners, civil, military, and religious ceremonies, advertisements, billboards, posters and chalked slogans, architecture, postage stamps, fairs, exhibitions and circuses, plays and films, photographs, paintings and cartoons, books, newspapers, pamphlets, circulars, broadsheets, leaflets, stickers, and every other form of the written word, fireworks and sky-writing, economic assistance programs, and indeed every conceivable means of communication between man and man.

The secondary instruments are the channels of communications, or means of distribution, by which the propagandist carries his material as embodied in the primary instruments to a distant or more extensive audience. They consist principally of newspaper presses, radio stations, postal and telegraph systems, roads and railways, theaters, education systems, publishing houses, and every kind of political, social or religious organization.

There are definite stages in planning the dissemination of propaganda. Having determined his objectives, the propagandist must decide on the material most likely to arouse the appropriate attitudes. At this stage he has to choose not only the general content of his message, but also the literary or artistic form in which it will be presented. This form may range from the calmly reasoned to the frankly scurrilous.

The propagandist's next consideration is the selection of the most suitable primary instruments to carry the message to the audience, Here he must consider the four basic criteria of successful propaganda—it must be seen, understood, remembered and acted upon.[4] He must make sure that not only is his propaganda accessible to his audience, but that they do in fact see it against a back-

ground of competing influences, that having seen it they will take from it the impression the propagandist intended to convey, and that the impression will remain with them long enough for them to act upon it. This means that the propagandist must take into account the size and the broad intellectual level of his audience, the existing attitudes of the audience to both the situation envisaged by the propagandist and to the propagandist himself, the extent to which the audience has access to the various media of communication, and the presence of competing propaganda or other non-propaganda influences.

That is to say, taking the size and intellectual level of the audience first, a street-corner meeting, appropriate enough in elections at ward level, would not be the best way to reach the nation's housewives, any more than a newspaper would be a practical means of reaching an illiterate peasant population. Normally, a government propagandist, with the entire resources of the state at his disposal, will adopt several techniques, each adding to and strengthening the others. The radio might be used first to get the material to as many people as quickly as possible, giving it that sense of urgency which a radio message can convey. The newspaper would follow more slowly, confirming and amplifying the original statement and at the same time presenting it in a more durable form. Once interest is aroused in this way, the work of influencing attitudes might then be further consolidated by a series of public meetings and workers' discussion groups explaining the importance of the earlier announcements.

The existing attitude of the audience to the propagandist and his message must also be considered. Open Russian propaganda to the United States, for example, suffers the disadvantage that most of it is rejected simply because of its Russian origin. The Russian propagandist knows that the first reaction to his every proposal and suggestion will be to dismiss it as a "Communist propaganda stunt.". . .

The presence of competing propaganda has also to be taken into account in selecting the primary instruments of communication. The nature of

THE TECHNIQUES OF PROPAGANDA
Terence H. Qualter

competing propaganda probably has an even greater effect on the selection and styling of material. The chief concern of the propagandist in these circumstances is to avoid exposing himself to counter-propaganda by a rival who possesses vastly superior resources in any particular means of communication. Competition also comes from many non-political sources: the billboard urging us to "Vote Smith for Progress and Prosperity" may seem a powerful piece of work in the campaign office, but it may not even be noticed amidst twenty others crying the virtues of soaps, motels, gasoline, and beer; the politician speaking on a natonwide network may go unheard if the local station is broadcasting the "Top Tunes of Today." Within dictatorships it is possible to avoid competition more easily than in a democracy. Hitler, for example, had no fear that the German people might prefer another program when he wished to speak to them. There was no other program.

> When Hitler speaks the people of Germany must listen wherever they are. Factory sirens blow, there is a minute or two of silence, and then the voice bursts forth. Loudspeakers in public places relay the speech; not to listen, or appear to listen, is disloyalty. The penetration of politicised radio into the entire national consciousness is then complete, its power inescapable.[5]

The selection of the primary instruments of propaganda is governed by one further factor, the availability of the secondary instruments: the printing presses, the radio stations, the paper supplies, the meeting halls, and so on, possession of which controls the planning of any propaganda campaign. The legal right to disseminate ideas through the primary instruments of propaganda, a "free press" or "freedom of assembly," has little real value unless there is also reasonable access to the secondary instruments. As Bertrand Russell once pointed out,[6] there is no equality of propaganda in a society where the press, radio stations and film studios are available to only one economic class. The 1936 Constitution of the Soviet Union guarantees freedom of speech, of the press, of assembly and mass

meeting, and of street processions and demonstrations, but it then restricts the effect of this guarantee "by placing at the disposal of the toilers and their organizations printing presses, stocks of paper, public buildings, the streets, means of communication and other material requisites for the exercise of these rights."[7] Free speech is a privilege of the Communist party and those organizations in which the Communist party provides the leadership.

Apart from the principles which apply to propaganda in general, there are a number of problems peculiar to each of the various media of communication that can be considered here under a few broad headings. . . .

RADIO

In two respects radio broadcasting demonstrates its supremacy over all other media of communication. It is immediate and it is universal, being bounded by neither time nor space. It is immediate in the sense that there is no time lag between the speaking and the hearing of the message. A broadcast address by the President of the United States to Congress would be heard by listeners in London and Rome before some of those actually watching the President speak.

Broadcasting is universal because it cannot easily be stopped at national frontiers. "Jamming" is at best an uncertain device, while the resort to "jamming" is in itself an admission of weakness. Even in so rigid a dictatorship as that of Nazi Germany, it was found impossible to prevent people listening regularly to Allied news broadcasts. At one stage in 1944, the BBC was broadcasting nearly 230 news bulletins a day beamed to every part of the world in forty-eight different languages.[8] The United States was slower in entering into international broadcasting propaganda campaigns, but by 1950 the *Voice of America*, which is under the control of a division of the State Department, was broadcasting daily in twenty-four languages.[9]

At one time it was imagined that the international character of radio would make it an instrument of universal peace and good will. In 1935, for example, two psychologists wrote that "Any device that carries messages instantaneously and inexpensively to the farthest and most inaccessible regions of the earth, that penetrates all manner of social, political, and economic barriers, is by nature a powerful agent of democracy."[10] Despite the extensive use of radio as an international propaganda medium by the Soviet Union and the speed with which the Nazis made use of the unique political potentialities of radio to impress the power and permanence of their regime upon the German people, this naïvely optimistic view persisted probably until 1939, after which time such idealism died. Radio is now accepted by all the major states as a legitimate instrument of power politics. It has become "the most powerful single instrument of political warfare the world has ever known. More flexible in use and infinitely stronger in emotional impact than the printed word, as a weapon of *war waged psychologically* radio has no equal. . . ."[11]

TELEVISION

Television introduces several further problems for the propagandist. The first of these is that the television viewer must pay more attention to the program than need the radio listener. Most of us are familiar with the ease with which the modern student is able to read and write against the background of radio music, but most of those who have attempted to combine studying with viewing will admit that television is a more demanding distraction. While it commands the attention of the viewer, however, television makes fewer demands upon his mind and imagination. Something that can be seen and heard is clearly much easier to follow and understand than something which can merely be heard. Television is thus an unusually potent instrument of public-opinion control. It first captures its audience and then relaxes it to the extent, in extreme cases, of complete intellectual lethargy. Its appeal is intimate, personal and dramatic. A television show is, however, extremely

costly to produce, which means that those responsible for it exert themselves to make it as near perfect as possible, in the technical sense at least. . . .

While radio still dominates in the sphere of international communication, its role in internal affairs has been taken over by television in the technically advanced countries. This is not to say that domestic radio is declining. Indeed, statistics show that even in such a television-oriented country as the United States, the number of radio sets in use continues to rise year by year. But radio broadcasting has changed in character. In many homes there are several radios, including portable transistor sets, but these are intended primarily to provide a local news service and a background of popular music for other activities. Television has come to be the chief source of commentaries, films, documentaries, plays and other programs that might influence opinions.

Despite a great mass of literature about the social significance of radio and television, our knowledge of the actual effect of these media on public behavior is limited. While generalizations of the enormous social impact of sight and sound broadcasting on our social and economic life are commonplace, and probably for the most part valid, they should still be treated with some reserve. It would perhaps be safer to regard all observations of this kind as reasoned probabilities rather than as authoritative conclusions.

There are other forms of spoken-word propaganda, most of them, however, operating on a relatively small scale and over a short period of time. Perhaps the most important is the deliberate circulation of rumors, particularly those that spread slander and gossip about some candidate for office. This can be an exceptionally vicious form of propaganda made doubly unattractive by the fact that those responsible for the rumors usually manage to remain undetected, if not unsuspected. Rumors have, however, the disadvantage that, once put into circulation, they are uncontrollable. A rumor that becomes distorted, as most rumors quickly become,

THE TECHNIQUES OF PROPAGANDA
Terence H. Qualter

may have effects quite contrary to those originally intended.

Rumors circulate most rapidly and are listened to most attentively in an atmosphere of crisis or emergency, or when important events are taking place but where those concerned have no clear picture of what is happening. Rumors circulate widely during air raids, floods, riots, among crowds waiting for some event, in prisons, among the spectators at accidents and fires; in short in all sorts of events where the situation is tense, but where official news is lacking.[12] One of the functions of the German "Fifth Column" agents in France in 1940 was to spread rumors which would disrupt morale and create panic. In the absence of up-to-date authoritative news, the rumors largely succeeded in their purpose. The disorder and confusion they caused then stimulated the spontaneous circulation of other rumors which further intensified the disorder and confusion. A number of experiments[13] have shown that, once a rumor gains some credence in a time of intense emotional stress, there will be many who will continue to believe in it and to reject official denials issued in a calmer atmosphere.

There are several other ways in which spoken propaganda can be disseminated: through telephones, public address systems, loudspeaker vans, phonograph records and so on; but none of these introduce any major problems not covered by what has already been written here. There is, therefore, no need to describe them in detail. . . .

THE PRESS

Newspapers are perhaps the most pervasive carriers of news and opinion. They are cheap, readily available, and, apart from the Sunday editions of some American papers, they do not take long to read. The prime service of the daily newspaper is usually stated as the giving of information about, and the interpretation of, public affairs. The term "public affairs" is loosely applied to events ranging from local crime to international war. Surveys have shown us,[14] however, that the newspaper serves several other functions which, to many readers, are far more important than its news content. Such informational services as television and theater programs, shipping notices, stock exchange reports, and super-market advertisements have become valuable aids to everyday life. The "comics," and magazine features, are read for entertainment. The newspaper's personal columns, social notes, birth, death, and marriage notices, and human interest stories provide some readers with a highly valued form of social contact.

One of the most obvious implications of these varied motives for reading newspapers is that a paper's circulation is not necessarily a measure of its political influence. It is not unknown, for example, for large numbers of people to subscribe to a newspaper whose politics they reject, and whose political commentaries they never read, but which provides an unusually thorough coverage of all sporting events. Many politically-oriented newspapers recognize this and deliberately try to build up circulation through popular features in the hope that at least a few new readers will be attracted to, and perhaps influenced by, its political commentaries.

One of the greatest advantages of the newspaper as a propaganda medium is that it is possible to direct appeals to different reading publics in the style and language most likely to appeal to that public. This is particularly noticeable in a dictatorship where one authority determines the policy to be followed by all newspapers, even though it might allow considerable editorial discretion in the manner in which that policy is interpreted for the readers. In Nazi Germany, for example, the once highly respected *Frankfurter Zeitung* and the party paper *Der Angriff* both gave unqualified support to the Nazi regime although their journalistic styles were as far apart as those of *The Times* and the *Daily News* in New York. Even within the democracies, the propaganidst for any one party or pressure group has to recognize that each newspaper has its own relatively distinct reading public, that most readers rarely see a newspaper other than the ones to which they regularly subscribe, and that if his propaganda is to have its maximum effect, it must be adapted to the journalistic tastes of a particular group of readers. Journalistic treatment varies not only between papers, but often from section to section of the one paper. The clichés of the editorials are generally more ponderous and moralistic than those of the foreign news page, while domestic news is written in a manner quite distinct from that of the financial columns. The popular newspaper has developed a vocabulary and literary style distinctively its own, designed to arouse the appropriate reaction. The cliché thus becomes, not a mark of laziness or ignorance, but an essential tool in newspaper communication. Carefully selected, it will almost automatically elicit the desired response from the casual reader. It has, of course, a greater influence on the large proportion of readers who do no more than skim the headlines and the main points of a story. The constant repetition of the same phrases to cover certain situations or to convey certain impressions saves the reader the effort of thought and interpretation. When he reads that "reformers are trying to bring order out of chaos," or that "so-called reformers would sacrifice the solid achievements of the past," he is likely to react to these familiar phrases in familiar ways. His attitude to the new situation will tend to be governed by his attitude to the situations to which they have been applied in the past.

Any doubts that even the news columns have propaganda significance can be settled by comparing the way in which several papers react to the one story. Each paper will make its own decision on the importance of the story—a decision which will be reflected in the page on which the story appears, its position on that page, and the size and style of type used in the headlines. Devices such as special type, illustrations or unusual layout may all serve to attract the readers' attention. Other factors include the length of the story, the manner in which it is rewritten and the extent to which its importance is emphasized by editorial comment and background feature articles. A report of new developments in,

say, the Berlin situation, reported briefly but factually on page five of one paper, will make a very different impression if rewritten and featured on page one with the blackest of banner headlines, commented on in the first leader, and supported by a human-interest story on life in Berlin today.

At one time it was customary to distinguish the expression of opinion on the editorial pages of a paper from the straightforward presentation of facts on the news pages. With the growing appreciation of the extent to which opinion governs the selection and manner of presentation of news, it has been concluded that this division is unrealistic and it is now generally admitted that the news columns can also contain propaganda. This is especially true of news magazines such as *Time* and *Newsweek* where the selection and presentation of news items is an expression of editorial policy. But while this blending of news story and editorial comment is common, another surprising feature of the American press is the frequency with which editorial policy seems to be at odds with the selection of news. This was particularly noticeable during the period of the New Deal, when a great many papers that consistently attacked editorially the policies of President Roosevelt were prepared to report the successes and popular achievements of the New Deal on their news pages.

Other forms of press propaganda are the paid advertisements on political themes by organizations such as the American Independent Electric Light and Power Companies or the Committee for Constitutional Government; and the free copy supplied to newspapers by the public relations offices of the various interested groups in the community.[15] Another form is the cartoon which by selection, simplification, and the use of familiar symbols such as the GOP Elephant, John Q. Public, Colonel Blimp, *etc.*, is able to reduce a complex situation to a single emotional reaction. For this reason, the cartoon is one of the commonest and (in skilled hands) most effective forms of printed propaganda. It is the almost universal practice of modern newspapers to publish at least one political

THE TECHNIQUES OF PROPAGANDA
Terence H. Qualter

cartoon in every issue, and some cartoonists such as Low in England or Herblock in the United States have a tremendous reputation and influence, their cartoons being frequently reproduced in other papers even in other parts of the world. The comic strips, the Letters to the Editor, and the feature articles are additional sources of newspaper propaganda, especially for pressure groups and individuals who can in this way appeal to a wider public.

The press is the cheapest form of printed propaganda and in the long run the most important. Despite the enormous advances of radio and television, the newspaper is still the major source of political news and commentary in all civilized countries. The newspaper makes up for its lack of immediacy, compared to radio, by its durability and a largely self-created reputation of being the traditional crusader for the liberties of the people against the tyranny of Government. Further, the radio is thought of primarily as a form of entertainment, so that the news and comment that fill the bulk of the newspaper's columns (apart from the advertisements) are given a relatively minor place in radio programming. It is therefore unlikely, as long as there is a high percentage of literacy, that the newspaper will be replaced as the most important instrument for the communication of propaganda. . . .

[1] M. Ostrogorski, *Democracy and the Organization of Political Parties* (New York: Macmillian, 1908), II, p. 334.

[2] The question of emotional transfer is more fully treated by R. Dodge, "Psychology of Propaganda," *Religious Education*, XV (1920), pp. 241–52.

[3] For some illuminating examples of the failure to communicate see M. F. Herz, "Some Psychological Lessons from Leaflet Propaganda in World War II," *Public Opinion Quarterly*, XIII (1949), pp. 471–86.

[4] This slogan is, I regret, not original, but I have long forgotten the source.

[5] C. Saerchinger, "Radio as a Political Instrument," *Foreign Affairs*, XVI (1938), p. 251.

[6] B. Russell, *Free Thought and Official Propaganda* (London: Watts, 1922), pp. 33–40.

[7] *Constitution of the U.S.S.R.* Art. 125.

[8] T. O. Beachcroft, *British Broadcasting* (London: Longman, 1948), p. 20.

[9] U. S. State Department, Office of International Information and Education Exchange, *The World Audience for the Voice of America* (1950), pp. 2–9.

[10] H. Cantril and G. W. Allport, *The Psychology of Radio* (New York: Harper & Bros. 1935), p. 20.

[11] C. J. Rolo, *Radio Goes to War* (New York: G. P. Putnam, 1940), p. 11.

[12] For a fuller treatment of this theme see G. Allport and L. Postman, "The Basic Psychology of Rumour," in W. Schramm (ed.), *The Process and Effects of Mass Communication* (University of Illinois Press, 1935), pp. 141–55.

[13] See Allport and Postman, *op. cit.*, and R. H. Knapp, "A Psychology of Rumour," *Public Opinion Quarterly*, VIII (1949), pp. 22–37.

[14] See, for example, B. Berelson, "What Missing the Newspaper Means," in Lazarsfeld and Stanton (eds.), *Communications Research 1948–49* (New York: Harper & Bros., 1949), pp. 111–29.

[15] The manner and extent to which public relations men rely on the press is discussed at length by C. S. Steinberg in *The Mass Communicators* (New York: Harper & Bros., 1958).

Reprinted from Quarterly Review of Economics and Business *(Spring, 1971), pp. 39–52. Used by permission of publisher and author.*

Mind Management: Mass Media in the Advanced Industrial State

HERBERT I. SCHILLER

THOUGH we would like to believe that a "free man" existed in some distant time or clime, the ordering and restraint of most human beings has been the typical situation in the past as well as in the present. It has been achieved in different ways depending on the character of the society, the state of the arts, and the resources available. The main objective generally has been to reserve as much of the social product as possible for a privileged minority while leaving enough to ensure the continued labor of the less fortunate majority. Scarcity, abetted by physical coercion, was the most dependable regulator of human conduct for thousands of years. In the last few centuries, coincident with the rise of modern industry, a more sophisticated system of control and subordination has developed. The emergence of the market society has permitted a relatively unfettered social condition, but one which has left ordinary working people totally dependent on a wage income derived from an ever uncertain employment.

Though this form of industrialization has not yet penetrated every corner of the globe, it is already changing the character of those places in which it has reached its highest development. In the United States especially and increasingly in Western Europe and Japan, the industrial state is moving, if not on to an entirely new course, at least in a direction significantly different from that which it traveled during its early growth and maturation. Productivity of labor has soared and the enlarged social product, reflecting the anarchy of its creation, has become increasingly indigestible, though still extremely unevenly distributed.

At the same time, with greater awareness of its weaknesses and its needs arising from the social disasters of the first third of the 20th century, the Western industrial system reluctantly has sought and accepted state intervention to keep it functioning without calamitous interruptions. Correspondingly, with increased regulation and control have come governmental bureaucracies and an ever widening stratum concerned with economic (and political) equilibria. The advanced system has brought with it, also, a heavier reliance on technology and on those trained to invent, produce, and work with the more complex equipment and processes.

After the second World War the American economy became the first to move across the great divide signifying that a larger part of the labor force was employed in services than in production. Clerical, sales, managerial, and service workers now outnumber manufacturing, agricultural, and other production workers. The trend is continuing, if not accelerating, and the consequences, in the first appraisal, seem more psycho-cultural than economic.

Peter Drucker describes the employee in this new situation as a "knowledge worker . . . the successor to the employee of yesterday, the manual worker, skilled or unskilled." Drucker notes that "This is a very substantial upgrading," but "it also creates," he believes, "an unresolved conflict

MIND MANAGEMENT: MASS MEDIA IN THE ADVANCED INDUSTRIAL STATE
Herbert I Schiller

between the tradition of the knowledge worker and his position as an employee. Though the knowledge worker is not a 'laborer' and certainly not a 'proletarian,' he is still an 'employee.'"[1]

This, according to Drucker, creates serious problems because the knowledge worker

> sees himself as just another "professional," no different from the lawyer, the teacher, the preacher, the doctor, the government servant of yesterday. He has the same education. He has more income.[2]

Yet he remains an order-receiver, filling an obscure box on the organization chart of the large social organization of labor and disenchanted with the narrow options, beyond income, that his extra education has afforded him. Furthermore, he is more cognizant than his earlier counterpart of at least the general contours of his cultural condition. There appears consequently, a very new dilemma in the advanced market-directed industrial state. Drucker puts it this way:

> The clash between the expectations in respect to knowledge jobs and their reality will become sharper and clearer with every passing year. *It will make management of knowledge workers increasingly crucial to the performance and achievement of the knowledge society . . .* It is likely to be *the* social question of the developed countries for the twentieth and probably for the twenty-first century.[3]

Curiously, Edward H. Carr, viewing the same industrial scene from what might be termed in a very general sense a socialist perspective, comes to a conclusion that is not incompatible with Drucker's, but Carr hopes for a less manipulative future. He writes,

> The social habits and labour incentives of the pre-industrial period cannot be resumed. But all that we have yet succeeded in doing is to destroy the philosophy, habits and incentives which for a century past have made the wheels of industry turn, without putting anything in their place. The task ahead is nothing less

than the creation of a new philosophy which will furnish an incentive and a reinforcement for a new social habit of work.[4]

For Drucker, who seems not to be unhappy with the social order, the task ahead is one of applied psychology. Carr's hopes rest ultimately on a fundamental restructuring of society's purposes and social organization.

The instrumentalities for "managing" the knowledge workers, Drucker acknowledges, are still to be forged. But significantly, the means for handling the manual workers and not-so-highly educated groups in the advanced industrial state are very well known, very effective, and continuously applied. The mass media, with radio and television leading the way, are enormously powerful levers of manipulation and control over the *traditional* working force in the US, and apparently in western European industrialized economies as well. Moreover, the evolution of the industrial state to a condition of total automation and computerization, with only knowledge workers in the labor force, is still many decades away. A numerically significant conventional working force continues, therefore, to be processed daily in the mass thought and attitudinal baths of the prevailing order. And advertising, which has stimulated wants so effectively (and encouraged labor thereby to work overtime for the satisfaction of those wants), undergirds the powerful standard-of-living ideology that provides the mass support for the industrial system as it now operates in the United States.

The entire informational apparatus—from the mass media, which are literally conduits of commercialism, and the opinion polls run largely by marketeers, to the formal educational system and the paraeducational structures provided by business, government, and the military—functions to produce popular acceptance of the goals and the values of the "goods economy."

So remarkably successful is this undertaking that it often requires the careful attention of the viewer or listener to detect when the selling message has stopped and the "recreational" material has begun in most broadcast programming. Some observers of the social scene are doubtful that this condition of omnipotent conditioning can be overcome. George Lichtheim, for example, denies that the working class has been "corrupted" by "the desire to possess consumer goods" but nevertheless concludes that equality and social decision-making are not highly prized by the popular majority who are instead "overwhelmingly concerned with simple economic issues: specifically, guaranteed full employment **and a** steady rise in living standards."[5]

Raymond Williams, writing about Britain as that nation moves into the 1970s, notes much the same characteristic in the general population there and tries to account for its existence:

> . . . there is a kind of stabilized poverty and neglect, and the creation of new forms of essentially orderly control and direction, toward narrowed social ends; with at the edge, and now quite virtuously displayed, the power of the state and the law ready to deal with protesting minorities. This is the order we are invited to celebrate, to make marginal choices inside. Its whole point is the distancing, the displacement and the manipulation of conflicts, and the direction of the society toward false definitions which are repeated so often as to seem the only condition of sanity. Any other possibilities not only seem, but in the short term are, impractical—so impractical that only the young can believe in them.[6]

We are rediscovering that the power to define reality and to set the social agenda for the community-at-large is the key to social control—a point noted by both Jerry Rubin, who writes that "The power to define is the power to control,"[7] and Senator Fulbright, who states that "Communication is power, and exclusive access to it is a dangerous, unchecked power."[8] Definitional control in America has been held securely (at least until recently) by the controllers of the mass media and their ancillary services of public relations (PR), advertising, opinion polling, and the many paraeducational forms and structures.

What people see and read and hear, what they wear, what they eat, where they go, and what they believe they are doing are now functions of an informational system which sets tastes and values according to its own self-reinforcing market criteria. In an earlier time, economic impoverishment established the criteria.

Daniel Bell calls knowledge "a strategic resource" and "as with all resources, the question becomes, who will control it, who will make the necessary decisions about allocations?" He seeks a

> balance of knowledge and power to spell out the technical components and the dimensions of cost; to widen the options and to specify the moral context of choices so that decisions may be made more consciously and with a greater awareness of responsibility.[9]

But of course it is the failure to achieve this condition that depresses so many. The ability to use knowledge morally and humanistically so that all the consequences of decision-making may be available for prior scrutiny is precisely the capability that the system of control in the advanced market-directed industrial state, especially so far as the mass media are concerned, does its best to curtail. It does so not because the decision-makers are deliberately malevolent, but because long-term social considerations are invariably at odds with short-term advantage, and a market economy is based on the immediate realization of self-interest.

The mechanics of the system-at-large, moreover, become deeply internalized in the values and thinking of people who have been schooled early and repeatedly to translate their personal conditions into a national calculus of short-run payoffs. This is now recognized as the situation and mind set of so-called "middle America." It does *not* describe, however, the condition of some of the newer adherents to, or the trainees of, the knowledge labor force. This group, a numerous and growing contingent (the university student population alone is now more than half the size of the nation's employment of production workers in manufacturing), has begun to create a very different system of social

MIND MANAGEMENT: MASS MEDIA IN THE ADVANCED INDUSTRIAL STATE
Herbert I. Schiller

measurement. So much so, in fact, that the issue that Drucker foresees as the problem of the future, the "manageability" of the knowledge worker/trainee, is already the crisis of the present.

Whatever the perspective, there is no denying that among the youth with more education and higher family income a deeply felt hostility to the commercialized information/recreation society has emerged. William McGill, president of Columbia University, estimates that "anywhere from a third to a half of the students today fall into the alienated group."[10] A study transmitted to the President's Commission on Campus Unrest found that "almost all college students believe some form of confrontation 'is necessary and effective' in changing society," and "three quarters of the students agreed with the statement that 'basically, the United States is a racist society.'"[11] Staughton Lynd sees it this way:

> Education tries to shape the young for (this) unmanly and inhuman adult work-life, and so itself becomes a target. The rapid expansion of higher education since the end of World War II came about because of technological change in industry. Automatized and computerized industry require more and more young men and women who have white-collar skills but behave with the docility expected of blue-collar workers. The thrust of the multiversity in which so many of our 7 million college students are trained is toward skilled obedience. The student, like the worker he is intended to become, uses his mind as well as his hands, but not creatively, not at his own initiative, still within limits set by orders coming down from above. That is what modern higher education is like, too. And the students tell those who give them orders to practice being foremen on someone else. In their own words, they refuse to be bent, folded, spindled, and mutilated.[12]

Labeling the repudiation of standard American values a "counter culture," Theodore Roszak[13] and others attribute the swelling youthful opposition to the rigidities and conformities imposed on society by technology. Roszak attacks the manipulative culture as the inevitable outgrowth of a rampaging technology. The specific social organization that determines the character of the technology and its

applications is regarded as irrelevant in this view. Ironically, the breakaway culture that Roszak supports is itself subject to the same distortions that the "straight" society suffers from its absorption with technology. Youth's new "life style" has become a profitable activity. Rock festivals, record promotions, cult foods, beads, and costumes become enterprise ventures for hip capitalists and "liberation" itself becomes a salable commodity. The "movement" becomes the market. Apparently it is not technology alone but certain types of criticism of industrialism as well that succumb to a specific social system.

Still, the indigenous American "cultural revolution" with all its vulnerabilities and dependencies undermines the traditional values of conventional society. Work, discipline, hierarchy, and repression are under continuous attack, and often the private enterprisers who use the new outlook and style for routine profit-making contribute to the unraveling of the social order and to the freeing of emotional currents whose direction no one can safely predict.

Automatic instrumentation which may eventually dispense altogether with ordinary human labor is imminent (in a historical sense, at least), and the awareness of the possibility of permanent escape from the traditional coercive nature of work has already permeated youthful consciousness. Since the underlying institutional arrangements give no sign of adapting to this entirely new technological capability, the conflict has broken out on the personal behavioral (cultural) level, concealing, and for the time being denying, the deeper economic-social issues that are at the base of the cultural revolt.

For the moment, the nation seems to have "lost" its youth to a hedonistic nihilism with undertones of violence and irrationality. But it is the unyielding socio-economic order, buffeted by an exploding technology yet resistant to structural change, which explains the widening disarray.

An increasing number of the knowledge workers/trainees are unable to accept the premises of the goods economy. Their schooling and their experi-

MIND MANAGEMENT: MASS MEDIA IN THE ADVANCED INDUSTRIAL STATE
Herbert I. Schiller

ence, limited as they may be, have raised doubts about a society which puts everything on sale and, despite its assertions to the contrary, values the human being only as an afterthought. Ironically, the mass media are the sources of this subversive revelation. The same radio-television which produces or at least reinforces the thinking of the "hard hats," also convinces many youths, whose backgrounds permit them to sample more fully the offerings of the consumer society, of the vacuity and the personal destructiveness of the system's values. The $20 billion private annual advertising budget has done an effective, if unintentional, job of awakening those whose perceptions have escaped total distortion at an early age to the true character of the American Way.

I.

This then is the growing dilemma of media managers in the United States today. Laissez faire in media matters solidifies the age-income split in the nation and makes the knowledge trainees less and less "manageable." Interventionism brings with it uncertainty and the possibility of deeper, though latent, social conflicts. The increasingly tense social condition, however, precludes laissez faire. We are encountering, therefore, the first indications of deliberate governmental intervention in the national information process. Communications decisions are becoming more political and consequently less commercial, though, of course, this is still a very uneven process. The trend has been observed and reported, optimistically it seems, as a source of future commercial business. A McGraw-Hill Publishing Company functionary foresees, for instance,

> . . . that government, which has to govern more and more by voter consent, will come into communications in a big way, learn to speak the language of the people, and use advertising to sell its "product." [14]

For this to occur without creating widespread fear and anxiety in the nation requires first of all popular enlightenment on the derelictions of the commercial mass media. And this has been the special contribution of Mr. Agnew. His indictment of the media is an introductory effort to accustom the nation to overt governmental intervention in the informational process because the commercial communications system cannot be trusted. Accordingly, we get a surprisingly frank, if only partly accurate, critique of the private media, which have hitherto had little difficulty in passing as an objective recreational and news system. Now we are informed by the Vice President that there is network control of news and programming, a situation in which

> the news that 40 million Americans receive each night is determined by a handful of men responsible only to their corporate employers and is filtered through a handful of commentators who admit to their own set of biases. . . . [There is] a virtual monopoly of a whole medium of communications . . . [There is a] trend toward monopolization of the great public information vehicles [newspapers] and the concentration of more and more power in fewer and fewer hands . . . [And, consequently,] the time for naive belief in their press and network neutrality is gone. [15]

Certainly, the picture is not overdrawn, although Agnew, ignoring a very rich historical record of similar criticism from a different perspective, seems to feel that he is the first to have called attention to these conditions. [16]

If anything, the control of the nation's informational apparatus is even more tightly held than Agnew suggests. It is not only a matter of the influence of the *New York Times* and the *Washington Post*, important as those organs of opinion are. So far as the press is concerned, the lack of competing voices has now reached an almost unsurpassable point. One longtime observer of these matters writes:

> Whereas in 1880 only 38% of U.S. cities were single daily cities, and only one city had a single-ownership combination, *today 85.6% of the cities have only one daily*. If the 150 cities with two dailies under a single ownership and the 21 cities with two dailies in joint-operating arrangements are added to the 1,284 single daily cities, *the number of cities without commercially*

MIND MANAGEMENT: MASS MEDIA IN THE ADVANCED INDUSTRIAL STATE
Herbert I. Schiller

competing local dailies rises to 97% of the total. In only 45 of the 1,500 daily newspaper cities today are there two or more commercially competing dailies, and in only three of these 45 cities are there more than two ownerships of daily newspapers of general content and circulation.[17]

Broadcasting facilities are no less concentrated. Though there are over 680 commercial TV stations and more than 6,200 commercial radio stations in the country, control is heavily pyramided through chain ownerships, mixed media holdings (newspapers owning stations) and, most importantly, the funneling of most of television programming through three networks, with one or another of which nearly every local station is affiliated.[18] Furthermore, in television, the newest and most compelling communications medium, a narrow base of control has existed from the outset. Those who received the first licenses granted in 1951 by the Federal Communications Commission have remained at the center of the profit making and have led the way in concentrating holdings.[19]

Normal market mechanics have produced an industrial structure in the mass media which is indistinguishable from other business sectors. Agnew calls attention to this also:

> Should a conglomerate be formed that tied together a shoe company with a shirt company, some voice will rise up righteously to say that this is a great danger to the economy and that the conglomerate ought to be broken up. But a single company, in the nation's capital, holds control of the largest newspaper in Washington, D.C., and one of the four major television stations, and an all-news radio station, and one of the three major national news magazines . . .[20]

In brief, the mass media, and broadcasting in particular, are highly profitable commercial enterprises. Across the board, taking the high earners with the low, television is a vast money-making machine.[21]

Higher profitability and easier access to congressional favor give media owners a very privileged position in the economy. But even more significant is the indispensable support that the media provide to the commercial-financial system in general, reinforcing market objectives at every turn.

Why then should the vital informational apparatus of the managerial-industrial order be attacked by governmental leaders recruited from and beholden to corporate enterprise? Why can it not be relied upon to do what it always did well in the past—secure the firm attachment of its national audience to the status quo? Ordinary market mechanics offer a partial explanation. Further reason rests, it seems, in the rapidly shifting nature of the political-social climate in the United States. Consider first the commercial factor.

II.

There is no disagreement on the enormous contributions the mass media make in the furtherance of American commodity production and distribution. TV moves goods best, according to Arthur Nielsen, founder of the well-known marketing research organization.[22] J. K. Galbraith also has observed that the industrial system would be a shambles without the consumer goods image-creating machinery of the home screen.[23] A consequence of the total involvement of the popular informational-entertainment channels with marketing is that even the news reports and informational programs are treated as commodities. Sir William Haley, former director-general of the British Broadcasting Corporation, put it this way: "Like so much else in American life today, it [the news] comes second to salesmanship. News, is, in fact, being used as a kind of entertainment."[24]

Newscasters and commentators are first of all salesmen. Viewers are sought as competitively for the news slots as for any other program because commercials have to be sold to sustain the "show," and more importantly, if viewers are lost at 6 P.M. to a rival newscaster, they may be lost for the high-priced prime-time hours of subsequent programming as well. So news operates under the same commercial imperatives as the rest of the schedule.

MIND MANAGEMENT: MASS MEDIA IN THE ADVANCED INDUSTRIAL STATE
Herbert I. Schiller

The result inevitably is a continuing frenetic search by the programmers for excitement, sensation, and action in the reportage. What affords more opportunity in this direction than the most cataclysmic daily events of this era? Furthermore, the social order appears to be coming apart at the seams, as both new and generations-old troubles cumulate, surface, and press for resolution. Urban decay, the draft, racism, environmental pollution, and the war are the everyday conditions of life for tens of millions of people. The cameras, microphones, and pencils of the mass media journeyman would have to be incredibly inept to overlook entirely such powerful raw material of social upheaval.

The actual conditions of society and the commercial motivation of attracting and holding an audience combine to provide the nightly viewer-listener with at least some glimmering of a disintegrating status quo. The picture obviously is not pretty. Hence the rising clamor from a multiplying host of adherents to the way things used to be to stop "manufacturing" or "distorting" reality. Here is the backdrop to the storm of conservative outrage against the televised violence of the Chicago police at the Democratic National Convention in the summer of 1968.

What is occurring now is the open repudiation not only of the hallowed principle of full news coverage, which in fact rarely if ever has been seriously implemented in the media, but also of the commercial rule of keeping the level of excitement sufficiently high to attract an audience. Spiro Agnew admonishes:

> . . . And in the networks' endless pursuit of controversy, we should ask: What is the end value—*to enlighten or to profit*? What is the end result—to inform or to confuse? How does the ongoing exploration for more action, more excitement, more drama serve our national search for *internal peace and stability*?[25]

Apparently the threat to the social order is sufficiently grave in this Administration's view to call into question what the nation generally has prized most, the quest for profitability.

But failing far-reaching structural change, it is traditional status quo behavior to conceal if possible, cosmeticize if necessary, and in any case minimize, the extent of the social disarray. In this period of communications saturation—almost every American home possesses at least one radio and television set, some have two and three of each—this requires, to be even minimally effective, a massive control and minipulation. It is just such an effort that recent governmental statements and actions herald and spotlight. Actually the process predates the Vice-President's intervention and has been well under way for several years.

The generalized condition of the information system invariably has been commercial, self-selective, and, in the main, reactionary. Furthermore, this was achieved very effectively *without* central direction, by structures which operated with implicit generalized assumptions common to all property-holders, media-controllers certainly not excepted. What is different now is not only a matter of degree, but the introduction of explicit manipulatory methods.

Consider, for instance, radio-television's performance after Martin Luther King's murder. The industry's trade magazine described it this way:

> Television and radio emerged with new esteem last week from what may have been the stormiest ten days of news coverage in their history.[26]

What merited this self-congratulation? In the words of *Broadcasting* again, "a spot survey of some stations in several of the major markets where civil disorders occurred showed that at the local level the theme was 'restraint'" (p. 25). And how was this "restraint" exercised in practice? In Baltimore, for instance, a news director said "films of police firing on snipers, white men with guns in the trouble area and black militants making inflammatory statements weren't used." In the New York area, station officials "emphasized that views of militants were reported but not generally as voiced by them" (p. 26). Television in some cities ran movies day and night. And *Variety* reported

MIND MANAGEMENT: MASS MEDIA IN THE ADVANCED INDUSTRIAL STATE
Herbert I. Schiller

with some astonishment how many black faces were seen on the home screen for one week after King's death, only to vanish once the passions subsided.

The media, largely abandoning their never widely fulfilled function as informational sources, were used deliberately for diversion, sedation, and pacification.

> In Washington, D.C., officials turned to a 34-year-old Negro singer whose ability to work up an audience had long been established. Before TV cameras and radio microphones, James Brown poured his soul into a message urging an end to the disorders in the city . . . "Go home, look at TV. Listen to the radio. Listen to some James Brown records."[27]

Still more significantly, voluntary agreements among broadcasters to hold back news on racial troubles as well as compacts with police agencies to delay or even withhold information on urban disorders are multiplying. A survey conducted by one media journal disclosed that

> about one quarter of all stations [TV] subscribe to some kind of such agreement. The larger stations (those with $3 million or more in annual revenue) reported the largest number of such compacts, which is not surprising considering the prevalence of disorders in the large cities. Nearly 39 percent of large station respondents reported operating under some kind of pact or informal agreement.[28]

An example of a tie-in between broadcasters and police is also reported.

> Stations in Indianapolis follow the "Omaha Plan" which provides that when a "Code 30" is announced by police, news media agree to withhold the release of the story for 30 minutes but can continue to cover it for information. WFBM-TV said that successive Code 30s can be called by police but WISH-TV understands the agreement to mean that only a second 30-minute blackout can be called by police after which each station is free to cover the story.
> Some agreements go so far as to ban broadcast news while a disorder is in progress. Others require

media not to mention the location of the disturbance. Memphis is an example of the latter.[29]

Coordinated news control is being institutionalized on a private as well as on a governmental basis. Expecting a troubled fall (1970), the National Association of Broadcasters in "an unprecedented call" advised its members "to be especially careful in their news coverage" of desegregation and campus unrest. The recommendation for news management was encased in reassuring language:

> It is not the purpose of the NAB to intrude into the processes of news gathering and responsible reporting or the full flow of freedom that must underpin all of our industry's information efforts. Rather, we would sound the alert before the fact to urge you to anticipate any eventuality that might arise. We hope with you that reason and domestic tranquility prevail, but if they do not, we must be ready. Broadcast journalism is now the cornerstone of our broad service to the public and our responsibilities are therefore of the highest order as we present the news of the day.[30]

Contrary to Vice-President Agnew's argument that the media have given protestors disproportionate coverage, there has been a calculated effort at the highest level of policy-making to mute the criticism and, wherever possible, to ignore it, even when the numbers and personalities in the rallies were major newsworthy events by any professional criteria of measurement. *Variety* reported that "The massive Washington, D.C. and San Francisco anti-war marches and rallies (Nov. 15, 1969) received no live or special coverage from the networks." The paper observed that "one objective of Veepee Spiro T. Agnew's high-voltage blast at network news operations last week was to squelch, if possible, any extensive moratorium coverage. He needn't have bothered."[31] The networks had no intention of covering the meetings live in the first place. But this was not a new development. *Variety* interviewed at network spokesman who

> recalled a similar situation with the 1967 Pentagon March when the Johnson Administration was appeased

without public outburst. NBC News was definitely planning live coverage of the march when CBS News presented the proposition that they all eschew live coverage. NBC went along. Also contacted was ABC, and there was a coverage blackout of an event which was at least newsworthy enough to win Norman Mailer a Pulitzer prize for his book about it.

The situation is deteriorating rapidly and the *Variety* reporter concludes that

. . . there are a complexity of factors working against network news before a high government official comes along to bully them via their own facilities. Generally conservative and profit-oriented network managements have no sympathy for extra and controversial coverage. Even more conservative affiliates can be downright hostile to issue-oriented TV reportage. Tough newsmen have been weeded out of the network news departments over the last few years. And then there was the public uproar when the Chicago Convention's chaotic reality ran contrary to network TV's constantly grinding fantasies about such things as law and order.[32]

Examples of the media's voluntary, widespread knuckling-under to pressure are too numerous to detail. A few of the more egregious recent instances include Johnny Carson's Tonight show tabooing Ralph Nader's appearance;[33] a satirical album, "The Begatting of the President," banned on several commercial stations;[34] Lawrence Ferlinghetti's "Tyrannus Nix" taped by the poet for National Educational Television and sharply trimmed by NET without Ferlinghetti's knowledge or permission;[35] and a special presidential briefing for top executives and editors of 38 selected television and newspaper organizations, to which the *New York Times* and the *Washington Post*, both outspoken critics of the Administration's Cambodia venture and general Indochina policy, were not invited."[36]

III.

The deteriorating national informational condition goes well beyond the individual episodic

censorship pressure of high bureaucrats. Executive manipulation of the media, limned brilliantly by Joe McGinnis in *The Selling of the President, 1968*, has developed into a fine art. Nowhere else is the ideational environment so effectively packaged as at the national level. The *New York Times*, singled out for attack by the present Administration, reported some of the techniques utilized to create a controlled informational perspective. It described top-level briefings of news executives, designed to bypass the less cooperative Washington press corps, personal presidential visits to especially receptive newspaper editors, packaged press releases nationally distributed to 1,200 editorial writers and radio and television news directors and, most important of all, the elaborately arranged presidential press conference, nationally televised. The *Times* noted that

he [Nixon] selects the reporters who will ask the questions. As every President has, Mr. Nixon has questions he wants to answer planted in the press. Moreover, few reporters, knowing the camera is on them, have shown themselves adept at asking sharp questions.[37]

Presidential public relations also are applied to the media journeymen. Mike Royko, Chicago-based columnist, wondered first why he was asked to a presidential social event, and then, what was the purpose of his five-minute chat with the President on the receiving line. He mused:

And the President was there, straining his mind and using time, in the capacity of a salesman, or a public relations man. Through a handshake and an exchange of pleasantries, we were all to go away thinking more highly of his foreign policies. . . . That's what I mean about it being a strange way to run a country. . . . I think he ought to forget about selling and just demonstrate that the product works.[38]

Still another instrument of the developing public-opinion manipulation are the omnipresent polls. Opinion surveys are employed increasingly to create the atmosphere that the information managers at

MIND MANAGEMENT: MASS MEDIA IN THE ADVANCED INDUSTRIAL STATE.
Herbert I. Schiller

the highest level seek. Often, a follow-the-leader effect is generated from the responses to carefully structured questions that embrace implicit political conclusions. The origin of and support for most of the surveying is generally obscure though the most prestigious names in public opinion sounding are employed. No one can estimate the full extent to which independent survey firms are enlisted by the government for the latter's purposes but the following passage from a United States Information Agency (USIA)-produced film, *The Silent Majority* is suggestive of the ties that now exist:

> *Correspondent:* For the last 33 years the American Institute of Public Opinion has been a respected reporter of American attitudes. The Institute—known as the Gallup Poll—has pioneered techniques of public sampling, and has refined the methods of research which are used all over this country and by foreign opinion research organizations in all parts of the world . . . George Gallup is president of the Gallup Poll organization. Today, we'd like to question him about one of his most recent polls.
> *Correspondent:* On November 3rd President Nixon spoke to the people of the United States about his policy on Vietnam. He mentioned a "silent majority" of Americans who, he felt, supported his position. What did your organization do following that speech?
> *Mr. Gallup:* Well, immediately following the speech we had a squad of well-trained telephone interviewers contact 500 people across the country and then the results came in the same night, of course, and we collected them the next day and wired the results off to our newspapers at one o'clock on Tuesday.[39]

The close association of the Gallup Poll with the presidential message and then the utilization of the poll's results along with the poll director's comments for official (and rapid) distribution overseas by the United States Information Agency indicate a relationship which can hardly instill confidence about the independence of the information and opinion-taking process. Besides, the employment of private nongovernmental survey firms in USIA overseas polling of foreign nationals' attitudes is publicly acknowledged.[40]

Domestically, the connections between governmental authorities and polling companies are a totally uncharted area, but one whose usefulness for manipulation can hardly be overstated.

Even when the polls are not being utilized for deliberate mind management, their impact may have that effect nonetheless. Joseph Klapper, director of social research for the Columbia Broadcasting System, observes that

> . . . There is another area in which mass communication is extremely effective, and *that is in the creation of opinion on new issues*. By "new issues" I mean issues on which the individual has no opinion and on which his friends and fellow group members have no opinion. The reason for the effectiveness of mass communication in creating opinions on new issues is pretty obvious: *The individual has no predisposition to defend, and so the communication falls, as it were, on defenseless soil*. And once the opinion is created, then it is this new opinion which becomes easy to reinforce and hard to change. This process of opinion creation is strongest, by the way, when the person has no other source of information on the topic to use as a touchstone. He is therefore the more wholly dependent on the communication in question.[41]

How could the opinion polling process be better described? Questions that in themselves are value judgments, or informational perspectives, create the attitudinal framework into which the respondent is pressed by his very participation in the process. More significantly, the impact goes well beyond the poll participant. The nation at large is brought into the arena when the poll is published or broadcast.

Much the same conclusion is reached by another writer who notes that

> we must realize that preferences reported in sample surveys, electronic or otherwise, are often very different in nature than those actively volunteered when citizens participate. The opinions expressed in polls are frequently shallow responses to problems to which the respondent has never given much thought. The saliency of the issue to him may be low and the opinion is likely to be based on little or no information.[42]

The passive polling process, therefore, is apt to be an instrument for opinion creation, not only for the directly participating respondents but, more significantly, for the millions who are told what national sentiment is supposed to be on such question.

The controlled informational environment domestically has its international extension in the expanding communications activities of governmental agencies, the USIA in particular. Still it is important to remember that mind management begins at home and the United States public is the first beneficiary/victim of controlled information. A glimpse of the scale of operations now undertaken is hinted at with respect to preparing the public for foreign military interventions or new departures in foreign policies, as, for instance, the formulation of the Truman Doctrine in 1947 and the Vietnamese intervention in the mid-1960s.

Howard K. Smith, the news commentator, told a congressional hearing:

> Senator Vandenberg suggested to President Truman if he wanted to take such a drastic step as commit America to the defense of Greece and Turkey, "If that is what you want to do, Mr. President, you had better go before Congress and scare the hell out of the American people," and Truman did it.
>
> [Congressman] Fascell: He scared Congress, too.
>
> Mr. Smith: In July 1965, when the decision was made to go into Vietnam in force, it was discussed at great length in Cabinet meetings, and in National Security Council meetings, and smaller meetings, whether or not to try to scare hell out of the people, and the decision was deliberate not to do so.[43]

Whichever way decision-makers move in any particular situation, the central and unprecedented fact is that information control has become part of national policy. The techniques of ideational packaging have become instruments for manipulating popular support for (or at least indifference to) governmental actions.

This may help to explain the seemingly paradoxial condition wherein no other nations (with the possible exception of the Scandinavian countries) approach United States gross informational levels as measured by radio and television set ownership and use, and yet, according to Senator Stuart Symington, ". . . the public in this country often knows less than much of the rest of the world."[44]

IV.

In fact, it cannot be emphasized too strongly that there appears to be a new direction in domestic informational activities. The communications editor of the *Saturday Review* refers to a "Coming Age of News Monopoly" and writes that "we feel we must at the very least put up storm-warning flags before the hurricane of fascism, monopoly, one-man rule, and press gag engulfs our democracy."[45] Unreservedly commercial in the past, and assuming matter-of-fact support of the social-industrial order as the natural consequence of their activities, the media and ancillary informational services today are being pushed, as well as moving on their own, onto a directly manipulative path, The growth of a large knowledge industry work force suggests to the country's media managers the necessity for an ever widening control of the informational and cultural environment. At the same time, increasingly explosive social and political issues provide a daily atmosphere of crisis, and if the media reflect even a small portion of this reality, passions are further enflamed and powerful custodians of the status quo, including the President, are aroused to fury and intimidation.

Accordingly, a deliberate movement is developing at influential levels of government, moving beyond manipulation, to restrict, censor, and anesthetize the most widely used communications channels. The *New York Times* reports, almost matter-of-factly, that the President has already appointed "the nation's chief censor, a private citizen now on standby duty who would assume office in a national emergency." A "little-known" plan has been in existence, according to the *Times*, for several years, which permits the President to

MIND MANAGEMENT: MASS MEDIA IN THE ADVANCED INDUSTRIAL STATE
Herbert I. Schiller

decree a national emergency without congressional approval and institute press censorship.[46] It is still too early to predict whether these multiplying efforts will succeed. Some countervailing forces are also operative. Concentrated as the main sources of information are, alternative channels, far weaker and with much narrower constituencies, do exist. Campus newspapers, "free" presses, a few listener-supported radio stations, underground movies, some rock albums, and even certain circulation periodicals which survive only because

they print provocative material, are some elements that resist "coordination" and still serve the purpose of free inquiry. Unfortunately, most of these channels are reaching only a very limited stratum of the population—the young, the university-enrolled, and for the most part, the well-to-do segment. The split in the national community is deepening, therefore, along informational as well as age, employment, racial, and political lines. It remains to be seen what will emerge from these fragments.[47]

[1]Peter Drucker, *The Age of Discontinuity* (New York: Harper, 1968), p. 276.

[2]Ibid.

[3]Ibid., pp. 277–78 (italics added only in the second sentence).

[4]Edward H. Carr, *The New Society* (Boston: 1957), p. 53.

[5]George Lichtheim, "What Socialism Is and Is Not," *New York Review of Books*, 9 April 1970, p. 44.

[6]Raymond Williams, "Saying 'No' to Labor," *Nation*, 15 June 1970, pp. 710–12.

[7]Jerry Rubin, *Do It* (New York: Simon and Schuster, 1970), p. 142.

[8]*New York Times*, 5 August 1970.

[9]Daniel Bell, "The Balance of Knowledge and Power," *MIT Technology Review*, June 1969, pp. 43–44.

[10]*New York Times*, 5 August 1970.

[11]*Los Angeles Times*, 21 September 1970, Part I, p. 3.

[12]Staughton Lynd, "Again—Don't Tread On Me," *Newsweek*, 6 July 1970, p. 31.

[13]Theodore Roszak, *The Making of a Counter Culture* (New York: Anchor, 1969).

[14]*Advertising Age*, 8 June 1970, p. 44.

[15]*New York Times*, 14 and 21 November 1969.

[16]"The questions I'm raising here tonight should have been raised by others long ago. They should have been raised by those Americans who have traditionally considered the preservation of freedom of speech and freedom of the press their special provinces of responsibility." *New York Times*, 14 November 1969.

[17]Statement of Raymond B. Nixon, in US Senate, Sub-committee on Antitrust and Monopoly, Hearings, *The Failing Newspaper Act*, 90th Cong., 2nd Sess. (Washington: US Government Printing Office, 1968), pp. 2841–42.

[18]Bryce Rucker, *The First Freedom* (Carbondale: Southern Illinois University Press, 1968), pp. 140–57.

[19]"The Rich Rewards of Pioneering . . . ," *Television*, March 1968, pp. 27–51.

[20]*New York Times*, 21 November 1969.

[21]"The Rich Rewards of Pioneering . . . ," pp. 27–51.

[22]Arthur C. Neilsen, Sr., "Greater Prospects Through Marketing Research," Speech before the Newcomben Society, Chicago, 30 April 1964.

[23]J. K. Galbraith, *The New Industrial State* (Boston: Houghton, 1967).

[24]William Haley, "News and Documentaries on U.S. Television," in Marvin Barrett, ed., *Survey of Broadcast Journalism, 1968–69* (New York: Grosset, 1969), p. 60.

[25]*New York Times*, 14 November 1969. Italics added.

[26]*Broadcasting*, 15 April 1969, p. 23.

[27]Ibid.

[28]*Television Age*, 23 September 1968, p. 29.

[29]Ibid., p. 29.

[30]*Broadcasting*, 31 August 1970, p. 57.

[31]*Variety*, 19 November 1969, p. 1.

[32]Ibid., p. 47.

[33]*Variety*, 12 August 1970, p. 31.

[34]*Variety*, 29 July 1970, p. 1.

[35]*Variety*, 31 December 1969.

[36]*New York Times*, 27 June 1970.

[37]*New York Times*, 24 August 1970.

[38]*Los Angeles Times*, 20 September 1970, Sec. e, p. 3.

[39]*New York Times*, 20 November 1969.

[40]See Edith Marie Bjorkland, "Research and Evaluation Programs of the U.S. Information Agency and the

Overseas Information Center Libraries," *Library Quarterly,* October 1968, p. 414.

[41] US House of Representatives, Subcommittee on International Organizations and Movements, *Modern Communications and Foreign Policy,* 90th Cong., 1st Sess. (Washington: US Government Printing Office, 1967). pp. 60–61. Italics added.

[42] Norman H. Nie, "Hello Central, Give Me Heaven," *University of Chicago Magazine,* Vol. 62 (May/June 1970), p. 4.

[43] US House of Representatives, Subcommittee on International Organizations and Movements, *The Future of United States Public Diplomacy,* 90th Cong., 2nd Sess. (Washington: US Government Printing Office, 1968), p. 54.

[44] Stuart Symington, "Congress's Right to Know," *New York Times Magazine,* 9 August 1970, p. 7.

[45] Richard L. Tobin, "The Coming Age of News Monopoly," *Saturday Review,* 10 October 1970, p. 51.

[46] *New York Times,* 9 October 1970.

[47] Addressing himself to some of the same issues considered in this article, Federal Communications Commissioner Nicholas Johnson believes that "the examination and close study of television as a power phenomenon in American politics should occupy some of the best minds in the U.S. and elsewhere for some time." Remarks prepared for delivery as the keynote address to the International Association of Political Consultants Annual World Conference, The Royal Garden Hotel, London, England, 14 December 1970, page 37.

Reprinted from Don't Blame the People *(Los Angeles: Diversity Press, 1971), pp. 180–88, 198–200. Used by permission of publisher and author.*

Propaganda in the United States

ROBERT CIRINO

THE agencies of news media unanimously cooperate to put over the idea that the term "propaganda" correctly applies only to Communist produced news. Whenever the claims of the North Vietnamese, the Viet Cong, the Russians or the Chinese are announced, correspondents characterize the message as propaganda. Hardly an hour passes without the term being used to describe "enemy" claims. In 1969 NBC showed a film of the Russian-Chinese border dispute produced by Communist China.[1] Instead of finding a Chinese translator to interpret the audio portion, NBC had one of its own correspondents narrate the film. He repeatedly used the word propaganda to describe the film and explained in detail, while the film was being shown, the actual photographic techniques of implanting a bias favorable to the Chinese:

> The shots are angled to make it look as though. . . .
> That scene was repeated to make everyone see how. . . .
> An old fashion 'freeze frame' makes them look. . . .

To make sure the audience didn't forget one moment that it was watching Communist propaganda, the statement:

FILM FROM COMMUNIST SOURCES

was repeatedly shown at the bottom of the screen.

News media are doing their job when they correctly reveal the sources of their information. And the term propaganda certainly does correctly describe the information output of Communist news agencies. The only criticism that can be made of U.S. news media's handling of Communist information sources is that U.S. correspondents substitute their dialogue for the original. This is a hidden technique of implanting bias in itself. It is also an insult to the American people to treat them as if they must be protected from the original words of Communists even after the source is made clear.

The media are not always so conscientious about identifying the source of their information — especially when this information emanates from the propaganda arm of the Pentagon. Many television stations show Pentagon produced film of action in Vietnam without identifying the source. When U.S. Army officers in Vietnam are interviewed to supply much of the dialogue for network film coverage of Vietnam, the audience isn't warned that they are getting a one-sided view, nor are Pentagon news releases ever termed "propaganda" by U.S. correspondents. Most U.S. correspondents writing about Vietnam support the presence of the United States in Vietnam and oppose an immediate and orderly withdrawal of all U.S. troops. When their interpretive reports on Vietnam are shown or published there is no warning to audience or readers that the news item represents a point of view favorable to the Pentagon. In contrast, articles written by Australian journalist Wilfred Burchett, a Communist, are introduced by conspicuous notices identifying his point of view. As the *Los Angeles Times* warned its readers, this article "presents a Communist viewpoint and should be read in that light."[2]

This double standard of news treatment, identifying and classifying only the other side's news releases as propaganda, has been successful in making propaganda a bad word—and a word never to be applied to the news output of U.S. commercial news agencies.

This myth conveniently prevents the American public from focusing attention on the situation that makes propaganda important to begin with. The real question is whether the public is receiving one-sided propaganda or propaganda from all viewpoints—a situation where one news agent of propaganda can balance off and expose propaganda techniques used by news agencies advocating opposing viewpoints. In the Communist world the public is unquestionably propagandized because there is no counter propaganda. But Americans are also being propagandized because there are no news agencies in the mass media who use the tools of propaganda to advance viewpoints which are fundamentally at odds with those of the establishment oriented media owners. How often does one network expose the propaganda techniques of its competitor or advocate, with its use of hidden bias, opposite priorities and policies?

The myth that only the other side uses propaganda is limiting in another aspect that is relevant to the one-sided presentation of news. It doesn't deal with the decided bias that is introduced into the media by technical or financial requirements of the communication system, a bias we've explored earlier. There is little competing bias to counter such bias either in Communist countries or in the United States. As a result, all the people of the world are in a state of being propagandized by the very technical and financial nature of modern communications. This explains in part why newspapers and news programs around the world feature moon shots, transplant operations and accidents while ignoring the less dramatic and palpable problems of illiteracy, the brain

drain, pollution, population increase, disparity between the rich and the poor, and arms proliferation. . . .

THE IMPORTANCE OF PROPAGANDA

Any attempt to influence public opinion can be considered propaganda of one sort or another. Some propagandists employ facts and history responsibly; others falsify or ignore facts and distort history. Some propagandists allow for at least the possibility of real choice and participation in opinion-making on the part of their audience; others try their best to keep people from thinking on their own. Propaganda is used to further good causes as well as bad causes, peace as well as war, brotherhood as well as hate. The use of hidden techniques of implanting bias by those who control mass media in the United States is a form of propaganda. That it is used to further establishment policies and priorities can be seen readily. The question we take up here is this: How important is propaganda in shaping American politics and society?

First, let us examine the matter of editorial support of presidential candidates. In twenty out of forty-two presidential elections the candidate supported by the press has lost the election.[3] Those who control access to media often claim that this is proof that there is little advantage in controlling the means of producing bias. If this control was a significant advantage, claim the owners, candidates supported by the owners would always win elections. This shaky reasoning ignores three very important factors that must be considered when trying to determine the effects of attempts to influence public opinion. First, it fails to take into consideration how an election would have turned out had press support been the opposite of what it was. President Harry Truman had the support of only 10 percent of newspaper circulation compared to Thomas E. Dewey's 78 percent. Truman won by a relatively small margin. Would he still have won by only

PROPAGANDA IN THE UNITED STATES
Robert Cirino

a small margin if he had 78 percent support and Dewey 10 percent? What is remarkable in this election is not that Truman won without press support, but that a candidate such as Dewey was able to get close to forty percent of the vote. Through its use of propaganda, the press was able to convince millions of poor and middle-class people that their interests were the same as the very wealthy whom Dewey represented. One factor that helped Truman win despite news media's massive editorial opposition and pro-Dewey bias was the Democratic advantage over the radio; confident of victory, the Republicans allowed the Democrats to outspend them in purchasing radio time.

John Kennedy won in 1960 by a very small margin and he also had little press support—only 16 percent of newspaper circulation compared to 71 percent for Richard Nixon. The question is by how much more might John Kennedy have won had he been backed by 71 percent of the press instead of 16 percent? The 1964 election may suggest some answers. In this unusual election the more conservative candidate, Barry Goldwater, was deserted by the traditionally Republican press. For the first time the more liberal candidate was favored by the press. The election resulted in the most lopsided victory ever recorded in a presidential election in modern times. The next largest margins of victory ever achieved at the polls occurred during the depression years of 1932 and 1936 when enough of the conservative press supported the more liberal Franklin D. Roosevelt to give him 40 and 36 percent press support instead of the usual 10 to 15 percent received by the Democrats.[4]

Second, in addition to having newspaper support, the more conservative candidate has usually had considerably more money to spend for political advertisements in newspapers and over radio and television. If this propaganda advantage had been reversed, giving the more liberal candidate like Hubert Humphrey more money for propaganda, it too, may have significantly affected the margin of victory or defeat. Candidate Humphrey was sure that his financial handicap influenced the outcome of the 1968 election:

> Equal time access to television is an empty concept if the time must be bought. And without question there must be a better way, a better system, to guarantee equal access of candidates and parties to the television viewers of America.
>   . . . Elections ought not to be decided on the basis of who has the most money.
>   There is no surer way to corrupt American life and American politics than to have the great decision of this nation as to who will be its leader and its sense of direction determined by the size of a checkbook or a bank account.
>   It's wrong; it is wrong, wrong, wrong to have to go around seeking large contributions from the few rich in order to conduct a campaign which you say is for many. Can't do it. It's wrong.[5]

Humphrey did all this complaining because Richard Nixon received three times as much money as he did and outspent him $12.6 million to $7.1 million on broadcasting alone. For the 1970 elections Democratic candidates were even at more of a financial disadvantage: figures released in October 1970 showed that the Republicans received $18.3 million in contributions compared to the Democrats $3.5 million.[6]

The third factor ignored by owner interpretation of election results is much more significant than the first two. This is the effect of consistent and long term use of propaganda to create views of the world and attitudes which favor conservative priorities and politicians. Constant and subtle use of bias over hundreds of years has created racism, chauvinism, respect for the right, contempt for the common laborer and the poor, and respect for religious leaders no matter how shortsighted or inhuman their use of political power is. At election time these basic attitudes are more important than political advertisements or the momentary endorsement of the press. If overnight all the mass media agents in the South supported politicians running on platforms of complete

racial equality, they could still not prevent seg-
regationists from winning the elections.

This long term bias on the part of news agencies
might in some cases explain seemingly paradoxical
political events. For example, until very recently
the *Los Angeles Times*, through the use of blatant
bias, had helped create racist and reactionary
attitudes toward labor and the black man. When
in 1968 the *Times* took the bold step of endorsing
for mayor a black man, Tom Bradley, against
Sam Yorty, a man who seemed to appeal to white
racists, its position was rejected by the majority
of voters. The *Times* long-term ultra-conservative
propaganda had been too successful even for a
Los Angeles Times that had become less conservative.

In recent times the *New York Times* has been
a strong advocate of abortion reform for the
state of New York, but the voters continued to
elect politicians who defeated abortion reform
year after year until 1970. The *New York Times* can
take most of the blame for the previous defeats
of abortion reform legislation. Their long term
propaganda glorifying church leaders and doctrines
has helped create in the public mind a respect
for dogmatic church leaders and politicians—the
very ones who have turned archaic and inhumane
church dogma into laws which demand obedience
from all citizens no matter what their religious
beliefs. A newspaper can reverse political direction
in midstream, but a human being doesn't so
easily change his basic attitudes.

If, as some owners claim, control of the means
of creating propaganda is no great advantage,
why are dictators, politicians and advertisers
so concerned with who gets access to mass media?
Would advertisers spend up to $70,000 for one
minute of access to television if it had only lttle
power to affect attitudes and behavior? Would
Spiro Agnew make such a fuss just because of a
few mildly critical comments about President
Nixon's half hour political speech? Would
President Nixon's media advisors have gone to
all the fuss that Joe McGinnis details in his book
The Selling of the President if the use of hidden

bias was not important? Of course not; none of
these people would have put the money and effort
they did into creating a favorable bias if it didn't
pay off. In fact the reason that dictatorships in
communist countries, as well as in South Vietnam,
Spain, Greece and Brazil, are able to continue in
power is that they control completely the means
of creating propaganda through the mass media.

Governor Nelson Rockefeller's successful 1966
campaign for re-election demonstrates the powerful
effect that a propaganda advantage can have. In
early 1966, only 25 percent of the potential voters
gave the Governor a favorable rating. The situation
seemed hopeless. But instead of dropping out of
the picture as friends advised, he hired a famous
advertising agency to launch a campaign through
the mass media. They made 35 different commercials—many of them indistinguishable from items
on news programs—and had them shown more
than 700 times. Nelson Rockefeller out-spent his
opponent, Frank O'Connor, $4.3 million to $278,000
—a 15 to 1 advantage. It worked: by September his
favorable rating had gone up to 36 percent and in
November he was re-elected.[7] In his 1970 election
victory four years later, Rockefeller outspent his
opponent Arthur Goldberg by a 5 to 1 margin.

"Buying" elections by outspending opponents by
huge margins is not an isolated phenomenon. In
the 1970 primaries, Senatorial candidates Howard
Metzenbaum in Ohio, Richard Ottinger in New
York and Lloyd Bentsen in Texas won elections in
which they outspent opponents by as much as ten
to one. In order to prevent such an enormous advantage, Congress in October 1970 sent to the
President a bill that would have limited somewhat a
wealthy candidate in being able to purchase more
broadcast time than his opponent. President Nixon's
veto of the bill (on the grounds that it discriminated
against broadcasters in not also putting limits on
money spent for political ads in newspapers and
magazines) no doubt pleased the broadcast industry as much as it pleased the wealthy candidates
and campaign contributors who can afford to pay
for television and radio commercials.

PROPAGANDA IN THE UNITED STATES
Robert Cirino

Even though it appears obvious that the use of propaganda has considerable effect on public attitudes and behavior, the owners of media are still able to minimize its importance because it is extremely difficult to prove scientifically the exact effect of attempts to influence public opinion. No election could be held over again, reversing the newspaper endorsements, advertising money or long term use of bias. The results of such a hypothetical election can only be guessed at. Furthermore, there are other uncontrollable and unmeasurable factors which may influence people's attitudes very significantly. The unemployment and poverty of millions of Americans during the depression was a factor that helped Franklin D. Roosevelt get elected. The poor knew things were bad and had come to suspect the intentions of big business despite a more optimistic view presented by the Republican press. In Cincinnati, after a six-month propaganda campaign designed to increase support for the United Nations, the percentage of people supporting the United Nations was found to have decreased. It was reasoned that one of the causes for this decrease was that decisions and actions by the United Nations during this period were unpopular and thus offset the pro-UN propaganda.[8] The use of propaganda in mass media has its limitations: it would be impossible to convince a starving person he has plenty to eat. The propagandist won't even try to do this; instead, he will try to tell him who and what is to blame for his hunger or find spurious comparisons for him to rest in, such as "you're less hungry than you were ten years ago," or "the people overseas are worse off." But whoever actual conditions and events may tend to favor, it is still a great and unfair advantage for one politician to have more press support, money and access to media than his opponent. It is a situation that can't possibly be made consistent with the American idea of a fair election in a democratic society. That the people accept the situation seems to me an example of the success and power of mass media propaganda.

While communication experts may disagree on whether or not public opinion can be significantly changed by a particular public relations or election campaign, they have all agreed that a few underlying principles hold true in all situations involving persuasion and public opinion. There are two types of propaganda campaigns aimed at influencing people's opinions and behavior. One is a short term campaign, such as a project aimed at getting people now or in the near future to buy a product, to vote for a certain candidate or to demonstrate in the streets. The other type of campaign is a long term project designed not to affect any immediate action but to form or modify, over a period of many years, the basic values and self concepts of individuals and society. Professor Michael Choukas, in his book *Propaganda Comes of Age*, considers the short term effort as tactical propaganda and the long term effort as strategic propaganda.[9]

Tactical propaganda is sometimes successful at changing ideas that are not too important to a person, but it will in very few if any cases change ideas that are an integral part of an individual's self concept—his nuclear self. Propaganda attempting to change overnight a person's belief in God or white supremacy will fail, but that aimed at changing a person's belief in birth control or the Ku Klux Klan has a chance of succeeding because the person can change his ideas on these topics and still continue to believe in God or white racism.

It is much easier to persuade people to hang on to their present ideas and attitudes than to change them. In other words, those advocating the status quo have an easier job than those advocating change of any kind. In addition, attitudes which are reinforced by social groups like family, church, club, military organization, school, or society at large are much more resistant to change than attitudes that play no part in a person's social interactions.

While tactical propaganda will fail to change a person's basic attitudes, strategic propaganda carried on for years can be successful in developing, modifying or changing an individual's fundamental beliefs and self concept. Media owners' capacity to produce this kind of propaganda gives them their real power—much more potent a force than the power to endorse a particular candidate or help him with biased presentation of photographs at election time. Through their strategic or long term use of bias they can create basic public attitudes that will insure that both candidates—whoever they may be—will be acceptable to them. Candidates who advocate policies fundamentally at variance with the attitudes created over a long period of time by media owners will be lucky to poll 5 percent of the vote. Gilbert Seldes, media critic, describes the process of influencing basic ideas through the media as

> the slow daily and weekly creation of a climate favorable to certain ideas, the unnoticed gentle nudges and pressures that turn people in one direction rather than another, the constant supply of images to populate our subconscious minds.[10]

In the process of shaping attitudes that serve their own special interests, the media owners have created, sustained and confirmed racism, an unthinking patriotism, self blinding anti-communism and an acceptance of a communication system that prevents real competition between conflicting viewpoints. These undemocratic ideas have been implanted so deeply in Americans' concept of themselves that the ideas are highly resistant to propaganda aimed at changing them. J.H.C. Brown, in his book *Techniques of Persuasion*, states: "The most difficult thing in the world is to change minds in directions which conflict with the attitudes deeply embedded in the nuclear self."[11] The resistance is natural; it is based on man's instinct for survival. If man accepts ideas which destroy his value system—no matter how distorted his values may be—he has nothing left to live for. To destroy a person's self concept without replacing it with another, reinforced by the approval of social groups, is to risk destroying the person himself. In his book Brown includes many fascinating examples of

how individuals made dramatic changes in their opinions regarding religion or social philosophies, but in each case there was a substitute system of belief that the individual could adopt in place of the old one.

Over a long period of time basic attitudes may be modified by strategic propaganda, but since all the means of creating strategic as well as tactical propaganda are in the hands of those who don't want basic changes, there is little hope for the creation of attitudes that will demand a basic realignment of priorities in America. Establishment ideas have been made even more resistant to change as the result of the media owners success in convincing the family, school, military, and church to reinforce these ideas in group situations. Nothing else can explain or exonerate the American peoples' acceptance of the racism, self-blinding anti-communism, censorship by mass media and the distorted priorities that the establishment has found so profitable. Nothing else can explain why the American people often choose very conservative individuals such as George Wallace, Spiro Agnew, Ronald Reagan, Everett Dirkson, Pope Paul and the Reverend Billy Graham to be on the list of the ten most admired men in the world while solid liberal or moderate liberal individuals such as Ernest Gruening, George McGovern, Eugene McCarthy, Paul Douglas, Father Groppi and Malcolm Boyd seldom make the top ten.

Research has indicated that intelligence is not an important factor in whether a person can be easily persuaded or not. What appears to be important is how inadequate a person feels.[12] Perhaps it is not entirely an accident that the poor, the laborer and the ordinary middle class workers are pictured in the media in such a way as to make them feel inadequate. The rich, the corporate owners and managers, the military and the establishment politicians, by comparison, are idolized even if they are unethical. The feeling of inadequacy that the ordinary man unconsciously picks up from images produced by the media make him easy prey for

PROPAGANDA IN THE UNITED STATES
Robert Cirino

both tactical and strategic propaganda efforts. This partly explains the biggest miracle accomplished by media owners—the turning of the laborer and middle class against the hungry, poor, black and brown. It is the laborer and the man of the middle class who violently opposes welfare to the poor while supporting the giving billions of dollars of "welfare" to the very rich in the form of subsidies, tax privileges and wasteful or unnecessary defense contracts. As Jacques Ellul points out, while the middle class is highly resistant to tactical propaganda urging agitation for some new cause, they are "ideal prey" of *integration* propaganda, the term Ellul uses to describe strategic propaganda.[13]

The voting behavior of the common American and the ease with which he is persuaded to vote for establishment priorities that are detrimental to his and his country's well being leads many liberals and scholars to doubt the reasoning ability and good sense of the common man. They claim that even if there was equal competition among varying viewpoints, the people would vote for establishment priorities and politicians. This may be true from a limited viewpoint, but no real test of the common man's capabilities can be conducted until all viewpoints have an equal chance to employ techniques of implanting bias on a long term or strategic basis. Competition among viewpoints is only fair when each position on the political spectrum has had a chance to affect the individual's basic nuclear attitudes from the first time he is exposed to the media. To grab a person at twenty, thirty or fifty-years-old, after he has been exposed to only establishment viewpoints, and expect him to choose intelligently among all viewpoints—when he has just then and for the first time seen them presented on an equal basis—is to ignore the basics of persuasion.

These are fundamentals that the conservatives understand much better than the liberals because of their experience in using and monopolizing the tools of propaganda that come with ownership of mass media.

---

[1]NBC, *Huntley-Brinkley*, July 9, 1969.

[2]*Los Angeles Times* and *New York Times*, February 11, 1967.

[3]Nathan Blumberg. *One Party Press*, University of Nebraska Press, 1954, p. 11.

[4]*New York Times*, November 10, 1944, pp. 1, 11.

[5]UPI, *Stars and Stripes*, Fulda, Germany, February 3, 1969, p. 8.

[6]*Los Angeles Times*, January 15, 1970, p. 2 and October 28, 1970, p. 2.

[7]Robert MacNeil, *The People Machine*, Harper & Row, N.Y., 1968, p. 209.

[8]Irwin Ross, *The Image Merchants*, Doubleday & Company, Inc., Garden City, N.Y., 1959, p. 265.

[9]Public Affairs Press, 1965, Chapter 12.

[10]*The Great Audience*. Viking Press, N.Y., 1950, p. 139.

[11]Penguin Books, Baltimore, Maryland, 1963, p. 222.

[12]Joseph Klapper, *The Effects of Mass Communications*, Free Press, N.Y., 1960, p. 95.

[13]Jacques Ellul, *Propaganda*, Alfred A. Knopf, N.Y., 1965, p. 112.

C. Are the Media Revolutionary? McLuhan's Message

The remaining selections deal with the theories of H. Marshall McLuhan. He argues more strongly than any other media scholar that the mass media have a thoroughgoing, indeed, revolutionary, impact on mass society. His approach to the media is often ignored by serious media scholars. He has invented his own terminology, methodology, and literary style to produce a new model for understanding media which cannot, he claims, be judged in literary terms; that is, by what he calls "linear" reasoning and logic.

The validity and usefulness of this new approach has been acclaimed by disparate enthusiasts. Radical youth may like it because it proclaims them to be qualitatively (psychically) different from their seniors, who continue to plod along with their linear, print-oriented thought patterns. Advertising men, despite the fact that McLuhan's first book was a scathing attack on them, find his later de-emphasis of media content a perfect ideology to excuse their practices, even if it does not fully justify them.[1] But outside a small band of ardent McLuhanites he has been largely ignored by conventional scholars. As with Marx's followers, McLuhan's following seems to respond to the seductive nature of a simple, all-encompassing explanatory scheme. In this case, McLuhan has substituted media characteristics for the Marxist relations of production. With his theory McLuhan

can interpret history, explain contemporary events, and predict the outlines of the future.[2]

As with Marx, however, it is not necessary to adopt the whole system in order to find it useful. What McLuhan has to say on specific aspects of the media may still be worth examining individually. Thus his views on media content, differences between types of media, and the world context of communication are briefly considered here.

McLuhan's thoughts on the content of media are put strongly and succinctly as follows:

> Our conventional response to all media, namely that it is how they are used that counts, is the numb stance of the technological idiot. For the 'content' of a medium is like the juicy piece of meat carried by the burglar to distract the watchdog of the mind. . . The effect of the movie form is not related to its program content.[3]

Boulding has formalized this in his statement that "a social system is largely structured by the nature of the media in which communications are made, not by the content of these communications."[4] It is true that there are what might be called "first

[1] H. Marshall McLuhan, *The Mechanical Bride: Folklore of Industrial Man* (New York: The Vanguard Press), 1951.

[2] H. Marshall McLuhan, *The Gutenberg Galaxy: The Making of Topographic Man* (Toronto: University of Toronto Press), 1962. Present and future are the subjects of his *Understanding Media* and (with Quentin Fiore), *The Medium is the Message* (New York: Random House, 1967).

[3] *Understanding Media*, quoted by H. Rosenberg in G. E. Stearn, ed., *McLuhan: Hot and Cool* (New York: Dial Press, 1967), p. 198.

[4] K. Boulding in G. E. Stearn, ed., *op. cit.*, p. 59.

304

PART V: MASS MEDIA, MASS SOCIETY, AND MASS CULTURE
C. Are the Media Revolutionary? McLuhan's Message

order" consequences of changing from one media to another. The printing press and television network undoubtedly have had an impact that transcends their content, and this is the impact that McLuhan emphasizes to the exclusion of "lesser" media effects.

Such a grand theoretical view, however, overlooks many important details, even if these are not of world historical significance. Nazi Germany, for example, was not particularly unique in its media structure, for several other nations possessed close approximations to its print-radio media mix. But surely the differences in media systems and content made Germany sufficiently different from Britain, the United States, and France to make it a qualitatively unique environment. If, for example, Jews had been able to determine the content of the Nazi media, is it not possible that the outcome for them might have been different? Can we completely discount the numerous studies of media content, several of which are included in this volume, and claim that it makes no difference whether gangster films or ballet, exhortations to consume or do-it-yourself programs are shown on television? Clearly the advertising followers of McLuhan think that content counts, and the seller of merchandise backs this conviction with his money.

McLuhan does have one useful statement on content. He claims epigrammatically that "it's misleading to suppose there's any basic difference between education and entertainment."[5] This could be interpreted as meaning "anything goes," or "the medium is the message," but in context the statement was directed as the educational purist. McLuhan's point is that people are educated by their entertainment, the things that they enjoy. But this, apparently, should accentuate the importance of content, for by this interpretation the banal and trivial entertainment that is so common today actually is educating the public.

While conventional students of communication stress the content of the media, McLuhan stresses the differences between the media. His major distinction is between what he calls "hot" and "cool" media. The former do not require much participation by the recipient but the latter do. The designation of a medium is crucial since McLuhan claims that its impact ". . . on the structure of society depends very much on its temperature."[6] Boulding has conceded that there are qualitative differences between face-to-face communication, print, radio, and television. But he doubts that simplistically labeling television "cool," while designating print as "hot," in the McLuhan fashion can serve much purpose. It does of course suggest easily distinct historical periods and thus fits nicely into McLuhan's scheme of media revolutions, of a society being totally changed by a newly invented medium. Since both speech (primitive communication) and television are classified as "cool," the McLuhan cycle is closed — in his words we are returning to the "tribal village."

The modern world is dealt with ambiguously because of the classification scheme devised by McLuhan. He recognizes that the contemporary media network is entirely new, but he then develops this insight in the part metaphorical, part scientific idea of a return to primitivism. One of McLuhan's admirers comments on this in the following way:

A whole generation in America has grown up in the T.V. environment, and already these millions of people, twenty-five and under, have the same kind of sensory reactions as African tribesmen. The same thing is happening all over the world. The world is growing into a huge tribe, a . . . *global village*, in a *seamless web* of electronics.[7]

[6] K. Boulding in G. E. Stearn, ed., *op. cit.*, p. 60.
[7] Tom Wolfe, "suppose he is what he sounds like, the most important thinker since newton, darwin, freud, einstein, and pavlov [sic] — what if he is right?" [Article title appears in lower case. The subject pronoun refers to McLuhan.] in G. E. Stearn, ed., *op. cit.*, p. 19.

[5] *Ibid.*, p. 116.

305

PART V: MASS MEDIA, MASS SOCIETY, AND MASS CULTURE
C. Are the Media Revolutionary? McLuhan's Message

Or as McLuhan has said, "we live in a single constricted space resonant with tribal drums."[8] Very heady stuff, indeed! But what does it all mean?

The TV generation, we are told, is like pre-literate man, but the analogy cannot be pushed too far. (McLuhan of course doesn't spell out his arguments in linear or logical form.) True, today's youth rely more on sound and sight for their communication than did the preceding "print" generation, and in this sense they may resemble more closely the primitives. But not only can they converse (the primitives' only mode), read print, and hear radio (as did their parents), they also participate in the highly technical and de-cidedly non-primitive (one-way) communication medium, television.

And what is the global village into which we will be (or have been, for McLuhan is unclear on this point) re-tribalized? Clearly it cannot be a return to a social life dominated by face-to-face oral patterns of communication. It represents, at best, the notion of an international audience made possible by electronic communications, to which the world's real tribesmen can "plug in" without going through the stage of literacy. The unifying factor may be the modern media, but the messages they carry are not in fact universal. Thus there are quarrels in our "village," e.g., the Cold War, that cannot be automatically settled simply by expanding world communication networks.

That McLuhan's grasp of the international setting is rudimentary may be illustrated by the following passage in which he maintains his position that the media have effects *sui generis*. Here, though, he is apparently less sure of the desirability of the "global village"; indeed, he would rather postpone its development:

[8]T. Wolfe, quoting McLuhan, in *op. cit.*, p. 18.

If TV was simply eliminated from the United States scene, it would be a very good thing. Just as radio has a most malignant effect in Africa or [sic] Algeria, or China—in highly auditory cultures, radio drives these people nearly mad with paranoia and tribal intensity—TV, in a highly visual culture, drives us inward in depth into a totally non-visual universe of involvement. It is destroying our entire fabric of society in a short time. If you understand its dynamics, you would choose to eliminate it as soon as possible. TV changes the sensory and psychic like. It is an oriental form of experience, giving people a somber, profound sense of involvement.[9]

The new experience is not literally "oriental," as McLuhan claims, but entirely novel. There are, indeed, worldwide communications systems that by their structure and content can have very real consequences for the economic development of countries. But the effects of these media systems are clearly the result of their content, not merely their form, as McLuhan implies.[10]

The selection by McLuhan included here out-lines his central thesis. He uses literary examples to illuminate the revolutionary impact of the new media technologies which become "extensions" of our senses. The two articles which follow are critiques of McLuhan's work. Harold Rosenberg is generally favorable and stresses the imaginative, or, as he says, "illuminating" aspects of it. Thelma McCormack, however, responds with a much less enchanted evaluation. She finds his approach simplistic, naive, and dangerous in its ideological implications. Like all theories—and particularly ones from oracles like McLuhan—we should use this one with caution.

[9]H. Marshall McLuhan, in an interview with G. E. Stearn, *op. cit.*, p. 301.

[10]See Alan Wells, "Communications and Development: The Relevance of Media Content," *Sociological Quarterly* (Winter, 1971) pp. 95–99.

The Medium Is the Message

H. MARSHALL MC LUHAN

IN A culture like ours, long accustomed to splitting and dividing all things as a means of control, it is sometimes a bit of a shock to be reminded that, in operational and practical fact, the medium is the message. This is merely to say that the personal and social consequences of any medium—that is, of any extension of ourselves—result from the new scale that is introduced into our affairs by each extension of ourselves, or by any new technology. Thus, with automation, for example, the new patterns of human association tend to eliminate jobs, it is true. That is the negative result. Positively, automation creates roles for people, which is to say depth of involvement in their work and human association that our preceding mechanical technology had destroyed. Many people would be disposed to say that it was not the machine, but what one did with the machine, that was its meaning or message. In terms of the ways in which the machine altered our relations to one another and to ourselves, it mattered not in the least whether it turned out cornflakes or Cadillacs. The restructuring of human work and association was shaped by the technique of fragmentation that is the essence of machine technology. The essence of automation technology is the opposite. It is integral and decentralist in depth, just as the machine was fragmentary, centralist, and superficial in its patterning of human relationships.

The instance of the electric light may prove illuminating in this connection. The electric light is pure information. It is a medium without a message, as it were, unless it is used to spell out some verbal ad or name. This fact, characteristic of all media, means that the "content" of any medium is always another medium. The content of writing is speech, just as the written word is the content of print, and print is the content of the telegraph. If it is asked, "What is the content of speech?," it is necessary to say, "It is an actual process of thought, which is in itself nonverbal." An abstract painting represents direct manifestation of creative thought processes as they might appear in computer designs. What we are considering here, however, are the psychic and social consequences of the designs or patterns as they amplify or accelerate existing processes. For the "message" of any medium or technology is the change of scale or pace or pattern that it introduces into human affairs. The railway did not introduce movement or transportation or wheel or road into human society, but it accelerated and enlarged the scale of previous human functions, creating totally new kinds of cities and new kinds of work and leisure. This happened whether the railway functioned in a tropical or a northern environment, and is quite independent of the freight or content of the railway medium. The airplane, on the other hand, by accelerating the rate of transportation, tends to dissolve the railway form of city, politics, and association, quite independently of what the airplane is used for.

Let us return to the electric light. Whether the light is being used for brain surgery or night baseball is a matter of indifference. It could be argued that these activities are in some way the "content" of the electric light, since they could not exist without the electric light. This fact merely underlines the point that "the medium is the message" because it is the medium that shapes and controls the scale and form of human association and action. The content or uses of such media are as diverse as they are ineffectual in shaping the form of human association. Indeed, it is only too typical that the "content" of any medium blinds us to the character of the medium. It is only today that industries have become aware of the various kinds of business in which they are engaged. When IBM discovered that it was not in the business of making office equipment or business machines, but that it was in the business of processing information, then it began to navigate with clear vision. The General Electric Company makes a considerable portion of its profits from electric light bulbs and lighting systems. It has not yet discovered that, quite as much as A.T. & T., it is in the business of moving information.

The electric light escapes attention as a communication medium just because it has no "content." And this makes it an invaluable instance of how people fail to study media at all. For it is not till the electric light is used to spell out some brand name that it is noticed as a medium. Then it is not the light but the "content" (or what is really another medium) that is noticed. The message of the electric light is like the message of electric power in industry, totally radical, pervasive, and decentralized. For electric light and power are separate from their uses, yet they eliminate time and space factors in human association exactly as do radio, telegraph, telephone, and TV, creating involvement in depth.

A fairly complete handbook for studying the extensions of man could be made up from selections from Shakespeare. Some might quibble about whether or not he was referring to TV in these familiar lines from *Romeo and Juliet:*

> But soft! what light through yonder window breaks?
> It speaks, and yet says nothing.

In *Othello*, which, as much as *King Lear*, is concerned with the torment of people transformed by illusions, there are these lines that bespeak Shakespeare's intuition of the transforming powers of new media:

> Is there not charms
> By which the property of youth and maidhood
> May be abus'd? Have you not read Roderigo,
> Of some such thing?

In Shakespear's *Troilus and Cressida*, which is almost completely devoted to both a psychic and social study of communication, Shakespeare states his awareness that true social and political navigation depend upon anticipating the consequences of innovation:

> The providence that's in a watchful state
> Knows almost every grain of Plutus' gold,
> Finds bottom in the uncomprehensive deeps,
> Keeps place with thought, and almost like the gods
> Does thoughts unveil in their dumb cradles.

The increasing awareness of the action of media, quite independently of their "content" or programming, was indicated in the annoyed and anonymous stanza:

> In modern thought, (if not in fact)
> Nothing is that doesn't act,
> So that is reckoned wisdom which
> Describes the scratch but not the itch.

The same kind of total, configurational awareness that reveals why the medium is socially the message has occurred in the most recent and radical

THE MEDIUM IS THE MESSAGE
H. Marshall McLuhan

medical theories. In his *Stress of Life,* Hans Selye tells of the dismay of a research colleague on hearing Selye's theory:

> When he saw me thus launched on yet another enraptured description of what I had observed in animals treated with this or that impure, toxic material, he looked at me with desperately sad eyes and said in obvious despair: "But Selye, try to realize what you are doing before it is too late! You have now decided to spend your entire life studying the pharmacology of dirt!"

As Selye deals with the total environmental situation in his "stress" theory of disease, so the latest approach to media study considers not only the "content" but the medium and the cultural matrix within which the particular medium operates. The older unawareness of the psychic and social effects of media can be illustrated from almost any of the conventional pronouncements.

In accepting an honorary degree from the University of Notre Dame a few years ago, General David Sarnoff made this statement: "We are too prone to make technological instruments the scapegoats for the sins of those who wield them. The products of modern science are not in themselves good or bad; it is the way they are used that determines their value." That is the voice of the current somnambulism. Suppose we were to say, "Apple pie is in itself neither good nor bad; it is the way it is used that determines it value." Or, "The smallpox virus is in itself neither good nor bad; it is the way it is used that determines its value." Again, "Firearms are in themselves neither good nor bad; it is the way they are used that determines their value." That is, if the slugs reach the right people firearms are good. If the TV tube fires the right ammunition at the right people it is good. I am not being perverse. There is simply nothing in the Sarnoff statement that will bear scrutiny, for it ignores the nature of the medium, of any and all media, in the true Narcissus style of one hypnotized by the amputation and extension of his own being in a new

technical form. General Sarnoff went on to explain his attitude to the technology of print, saying that it was true that print caused much trash to circulate, but it had also disseminated the Bible and the thoughts of seers and philosophers. It has never occurred to General Sarnoff that any technology could do anything but *add* itself on to what we already are.

Such economists as Robert Theobald, W. W. Rostow, and John Kenneth Galbraith have been explaining for years how it is that "classical economics" cannot explain change or growth. And the paradox of mechanization is that although it is itself the cause of maximal growth and change, the principle of mechanization excludes the very possibility of growth or the understanding of change. For mechanization is achieved by fragmentation of any process and by putting the fragmented parts in a series. Yet, as David Hume showed in the eighteenth century, there is no principle of causality in a mere sequence. That one thing follows another accounts for nothing. Nothing follows from following, except change. So the greatest of all reversals occurred with electricity, that ended sequence by making things instant. With instant speed the causes of things began to emerge to awareness again, as they had not done with things in sequence and in concatenation accordingly. Instead of asking which came first, the chicken or the egg, it suddenly seemed that a chicken was an egg's idea for getting more eggs.

Just before an airplane breaks the sound barrier, sound waves become visible on the wings of the plane. The sudden visibility of sound just as sound ends is an apt instance of that great pattern of being that reveals new and opposite forms just as the earlier forms reach their peak performance. Mechanization was never so vividly fragmented or sequential as in the birth of the movies, the moment that translated us beyond mechanism into the world of growth and organic interrelation. The movie, by sheer speeding up the mechanical, carried us from the world of sequence and connections into the world of creative configuration and structure. The message of the movie medium is that of transition from lineal connections to configurations. It is the transition that produced the now quite correct observation: "If it works, it's obsolete." When electric speed further takes over from mechanical movie sequences, then the lines of force in structures and in media become loud and clear. We return to the inclusive form of the icon.

To a highly literate and mechanized culture the movie appeared as a world of triumphant illusions and dreams that money could buy. It was at this moment of the movie that cubism occurred, and it has been described by E. H. Gomrich (*Art and Illusion*) as "the most radical attempt to stamp out ambiguity and to enforce one reading of the picture—that of a man-made construction, a colored canvas." For cubism substitutes all facets of an object simultaneously for the "point of view" or facet of perspective illusion. Instead of the specialized illusion of the third dimension on canvas, cubism sets up an interplay of planes and contradiction or dramatic conflict of patterns, lights, textures that "drives home the message" by involvement. This is held by many to be an exercise in painting, not in illusion.

In other words, cubism, by giving the inside and outside, the top, bottom, back, and front and the rest, in two dimensions, drops the illusion of perspective in favor of instant sensory awareness of the whole. Cubism, by seizing on instant total awareness, suddenly announced that *the medium is the message*. Is it not evident that the moment that sequence yields to the simultaneous, one is in the world of the structure and of configuration? Is that not what has happened in physics as in painting, poetry, and in communication? Specialized segments of attention have shifted to total field, and we can now say, "The medium is the message" quite naturally. Before the electric speed and total field, it was not obvious that the medium is the message. The message, it seemed, was the "content," as people used to ask what a painting was *about*. Yet they never thought to ask what a melody was about, nor what a house or a dress was about. In such matters, people retained some sense of the whole pattern, of form and function as a unity. But in the electric age this integral idea of structure and configuration has become so prevalent that educational theory has taken up the matter. Instead of working with specialized "problems" in arithmetic, the structural approach now follows the lines of force in the field of numbers and has small children meditating about number theory and "sets."

Cardinal Newman said of Napoleon, "He understood the grammar of gunpowder." Napoleon had paid some attention to other media as well, especially the semaphore telegraph that give him a great advantage over his enemies. He is on record for saying that "three hostile newspapers are more to be feared than a thousand bayonets."

Alexis de Tocqueville was the first to master the grammar of print and typography. He was thus able to read off the message of coming change in France and America as if he were reading aloud from a text that had been handed to him. In fact, the nineteenth century in France and in America was just such an open book to de Tocqueville because he had learned the grammar of print. So he, also, knew when that grammar did not apply. He was asked why he did not write a book on England, since he knew and admired England. He replied:

One would have to have an unusual degree of philosophical folly to believe oneself able to judge England in six months. A year always seemed to me too short a time in which to appreciate the United States properly, and it is much easier to acquire clear and precise notions about the American Union than about Great Britain. In America all laws derive in a sense from the same line of thought. The whole of society, so to speak, is founded upon a single fact; everything springs from a simple principle. One could compare America to a forest pierced by a multitude of straight roads all converging on the same point. One has only to find the center and

THE MEDIUM IS THE MESSAGE
H. Marshall McLuhan

everything is revealed at a glance. But in England
the paths run criss-cross, and it is only by travelling
down each one of them that one can build up a
picture of the whole.

De Tocqueville, in earlier work on the French
Revolution, had explained how it was the printed
word that, achieving cultural saturation in the
eighteenth century, had homogenized the French
nation. Frenchmen were the same kind of people
from north to south. The typographic principles
of uniformity, continuity, and lineality had overlaid
the complexities of ancient feudal and oral society.
The Revolution was carried out by the new
literati and lawyers.

In England, however, such was the power of
the ancient oral traditions of common law, backed
by the medieval institution of Parliament, that
no uniformity or continuity of the new visual print
culture could take complete hold. The result was
that the most important event in English history
has never taken place; namely, the English
Revolution on the lines of the French Revolution.
The American Revolution had no medieval legal
institutions to discard or to root out, apart from
monarchy. And many have held that the American
Presidency has become very much more personal
and monarchical than any European monarch ever
could be.

De Tocqueville's contrast between England
and America is clearly based on the fact of typography and of print culture creating uniformity
and continuity. England, he says, has rejected
this principle and clung to the dynamic or oral
common-law tradition. Hence the discontinuity
and unpredictable quality of English culture. The
grammar of print cannot help to construe the
message of oral and nonwritten culture and
institutions. The English aristocracy was properly
classified as barbarian by Matthew Arnold because
its power and status had nothing to do with literacy
or with the cultural forms of typography. Said
the Duke of Gloucester to Edward Gibbon upon
the publication of his *Decline and Fall:* "Another
damned fat book, eh, Mr. Gibbon? Scribble,
scribble, scribble, eh, Mr. Gibbon?" De Tocqueville

was a highly literate aristocrat who was quite able
to be detached from the values and assumptions
of typography. That is why he alone understood
the grammar of typography. And it is only on
those terms, standing aside from any structure or
medium, that its principles and lines of force can
be discerned. For any medium has the power of
imposing its own assumption on the unwary.
Prediction and control consist in avoiding this
subliminal state of Narcissus trance. But the
greatest aid to this end is simply in knowing that
the spell can occur immediately upon contact, as
in the first bars of a melody.

A Passage to India by E. M. Forster is a dramatic
study of the inability of oral and intuitive oriental
culture to meet with the rational, visual European
patterns of experience. "Rational," of course, has
for the West long meant "uniform and continuous
and sequential." In other words, we have confused
reason with literacy, and rationalism with a single
technology. Thus in the electric age man seems
to the conventional West to become irrational. In
Forster's novel the moment of truth and dislocation
from the typographic trance of the West comes
in the Marabar Caves. Adela Quested's reasoning
powers cannot cope with the total inclusive field
of resonance that is India. After the Caves: "Life
went on as usual, but had no consequences,
that is to say, sounds did not echo nor thought
develop. Everything seemed cut off at its root
and therefore infected with illusion."

A Passage to India (the phrase is from Whitman,
who saw America headed Eastward) is a parable
of Western man in the electric age, and is only
incidentally related to Europe or the Orient. The
ultimate conflict between sight and sound, between
written and oral kinds of perception and organization of existence is upon us. Since understanding
stops action, as Nietzsche observed, we can moderate the fierceness of this conflict by understanding the media that extend us and raise
these wars within and without us.

Detribalization by literacy and its traumatic
effects on tribal man is the theme of a book by
the psychiatrist J. C. Carothers, *The African Mind*

in *Health and Disease* (World Health Organization, Geneva, 1953). Much of his material appeared in an article in *Psychiatry* magazine, November, 1959: "The Culture, Psychiatry, and the Written Word." Again, it is electric speed that has revealed the lines of force operating from Western technology in the remotest areas of bush, savannah, and desert. One example is the Bedouin with his battery radio on board the camel. Submerging natives with floods of concepts for which nothing has prepared them is the normal action of all of our technology. But with electric media Western man himself experiences exactly the same inundation as the remote native. We are no more prepared to encounter radio and TV in our literate milieu than the native of Ghana is able to cope with the literacy that takes him out of his collective tribal world and beaches him in individual isolation. We are as numb in our new electric world as the native involved in our literate and mechanical culture.

Electric speed mingles the cultures of prehistory with the dregs of industrial marketeers, the non-literate with the semiliterate and the postliterate. Mental breakdown of varying degrees is the very common result of uprooting and inundation with new information and endless new patterns of information. Wyndham Lewis made this a theme of his group of novels called *The Human Age*. The first of these, *The Childermass*, is concerned precisely with accelerated media change as a kind of massacre of the innocents. In our own world as we become more aware of the effects of technology on psychic formation and manifestation, we are losing all confidence in our right to assign guilt. Ancient prehistoric societies regard violent crime as pathetic. The killer is regarded as we do a cancer victim. "How terrible it must be to feel like that," they say. J. M. Synge took up this idea very effectively in his *Playboy of the Western World*.

If the criminal appears as a nonconformist who is unable to meet the demand of technology that we behave in uniform and continuous patterns, literate man is quite inclined to see others who cannot conform as somewhat pathetic. Especially

the child, the cripple, the woman, and the colored person appear in a world of visual and typographic technology as victims of injustice. On the other hand, in a culture that assigns roles instead of jobs to people—the dwarf, the skew, the child create their own spaces. They are not expected to fit into some uniform and repeatable niche that is not their size anyway. Consider the phrase "It's a man's world." As a quantitative observation endlessly repeated from within a homogenized culture, this phrase refers to the men in such a culture who have to be homogenized Dagwoods in order to belong at all. It is in our I.Q. testing that we have produced the greatest flood of misbegotten standards. Unaware of our typographic cultural bias, our testers assume that uniform and continuous habits are a sign of intelligence, thus eliminating the ear man and the tactile man.

C. P. Snow, reviewing a book of A. L. Rowse (*The New York Times Book Review*, December 24, 1961) on *Appeasement* and the road to Munich, describes the top level of British brains and experience in the 1930s. "Their I.Q.'s were much higher than usual among political bosses. Why were they such a disaster?" The view of Rowse, Snow approves: "They would not listen to warnings because they did not wish to hear." Being anti-Red made it impossible for them to read the message of Hitler. But their failure was as nothing compared to our present one. The American stake in literacy as a technology or uniformity applied to every level of education, government, industry, and social life is totally threatened by the electric technology. The threat of Stalin or Hitler was external. The electric technology is within the gates, and we are numb, deaf, blind, and mute about its encounter with the Gutenberg technology, on and through which the American way of life was formed. It is, however, no time to suggest strategies when the threat has not even been acknowledged to exist. I am in the position of Louis Pasteur telling doctors that their greatest enemy was quite invisible, and quite unrecognized by them. Our conventional response to all media, namely that it is how they are used that counts,

THE MEDIUM IS THE MESSAGE
H. Marshall McLuhan

is the numb stance of the technological idiot. For the "content" of a medium is like the juicy piece of meat carried by the burglar to distract the watchdog of the mind. The effect of the medium is made strong and intense just because it is given another medium as "content." The content of a movie is a novel or a play or an opera. The effect of the movie form is not related to its program content. The "content" of writing or print is speech, but the reader is almost entirely unaware either of print or of speech.

Arnold Toynbee is innocent of any understanding of media as they have shaped history, but he is full of examples that the student of media can use. At one moment he can seriously suggest that adult education, such as the Workers Educational Association in Britain, is a useful counterforce to the popular press. Toynbee considers that although all of the oriental societies have in our time accepted the industrial technology and its political consequences: "On the cultural plane, however, there is no uniform corresponding tendency." (Somervell, I. 267) This is like the voice of the literate man, floundering in a milieu of ads, who boasts, "Personally, I pay no attention to ads." The spiritual and cultural reservations that the oriental peoples may have toward our technology will avail them not at all. The effects of technology do not occur at the level of opinions or concepts, but alter sense ratios or patterns of perception steadily and without any resistance. The serious artist is the only person able to encounter technology with impunity, just because he is an expert aware of the changes in sense perception.

The operation of the money medium in seventeenth-century Japan had effects not unlike the operation of typography in the West. The penetration of the money economy, wrote G. B. Sansom (in *Japan*, Cresset Press, London, 1931) "caused a slow but irresistible revolution, culminating in the breakdown of feudal government and the resumption of intercourse with foreign countries after more than two hundred years of seclusion." Money has reorganized the sense life of peoples just because it is an *extension* of our sense lives. This change does not depend upon approval or disapproval of those living in the society.

Arnold Toynbee made one approach to the transforming power of media in his concept of "etherialization," which he holds to be the principle of progressive simplification and efficiency in any organization or technology. Typically, he is ignoring the *effect* of the challenge of these forms upon the response of our senses. He imagines that it is the response of our opinions that is relevant to the effect of media and technology in society, a "point of view" that is plainly the result of the typographic spell. For the man in a literate and homogenized society ceases to be sensitive to the diverse and discontinuous life of forms. He acquires the illusion of the third dimension and the "private point of view" as part of his Narcissus fixation, and is quite shut off from Blake's awareness or that of the Psalmist, that we become what we behold.

Today when we want to get our bearings in our own culture, and have need to stand aside from the bias and pressure exerted by any technical form of human expression, we have only to visit a society where that particular form has not been felt, or a historical period in which it was unknown. Professor Wilbur Schramm made such a tactical move in studying *Television in the Lives of Our Children*. He found areas where TV had not penetrated at all and ran some tests. Since he had made no study of the peculiar nature of the TV image, his tests were of "content" preferences, viewing time, and vocabulary counts. In a word, his approach to the problem was a literary one, albeit unconsciously so. Consequently, he had nothing to report. Had his methods been employed in 1500 A.D. to discover the effects of the printed book in the lives of children or adults, he could have found out nothing of the changes in human and social psychology resulting from typography. Print created individualism and nationalism in the sixteenth century. Program and "content" analysis offer no clues to the magic of these media or to their subliminal charge.

Leonard Doob, in his report *Communication in Africa*, tells of one African who took great pains to listen each evening to the BBC news, even though he could understand nothing of it. Just to be in the presence of those sounds at 7 P.M. each day was important for him. His attitude to speech was like ours to melody—the resonant intonation was meaning enough. In the seventeenth century our ancestors still shared this native's attitude to the forms of media, as is plain in the following sentiment of the Frenchman Bernard Lam expressed in *The Art of Speaking* (London, 1696):

> 'Tis an effect of the Wisdom of God, who created Man to be happy, that whatever is useful to his conversation (way of life) is agreeable to him . . . because all victual that conduces to nourishment is relishable, whereas other things that cannot be assimilated and be turned into our substance are insipid. A Discourse cannot be pleasant to the Hearer that is not easie to the Speaker; nor can it be easily pronounced unless it be heard with delight.

Here is an equilibrium theory of human diet and expression such as even now we are only striving to work out again for media after centuries of fragmentation and specialism.

Pope Pius XII was deeply concerned that there be serious study of the media today. On February 17, 1950, he said:

> It is not an exaggeration to say that the future of modern society and the stability of its inner life depend in large part on the maintenance of an equilibrium between the strength of the techniques of communication and the capacity of the individual's own reaction.

Failure in this respect has for centuries been typical and total for mankind. Subliminal and docile acceptance of media impact has made them prisons without walls for their human users. As A. J. Liebling remarked in his book *The Press,* a man is not free if he cannot see where he is going, even if he has a gun to help him get there. For each of the media is also a powerful weapon with which to clobber other media and other groups. The result is that the present age has been one of multiple civil wars that are not limited to the world of art and entertainment. In *War and Human Progress*, Professor J. U. Nef declared: "The total wars of our time have been the result of a series of intellectual mistakes . . ."

If the formative power in the media are the media themselves, that raises a host of large matters that can only be mentioned here, although they deserve volumes. Namely, that technological media are staples or natural resources, exactly as are coal and cotton and oil. Anybody will concede that society whose economy is dependent upon one or two major staples like cotton, or grain, or lumber, or fish, or cattle is going to have some obvious social patterns of organization as a result. Stress on a few major staples creates extreme instability in the economy but great endurance in the population. The pathos and humor of the American South are embedded in such an economy of limited staples. For a society configured by reliance on a few commodities accepts them as a social bond quite as much as the metropolis does the press. Cotton and oil, like radio and TV, become "fixed charges" on the entire psychic life of the community. And this pervasive fact creates the unique cultural flavor of any society. It pays through the nose and all its other senses for each staple that shapes its life.

That our human senses, of which all media are extensions, are also fixed charges on our personal energies, and that they also configure the awareness and experience of each of us, may be perceived in another connection mentioned by the psychologist C. G. Jung:

> Every Roman was surrounded by slaves. The slave and his psychology flooded ancient Italy, and every Roman became inwardly, and of course unwittingly, a slave. Because living constantly in the atmosphere of slaves, he became infected through the unconscious with their psychology. No one can shield himself from such an influence (*Contributions to Analytical Psychology*, London, 1928).

Reprinted from The New Yorker *(February 27, 1965), pp. 129–36. Reprinted by permission;* © *1965, The New Yorker Magazine, Inc.*

Philosophy in a Pop Key

HAROLD ROSENBERG

UNDERSTANDING MEDIA (McGraw-Hill) has a dry, professional-sounding title, suggesting a handbook on magazines and television for advertising men, in particular those charged with buying space and time. It was written, however, by Professor Marshall McLuhan, director of the Center for Culture and Technology at the University of Toronto and author of "The Mechanical Bride" and "The Gutenberg Galaxy," whose conception of pop culture is no more conventional than an electronic opera. McLuhan is more likely to write a manual for the angels than for Madison Avenue. "Understanding Media" carries the subtitle "The Extensions of Man," which alerts readers at the start that more is at issue in this book than the relative merits of news and entertainment packages. We all know that radio, the movies, the press do things to us. For McLuhan they also *are* us: "They that make them," he quotes the Psalms, "shall be like unto them." So "Understanding Media" is nothing less than a book about humanity as it has been shaped by the means used in this and earlier ages to deliver information.

McLuhan's account of the effects of the media upon the human psyche lies between fact and metaphor. The instrumentalities through which words, images, and other human signals reach us transform our bodies as well as our minds. Our eyes are bulged out by vacuum tubes, our ears elongated by transistors, our skin ballooned by polyesters. ("Clothing and housing, as extensions of skin and heat-control mechanisms, are media of communication.") In his first book, "The Mechanical Bride,"

published a dozen years ago and unmistakably inspired by Duchamp's erotic apparatuses, McLuhan dealt with the pop creations of advertising and other word-and-picture promotions as ingredients of a magic potion, "composed of sex and technology," that was populating America with creatures half woman, half machine. "Noticed any very spare parts lately?" he inquired in a subhead of his title chapter. The legs, bust, hips of the modern girl have been dissociated from the human person as "power points," McLuhan claimed, reminding the reader that "the Hiroshima bomb was named 'Gilda' in honor of Rita Hayworth." Man, to McLuhan, often appears to be a device employed by the communications mechanisms in *their* self-development. "Any invention or technology," he writes in "Understanding Media," "is an extension or self-amputation of our physical bodies, and such extension also demands new ratios or new equilibriums among the other organs and extensions of the body. There is, for example, no way of refusing to comply with the new ratios or sense 'closure' evoked by the TV image."

In McLuhan's "The Gutenberg Galaxy," the analysis of how the human organism has been remodelled by a single communications medium is turned into a full-scale interpretation of Western history. The outstanding characteristics of life in Europe and America from the Renaissance to the turn of the twentieth century are traced to the invention of movable type and the diffusion of the printed word. The streaming of letters across a page brought into being an "eye culture" that found symbolic representation in "King Lear," with its blindings and its wanderers stripped naked by the storm. (McLuhan got his Ph.D. in English at Cambridge.) With Gutenberg began the technological acceleration of history that has made constant change the norm of social life. The portability of books, McLuhan says, allowed "alphabetic man" to feed his intellect in isolation from others, thus introducing individualism and the Hamlet-like division between knowing and doing, as well as split personality ("Schizophrenia may be a necessary consequence of literacy") and the conflict between the ego and its environment. The separation of seeing from the other senses and the reduction of consciousness to sight-based concepts were compensated for by the emergence of the world of the unconscious. The fixed position of the reader vis-à-vis the page, says McLuhan, inspired perspective in painting, the visualization of three-dimensional objects in deep space, and the chronological narrative. The uniformity and repeatability of the phonetic bits that make up a line of type strengthened mechanistic philosophies, serial thinking in mathematics and the sciences, and ideas of social levelling, and they were the model for the assembly line. In replacing vernacular with mass media, print generated the centralizing forces of modern nationalism: "The citizen armies of Cromwell and Napoleon were the ideal manifestations of the new technology."

"Understanding Media" is McLuhan's goodbye to Gutenberg and to Renaissance, "typographic" man; that is, to the self-centered individual. As such, it takes its place in that wide channel of cultural criticism of the twentieth century that includes writers like T. S. Eliot, Oswald Spengler, D. H. Lawrence, F. R. Leavis, David Riesman, Hannah Arendt. "Understanding Media," McLuhan's most neatly ordered and most comprehensive book, is an examination of how the eye-extended, print-reading individualist of the past five centuries is in our time undergoing metamorphosis under the bombardment of all his senses by new electronic media, the first of which was the telegraph. With the loss

of the monopoly of the column of type has come the breakup of its peruser, and with this a landslide of all print-based social and art forms; e.g., the mechanical assembly lines gives way to automation, and perspective in painting to two-dimensional, over-all composition. Thus the changeover of media is synchronized with revolutionary phenomena in production and in cultural life and with an extreme crisis of values.

Of all crisis philosophers, McLuhan is by far the coolest. Though his notion of the "externalization" or "numbness" induced in the consumer of today's popular culture accords with Eliot's "hollow men," Riesman's "other-directedness," and Arendt's "banality," he is utterly unsympathetic to any concept of "decline." The collective trance of his contemporaries is to his mind a transitional phenomenon—one that recurs in all great historic shifts from one dominant medium to another. Current unfeeling and anxiety parallel states prevalent in the early Renaissance, when the printed document was replacing the hand-written script. Regarding us all in this light, McLuhan is immune to despair; in his terms, the theory that the modern world is a cultural wasteland is meaningless. What, he might ask, makes the inwardness of yesterday preferable to the shallowness of tomorrow, if both are by-products of more or less effective devices for conveying information? As the phonetic alphabet carried man from tribalism to individuality and freedom, the new electric media are taking him beyond "fragmented, literate, and visual individualism." If man today is part machine, this is not an effect of the Industrial Revolution. Technologies have been a component of human living for three thousand years, and our loftiest feelings have derived from that segment of us that is least ourselves: "By continuously embracing technologies, we relate ourselves to them as servo-mechanisms. That is why we must, to use them at all, serve these objects, these extentions of ourselves, as gods or minor religions. An Indian is the servo-mechanism of his canoe, as the cowboy of his horse or the executive of his clock." In line with Toynbee (the

PHILOSOPHY IN A POP KEY
Harold Rosenberg

idea of the Eskimo as a merman, the cowboy as a centaur, is his), McLuhan has superseded Marx's "fetishism of commodities" with a fetishism of the medium to explain the forms of belief by which men have been governed in various epochs. Societies in which the sacred played a greater role than it does in ours were simply those ruled by media of communication more primitive than the visual. "To call the oral man 'religious,'" McLuhan observed in "The Gutenberg Galaxy," "is, of course, as fanciful and arbitrary as calling blondes bestial."

McLuhan, then, is a modernist to the hilt; his own "sacred" touchstones are Cézanne and abstract art, the new physics, "Finnegans Wake." His is the kind of mind that fills with horror the would-be conservator of values (a Leavis, a Yeats, a Lukács). He is not tempted in the slightest to dig in at some bygone historical moment. Accepting novelty as inevitable, he is not only a modernist but a futurist. In his latest mood, he regards most of what is going on today as highly desirable, all of it as meaningful. His position is to be inside change; he is given over to metamorphosis on principle. The present worldwide clash between the new and the old arouses him to enthusiasm, since "the meeting of two media is a moment of truth and revelation from which new form is born." It is this appreciation of innovating forms that distinguishes McLuhan from other writers on popular culture. Instead of discovering menace in the chatter of the disc jockey and the inanities of the commercial, or relief in New Wave films or in Shakespeare and ballet on TV, McLuhan probes beyond the content of the media to the impact of each medium itself as an art form. What takes place at any moment in the rectangle of the comic strip or on the screen of the TV set may not be worth serious reflection. But as you look, or look and listen, in the particular way demanded by the comic strip or the television image, something is slowly happening to one or more of your senses, and through that to your whole pattern of perception—never mind what gets into your mind. Hence the first axiom of "Understanding Media" is "The medium is the message." Radio tells us about bargains in second-

hand cars, the great books, the weather, but the ultimate effect of radio is that, day after day, it is displacing reading and reintroducing on a new, technological level the oral communication of pre-literate societies—or, as McLuhan calls it, "the tribal drum." The effect of a tale differs depending on whether we read it, hear it, or see it on the stage. McLuhan therefore ridicules the reformist idea that changes in programming could alter the cultural mix now produced by the popular arts. "Our conventional response to all media, namely that it is how they are used that counts, is the numb stance of the technological idiot. For the 'content' of a medium is like the juicy piece of meat carried by the burglar to distract the watchdog of the mind. . . . The effect of the movie form is not related to its program content." In fact, McLuhan suggests that one medium always uses another medium as its subject matter: "The content of the press is literary statement, as the content of the book is speech, and the content of the movie is the novel." Whether or not this is so in every case, it provides a suggestive description of much contemporary art—for example, that of Rauschenberg, who through photographs and silk-screen reproductions makes news the content of painting.

A remarkable wealth of observation issues from the play of McLuhan's sensibility upon each of today's vehicles of human intercourse, from roads and money to games and the computer. After "Understanding Media," it should no longer be acceptable to speak of "mass culture" as a single lump. Each pop form, this work demonstrates, has its peculiar aesthetic features: the comics, a crude woodcut style; TV, a blurred "iconic" image shaped by the eye of the viewer out of millions of dots (in contrast to the shiny completed image of movie film). A further aesthetic complexity of the popular media pointed out by McLuhan lies in their division into "hot" and "cool." The hot medium, like radio and newspapers, is aggressive and communicates much information, while the cool, like TV and the Twist (also open-mesh stockings and dark glasses), is reticent and tends to draw its audience into participation. The varieties of aesthetic influences by which modern man is showered ought to dissolve the belief, prevalent among intellectuals, that today's man in the street, in contrast to the peasant or the bushman, has been cut down to a bundle of simple reflexes.

Responding to the man-made forms that flow continually through our senses, McLuhan arrives at happy conclusions for the future. No, man is not being impoverished by packaged cultural commodities. On the contrary, it was the split personality created by the book who was deprived of sensual self-realization: "Literacy is itself an abstract asceticism that prepares the way for endless patterns of privation in the human community." Though the shock of the sudden passage from mechanical to electrical technology has momentarily narcotized our nerves, integral man is in the process of formation. For the first time in history, the media are providing us with extensions not of one or more sense organs but of our sense structure as a whole, "since our new electric technology is not an extension of our bodies but of our central nervous systems." The mechanical age is departing, and with it the division of man within himself and his separation from his fellows. "Synesthesia, or unified sense and imaginative life, had long seemed an unattainable dream to Western poets, painters, and artists in general. They had looked with sorrow and dismay on the fragmented and impoverished imaginative life of Western literate man in the eighteenth century and later. . . . They were not prepared to have their dreams realized in everyday life by the aesthetic action of radio and television. Yet these massive extensions of our central nervous systems have enveloped Western man in a daily session of synesthesia." Instant communication through the electric media, McLuhan goes on to argue, is ending the age-old conflict between city and country; by "dunking entire populations in new imagery" and bringing them together in the "global village," it is eliminating, too, the conditions that make for war.

In sum, McLuhan has built a philosophy of history on art criticism, which he has directed not at styles in literature, painting, or architecture but at the lowly stuff of everyday life. In doing this, he has also sought to recast the meaning of art and literature since the Renaissance by finding in Shakespeare, Pope, or Blake "galaxies" of meaning related to the aesthetics and metaphysics of print. He has experimented with form in his own writings; that is, he has tried to function as an artist. "The Mechanical Bride" was a kind of early pop art, with a layout like a museum catalogue and with headlines, clips of advertising art, comic-strip boxes. "The Gutenberg Galaxy" and "Understanding Media" regard the human habitation as an enormous art pile, a throbbing assemblage of things that communicate, and they try to make it comprehensible by means of a mosaic of exhibits and comments that the author's "circulating point of view" has assembled from widely separated fields; McLuhan is attempting to imitate in his writing the form of the TV image, which he describes as "mosaic." The effort to develop an open, expressive social-science investigation in place of the customary learned research report may in time produce important results; McLuhan's version of this new form has the virtue of allowing the author to pick up bits of observation (e.g., that girls in dark glasses are engaged in "cool" communication) that are usually excluded, and it also enables him to bring into focus a remarkable spread of information (e.g., the measurement of time by smell among the ancient Chinese and among modern brain-surgery patients). McLuhan's concern for style tempts him into discharges of epigrams, wisecracks, and puns. These have abated in "Understanding Media," but the chapter titles are still haunted by gags ("Money: The Poor Man's Credit Card," "The Photograph: The Brothel-Without-Walls"). Some of this wit is low-grade ("Movies: The Reel World") even if we consider bad puns to be in keeping with the pop spirit. However, formulas like "If it works it's obsolete," to suggest the rate of change in media, and "Today, even natural resources have an informational aspect," more than balance the account.

McLuhan, then, is a kind of artist, and his quick leaps from datum to axiom ("Take off the dateline, and one day's paper is the same as the next") are

PHILOSOPHY IN A POP KEY
Harold Rosenberg

often aesthetically pleasurable. In his communica-
tions-constructed world, the artist is the master
figure—in fact, the only personage whom he differ-
entiates from the media-absorbing mass. The artist,
McLuhan believes, anticipates the changes in man
that will be wrought by a new medium and through
his work adjusts the collective psyche to it. Thus
the artist provides an antidote to the numbness
induced by changeover. Painting has long since
gone beyond being a merely visual medium; praising someone for having a "good eye," as if a modern
painting were an object to be taken in by a single
sense, is tantamount to praising him for being out
of date. A Kandinsky or a Mondrian is actually
apprehended through a "resonating interplay" of
the whole keyboard of sense and consciousness; no
wonder that eye-trained people continue to ask,
"What does it mean?" One of McLuhan's most
valuable contributions is to help dissolve the craft-
oriented concept that modern art works still belong
in the realm of things contemplated instead of
being forces active in "the unified field of electric
all-at-onceness" of tomorrow's world community.

Unfortunately, despite his insights into form,
McLuhan's organization of his own ideas is far
from first-rate. As a composition, "Understanding
Media" is often out of control; "circular" perspective becomes synonymous with going round in
circles. Endlessly repetitious, the book, for all its
rain of bright intuitions, creates a total effect of
monotony. This repetitiousness probably reflects
McLuhan's uneasiness about his ability to make
himself clear. For there are in his thesis inherent
ambiguities. Given the advanced nature of the
electric media, the implication is that older forms,
like the book and the stage, are obsolete and that
film and comic strip are the art forms of the future.
In clinging to a sense extension (the eye) that has
been surpassed, the novelist is a reactionary—
except for the beatnik who gives readings in coffee-
houses. Even being an individual is retrogressive, so
turn the dial and slip into the new global kraal.
Much as McLuhan lauds the artist, he has pitted
the pop media against him, in disregard of the

fact that the masterpieces of this century have been
paintings, poems, plays, not movies or TV shows.
The point is that while McLuhan is an aesthete, he
is also an ideologue—one ready to spin out his
metaphor of the "extensions" until its web covers
the universe; if clothes are media, and trees and
policemen are, too—if, in short, all of creation
"speaks" to us—McLuhan is discussing as media
what used to be called "Nature," and his notion of
the "sensuously orchestrated" man of the future is
a version of the pantheistic hero. He is a belated
Whitman singing the body electric with Thomas
Edison as accompanist. Yet to expect Adam to step
out of the TV screen is utopianism of the wildest
sort. For McLuhan, beliefs, moral qualities, social
action, even material progress play a secondary role
(if that) in determining the human condition. The
drama of history is a crude pageant whose inner
meaning is man's metamorphosis through the
media. As a philosophy of cultural development,
"Understanding Media" is on par with theories that
trace the invention of the submarine to conflicts in
the libido or the decline of the handicrafts to the
legalization of interest on loans.

"Usury," Ezra Pound wrote in the "Cantos,"

. . . rusts the man and his chisel
It destroys the craftsman, destroying
craft;

    Azure is caught with cancer.

McLuhan has taken with deadly literalness his
metaphors of the media as extensions of the body
and of a nervous system outside ourselves. "Man
becomes, as it were, the sex organs of the machine
world, as the bee of the plant world, enabling it to
fecundate and to evolve ever new forms." His
susceptibility to figures of speech leads him to
describe possibilities of technological innovation as
if they were already achieved facts. In his world,
money and work are things of the past; we live on
credit cards and "learn a living" as managers of
computers, and the struggle, backwash, surprise of
real events are somnambulistically brushed away.
The chilly silence of science fiction reigns over a
broad band of McLuhan's temperament.

These deficiencies might be decisive were there to arise a McLuhan "school" of cultural interpretation through media analysis. If one judges McLuhan as an individual writer, however, what remain paramount are his global standpoint and his zest for the new. As an artist working in a mixed medium of direct experience and historical analogy, he has given a needed twist to the great debate on what is happening to man in this age of technological speedup. Other observers have been content to repeat criticisms of industrial society that were formulated a century ago, as if civilization had been steadily emptied out since the advent of the power loom. As against the image of our time as a faded photograph of a richly pigmented past, McLuhan, for all his abstractness, has found positive, humanistic meaning and the color of life in supermarkets, stratospheric flight, the lights blinking on broadcasting towers. In respect to the maladies of de-individuation, he has dared to seek the cure in the disease, and his vision of going forward into primitive wholeness is a good enough reply to those who would go back to it. "Understanding Media" is a concrete testimonial (illuminating, as modern art illuminates, through dissociation and regrouping) to the belief that man is certain to find his footing in the new world he is in the process of creating.

Reprinted from Canadian Literature *(Autumn, 1964), pp. 55–60. Used by permission of the author and publisher.*

Innocent Eye on Mass Society

THELMA MC CORMACK

I USED to think that Marshall McLuhan was an innocent who had discovered depth psychology and called it "television." Since depth psychology is as good an approach as any to the mass media, a great deal better than some, McLuhan, with all his mannerisms was working in the right direction. This impression is borne out in *Understanding Media* where what he has to say about the mass media of communication is contrived, autodidactic, amusing, occasionally right and occasionally dangerous. But below the surface of his comments about the media is an insight and system which bear serious attention whether one is interested in the media or not. McLuhan has now gone well beyond discovering depth psychology; he has discovered mass society.

The metaphors he draws upon are from pre-literate societies. In particular, he is entranced by the group cohesion and group consciousness of an "oral" culture, a term which summarizes a closed, static, tradition-bound social structure where relationships are face-to-face, where there is scarcely any individual differentiation and only a rudimentary division of labour. In urban industrialized societies, consensus on such a scale is an artifact, achieved by the sacrifice of critical judgement, sustained internally by anxiety and externally by manipulation. To paraphrase McLuhan's most famous dictum: the medium is history: the message is the mass movement.

Content of the media is irrelevant, according to McLuhan. Thus he refuses to be drawn into discussions of Kitsch and popular culture that have so engaged intellectuals in recent years. By "content,"

he means the manifest content of any particular news story, feature article, TV documentary, etc. The real stuff of the media are not facts, opinions, concepts, but the structure of symbols that emerge cumulatively. Imagine the American constitution rewritten by Joyce and analysed through structural linguistics and you have approximately what McLuhan regards as the substance of the media. Imagine, also *Finnegan's Wake* rewritten by Thomas Jefferson and analysed by John Stuart Mill and you have the mistake McLuhan thinks we make.

Our mistake belongs to the age of mechanical technology which produced individualism, scientific detachment, democratic pluralism, nationalism, the sequential analysis of cause and effect, the class struggle, competition, the market mechanism, critical intelligence, a rational approach to social change and a high degree of self conscious awareness. All of them divisive. Electronic technology of the twentieth century is unifying, communal, demanding commitment and involvement. It submerges individual personality, obliterates social differences and de-nationalizes the world, restoring the ethos of the oral society. The great modern revolution for McLuhan, seen most clearly in the mass media of communication, is the shift from divisive to unifying ways of perceiving and organizing experience, from "explosion" to "implosion."

No field of science I know of has not moved in the direction of configurational concepts, and in that sense McLuhan is a popularizer of contemporary science though he appears to be unaware of these developments. His hypothesis, however, that technology is responsible for this historical change is something else again. It is legitimate to regard technology as a casual variable, but its weight in relation to other factors, material and non-material, in the social matrix, and the precise nature of its social and psychological impact, direct and indirect, are exceedingly complex problems. For McLuhan, however, this is not a provisional hypothesis. Technology is the Prime Mover, and everything large or small, becomes its consequences. Wherever he looks, from ladies' hair-does to weapons, he finds corroboration.

The immediate model for this is depth psychology where all behaviour awake or asleep, trivial or important, accidental or planned, express the motivational key; a key, moreover, which we do not, will not, cannot consciously recognize. McLuhan draws upon this model further by locating the source of technology within the individual. Technology is nothing more than the externalization of our feet, hands, eyes, brain, skin, teeth, etc. The correspondences he establishes between body and machine are cruder and more arbitrary than those of a Freudian since McLuhan is not guided by a theory of motivation, least of all by one based on conflict. For Oedipus, he offers Narcissus who having created his own image fails to recognize it.

The Narcissus myth eliminates the dichotomy between consumer and producer just as the modern economy eliminates the price mechanism. The "audience" of the media is not the consumer; it is the producer. We are not sold General Motors cars in McLuhan's system; we are shareholders, producers of transportation. Looked at one way, he is simply saying that audiences are not passive, that communication is a reciprocal process, and the fact that communication is now mediated, conducted through a technology, does not alter this. This is one of the cornerstones of current media research, and it is characteristic of the older media as well as the newer ones. We not only select the books we read, but read into them and read out anyting that is threatening. Looked at another way, this is an argument for public ownership of the media, for it

is, as McLuhan says, as absurd for us to "lease" to others the media of communication as it would be to "lease" speech.

Either way, this new producer role does not solve any better than the old consumer role the problem — no problem to primitive societies — of how we control the media. Being told that we own or produce the media of communication can be as politically disingenuous as Henry Luce's concept of "the people's capitalism," as dishonest as thinking that letters to the Soviet press or, closer to home, open-line radio where the housewife and folksy disc jockey exchange generalities are genuine forms of participation. McLuhan does not suggest that these problems constitute another area of inquiry or that they do not properly belong in a general theory of communication. On the contrary, to raise them at all, he maintains, is to misunderstand the media. This is not arrogance on his part, for it is inherent in this theory, essentially an historical theory, that these and similar questions belong to an earlier epoch.

Much of McLuhan, including his style and his penchant for anthropology, is reminiscent of Veblen who similarly began his analysis with technology and expected that its rational logic would spread to the business class and ultimately throughout social life. Engineers were Veblen's vanguard of the revolution. Instead, we got the "managerial revolution," for Veblen, like McLuhan, underestimated our capacity to use technology without being influenced by it. Technological determinism, like all forms of determinism, is never able to cope with discrepancies and must rush in concepts like Ogburn's "cultural lag," Marx's "false consciousness," and McLuhan's psychic shock or "numbness."

Historical determinism is the mystique of all modern ideologies. However, what distinguishes the ideologies of mass society is their response to alienation, their disillusionment with the democratic "left," their idealization of provincial anti-intellectual and anti-secular values. They combine, as J. L. Talmon says, two contradictory notions: social cohesion and self expression. McLuhan and

INNOCENT EYE OF MASS SOCIETY
Thelma McCormack

McCarthy, vastly different in every other respect, intuitively grasped the same thing. McLuhan is not interested in restoring the values of a secular-rational cosmopolitan *Anschauung*, for it destroys the cohesion of tribal life and is as obsolete as the assembly line in an age of automation.

The more passive, alienated and uncommitted we are, the more we yearn for, the more strongly we respond to ideologies of "effectiveness" provided they make no demands on us. The most successful ideology is the most ambiguous one which we structure ourselves with our infantile and wish fulfillment fantasies. Applying this principle to the media, McLuhan distinguishes between "hot" media, like print and radio which are highly structured, and "cold" media, like TV which are relatively unstructured. The latter, he claims, involve us; the former, do not.

Actually, they both involve us, but in different ways, the difference being the distinction between "identification"—when you cry with the martyred Elsie who is forced to play the piano on the Sabbath—and "projection"—when you see your mother's face in the clouds. Identification is the mechanism of social learning; it is growth, strengthening and broadening the ego. Projection is regression, the absence of controls and capacity for problem-solving. When McLuhan talks about "involvement," he means projection. For the alienated with their impoverished or damaged egos, projection is the only means of involvement. It goes a long way toward explaining why changes in a party line scarcely disturb the true adherent, and why, as Lasswell pointed out many years ago, logical consistency is not the criterion of ideology. The race is to the vaguest.

McLuhan goes even further, equating projection or "participation in depth" with "maturity." As he describes "participation in depth" it is the furthest extreme from introspection, the latter being private, inner directed, self critical, leading to a sense of apartness, a capacity to live comfortably with relative truths, to resist group pressure, and, if necessary to endure isolation. McLuhan's definition of "maturity" is "belief," collective belief.

All historical determinism faces the problem of leadership. According to McLuhan, the group best qualified to lead us into the Promised Land are the artists who "can show us how to 'ride with the punch'." Taken at face value, this is a puzzling choice to make since no group has had a sorrier record in the past century for its inability to understand or accept technology than artists. The explanation lies, I think, in understanding that McLuhan is talking not so much about artists as about art. He is attempting here to develop an aesthetic theory which abolishes the distinctions usually made between (1) "highbrow" and "lowbrow" art; and (2) "lowbrow" and "folk" art. In his system, folk art and popular art ("lowbrow") become the same, a rationale that Marxist writers used to give years ago for going to Hollywood. In a limited sense, he and they are right. Structurally, popular art and folk art are both highly simplified and repetitive. They may move us at the level of universal archetypal images. Both have a social function; in the case of folk art or religion, it is to provide the closure of ritual. But, if in mass society, there is, as Malraux says, no "folk," the closure is delusional; its function is escape or pseudo-closure, harmless enough under certain circumstances, even necessary, but disastrous as a fixation and dangerous in a period of confusion and rapid social change which calls for the highest degree of political intelligence.

The distinction between "highbrow" and "lowbrow" art is minimized by recognizing that great art, too, tells us something about the "human condition." The distinction becomes even more blurred by art styles which have no cognitive content and communicate solely by involving us. In McLuhan's system, then, there is no difference between abstract art and a television screen. "Pop art" which is, on the one hand, a parody of folk art, and, on the other hand, a parody of what we have traditionally meant by the term "creative" carries this to its logical conclusion. Aesthetic theory thus becomes the science of communication. It is as if we were asked to judge art by the same criteria we would use in judging snapshots of our children, and if this sounds foolish, it is no more so than the reverse fallacy which intellectuals usually make in approaching the media; that is, to judge family snapshots by the same criteria they would use for judging art.

When McLuhan turns to the specific media of communication, he runs into difficulty. First, because he is forced to deal with "content" in the same terms as anyone else does, e.g. "the success theme." Second, because it is almost impossible to isolate what is unique about a medium from the policies of the people who run it. For example, the diffuseness of TV, its avoidance of controversial subjects, may have as much to do with the costs of TV and the cautiousness of TV executives as it does with the intrinsic nature of the medium. We can be sure it will become even "cooler" with colour. Radio, he tells us, is a "hot" medium and so can deal with ideas, personalities (Hitler, Fred Allen) and empirical data (the weather). At the same time, since it is an electronic medium, it is intimate and tribal, or, as we are more apt to say, it is the intellectuals' ghetto, just exactly what we have been hearing from TV executives. Is it because they understand the medium and we do not? Finally, whatever distinctions may be made among the different media, the distinction between "hot" and "cold" breaks down. All of the media, taken together or separately, are nothing if not flexible; radio and print are as capable of surrealism as realism; the seven types of ambiguity are as much in poetry as they are in television.

Still, McLuhan is a God-send to the TV producer who because he is often young wants recognition and who because he is an *arriviste* to the media wants status. In McLuhan he can find a basis for claiming that TV is unique, different from the older media; above all, different from print. Long impatient with the psychological ineptitude of most

do-good preachy broadcasting and equally frustrated by the complexities of modern thought, he finds in McLuhan a mandate to experiment without worrying too much about "content." His banner is television for television's sake.

Watching TV is a revelation. More and more public affairs programmes resemble Rorschach cards, each one different but no objective content in any; each one involving us, but leaving us none the wiser as citizens. One politician differs from another in the way one piece of abstract art or one page of Joyce differs from another. Just how cynical this is is revealed by McLuhan's suggestion that had Jack Paar produced Nixon the election results might have been different. As it was, Kennedy with his more diffuse image was better suited to the medium. In other words, McLuhan is saying that TV depersonalizes and de-intellectualizes politics. The depersonalization of politics could be the hopeful start of politics based on issues in which the elected representative is held accountable for his ideas rather than his morals or character. But a de-intellectualized politics is its antithesis. Combined, they are the politics of ideology in mass society, an ill wind that blows some good to the young eager TV producer who thinks that political theory is in the hand-held camera.

TV producers are not the only ones to welcome McLuhan. Canadians in general have become more susceptible to the charms of an intellectual exploring the cultural demi-monde without the usual class biases. It is an attractive egalitarian avant-garde image for a country that has not yet had its Whitman, Sandburgs, or Pounds; a country that has only begun to face the fact that it is urban and industrialized, its quickest and best minds straining at the leash to break away from an intellectual Establishment which has been singularly obtuse, Mandarin-minded and peculiarly punitive. Bright young men will find in McLuhan's enthusiasm for the media a populist realism, his distrust of intellectualism a revolt against dead scholarship and the demands of specialization, his approach

INNOCENT EYE ON MASS SOCIETY
Thelma McCormack

through technology an unsentimental toughness, his removal of the issue from a context of values a liberation from petty Philistine censors, his rejection of social criticism a long overdue break with the tiresome futile leftish politics of the thirties. It is an ideal formula for the 1960s, and to his disciples— and they are legion—McLuhan is a prophet. From a longer perspective, he is the first, original, genuine Canadian *ideologue* of mass society, but his sense-ratios were shaped by the irrationalism, determinism, and folk romanticism of the nineteenth century.

THE MEDIA AND PUBLIC ISSUES

Part VI

PART VI / THE MEDIA AND PUBLIC ISSUES

INTRODUCTION

Several of the topics dealt with so far, such as commercialization, regulation, and the concentrated ownership of the media, together with the overall shaping of our life styles and values, are of central importance for understanding mass media. They have not, however, been articulated as public issues. That is, the general public and specific interest groups are largely unaware or indifferent to their impact. Two general issues that have attracted public notice are the topics for this final selection of readings. The first concerns the part played by broadcasting and the press in fostering the crime and violence which many citizens feel increasingly characterizes American society. This concern has stimulated debate in Congress and the FCC, and it has led to a growing demand for research on violence. The second issue centers on the political use of the media, their potential for propaganda, manipulation, and the distortion of democratic processes. Some aspects have been openly debated. For example, Congress has already passed a bill limiting campaign expenditures—it was vetoed by President Nixon—and the FCC has promulgated the fairness doctrine.

A. Crime and Violence

The first two selections deal with the direct impact of the media on the legal system. Cohn notes that television in particular has closely followed social movements and demonstrations in its efforts to cover and, indeed, "make" news. The television journalist has therefore become a key "insider," one who is in great demand by the government for prosecuting illegal acts covered by the media. Film footage is subpoenaed. Broadcast material is readily given, but reporters have objected to providing "out-takes," i.e., the often confidential material not used publicly. Demands for this material raises important constitutional issues and goes to the heart of the journalist's role: Is he to be a privileged enquirer who may keep illegal activities confidential for the sake of "inside" reporting, or must he be a planted government agent?

Carolyn Jaffe's article investigates a similarly volatile issue, the degree to which pre-trial publicity interferes with justice. No trial, of course, is completely objective. Racial attitudes, for example, and other pre-existing dispositions toward the accused cannot be eliminated, even though jury selection procedures can minimize bias considerably. The newsman's dilemma is that of either telling all he knows as soon as he knows it, thereby making the selection of an unbiased jury impossible, or holding back information until after the trial. The former leads to "trial by the press" and is common for "sensational" crimes of violence and the crimes of the poor. Since news must "sell" there are built-in pressures for this type of reporting. White collar and corporate criminals, however, since they are less "news-worthy," are usually better protected.

The remaining articles each deal with the relationship of the media to violence. Bandura reports a study that investigated the effects of violent television programming on children, a study that helped precipitate the current debate on the subject. The networks, of course, claim that their programming is not harmful, and NBC and ABC are both currently sponsoring research to support their position.[1] Bandura's laboratory research showed that viewing violence reduced inhibitions on aggression and taught the child how to be aggressive.[2] This apparently holds for adults too, for most TV viewers know how to commit murder, elementary forms of torture, etc., even if they don't practice them. The mass media effects, together with novels and handed-down nursery tales and folklore, and perhaps more important in the formation of a climate of violence than in triggering it directly. One of the mysteries of our culture is that we are preoccupied with violence (horror films are often rated G.P.) which we deplore, while we ban treatment of explicit

[1]For a critique of the NBC study which claims that it is not likely to discover harmful effects see Rose K. Goldsen, "NBC's Make-Believe Research on TV Violence," *Trans-action* (October, 1971), pp. 28–35. J. Ronald Milavsky and Allen H. Barton responded with "In Defense of NBC" Violence, *Trans-action*, January 1972, pp. 30–31.

[2]The network studies and Seymour Feshback and Robert D. Singer in their book *Television and Aggression* (San Francisco: Jossey-Bass, 1971) are concerned with *direct* effects on behavior.

sex ("skin" movies are X rated) which we are urged to enjoy in its context.

News coverage of violence and social disorders is discussed by Terry Ann Knopf. Bad handling of news can contribute to the worsening of tense situations. In recent years steps have been taken to prevent this, but distortion, bias, and inflammatory treatment of news is still a major problem. Careful reporting is essential, although it alone is not sufficient for a responsible press because there may be situations in which suppression of news is in the public interest, and arrangements with police to bring this about are common.[3] Whether

[3]For a description of early riot coverage and some of the problems of "managed" news see David L. Paletz and Robert Dunn, "Press Coverage of Civil Disorders: A Case Study of Winston-Salem, 1967," *Public Opinion Quarterly* (Fall, 1969), pp. 328–345.

this censorship conflicts with the public's "right-to-know" is clearly an agonizing decision for the newsman to make.

Singer's article treats the effect of news broadcasting in a specific crisis situation, the Detroit riot of 1967. From his interviews with 500 males arrested in the disturbances he concludes that the media did not add greatly to the riot. Just knowing that it was happening was sufficient to induce the rioters to join in. Immediate coverage did not lead the participants to violence, but from coverage of previous riots they had probably learned the "appropriate" behavior. (National Guardsmen, police, and the citizen-at-large, of course, also have notions of what to do in a riot without ever having been actually involved in one.) The media, then, didn't cause the riots, but they unavoidably added to the climate of violence.

Reprinted from The Alfred I. duPont Survey of Broadcast Journalism 1969–1970, *edited by Marvin Barrett (New York: Grosset &* *Dunlap, 1970), pp. 122–28. Copyright © 1970 by The Trustees of Columbia University in the City of New York. Published by Grosset &* *Dunlap, Inc.*

Subpoenas: Should Reporters be Forced to Tell What They Know?

MARCUS COHN

NEWSPAPER publishers, editors, and reporters are understandably schizophrenic about recent constitutional law developments. They loved the Supreme Court when it expanded the parameters of the First Amendment — and almost eliminated libel suits — in *New York Times* v. *Sullivan* and a number of cases that followed. They grumbled when the Court held that their conduct (along with that of television cameramen) had made it impossible for Dr. Sam Sheppard to receive the kind of trial guaranteed to him by the Constitution and commented that "unfair and prejudicial news" coverage of criminal trials had "become increasingly prevalent."

But broadcasters and their reporters haven't even had the pleasure of ambivalence. They were downright distraught when, in the *Billie Sol Estes* case, the Court held that television cameras in the courtroom violated a defendant's Sixth Amendment rights to have a fair trial and then last year held in the *Red Lion* case, which sustained the FCC's Fairness Doctrine, that the First Amendment right was that "of the viewers and listeners, [and] not the right of the broadcasters."

At the very time that these developments in constitutional law — one protecting and one spanking the media — were taking place, newspapers and television stations were becoming more and more caught up in society's current convulsively volatile social problems. Their aggressive involvement was accentuated by the fact that a new breed of reporters — young, bright, sensitive, and personally involved in social issues — had entrées and relationships with the social activists of our time, which the old establishment did not seem to have.

Today's big social issue stories do not deal with the graft and corruption of government officials, but with social movements involving large numbers of people who, in their collectivity and joint action, cause news to occur: the 1968 Democratic Convention in Chicago, the several recent mass rallies in Washington, the Woodstocks, and the frequent political and social protest marches around the country. The very nature of what the participants do in those events lends itself to pictorial reporting. Indeed, what any one of them *says* becomes comparatively unimportant. What they *do* becomes the important event and, thus, the television camera becomes a more meaningful messenger of the news than do the notebook and pencil.

Every lawyer knows that, given a choice of oral testimony, on the one hand, or photographic evidence, on the other, the latter is always more persuasive to a jury. Consequently, it was quite logical, as more and more television cameramen showed up at the scenes of social protest, for prosecuting attorneys later to want to secure and present to grand juries the photographs and the motion pictures that they had made of the alleged crime. These films had two functions. In the first place, they were able vividly to portray the *act* itself and, secondly, they could positively identify

SUBPOENAS: SHOULD REPORTERS BE FORCED TO TELL WHAT THEY KNOW?

Marcus Cohn

the person involved in the act. The work product of the television reporter became, in a real sense, the best evidence of what had occurred and certainly far better than the notes of the newspaper reporter or the oral testimony of one of the participants in the event.

And if the number and frequency of "political crimes" increases, it will only be natural for the prosecutor to want to see and be even more dependent upon the films shot by television cameramen.

Although during the past seventy-four years, seventeen state legislatures have dealt with and attempted to resolve by various types of legislation the limits to which a state grand jury could subpoena newspaper reporters (and in a few instances broadcasting reporters), federal grand juries have had no comparable legislative guidance. Moreover, the Supreme Court has never had the occasion either to discuss or decide the issue.

Most of the recent prosecutions for activities arising from the social stresses of our time have been in federal courts. Thus, who appears and what notes, photographs, tapes, and films he is required to bring with him are questions decided by the United States Attorney.

The prosecutor normally has very little difficulty in securing that portion of television tapes which were actually telecast or that portion of the news reporter's story which was published. The problem arises when he desires to have the television "out-take" (the portion of the film which was not televised, generally constituting the bulk of what was actually recorded) and the notes or tapes of the newspaper reporter.

Until recently, reporters in most cases were able to negotiate successfully with the prosecutor and narrow the scope of the subpoena.

However, during the past several years, the attitude of prosecuting attorneys has toughened. They have taken to subpoenaing reporters more often; the desired testimony has dealt with information given in confidence and never published or exhibited; and the information has come from

reporters' peers who have been protesting against the establishments. Reporters were being asked to betray friends. They began to resist these command performances and to raise a number of questions.

If, indeed, it is true that the First Amendment protects reporters not only against direct interference by the government, but also — to use the Supreme Court's words in the *Dombrowski* case — any act which would have a "chilling effect" upon the opportunity to gather and publish news, then *any* subpoena which required the revelation of *any* information given in confidence was unconstitutional. To give it would not only drop the informer's temperature, but would freeze him into complete silence. Earl Caldwell, the reporter of the New York *Times* who has covered the Black Panther movement extensively, has refused even to appear before a grand jury, pursuant to a subpoena, even though a federal district judge has told him that he may have the advice of counsel throughout the proceedings and come back to the Court for protection in the event the jury's questions require him to reveal confidential sources of information. Caldwell replied that once he sets foot in the grand jury room, he has cracked the cement of confidentiality and his informants will no longer trust him. This, in turn, will make it impossible for him to exercise his First Amendment right to gather news.

When the subpoena proponents argue that total truth in the "market place" is as important in the judicial as it is in the political process, the media reply that society has historically recognized that individual liberties and rights sometimes take precedence over the jury's or the judge's right to know. A number of these barriers to the revelation of all the facts are constitutionally protected in the Fifth and other constitutional amendments. Moreover, society made a decision a long time ago to protect the communications between a lawyer and his client, a doctor and his patient, and the clergyman and his parishioner.*

If a reporter does not have this constitutional protection, then, in order to protect his own dignity

SUBPOENAS: SHOULD REPORTERS BE FORCED TO TELL WHAT THEY KNOW?
Marcus Cohn

and to be certain that confidential communications remain confidential, he will destroy all memoranda, photos, and films once his story has been written and his photograph or film exhibited. Because normally the television reporter shoots far more footage than he will ever use and stores most of the rest for future use and reference, the net result will be that broadcasters may be driven to destroy large libraries of current events and deprive society of historical documentation they would otherwise have.

And then, lastly, reporters point out that if it is common knowledge that their notes and their films are always subject to examination by a grand jury, they will be subject to harassment by their normal sources because, in the eyes of the disadvantaged, they have become spies for the police and the very notes, photographs, and films, become symbols of oppression and, thus, should be destroyed.

The prosecutor's reply to these arguments is basically quite simple: I've got a job to do. I want to give the grand jury all the information available. As long as a reporter does not have the protection of a statute which gives him the right to refuse to testify, then he has an obligation to give the grand jury any information which may have a bearing on its investigation.

Putting aside the prosecuting attorney's desire to justify his pay check, there are basic and fundamental issues posed to society if newsmen may decide for themselves whether they should testify before a grand jury. If newsmen may successfully resist grand jury subpoenas on the ground of confidentiality, then what is to preclude them from invoking the same privilege when a *defendant* in a criminal case subpoenas them in order to establish his innocence under *his* guaranteed Sixth Amendment right to a fair trial? The civil libertarians who now cry for the protection of the reporter, because his confidants have been society's social critics, may find themselves denying justice to those very same social critics seeking the testimony of the reporter who stands on his constitutional rights.

Moreover, the Fifth Amendment explicitly recognizes the function and purpose of the grand jury. It was placed there for the protection of people who are suspected of crimes. Its existence has made it mandatory that indictments be issued by a legally constituted body whose members reside in the area where the crime occurred. The jury members hear and sift all the available evidence before issuing an indictment rather than, as in pre-Constitution days, a single magistrate issued the indictment merely because the prosecutor requested him to do it. Any interpretation of the First Amendment which would give reporters the right to decide whether they wish to testify before a grand jury weakens that system and could result in the indictment of innocent people.

On February 5, 1970, Attorney General Mitchell issued a two-and-a-half page double-spaced statement in which he announced that henceforth the Justice Department would be willing to negotiate the scope of subpoenas to the press prior to their issuance and be willing to discuss modifications afterward. It referred to the "press" eleven different times. Neither radio, television, nor broadcasting was mentioned once. It ended with the prayer that "this policy of caution, negotiation and attempted compromise will continue to prove as workable in the future as it has in the past." Putting aside the question of its past workability, obviously the Attorney General's prayer for the future went unanswered. Six months later (August 10) he delivered a twenty-six-page address on the same subject to the American Bar Association, in which he referred to all the media. In it he indicated a far greater concern over the issue, set forth a detailed series of guidelines for those responsible for the issuance of subpoenas, and adopted a procedure where subpoenaed reporters could appeal their cases directly to him.

In essence, the guidelines require the United States Attorney to attempt to obtain the desired information from non-press sources before subpoenaing the press. Failing this, the prosecutor is now required to confer ahead of time with the

SUBPOENAS: SHOULD REPORTERS BE FORCED TO TELL WHAT THEY KNOW?

Marcus Cohn

reporter whom he proposes to subpoena and attempt to negotiate a mutually satisfactory scope for the subpoena. If the negotiations fail, then the prosecutor must request the Attorney General's approval before issuing the subpoena.

The principles which will guide the Attorney General's decision on whether or not to issue the subpoena are: that there is reason to believe that a crime has been committed; that the information requested is "essential" to a successful investigation; that the government tried unsuccessfully to get the information from non-press sources; and that, "wherever possible," the subpoena should be directed at "material information regarding a reasonably limited subject matter." The subpoena should cover only a "reasonably limited time period" and should avoid the requirement of producing "a large volume" of unpublished material. "Normally," the subpoena should be limited to verification of published information and circumstances relating to its accuracy.

These vague and amorphous expressions of concern are extended even further in the pen-ultimate standard. The Attorney General promises to exercise "great caution" in subpoenaing un-published information where an "orthodox" First Amendment defense is raised or where a "serious claim" is made that the information was received on a confidential basis.

"Great," "orthodox," and "serious" allow for tremendous latitude of non-appealable inter-pretations. Indeed, they may vary dramatically from time to time, and the intensity of the "sensitivity" with which they are to be administered will, of course, depend upon *who* is the Attorney General.

The intensity with which broadcasters and their news reporters will assert First Amendment rights when subpoenaed by grand juries—despite the Mitchell statement—must be viewed in the context of the total present political climate. Vice President Agnew has repeatedly warned the federally licensed broadcasters that their behavior was less than desirable because they overexposed socially disruptive movements and personalities.

FCC Chairman Burch has endorsed what the Vice President said. Although there is no hard evidence that broadcasters have been intimidated by what Mr. Agnew said, nevertheless, there can be little doubt that they will want to give thought to the question of whether they should compound the administration's antagonism toward them by now defying grand jury subpoenas.

The ominous character of the Vice President's scolding of the television industry takes on added significance in light of the fact that the Attorney General, in his recent twenty-six-page peace-making guidelines which established the criteria under which newspapermen might be subpoenaed before grand juries, specifically limited the guidelines to the "press." Indeed, in his speech he asked the question whether there shouldn't be "a distinction among different categories of media." He did not explain why radio and television might be treated any differently than the press, but obviously he also had been reading the Vice President's speeches. He knew of one distinction: newspapers are not licensed by the federal government, whereas broadcasting stations are. Merely by raising the question, there is an intimation that broadcasters would be more intimidatable than newspapers.

In the spring of this year—just after the Attorney General issued his two-and-a-half-page statement on the subject—legislation was introduced in the House (Congressman Ottinger and twenty-one cosponsors) and in the Senate (Senator McIntyre and nine co-sponsors) which would drastically limit the subpoenaing of reporters from *any* of the media. It refers specifically to radio and tele-vision. It would prohibit all such subpoenas (whether issued by a grand jury, a court, an agency or department of the federal government, or Congress itself) except under very limited and precisely defined circumstances: when the con-fidential *information* itself had been made public by the person who had the right to claim the privilege; where the disclosure of the *source* of an alleged slander or libel was needed by a defendant in order to assert a defense in a civil

SUBPOENAS: SHOULD REPORTERS BE FORCED TO TELL WHAT THEY KNOW?
Marcus Cohn

suit; and when the details of secret sessions, such as that of a grand jury, are published. The privilege would not apply to either the source or the information, when the inquiring body deals with a question involving a "threat of foreign aggression." However, in such a situation there must first be a determination by a federal district court that the exception is applicable.

There is a question whether Congress can constitutionally include broadcast reporters in such legislation. If *Red Lion* really means what it says and it is the public, rather than the broadcaster (a mere licensee of the federal government), who has First Amendment rights, then one of the constitutional issues which must ultimately arise is whether the broadcast reporter can claim any kind of First Amendment protection when he is subpoenaed by a grand jury—whether or not he is included in the proposed legislation.

Hearings on these pending bills may provide the very kind of study which is urgently needed. There has never been a national formalized discussion of the issue. The results of the hearings may also have the effect of stimulating the thirty-three states which have not, as yet, adopted any legislation on the matter to face up to the problem and to do something about it.

In his August, 1970 ABA speech, the Attorney General made a point of saying that he would not oppose legislative guidelines. That is understandable. Legislation would take him and the administration off the hot seat.

---

*Of course, in these cases the "informant" (the client, patient or parishioner) is seeking personal help and guidance—he wants to save his own skin or soul—and, at least for the time being, is totally unconcerned with what relationship, if any, his problem has to any major social issue.

Reprinted by special permission of The Journal of Criminal Law, Criminology and Police Science *(Northwestern University School of Law). Copyright © 1965, Volume 56, Number 1, pp. 1–17. Original documentation omitted.*

Fair Trials and the Press

CAROLYN JAFFE

In the exercise of their constitutional right to freedom of the press, news media publish information concerning criminal cases. In the exercise of his constitutional right to a fair trial, every criminal defendant may demand trial by an impartial jury. Often, however, publicity exposes potential or actual jury members to information which is not eventually admitted in evidence at the trial. By thus enabling the jury to consider incompetent material, publicity can be prejudicial to the defendant, with the result that he is unable effectively to exercise his right to a fair trial. Frequent conflict between these fundamental rights constitutes a serious problem to the administration of criminal justice and raises the question of how the criminal defendant's right to a fair trial can be preserved without infringement of the equally important right to freedom of the press. A third right is also concerned whenever this conflict occurs—that of the prosecuting government to perform one of its vested functions, the administration of criminal justice.

In an effort to formulate a solution to this increasingly serious problem, these articles will review the elements of these three distinct rights: that of the defendant to a fair trial, that of the government fairly to administer criminal justice, and that of the news media to freedom of the press; will attempt to define what is meant by the phrase "prejudicial publicity"; and will analyze the efficacy of existing methods of attempting to deal with the problem in the light of their respective effects on the co-existing and conflicting rights sought to be preserved.

I: AN IMPARTIAL JURY

The United States Constitution entitles every defendant in a federal criminal action to a fair trial by an impartial jury. Although the Constitution does not require the states to provide trial by jury, every state by its own constitution guarantees jury trials in criminal cases. The Constitution does require, however, that whatever methods a state elects to use for disposition of criminal cases must be in accordance with due process of law, if the jury system is used, the jury must be impartial. Consequently, defendants in state as well as federal criminal prosecutions possess a right to trial by an impartial jury.

To satisfy federal constitutional requirements, the jury must meet the federal constitutional standard in state as well as federal criminal cases. Since this standard is not specified in the Constitution, it has been variously fashioned by the courts. "Impartiality is not a technical conception. It is a state of mind. For the ascertainment of this mental attitude of appropriate indifference, the Constitution lays down no particular tests and procedure is not chained to any ancient and artificial for-

FAIR TRIALS AND THE PRESS
Carolyn Jaffe

mula." Because "The theory of our system is that conclusions to be reached in a case will be induced only by evidence and argument in open court, and not by any outside information, whether of private talk or public print," the basic question in resolving the issue whether a trier of fact possesses this "mental attitude of appropriate indifference" is whether he has the ability to decide the facts in a criminal case solely on the basis of the evidence presented in court. Obviously a juror with this ability is the impartial juror required by the federal constitutional standard. And since, within the scope of this paper, impartiality of the jury is the determinant of whether or not a given trial was fair, nothing less than trial before a jury composed of such impartial jurors is a fair trial. The problem of how to establish the existence of this ability entails both the substantive test of impartiality used and the procedure for applying the test.

Until recently, with but a few exceptions, the substantive test of whether a juror is sufficiently impartial has been whether he testifies that he can render a fair and impartial verdict based solely on the evidence presented at the trial. If this criterion is met, a juror is not challengeable for cause, nor is his presence on the jury grounds for mistrial or continuance merely because he has been exposed to prejudicial articles or broadcasts, even if he admits that he has formed an opinion as to the guilt or innocence of the accused. Recognizing the intricacies and frailties of human nature, the federal courts and a few state courts have recently held this test an inadequate measure of impartiality, with the result that a juror with preconceived opinions of an accused's guilt may be found partial if his declaration of inpartiality, sincere thought it may be, is objectively untenable in the light of his exposure to extrajudicial information about the case. The following statement by the Supreme Court of Florida is illustrative:

"[A] juror's statement that he can and will return a verdict according to the evidence submitted and the law announced at the trial is not determinative of his competence [impartiality], if it appears *from other statements made by him or from other evidence* that he is not possessed of a state of mind which will enable him to do so."

Generally, the defendant complaining that his trial was unfair due to prejudicial publicity bears the burden of proving actual rather than speculative prejudice. While speculative prejudice is established upon proof of the existence of a condition which might result in prejudice, actual prejudice is not established unless it is proved that at least one juror in fact formed an opinion which influenced his verdict. The "actual prejudice" test compelled affirmance in two recent cases where, although newspapers containing highly prejudicial material were found in the jury room, the defendant failed to prove that any juror read the articles.

However, it has been held that when potentially prejudicial material has been publicized, a presumption of prejudice arises. For example, in *Commonwealth v. Crehan*, the Massachusetts Supreme Court presumed prejudice because the jury was allowed to separate, and since the trial court denied defendant's motion to poll the jury after damaging articles were published, it was impossible to rebut the presumption of prejudice. In *Rideau v. Louisiana*, where a film of defendant's interrogation by a group of local police officials and his confession were broadcast on several occasions over a local television station, the United States Supreme Court reversed defendant's state murder conviction without even using the transcript of the voir dire examination to ascertain whether any juror had seen the film. The Court held that the highly prejudicial nature and wide dissemination of the film rendered a fair trial in that locality impossible, and therefore examination of the voir dire was unnecessary. In *Irvin v. Dowd*, the first Supreme Court case upsetting a state conviction on prejudicial publicity grounds, the Court had found the jury not sufficiently impartial after carefully considering the voir dire. The *Rideau* case is the first in which the Supreme Court has reversed a state conviction on proof of speculative prejudice.

Because a trial judge has broad discretion in such matters, an appellate court will not overturn a finding of impartiality unless error is so manifest that the judge's action amounts to an abuse of that discretion.

With this background in mind, we must now try to define exactly what is the "prejudicial publicity" which can operate to deprive a defendant of that impartial jury to which his federal constitutional right to a fair trial entitles him.

II: WHAT IS "PREJUDICIAL PUBLICITY"?

The trier of fact in a criminal case must reach its conclusions as to a defendant's guilt only on the basis of evidence presented in open court, and not on any outside influence. A jury failing to accomplish this task does not meet federal constitutional standards of impartiality, and the trial at which the jury is not properly impartial is not "a fair trial" within the federal constitutional requirement. Within this framework, the publicity with which we should be concerned is publicity which, if read or heard by potential or actual jurors, may reasonably be used by them in deciding the issue whether a criminal defendant is guilty, and which might not be admitted as evidence at his trial. If jury members are exposed to such material and the material is not eventually admitted as evidence, then the defendant's right to a fair trial will have been violated in that the jury had the opportunity to consider matters not presented in open court in determining his guilt.

For example, in *Marshall v. United States*, defendant was on trial for unlawfully dispensing drugs in violation of a federal statute. Seven members of the jury admitted having read news articles containing facts relating to defendant's prior convictions for practicing medicine without a license. The trial court had held evidence of these convictions inadmissible on the ground that it was irrelevant to the issues in the case and would be prejudicial to defendant. In the exercise of its supervisory power over the lower federal courts,

the United States Supreme Court reversed Marshall's conviction, stating: "[The jurors were exposed] to information of a character which the trial court ruled was so prejudicial it could not be directly offered as evidence. The prejudice to the defendant is almost certain to be as great when that evidence reaches the jury through news accounts as when it is a part of the prosecution's evidence."

On the other hand, where the text of defendant's confession was published before trial, the United States Supreme Court affirmed his state conviction on the ground that since the confession was subsequently admitted in evidence, defendant was not prejudiced by the publication. Moreover, where a jury was exposed to publicity containing proffered testimony which the trial court had excluded merely on grounds of irrelevance rather than because of its prejudicial nature, the Alaska Supreme Court affirmed defendant's conviction.

The case law follows the general test outlined above — if material, read or heard by jurors, was likely to influence their decision as to a defendant's guilt, and if the material was not admitted as evidence, then the material was prejudicial to that defendant's right to a fair trial.

Six categories of material appear to meet this general test: (1) Confessions; (2) Prior criminal activities; (3) Incriminating tangible evidence; (4) Statements of persons who may not actually testify; (5) Reports of proceedings from which the jury has been excluded; and (6) Miscellaneous inflammatory material which may sway a jury's sympathies against a defendant.

(1) *Confessions.* No defendant can be convicted upon evidence which includes an involuntary confession, regardless of the truth of the confession, and regardless of independent evidence sufficient to sustain his guilt. Moreover, federal courts must exclude certain voluntary confessions as well, if they resulted from prohibited official activity.

Since the jury must not consider the fact that a defendant has confessed or the contents of his confession unless and until that confession is held admissible, a defendant whose purported confession is published and then not admitted in evidence, whether because not offered or because found inadmissible, is certain to be prejudiced by such publication. Reports that a defendant has offered or attempted to enter a plea of guilty or of *nolo contendere* are tantamount to reports that he has admitted guilt, and thus should be treated the same as publicity concerning confessions. It would be extremely naive to expect a juror who has read or heard a statement referring to a defendant as a "confessed killer," or has read or heard that a defendant has confessed or the purported contents of his confession, to put this out of his mind merely because no confession was admitted in evidence and he was told to consider only evidence admitted in court.

That in many cases confessions are properly admitted does not in any way vitiate the prejudice suffered by the defendant whose confession, though not admitted in evidence, was publicized. Nor can the general pre-admission publication of confessions be justified by maintaining that it would serve to relieve the public hysteria which often follows an unsolved crime of violence, unless we are willing to cite the desire for public complacency as a rationale for the denial of a fundamental constitutional right.

(2) *Prior criminal activities.* Evidence of a defendant's alleged criminal activities unrelated to the crime for which he is being tried is ordinarily inadmissible in court.

> "The state may not show defendant's prior trouble with the law [or] specific criminal acts . . . even though such facts might logically be persuasive that he is by propensity a probable perpetrator of the crime. The inquiry is not rejected because character [as evidenced by prior criminal activities] is irrelevant; on the contrary, it is said to weigh too much with the jury and to so overpersuade them as to prejudge one with a bad general record and deny him a fair opportunity to defend against a particular charge."

Unless one of the few exceptions to this general rule can be invoked, admission of such evidence constitutes prejudicial, reversible error. For example, in a rather extreme holding, the Fourth Circuit recently granted a state convict's petition for habeas corpus on the ground that the jury's improper knowledge of defendant's prior convictions in and of itself constituted a denial of his federal constitutional right to a fair trial.

Since evidence of prior arrests, convictions, and pending indictments and accusations of crimes unrelated to the offense charged are all likely to cause the jury, probably through conscious or subconscious use of a "leopard never changes its spots" thought process, to believe that defendant committed the crime charged, publication of such material is reasonably certain to be prejudicial if not later admitted.

(3) *Incriminating tangible evidence.* No criminal defendant can be convicted by means of evidence obtained in violation of the constitutional prohibition against unreasonable search and seizure. If the fact that incriminating tangible evidence has been discovered is published in such a way that the defendant is connected with the commission of a crime, he will be prejudiced unless the evidence is found to have been lawfully obtained and is admitted against him at the trial. A defendant can be equally prejudiced by such publicity concerning tangible evidence which may prove inadmissible by reason of some non-constitutional evidentiary rule. If, however, the discovery of evidence is publicized without connecting any particular person to the crime, it is not prejudicial to a defendant even if, for some reason, the evidence is not subsequently admitted. For example, if police discover the "murder weapon," publication of that fact alone would not be prejudicial, while publication of the fact that they found it in the possession of the defendant would be.

(4) *Statements of persons who may not actually testify.* Since every criminal defendant has a federal

constitutional right to be confronted by and to cross-examine his accusers, a defendant may be prejudiced for inability to exercise the right if the news media publish an extra-judicial statement made by a person not subsequently called as a witness against him. Such statements may independently tend to lead a juror to believe that the defendant committed the crime charged, *e.g.*, statements of "experts" regarding the results of polygraph tests, ballistics tests, and other scientific evidence, identification by "eye-witnesses," statements of official opinion that defendant is guilty, statements which might not qualify as dying declarations, and the like; or, such statements could reasonably tend to discredit an accused's possible defense without actually incriminating him, *e.g.*, statements impeaching the credibility of defense witnesses, or indicating that a defendant pleading insanity is actually sane.

(5) *Reports of proceedings from which the jury has been excluded.* Since a judge's exclusion of the jury from a court proceeding is generally based on the probability that the proceeding will contain information the jury is not entitled to know, publication of occurrences which take place during such proceedings is very likely to be prejudicial to a defendant. Most proceedings of this nature are hearings at which the trial court rules on the admissibility of evidence or confessions. Only if and when the evidence or confession is admitted can the proceedings on which that determination was based be published without probable prejudice to the defendant.

(6) *Miscellaneous inflammatory material.* Material in this category may consist of "human interest" interviews with the victim or his family, publication of the fact that a murder victim's estate is to be disposed of, editorials or factual reports concerning a "crime wave," or reports of the greater deterrent nature of capital punishment as compared with prison sentences. This type of material tends to be inflammatory—that is, to cause the jury to want to

convict—and thus to be prejudicial to whomever happens to be the defendant, not because he is any particular person about whom publicity has been disseminated, but merely because he is the defendant. For example, members of the jury which found a defendant guilty of murder and sentenced him to 299 years in prison later admitted that they had been influenced by articles concerning the then-pending proposed parole of Nathan Leopold.

It can be argued that, since material of the kinds enumerated tends to disclose The Truth, their publication should be encouraged. However, even if a coerced confession is true, and even if unconstitutionally seized evidence would conclusively establish a defendant's guilt, the United States Constitution as interpreted by the United States Supreme Court will permit no state or federal court in America to convict on such evidence. While conceding that evidence of previous criminal activities is not irrelevant and, in fact, is independently probative of present guilt, courts generally refuse to admit such evidence because of its extremely prejudicial nature. Surely only a perverted form of justice would permit jurors to be aware via news media of information which that same justice forbids those jurors to take cognizance of in open court.

III: EXISTING METHODS

Accepting the above general definition of prejudicial publicity and tentative characterization of specific kinds of material which may be prejudicial, we must now examine the means which have been used in an attempt to prevent defendants from being convicted by juries influenced by such material. In evaluating each method, its effect upon each of the three co-existing interests—of the defendant, the government, and the news media—will be considered.

Methods currently available to American courts for the purpose of attempting to solve the free press-fair trial dilemma are: (1) issuing contempt

FAIR TRIALS AND THE PRESS
Carolyn Jaffe

citations against those responsible for publication of prejudicial information; (2) granting of trial level procedural reliefs designed to prevent a biased jury from rendering a verdict; (3) use of cautionary instructions to prevent or erase the harmful effects of prejudicial publicity; and (4) reversing convictions resulting from trials unfair because of prejudicial publicity.

(1) *Contempt citations.* Contempt citations against those responsible for the publication of prejudicial information have been little used by American courts because of their general reluctance to apply the doctrine of constructive contempt. Used with much success in Great Britain, this doctrine allows a court to punish as contempt any act which interferes with proceedings before it even though that act did not take place in or in the immediate vicinity of the court.

Perhaps the reason for rejection of this concept is that constructive contempt is almost invariably committed by publication, and its exercise is regarded by the press, radio, and television as violative of the federal constitutional guarantee that neither federal nor state action may abridge freedom of speech and of the press. While freedom of the press protects almost absolutely against prior restraint, the government may take corrective action to punish past misconduct—such as issuing a contempt citation—if, under the circumstances, the words uttered or published create a "clear and present danger that they will bring about the substantive evils that Congress [or the state] has a right to prevent." Interference with the fair administration of justice, such as by publication of material which presents a clear and present danger to the fairness of a particular trial, is an evil which the government has a right to prevent. Freedom of the press has been held subject to restriction where there was a clear and present danger that its exercise would cause serious political, economic, or moral injury to the government, would impede the performance of governmental duties, or would endanger the foundations of organized govern-

ment. A fair judicial system surely is one of the foundations of our government, and maintenance of such a system a governmental duty. The United States Supreme Court has expressly recognized "the conceded authority of courts to punish for contempt when publications directly tend to prevent the proper discharge of judicial functions."

The Supreme Court, though, has never affirmed a contempt citation issued for a contempt committed by publication. However, in reversing three cases in which newspapers had been held in contempt for the publication of prejudicial material, the Court based its decisions not on the per se invalidity of holding newspapers in contempt, but rather on the absence of a "clear and present danger" to the orderly administration of the judicial process in the cases in question. It should be noted that these three cases were not tried before juries. It has been suggested that the danger of impeding the judicial process via prejudicial publications is substantially lessened where the case is tried by a judge, a law-trained man regarded as capable of being objective, rather than before a jury of impressionable laymen. In *Wood v. Georgia*, a recent contempt by publication case involving publication of a sheriff's statements designed to influence a grand jury, the United States Supreme Court reversed for lack of a clear and present danger, noting that the instant case did not involve a criminal trial pending before a jury. This dictum indicates that, presented the proper case of dissemination of prejudicial material regarding a criminal case pending before a jury, the Supreme Court would affirm a contempt conviction.

The purpose of freedom of the press is to "assure unfettered interchange of ideas for the bringing about of social changes desired by the people," and this right thus is essential to our system of government. Arguably, only publications consistent with the legitimate purpose of freedom of the press are entitled to its full protection. In an analogous situation, freedom of the press does not extend to confidential government documents, since disclosure to the press of secret government information could seriously undermine the ability of the various branches of government in discharging their constitutionally defined responsibilities. Use of the freedom of the press which results in the denial of a defendant's right to a fair trial and prejudices the outcome of a criminal case seems a perverted exercise of that right, and repugnant to its purpose. For example, consider Mr. Justice Frankfurter's pointed observation:

> In securing freedom of speech, the Constitution hardly meant to create the right to influence judges or juries. That is no more freedom of speech than stuffing a ballot box is an exercise of the right to vote.

The fair comment which serves the purpose of freedom of the press does not include material published with the intent to influence the result of a criminal trial. Moreover, material published without such intent but nonetheless reasonably certain to have that incidental effect constitutes a "clear and present danger" under a fair interpretation of that test, since the danger lies in the probable effect of publication.

Use of the contempt power to punish a contempt committed by publication of prejudicial material would seem to be constitutional so long as the clear and present danger test was met, because the action would not impose prior restraint, and the publication would be of a nature inconsistent with the purpose of freedom of the press.

Another reason for judicial reluctance to exercise the inherent contempt power may rest upon the position of most of our judges as elected officials dependent on the press for political support. A further reason may be judicial ignorance that the inherent contempt power extends beyond the power to cite for contempt those who scandalize the court.

Although it is essential to our system of government that no person be convicted but by an impartial jury, it is just as essential that no organ of public sentiment be effectively prohibited from making fair comment on that government. Only publications not constituting fair comment as defined above would be contemptuous, but limited restrictions with fair and reasonable beginnings may eventually compound into an oppressive whole. Use of the contempt power may thus projectively undermine freedom of the press even if it would not presently violate that freedom.

Furthermore, what does it help a particular convicted defendant that the newspaper which helped to convict him has been held in contempt? And future defendants will not be aided by present contempt citations unless definite standards of contemptuous conduct are established; in absence of such standards, punishment for contempt lacks deterrent effect. The prosecuting government's interests are also neglected by use of the contempt power, because so long as this process is not uniformly applied according to some standards, it serves no deterrent function and thus does not tend to help secure the effective enforcement of justice in the long run.

(2) *Trial level remedies.* Various remedies designed to prevent a defendant from being tried by a prejudiced jury are available at the trial level. Included are motions for dismissal of a prospective or impanelled juror for cause, for declaration of mistrial, for continuance, for change of venue, and for new trial. Failure to grant the requested relief is reversible error only where a defendant has been prejudiced thereby and where such failure amounts to an abuse of discretion. However, these remedies fail to protect defendants' rights and the corollary sovereign rights simply because they are so seldom granted, probably due to the nebulous nature of impartiality and the trial court's broad discretion as to disposition of such motions. Another reason these procedures are ineffective is that, if granted, such remedies as change of venue, continuance, and even new trial, will be unable to assure a fair trial if

FAIR TRIALS AND THE PRESS
Carolyn Jaffe

widespread and intense publicity concerning the trial continues to be disseminated. Even when granted, these motions have little tendency to deter future publication of prejudicial material.

It would appear that the trial level technique of sequestering the jury (*i.e.*, keeping the jurors "locked up" during the course of the trial) is the most effective way to prevent the defendant's being prejudiced by publicity appearing after the jury has been impanelled. This method has been infrequently employed, however, perhaps because of a desire to avoid coercing the unhappily confined jurors to concur in a hurried verdict. However in a recent case the Seventh Circuit approved the trial judge's sua sponte sequestration of the jury for the purpose of protecting defendant from the effects of prejudicial publicity over defendant's contention that this action resulted in a coerced verdict against him. Furthermore, sequestration requires large expenditures by the state.

(3) *Cautionary instructions.* Where the trial court instructs the jury not to read or listen to accounts of the case which may appear during the course of the trial or not to consider any matters other than evidence presented at the trial, appellate courts generally presume that the instructions were effective and thus find no prejudice due to pre-trial publicity or publicity appearing during the trial; accordingly, failure to give cautionary instructions has been held to constitute reversible error.

However, for several reasons, preventive cautionary instructions nonetheless fail to protect a defendant's right to a fair trial and the sovereign's right to preserve the orderly administration of justice by giving him a fair trial. First, they cannot protect against the possible effects of pre-trial publicity, simply because of the time element. Second, jurors may disregard preventive cautionary instructions and fail to admit it for fear of reprisal by the court. For example, in *Smith v. United States*, a prejudicial article was published after cautionary instructions had been given. Upon

defense counsel's request that despite the instructions the jury be polled as to whether any had read the article, the court addressed the jury as a whole as follows: "'[I]f any juror violated the instructions of the court and read the article . . . hold up your hands.'" A better procedure involving the private interrogation of individual jurors is outlined by Judge Kiley in *United States v. Accardo*. Third, these instructions may call to a juror's attention articles which might otherwise have gone unnoticed. Corrective cautionary instructions are likely to be ineffective for the third reason above, and also because of the difficulty, if not impossibility, for a juror not to be at least subconsciously influenced by extra-judicial matters to which he was exposed despite honest efforts to remain fair and impartial and to discharge his oath.

Exposure to extra-judicial matters not in evidence at the trial may cause a juror subconsciously to resolve disputed issues of fact against the defendant even though that juror is not in fact deciding defendant's guilt on the basis of consciously considered facts gained other than at the trial. Moreover, extra-judicial exposure to matters which are subsequently admitted in evidence may lead a sincere juror to resolve disputed issues of fact, and, perhaps more importantly, issues of credibility of witnesses, against defendant. The pre-admission exposure may well cause a juror to give more weight to the evidence than he would if his first and only contact with the matter were as evidence in court.

(4) *Reversal of Convictions.* Many factors are considered by reviewing courts in determining whether a judgment of conviction should be overturned on prejudicial publicity grounds. Invariably the reversible error alleged by appellant will be denial of a fair trial occasioned by the trial court's failure or refusal to grant trial level remedies or cautionary instructions. Hence, the issues reviewing courts discuss tend to establish the presence or absence of prejudice.

State or Federal Convicting Court. The question whether the conviction was rendered in a state or federal court is peculiar to the federal courts, since only a federal court can hear cases which originate in both federal and state courts. If the conviction was rendered in a federal court, the United States Supreme Court can reverse in exercise of its general supervisory power over the lower federal courts. When a federal court is reviewing a state conviction, however, habeas corpus can be granted or reversal ordered only if the defendant was denied a fair trial in violation of due process. However, the fact that the 1963 case of *Rideau v. Louisiana* allowed speculative proof of prejudice to establish that the constitutionally compelled impartiality requirement was not met by the state jury indicates that the state-federal distinction will seldom be meaningful in cases to come.

Admissibility of Information Complained of. Publicity relating facts unfavorable to a defendant which are inadmissible as evidence at the trial is very likely to be prejudicial, since a juror who reads such publicity will have been exposed to evidence not introduced at the trial, and might consider such facts in his deliberations. Conversely, if information published prior to trial is subsequently admitted, defendant cannot successfully allege that the publicity prejudiced his rights. The rule in the federal courts, controlled by *Marshall v. United States*, requires reversal where the jury was extra-judicially aware of information inadmissible because of its prejudicial nature, not simply because of some evidentiary rule.

Time Between Publication and Trial. Although it is difficult to measure so subjective a thing as impartiality—admittedly a state of mind—on an objective scale, some courts have attempted to do so. If a relatively long period of time has elapsed between publication of the material complained of and time of trial, a reviewing court is not likely to find prejudice.

Action Taken by Defense Counsel Prior to or During Trial. If defense counsel fails to move the court to interrogate the prospective jurors on voir dire, or the impanelled jurors during the trial, as to whether they read the articles complained of, and if so whether they were prejudiced thereby, most reviewing courts will not disturb the result. It has been recognized, however, that such questioning may be harmful to a defendant's cause. For example, in *Briggs v. United States*, defendant moved for a mistrial, but declined to accept the trial court's offer to interrogate the jury. Reversing the conviction rendered after the trial court refused to declare a mistrial, the Sixth Circuit stated, "It could very well be that questioning the jury would be more prejudicial than helpful. We do not believe that appellant was required to agree to such questioning in order to preserve his contention that [he] was entitled to a mistrial." In another case, defense counsel suggested voit dire questions designed to elicit the existence of prejudice without alerting jurors to prejudicial material. The trial court's insistence on asking questions in such a form as to make the jurors aware of the material constituted one ground for reversal.

Failure of a defendant to exhaust his peremptory challenges, to challenge for cause, or to move for continuance, change of venue, or mistrial, though not usually precluding the appellate court from deciding the issue of impartiality, may lead the court to infer that the articles complained of did not in fact generate such widespread and lasting prejudice as the defendant would like the court to believe.

Source and Intent of the Information. If the information contained in the publicity complained of was instigated solely by the press, federal and state reviewing courts have been less likely to reverse than if an agent of the prosecuting government was responsible for dissemination. Indeed, the "state action" concept of due process seems especially applicable to support federally compelled reversal of state convictions contaminated by publicity promulgated by an officer of the state. However, in *Rideau v. Louisiana*, where

FAIR TRIALS AND THE PRESS
Carolyn Jaffe

the United States Supreme Court reversed defendant's state murder conviction on prejudicial publicity grounds, the Court expressly disclaimed reliance on state action as to promulgation of the prejudicial broadcasts, stating that, although it appeared that local officials probably had prompted the filmed interview, "the question of who originally initiated the idea . . . is . . . a basically irrelevant detail." The state action held by the Court to have deprived defendant of his federal rights was the state trial court's refusal to grant his motions for change of venue. This notion utilized by the *Rideau* court—that it is the prejudicial effect of an occurrence upon the defendant rather than the identity or motive of the person who caused the event which is the sole determinant of whether defendant's trial was fair, and that the trial court's failure to cure the effects of the prejudicial occurrence constitutes "state action" for due process purposes—would seem to eradicate any previously persisting distinction between prosecution-generated publicity and publicity emanating from other sources.

In short, reviewing courts are slow to reverse convictions attacked on prejudicial publicity grounds, mainly because it is extremely difficult, as a practical matter, to prove prejudice. Even in the case where the rights of a particular defendant are vindicated by reversal of his conviction, this method is an incomplete solution. Reversal of

a few convictions influenced by prejudicial publicity will have little, if any, deterrent effect upon promulgation of like material in subsequent cases. Further, the right of the prosecuting government fairly to administer criminal justice and to protect its citizens is entirely neglected by this "solution." Where the publicity which occasions reversal and remand emanates without participation of any government official, the government has been unjustly "punished"—by the trouble and expense of a new trial, or, if retrial is impossible as a practical matter or because the appellate court reversed without remand, by the danger that one who may be a criminal remains at large—while the guilty press is allowed to go free. And, as we have seen, the method which would punish the press by contempt is rarely resorted to.

Summary. It appears that the above methods, as currently practiced by American courts, are inadequate solutions to the freedom of the press-fair trial conflict, for the following brief reasons: (1) contempt, because of disuse; (2) trial level reliefs because of disuse and lack of deterrent effect; (3) cautionary instructions, because of human nature; and (4) reversal, because of disuse, failure to protect sovereign rights, and lack of deterrent effect.

Reprinted from Look *(October 22, 1963), pp. 46–52. Used by permission of the publisher. Copyright © 1963 by Cowles Communications, Inc.*

What TV Violence Can Do to Your Child

ALBERT BANDURA

IF PARENTS could buy packaged psychological influences to administer in regular doses to their children, I doubt that many would deliberately select Western gunslingers, hopped-up psychopaths, deranged sadists, slapstick buffoons and the like, unless they entertained rather peculiar ambitions for their growing offspring. Yet such examples of behavior are delivered in quantity, with no direct charge, to millions of households daily. Harried parents can easily turn off demanding children by turning on a television set; as a result, today's youth is being raised on a heavy dosage of televised aggression and violence.

Testimony in recent U.S. Senate hearings revealed that the amount of violence in television programs has increased substantially over the years. One network executive claimed that this rise in violent action-adventure programs reflects nothing more than technological advances in photography; new films and camera techniques, he said, make it possible to catch action that previously went unrecorded. Other investigators, however, charged that some television shows deliberately used brutality to attract and hold a larger audience.

What happens to a child who watches aggressive personalities on television slug, stomp, shoot and stab one another?

Spokesmen for the broadcasting industry generally claim that television has no demonstrable ill effect on viewers. Many mental-health workers and a large segment of the general public assume that exposure to violence can be cathartic—i.e., as children identify with the aggressor, their pent-up hostile feelings are drained away—and that television thus serves as a harmless cultural pacifier. A minority considers television a demonic influence that must be stamped out completely.

Several widely circulated survey studies contend that televised violence has neither harmful nor beneficial effects, except perhaps on highly insecure and emotionally disturbed children. It is surprising how this view has won uncritical acceptance, particularly because it is based on little more than findings from public-opinion polls and survey questionnaires that seldom, if ever, directly examine the *children's* attitudes and social behavior.

If you wished to assess the full effect of a particular medicine on children's physical health, you would hardly do it by soliciting opinions from parents, teachers and self-defined "experts."

Precise information can come only through carefully controlled laboratory tests in which the children themselves participate. For this reason, we recently conducted a series of experiments at the Stanford psychological laboratories to provide some real basis for evaluating the impact of televised aggression on preschool children.

We designed a series of experiments to test the extent to which children will copy aggressive patterns of behavior, when these patterns are shown by adult models in three different situations: in real life, on film and as cartoon characters on film.

WHAT TV VIOLENCE CAN DO TO YOUR CHILD
Albert Bandura

The first group observed real-life adults. An experimenter brought the children, one by one, into a test room. In one corner, the child found a set of play materials; in another corner, he saw an adult sitting quietly with a set of tinker toys, a large, inflated plastic Bobo doll and a mallet. Soon after the child started to play with his toys, the adult model began attacking the Bobo doll in ways that children rarely would. For example, the adult sat on the doll and punched it repeatedly in the nose, pummeled its head with the mallet, tossed it up in the air aggressively and kicked it around the room while saying things like "Sock him in the nose!" "Hit him down!" "Throw him in the air!" "Kick him!"

The second group of children saw a movie of the adult model beating up the Bobo doll. The third group watched a movie—projected through a television console—in which the adult attacking the doll was costumed as a cartoon cat. Children in the fourth group did not see any aggressive models; they served as a control group. This gave us a basis of standard behavior to compare with the actions of the groups who were exposed to the aggressive models.

At the end of 10 minutes, the experimenter took each child to an observation room, where we recorded his behavior. For reasons that I will explain later, we mildly annoyed each child before he came in.

The observation room contained a variety of toys. Some could obviously be used to express aggression, while others served more peaceful purposes. The "aggressive" toys included a mallet, dart gun and the three-foot Bobo doll. The "non-aggressive" toys included a tea set, crayons and coloring paper, dolls, cars and trucks and plastic farm animals. Each child spent 20 minutes in the room, and his behavior was rated by psychologists observing through a one-way mirror.

The results leave little doubt that exposure to violence heightens aggressive tendencies in children. Those who had seen the adult model attacking the Bobo doll showed approximately twice as much aggressiveness in the observation room as did those in the control group.

We reached two important conclusions about the effect of aggressive models on a child.

1. The experience tends to reduce the child's inhibitions against acting in a violent, aggressive manner. .

2. The experience helps to shape the *form* of the child's aggressive behavior. Most of the cildren from the first three groups sat on the Bobo doll and punched its nose, beat it on the head with a mallet, tossed it into the air and kicked it around the room. And they used the familiar hostile remarks, "Hit him down!" "Kick him!" and so forth. This kind of conduct was rare among children in the control group.

Our observations led us to a third, and highly significant conclusion. We noticed that a person displaying violence on film is as influential as one displaying it in real life. The children were not too inclined to give precise imitations of the cartoon character, but many of them behaved like carbon copies of both real-life *and* film models. From these findings, we must conclude that televised models are important sources of social behavior and can no longer be ignored as influences on personality development. As audio-visual technology develops, television will become even more influential.

I would like to make one point clear: A child who watches violence on a screen is not necessarily going to attack the first person he sees. But if he is provoked enough on some future occasion, he may very well copy aggressive patterns of behavior that he has learned from a pictorial medium like television. This is clearly illustrated by an episode in which a boy was seriously wounded during the reenactment, with a friend, of a switchblade knife fight seen in a television rerun of the movie *Rebel Without a Cause*. The impact of the scene upon the boys did not become apparent until the day after the program, when one of them adopted the James Dean role and challenged his friend to a fight. Only after the fight had begun did the *Rebel*-style knife play emerge.

That is why we deliberately irritated each child in our experiment before he entered the observation room. We wanted to see if the children who had viewed aggressive models would display more aggression than those in the control group after all were exposed to the same degree of annoyance. They did.

In assessing the influence of televised violence on viewers' behavior, however, we must distinguish between *learning* and *doing*. Though children readily learn patterns of social behavior from television programs, they do not copy indiscriminately the behavior of television characters, even those they like best. There are at least two reasons for this:

1. Children rarely have access to the weapons necessary for showing off what they have learned. If they had switchblades, blackjacks and six-shooters, it is safe to predict that the incidence of tragic imitative aggression connected with television viewing would rise sharply.

2. Most parents quickly suppress any learning that conflicts with what they consider desirable conduct. This is particularly true of verbal affectations that arise frequently, are irritating to parents and can be readily identified as television-produced.

Therefore, the impact of television can be isolated and measured precisely only when parental influences are removed and the children are given the instruments they need to reproduce behavior they see on television. These are the conditions we achieved in the laboratory. No one should forget, however, that television is but one of several important influences on children's attitudes and social behavior, and other factors undoubtedly heighten or suppress its effects.

PUNISHING THE BAD GUY

Most people believe an ethical ending to a program, in which the bad guy is punished, will erase or counteract what a child learns from exposure to aggressively antisocial models. To test this assumption, I conducted another experiment.

One group of nursery-school children watched a movie, again projected through a television console, in which Rocky, the villain, seizes all of Johnny's favorite toys. He kicks him and hits him with a baton and finally takes the toys in a big sack. In this version, aggression pays off handsomely.

A second group of children saw the same program with a punishment ending added to show that aggression does not pay. As Rocky tries to seize the toys, Johnny overpowers him and thoroughly thrashes him.

We tested the two groups of children to see how much they behaved like Rocky. Children in the first group—who saw Rocky's aggressive behavior rewarded—readily imitated his physical violence and his hostile remarks. Children in the other group—who saw him punished by Johnny—showed very little imitative aggression. We then asked each child to evaluate the behavior of Rocky and Johnny, and to decide which of the two characters he would prefer to copy. The replies were both interesting and surprising.

As might be expected, children who had seen Rocky punished for his aggressive behavior rejected him as a person to emulate. Also, as expected, most of those who had seen Rocky's aggression pay off said they would copy him.

What did surprise us, however, was the discovery that all the children were highly critical of the way in which he behaved ("Rocky is harsh," "Mean," "He whack people"). Their comments indicate that they imitated Rocky, not because his aggression was intrinsically desirable, but because it paid off ("Rocky beat Johnny and chase him and get all the good toys." "He was a good fighter. He got all the good toys"). One little girl provided a striking example of how a child will adopt objectionable patterns of conduct if they prove successful. She denounced Rocky for the way in which he grabbed Johnny's toys. Nevertheless, at the end of the experimental test

WHAT TV VIOLENCE CAN DO TO YOUR CHILD
Albert Bandura

session—during which she exhibited much of Rocky's aggressive behavior—she turned to the experimenter and asked, "Do you have a sack here?"

This experiment involved only a single episode of aggression that was rewarded or punished. In most television shows, the bad guy typically wins power over important resources and amasses considerable material rewards through a whole *series* of aggressive exploits. For example, he may gain control over grazing land, water supplies, gold mines, steers, nightclubs, blondes, the constabulary and perhaps the whole town. Generally, he is not punished until just before the last commercial—and punished only once—whereas he has probably succeeded several times during the program. Such punishment of the villain at the end may have only a weak inhibitory effect on the child viewer. In the learning process, immediate rewards have much more influence on a child than delayed punishment.

Although seeing the televised villain punished may discourage children from copying his antisocial behavior immediately, it does not erase from their minds the methods of aggression that they have learned.

In a related experiment, three separate groups of children observed a model's aggression rewarded, punished or left without consequences. When tested, children who saw the model punished displayed less imitative aggression than the other two groups. Then we offered all the children attractive rewards if they would reproduce the model's behavior. The introduction of rewards completely wiped out the differences between the three groups of children. They *all* reproduced with considerable accuracy the model's physical and verbal aggression.

From these findings, we can conclude that if children see the bad guy punished, they are not likely to imitate his behavior spontaneously. But they do acquire—and retain—concrete information about *how* to behave aggressively, and punishment of the bad guy does not make

them forget what they have learned. They may put his knowledge into practice on future occasions, if they are given enough provocation, access to the necessary weapons and the prospect of sufficiently attractive rewards.

EFFECTS ON ADULTS

Are the effects of televised violence revealed in these experiments confined to children? The answer is no, according to a recent study by Dr. Richard H. Walters at the University of Toronto. Grown-ups can be just as deeply influenced by exposure to aggression.

Dr. Walters asked a group of adult males and adolescent boys to help in a study of the effects of punishment on learning. The participants could give an electric shock to a "learner" every time he made a mistake on a test. They could vary the length and intensity of the shock. Before the test began, each sampled a few shocks to become familiar with the different pain levels.

The learner then proceeded to make intentional mistakes, and Dr. Walters measured the length and strength of the shocks he duly got. (Unknown to the participants, the electrodes were disconnected, and the learner felt no pain.)

In the second step of the study, half the participants watched the switchblade scene from *Rebel Without a Cause*, while the other half saw a short film about picture making. Then they all repeated the shock-administration test.

Those who had seen the picture-making film administered relatively weak shocks. But the *Rebel* group gave longer, more powerful shocks. Indeed, if the electrodes had been connected, they would have caused considerable pain. Moreover, this group showed a pronounced increase in aggressiveness and hostility on an objective personality test.

All the laboratory studies that I have reported deal with the immediate impact of a single exposure to aggression on the viewer's attitudes and conduct. While the questions about immediate effects have been clarified to some extent, we need much

more research on the cumulative impact of
television, and the way in which the medium
combines with other beneficial or adverse influences
in the shaping of people's thoughts and acts.

But what about those immediate effects? We
now see clearly that violence on a television or
movie screen affects viewers by:

1. Reducing their inhibitions against violent,
aggressive behavior.

2. Teaching them *forms* of aggression—that is,
giving them information about how to attack
someone else when the occasion arises.

And, third, let us keep in mind that the ethical
ending, in which the villain is punished, may
keep viewers from reproducing villainy right
away, but does not make them forget how to do
it. The ethical ending is just a suppressor of
violence; it does not erase.

Since the amount of time that children are
exposed to television makes it one of the most
important influences in their lives, these laboratory
findings do not present a pretty picture—unless
our society is interested in increasing the aggressive
tendencies of a growing generation.

Reprinted from Columbia Journalism Review *(Spring, 1970), pp. 17–23. Used by permission of publisher and author.*

Media Myths on Violence

TERRY ANN KNOPF

SEVERAL years ago a resident of a small Northern town kept insisting to a local newspaper reporter that a policeman had been shot and killed during a racial disturbance there. The reporter checked and rechecked but was unable to substantiate the story. In fact a policeman had been killed, but in another city. The man simply had heard a garbled version of the story—not an unusual occurrence in the confusion that prevails during crises.

Crisis situations increase the need for news. During most serious disturbances, news media are bombarded with calls from anxious citizens wanting information, clarification, verification of what they have heard. So important is the flow of news through established channels that its continued absence can help precipitate a crisis. In 1968 in Detroit the absence of newspapers during a protracted strike helped create a panic: there were rumors in the white community that blacks were planning to blow up freeways, kill suburban white children, and destroy public buildings; in the black community, that white vigilantes were coming into the area to attack the residents. Gun clubs sprang up in the suburbs; black leaders urged preparation of survival kits. On March 7—nearly four months after the strike began—Mayor Cavanagh had to go on TV to plead for calm.

As racial disorders have become a familiar part of the national scene the media have demonstrated a growing awareness of their responsibilities and a healthy willingness to experiment with new policies and procedures. Technical improvements also have been made. The City of Detroit, for example, has built a press room large enough for 150 people, with independent telephone lines. Operational techniques have been modernized—the Pittsburgh police, among others, have on occasion provided a helicopter for the press. And central headquarters or "press centrals" have been established to help eliminate conflicting reports. Moreover, a number of cities have adopted or revised guidelines for reporting. These guidelines—sometimes formal, sometimes informal—urge that unnecessary interpretation be minimized, rumors be eliminated, unverified statements be avoided, and superlatives and adjectives in "scare" headlines be excluded. One set of guidelines put the matter simply: "Honest and dispassionate reporting is the best reporting."

In accordance with these guidelines, newspapers have tended to move away from the "shotgun" approach—the front-page buildup, complete with splashy pictures and boxscores of the latest "riot" news. Dramatic but meaningless predictions have also largely disappeared. In May, 1967, *U.S. News & World Report* declared that Newark was "not expecting trouble," while Cleveland was voted the city "most likely to explode—again." Cleveland failed to erupt in 1967, but Newark experienced one of the most massive outbursts in our country's history. This kind of journalism is much less common today.

There is also evidence of greater sympathy and sensitivity toward blacks. How far have we come? Consider the following comment from the New

MEDIA MYTHS ON VIOLENCE
Terry Ann Knopf

York *Times* on July 23, 1919, concerning the violent disorder in Washington, D.C.:

> The majority of the negroes (sic) in Washington before the great war were well behaved. . . . More of them admitted the superiority of the white race, and troubles between the two races were undreamed of. Now and then a negro intent on enforcing a civil rights law would force his way into a saloon or a theatre and demand to be treated the same as whites were, but if the manager objected he usually gave in without more than a protest.

These changes represent considerable improvement. But serious problems remain. Glaring instances of inaccuracy, exaggeration, distortion, misinterpretation, and bias have continued at every level—in newspapers and newsmagazines large and small, Northern and Southern, liberal and conservative.

The wire services are probably the most underexamined segment of the media, although as much as 90 per cent of the news in some newspapers on a given day may come from the wires. One error in a wire service report from one city may be repeated in hundreds of newspapers and newscasts. In York, Pa., in mid-July, 1968, for instance, incidents of rock- and bottle-throwing were reported. Toward the end of the disturbance UPI in Harrisburg asked a stringer to get something on the situation. A photographer took a picture of a motorcyclist with an ammunition belt around his waist and a rifle strapped across his back. A small object dangled from the rifle. On July 18, the picture reached the nation's press. The Washington *Post* said:

> ARMED RIDER—Unidentified motorcyclist drives through heart of York, Pa., Negro district, which was quiet for the first time in six days of sporadic disorders.

The Baltimore SUN used the same picture and a similar caption:

> QUIET, BUT . . . An unidentified motorcycle rider, armed with a rifle and carrying a belt of ammunition, was among those in the heart of York, Pa., Negro district last night. The area was quiet for the first time in six days.

The implication of this photograph was clear: The "armed rider" was a sniper. But since when do snipers travel openly in daylight completely armed? Also, isn't there something incongruous about photographing a sniper, presumably "on his way to work," when according to the caption the city "was quiet"? Actually the "armed rider" was a sixteen-year-old boy who happened to be fond of hunting groundhogs—a skill he had learned as a small boy from his father. On July 16, as was his custom, the young man had put on his ammo belt and strapped a rifle across his back, letting a hunting license dangle so that all would know he was hunting animals, not people. Off he went on his motorcycle headed for the woods, the fields, the groundhogs—and the place reserved for him in the nation's press.

More recently, an AP man in Dallas filed a story on a student takeover at Southern Methodist University. The Fort Worth *Star-Telegram* in its evening edition last May 2 put the story on the front page and gave it a banner headline:

BLACKS SEIZE OFFICE OF S.M.U.'S PRESIDENT

Police Are Called to Stand By

> DALLAS (AP)—Black students with some support from whites took over the office of the president of Southern Methodist University today and swore to remain until their demands are met. . . .
>
> Reports from the scene said from thirty to thirty-five students were in control of [President] Tate's office.
>
> The takeover occurred during a meeting of Tate and a campus organization, the Black League of Afro-American and African College Students.

The story had one major flaw—it wasn't true. While about thirty-five students had met with the university president, they were not "in control" of his office; nor had they "swore to remain" until

MEDIA MYTHS ON VIOLENCE
Terry Ann Knopf

their demands were met. No such "takeover" had occurred. Glen Dromgoole, a staff writer for the *Star-Telegram*, later reported what really happened. The black students had met with the president for more than five hours discussing recent demands. The talks were more friendly than hostile. (At one point hamburgers were brought in.) By the end of the meeting, agreement had been reached on most of the issues. Apparently the wire service reporter had accepted the many rumors of a student takeover.

Martin Hayden of the Detroit *News* has suggested "an almost mathematical relationship between the level of exaggeration and the distance of news transmission." Edwin Guthman of the Los Angeles *Times* maintains that the early wire service report "is at the crux of the news media's problem." However, it is more likely that instances of misreporting remain a problem at *every* media level. The Lemberg Center for the Study of Violence, in investigating twenty-five incidents in which the news media had alleged sniping, found that, along with the wire services, local and nationally known newspapers bore a heavy responsibility for imprecise, distorted, and inaccurate reporting.

While treatment of racial disorders is generally more restrained today, the news media continue to overplay the more violent or sensational aspects of a story. The central media concern during the disorder at Cornell University last April, for example, was the emergence of the blacks from the student union. A picture of the students carrying rifles and shotguns, splashed across the nation, had a distorting effect on public opinion. The New York *Times* put the picture on page 1, and *Newsweek* used it on its cover the following week. Certain facts were largely ignored: prior to the disorder a cross had been burned in front of a black women's dormitory; the students had heard radio reports that carloads of armed whites were moving toward the campus; when the students emerged from the building their guns weren't loaded. What was basically a defensive response by a group of frightened students came across in the media as a terrorist act by student guerrillas.

Aspects of the disorders are dramatic and do merit extensive coverage. But the media still tend to equate bad news with big news and to confuse the obvious with the relevant. Thus when sixty-five students at Brandeis University took over a building last year it rated a story on the front page of the New York *Times*—despite the fact that there was no violence, that classes continued, and that the university suffered only minor inconvenience. I was on campus then. My only recollection of anything unusual was that on the first day or two an attendant asked to see my identification, and for the next week and a half I noticed large numbers of reporters, press cars, cameras, and other equipment. I sometimes wondered if there weren't more reporters outside than students inside the building.

The *Times*, along with most newspapers, missed the unusual climax at Brandeis. In a war of nerves with the students, President Morris Abram showed consummate skill in handling the situation, remaining flexible on the issues, mobilizing the support of the student body and faculty, and, above all, refusing to call in police. Eleven days after the crisis had begun the students quietly left the building—a dramatic victory for the Brandeis community, a dramatic example of how to handle a university crisis in contrast to fiascoes at Columbia and San Francisco State. Yet the students' departure merely merited a *Times* story about three inches long, well off the front page.

Disparities between the headlines and news stories are another problem. Often much less occurs in the story than the headline would indicate. Last year, for example, some concerned parents in Jacksonville, Fla., removed their children from Kirby Smith Junior High School after a local radio station had broadcast an exaggerated report of a fight between black and white students. The school principal later indicated that "classes continued and there was no panic." Nevertheless the

MEDIA MYTHS ON VIOLENCE
Terry Ann Knopf

Miami *Herald* headlined its story last April 25: MOMS MOB SCHOOL AFTER RIOT 'NEWS.' Sometimes no violence occurs in the story, dramatic headlines to the contrary. A story appearing in the Boston *Globe* last May 10 told of a peaceful rally by a small group of students at a local theological seminary. According to the *Globe*, the rally was "brief and orderly." But the headline above the story read NEWTON CAMPUS ERUPTS.

The use of the word "riot" presents another problem because it has no precise meaning in terms of current disorders. *Webster's* defines a "riot" as a "tumultuous disturbance of the public peace by three or more persons assembled together and acting with a common intent." The difficulty is that "riots" have become so frequent and come in so many sizes and shapes as to render the word meaningless. There is something ludicrous about lumping together as "riots" Detroit, with forth-three deaths, 7,000 arrests, and $45 million in property damage, and an incident in which three people break a few store windows. Yet this is precisely what the news media still do. The continued media use of the term contributes to an emotionally charged climate in which the public tends to view every event as an "incident," every incident as a "disturbance," and every disturbance as a "riot." Journalists would do well to drop the word from their vocabulary altogether.

No law says the media have to interpret and not simply report the news, but having assumed this responsibility they have an obligation to make reasonable judgments based on careful analysis. Unfortunately, journalistic attempts in the direction of social science research have been rather amateurish, particularly where new trends and patterns are concerned. The case of the Cleveland "shoot-out" is a good example. On July 23, 1968, an intense gun battle broke out between the police and a group of black nationalists led by Ahmed Evans. Before the disorder was over 16,400 National Guardsmen had been mobilized, nine persons had been killed, and there was property damage estimated at $2.6 million. The Cleveland

Press on July 24, 1968, compared the violence to guerrilla activity in Vietnam:

> . . . it didn't seem to be a Watts, or a Detroit, or a Newark. Or even a Hough of two years ago. No, this tragic night seemed to be part of a plan.

A reporter writing in the New York *Times* of July 28, 1968, stated:

> It marks perhaps the first documented case in recent history of black, armed, and organized violence against the police.

More recent reports have revealed that the "shoot-out" was something less than a planned uprising and that the situation was considerably more complicated than indicated initially. Unfortunately, following the events in Cleveland, disorders in which shots may have been fired were immediately suspected by the press of being part of a "wave." A series of errors involving a handful of cities became the basis of a myth—that the pattern of violence in 1968 had changed from spontaneous to premeditated outbreaks. Few of the nationally known newspapers and newsmagazines attempted to verify sniping reports coming out of the cities and over the wire services; few were willing to undertake independent investigations; and far too many were overly zealous in their assertions of a new "trend" based on limited and unconfirmed evidence. Unwittingly or not, the national media had constructed a scenario on armed uprisings.

Although having more time to check and verify reports than daily newspapers, the newsmagazines were even more vocal in their assertions of a "new pattern." On September 13, 1968, *Time* took note of an "ominous trend" and declared that the violence "appears to be changing from spontaneous combustion of a mob to the premeditated shoot-outs of a far-out few." The story went on to indicate that "many battles" had begun with "well planned sniping at police." Nearly a year later, on June 27, 1969—long after investigation by a task

MEDIA MYTHS ON VIOLENCE
Terry Ann Knopf

force of the National Commission on the Causes and Prevention of Violence, by the Lemberg Center, and by the New York *Times* (which reversed itself on the Cleveland question) had cast serious doubt about premeditated outbreaks in Cleveland and elsewhere — *Time* still was talking about the possibilities of a "guerrilla summer" and reminding its readers of the time in Cleveland when "police were lured into an ambush." Once started, myths are difficult to extinguish.

The most recent myth created by the media involves an alleged "shift" in racial disturbances from large to small cities. Last July 25 a syndicated reporter for the News Enterprise Association (NEA) noted:

> The socially sizzling summer has begun — but unlike recent history, it seems to be the minor, not the major, cities which are sweltering.

In an article entitled "Riots, 1969 Style," *Newsweek* declared on August 11:

> . . . the traditional riot scenario is still being played out this summer — with one major difference. This season the stage has shifted from the major population centers to such small and disparate communities as Kokomo, Ind., Santa Ana, Calif., Cairo, Ill., Middletown, Conn., and Farrell, Pa.

Last September 9 the New York *Times* captioned a picture:

> NEW RIOT PATTERN: Rioting in Hartford, Conn., last week . . . underscored the fact that smaller cities this summer have had more racial trouble than the big ones.

Similar stories appeared about the same time in scores of other newspapers, including the *Wall Street Journal*, the Baltimore *News American*, the Woburn, Mass., *Times*, and the Pittsburgh *Press*.

In fact, racial disorders occurring over the past few years — not just this past summer — have been concentrated in smaller cities. About 75 per cent of all outbreaks recorded in 1968 by the Lemberg

Center's Civil Disorder Clearinghouse occurred outside the 100 largest cities. For the first six months of 1969 and also for the summer no appreciable change in the percentage was noted. Furthermore, many of the cities cited as prototypes of this latest "new pattern" — Hartford and Middletown, Conn., Cario, Ill. — have had disorders in previous years. The difference is that such outbreaks were completely overshadowed by a few enormous outbreaks in large cities such as Newark and Detroit.

Discovering the origin of these and other myths would be useful — a faulty wire service report, an inept reporter, an unreliable source. But aside from the fact that such a task would be almost impossible, it would miss a central point — that the system of reporting ensures that errors of fact and interpretation may be repeated, compounded, and reformulated as myths. In recent years the various components of the media have become extremely intertwined and dependent upon one another. The wire services, the nationally known newspapers, and the newsmagazines feed one another news and information. While the system undoubtedly speeds the flow of news to the public, it has encouraged a parrot-like character in which the various media segments tend to reproduce rather than examine one another's views.

In this respect the New York *Times'* caption proclaiming a NEW PATTERN assumes greater significance. Prior to its appearance in the *Times*, I talked with Jack Rosenthal, who had been working on a story on the relatively cool summer. When the subject of a new "shift" in violence came up I indicated that such allegations were false and misleading. Rosenthal wrote a thoughtful story, dwelling on police-community relations, civic programs, and the new community spirit among blacks. His story made no mention of a "new riot pattern." Apparently the caption writer had paid more attention to what *Newsweek* and the *Wall Street Journal* were saying than to his colleague at the *Times*.

The failure of the media to tell the complete story in the case of Cornell or the right story in the case of Cleveland goes beyond a lack of initiative or an inclination to sensationalize. It also indicates a bias—one which, notwithstanding Vice President Agnew's declarations, cuts *across* political and geographical lines. The media are no more aware of this bias than is the general public aware of its own. In part, we could call it a class bias in that those who comprise media staffs—reporters, editors, headline writers, etc.—are part of the vast American middle class and, as such, express its views, values, and standards.

Both the general public and the media share the same dislike of protestors; both are unable to understand violence as an expression of protest against oppressive conditions; both prefer the myth of orderly, peaceful change, extolling the virtues of private property and public decorum. People are expected to behave in a certain way; they just don't go around yelling and cursing or throwing rocks. Both will grant that it took a revolution to secure our independence and a civil war to end slavery (at least officially), but that was all long ago and somehow different. The bias also has elements of racism in that color is never far from the surface. It is difficult to say where the class bias begins and racist bias ends. These elements are inseparable and reenforce each other, and both manifest themselves in the thinking of the public and media alike.

A growing body of research shows that racial disorders are a part of the social process. The process includes an accumulation of grievances, a series of tension-heightening incidents such as police harassment, and a precipitating event such as an arrest which crystallizes the tensions and grievances that have mounted—the "last straw" that triggers the violence. The "typical rioter" is young, better educated than the average inner-city black, and more dissatisfied. He wants a better job but feels that prospective employers will discriminate against him. He is likely to be a long-term resident of the city. (In a survey in Detroit, 90 per cent of those arrested were from Detroit, 78 per cent lived in the state, and only 1 per cent lived outside the state.) He is extremely proud of

his race and is politically conscious. He is more interested in and informed about politics than blacks who are not involved in a disorder. He is also more inclined toward political activism. (In one survey, nearly 40 per cent of the participants in the disorder—as compared to only about 25 per cent of the nonparticipants—reported having been involved in civil rights activity.) Finally, he receives substantial support from the rest of his community, which does not participate but regards the violence as necessary and beneficial.

As important as the findings in these studies are, they have made virtually no impact on the vast majority of the public. Most Americans continue to believe that violence is caused by a tiny and insignificant minority, that "outside agitators" and "criminal elements" are mainly responsible for isolated outbursts that have little or no social significance. Intellectuals must share a portion of the blame for this situation. Having completed their studies, they have been notoriously reluctant to roll up their academic shirtsleeves and assume leadership in presenting their ideas to the public. There is a trace of condescension in their assumption that good ideas from above will somehow trickle down to the "masses of asses," as one academic I know calls them.

Greater responsibility for the failure to confront the public's resistance rests with the news media. They have failed to commit their power and prestige on behalf of such studies. They have failed to place the ideas before the public and push for reform in an aggressive, effective manner—settling for a splash of headlines and stories initially, and little followup. Instead the media have opted for the status quo, reflecting, sustaining, and perpetuating outworn beliefs of their predominantly white audience.

Historically the notion of plots and conspiracies has always had great currency in this country—and in other countries, too. Prior to the Civil War, Southerners frequently viewed abolitionists as "outside agitators" trying to stir up the happy slaves. Violent interracial clashes during World War I were said to have been instigated by the

MEDIA MYTHS ON VIOLENCE
Terry Ann Knopf

Bolsheviks, and the outbreak in Detroit in 1913 was attributed to an "Axis plot." The current wave of disorders has been blamed on individuals such as Stokely Carmichael and H. Rap Brown or, for those who like a more international flavor, "Communist infiltrators." In a survey of six Northern cities by the Lemberg Center, 77 per cent of all whites interviewed believed that "outside agitators" were a major contributing cause of disorders. When Los Angeles Mayor Sam Yorty recently blamed a rash of school disorders on a conspiracy of the Black Student Union, the Students for a Democratic Society, Communist sympathizers, and the National Council of Churches, he was following a long—though not very honorable—tradition.

Such allegations are usually made without a shred of evidence, except for an occasional "someone told me so." Nevertheless the media have frequently taken their cues from the public in formulating and circulating such reports. Misinterpretations of the events in Cleveland, along with assertions of a "new pattern" of premeditated violence, are blatant examples of this form of bias. But more often the bias is expressed in more subtle ways. For example, when rumors circulated that "outside agitators" were involved in a disturbance in Omaha, Neb., a news story appearing in the Arkansas *Gazette* last June 27 made reference to the rumors but also mentioned that the mayor had no evidence to support such reports. Yet, the headline about the story read: 'OUTSIDERS' LINKED TO OMAHA RIOTING.

A look at the way in which the disorders are written up reveals, tragically, that the majority of the media and the public share essentially the same view of the violence—as meaningless, purposeless, senseless, irrational. Media treatment of the disorders following the assassination of Rev. Martin Luther King, Jr., illustrates the point. The sense of loss and injury among blacks at the time of the assassination was extremely great—

far greater than among whites. The unprecedented wave of disorders—approximately 200—was expressive of the anger, bitterness, resentment, frustration that black people everywhere felt.

How did the media handle the disorders? Stories in just two newspapers analyzed—the Buffalo *News* of April 9, 1968 (the day of Dr. King's funeral), and the Trenton *Times-Advertiser* one day later—are fairly typical. No attempt is made to place the violence in a social context. The reference to the assassination of Dr. King is perfunctory, with only a passing mention of his funeral and a few shouts about his death. Value-laden words receive unusual emphasis. The participants are "marauders," not men; they "rove" instead of run; they move in "gangs," not groups; they engage in "vandalism," not simply violence.

We have all grown so used to viewing blacks as stereotyped criminals that it is difficult to picture them in any other role; hence such frequent press concoctions as "roving gangs," "roving vandals," "roving gangs of rampaging teenagers," or, for variety, "a window-smashing rampage of roving gangs of Negro youths." The New York *Times* assertion last July 1 that "roving bands of ruffians" were involved in a disturbance in Middletown, Conn., seems somewhat feeble by comparison. The effect of such treatment by the media is to pander to the public's prejudice, reenforcing stereotypes, myths, and other outmoded beliefs. The media not only frighten the public but confuse it as well.

And let us not forget the effects on the news media. The proliferation of underground newspapers, radical publications, black journals, as well as underground radio stations on FM bands held by churches and universities, indicates that the media are failing to reach certain groups, and that they still lack sensitivity, sophistication, and skepticism commensurate with their important and strategic position.

Reprinted from Public Opinion Quarterly *(Summer, 1970), pp. 236–45. Used by permission of publisher and author.*

Mass Media and Communication Processes in the Detroit Riot of 1967

BENJAMIN D. SINGER

A GREAT deal has been written in recent years about mass media contributions to urban disturbances. Oberschall has suggested preparticipants in Watts used television to monitor locations for looting and police activity in specific areas;[1] Conot has asserted television coverage helped stimulate potential looters as well as providing locations;[2] various sources have suggested media coverage, particularly television, was important in helping to create a riot culture as well as stimulating the spread of disturbances.[3] Other sources have addressed themselves to the role of interpersonal sources in spreading "the message" of a disturbance.[4]

If, indeed, the mass media, particularly television, provide directions for participating in riots and serve to change the viewer's frame of reference toward riots, making these more acceptable over time through sheer repetition, then they perhaps exert such effects in two ways: (1) between cities, by demonstrating "how" in advance and building expectations that "our city will be next," or "our turn hasn't come yet," etc., and (2) within cities, helping to enlarge a disturbance in progress.

In spite of the interest in this area (and without denying the underlying problems and grievances of the Negro communities involved), very little has been done empirically to gauge the relevance of communication factors in urban riots. Most statements have been polemical in nature, or

observations by journalists; or, as in the case of the Kerner Report, have tried to measure what was presented on television, rather than viewers' reactions. The present analysis focuses on the media and communications behavior of a group of persons arrested during the 1967 Detroit riot. The paper describes their past exposure to riots on television and the process by which they were informed of the Detroit riot prior to their alleged participation.

Between July 31 and August 4, 1967, interviews were conducted in the jails, internment locations, and prisons in Detroit and outlying areas where persons charged with participating in the Detroit riot were being held. The essentially open-ended interview guide concerned itself with socioeconomic chracteristics of the respondent, attitudes toward civil rights, Negro leadership and riots, and "communication" variables—types of mass media exposure and interpersonal communication patterns. The interviewers were Negro males, most with college degrees and some form of interviewing or similar experience. The sample consisted of 499 Negro males who had been distributed in the order of their arrival to detention facilities depending upon available space.

The 499 interviews represented approximately a ten per cent sample of arrested Negro males, who made up the overwhelming majority of those arrested. The distribution of charges levied against

MASS MEDIA AND COMMUNICATION PROCESSES IN THE DETROIT RIOT OF 1967
Benjamin D. Singer

the sample closely approximates that of charges against all males arrested, which is an important test of the representativeness of the sample.[5]

EXPOSURE TO TELEVISED RIOTS

Television, other research has indicated, is the most important mass medium for black America.[6] In our sample, television ranked ahead of newspapers and radio as a medium for finding out about riots in our cities. It is perhaps the most likely way in which individuals acquire their knowledge of leaders, particularly the nationally known militants. The overwhelming majority (approximately 75 per cent) were able to report specific riots they had witnessed on television.

If television is implicated in the disturbances, and particularly the intercity spread, we might ask how it functions in this regard. The kind of stimulus value carried by televised riot sequences depends first on the perceived content; it is, in fact, not the *objective* content as revealed by various content counts but rather the *viewer's definition of the situation* which is critical. We attempted to assess this by asking those arrested, "What were most of the people doing in these race riots (seen on television)?"

Examination of Table 1 reveals that respondents reported approximately 50 per cent of the time

viewing violent acts, including police brutality, arson, throwing rocks, fighting, screaming, killing, shooting, etc. Looting was mentioned only 21 per cent of the time. Thus, the opportunity for material gain was perceived less than half as often as actions presumably more changed with affective content. Respondents characterized past disturbances shown on television as involving violence more often than any other phenomenon; this is particularly significant when compared with the small number (5 per cent) who recalled presumably legitimate attempts by authorities to control crowds.

While there will inevitably be debate concerning the meaning of this finding, we can focus upon its manifest appearance and ask whether the perception of violence, as opposed to property offenses, increases the identification of the viewer with the participants on the screen; we can ask whether the perception of violence suggests a greater intensity and excitement for the potential participant; and we can ask whether the sight of violence, as opposed to, e.g., property crimes, operates more to change norms in the direction of acceptance of riots as justified. While no answer at this point can be definitive, Table 2 provides information concerning the feelings that our respondents reported experiencing while viewing televised riots.

As shown in Table 2, over one quarter felt anger at whites or police or were happy with the attacks shown as directed at whites or white authorities; 49 per cent indicated varying degrees of disturbance at the sight or suggested riots ought not to be televised; only 12 per cent indicated sheer indifference or ambivalence to televised riots. Thus, respondents do appear to indicate a high degree of emotional involvement with television sequences of this nature. This may be more important than the Kerner Commission's report that less than five per cent of scenes broadcast on racial problems or riots for three days before and three days after a riot in a given city were of "actual mob action, or people looting,

TABLE 1

Perceptions of What People Were Doing in Televised Riot Sequences

Perception	Percentage of Responses
Violent acts against persons	49.8%
Looting	21.1
Property destruction	6.5
People running, standing, milling	10.2
Arrests, crowd control	5.2
Peaceful demonstrations, other responses	7.2
Total (some respondents gave more than one answer)	100.0% (650)

TABLE 2

Reaction to Televised Riots

Respondent's Reaction	Percentage of Responses
Disapproval, sadness, disgust or opposed to televising of riots	48.9%
Feels whites responsible, resentment at authorities or community, happy with rioting	26.1
Indifference or ambivalence	12.3
Intellectualizes about cause or prevention of riots	3.1
Has never seen TV riots, don't know, and other	9.8
Total	100.2% (499)

sniping, setting fires or being injured or killed."[7] Television needs to be re-examined with regard to what people perceived and were affected by.

COMMUNICATION PROCESSES IN THE DETROIT RIOT

The preceding section dealt with past television exposure. Presumably such exposure is a factor in what has been described as "riot culture." It would contribute to intercity spread. However, of major importance is the process by which knowledge about the Detroit disturbance was communicated to those charged with participating. First, a brief description of the setting and sequence of the disturbance will be presented.

At 3:45 A.M. on Sunday, July 23, Detroit police conducted a raid on a drinking and gambling club on Twelfth Street which was operating after legal closing time, arresting some 82 persons. Approximately two hundred spectators watched the proceedings, some of whom voiced indignation at the raid. A few minutes after 5 A.M., an empty bottle crashed into one of the police car windows, to be followed by other missiles. Meanwhile, word spread that the police were using excessive force; a few hours later the crowds had swelled to thousands and window smashing and looting

began.[8] At 8 A.M. several radio stations first reported the disturbance[9] and the first television report of it was carried at 2 P.M. According to one news director, "At least one radio station transmitted a voice report of a 'race riot' to its network, which in turn aired it across the country. Some of these early radio reports left the impression that the scene was worse than it really was during the early hours. The reports apparently had less inflammatory effect than they might have because of the relatively small radio audience early Sunday."[10]

The first television announcement was made by CKLW-TV at 2 P.M. "Violence broke out in west side Detroit early this morning when police raided a west side blind pig. A police lieutenant was hit with a rock, and one man was stabbed, as hundreds brawled for five hours." Another station, WXYZ-TV, falsely reported a policeman had been killed and WWJ-TV was reported to have alarmed thousands of persons by falsely reporting an anonymous phone tip to the effect that the rioters were spreading to the suburbs.[11] With time, the TV reports grew more detailed and by 7:30 P.M., CKLW-TV was reporting on shooting, blazing fires, rioters stoning firemen, etc.

When a disturbance begins in a given city, it is enlarged through communication of two kinds: the interpersonal network—a very highly developed network of communications within the black community which operates on a word-of-mouth basis; and the local mass media, initially the broadcast variety. The potential participant is informed by someone else who may know of the disturbance firsthand or because someone else told him or because the mass media informed him; or the participant may have direct or mass media knowledge about the riot. The scheme, in part empirically derived, for categorizing knowledge about the riot, is set forth below:

I. Direct Experience
  1. On the scene
  2. Heard noise from house or other location or saw activity

MASS MEDIA AND COMMUNICATION PROCESSES IN THE DETROIT RIOT OF 1967

Benjamin D. Singer

II. Interpersonal Network
    1. Another individual told him in person
    2. Another individual telephoned him
III. Mass Media
    1. Radio
    2. Television
    *3. Newspapers
    *4. Publicly distributed or placed handbills

The interpersonal network may merely be later links in a chain that begins with either direct experience or the mass media. We do not know how the "other individual" happened to hear of the disturbance; furthermore, various combinations of the three knowledge routes are possible. Since the overwhelming majority of those who were participants in the Detroit disturbance were not present at the assumed precipitating incident (the raid on the blind pig), they heard about the riot through one of several means: direct experience, interpersonal communication, or the mass media. We are now going to examine the data concerning the method or medium by which respondents heard of the riot, the message (what they heard), and the relationship between the specific medium and the kind of message heard.

HOW RESPONDENTS FOUND OUT ABOUT THE RIOT

As Table 3 indicates, the leading channel of information for those arrested was interpersonal communication, with 48 per cent finding out from another person. Following this, 27 per cent found out through some form of direct experience—through being present at the riot scene or hearing the commotion or seeing it from some distance. Broadcasting (mass media) informed another 26 per cent. As indicated earlier, our data do not reveal where the secondary source (interpersonal) received his information, but we must assume that the first stage of the process by which the word "got out" in the community was either direct experience or broadcast media,

*Neither newspapers nor handbills were mentioned by those in our sample.

TABLE 3

Channels through Which Those Arrested Found out about Detroit Riot

Channel	Percentage of Responses
Direct experience	26.9%
Interpersonal: Phone	8.8
Interpersonal: Person	39.0
Radio	16.5
Television	9.0
Total	100.2% (491)

which were nearly equal as a source (27 per cent and 26 per cent respectively). The way in which the news first entered the Negro community is treated as the primary source—and the two channels would be either mass media or direct experience of an individual; from there, interpersonal channels take over with great effect. Table 4 provides data suggesting that the broadcast media were the most important primary source by which the information entered the black community.

The majority of individuals who found out about the riot through broadcast media or telephone then told another person; only 37 per cent of those who heard about the riot from another person told another; and finally, the smallest proportion, 28 per cent of those who were at the scene, then told another. In general, this suggests that the most powerful sources for spreading the news of the riot were the broadcast

TABLE 4

Relationship between Source of Information and whether Arrestee Informs Another Person of Riot

Channel	Percentage Informing Another
Television	51%
Radio	54
Phone	51
Person	37
At scene	28
Total	39% (499)

media if the communication behavior of those arrested was typical of other members of the black community.

WHAT RESPONDENTS HEARD: THE MESSAGE

Table 5 indicates the relative frequency with which different messages were heard. The news that the police had, perhaps unjustly or brutally, raided a blind pig was reported by only 5 per cent of the respondents, and thus it may not have been in general an important motivational element in causing individuals to enter the riot scene; that there were fires and looting were more frequently mentioned. The fact that police were on the scene taking repressive action was mentioned only 5 per cent of the time, as was the fact that a curfew had been established.

TABLE 5

Content of Riot Messages Reported

Message	Percentage of Responses
Riot (general)[a]	17.2%
Riot on 12th Street[b]	52.1
Police actions[c]	5.0
Looting, stealing	15.0
Arson	15.6
Streets blockaded	2.0
Curfew	5.0
Blind Pig raided	5.4
Ideological statement[d]	2.2
No response	1.4
Total (some respondents gave more than one answer)	120.9% (604)

[a] "Riot (general)" is a simple statement that a riot or civil disturbance was in progress, without indicating a location.
[b] "Riot on 12th" includes all statements indicating a location.
[c] "Police action" includes activities by the National Guard; the message usually indicated arrests, shooting, or police brutality.
[d] Ideological statements are those with a further message, often of a polemical nature, such as "Detroit police picking on Negroes again," "The riot has finally come to Detroit," etc.

We can assert, then, if the characteristics of the message reported to us influence the decision to go to the scene, that merely knowledge of a disturbance and its location are sufficient to initiate this action for the majority of individuals arrested, with the general riot statement being next most frequent and the messages concerning looting (presumably an opportunity statement) and arson following in importance.

Each channel or medium has characteristics of its own which may be responsible for the kind of message presented, or, on the other hand, the content of the message as "received" by the audience. Table 6 indicates the content of the message by the source or medium. Although the message in all cases most often referred in general terms to the riot or its location, looting was mentioned more frequently by broadcast media than on any other channel. In addition, the possibly emotion-charged report of the precipitating incident, the blind pig raid, was also mentioned more often by the broadcast media. On the other hand, these media more often mentioned the curfew that had been imposed; this was a subject more rarely mentioned during interpersonal transmissions of news.

Although the cells are small, the data are suggestive. The message in the case of all channels most often refers to the riot location. Interpersonal channels more often than mass media specify the location of the rioting. The broadcast media, on the other hand, focus more on control measures (police taking repressive measures, the establishment of the curfew), on the precipitating incident (the blind pig raid), and on the looting which is occurring.

In any case, the data suggest that the population was already primed as a result of personal experiences in the ghetto and televised prior riots and other media presentations. The focus on the blind pig raid by broadcast media, the curfew warnings and statements about the presence of police did not seem significant, not nearly as much as knowing the location of the "action."

MASS MEDIA AND COMMUNICATION PROCESSES IN THE DETROIT RIOT OF 1967
Benjamin D. Singer

TABLE 6

Messages by Different Media

Message	Radio	Television	Telephone	Person
Riot (general)	11.0%	11.9%	21.8%	18.7%
Riot on Twelfth St.	32.1	22.0	45.5	44.4
Police actions	3.6	10.2	3.6	2.1
Looting, stealing	16.5	18.6	10.9	11.2
Arson	14.7	10.2	12.7	12.4
Streets blockaded	1.8	0.0	1.8	2.1
Curfew	8.3	11.9	1.8	2.9
Blind Pig raided	7.3	11.9	0.0	3.3
Ideological statement	0.9	1.7	0.0	2.9
No response	3.7	1.7	1.8	0.0
Total	100.0%	100.0%	100.0%	100.0%
N (Messages)	109	59	55	241

CONCLUSION

This paper has addressed itself to an area which has not received much research attention— the role of communication factors in riots. The present findings suggest that different media perform different functions. Television appears particularly important at the interurban level, as the most frequently mentioned means by which individuals learned of past riots. A substantial proportion of individuals reported violent aspects of past televised riots (in contradistinction to the implications of the Kerner Commission's findings) and were angry or disturbed by what they had seen; and it seems likely that this affective aspect, along with routine "instructions" on how a riot is conducted *when it arrives*, contributed substantially to the riot readiness of a large number of individuals.

A great deal of emphasis, most of it speculative, has been placed on the diffuse function of television in spreading a disturbance, but it is valuable to distinguish between television as an interurban and an intraurban force. In Detroit, television's pictorial qualities were not particularly important. When a disturbance finally begins in the individual's city, the precipitating incident and its affective connotations appear to be relatively unimportant components of the transmitted message. Just the knowledge that "there's a riot on," and its location, are sufficient to set the final stage for possible participation. At this point in time, interpersonal communication and broadcast media, particularly radio, transmit the message, which need not be elaborate or emotional but merely need inform individuals of the beginning of the riot and its location.

---

[1] Anthony Oberschall, "The Los Angeles Riot of August, 1965," *Social Problems*, Vol. 15, 1968, pp. 322–341.

[2] See Robert Conot, *Rivers of Blood, Years of Darkness*, New York, Bantam, 1967, pp. 97, 226, and 244 concerning the role of the mass media in the Watts disturbance of 1965.

[3] The "technological" aspect of riot culture is penetratingly analyzed by Lee Rainwater in "Open Letter on White Justice and the Riots," *Trans-Action*, Vol. 4, No. 9, September 1967, p. 27. Among the many statements critical of the mass media's role, see Drew Pearson and Jack Anderson, "The Almighty Eye," *New York Post*, April 17, 1968, and Allen C. Brawnfeld, "Television and the Big City Riots," *The American Legion Magazine*, Vol. 83, December 1967, pp. 6–8.

[4] Concerning interpersonal means of communication, Fred Powledge has asserted: "We know that riots occur,

by and large after sudden relatively minor confrontations with persons of authority — the cops. We know that word of these confrontations is often magnified and carried by rumor at high speed through the Negro community. There is probably a better system of internal communications in the ghetto than in the National Guard. During the early hours of a riot, it functions like lightning." "What We Failed to Learn," *New Leader,* August 14, 1967, p. 5.

[5]For further details on the methodology, see B. D. Singer, R. W. Osborn, J. A. Geschwender, *Black Rioters,* Lexington, Mass., D. C. Heath, forthcoming, ch. 1.

[6]Bradley S. Greenberg and Joseph R. Dominick, *Communication among the Urban Poor: Television Usage, Attitudes, and Functions for Low-Income and Middle-Class Teenagers,* Lansing, Michigan State University, Department of Communication, 1968.

[7]*Report of the National Advisory Commission on Civil Disorders,* New York, Bantam, 1968, p. 369.

[8]*Ibid.,* p. 48.

[9]Personal correspondence to Benjamin D. Singer from Robert J. McBride, WJBK-TV, Detroit, March 20, 1968.

[10]*Ibid.*

[11]*Newsweek,* August 14, 1967, p. 78.

B. The Political Uses of the Media

The instruments of mass communication in the modern world have an enormous potential for shaping politics, as we have already seen in the previous section on propaganda. This is particularly obvious in totalitarian countries, in which the media are under direct political control. The uses in our own society are less obvious but are real enough to have caused considerable public concern in recent years. This issue includes political bias and control, the effect of the media on campaigns, and the long range implications for the political system.

Mendelsohn and Crespi give an overview of the problem. They trace the growing use of the media by President Roosevelt and his successors and the changes this has wrought. Personality, "images," and celebrity have replaced political experience, issues, and integrity in the political arena. At the same time, access to the media has spelled political strength. The executive thus has a distinct advantage over the legislative branch, for the President is a personality who can project a single, human image, while Congress is a body of a few hundred disputatious men, many of them unknown to the general public. Personality politics is based on media exposure, hence the escalation of election expenses, the increasing employment of marketing techniques, and the emergence of what Mendelsohn and Crespi call the "pseudo campaign."

The excerpt from Joe McGinniss' book describes from ground level the production of a campaign

"advertisement" in 1968. The guiding forces in Nixon's campaign came from show business, marketing, and public relations. It is clear that the Nixon team was not dealing with deep political ideas, rather they were applying professional advertising skills to the campaign. Of course, this style of campaign is not limited to President Nixon, nor the Republican Party; most candidates for major office use similar techniques of persuasion. In so doing, emphasis falls on images and personality—show business celebrities thus become prime political material—while party platforms and ideologies fade into insignificance.

A related problem arises once the politician is in office. The newsman must often rely on him for his news—the President, of course, can "make news" whenever he pleases—and this puts considerable potential for manipulation in the politician's hands. To a degree all influential personages, elected or not, have this power. If a newsman offends them they will not co-operate with him in the future. A blunt, crusading newsman is likely to become an unemployed one. Hedrick Smith demonstrates this idea in his analysis of Presidential news conferences, which, he finds, are usually very tame affairs. Here we see the nation's top office holder being quizzed by men who must stay in some favor if they wish to pursue their work in Washington or even be called on again for a question. Smith suggests various ways to improve the depth of questioning, but only anonymity of the newsman or bringing in a high status questioner, such as a senator or opposition party leader, is likely to upgrade the conferences appreciably.

The final two selections deal with the complaints made by the executive branch concerning media bias. The issue was raised by Vice President Agnew in November, 1969, during which time he was given extensive news coverage and drew a wide range of responses. Those of Balk and longtime network insider Friendly are two of the most thoughtful replies. Friendly finds crit-icism of the media in order, but for reasons completely opposite from those of Agnew. The issue of concentration in the media is relevant to commercial programming, not to news teams (which after all, must be concentrated in Washington since that's where the government is); and there is too little, not too much news analysis. Balk points out that the media are in fact generally conservative, not radical-liberal as Agnew charged. He acknowledges that broadcasting credibility is indeed questionable but for a very different set of reasons.

Reprinted from Polls, Television and the New Politics *(Scranton, Pa.: Chandler, 1970), pp. 265–93.* © *1970, Chandler Publishing Company. Used by permission.*

Television, Personality Cults and the Pseudo Campaign

HAROLD MENDELSOHN AND IRVING CRESPI

IT IS in the area of building the public's imagery of political leaders and the political process that television's impact on American politics has been felt most strongly. The introduction of the "personality" ingredient into the selection and election (or rejection) of national political candidates begun by F.D.R.'s assiduous use of radio has become a most significant development in our contemporary age of television. . . .

What television accomplishes most effectively is the shaping of the viewers' images of national political figures, both as those figures perform in office and as they project themselves in bidding for office. Thus, television has provided the electorate with a new set of criteria which enable viewers to shape expectations of what an American President should be and help them to make judgments of a particular President as he is. These criteria are not lost upon seekers or holders of high political office. Considerable anxiety about the projection of the "right" television image to the electorate is exhibited by politicians in the knowledge that a "correct" projection can make them successful, while the "wrong" projection can doom them to failure.

The following excerpt from a *New York Times* interview with Mrs. Lyndon B. Johnson touches on the former First Family's concern with the televised public projection of Mr. Johnson's Presidential image:

[Q] Do you think that the news media like radio and television project the President as you see him? You know, some people's personality comes over on television very accurately, others don't.

[A] I do think that he is at his best in a small group of people where he simply talks straight from the heart. There's a pungency and a color and a humor and a force in meetings of that sort, and it may be equally as good in a face-to-face confrontation with a larger group. It is somewhat diluted and restricted when it gets to the mechanics of TV and the great invisible audience. I do not think it is quite as good as face to face. I think it's perhaps because he's used to and likes that bond of looking at people and feeling their response. Nevertheless, I have seen him lots of times on TV when I thought, "That is the real flavor of the man coming through."

[Q] Why at times doesn't that flavor come through?

[A] I simply think that the sheer mechanics and the absence of the audience make it somewhat more difficult for some people. He's a human man and not a machine man.

[Q] Do you think he is somewhat afraid of these machines?

[A] No, not at all. He just is not responsive to them. He responds to humans.[1]

President Johnson's difficulties with mastering the communicative power of the television medium has been underscored by the former Chief Executive himself, and in Eric Goldman's phrase, this failure to take advantage of the medium effectively con-

TELEVISION, PERSONALITY CULTS AND THE PSEUDO CAMPAIGN
Harold Mendelsohn and Irving Crespi

tributed substantially to "the tragedy of Lyndon Johnson."

The capability of television to project relatively unknown politicians into full-blown national figures was first realized as early as 1951 when the hearings of the Senate's Special Committee to Investigate Crime in Interstate Commerce — the so-called Kefauver Committee — were aired on network television. With national television reaching audiences ranging from twenty to thirty million viewers, "Estes Kefauver, as chairman of the committee looking into the activities of organized crime in the United States was raised by the magic eye from the status of just another United States Senator to the very verge of the Presidency, from being an interesting 'comer' from Tennessee to a pinnacle of national popularity and international interest."[2]

Although the televised Kefauver hearings gave viewers some impressions of the extent of criminal activities in the United States, it did not accomplish much in implementing its manifest function — the generation of new crime control legislation. Instead, the hearings fulfilled two quite unexpected latent functions. First, they demonstrated that politics, as viewed in progress on television, can project the necessary dramatic elements for affording entertainment. Second, because viewers can become involved (even though vicariously) in an unfolding political process as it appears to be actually happening, they can experience the same identifications with hero figures and vent the same kinds of emotions against villainous characters as they would in witnessing fictionalized dramas.

Here lies the true political power of television. Whereas the print media can merely describe the results of complex political-legal processes such as United States Senate hearings, testimony, and cross-examination of witnesses, television allows the viewers to literally *see these processes in action.* How the various participants (the actors) in such a process comport themselves soon becomes a measure of the men themselves. These public judgments quickly become crystallized into

psychological sets — composed of sentiments, attitudes, and opinions — the sum total of which emerge as "images." Generally these images or impressions revolve about a man's physical appearance, his poise, assertiveness, determination, reaction to pressure, and all the various complex attributes that go into making up his particular "style." As already stated, when a man's style and role participation match the peculiar exigencies of the television medium he can be launched as a prominent political personality quite literally overnight. This happened in 1964 when an obscure motion-picture actor took to the television air waves several nights before Election Day with an impassioned plea for Californians to cast their ballots for Barry Goldwater. The very next day Ronald Reagan was launched into the political waters that won him the governor's chair in California and then propelled him as a serious contender for the Presidency of the United States in 1968.

, The ability of television to push political personalities into national prominence was realized all too well by Senator Joseph McCarthy when, as Chairman of the Senate Permanent Subcommittee on Investigations, he began what we now commonly refer to as the "Army-McCarthy hearings" on television on April 23, 1954. The Senator's guess that television would provide him with a massive public sounding board was realized on the very first day of the activities when fully 63 percent of all the TV sets in New York City were tuned into the hearings.

What McCarthy did not realize, however, was that both in his personality and in the highly unorthodox manner in which he conducted himself lay the ingredients for the emergence of a highly negative image of the man. . . . The results were disastrous for McCarthy. Instead of emerging as a tough, patriotic, anti-Communist dragon-slayer, McCarthy's image as projected on the television screen, came through as an unshaven, ill-mannered, nasty, unprincipled, brow-beating bully. The Army-McCarthy hearings sounded the

TELEVISION, PERSONALITY CULTS AND THE PSEUDO CAMPAIGN

Harold Mendelsohn and Irving Crespi

political death-knell for Wisconsin's then junior Senator. Laymen and politicians alike experienced their first realization of the boomerang power of television to tear down a political personality. The demonstration in the televised Kefauver hearings of television's build-up power, it was soon realized, told only part of the story.

Wedged in between the 1951 Kefauver hearings and the Army-McCarthy hearings of 1954 was the national Presidential campaign of 1952. Twenty-seven million Americans in that year, from the vantage point of their living-rooms had the opportunity to take an intimate glimpse into the selection of a President from the preconvention primaries right through to the final vote tallies.

As matters finally developed, the 1952 campaign boiled down to a "personality" battle between a revered, simplistic, avuncular, war-hero General and an urbane, intellectual, unknown, divorced Governor of Illinois. Television was the major weapon that was used in this battle. . . .

Just as F.D.R.'s use of radio in political campaigning drastically altered the traditional process of selecting a President, so the new television medium in 1952 rendered unique and lasting changes in this process. . . .

While Stevenson, in 1952, attempted to encourage voters to address themselves to rational considerations of the issues, he only succeeded in pinning the high-brow, "egg-head" label on himself. In contrast, Eisenhower focused least of all on political matters and mostly on his own personal, folksy image by appealing to voters who, as Hyman and Sheatsley point out, "placed less emphasis on ideology and more emphasis on personal qualities in their choice of a candidate."[3]

In a study of what images of the two candidates emerged during the 1952 campaign, Ithiel de Sola Pool concluded that "*both* candidates were regarded as fine and great men by people on *both* sides of the political fence . . . It was not a struggle of good versus evil but of good versus good."[4]

Pool found that the predominant images of Eisenhower held by his supporters as a consequence of exposure to the mass media during the campaign (expressed by over 70 percent of the sample studied) was that the General was good-natured, sincere, honest, cheerful, and clear-headed. Even majorities of the Stevenson supporters (over 50 percent) who were surveyed believed Eisenhower to be likeable and good-natured.

In contrast, over 70 percent of the Stevenson supporters studied considered the Illinois candidate to be clear-headed, sincere, brilliant, likeable, honest, and refined. Eisenhower advocates thought Stevenson to be clear-headed mainly (in over 50 percent of the cases). Thus, where Eisenhower warmed up his previous public image as a tough soldier, Stevenson succeeded in converting himself into a potent *intellectual* political power from a starting point of near anonymity. In 1952—during a period in our history when an alleged "mess in Washington" was supposed to have dominated the national political vista—the times apparently were not such as to warrant the electorate to respond positively to the egg-head approach to politics.

It is important to note here that in the United States in 1952, the mass media, and television in particular, began to focus voters' attention on personalities and away from the issues in national political campaigns, a trend which became most discernible in 1968. From 1952 on, the national political wars were waged on the basis of the very good guys versus just the good guys or versus the bad guys, as the case may be. James Reston noted in *The New York Times* on October 30, 1958, "Instead of the old-fashioned emphasis on what a candidate thinks, or what he says, the emphasis now seems to be on how he looks, especially on television, and on what kind of personality he has."

What radio was for Franklin D. Roosevelt in 1932, television was for John F. Kennedy in 1960. As Theodore White, the chronicler of the 1960 national election observed, television had rendered "a revolution in American presidential politics." By that year nearly nine out of ten American homes (40,000,000, or 88 percent) were equipped with at least one television receiver. The new importance of television as a political device was noted in the expenditures that both parties were to make for national network broadcast time on television—$3,006,100 ($1,900,000 spent by the Republicans, and $1,106,000 by the Democrats). Outlays for national radio network time during the 1960 campaign were to be cut by no less than 75 percent. It was clear that the new Presidential candidate had to be blessed with an abundance of funding as well as with personal appeal.

Mr. Kennedy entered the 1960 Presidential lists with a mixed set of positive attributes and negative handicaps. On the positive side he was youthful, independently wealthy, articulate, physically attractive, and he was bestowed with a personality that was fresh, charming, and free of the stilted politician's posture. In describing his reaction to Senator John F. Kennedy in 1959, Douglas Cater wrote,

> . . . he shows a restraint of manner that is unusual among politicians. Both in public and private conversation he eschews cliché with the contempt of a man for whom words are precise instruments. He does not retreat behind the high wall of pomposity that most politicians erect on occasion to protect themselves from interlopers.[5]

It was clear from the start that John F. Kennedy possessed all the "cool" attributes that television required for projecting a positive image.

On the negative side, Mr. Kennedy's Catholic persuasion and Irish-American background were considered to be definite political handicaps. His opponents would try to turn his youthfulness into an image that denoted "lack of experience," and his Boston Brahminism could be used to identify him with the "privileged classes."

John Kennedy's task was clear in 1960—above all he had to establish himself as a *serious* contender for the Presidency of the United States. He had to convince the electorate that he could and would be a strong Chief Executive. The image he wished the public to develop of him was sketched in early 1960 by Mr. Kennedy himself in an address before

the National Press Club when he suggested that contemporary Americans needed

> . . . a vigorous proponent of the national interest—not a passive broker for conflicting private interests. They demand a man capable of acting as the commander-in-chief of the grand alliance, not merely a bookkeeper who feels that his work is done when the numbers on the balance sheet come out even. They demand that he be head of a responsible party, not rise so far above politics as to be invisible—a man who will formulate and fight for legislative policies, not be a casual bystander to legislative process.

Kennedy accomplished the projection of this image through public encounter with opponents within the Democratic party in the Wisconsin and West Virginia State Primaries; through his appearances before Protestant ministerial and lay groups in which he outlined explicitly his position on the separation of church and state; through his performance at the Democratic Nomination Convention; and, perhaps most importantly of all, through the way he conducted himself during the tradition-breaking Nixon-Kennedy "Great Debates." All this was made available to multitudes of television viewers throughout the land.

Although political observers and researchers alike agreed that neither Mr. Kennedy nor Mr. Nixon "won" the Great Debates in terms of influencing opposition votes, the four televised confrontations accomplished two major objectives. The first was the direct involvement of the electorate once again in an important part of a political process as it actually occurred. Audience measurements tallied the viewership of the first debate at between 70 and 75 million, of the second debate at between 51 and 62 million, of the third at between 48 and 60 million, and the fourth at between 48 and 70 million.

The second over-all effect of the Great Debates was the elevation of John F. Kennedy as a serious Presidential contender in his own right. Democrats became convinced that with Mr. Kennedy as their standard bearer the possibility of a November

TELEVISION, PERSONALITY CULTS AND THE PSEUDO CAMPAIGN

Harold Mendelsohn and Irving Crespi

victory was real. Republicans came to the realization that they indeed had a tough battle on their hands. That the debates helped to crystallize allegiances in J.F.K.'s own party was evidenced after the first encounter with Nixon on September 26, 1960. The very next day the "Ten Southern Democratic governors" relayed a telegraphed message to Mr. Kennedy proclaiming, "We the undersigned Governors . . . wish to congratulate you on your superb handling of Mr. Nixon and the issues facing our country. It is the consensus of the Governors . . . that the masterful way in which you controlled this debate further accelerates the movement to the Kennedy-Johnson and Democratic ticket." How many heretofore "undecided" Democratic voters left their television sets that night with the same feeling is unknown.

In a November 5, 1960 *Nation* article titled "Asking for a Job," Alan Harington summed up the broad impacts of the Great Debate encounters on voters' assessments as primarily those of the candidates' projected television personalities:

> . . . A political speech made before an admiring audience that will surely applaud the candidate, or a cozy chat issuing from his library, has never given us an approximation of the whole man. Now thanks to the Kennedy-Nixon TV confrontations, we are appreciably closer to the valid, intuitive "take," the wholly human—even though sometimes mistaken—feeling we have about someone whom we are going to accept or reject for a job.

After his elevation to the Presidency, Kennedy used the device of the televised, "spontaneous" press conference to reach the people directly, much as Franklin Roosevelt used radio to accomplish similar purposes through his fireside chats. The new President's charisma, developed in his televised precampaign and campaign performances, accompanied him into the White House. It was estimated that some 65 million people viewed President Kennedy's first televised news conference.

The televised news conferences helped to reinforce the charismatic attributes that previously were merely in embryo. Suddenly television brought forth an exciting new star in the nation's political firmament. The cult of the Kennedy personality was developing through the unprecedented attention that the mass media was giving both to the President and to members of his family. . . .

Television had presented America with a new genuine political hero. The power of this new personality was used once again to strengthen the office of the President, to weaken traditional party encumbrances, and to promote the officeholder's own programs and aspirations.

In its ability to create in its audience the illusion of involvement through what Horton and Wohl term "para-social interaction," televised presentations of President Kennedy seemed to create more and more public curiosity about the man as more and more was written and broadcast about him. Although neither the media nor the public seemed to be sated with the abundant coverage that Mr. Kennedy was accorded, a certain degree of alarm began to be voiced regarding the "dangerous" precedent that was being set. It was argued that overemphasis on the "trivia" of the President's life might very well divert the public from the pursuit of the "serious" aspects of politics. . . .

In our own time, then, television has created new political experiences for the electorate which are not fully understood. Because these experiences are emotional rather than purely cognitive they have powerful impact upon the election process, particularly in the selection of candidates for national office. As the voter is embroiled in the daily unfolding of the political process on the TV screen, he develops over time his own subjective, private percepts of the process and of its participants. The development of these percepts occurs quite imperceptibly and unconsciously. In McLuhan's words, "Everybody experiences far more than he understands. Yet, it is experience rather than understanding that influences behavior."

The television build-up of political personalities is the major new mass-communications effect upon contemporary politics in our time. As yet we have not been able to measure what this will do to our future political lives. Mendelsohn has attempted several speculations:

> . . . we should [now] expect a new breed of politicians. They will not necessarily be a bunch of well-poised, good-looking, vacuous types, as some observers have conjectured; nor will it be impossible for an ugly man to become President, as some have warned. The recent emergence of Hollywood actors on the political scene reflects a rather crude temporary response to the demands of television in contemporary politics. Rather, we can expect the new generation of politicians to respond to the "low intensity" demands of the TV medium in order to procure the greatest possible degree of viewer involvement well before the national conventions are convened officially. Regardless, then, of whether they fit the Cary Grant or the Anthony Quinn pattern, the professionals of tomorrow must project a "cool" image.
>
> This image will be cultivated and polished over considerable periods of time—during which every opportunity for television exposure will be exploited. Testing grounds for developing this particular sort of imagery will be young audiences who . . . are peculiarly sensitive to the televised mode of political communication.[6]

Between the appearances of *The Making of the President 1960* and *The Making of the President 1964*, a political event of the gravest tragic importance occurred—the assassination of President John F. Kennedy. No American can forget the incredible experience of an entire nation participating in this disastrous event through a medium of mass communication—television. Reports published by the Nielsen Audimeter Service, a television audience measurement service, revealed that in New York City, which comprises 10 percent of all the television households in America, 70 percent of the television households had tuned in to view the arrival of the late President's body at Andrews Air Force Base in Washington, D.C. on the night of his murder, Friday, November 22, 1963. Throughout the next day, Saturday, November 23, estimates indicate that nearly 50 percent of all the households in

the United States had their television receivers tuned in, marathon fashion, for nearly twelve hours. On Sunday, November 24, during the ceremonies in the Capitol Rotunda, it is estimated that 85 percent of all the TV homes in the United States were tuned in, and on the following day, Monday, November 25th, an unbelievable 93 percent of all television households in the United States—representing more than 100 million persons—became witness to the funeral and burial services for President Kennedy via television.

Television's ability to involve the nation in near-total, psuedo participation in a calamitous national political event was demonstrated as it had never been before. Theodore White noted two important consequences of this psuedo participation by the American people:

> The political result of this participation, of this national lament, was a psychological event which no practical politician will ever be able to ignore. Out of it began the Kennedy myth and the Kennedy legend . . .
>
> Beyond the beginning of the myth one must stress another political result . . . By concealing nothing; by sharing all; by being visible when their private natures must have craved privacy, Jacqueline Kennedy first above all, then the grief-stricken Kennedy family, then the new President permitted television to give strength and participation to the citizens.[7]

Well before the 1964 national election, then, it was clear that the personalities of a popular, martyred President and his successor, as projected primarily through television coverage of the assassination, would play significant roles in the contest that was to occur a year later.

In assuming the Presidency upon Mr. Kennedy's death, Lyndon B. Johnson afforded the nation the essential reassurance that no doubt played a critical part in his 1964 victory. First of all, by virtue of the quiet, steadfast manner in which he took the reins of government, he demonstrated both ability and stability at a time when such traits were critically necessary to the tranquility

TELEVISION, PERSONALITY CULTS AND THE PSEUDO CAMPAIGN
Harold Mendelsohn and Irving Crespi

of a nation that had experienced a brutal sense of
loss, despair, and anxiety. Theodore White
writes,

> There is no word less than superb to describe the
> performance of Lyndon Baines Johnson as he became
> President of the United States [upon the death of
> President Kennedy].
>   All the accounts of his behavior through the week of
> the tragedy—his calm, his command presence, his
> doings, his unlimited energies—endow him with
> superlative grace. Yet such stories limit the tale only
> to his positive deeds. To measure the true quality of
> his take-over, one must consider not only these
> positive acts, but what did *not* happen. So much
> might have gone wrong—yet did not.[8]

Second, President Johnson, during the period in
which he assumed the Presidency in 1963, did
nothing to abrogate the Kennedy legend that was
emerging and becoming full-blown with unsur-
passed rapidity and over-all public acceptance.
Johnson indeed pledged to continue the Kennedy
orientation to politics, and in actuality both
exploited and reinforced the legend simultaneously.

Against this backdrop, the Republican party in
1964 presented the junior Senator from Arizona,
Barry Goldwater, for consideration by the
American electorate. From the very moment of
his nomination, Mr. Goldwater suffered a severe
image problem with the voters—a problem which
stemmed primarily from the personality of the
man plus the rigid ideological stance he assumed.
This image was both projected and reinforced in
rather negative terms throughout the 1964 Presidential campaign by television and the other media
of mass communication.

Goldwater used rough-house tactics at the
Republican National Convention in 1964. He
obstinately refused to accommodate to the Party's
moderates. This refusal was reinforced by the
capstone pronouncement in his acceptance
speech—"Extremism in the defense of liberty
is no vice . . . Moderation in the pursuit of

justice is no virtue!" He suggested the possible use
of low yield nuclear weapons in Vietnam. He
questioned social security funding. And he publicly
mused about the possible sale of the Tennessee
Valley Authority. All of these factors served to
fashion an image of the Republican candidate as
a hard-nosed, irresponsible, trigger-happy,
calloused, militaristic, anti-civil-rights politician who
represented a dangerous threat to all that the
legendary John F. Kennedy had sacrificed his life
for.

Where Johnson offered continuity in the tradition of Kennedy, Goldwater presented the
possibility of an abrupt and explicit break with
that tradition. Where Johnson offered social
progress in the Kennedy manner, Goldwater
offered what appeared to be a regression from
Kennedy's social concerns. Where Johnson offered
an image of reassurance, ability, and stability,
Goldwater offered untried ideology, radical change,
and a seemingly careless and casual approach to
government that conflicted sharply with the
Kennedy style.

Nor did the rather massive television campaign
launched by the Goldwater forces seem to be able
to rescue what was rapidly solidifying into a
disastrous image for the Arizonan. (The Republicans are estimated to have spent $12,800,000
for national radio-TV time in 1964 as compared to
$5,100,000 expended by the Democrats.) Although
five major television network half-hour programs
designed to project the Goldwater image in more
favorable terms were presented during October
and on Election Eve, 1964, the largest number of
viewers attracted to any one of these offerings
never topped the 7 million mark. Contrast this
to the estimated 100 million viewers who witnessed
the Kennedy-Nixon debates just four short years
before.

The utilization of television in the 1964
campaigns once again drove home the risks that
are involved in "hotting up" the medium with
political ideologies and with the old fashioned
images of the so-called conservative brand of

TELEVISION, PERSONALITY CULTS AND THE PSEUDO CAMPAIGN

Harold Mendelsohn and Irving Crespi

politics (for example, explicit super-patriotism). The 1964 campaigns also pointed up television's inability to project a favorable image of a candidate whose disfavor with the electorate had become hard reality by virtue of the man himself and his rigid adherence to his stand. As Theodore White put it, "The fundamental Goldwater problem was himself."

Even before convention time in 1964, a top aide to Barry Goldwater, Richard Kleindienst, commented on the Senator's reluctance to place himself completely in the hands of the image-makers, even though it appeared that his candidacy might have benefited substantially from doing so:

> The advertising people just love to get their hands on a guy like this. They treat him like a block of wood, cutting him into the shape they want. Barry just won't put up with that. If it means losing the nomination because he won't adopt the image they want, then he'll lose.[9]

What Goldwater appeared to be saying to the electorate in 1964 was, "If you don't like me the way I am, to hell with you." By the time 1968 rolled around, Richard Nixon in effect was promising the American voter, "If you don't like me the way I am, I'll change."

The lessons of 1964 were not ignored as 1968 began. Enmeshed in the complex events relating to America's participation in its most unpopular foreign war and to its internal upheavals, and overwhelmed by his admitted difficulties in turning the image-building, sustaining power of television to communicate with the electorate effectively, the hero of 1963-1964 became the villain of 1968. Rather than risking a Goldwater-like humiliation at the polls, President Johnson withdrew voluntarily from the 1968 Presidential race. It can be said perhaps that in 1968, the "fundamental Johnson problem was himself."

Richard Nixon was far more optimistic about overcoming his particular image. Burdened by past allegations of opportunism, of conservatism (and even reactionary orientations), of allegiance to the special interests of Wall Street, of a propensity to "shoot from the hip," and by his actual record as a political "loser," Mr. Nixon unabashedly and straightforwardly presented himself to the American electorate in 1968 as "the new Nixon." The new Nixon image was to be projected primarily through the medium of television, the instrumentality by which the 1968 Republican candidate had in the past experienced both his greatest triumph—the famous "Checkers" performances—as well as his deepest humiliation— the "Great Debates" against John F. Kennedy.

Nixon's effort to put across the new Nixon together with the poignant attempt of his opponent, Hubert Humphrey, to convince the electorate that the latter was indeed "his own man," both efforts primarily taking place via the television route, ushered in a new and strangely frightening development in American politics— the pseudo campaign.

TELEVISION AND THE EMERGENCE OF THE PSEUDO CAMPAIGN

On the national level, with the advent of television as a major means of political communication came a ritualistic, stylized orientation to national political campaigning, the product of which looks like the genuine, honest-to-goodness, real thing, but in essence is not. The psuedo campaign as presented by television merely simulates political reality, but it is as far from the real thing as the girl in the Revlon ad is from the bucolic young creature next door.

In the psuedo campaign candidates appear to be chosen by explicitly observable democratic processes of selection taking place before the television cameras on the floors of the conventions, when in actuality all the selective action takes place behind closed doors, where the cameras are barred. The campaign trail looks as if the candidates are addressing themselves to vital issues of the day in every nook and cranny of the land, but, in fact, most of those pathways are carefully

TELEVISION, PERSONALITY CULTS AND THE PSEUDO CAMPAIGN
Harold Mendelsohn and Irving Crespi

prearranged and are "coordinated" to the demands of nighttime television news shows whose deployment of equipment and reporters dictate to a large degree where a candidate goes and when he will appear. Additionally, what the candidate says must be carefully tailored to fit the cleverly captioned three-minute "lead story" that can be easily inserted into those very same news programs. The spontaneous reaction of the crowd is the lifeblood of actual campaigning, and in the psuedo campaign the crowds are paraded before the television cameras with their "spontaneous" reactions properly cued in to be filmed. The psuedo campaign thrives on the visual "body count" because, if the candidates themselves appear dull and uninteresting, at least the "crowd" can be made to appear visually stimulating. Instead of spending substantial amounts of time in solely elucidating the issues involved, the positions taken, and the specific actions they intend to put in motion after Inauguration Day, candidates are compressed into ten-, twenty-, thirty-, and sixty-second commercials that hawk their attributes much as if they were frozen fruit pies. . . .
The overwhelming demands of television for individuals skilled in its use and application in entertainment, news, and particularly in the mass-persuasion process has introduced a new breed—The "campaign strategists"—into the political process in the United States. The new campaign strategist is generally a man versed in the arts of advertising and public relations. He usually has some knowledge of the structures and functions of the mass media; is generally an amateur psychologist dabbling in the intricacies of individual "motivations" and mass behavior. He is familiar with the techniques of show business; has vague insights into the workings of public-opinion polls and into some of the grosser aspects of sociological research; and, above all, is not embarrassed to be cast in the role of an overt manipulator (or aspiring manipulator) of public opinion on behalf of paying clients who are determined to win an election. More often than

not all these attributes do not reside within one man, but are found to be distributed with more or less abundance among the bevy of campaign management and consulting firms that has sprung up with amazing proliferation throughout the nation during the past two decades. . . .
By 1964 the resort to television commercials as campaign instrumentalities had escalated to major proportions. Theodore White reports in his coverage of that campaign that throughout the year 1964 fully 29,300 TV commercials on behalf of candidates were repeated over and over again as were some 63,000 on-air radio commercials. These figues contrast sharply with the 9,000 political commercials that were repeatedly telecast and the 29,000 spots that were broadcast over radio throughout the year 1960.
In order to mount campaigns of such magnitudes, Presidential campaigners have begun to rely more and more heavily upon the resources, know-how, and counsel of professional advertising and counseling agencies. Thus, for example, some sixty professional advertising men from a large variety of agencies such as J. Walter Thompson; William Esty Company; Ketchum, McLeod and Grove; Young and Rubicam; Ted Bates and Company, under the overall management and administrative supervision of Fuller and Smith and Ross serviced the advertising needs of the 1968 Republican Presidential contenders. The switching of agencies in midstream by the 1968 Democratic ticket made front page news in the advertising media trade press in October of that year. The Humphrey-Muskie account was moved from Doyle, Dane, and Bernbach and was set up in a newly formed operation, Campaign Planners Associates, an offshoot of Lennen and Newell. An estimated twenty-five professionals serviced the account at Campaign Planners Associates.
In actuality, advertising agencies afford political campaigns a variety of prosaic services that are concerned mostly with the purchase of advertising time on the electronic media and space in print. The "brains" and "creative" influences for the

TELEVISION, PERSONALITY CULTS AND THE PSEUDO CAMPAIGN

Harold Mendelsohn and Irving Crespi

actual advertising strategies and content are provided by specialists who may or may not be employed by a standard advertising agency. In a lead article in *The New York Times Magazine* of October 13, 1968, titled "Joe Napolitan Packages Candidates: Selling the Product Named Hubert Humphrey," Thomas J. Fleming explains the set-up for the Democratic national candidacies:

> Joseph Napolitan is the former public-relations partner of Larry O'Brien, whom Hubert Humphrey installed as head of the Democratic National Committee after the Chicago convention. O'Brien, the man behind Humphrey's successful nomination drive, and the political engineer of the Kennedy 1960 victory and the Johnson 1964 triumph, had Napolitan on the job within a week, installed in an office next to his own at National Committee headquarters in Washington. Doyle, Dane Bernbach were out the door a week later.
>
> . . . To fire it some nine weeks before Election Day with the Nixon radio and television campaign already achieving a steam-roller impact would seem at first either an act of high courage or sheer madness on Joseph Napolitan's part.

Napolitan is quoted as proclaiming "I am the only one ordering stuff. Campaign Planners are mostly just buying time."

Backing up Napolitan were so-called creative units among which were such groups and individuals as Tony Schwartz, described by Fleming as the "American advertising world's acknowledged King of sound . . . a disciple of Marshall McLuhan"; Vision Associates, film producers; Harry Muheim, a television-film writer; and Shelby Storck, a producer of motion pictures.

One recent political outcropping worth mentioning here is the full-blown emergence of campaign news as reported assiduously in the trade press of both the advertising and the media industries. To the advertising and media fraternities Presidential campaigns represent substantial business, both in terms of actual cash and attendant prestige value. The contemporary student of the new politics would do well to refer himself to such sources as *Advertising Age* and *Broadcasting* during the course of Presidential campaigns along with the more orthodox *New York Times* (do not by-pass the daily advertising and television columns) and the *Wall Street Journal*.

Preliminary figures released by the Federal Communications Commission on January 2, 1969, reveal that in 1968 the Republicans spent an estimated $2.5 million on television commerical announcements, and the Democrats spent $844,313 for *national network "spot" time alone*. These figures are a bare minimal estimate since they do not include monies spent on behalf of national candidates by various business interests, labor unions, and the like. They exclude expenditures to local television that is not affiliated with any of the three national networks. And these figures do not include expenditures for talent, production, and placement on television by advertising agencies (costs for the production of one sixty-second commercial alone average about $20,000). Similarly excluded from these estimates are expenditures for radio commercials and print advertisements on behalf of the candidates.[10]

The same FCC report indicated that the 1968 expenditures for all *political advertising time on national network television* alone reached an unprecedented high of $5 million on behalf of the Republican national ticket and $3 million on behalf of the Democratic national ticket. Again, these estimates represent a bare minimum for the reasons cited. Ed Dowling, writing in the November 30, 1968 issue of *The New Republic*, put the estimates for televised political advertising into a more realistic perspective when he noted, "According to one informed estimate, Nixon spent $10.5 million on TV this fall; Humphrey, $9 million; and the grand total for all political spending is put at $67.5 million."

Harry S. Ashmore supports Dowling's estimate of television expenditures by the national candidates in 1968:

> For the relatively brief period of the general election campaign Richard Nixon mounted the most expensive

TELEVISION, PERSONALITY CULTS AND THE PSEUDO CAMPAIGN

Harold Mendelsohn and Irving Crespi

effort in history—one that ran well over twenty million dollars, with more than half of it going directly into television and most of the remainder devoted to co-ordinated management and sales techniques geared to the TV campaign. During the eight weeks preceeding the election, the Washington Post calculated, Mr. Nixon's candidacy involved a dollar outlay far exceeding that for the leading commercial TV offering, Chevrolet, which spent only thirty million dollars during all of 1967. Mr. Nixon's agency even signed him on (along with Coca-Cola, Schlitz, Goodyear, Ford, Texaco, Pan American, and Reynolds Metals) as a sponsor of the broadcasts of the Olympic Games from Mexico City.

With the last minute surge of contributions that followed his spectacular rise in the public opinion polls Hubert Humphrey pushed his television spending up into the Nixon range. George Wallace came in for an officially recorded campaign expenditure of 4.7 million.[11]

On September 3, 1969, The Federal Communications Commission issued its final report on radio-television expenditures during the 1968 general elections. As usual, the data related reported expenditures for air time alone. Also, the figures are confusing due to the fact that different bases are used for their various computations.

If we take into account all the money that was reported to have been spent to purchase both television and radio time on behalf of all gubernatorial, senatorial, and Presidential races during the entire year of 1968 (including the primaries) we arrive at a grand total of $58,900,000. This is up $24,300,000 from the 1964 grand total of $34,600,000. The expenditures for television air time alone during the general election of 1968 on behalf of all gubernatorial, senatorial, and Presidential candidates equalled $27,087,027 as compared with the total of $17,496,405 that was reported in 1964 and the $6,635,946 total in 1956. Here, Republicans are reported to have spent $15,182,298 for television air time on behalf of all their gubernatorial, senatorial, and

Presidential candidates; Democrats, $10,423,517; and the American Independent Party, $1,481,212.

Now if we look at the total amount of money spent for both radio and television air time for the major Presidential tickets alone we see that the Republicans spent $12,129,082; the Democrats, $5,965,474; and the American Independent Party, $1,697,765.

To many and, very importantly, to those in the advertising-campaign management world, the outcome of the 1968 national election was simply a matter of which advertising giant outspent the other. *Advertising Age*, a major trade paper in the advertising business, noted on February 20, 1969:

> How did Richard Nixon win the Presidency? Partly. at least, because he outspent the competition in advertising. The extent to which that was true was again pointed up today with the Television Bureau of Advertising's release of 1968's biggest clients in network tv. Nestled among the top 100, in 79th place, between Schlitz Brewing Co. and Monsanto is United Citizens for Nixon-Agnew with an estimated net time and talent budget of $3,922,600. In addition, $175,000 was reported by the Nixon for President Committee.
>
> Hubert Humphrey, the Democratic runnerup, was in 109th place, bracketed between Sperry Rand Corp. and and Standard Oil Co. of New Jersey. His budget: $2,826,000.
>
> Third party hopeful George Wallace didn't even make the first 200. He ranked 227th with an appropriation of $701,600. New York's Governor Nelson Rockefeller never reached the Presidential starting gate in the campaign, but he was third in terms of network TV dollars spent. An outlay of $852,800 placed him No. 210 in the ranking.
>
> Spending for other politicos in network TV: Citizens for (Sen. Eugene) McCarthy, $141,000; Citizens for (Gov. Ronald) Reagan, $45,000.

Small wonder, then, that, as Robert MacNeil points out, "Broadcasters are quite happy with the trend. Short spots keep the politicians happy, do not annoy audiences by interrupting their entertainment, and make money."[12]

Whether or not televised political commercials actually affect the voter directly in terms of altering his choices is open to question—a question to which serious researchers have yet to address themselves.

Political television advertising has certainly demeaned the Presidential campaign so that only remnants of dignity are visible any longer. Under these circumstances candidates become de-humanized and are considered to be "products" suitable for clever "packaging" and "merchan-dizing."[13] Carroll Newton, long-time Republican campaign strategist, has put forth the basic formula for marketing the Presidential candidate: (1) through testing and research develop various appealing aspects of the "product"; (2) determine through motivation and attitude research what voters like and dislike about it; and (3) develop mass communications strategies and tactics which emphasize what is liked, and either change or play down what is reacted to unfavorably.[14]

There is no quarrel that such tactics may indeed be suitable for the marketing of the numerous commodities and services that are considered to be vital to the economy of the United States. After all, there is very little consequence (other than to the advertisers) if we reach for the shiny red package rather than the equally shiny green one at the local supermarket.

But what happens when contenders for the highest office in the land are handled similarly? Are not our sensitivities regarding the significance of that office dulled by such exposure? Are not our expectations of the qualities a man needs to fill that office properly distorted and truncated? Is not our reaction to exposure to thousands upon thousands of paid political commercials and other fare similarly contrived one that leaves us with the impression that we are being fully and realistically informed when in essence we are not at all being made truly knowledgeable about the persons, issues, and events that literally have the poten-tiality of destroying us?

Writing in the *TV Guide* of October 22, 1966, Arthur Schlesinger Jr. sounded this ominous warning:

> This development can only have the worst possible effect in degrading the level and character of our political discourse. If it continues, the result will be the vulgarization of issues, the exaltation of the im-mediately ingratiating personality and, in general, an orgy of electronic demagoguery. You cannot merchandise candidates like soap and hope to preserve a rational democracy.

Mr. Schlesinger is not alone in recognizing the hazards that are posed by the contemporary trend in political advertising. Advertising men themselves are becoming alarmed. Addressing the Chicago Advertising Club on October 29, 1968, Don Nathanson, president of North Advertising Agency (which was involved in Adlai Stevenson's Presidential trials) appealed to his colleagues in advertising to "join in working diligently to make sure that evil men do not rise to power on the power of a broadcast . . . We need," he added, "advertising agencies of high moral purpose who will shun becoming accomplices of a man with evil intent."

Again, it must be pointed out that it is not our purpose to develop a conspiratorial theory of political communications here. It is profoundly difficult, if not entirely impossible, to put the blame for this state of affairs at the feet of any specific individuals, groups, or institutions. In contemporary politics it is sufficient to note that the television medium has indeed displaced the message, and that, as a consequence, we have entered into a new, bewildering, and perhaps even threatening phase of politics.

Today's television fare is made up of heavy doses of entertainment intertwined with smaller doses of news and advertising. In tune with the demands of TV's realistic entertainment demands, political campaigning is becoming more and more "enter-taining" as the years go by. In all aspects of the contemporary national campaign can be found a

TELEVISION, PERSONALITY CULTS AND THE PSEUDO CAMPAIGN
Harold Mendelsohn and Irving Crespi

definite "show biz" flavor. Candidates make brief "personal appearances" as guest stars on popular entertainment programs; news coverage of their activities are heavily flavored with entertainment values; and, when possible, candidates perform as feature stars of their own shows. This turn of events has, for one thing, "made drama critics out of political writers," according to Harry S. Ashmore.

On the critical night before Election Day, 1968, the voters of America were given the opportunity of viewing either the Humphrey-Muskie spectacular on the ABC network or the Nixon special (Spiro T. Agnew, the controversial Republican vice-presidential contender, was conspicuously absent from the proceedings) on the NBC network.

The Humphrey-Muskie show was considerably more earthy than was the restrained and more "dignified" (in other words, dull) Nixon opus. More than forty show-business celebrities encircled the beaming Democratic candidates—among whom were such notables as Buddy Hackett, Johnny Carson, Paul Newman, Bill Cosby, and Nancy Sinatra. Both Democratic candidates exchanged meaningless pleasantries and gags with the show people in a last desperate appeal to the American electorate. In contrast, the Nixon special placed heavy emphasis on wholesomeness, and, instead of the usual show business accoutrements that signify big-time television variety entertainment, Mr. Nixon was surrounded by attractive girl-next-door type young ladies (including the two Nixon daughters). Questions that were phoned in from viewers were delicately relayed to the candidate by an admiring, reverent, and equally wholesome former football coach.

All candidates featured on the two televised marathons on Election Eve were attempting to project the imagery of "regular guys"—likeable, oriented to youth, and men of humor. Nixon's appeal was directed to the sedate middle majority whom he had labelled as having been "forgotten." Humphrey and Muskie were making a blatantly

apparent pitch to the McCarthy hold-outs and to the Wallace defectors with their down-to-earth, "contemporary" orientation. To the discerning observer, both shows resembled exercises in the theatre of the absurd.

Rather than gaining specific information in depth regarding the candidates' policies and plans directly from the candidates during the few remaining hours prior to Election Day, American voters were offered a heavy tray of entertainment-laden goodies—all looking attractive and sugary, filled with what advertising men refer to as "appetite appeal" and "beauty footage"—but received very little in the way of real nourishment. Once again, it is highly unlikely that much direct influence upon the voters occurred that evening. There is very little doubt, however, that the traditional, libertarian democratic process which rests upon the public's need for meaningful enlightenment rather than upon diverting amusement was not enhanced in any manner on Election Eve, 1968.

Robert Lewis Shayon's pertinent though melancholy observations serve as a serious admonition to us all:

> The comic and the candidate mixing fun and issues in a sort of Hellzapoppin, symbolized the leading edge of the love affair between TV and politics that steadily grows hotter every four years. Where are we heading?
> . . . Certainly we have not yet attained the apogee of the show biz-politics orbit. Some people worry about demagogues with huge budgets and Madison Avenue savvy winning Presidential power in the future. The worriers suggest voluntary advertising agency-network-party guidelines for a more honest pattern of TV campaigning. But as TV pulls the candidates nearer to voters, the candidates tend to draw back from close scrutiny, and to place symbols of themselves between the voters and the real men. The sad prospect is more manipulation and less restraint.[15]

Unless the current trend is checked, we can expect more and more that the new politics will exploit the voters' penchants for seeking pleasure rather than "work" from their communications environment. By providing ever-increasing amusement and ever-decreasing information, the "game of politics" as it has come to be played in the United States today may become a deadly one.

This state of affairs poses an awesome ethical question for American democracy. We know that the voter need not be appealed to cognitively; and we know he does not behave in a purely cognitive, rational manner as far as politics go. In fact, there is considerable evidence that indicates that noncognitive, emotional appeals serve far more effectively in predisposing voters to a particular partisan posture. Given this knowledge, do candidates, campaign managers, party workers, and media executives use the nonrational techniques of mass persuasion that are readily available for the benefit mostly of the candidates, or do they pursue the less effective, but seemingly more responsible course of appealing to the voter in his role as Homo sapiens?

[1] H. Brandon, "A Talk With the First Lady," *New York Times Magazine* (September 10, 1967), p. 160.

[2] B. Rubin, *Political Television* (Belmont, California: Wadsworth Publishing Co. Inc., 1967).

[3] H. Hyman, and P. B. Sheatsley, "The Political Appeal of President Eisenhower," *Public Opinion Quarterly* (Winter 1953–54), p. 459.

[4] Ithiel de Sola Pool, "TV, a New Dimension in Politics," in E. Burdick and A. J. Brodbeck, eds., *American Voting Behavior* (Glencoe: Free Press, 1957), p. 248.

[5] Douglas Cater, "The Cool Eye of John F. Kennedy," *The Reporter* (December 10, 1959), p. 27.

[6] Harold Mendelsohn, "TV and Youth: A New Style for Politics," *The Nation* (June 6, 1966), p. 671.

[7] Theodore H. White, *The Making of the President 1964* (New York: Signet Books, 1966), p. 25.

[8] *Ibid.*, p. 45.

[9] Quoted in Robert MacNeil, *The People Machine: The Influence of Television on American Politics* (New York: Harper and Row, Publishers, 1968), p. 204.

[10] The FCC revealed that some $700,000 was expended for the purchase of national network television time alone on behalf of the George Wallace candidacy, but the Commission's report did not break down this figure in terms of expenditures for network commercials. Under present circumstances relating to disclosure of campaign expenditures it is impossible to derive accurate tallies of actual costs for any candidate.

[11] Harry S. Ashmore, "Electoral Reform: What Can Be Done When Everybody Loses?" *The Center Magazine* (Santa Barbara, California: a publication of The Center for the Study of Democratic Institutions, January, 1969), p. 6.

[12] MacNeil, *op. cit.*, p. 195.

[13] The speculation that candidates in the 1968 Presidential election were being "merchandised" has been given sound substance by Joe McGinniss in his well-documented book, *The Selling of the President 1968* (New York: Trident Press, 1969). [See the selection which follows — Ed.]

[14] MacNeil, *loc. cit.*, p. 197.

[15] Robert Lewis Shayon, "The Show-Biz-Politics Scene," *Saturday Review* (December 7, 1968), p. 61.

Reprinted from The Selling of the President, 1968 *(New York: Trident Press, 1969), pp. 62–72, by permission of Trident Press,*
a division of Simon & Schuster, Inc. Copyright © 1969 by Joemac Inc.

The Antiseptic Campaign

JOE MC GINNISS

ｌAM not going to barricade myself into a television studio and make this an antiseptic campaign," Richard Nixon said at a press conference a few days after his nomination.

Then he went to Chicago to open his fall campaign. The whole day was built around a television show. Even when ten thousand people stood in front of his hotel and screamed for him to greet them, he stayed locked up in his room, resting for the show.

Chicago was the site of the first ten programs that Nixon would do in states ranging from Massachusetts to Texas. The idea was to have him in the middle of a group of people, answering questions live. Shakespeare and Treleaven had developed the idea through the primaries and now had it sharpened to a point. Each show would run one hour. It would be live to provide suspense; there would be a studio audience to cheer Nixon's answers and make it seem to home viewers that enthusiasm for his candidacy was all but uncontrollable; and there would be an effort to achieve a conversational tone that would penetrate Nixon's stuffiness and drive out the displeasure he often seemed to feel when surrounded by other human beings instead of Bureau of the Budget reports.

One of the valuable things about this idea, from a political standpoint, was that each show would be seen only by the people who lived in that particular state or region. This meant it made no difference if Nixon's statements—for they were not really answers—were exactly the same,

phrase for phrase, gesture for gesture, from state to state. Only the press would be bored and the press had been written off already. So Nixon could get through the campaign with a dozen or so carefully worded responses that would cover all the problems of America in 1968.

And, to carry it one step sideways, it made no difference either if the answers varied—in nuance—from state to state. No one, unless he traveled a lot, would hear any statement but the one designed for him. So, a question about law and order might evoke one response in New England and a slightly different one in the South. Nothing big enough to make headlines, just a subtle twist of inflection, or the presence or absence of a frown or gesture as a certain phrase was spoken. This was what the new politics was to Frank Shakespeare. And he did all he could to make sure Richard Nixon's definition would be the same.

Roger Ailes, the executive producer of the Mike Douglas Show, was hired to produce the one-hour programs. Ailes was twenty-eight years old. He had started as a prop boy on the Douglas show in 1965 and was running it within three years. He was good. When he left, Douglas' ratings collapsed. But not everyone he passed on his way up remained his friend. Not even Douglas.

Richard Nixon had been a guest on the show in the fall of 1967. While waiting to go on, he fell into conversation with Roger Ailes.

"It's a shame a man has to use gimmicks like this to get elected," Nixon said.

"Television is not a gimmick," Ailes said.

Richard Nixon liked that kind of thinking. He told Len Garment to hire the man.

Ailes had been sent to Chicago three days before Nixon opened the fall campaign. His instructions were to select a panel of questioners and design a set. But now, on the day of the program, only six hours, in fact, before it was to begin, Ailes was having problems.

"Those stupid bastards on the set designing crew put turquoise curtains in the background. Nixon wouldn't look right unless he was carrying a pocketbook." Ailes ordered the curtains removed and three plain, almost stark wooden panels to replace them. "The wood has clean, solid, masculine lines," he said.

His biggest problem was with the panel. Shakespeare, Treleaven and Garment had felt it essential to have a "balanced" group. First, this meant a Negro. One Negro. Not two. Two would be offensive to whites, perhaps to Negroes as well. Two would be trying too hard. One was necessary and safe. Fourteen percent of the population applied to a six- or seven-member panel, equaled one. Texas would be tricky, though. Do you have a Negro *and* a Mexican-American, or if not, then which?

Besides the Negro, the panel for the first show included a Jewish attorney, the president of a Polish-Hungarian group, a suburban housewife, a businessman, a representative of the white lower middle class, and, for authenticity, two newsmen: one from Chicago, one from Moline.

That was all right, Roger Ailes said. But then someone had called from New York and insisted that he add a farmer. A farmer, for Christ's sake. Roger Ailes had been born in Ohio, but even so he knew you did not want a farmer on a television show. All they did was ask complicated questions about things like parities, which nobody else understood or cared about. Including Richard Nixon. He would appoint a secretary of agriculture when he won, yes, but why did he have to talk to farmers on live television in the campaign?

Besides, the farmer brought the panel size to eight, which Ailes said was too big. It would be impossible for Nixon to establish interpersonal relationships with eight different people in one hour. And interpersonal relationships were the key to success.

"This is the trouble with all these political people horning in," Ailes said. "Fine, they all get their lousy little groups represented but we wind up with a horseshit show."

There was to be a studio audience—three hundred people—recruited by the local Republican organization. Just enough Negroes so the press could not write "all-white" stories but not enough so it would look like a ballpark. The audience, of course, would applaud every answer Richard Nixon gave, boosting his confidence and giving the impression to a viewer that Nixon certainly did have charisma, and whatever other qualities he wanted his President to have.

Treleaven and his assistant, Al Scott, came to the studio late in the afternoon. They were getting nervous. "Nixon's throat is scratchy," Treleaven said, "and that's making him upset." Al Scott did not like the lighting in the studio.

"The lights are too high," he said. "They'll show the bags under RN's eyes."

Then there was a crisis about whether the press should be allowed in the studio during the show. Shakespeare had given an order that they be kept out. Now they were complaining to Herb Klein, the press relations man, that if three hundred shills could be bussed in to cheer, a pool of two or three reporters could be allowed to sit in the stands.

Shakespeare still said no. No *newspapermen* were going to interfere with his TV show. Klein kept arguing, saying that if this was how it was going to start, on the very first day of the campaign, it was going to be 1960 again within a week.

Treleaven and Ailes went upstairs, to the WBBM cafeteria, and drank vending machine coffee from paper cups.

"I agree with Frank," Ailes said. "Fuck 'em. It's

THE ANTISEPTIC CAMPAIGN
Joe McGinniss

not a press conference.

"But if you let the audience in . . ."

"Doesn't matter. The audience is part of the show. And that's the whole point. It's a television show. Our television show. And the press has no business on the set. And goddammit, Harry, the problem is that this is an electronic election. The first there's ever been. TV has the power now. Some of the guys get arrogant and rub the reporters' faces in it and then the reporters get pissed and go out of their way to rap anything they consider staged for TV. And you know damn well that's what they'd do if they saw this from the studio. You let them in with the regular audience and they see the warmup. They see Jack Rourke out there telling the audience to applaud and to mob Nixon at the end, and that's all they'd write about. You know damn well it is." Jack Rourke was Roger Ailes's assistant.

"I'm still afraid we'll create a big incident if we lock them out entirely," Treleaven said. "I'm going to call Frank and suggest he reconsider."

But Shakespeare would not. He arranged for monitors in an adjacent studio and said the press could watch from there, seeing no more, no less, than what they would see from any living room in Illinois.

It was five o'clock now; the show was to start at nine. Ray Voege, the makeup man, borrowed from the Johnny Carson Show, had arrived.

"Oh, Ray," Roger Ailes said, "with Wilkinson, watch that perspiration problem on the top of his forehead."

"Yes, he went a little red in Portland," Ray Voege said.

"And when he's off camera, I'd give him a treated towel, just like Mr. Nixon uses."

"Right."

Ailes turned to Jack Rourke, the assistant. "Also, I'd like to have Wilkinson in the room with Nixon before the show to kibitz around, get Nixon loose."

"Okay, I'll bring him in."

Then Treleaven and Scott went back to the Sheraton Hotel for dinner. Ailes stayed in the studio to rehearse the opening with the cameramen one more time. There was nothing he could do about what Nixon would say or would not say, but he did not want anyone turning off before the hour was over because the program was dull to watch.

The set, now that it was finished, was impressive. There was a round blue-carpeted platform, six feet in diameter and eight inches high. Richard Nixon would stand on this and face the panel, which would be seated in a semicircle around him. Bleachers for the audience ranged out behind the panel chairs. Later, Roger Ailes would think to call the whole effect, "the arena concept" and bill Nixon as "the man in the arena." He got this from a Theodore Roosevelt quote which hung, framed, from a wall of his office in Philadelphia. It said something about how one man in the arena was worth ten, or a hundred, or a thousand carping critics.

At nine o'clock, Central Daylight Time, Richard Nixon, freshly powdered, left his dressing room, walked down a corridor deserted save for secret service, and went through a carefully guarded doorway that opened onto the rear of the set.

Harry Treleaven had selected tape from WBBM's coverage of the noontime motorcade for the opening of the show. Tape that showed Richard Nixon riding, arms outstretched, beaming, atop an open car. Hundreds of thousands of citizens, some who had come on their own, some who had been recruited by Republican organizations, cheered, waved balloons and tossed confetti in the air. One week before, at the Democratic convention, it had been Humphrey, blood, and tear gas. Today it was Nixon, the unifying hero, the man to heal all wounds. No disorder in his crowds, just dignified Republican enthusiasm, heightened a notch or two by knowledge of the inevitable comparisons between this event and those from the previous week. If the whole world had been watching then, at least a fair portion would see this on the network news. Chicago Republicans showed a warm, assured, united front. And Harry Treleaven picked only the most magical of moments for the opening of his show.

Then the director hit a button and Bud Wilkinson appeared on the screen. And what a placid, composed, substantial, reassuring figure he was: introducing his close personal friend, a man whose intelligence and judgment had won the respect of the world's leaders and the admiration of millions of his countrymen, this very same man who had been seen entering Jerusalem moments ago on tape: Richard Nixon.

And the carefully cued audience (for Jack Rourke, the warmup man, had done his job well) stood to render an ovation. Richard Nixon, grinning, waving, *thrusting,* walked to the blue riser to receive the tribute.

It was warmly given. Genuine. For Nixon suddenly represented a true alternative: peace, prosperity, an end to discord, a return to the stable values that had come under such rude and unwarranted attack. Nixon was fortification, reaffirmation of much that needed to be reaffirmed. They needed him now, these Republicans, much more than they had in 1960. Then they were smug; and they did not especially like him. They toyed with him, as a small boy would poke a frog with a stick. They made him suffer needlessly, and, in the end, their apathy had dragged a nation down. Now, on this night, this first night of his campaign to restore decency and honor to American life, they wanted to let him know they cared. To let him know 1960 would not happen again.

He looked toward his wife; the two daughters; Ed Brooke, the most useful Negro he had found; Charles Percy, the organization man; and Thurston Morton, resigned if not enthusiastic. They sat in the first row together.

Then, eagerly, forcefully, strong, confident, alive, he turned toward the panel to begin.

He was alone, with not even a chair on the platform for company; ready to face, if not the nation, at least Illinois. To communicate, man to man, eye to eye, with that mass of the ordinary whose concerns he so deeply shared; whose

values were so totally his own. All the subliminal effects sank in. Nixon stood alone, ringed by forces which, if not hostile, were at least—to the viewer—unpredictable.

There was a rush of sympathy; a desire—a need, even—to root. Richard Nixon was suddenly human: facing a new and dangerous situation, alone, armed only with his wits. In image terms, he had won before he began. All the old concepts had been destroyed. He had achieved a new level of communication. The stronger his statement, the stronger the surge of warmth inside the viewer. *Received impressions.* Yes, this was a man who could lead; infinitely preferably to the gray and bumbling Johnson; the inscrutable, unsuccessful Rusk. A man who—yes, they remembered, even through the electronic haze—had stood up to Khrushchev in the kitchen. And, it was obvious now, who would stand up to Jerry Rubin in the street.

His statements flowed like warm milk, bathed the audience, restored faith in the Founding Fathers, rekindled the memory of a vigorous Eisenhower, of ten, of fifteen years before. *"The American Revolution has been won,"* he had said in his acceptance speech in Miami, *"the American Dream has come true."*

Morris Liebman, the Jewish attorney, asked the first question: "Would you comment on the accusation which was made from time to time that your views have shifted and that they are based on expediences?"

Richard Nixon squinted and smiled. "I suppose what you are referring to is: Is there a new Nixon or is there an old Nixon? I suppose I could counter by saying: Which Humphrey shall we listen to today?"

There was great applause for this. When it faded, Richard Nixon said, "I do want to say this: There certainly is a new Nixon. I realize, too, that as a man gets older he learns something. If I haven't learned something I am not worth anything in public life.

"We live in a new world. Half the nations in the world were born since World War Two. Half

THE ANTISEPTIC CAMPAIGN
Joe McGinniss

the people living in the world today were born since World War Two. The problems are different and I think I have had the good sense—I trust the intelligence—to travel the world since I left the office of Vice President and to bring my views up to date to deal with the new world.

"I think my principles are consistent. I believe very deeply in the American system. I believe very deeply in what is needed to defend that system at home and abroad. I think I have some ideas as to how we can promote peace, ideas that are different from what they were eight years ago, not because I have changed but because the problems have changed.

"My answer is, yes, there is a new Nixon, if you are talking in terms of new ideas for the new world and the America we live in. In terms of what I believe in the American view and the American dream, I think I am just what I was eight years ago."

Applause swept the studio. Bud Wilkinson joined in.

The farmer asked a question about farming; the Polish-Hungarian delivered an address concerning the problems of the people of eastern Europe. His remarks led to no question at all, but no matter: Richard Nixon expressed concern for the plight of eastern Europeans everywhere, including northern Illinois.

Then Warner Saunders, the Negro, and a very acceptable, very polite one he seemed to be, asked, "What does law and order mean to you?"

"I am quite aware," Richard Nixon said, "of the fact that the black community, when they hear it, think of power being used in a way that is destructive to them, and yet I think we have to also remember that the black community as well as the white community has an interest in order and in law, providing that law is with justice. To me law and order must be combined with justice. Now that's what I want for America. I want the kind of law and order which deserves respect."

John McCarter, the businessman, asked about Spiro Agnew. Nixon said, "Of all the men who I considered, Spiro Agnew had the intelligence, the courage and the principle to take on the great responsibilities of a campaigner and responsibilities of Vice President. And who also had the judgment so that if anything happened, the President of the United States could sit in that chair and make decisions that need to be made that would make the difference between war and peace and that I would have confidence in him." Then he called Agnew "a man of compassion."

McCarter came back later wanting to know if Nixon thought the Chicago police had been too harsh on demonstrators in the streets.

"It would be easy," Nixon said, "to criticize Mayor Daley and by implication Vice President Humphrey. But it wouldn't be right for me to lob in criticism. I am not going to get into it. It is best for political figures not to be making partisan comments from the sidelines."

The show went on like that. At the end the audience charged from the bleachers, as instructed. They swarmed around Nixon so that the last thing the viewer at home saw was Nixon in the middle of this big crowd of people, who all thought he was great.

Treleaven plunged into the crowd. He was excited; he thought the show had been brilliant. He got to Nixon just as Nixon was bending down to autograph a cast that a girl was wearing on her leg.

"Well, you've got a leg up," Treleaven said.

Nixon stood up and grinned and moved away.

"Gee, that was sure a funny look he gave me," Treleaven said. "I wonder if he heard me. I wonder if he knew who I was."

Reprinted from The Atlantic Monthly *(August, 1970), pp. 65–67. Copyright © 1970 by Hedrick L. Smith. Reprinted with permission.*

When the President Meets the Press

HEDRICK SMITH

SOMETHING ought to be done to bring the presidential news conference back to life. It has never been as lusty or exalted an instrument of democracy as its apologists and practitioners would have wished. But rarely has a news conference been as pallid or synthetic a ritual as the one last May 8, the night the White House was girding for mass demonstrations against President Nixon's Cambodian decision and the killings at Kent State.

When the President strode into the subdued elegance of the East Room that evening to confront several newsmen, it was a moment of high drama. The nation was in agony. The campuses were aflame. The stock market was plummeting. Secretary of the Interior Walter Hickel's letter of distress to President Nixon had exposed a split high within the Administration. Members of Congress, angered at not having been consulted about sending U.S. troops into Cambodia, were rising to challenge or limit the President's war-making powers. Within hours, the White House itself would face a siege of protesters.

Rarely has a news conference promised so much but, alas, produced so little. That session in the East Room was a pale shadow of the passion and trauma of the nation. It was as real-life as a minuet, as illuminating as a multiplication table. President Nixon held the assembled reporters at bay as easily as Cassius Clay dabbling with a clutch of welterweights.

Vice President Agnew has raised the specter of a hostile press shading the news to suit its prejudices and unwilling to give the Nixon Administration a fair shake. But many outsiders, on campus and elsewhere, worry about the opposite risk: that when the President actually meets the press, he finds it too deferential, too compliant, too harassed, or too disorganized to pose him a real challenge or to raise a serious and sustained critique. This is one reason why, in an age when all institutions are being questioned, the cream of the Washington press corps are viewed by many young skeptics as lapdogs rather than watchdogs of the government.

The favorite analogy among Washington reporters is that the presidential news conference is the American counterpart to Parliamentary Question Time for the British Prime Minister and Cabinet. It is supposed to help fill a gap in the American Constitution, which made no provision for calling the Chief Executive before either Congress or the public to give some accounting of his Administration between elections.

But the analogy with Parliament is false. Question Time in the British House of Commons is a much more rigorous and risky affair. The exchange, often bristling with barbs takes place between two groups of equals, the Ins and Outs, the elected adversaries of a two-party system. An American presidential news conference is an unequal contest from the start, for no newsman

WHEN THE PRESIDENT MEETS THE PRESS
Hedrick Smith

can stand toe-to-toe with the President in the way that the Opposition Leader can face the British Prime Minister.

Question Time also has a number of built-in procedures which help put the government on the spot. The inquiries are frequently very detailed and highly informed for they are as much a measure of the intelligence and ingenuity of the questioners as they are a test of the government's policies and its ability. Generally, they are submitted and printed in advance; but it is the supplementaries, the surprise follow-up questions, that add zing to Question Time and make it perilous for a clumsy minister. In a flash it can veer into gladiatorial combat, real rough-and-tumble debate. Another important difference is that Question Time is a regular affair, with an hour set aside four days a week. Cabinet ministers take it in rotation; the Prime Minister steps in only on the most crucial issues. The questions are grouped by subject and taken one at a time. This makes for continuity, in contrast to the frenetic, grab-bag, jack-in-the-box scramble of the televised quiz shows at the White House.

The American press cannot play the role of an elected parliamentary opposition and debate the President. But it would profit by following a number of techniques from Question Time. At the May 8 conference, for example, many of the questions were vague or timid, possibly conjured up in some haste during the final minutes before the show went live. The net effect was more a fusillade of spitballs at 50 paces than a searching examination of the President's mood and motives at a moment of national crisis. Nothing caught Mr. Nixon offguard or prodded him to acknowledge a shred of responsibility for the turmoil that was rolling over the nation. To wit: One reporter noted that some people were saying the United States was headed for revolution or repression and asked the President's view: true or false? Another invited Mr. Nixon to tell the public about the isolation of the presidency. A third inquired whether the President thought the Vietnam War worthwhile. A fourth wanted to

know if the President was prepared to pursue a political settlement in Paris with fervor. A fifth asked for "comment" on the Hickel letter.

Any of these might have served well enough for a White House dinner guest with hours to chat with the President. But in the hothouse tautness of a news conference, cut to fit the TV schedule (one minute to answer each question), each was an easy and open invitation for Mr. Nixon to speechify or filibuster as he chose.

In fairness, there were—and always are—cunning efforts to probe the President's policies and frame of mind, but he deflected them, and other reporters failed to pursue them. About halfway through, for example, one dark-haired young man a few rows back recalled that Mr. Nixon, in his Inaugural Address, had promised to bring Americans together, to move from an era of confrontation to an era of negotiation, and to bring peace in Vietnam. "During the past two weeks it seems that we are farther than ever from those goals," the reporter observed; how could the President account for this failure? Mr. Nixon, smooth as a cue ball and about as communicative, pointed proudly to the arms talk with the Soviet Union as evidence of serious and peaceful intent. A rush of jumping bodies spared him from having to go on and deal with Indochina or the troubled campuses, and no one later called Mr. Nixon back to this aching, unanswered question.

Another reporter asked the President why he had said on April 20 that Vietnamization was going so well that he could pull 150,000 American troops out of Vietnam, and yet just ten days later had to announce that Vietnamization was so seriously threatened that he was sending American forces into Cambodia. When Mr. Nixon replied that increased enemy action in Cambodia made the difference, no one asked him to explain precisely how and why. Given the enemy raids into Vietnam from sanctuaries in Cambodia for the past several years, how were the actions of the previous ten days suddenly so menacing to Americans in Vietnam—unless the Nixon Administration was trying to save the Cambodian government or saw a military opening in Cambodia and decided to take advantage of it?

Some crucial questions were left unasked: Why hadn't Congress been consulted before the Cambodian assault? Had he usurped the warmaking powers of Congress by sending American troops into a new country? And if not, did he recognize any restraint that the Constitution or Congress could impose on his powers as Commander in Chief? Since there had been no Cambodian request for American intervention, how did he answer the charge that it violated Cambodian neutrality or the United Nations Charter? Or, on the domestic side: What precautions had the Administration taken to prevent another Kent State tragedy, say by restricting the use of live ammunition by the National Guard on campuses? And so on.

It is fashionable among Washington reporters to lament the decline of eloquence in the halls of Congress, to murmur that the coin of political debate has been cheapened. But evidently there has also been a decline in the calculated aggressiveness and perseverance of the press questioning the President. Few are the reporters who let fly blunt queries and then respectfully but firmly stand their ground before the President and their colleagues, demanding a responsive answer. It was not always thus. In November, 1962, several reporters closely hawked President Kennedy about the government's management of the news during the Cuban missile crisis. Three reporters pressed the President to relax administrative restrictions on the flow of news; finally one of them, Raymond P. Brandt of the St. Louis *Post-Dispatch*, persisted through five questions, forcing the President to explain how and when he would amend the news management policies. His tenacity produced a real dialogue.

An even more classic example of relentless group questioning came during the Eisenhower Administration. President Eisenhower was called upon to explain Attorney General Herbert Brownell's charge that the late Harry Dexter White, appointed by President Truman to the International Monetary Fund, was a communist spy, though a grand jury had previously refused to indict White on those charges. For almost the entire news conference—twenty questions—Mr. Eisenhower was pursued on this topic until, in the last two minutes, he asked to change the subject.

Many a White House regular has complained that the televised news conferences, initiated under Eisenhower and enshrined by Kennedy, are inevitably the President's show. Unquestionably the format favors him and handicaps the press. TV cameras draw an unwieldy crowd of several hundred reporters, and sheer numbers defeat the purpose of information dialogue.

The crucial flaw is the failure of the press corps as a group to develop important lines of questioning. Most reporters recognize that it is the second or third question, like gangtackling in football, that is likely to get results. If the President is to be enticed or provoked into some meaningful revelation, it usually takes a collective effort. But the White House news conference is a series of virtuoso performances.

The system, as now operated, puts the squeeze on the reporter, and President Nixon has tightened the vise by holding conferences while many newspapers are going to press in the evening hours. Some reporters have only minutes to file their stories. They must not only take detailed notes on the President's exact words but mentally organize their stories during the waning minutes of the news conference. Little chance is left for them to spot the holes in the President's earlier comments and to raise new questions. (One way of coping with these conflicting pressures is for large news organizations to send several reporters to the proceedings—one to follow the exchange and ask the pertinent questions, and the others to take notes and write stories.)

Finally, no White House regular is entirely free of some conflict of interest. He normally depends on the White House staff for much of his everyday news. This leaves the President's aides in excellent position to discipline him, if they wish, were he to ask too many impertinent questions of the President. No reporter welcomes the prospect of provoking the President's anger or scorn on national TV, where a large part of the audience is quickly hostile to any questioner who puts the President on the spot. Moreover, the White House regulars themselves live so much within the President's orbit that they rarely mix with people outside Washington or get a direct and palpable feel of the public's passions.

None of these ailments is brand-new, and none is of President Nixon's making. But Mr. Nixon has compounded them by becoming the most inaccessible President since Herbert Hoover. This adds to the hectic superficiality of the few news conferences that he does hold because reporters feel they have so much ground to cover. Inevitably when time is limited, the verbal melee is more confusing than ever.

No two Presidents have handled the press in the same way, though over the past four decades a loose tradition has been established — Mr. Nixon is quietly breaking it — that the President meets the press at least once every two weeks. That was the interval adopted by Woodrow Wilson when he instituted news conferences with the White House reporters of his day. Franklin D. Roosevelt was the most accessible of all recent Presidents, a beguiling master of the press, whom he invited into his office for wide-ranging give-and-take sessions twice a week (998 sessions in just over twelve years). Harry Truman cut it to once every ten days or so (324 in eight years), and Presidents Eisenhower, Kennedy, and Johnson each saw the collective press roughly every two weeks.

By comparison President Nixon has met with the press less than once a month (sixteen times in his first seventeen months — ten times on TV, six times off-camera and only one of those for direct quotation). The overall figures may be misleadingly generous, for he has been much less accessible this year than last. This from a President who sniped in his campaign at Lyndon Johnson with the ringing pledge that he would run an open

Administration because, Mr. Nixon said, 'The President cannot isolate himself from the great intellectual ferments of his time. On the contrary, he must consciously and deliberately place himself at their center."

Since the Cambodian venture, the President's isolation — his widely publicized penchant for going off with a yellow legal pad for solitary decision-making and speech-drafting — has become a matter of some concern. More news conferences are one answer. The press and public need, and by Mr. Nixon's own language are entitled to, a greater flow of give-and-take.

Some White House reporters have been pressing Mr. Nixon to hold regular, informal sessions, FDR-style, in his office. The President evidently feels more relaxed on these occasions, able to talk in greater depth, and the White House reporters find it easier to pursue questions in these smaller sessions. But there is no reason why the off-camera sessions cannot be vastly increased without cutting back on the televised news conferences that let the public view the President in the flesh.

Whether or not President Nixon does increase his press contacts, the basic responsibility for restoring the vigor of the White House news conference rests with the correspondents themselves. The rigor of the questioning itself is vital. Without sliding into malevolent heckling or the rasping cross-examination of a district attorney, newsmen can confront the President with more daring and tenacity than they have done recently.

Changes are also necessary in the format of the televised news conferences if they are to give us insights into the Nixon presidency. No reform is surefire, but the White House Correspondents Association might consider these steps: (1) limiting questions at certain crucial conferences to a single broad topic. This, for example, would have ruled out inquiries on the Middle East on May 8, leaving more time to plumb the Cambodian operation and its domestic repercussions; (2) alternatively, asking reporters to group all questions on the main topic of the day during the first half of the news conference, and leaving the remainder for any other kind of question; (3) establishing a firm tradition that each questioner can follow up his own inquiry at least once; (4) finding a new way to determine who gets the floor to replace the present jumping match. One approach would be for reporters to draw random-numbered slips as they enter the conference room and then ask questions in numerical order. Another approach is for the White House reporters to write out questions and submit them to a pool of four or five newsmen. This panel, basing itself on all questions received, could then engage in coordinated questioning of the President on one or two major topics in the first half of the conference, throwing open the final half to everyone else.

The hitch is that these suggestions cut into the Washington reporter's prized independence, the foundation stone of the present system. But chaos and superficiality are the price paid for that freedom. Some independence must be voluntarily surrendered if there is to be a more orderly and cunning pursuit of the President.

None of these reforms will guarantee candor, or newsworthy admission on the part of the President. But they will tax him where he is most vulnerable—in the need to honor his accountability to the nation.

Reprinted from Saturday Review *(December 13, 1969), pp. 61, 62, 75. Copyright 1969 Saturday Review, Inc. Used by permission of publisher and author.*

Some Sober Second Thoughts on Vice President Agnew

FRED W. FRIENDLY

IN DEFENDING Vice President Spiro Agnew, one of the most fair-minded men in the United States Senate said, "It is the pig that is caught under the fence that squeals." The analogy may be partly accurate, but the question is who is stuck under the fence—the broadcast journalist or the administration? Long ago, when broadcasting was fighting for its right to be responsible, Edward R. Murrow, then under attack, spoke words that might be paraphrased today: When the record is finally written it will answer the question, who helped the American people better understand the dilemma of Vietnam—the administration or the American journalist? History, of course, will decide that question. But I would suspect that in the struggle between the news media and the last two administrations, the record has been with the journalists.

The American people are worried about Vietnam, race, and youth, the three crucial stories of our time. What the Vice President of the United States is attempting to do is create doubts in the minds of the American public about the motivation and background of those charged with the responsibility of trying to understand and explain these complicated and sensitive controversies.

When Mr. Agnew asks, "Are we demanding enough of our television news presentations?" he is certainly asking a question that others, including many inside the profession, have asked for a generation. For some, the Vice President's question seemed to be about raised eyebrows, caustic remarks, and too much news analysis. For me, his speech was really about too little analysis. In fact, the Vice President may have provided a most valuable service in his Des Moines speech. He sharpened an issue that has been diffuse for too long, inviting us all to consider once again the state of broadcast journalism.

Agnew and I share the view that television journalism leaves something to be desired. We both fear the concentration of great power in a few individuals in the broadcasting industry. But we are apparently in profound disagreement on not only the nature of the network's coverage of President Nixon's Vietnam address, but even more importantly, on our crying need for more, not less, interpretive reporting. We require bolder, not blander illumination of the issues that divide men of reason.

Where Agnew went astray, in my view, was in his suggestion that the media ought somehow to be a conduit for the views of the government, or merely a reflector of public opinion. He was not the first nor the last high official to equate fairness and the possession of great power with the obligation of conformity.

The Vice President has forgotten history when he criticizes ABC's journalistic enterprise in arranging for Ambassador Averell Harriman to participate in the broadcast that followed Mr. Nixon's speech of November 3. I don't think President Kennedy rejoiced in having the

SOME SOBER SECOND THOUGHTS ON VICE PRESIDENT AGNEW
Fred W. Friendly

Republican Senator from Indiana, Homer Cape-
hart, critique his Berlin crisis speech of 1961
nor in having Ladd Plumley, president of the
National Chamber of Commerce, pursue him after
his controversial 1962 speech on the state of
the economy. How many times after a major
address did President Johnson have to listen to the
cutting remarks of Minority Leaders Everett
Dirksen and Gerald Ford? It was all part of the
democratic process. After all, the President had
had prime time on all three networks, and a
small measure of counter-fire from the loyal
opposition was hardly stacking the deck. In the
end of the day, perhaps ABC might not be faulted
for having invited Ambassador Harriman, an
experienced negotiator with the Hanoi government,
but rather for not having asked him enough
hard questions.

The Vice President doubts that President
Kennedy, during the Cuban missile crisis of 1962,
had his words "chewed over by a round table
of critics" immediately following his address to
the nation. Would the Vice President believe
Sander Vanocur, Ray Scherer, Frank McGee,
David Schoenbrun, Roger Mudd, George Herman,
Richard C. Hottelet, and Douglas Edwards?
The date on that was October 22, 1962. The Vice
President did not mention the Bay of Pigs, but
certainly he must remember the news analyses
and the GOP counter-briefings that followed.
President Kennedy, who earlier had called upon
broadcasters for self-censorship of the story in
the national interest, later told the managing editor
of *The New York Times* that revelation of the Bay
of Pigs plan might have saved the nation "a
colossal mistake."

A generation ago the most savage denounce-
ments against news analysis involved Senator Joseph
McCarthy. In an inflammatory speech in Wheeling,
West Virginia, in 1950 he declared there were
205 Communists in the State Department. Good
news analysis, in fact, good reporting, would have
required that the journalist not just hold up his
mirror to that startling event, but that he report

that the Senator had not one scrap of evidence to
substantiate so extravagant a claim. It took broadcasting several years during the McCarthy period
to learn that merely holding up a mirror could
be deceptive, as in fact holding up a mirror
to a riot or a peace march today can be deceptive.
It took the shame of the McCarthy period and
the courage of an Ed Murrow to elevate broadcast
journalism to a point where it could give responsible insights to issues such as those raised by
the junior Senator from Wisconsin.

For generations, editors and students of
journalism have tried to define news analysis and
interpretive reporting. The late Ed Klauber, one
of the architects of broadcast news standards,
offered the most durable description. I have
always kept it in my wallet, and I provide copies
to all my students at the Columbia Graduate
School of Journalism:

> What news analysts are entitled to do and should do
> is to elucidate and illuminate the news out of common
> knowledge, or special knowledge possessed by
> them or made available to them by this organization
> through its sources. They should point out the facts
> on both sides, show contradictions with the known
> record, and so on. They should bear in mind that in
> a democracy it is important that people not only should
> know but should understand, and it is the analysts'
> function to help the listener to understand, to weigh,
> and to judge, but not to do the judging for him.

If the Vice President would test the brief analyses
of November 3 against Mr. Klauber's criteria,
I think he might agree that the correspondents
did not cross the line in any attempt to make
up the viewer's mind on a course of action. Agnew
felt that the response to the President on November 3 was instant analysis. But it seems fair to
remind the Vice President that the administration
had provided correspondents with advance copies
of the speech for study earlier that evening,
and there had been a persuasive White House
briefing on the content. While the comments of the
correspondents were clearly appropriate, my own

SOME SOBER SECOND THOUGHTS ON VICE PRESIDENT AGNEW
Fred W. Friendly

personal opinion is that only those of Eric Sevareid and Marvin Kalb were probing and thoughtful. Kalb conceivably erred in not quoting pertinent paragraphs from the Ho Chi Minh letter that he believed were subject to different interpretation from that of the President.

Part of our Vietnam dilemma is that during the fateful August of 1964, when the Tonkin Gulf Resolution escalated the war, there was little senatorial debate worthy of the name, and there was a dramatic shortage of news analysis. If I am inclined to give the networks an A for effort and a B for performance the night of November 3, 1969, let me tell you that I give CBS News and myself a D for effort and performance on the night of August 4, 1964, when President Johnson, in his Tonkin Gulf speech, asked for a blank check on Vietnam. In spite of the pleas of our Washington bureau, I made the decision to leave the air two minutes after the President had concluded his remarks. I shall always believe that, if journalism had done its job properly that night and in the days following, American might have been spared some of the agony that followed the Tonkin Gulf Resolution. I am not saying that we should have, in any way, opposed the President's recommendations. But, to quote Klauber's doctrine of news analysis, if we had "out of common knowledge or special knowledge . . . [pointed] out the facts on both sides, [shown] contradictions with the known record," we might have explained that after bombers would come bases, and after bases, troops to protect those bases, and after that hundreds of thousands of more troops. Perhaps it is part of the record to note that Murrow, who understood the value of interpretive journalism from his years as a practitioner, and from his experience as director of the U.S. Information Agency, called minutes after the Johnson speech to castigate me and CBS for not having provided essential analysis of the meaning of the event.

One key aspect of the Vice President's speech did strike me as relating to the public interest as distinguished from the administration's political interest. This was his concern over the geographic and corporate concentration of power in broadcasting. Here he had the right target, but a misdirected aim. His criticism of broadcasters for centralization and conformity better describes the commercial system and its single-minded interest in maximum ratings and profits.

To some extent, it may be true that geography and working out of New York and Washington affect the views of Dan Rather of Wharton, Texas, Howard K. Smith of Ferriday, Louisiana, Chet Huntley of Cardwell, Montana, David Brinkley of Wilmington, North Carolina, Bill Lawrence of Lincoln, Nebraska, and Eric Sevareid of Velva, North Dakota. But I, for one, simply do not buy the Vice President's opinion that these responsible decision makers in news broadcasting and the professionals who work with them are single-minded in their views or unchecked in their performance. There is an independent, sometimes awkward complex of network executives, station managers, producers, and reporters whose joint production is the news we see. They represent a geographic, ethnic, and political profile nearly as far ranging as American society itself, with the tragic exception of blacks. The heads of the three major network news bureaus find their constituencies and their critics among the station managers they serve, the correspondents they employ, sponsors they lose, and in the wider public they please and occasionally disappoint. The news program emerges from a complicated system of argument, conflict, and compromise.

Beyond that, the record suggests that the best professionals recognize and acknowledge their limitations. Walter Cronkite was the first to admit that he erred in some of his reporting at the 1968 Democratic convention. It was David Brinkley, admitting that no reporter could always be objective but could only strive for fairness, who gave the Vice President a high visibility target. In his commentary of November 3, Eric Sevareid clearly noted that his views were "only the horseback opinion of one man and I could be wrong." Yet,

SOME SOBER SECOND THOUGHTS ON VICE PRESIDENT AGNEW
Fred W. Friendly

if the Vice President's aim was wild, his target of concentrated power is valid and endures. The "truth" of commercial broadcasting is that it maximizes audiences by maximizing profits. This system minimizes the presentation of hard news and analysis, leading the broadcast journalists into occasional oversimplification in the interest of time, overdramatization in the interest of impact.

If such distorting tendencies do exist, and I believe they sometimes do, the proper measure is not to subject the performance of professional journalists to governmental direction nor to majority approval. Rather, the task for government is to apply its leadership and authority to expand and diversify the broadcasting system and environment in which professional journalists work.

I do not see these public actions as inconsistent with or disruptive of the protections of the First Amendment. When Congress passed the Communications Act enabling the FCC to restrict a limited number of frequencies and channels to a limited amount of license-holders, everyone's freedom was slightly qualified because everyone cannot simultaneously broadcast over the same television channel. The Communications Act insisted that license-holders operate their franchise "in the public interest, convenience, and necessity." By every definition I have ever heard, that includes responsible news coverage. Selling cancer-giving cigarettes and not providing enough news and public affairs programing is certainly ample reason to reconsider a station's license, and doing so has nothing to do with the First Amendment. The FCC would be fulfilling long-standing national policy by demanding more, not less, public service broadcasting from the commercial systems, as well as by accelerating development of a publicly supported noncommercial alternative.

The Vice President quotes Walter Lippmann to make a case that the networks have hidden behind the First Amendment. He does not add that Mr. Lippmann's point was that this demonstrated the necessity for just such a competitive, alternate

system that most commercial broadcasters today support. Lippmann has also said that "the theory of a free press is that the truth will emerge from free reporting and free discussion, not that it will be presented perfectly and instantly in any one account." Public television, with national interconnection due in part to a new ruling by the FCC, now has a chance to make that "free reporting and free discussion" 25 per cent more widespread and more effective.

In the days since the Vice President's speech, I have been jarred by the strange coalition of Americans who find an assortment of reasons for identifying with parts of the Vice President's remarks. The mobilizers for peace don't like the way the peace march was covered or, as they put it, left uncovered. My Democrat friends point to the Humphrey defeat, which they say happened at the hands of the television cameras in Chicago. My journalism students at Columbia feel that time after time broadcasters of my generation misjudge the youth movement and the black movement. In the end, I have had to plead with these students to believe in the integrity of a Cronkite, a Smith, a Brinkley, and in the professionalism of their producers—men such as Les Midgley of CBS, Av Westin of ABC, and Wally Westfeldt of NBC. My defense has been only partly successful, and this has been with an audience generally quite hostile to the main trust of the Agnew attack. With sadness, I have painfully learned that the reservoir of good will that broadcast journalists could once rely on in time of crisis has now been partially dissipated.

Perhaps if the public knew that the broadcast newsman is fighting for longer news programs, fewer commercials, more investigative reporting, there might be a broader sense of identity.

The broadcast journalist knows how little news analysis appears on the air. Five or eight minutes after a major presidential address is not interpretive journalism as much as it is time to be filled to the nearest half-hour, or to the nearest commercial. He also knows that a half hour minus

SOME SOBER SECOND THOUGHTS ON VICE PRESIDENT AGNEW
Fred W. Friendly

six commercials is just not enough air time to present and analyze the news properly. Perhaps the broadcast newsman of today can no longer afford the luxury of abdicating his role in a decision-making process that now so clearly affects his profession and his standards. He is a far better newsman than the public ever sees and he has far more power to change the system than he and the public imagine.

For a long time the broadcasting companies have relied on the prestige of their news organizations to enhance their own corporate prestige, in fact, their very survival. The reputation of these newsmen is now at stake. They need to do their best, not their worst. They need to be seen at their most courageous, not to slip into timidity. This is not a time for public relations experts, although there will be a frantic search for a corporate line that will once again salvage the good name of broadcasting.

Television's battles will not be fought or won with the polemics of corporate handouts, First Amendment platitudes, or full-page ads. They will be won by what is on the air, and they will be lost by what is *not* on the air. It is later than many people think, and we all have Agnew to thank for reminding us.

Here we stand, with the image orthicon tube, the wired city, and the satellite the greatest tools of communication that civilization has ever known, while the second highest officeholder in the land implies that we use them less. Here we are in 1969, Mr. Vice President, with one leg on the moon and the other on earth, knee-deep in garbage. That's going to require some news analysis.

What the Vice President says is that he wants editorials (which network news divisions don't use) labeled for what they are. Certainly it is general custom to label news analysis and comment when it is taking place, and omission of that, even

under the pressure of time, is a mistake.

But Agnew ought to have labeled his speech for what it was. Did he want to encourage responsible journalism or did he wish to silence it?

The second salvo from the Agnew shotgun contained more buckshot and had even less precise aim. His facts were wobbly and subject to immediate rebuttal. He might have checked to see whether it was only the early out-of-town edition of *The New York Times* that missed the story of the 359 members of Congress who signed a letter endorsing the President's Vietnam policy. Making charges against the power of the *Times* and *The Washington Post* is the kind of anti-conglomerate philosophy usually identified with liberals. The Vice President jarred his own aim by being self-serving. His targets were only those organizations which he considered to be critical. The mighty complex that controls two of the largest newspapers in the nation—the New York *Daily News* and the Chicago *Tribune*, plus television and radio stations in those two cities and a lot more in other cities—was left unscathed, together with other media conglomerates that control huge circulations. Could the fact that hawks rather than doves fluttered atop those mastheads and transmitters have given them immunity?

Perhaps the journalist and the party in power are always destined to be on the outs. President Eisenhower was pretty sore with television news until he left office and became a big fan. President Kennedy was reading and watching more, and enjoying it less. President Johnson watched three sets and knew how to talk back to three talking heads at once, and the Nixon administration has let us know where it stands. It is my theory that, when the message from Des Moines or from the White House itself is always a valentine or a garland of flowers, television and radio will have failed their purpose.

Reprinted from the Columbia Journalism Review *(Winter, 1969–70), pp. 14–19.* ©. *Used by permission of author and publisher.*

Beyond Agnewism

ALFRED BALK

ALL inhabitants of the White House at some point become exasperated with the press. As James E. Pollard noted in *The Presidents and the Press*, George Washington (in the words of Thomas Jefferson) on one occasion became "much inflamed, got into one of those passions when he cannot command himself, ran on much about the personal abuse which had been bestowed on him . . ."; Andrew Jackson faced such press antagonism that he wooed newspapermen by placing some on government postmastership rosters; Franklin D. Roosevelt operated in so hostile a press environment that columnist Raymond Clapper commented, "No future politician looking for an alibi is going to have a ghost of a case trying to convince the country that he must curb free speech to get things done"; and John F. Kennedy confessed, "I am reading it more and enjoying it less."

Thus, when Vice President Spiro Agnew delivered his twin polemics against the media last November, it was not the fact that they conveyed White House displeasure with the press that was historic. They were significant, first, as the only time a U.S. official of so high a rank had devoted two consecutive prepared speeches to castigating the news media. Secondly, coupled with other actions, they seemed to constitute prominent elements in a developing political strategy, the ultimate objective of which was not clear at this writing. Further . . . the actions occurred against a backdrop of calculated "packaging" and insulation of Mr. Nixon from close questioning by reporters during his Presidential campaign.

For these reasons alone, Vice President Agnew's two anti-media speeches merit more than cursory analysis. But there are other reasons as well. One, certainly, is the noteworthy number of factual errors—along with errors of omission—they contain. Also, there is the exceedingly emotional level on which they appealed to some listeners. Both speeches were selective in the specific media organizations mentioned; both were sharply anti-Eastern; both were replete with what conservative columnist Ted Lewis of the New York *Daily News* characterizes as "red hot phrases." Consequently, several news media were deluged with the heaviest shower of hate communications since the McCarthy era.

Norman Isaacs, president of the American Society of Newspaper Editors, told of correspondents' "vicious" and "venomous" remarks about the "Jew-owned and Jew-dominated news media"; Robert Donovan of the Los Angeles *Times* noted that "yahoos are telephoning obscenities to television stations"; and New York *Post* columnist Pete Hamill revealed that "since Spiro Agnew opened his mouth, the mail has been . . . the real vicious stuff: they are going to kill my children; I am a 'Jew bastard' . . . Agnew is going to put me in a detention pen or under a rock; Hitler didn't gas enough of us. . . ."

Nonetheless, there was, to quote one editorialist, "a germ of truth" in the Vice President's remarks, and it is the sorting out of truth from partisan polemics that concerns us here. It is true, for example, that the conventional spot-news formula

BEYOND AGNEWISM
Alfred Balk

means that "bad news drives out good news"; that "in the networks' endless pursuit of controversy, we should ask: What is the end value—to enlighten or to profit?"; and, most emphatically, that "our knowledge of the impact of network news on the national mind is far from complete." It is also true that "many, many strong, independent [media] voices have been stilled in this country in recent years" and that "the American people should be made aware of the trend toward monopolization of the great public information vehicles." It is further true that Americans should ask themselves, "Are we demanding enough of our television news presentations"—and other news media as well?

But is it true, as Spiro Agnew seemed to be saying, that American news media have been politicized—that they have fallen under effective control of liberal zealots, to the detriment of fair reporting and analysis of other than liberal viewpoints? If this were true, certainly it would represent a genuine watershed in American journalistic history, for the news media as a class, by all available indices, always have tended toward the conservative. One indication of this is newspaper endorsements of Presidential candidates. When *Editor & Publisher* began tabulating daily newspaper endorsements in 1932, 52 per cent of newspapers responding were for Herbert Hoover, 40 per cent for Roosevelt, and 7 per cent uncommitted. Since then, Republican candidates consistently have won the majority of endorsements except in 1964, when 42.4 per cent of newspapers reporting to *Editor & Publisher* endorsed Lyndon Johnson, compared to 34.7 per cent for Barry Goldwater (the remainder were uncommitted). In fact, except for that election, no more than 17 per cent of U.S. dailies ever have supported a Democratic Presidential candidate since the Roosevelt era. In 1968, Richard Nixon won 60.8 per cent of reported endorsements; Hubert Humphrey, 14 per cent; George Wallace, 1.2 per cent; and 24 per cent were uncommitted.

Other indicators substantiate this basic conservatism. In the study "How Newspapers Use

Columnists" [*CJR*, Fall, 1964], for example, Ben Bagdikian found that of all syndicated columns used in dailies, only 37 per cent of the columns run were liberal—and only 1 per cent were "very liberal," contrasted to 29 per cent which were "very conservative." Of the papers using columns, more than half had an imbalance favoring conservatives, and among these "conservative-favoring" papers 85 per cent of the columns used were conservative. Concludes Bagdikian:

> On heated issues that are serious and contemporaneous—Medicare, fair employment practices, relations with China, for example—there is no healthy printed dialogue because only half of the mechanism exists in most places. . . . It is hard to reconcile the findings with the claim by Republican conservatives that the press has been hostile to conservative ideas. . . . The situation has resulted in curious behavior: the Democrats seem to be pleased if some columnists are on their side; Republicans, indignant if not all of them are.

One is reminded of A. J. Liebling's comparison of the London press—where the "fan of opinion" includes "Communists, Socialist, Liberal, and all shades of Conservative"—to New York City's, with a range "from conservative to reactionary." Most of all, one thinks of a comment by Robert U. Brown of *Editor & Publisher*—never accused of flaming liberalism—in a December 13 editorial:

> Is it possible that the onetime one-party press, the target of the late Adlai Stevenson because of its support of conservative candidates and issues, could all of a sudden become the liberal press, the target of those same conservatives it was once accused of favoring? Or are we in danger of dealing in slogans and generalities, just as the critics were in Stevenson's day?

Because broadcasters are subject to the Fairness Doctrine when opinions are offered, and none of the Big Three networks and few local stations endorse political candidates, similar indices of broadcasters' political leanings are unavailable. Still, given the many instances in which a publisher and local broadcaster are the same man, there seems no reason to assume any large disparity in the political profiles of management in the two media. And even if one accepts Frank Shakespeare's generalization that most editorial employees are more liberal than he and his politically compatible colleagues, it must be remembered that it is the owner who hires and fires, sets editorial policy, and encourages or discourages major reportorial undertakings.

Edward R. Murrow confirmed this when, despite his formidable professional stature, he was unable to gain a greater share of prime time and plentiful CBS-TV revenue for public affairs projects, and soon thereafter left. Floyd Knox, city editor of the Waterbury *Republican*, also confirmed this last October when, against his publisher's wishes on Vietnam Moratorium Day he ran a front-page list of Vietnam casualties from the Waterbury area — and, for this and previous transgressions, was fired. Also, at the Passaic-Clifton, N. J., *Herald News*, when managing editor Ted Hall defied his publisher's orders to cease investigating the prosecution of two murder cases — one of them involving charges against the son of a nearby suburb's newspaper publisher — Hall, too, was fired.

If media management as a class, with exceptions, remains basically conservative politically, however, it also is true, as noted by Theodore H. White, that publishers, at least, are becoming increasingly independent in partisan terms. This was illustrated by the unprecedented 1964 shift of editorial support away from Barry Goldwater, despite his capture of the GOP Presidential nomination. This independence also is reflected in such "split-ticket" endorsement records as that of the Riverside, Calif., *Press and Daily Enterprise*. In 1964, while declining to endorse either Johnson or Goldwater for President, it made its first Democratic endorsement for Senator in history, for Pierre Salinger. In 1966, it made its first Democratic endorsement for Governor, for Edmund "Pat" Brown. Then in 1968, while endorsing Richard Nixon for President, it approved Democrats for both the U.S. Senate and Congress.

Like all political definitions, furthermore, the terms "conservative" and "liberal" are relative. By what criteria, for instance, could George Wallace, Spiro Agnew, Nelson Rockefeller, Eugene McCarthy, and Tom Hayden agree on classifying someone as "conservative" or "liberal"? Is the John Birch Society "conservative," or "radical Right"? Is Nelson Rockefeller "conservative" or "liberal"? What are the Americans for Democratic Action — "radical"? If so, what are the Students for a Democratic Society — "revolutionary"? If so, then what are the Black Panthers — who, unlike the SDS, like to collect guns? And how do they differ from the Minutemen or some White Citizens Council units, which supposedly are at the other "end" of the political spectrum (which, of course, actually is more circular than linear)? The definitions or classifications operatively are really what the majority of Americans believe that they are.

How conservative are most Americans? Lloyd A. Free and Hadley Cantril did extensive attitude polling on this question and reported their findings in *The Political Beliefs of Americans* (Rutgers Press, 1968). They conclude in part:

In brief, about two-thirds of the public qualified as "liberal" with respect to the operational level of Government programs, and the category of "completely liberal" outnumbered the "predominantly liberal" by more than two to one. . . .

[On the other hand] the liberal consensus of Americans at the *operational* level . . . fades away when the views of the same representative sample of people are tapped at the *ideological* level. . . . . In view of actual practices at the operational level, Americans at the ideological level continue to pay lip service to an amazing degree of stereotypes and shibboleths inherited from the past.

What the educated man believes is likely to fall within this "liberal" (philosophically, not partisan) consensus. What the educated, informed journalist adopts as his frame of reference is also. If he is "professional" — a word Mr. Agnew unfortunately ignored, but one essential to any serious

BEYOND AGNEWISM
Alfred Balk

dialogue on journalism—the *majority* of the audience therefore will accept him as apolitical as a *reporter*, and will prefer as *commentators* and *editorialists* voices credible to those within the consensus (but not necessarily credible to fringe groups).

Thus logic dictates that the loudest, most persistent complaints about media bias are likely to come, not from the two-thirds of the electorate which constitute Free's and Cantril's national consensus, but rather from the fringes of the consensus. Hence, as former Kerner Commission aide David Ginsburg told a Pittsburgh conference on the media and minorities: "The problem is made harder by the fact that accusations of bias against the media are often based on the bias of the audience itself. What you and I might agree is neutral and objective, Strom Thurmond and a Black Panther might both believe is biased and lacking in credibility—for very different reasons."

In some instances, obviously, protests from the far Right or far Left are justified, as are those from politically disparate Negroes, Puerto Ricans, Mexican-Americans, and Indians; farmers, tenement dwellers, small businessmen, labor unionists, college students—any subgroup which, in a given situation, may not share society's dominant concerns and values. If enough such groups feel this dissatisfaction over the media, the social consequences can be unhappy indeed. For, as Zechariah Chafee emphasizes in *Government and Mass Communications:*

> The press then fails to satisfy the need for social health through adequate communications in order to relieve the stresses and strains and class antagonisms. A widespread belief in the unfairness of the media arises. . . .

This appears to be the situation extant in the United States now. Technology, urbanization, education, and other engines of rapid social change have at least temporarily fragmented American society. With this fragmentation and the disorientation inherent in rapid change have come heightened pressures on the news media. As columnist David Broder writes:

> That tiny undercurrent of anti-press emotion which General Eisenhower tapped when he invited the 1964 Republican convention delegates to express their scorn of "sensation-seeking columnists and commentators" has quickly become a flood. George Wallace found that newspaper editorial writers ranked right up there with those "pointy-headed guideline-writers who can't even park their bikes straight" as sure-fire targets. . . .
>
> The press is caught up in what John Gardner has called the crisis of our times—the necessity for institutional adaptation to the forces of change. . . . It is my impression that the adaptive response from the press has been perhaps more sluggish than that of any other major institution.

As a result, the news media face grave credibility problems. Both George Gallup and Louis Harris have attested to this from the same platform. In September, 1968, Gallup told a Public Relations and Media Symposium at the Waldorf Astoria in New York:

"Never in my time has journalism of all types—book publishing, television, radio, newspapers, magazines, movies—been held in such low esteem. . . . We have raised up a new kind of person in the United States during the last three decades. He's much better educated, more enlightened, and he's no longer satisfied with the obsolete practices, the tired formulas that we've handed down in the field of journalism, all designed for a different kind of person, brought up in an entirely different age."

A year later, at the next forum, Harris reported having quantified some of these sentiments in a poll for *Time:* "A high 72 per cent of the most educated people are the most distrustful of news out of Washington. . . . Scarcely more than a third of the public agree with the proposition that the way Washington is covered is a free press operating at its best. A majority of the college-educated simply refused to believe it. . . . The college-educated and the young professional people and newsmagazine readers feel most strongly that

. . . the TV camera can lie. . . ." Readers, he added, are concerned about "coloration," suspecting that publishers and some newsmen slant news toward "special" rather than the "public" interest.

Similarly, last August the *APME News*, summarizing a study by the Associated Press Managing Editors Association, reported that a "credibility gap exists for the press without question." It quoted the report:

> The respondents cited such shortcomings as editorial prejudice, half-told stories, inaccurate headlines, and insufficient attention to serious community matters.
>
> Nearly 90 per cent of the public officials and leaders felt that professional journalists should set up ethics committees to investigate press misconduct. . . . Seventy-seven per cent of the public officials and leaders favored the establishment of local press councils. . . .
>
> Officials and editors alike pointed to major causes of our credibility gap: failure to print corrections properly; inaccuracies in elementary facts; evidence of editorial prejudice by placement of stories, size of headlines, etc.; faulty headlines; half-told or misleading stories; influence of organized pressure groups and public relations specialists.

Is it, then, political bias and "blurring" of the reporting and comment functions which are at the root of media credibility problems, or something more? Perhaps underdevelopment of diverse media channels; declining access to forums in the media; obsolescent journalistic formats; inadequate understanding of how to report change; overemphasis on trivia, escapism, and commercialism at the expense of richer veins of our culture?

Indeed, does our present media structure serve the public interest? What are the trends?

John McLaughlin, S.J., in *America*, writes:

> Twenty-five per cent of all television stations are controlled by newspapers. *Every* commercial VHF television license in the top ten U.S. markets is controlled either by a network, a group owner or a metropolitan newspaper chain. In the top twenty-five television markets there are ninety-seven stations. Fifteen of these ninety-seven are network owned.

Over *one-half* of all television revenue ($1.13 billion) regularly goes to these fifteen stations and their network owners.

FCC Commissioner Nicholas Johnson declares:

> The average return on depreciated tangible capital investment [in broadcasting] runs about 100 per cent a year. Over 340 stations last year grossed in excess of $1 million per station. There is an active market for stations—capital gains providing an even more lucrative source of private profit . . . than the exorbitant revenues.

Atlantic, in July, 1969, devoted a section to the "American Media Baronies" [reprinted in Part I, editor] in which is discussed, among other points, a trend toward conglomeratism that has made CBS, for example, "owner of TV stations in five major cities, a record company, musical-instrument manufacturing companies, a book-publishing house, educational film producers, CATV systems, Creative Playthings toys, and the New York Yankees." *Broadcasting*, on December 22, reported on the FCC's having sent "pilot questionnaires" to parent firms of six major broadcast licensees. Travelers Insurance, one of the six, owns stations only in Hartford, Conn., but others own a dozen or more. They are:

> Avco Corp. . . . It manufactures airplane and industrial engines and parts, aircraft-frame components, missile and space products, defense and industrial electronics, weapons and ammunition, steel products, heating equipment, mechanized farm equipment, and financial services.
>
> Fuqua Industries, Inc. . . . It is in photo processing and trucking, manufactures agricultural equipment, power lawnmowers, metal buildings, mobile homes and land-clearing equipment, sells pleasure boats, and owns motion picture theaters and real estate.
>
> Chris-Craft Industries, Inc. . . . Its manufacturing interests include auto interior textile trim, cotton and jute pads, automotive carpet, foam rubber products, boats, and marine motors and chemicals.
>
> Cox Enterprises, Inc. . . . publishes newspapers [and] has a number of other interests—in common-carrier microwave facilities, television-program

BEYOND AGNEWISM
Alfred Balk

production and distribution; motion-picture production; trade journals, technical publishing, and wholesale auto auctions.

E. W. Scripps Co. . . . publishes newspapers [and] also owns 95 per cent of United Press International, which in turn owns United Features Syndicate, and has CATV interests. . . .

Raymond B. Nixon, in *Editor & Publisher* on June 1, 1968, reported that "the growth rate in the number of group-owned dailies over the last seven years has been the most rapid in U.S. history" and that 828 of some 1,700 dailies now are group-owned, representing 58 per cent of daily and 63 per cent of Sunday circulation. The Thomson Newspapers organization, he added, encompasses three dozen U.S. dailies, while Gannett, Scripps League, Newhouse, and Donrey Media all own from twenty-two to twenty-nine dailies; and nine groups own fifteen to twenty: Scripps-Howard, Ridder, Copley, Harte-Hanks, Lee, Freedom (Hoiles), Worrell, Perry, and Southern (Walls).

Forbes, on October 1, noted that *Editor & Publisher* samplings showed the average medium-city newspaper (circulation 53,800) "*netted* close to 14 per cent on revenues" while papers with a circulation of 250,000 or more made 22.4 per cent on revenues (before taxes)—compared to 5.8 per cent for all manufacturing industries (among which, for example, the drug industry earned only 9.5 per cent). The magazine added:

Monopoly is the key to profitability in the newspaper industry generally. . . . Problems? Every industry has problems. It can stand a few of them when it's as profitable as the newspaper industry.

Bigness, of course, is to some extent inevitable and is not necessarily evil if counterbalanced; and profitability is essential to survival of private business. But as Yale University president Kingman Brewster, Jr., said in a speech on December 6:

The concentration of economic power, opinion power, and political power creates a sort of closed loop. Politicians must raise money from corporations in order to pay the networks the enormous cost of television time. Corporate advertisers call the network tune. And the networks must curry favor with the successful politicians to assure their franchise. The open society seems to be closing—not by conspiracy, but by this mutual dependence. . . .

The opinion industry itself could be loosened up by a variety of ownership interest. . . . Why should a town be locked into a jointly owned newspaper and television station? We should also consider requiring advertisers or commercial networks to contribute a small percentage of their outlays or revenues to the financing of nonprofit community and educational television. . . . The ancient faith in the free competition of ideas and interests and viewpoints could be revived. But it will happen if, and only if, we make it our cause.

It is, it would seem, to these issues that laymen, media executives, and public officials must address themselves if the underlaying causes of press and broadcasting credibility problems are to be solved.

EPILOGUE

These readings have been primarily concerned with the contemporary media system in the United States. The selections on the whole — whether they were written by outsiders or people in the business have been critical of the media. This criticism, however, should be put in perspective. This can be done by looking at other media systems since the American commercial pattern is only one of several ways of using the mass media. The communist model, for example, is subject to almost total political control, which makes our own method look quite benign. The British Broadcasting Corporation and a truly national press in Britain offers an alternative system. British radio and television are used much more for educational and cultural uplift than are the sales oriented American media. Our newly established Corporation for Public Broadcasting follows this style, but it is still underfinanced.

The criticism, I believe, reflects more a feeling of the great potential of the media in this country, a potential that is only partially fulfilled, than a blanket condemnation of the entire industry. Television still employs considerable, though often frustrated, creative talent which, if freed from constraints, might provide the basis for a cultural renaissance in America. Its main obstacle is neither sponsors, nor censors but the current financial imperative to reach the largest possible audience. As more channels are opened they may cater to a more select audience for the trend, as in radio, is not necessarily toward massness.

Two new technological innovations are now available which may well revolutionize the media system. Communication satellites and cable television are already of considerable concern to the networks and media empires, which are struggling to establish their claims to these new and promising communication media. Satellites could technically transmit programs to and from any point on the globe, while cable TV theoretically can relay many stations and be linked to data retrieval systems or telephones.

H. L. Nieburg has sketched the formative years of Comsat, the controlling interest in satellite communications.[1] Like many other endeavors in the defense/space arena, the government, — because it relies on private contractors, is deeply entangled in the corporate world. Satellite technology was developed as a result of political pressures, corporate lobbying, and government expenditure. It was then turned over to a monopoly, Comsat, which is a consortium of established communications carriers with ATT the dominant partner, to run as a profit-making enterprise. The government, meanwhile, continues to subsidize and guarantee the profitability of the corporation. Why the benefits of such nationally financed enterprises should not accrue to the general public is one of the recurrent mysteries of the American political economy.

[1] See his *In the Name of Science* (Chicago: Quadrangle, 1970; rev. ed.), pp. 505–24.

Ralph L. Smith[2] has outlined the technology and potential of the coaxial cable for television service. Cable television (CATV) could and should provide the diversity and free flow of information that over-the-air broadcasting obviously fails to provide. But Smith finds that the established communications oligarchy consisting of the broadcasting networks and telephone companies threaten to dominate the new system. The former have already pressured the FCC to follow policies that protect network broadcasters who need it less than independent station operators. The dismal prospect is therefore that the "wired nation" will initially receive the same banal, centrally-controlled programming as before. This will be facilitated by local community authorities who continue to view mass communications as just another commercial proposition and who will settle for a small share of the bonanza profits of CATV.

What is needed to avert such control of these new technologies and the continued operation of the media along existing commercial and self-serving lines is strong public pressure. The citizen does have rights in this area, but they must be asserted if the media are to be free and serve the public. Nicholas Johnson and many other critics have attempted to bring about the necessary public awareness, and citizens groups are beginning to mobilize. This volume, I hope, will give some impetus, however small, to such awareness and action.

[2]See his "The Wired Nation," *The Nation* (May 18, 1970), pp. 582–606.

BIOGRAPHICAL INDEX OF AUTHORS

IRVING L. ALLEN is an associate professor in the Department of Sociology at the University of Connecticut. He received his Ph.D. from the University of Iowa and is active in communications research.

ALFRED BALK is the editor of the *Columbia Journalism Review*. He is the author of two books, *The Religion Business* and *The Free List: Property without Taxes*, and has also produced a documentary film narrated by Walter Cronkite.

ALBERT BANDURA is a professor of psychology at Stanford University. He earned a Ph.D. at the University of Iowa. He is the author or co-author of four books: *Adolescent Aggression, Social Learning and Personality Development, Principles of Behavior Modification*, and *Psychological Modeling*. He has done extensive research into questions of modeling and vicarious processing.

RAYMOND A. BAUER is Professor of Business Administration at the Graduate School of Business Administration, Harvard University. He is a past president of the American Association for Public Opinion Research and has held offices in several other professional associations. In 1970 he was Senior Consultant, National Goals Research Staff, at the White House. He is author or co-author of numerous articles and twelve books including *The Soviet Citizen, American Business and Public Policy*, and *Second Order Consequences*.

DAVID R. BOWERS is a professor of journalism at Texas A&M University. Previously he was executive editor and then assistant publisher of the *Daily Times* of Chester, Pennsylvania. He holds a Ph.D. from the University of Iowa and is the author of numerous articles in journals and trade publications.

RICHARD F. CARTER is professor of Communications at the University of Washington, Seattle. He holds a Ph.D. from the University of Wisconsin, and has previously taught there and at Stanford University. He teaches courses in theory and methodology as well

as conducting research relative to his theoretical formulations.

ROBERT CIRINO has taught in secondary schools and has been a truck driver and merchant seaman. He holds a master of secondary education degree from the University of Hawaii and is the author of a book entitled *Don't Blame the People*.

MARCUS COHN is professorial lecturer in law, Graduate School of Public Law, George Washington University. He holds an L.L.M. degree from Harvard Law School. He is a partner of the Washington law firm of Cohn and Marks and the author of various articles in the *Illinois Law Review, Georgetown Law Review*, and *The Reporter Magazine*.

IRVING CRESPI holds a Ph.D. from the New School for Social Research. He is executive vice president of the Gallup Organization which he joined in 1956. His articles have been published in sociological and mass communications journals.

HAL DAVIS is a former graduate student at Oregon University. He is now assigned to the Office of Information, Department of the Air Force, Washington, D.C.

MELVIN L. DE FLEUR is chairman of the Department of Sociology at Washington State University. He earned a Ph.D. at the University of Washington. He is the author of four books, including *Sociology: Man in Society* and *Theories of Mass Communication*. He is the author of numerous articles published in social science journals.

BRENDA DERVIN is currently lecturer, School of Library Science, Syracuse University, New York. She was previously Senior Research Assistant in the Department of Communications at Michigan State University, and Resident Lecturer-Coordinator for the MSU Communications Seminar for AID Sponsored Foreign Students. She holds a Ph.D. from Michigan State University. She has also worked as a Public Relations-Program

Development Specialist for the University of Wisconsin Center for Consumer Affairs, the American Home Economics Association, and other non-profit organizations concerned with poverty and development.

ELIZABETH BRENNER DREW is Washington editor of *The Atlantic Monthly*, and a free-lance writer. She has appeared on "Meet the Press" and "Face the Nation" and is the regular interviewer on "Thirty Minutes with . . . ," a penetrating interview program carried by the Public Broadcasting Service.

ROBERT ECK has worked for the past twenty-three years for the advertising agency Foote, Cone and Belding. His current interest is in Phoenician and Punic loan words in western European and other languages.

FRED FERRETTI was formerly a reporter, editor, and producer for NBC News, and a correspondent for the New York Herald Tribune. He has covered radio-TV and is currently on general assignment for the New York Times.

LEON FESTINGER is professor of psychology, New School for Social Research, New York City. He holds a Ph.D. degree from the State University of Iowa. He is the author of *A Theory of Cognitive Dissonance* and *Conflict, Decision and Dissonance* and more than sixty articles in psychological and related journals.

FRED W. FRIENDLY is advisor on television to the Ford Foundation and Edward R. Murrow Professor of Journalism at Columbia University. He is more widely known for his long career with CBS. He resigned as president of CBS News in 1966 over a dispute in which he insisted on the live television presentation of Senate hearings on the Vietnam war instead of re-runs of comedies. Friendly lost the dispute. While with CBS, Mr. Friendly was executive producer of "CBS Reports" and producer of "See it Now," two series of controversial broadcasts for which he won several broadcasting awards. Together with Edward R. Murrow, with whom he worked earlier in radio, Mr. Friendly represents the most courageous brand of journalism yet produced on television. His recent book *Due to Circumstances Beyond our Control . . .* describes his sixteen years at CBS, the dilemma that confronts commercial television today, and the hopes that he holds for non-commercial television, in which, through the Public Broadcast Laboratory, he is still active.

HYMAN H. GOLDIN is associate professor at Boston University's School of Public Communication. He holds a Ph.D. from Harvard University and was formerly the chief economist, Broadcast Bureau, Federal Communications Commission. He is a trustee for Action for Children's Television, a citizens' group, and public trustee of the Eastern Educational Network.

BRADLEY S. GREENBERG is Professor of Communications at Michigan State University. He holds a Ph.D. in Mass Communications from the University of Wisconsin. In 1971 to 1972 he was a consultant to the BBC research department, London, and Visiting Professor at the London School of Economics and Political Science. He is author of many articles and two books, *The Kennedy Assassination and the American Public*, and *Use of the Mass Media by the Urban Core*.

JOSE L. GUERRERO is with the Asian Institute of Management in the Philippines. He earned his Ph.D. and M.A. degrees in mass communication and journalism at the University of Wisconsin. He was a postdoctoral research associate at Cornell University and has taught at the University of the Philippines, the University of Hawaii, and the University of Washington. His current work is in the fields of national development and communication.

SIR WILLIAM HALEY was formerly editor of *The Times* of London, Director General of the BBC, and editor in chief of *Encyclopedia Britannica*. He studied U.S. television during a recent sixteen-month residence in this country.

DANIEL HENNINGER is a staff writer for the *National Observer* on consumer affairs, a position in which he formerly served the *New Republic* for three years. He has written on controversial aspects of auto insurance, food additives, blood transfusions, and the potential of air bags as future highway safety devices. He is one of the nation's best young investigative reporters.

WILLIAM H. HONAN is travel editor of the *New York Times*. He was formerly an editor of the *New York Times Magazine*, national affairs editor at *Newsweek*, and an editor for the *New Yorker*.

CAROLYN JAFFE is an Assistant Public Defender of Cook County, Illinois, now assigned as Chief Assistant Public Defender in charge of Juvenile Court Division. She received Bachelor and Master of Law degrees in criminal law from Northwestern University and served as law clerk to U.S. District Judge Julius Hoffman. She has assisted in editorial duties for the *Journal of Criminal Law, Criminology and Police Science*.

NICHOLAS JOHNSON is a member of the Federal Communications Commission. When appointed by President Johnson he was the youngest man ever to serve on the FCC and soon became its most controversial member. According to his publisher five broadcasters' associations have asked President Nixon to fire him. His scathing but constructive attacks on the media are outlined in his book *How to Talk Back to your Television Set.*

PAUL KLEIN is the president of Computer Television, Inc., which he founded in 1970. Previously he was vice president for audience measurement at NBC. Prior to his ten years with NBC he was research manager for the Doyle, Dane, Bernbach Advertising Agency in New York. He is also president of the board of trustees for Schools for the Future, a non-profit organization devoted to the eradication of illiteracy in the United States and the world.

TERRY ANN KNOPF is a research associate at the Lemberg Center for the Study of Violence at Brandeis University. She has written numerous articles on the media which have appeared in *Chicago Journalism Review, Columbia Journalism Review* and *Trans-action*. She is currently at work on a book about rumors and racial disorders; it will include a section on rumors disseminated by the news media.

HERBERT E. KRUGMAN is manager of public opinion research at the General Electric Company. He was formerly research vice president at the Marplan Division of the Interpublic Group of Companies, Inc. He received a Ph.D. from Columbia University and has been on the faculties of Yale, Princeton, and Columbia. He is a past president of the American Association for Public Opinion Research.

RUTH LIEBAN is currently active in assisting the East-West Center at the University of Hawaii. She has had a long career in the electronic media writing and directing radio programs for ABC, CBS, and NBC and producing programs for educational radio. She has traveled widely and has been engaged in government and voluntary work in China, Japan, Okinawa, and the Philippines. She has also been executive secretary for the Governor's Commission on the Status of Women in North Carolina and films officer for the North Carolina Film Board. Between 1965 and 1970 she was Washington Bureau Chief for the DuPont-Columbia Broadcast Survey and Awards.

LORING MANDEL is known primarily for his writing of network television programs and plays. In 1959 he won the Sylvania Award for the Best Original Drama, "Project Immortality." In 1968 he won the Emmy for Best Dramatic Writing with his "Do Not Go Gentle into That Good Night." He has written numerous works for CBS's Playhouse 90 and Studio One as well as works for motion pictures and the theater. Writing with inside experience, he is one of the industry's sharpest critics.

THELMA MC CORMACK is associate professor of sociology at York University, Ontario, Canada. Educated at the University of Wisconsin and Columbia University, she has written on a wide range of mass communications topics. She is currently completing a book on social theory and the mass media of communications.

JOE MC GINNISS has worked for several newspapers including the *Philadelphia Bulletin* and the *Philadelphia Inquirer*. His work has included a series of syndicated newspaper columns from Vietnam and numerous articles for magazines. He is author of *The Selling of the President* and a novel, *The Dream Team.*

H. MARSHALL MC LUHAN was born in Edmonton, Alberta, Canada, and studied at Manitoba University and Cambridge University, where he received his Ph.D. in English Literature. He has taught at the University of Wisconsin, the University of St. Louis, and Assumption University and St. Michael's College, University of Toronto, where he is now the Director of the Center for Culture and Technology. His numerous works have drawn wide acclaim and criticism and have made him the most controversial writer on the mass media.

HAROLD MENDELSOHN received his Ph.D. in sociology and psychology from the New School for Social Research. He is now a professor and chairman in the Department of Mass Communications, School of Communication Arts, University of Denver. He has wide experience in advertising and communications research. He is a frequent contributor to social research journals and books. He has either written or co-authored three books: *Mass Entertainment; Minorities and the Police;* and *Polls, Television and the New Politics*. He has also been active in community service television programming.

A. Q. MOWBRAY was trained in engineering, which he taught at the University of Illinois. He is now employed as special assistant to the managing director of the American Society for Testing and Materials, a National Standards-Writing organization. He is author of two books: *The Thumb on the Scale*, an account of the struggle to get truth-in-packaging legislation through Congress, and *Road to Ruin*, a polemic against the destruction of our cities and countryside that is being caused by uncontrolled highway building.

DONALD MULLALLY holds a Ph.D. and is assistant professor in the Department of Radio and Television, College of Communications, University of Illinois.

RAYMOND B. NIXON is an emeritus professor of journalism and international communications at the University of Minnesota. He has published more than a score of studies on media ownership trends in the

United States and abroad. From 1945 to 1964 he was editor of *Journalism Quarterly* and is former president of the International Association for Mass Communication Research. He has also been a working newspaperman and magazine editor.

THOMAS PEPPER is a correspondent in Japan for the *Baltimore Sun* and was formerly a reporter on the *Winston-Salem Journal.* He was studying Japanese at Columbia University on a Carnegie Corporation grant at the time his article was published by the *Nation.*

RONALD H. PYSZKA is assistant professor of communications at the University of Washington, Seattle. He earned his Ph.D. in communications at the University of Wisconsin, and has taught previously at the University of Illinois. He teaches courses in advertising and communications, primarily in the fields of advertising research and consumer behavior.

TERENCE H. QUALTER holds a Ph.D. from the London School of Economics. He is a professor of political science at the University of Waterloo, Ontario. He is the author of two books, *Propaganda and Psychological Warfare* and *The Election Process in Canada* as well as numerous articles in scholarly journals.

GALEN RARICK was a newspaperman for 10 years prior to earning a Ph.D. in Mass Communication Research at Stanford University. He has taught at the University of Oregon and is currently Professor of Journalism at Ohio State University. His publications focus primarily on newspaper topics.

HAROLD ROSENBERG is art critic for *The New Yorker.* He was a visiting professor at Southern Illinois University in 1965. In 1966 he was appointed professor of the Committee on Social Thought of the University of Chicago, and subsequently professor in the department of art. He is author of several books including *Act and the Actor* (New American Library), *The Anxious Object,* and *The Tradition of the New.* His books have been translated into French, Italian, and Japanese, and his work appeared in leading literary and art reviews in the United States and overseas.

HERBERT I. SCHILLER is a professor of communication at the Third College, University of California, San Diego. He was formerly editor of the *Quarterly Review of Economics and Business.* His numerous articles and reviews have appeared in leading periodicals. He is the author of *Mass Communications and American Empire.*

WILBUR SCHRAMM received his Ph.D. from the University of Iowa. He is Janet M. Peck Professor of International Communication, adjunct professor of education, and director of the Institute for Communi-

cation Research at Stanford University. He has been a consultant to several government agencies and foundations which have recognized his pre-eminence in communications research. He is the author of fourteen books on communications including *Television in the Lives of our Children, Mass Media and National Development, Responsibility in Mass Communication,* and *Classroom Out-of-Doors.*

AUBREY SINGER is head of Features Group, Television, with the British Broadcasting Corporation, which he joined in 1949.

BENJAMIN D. SINGER was formerly a newspaper writer and editor and advertising proprietor. He earned a Ph.D. from the University of Pennsylvania in 1965. He is now associate professor, Department of Sociology, University of Western Ontario. He is consultant to the Department of Communications in the Canadian government and to the Childrens' Psychiatric Research Institute in London. He is the author of *Black Rioters* and *The Sociology of Communication in Canada* and numerous journal articles.

HEDRICK L. SMITH is a correspondent at the Moscow Bureau of the *New York Times.* He has been a distinguished reporter specializing in foreign news coverage and race relations. He covered civil rights in the South for the *New York Times* and UPI in the early sixties and has written extensively on Vietnam. In addition to daily and monthly news stories he has contributed articles to the *Atlantic, Saturday Review,* and other magazines. He contributed four of the ten articles in the New York Times' book *The Pentagon Papers.*

LEE H. SMITH is a free-lance writer who formerly worked for the *San Juan Star,* Associated Press, and *Newsweek.* In 1970 he helped launch and became managing editor of *Black Enterprise,* a magazine for black businessmen. He is currently writing a comic novel set in the Caribbean.

MAX WALES is a professor of journalism in the School of Journalism at the University of Oregon.

MEL WAX was a newspaperman for twenty-five years. He worked first in New England then on the *Chicago Sun Times* and then for the *San Francisco Chronicle* for ten years. He is now public affairs director for KQED, the public television station in San Francisco. He was the creator of the station's program "Newsroom," which won the Peabody Award for the best news program in the United States. He also served as the mayor of Sausalito, California.

WILLIAM M. WEILBACHER is senior vice president of the advertising agency Dancer, Fitzgerald, Sample, Inc.

He was president of the Market Research Council for 970–1971. He is author of *Marketing Management Cases* and co-author of *Advertising Media* and *Marketing Research*. He has been an adjunct professor of marketing at the Graduate School of Business, New York University.

CHRIS WELLES was a reporter and business editor for *Life* magazine, business editor *Saturday Evening Post*, and is currently general editor of *Institutional Investor*. An article in the latter won him the G. M. Loeb Award in 1971 for distinguished writing on investment, finance, and business. He is co-editor of *The Money Managers*, author of *The Elusive Bonanza: The Story of Oil Shale*, and a frequent contributor to magazines and journals.

DAVID MANNING WHITE holds a Ph.D. from the University of Iowa and is currently chairman of the Division of Journalism and a research professor of journalism at Boston University. He has also worked as reporter, editor, and correspondent for both print and electronic media. He is author or editor of fourteen books including *Journalism in the Mass Media, From Dogpatch to*

Slobbovia, and *The Celluloid Weapon*, as well as numerous articles. He has served widely as a consultant and has been the editor of *Television Quarterly*, the journal of the Nataional Academy of Television Arts and Sciences.

GERHART D. WIEBE is Dean of the School of Public Communication at Boston University. He was formerly research executive and partner in Elmo Roper and Associates, and research psychologist and assistant to the president of the Columbia Broadcasting System. He is the author of *Casebook in Social Processes*. He has contributed chapters to five other books and articles to a broad range of magazines and journals.

WILLIAM A. YOELL holds a doctorate in psychology and is president of the Behavior Research Institute. He was an early pioneer (1941) in motivational research and in the development and application of behavioral or learning psychology to business problems (marketing). He has held various positions in marketing and research with such firms as Young and Rubicam, BBDO, and M&M Candy.